Rick Steves®

IRELAND

Rick Steves & Pat O'Connor

CONTENTS

Post-Pandemic Travels: Expect a Warm Welcome...and a Few Changes
Research for this guidebook was limited by the COVID-19 outbreak, and the long-term impact of the crisis on our recommended destinations is unclear. Some details in this book will change for post-pandemic travelers. Now more than ever, it's smart to reconfirm specifics as you plan and travel. As always, you can find major updates at RickSteves.com/update.

Welcome to Rick Steves' Europe

Travel is intensified living—maximum thrills per minute and one of the last great sources of legal adventure. Travel is freedom. It's recess, and we need it.

I discovered a passion for European travel as a teen and have been sharing it ever since—through my tours, public television and radio shows, and travel guidebooks. Over the years, I've taught millions of travelers how to best enjoy Europe's blockbuster sights—and experience "Back Door" discoveries that most tourists miss.

Written with my talented co-author, Pat O'Connor, this book covers the highlights of the entire island of Ireland, offering a balanced mix of exciting cities and great-to-be-alive-in small towns. And it's selective—there are plenty of manor-house gardens, but we recommend only the best ones. Our self-guided museum tours and city walks give insight into the country's vibrant history and today's living, breathing culture.

We advocate traveling simply and smartly. Take advantage of our money- and time-saving tips on sightseeing, transportation, and more. Try local, characteristic alternatives to expensive hotels and restaurants. In many ways, spending more money only builds a thicker wall between you and what you traveled so far to see.

We visit Ireland to experience it—to become temporary locals. Thoughtful travel engages us with the world, as we learn to appreciate other cultures and new ways to measure quality of life.

Judging by the positive feedback we receive from readers, this book will help you enjoy a fun, affordable, and rewarding vacation—whether it's your first trip or your tenth.

Have a grand holiday! Happy travels!

Rick Steves

IRELAND

Flung onto the foggy fringe of the Atlantic pond like a mossy millstone, Ireland drips with mystery, drawing you in for a closer look. You may not find the proverbial pot of gold, but you'll treasure your encounters with the engaging, feisty Irish people. The Irish culture—with its intricate art and mesmerizing music—is as intoxicating as the famous Irish brew, Guinness.

The Irish revere their past and love their proverbs, such as "When God made time, he made a lot of it." Ireland is dusted with prehistoric stone circles, burial mounds, and standing stones...some older than the pyramids, and all speckled with moss. While much of Europe has buried older cultures under new, Ireland still reveals its cultural bedrock. It's a place to connect with your Neolithic roots, even if you're not Irish.

The 300-mile-long island (about the size of Maine) is ringed with some of Europe's most scenic coastal cliffs. It's only 150 miles across at its widest point. No matter where you go in Ireland, you're never more than 75 miles from the sea. Despite being as far north as Newfoundland, Ireland has a mild maritime climate, thanks to the Gulf Stream. Rainfall ranges from more than 100 inches a year in soggy, boggy Connemara to about 30 inches a year in Dublin. Any time of year, bring rain gear. As Ireland's own Oscar Wilde once quipped, "There is no bad weather...only inappropriate clothing."

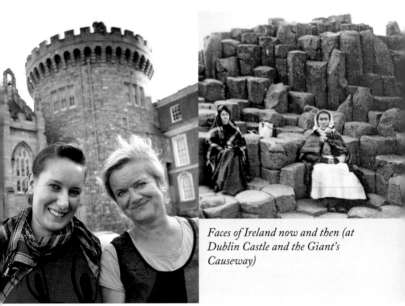

Faces of Ireland now and then (at Dublin Castle and the Giant's Causeway)

Though a small island, Ireland has had a large impact on the rest of the world. Geographically isolated in the damp attic of Dark Age Europe, Christian Irish monks tended the flickering flame of literacy, then bravely reintroduced it to the barbaric Continent. Ireland later turned out some of modern literature's greatest authors, including W. B. Yeats, George Bernard Shaw, Samuel Beckett, and Oscar Wilde. In the 1800s, great waves of Irish emigrants fled famine and colonial oppression, seeking new opportunities abroad and making their mark in the US and beyond. (Every Irish family seems to have a relative in America; about 50 million people claim Irish descent in North America alone.) And although peace now prevails in Northern Ireland, the religious and political conflict there long held the world's attention.

Northern Ireland (with 1.8 million people) is a province of the United Kingdom (like Scotland and Wales), while the Republic (with 5 million people and 80 percent of the land) is an independent nation. No visit to Ireland is complete without a look at both.

The Republic of Ireland boasts more sights, from the famous Book of Kells manuscript, prehistoric ruins, Celtic artifacts, and evocative monastic settlements to Iron Age

Traditional Irish Music

A *ceilidh* (KAY-lee) is an evening of music and dance...an Irish hoedown—and can be one of the great Irish experiences. You'll find traditional Irish music in pubs all over Ireland. "Sessions" (musical evenings) may be advertised events or impromptu (and quality can be hit or miss), but either way things get going at about 21:30—though Irish punctuality is unpredictable. Last call for drinks is just before midnight.

Pub music ranges from traditional instrumentals (merry jigs and reels) to ballads (songs of tragic love lost or heroic deeds done) to sing-along strummers. Sessions generally feature a fiddle, a flute or tin whistle, a guitar, and a bodhrán (BO-run, goatskin drum), sometimes joined by accordion or mandolin. Musical instruments from other regions have also become staples, including bouzoukis (from Greece) and banjos (from the southern United States); in the hands of a skilled Irish musician, the sounds and particularly the rhythms made by these instruments become distinctively Irish.

The music often comes in sets of three songs. The wind and string instruments embellish melody lines with lots of tight ornamentation. Percussion generally stays in the background. The *bodhrán* is played with a small, two-headed club; the performer stretches its skin by hand to change tone and pitch. More rarely, you'll hear the crisp sound of a set of bones: two cow ribs (boiled and dried) that are rattled in one hand like spoons or castanets, substituting for the sound of dancing shoes in olden days.

Watch the piper closely. The Irish cousin of Scottish Highland ▶▶▶

Irish dancing at a pub, accompanied by a bodhrán *player*

▶▶▶ bagpipes, the *uilleann* (ILL-in) pipes are played by inflating the airbag (under the left elbow) with a bellows (under the right elbow) rather than with a mouthpiece. *Uilleann* is Irish Gaelic for "elbow," and its sound is more melodic, with a wider range than Highland pipes. The piper fingers the chanter to create individual notes, and taps the chanter on his thigh to close the end and raise the note one octave. He uses the heel of his right hand to play chords on one of three regulator pipes. It takes amazing coordination to play this instrument well, and the sound can be haunting.

During your night out, it's worth staying until the wee hours for the magical moment when a rare *sean nós* (Irish for "old style") lament is sung to a hushed and attentive pub crowd. This slightly nasal vocal style may be a remnant of the ancient storytelling tradition of the bards whose influence died out when Gaelic culture waned 400 years ago. Stories—often of love lost, emigration to a faraway land, or a heroic rebel death struggling against English rule—are always heartfelt.

Sometimes a session hits all the right notes and the atmosphere is spellbinding. The drummer dodges the fiddler's playful bow. Sipping their pints, the musicians skillfully maintain a faint but steady buzz. The floor on their platform is stomped paint-free, and barmaids scurry artfully through the commotion, gathering towers of empty, cream-crusted glasses. Make yourself right at home, "playing the boot" (tapping your foot) under the table in time with the music. ▪▮

An uilleann *player entertains a pub crowd; fueled by beer*

ring forts. The country is bordered by green hilly peninsulas, craggy islands, and sheer cliffs rising up from the crashing waves of the Atlantic.

The people of the Republic of Ireland are known for the legendary "gift of gab," which has its roots in the ancient Celtic culture. With no written language (until the arrival of Christianity), the ancient Celts passed their history, laws, and folklore verbally from generation to generation. Even today, most transactions come with an ample side-helping of friendly banter. As an Irishman once joked, "How can I know what I think until I hear what I say?"

Listening to the thick Irish brogue, you'll get the fun sensation you're understanding a foreign language. But if you can't understand a thing, you're probably hearing Irish Gaelic, spoken in a Gaeltacht. These government-subsidized cultural preserves are found mostly in far western coastal regions (where English works, too).

The shamrock—used by St. Patrick to explain the concept of the Holy Trinity—is the most recognizable symbol of the Republic of Ireland. Another national symbol you'll see during your visit is the harp (on the back of Irish euro coins and reversed on every pint of Guinness). The Irish seem born with a love of music. Live music is a weekly (if not nightly) draw at any town pub worth its salt.

Northern Ireland is an underrated and often overlooked region that surprises visitors with its striking scenery and friendly people. Its coast boasts the alligator-skin volcanic

Prepared for rain; an Irish Gaelic sign for Dunquin reads "Míle Fáilte" (a thousand welcomes)

DÚN CHAOIN
Míle Fáilte

The serene, green Antrim Coast; raise a glass in Belfast's historic Crown Liquor Saloon

geology of the Giant's Causeway and the lush Glens of Antrim, while its interior is dominated by rolling hills of pastoral serenity and Lough Neagh, the UK's biggest lake.

An interesting hybrid of Irish and Scottish cultures, Northern Ireland is only 17 miles from Scotland at its closest point. The accents you'll hear in the North are distinctly different from their counterparts south of the border. With a population just a bit larger than that of Phoenix, it's small enough to have one phone book for the entire province, yet is twice as densely populated as the Republic to the south.

The people of the North generally fall into two categories: those who feel they're British (Unionists) and those who feel they're Irish (Nationalists). Those born in the North can choose which of the two passports they want. The turmoil of the Troubles—the decades-long conflict between Unionists and Nationalists, starting in the 1960s—has essentially ended, and Northern Ireland is now statistically one of the safer places in the Western world.

Today's Ireland is vibrant and cosmopolitan, yet warm and down to earth. Want to really get to know Ireland? Belly up to the bar in a neighborhood pub and engage a local in conversation. The Irish people have a worldwide reputation as witty, musical, moody romantics with a quick laugh and a ready smile. Come join them.

Ireland's Top Destinations

There's so much to see in Ireland and so little time. This overview breaks the country's top destinations into must-see sights (to help first-time travelers plan their trip) and worth-it sights (for those with extra time or special interests). I've also suggested a minimum number of days to allow per destination.

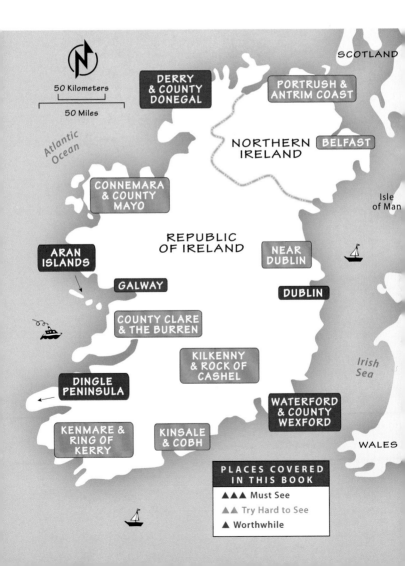

SCOTLAND

50 Kilometers

50 Miles

Atlantic Ocean

DERRY & COUNTY DONEGAL

PORTRUSH & ANTRIM COAST

NORTHERN IRELAND

BELFAST

Isle of Man

CONNEMARA & COUNTY MAYO

REPUBLIC OF IRELAND

ARAN ISLANDS

NEAR DUBLIN

GALWAY

DUBLIN

COUNTY CLARE & THE BURREN

KILKENNY & ROCK OF CASHEL

Irish Sea

DINGLE PENINSULA

WATERFORD & COUNTY WEXFORD

KENMARE & RING OF KERRY

KINSALE & COBH

WALES

PLACES COVERED IN THIS BOOK

▲▲▲ Must See
▲▲ Try Hard to See
▲ Worthwhile

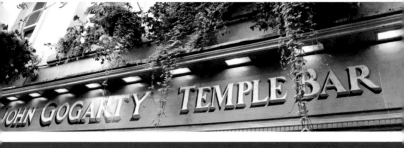

MUST-SEE DESTINATIONS

The island's top three destinations are Dublin, the capital city of the Republic of Ireland, on the east coast; the lush Dingle Peninsula on the west coast; and the rocky Aran Islands to the north, just off the coast of Galway. Each stop has a distinctly different flavor: from big-city Dublin and small-town Dingle to the remote and ancient Aran Islands. If you build your trip around these destinations, you'll get an unforgettable introduction to the best of Ireland.

▲▲▲Dublin (allow 2 days)
The bustling Irish capital offers fascinating tours (historical, musical, and literary), passionate rebel history (Kilmainham Gaol), treasured Dark Age gospels (starring the monk-illustrated Book of Kells), and intricate Celtic artifacts (National Museum of Archaeology). For evening fun, pub-hop through the rambunctious Temple Bar district, cocking your ear to seek out traditional music.

▲▲▲Dingle Peninsula (1-2 days)
My favorite fishing village, Dingle town, is a traditional Irish-music pub paradise. It's also a launchpad for a gorgeous loop drive (or bike ride) around Slea Head (the tip of the Dingle Peninsula), awash with striking scenery and a wealth of Celtic and early Christian sites.

▲▲▲Aran Islands (1 day)
Three windswept, treeless islands in the Atlantic are ringed by cliffs, crowned by striking ruins, and home to sparse villages of hardy fisherfolk. The island of Inishmore hosts the star attraction, the 2,000-year-old Dun Aengus fort, perching precariously at the edge of a sheer cliff.

Stone church on Dingle Peninsula; celebrating Bloomsday in Dublin; Dun Aengus perch; a Dingle pub

WORTH-IT DESTINATIONS

You can weave any of these destinations—rated ▲ or ▲▲—into your itinerary. It's easy to add some destinations based on proximity, but some out-of-the-way places can merit the journey, depending on your time and interests.

▲▲Near Dublin (1 day)

Of the varied sights near Dublin, the best is the Boyne Valley's ancient pre-Celtic burial mounds of Brú na Bóinne, with the majestic Norman castle in Trim nearby. Other choices are the green horse-racing pastures of the Irish National Stud, the graceful Gardens of Powerscourt, and the evocative monastic ruins of Glendalough.

▲▲Kilkenny and the Rock of Cashel (1 day)

These are the best two destinations in Ireland's interior: the medieval town of Kilkenny, with its narrow lanes, colorful facades, and stocky castle; and the Rock of Cashel, with its dramatic hilltop of church ruins, overlooking the Plain of Tipperary.

▲Waterford and County Wexford (1-2 days)

This gritty, historic port sparkles with the Waterford Crystal Visitor Centre. There's also a 12th-century lighthouse, the *Dunbrody* Famine Ship replica, the Irish National Irish Heritage park, and the Kennedy ancestral homestead.

▲▲Kinsale and Cobh (1-2 days)

County Cork has two quaint harbor towns: Kinsale, beloved by foodies, fun for strolling, and guarded by the squat Charles Fort; and the emigration hub of Cobh—the *Titanic's* last stop.

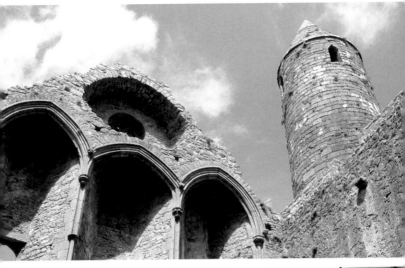

Brú na Bóinne (opposite); Rock of Cashel ruins; colorful Kinsale; bikers at Muckross House; shepherd with border collies

▲▲Kenmare and the Ring of Kerry (1 day)
The tidy town of Kenmare is the ideal home base for
side-stepping the throngs flocking to drive Ireland's most-
famous peninsula. The scenic loop route connects fairy
forts and villages, with options for a boat excursion to the
hermitage island of Skellig Michael.

▲▲County Clare and the Burren (1-2 days)
Ireland's western fringe has the breathtaking Cliffs of
Moher, the stony prehistoric landscape of the Burren, the
trad music crossroads of cozy Doolin, and the friendly town
of Ennis.

▲Galway (1 day)
This energetic university city has a thriving pedestrian street
scene and great people-watching pubs. For tourists, it's the
west coast's best home base for reaching the Burren, Aran
Islands, and Connemara region.

▲▲Westport and Connemara (1 day)
This region is a lushly green, hilly Irish outback of cottages,
lakes, and holy peaks, dotted with photogenic settlements
such as Cong, Kylemore Abbey, and the leafy riverside town
of Westport.

▲Donegal and the Northwest (half-day to 1 day)
Drivers will enjoy this far-flung section of the Republic and
its ruggedly beautiful landscape. The region's main town,
Donegal, has a striking castle.

▲Derry (half-day to 1 day)

This Northern Ireland town, which became a 17th-century British settlement encircled by stout town walls, is infamous as the powder keg that ignited Ireland's tragic "Troubles." Its insightful city history museum tells the tale.

▲▲Portrush and the Antrim Coast (1 day)

Portrush, an unpretentious beach resort, is the pleasant gateway to the geologic wonderland of the Giant's Causeway, the Old Bushmills Distillery, the cliff-edge ruins of Dunluce Castle, and the exhilarating Carrick-a-Rede Rope Bridge.

▲▲Belfast (1 day)

The no-nonsense capital of Northern Ireland has a walkable city center, stirring sectarian neighborhoods (best seen with a taxi tour), and the delightful riverside Titanic Quarter. Nearby is the charming Victorian seaside retreat of Bangor.

Ashford Castle in Cong (opposite); Galway picnic; crossing Carrick-a-Rede Rope Bridge; Belfast's City Hall

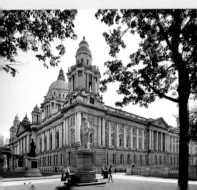

Planning Your Trip

To plan your trip, you'll need to design your itinerary—choosing where and when to go, how you'll travel, and how many days to spend at each destination. For my best general advice on sightseeing, accommodations, restaurants, and more, see the Practicalities chapter.

DESIGNING AN ITINERARY

As you read this book and learn your options…

Choose your top destinations.

My recommended itinerary (on page 20) gives you an idea of how much you can reasonably see in 21 days, but you can adapt it to fit your own interests and time frame. If you like what big cities have to offer—museums and nightlife—linger longer in Dublin. If trad music strikes a chord with you, your top stops are—in this order—Dingle, Doolin, Galway, Westport, and Dublin. Food lovers savor Kinsale.

If you're partial to prehistory, you can go back in time in the Burren, Brú na Bóinne burial tombs, and Aran Islands. Modern historians appreciate Belfast. If you're researching Irish roots, Cobh's a great place to start.

Drivers like to joyride around the Dingle and Kerry peninsulas and explore sights scattered throughout County Clare, Connemara, and the Antrim Coast. Nature lovers find inspiration at the Cliffs of Moher and the surprising rock formations of the Giant's Causeway. Photographers want to go everywhere.

Decide when to go.

Peak season (June through early Sept) is my favorite time to visit because of the longer days (with daylight from 4:30 until 22:30—Dublin is as far north as Edmonton, Canada). Note, though, that summer crowds have grown over the years, due partly to the cruise-ship industry, which affects mostly Dublin, the Cobh/Cork region, and Belfast.

Travel during "shoulder season" (mid-April through May, plus late Sept through Oct) offers fewer crowds, less competition, and all the tourist fun.

Winter travelers experience no crowds, soft room prices, colder rain, and shorter sightseeing hours (or sights open only on weekends, or even closed entirely Nov-Feb). Live music and pub crawls are limited to weekends. Winter weather can be chilly, dreary, and blustery, dampening the island's rural charm, though city sightseeing is fine.

No matter when you go, expect rain. Just keep on traveling and take full advantage of "bright spells." For weather specifics, see the climate chart in the appendix.

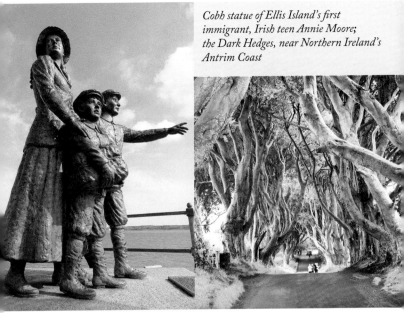

Cobh statue of Ellis Island's first immigrant, Irish teen Annie Moore; the Dark Hedges, near Northern Ireland's Antrim Coast

Ireland's Best Three-Week Trip by Car

Day	Plan	Sleep
1	Fly into Dublin	Dublin
2	Dublin	Dublin
3	Dublin	Dublin
4	Rent car at Dublin Airport, then drive through Glendalough	Kilkenny
5	Rock of Cashel	Waterford
6	Waterford	Waterford
7	Explore County Wexford and Cobh	Kinsale
8	Kinsale	Kinsale
9	Drive to Kenmare	Kenmare
10	Ring of Kerry	Dingle
11	Dingle Peninsula (Slea Head Loop)	Dingle
12	Blasket Island, Dingle town	Dingle
13	Cliffs of Moher, the Burren, Dunguaire Castle banquet	Galway
14	Aran Islands	Galway
15	Explore Connemara	Westport
16	Drive to Northern Ireland	Derry
17	Derry	Portrush
18	Explore Antrim Coast	Portrush
19	Drive to Belfast	Belfast
20	Drive to Boyne Valley sights	Trim
21	Return car and fly home from Dublin	

Notes: Spend your first three nights in Dublin, using buses and taxis, then pick up a car for the rest of this itinerary. For three weeks without a car, cut back on the recommended sights with the most frustrating public transportation (County Wexford, the Ring

Connect the dots.

Link your destinations into a logical route. Determine which cities you'll fly into and out of. Begin your search for transatlantic flights at Kayak.com.

Decide if you'll travel by car or public transportation. For the efficiency and freedom, I recommend driving. You won't need a car in big cities (park it), but a car is ideal for exploring regions, stopping wherever you like.

If relying on public transportation, you'll likely use a mix of Kerry, the Burren, Connemara, and the Boyne Valley). You can book day tours by bus for some of these areas at local TIs. For at least two people traveling together, taxis—though expensive—can work in a pinch if bus schedules don't fit your plans (e.g., Cork to Kinsale). If you have time for only one idyllic peninsula on your trip, I'd suggest the Dingle Peninsula over the Ring of Kerry. Small town Trim makes a mellow first- or last-night stop, offering access to Dublin Airport for car rentals.

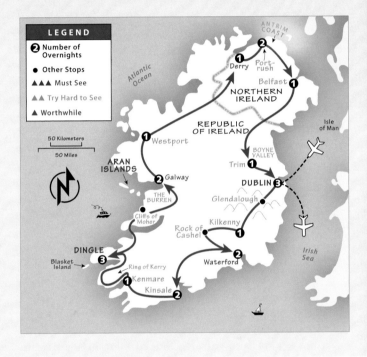

of trains and buses, and fill in transit gaps by taking minibus tours to outlying sights.

To determine approximate transportation times between your destinations, study the driving map in the Practicalities chapter, or train and bus schedules (see www.discoverireland.ie and select "Getting Around").

If your trip will include other European countries, check Skyscanner.com for intra-European budget flights.

Happy travels!

Write out a day-by-day itinerary.

Figure out how many destinations you can comfortably fit in your timeframe. Don't overdo it—few travelers wish they'd hurried more. Allow enough days per stop (see estimates in "Ireland's Top Destinations," earlier). Minimize one-night stands. It can be worth taking a late-afternoon drive or train ride to settle into a town for two consecutive nights—and gain a full day for sightseeing. Include sufficient time for transportation; whether you travel by car, train, or bus, it'll take you a half-day to get between most destinations.

Staying in a home base (like Dublin or Galway) and making day trips can be more time-efficient than changing locations and hotels.

Take sight closures into account. Avoid visiting a city on the one day a week its must-see sights are closed. Check if any holidays or festivals fall during your trip—these attract crowds and can close sights (for the latest, visit Ireland's tourist website, www.discoverireland.ie). Note major sights where advance reservations are smart or a free Rick Steves audio tour is available.

Give yourself some slack. Every trip—and every traveler—needs downtime for doing laundry, picnic shopping, people-watching, and so on. Pace yourself. Assume you will return.

Trip Costs Per Person

Run a reality check on your dream trip. You'll have major transportation costs in addition to daily expenses.

Flight: A round-trip flight from the US to Dublin costs about $900-1,500, depending on where you fly from and when.

Car Rental: Allow at least $250 per week, not including tolls, gas, parking, and insurance.

Public Transportation: For a three-week trip, allow $350 per person. Because Ireland's train system has gaps, a rail pass probably won't save you money, but buying train tickets online in advance can save as much as 50 percent.

AVERAGE DAILY EXPENSES PER PERSON

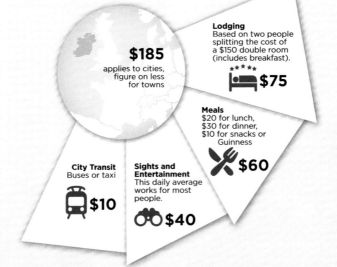

$185
applies to cities, figure on less for towns

Lodging
Based on two people splitting the cost of a $150 double room (includes breakfast).
$75

Meals
$20 for lunch, $30 for dinner, $10 for snacks or Guinness
$60

City Transit
Buses or taxi
$10

Sights and Entertainment
This daily average works for most people.
$40

Budget Tips

To cut your daily expenses, take advantage of the deals you'll find throughout Ireland and mentioned in this book.

Transit passes (for all-day or multiple-day usage) in bigger cities decrease your cost per ride. In Dublin and Belfast, using a hop-on, hop-off bus to get around isn't cheap, but it provides a live guide, a city intro-duction, and an efficient way to reach far-flung sights (cheaper than taxis and less time-consuming than city buses).

Avid sightseers consider two different sightseeing passes—the Heritage Card and the Heritage Island Visitor Attraction Map—that cover dozens of sights across Ireland (see "Sightseeing Passes," ▶▶▶

Rick Steves Ireland

▶▶▶ in the Practicalities chapter). On a smaller scale, some cities offer combo-tickets or passes that cover multiple museums. If a town doesn't offer deals, visit only the sights you most want to see, and seek out free sights and experiences (people-watching counts).

Some businesses—especially hotels and walking-tour companies—offer discounts to my readers (look for the RS% symbol in the listings in this book).

Book your rooms directly with the hotel. Some hotels offer a discount if you pay in cash and/or stay three or more nights (check online or ask). Rooms cost less outside of peak season (mid-June-Aug).

And even seniors can sleep cheap in hostels (some have double rooms) for about $30 per person. Or check Airbnb-type sites for deals.

It's no hardship to eat cheap in Ireland. You can get hearty, affordable meals at pubs and early-bird dinner deals at nicer restaurants. Cultivate the art of picnicking in atmospheric settings.

When you splurge, choose an experience you'll always remember, such as the Dunguaire Castle medieval banquet or a flight to the Aran Islands. Minimize souvenir shopping—how will you get it all home? Focus instead on collecting wonderful memories. ◼

Touring the Burren; a soaring sculpture (Rock of Cashel); a Dingle drive

BEFORE YOU GO

You'll have a smoother trip if you tackle a few things ahead of time. For more info on these topics, see the Practicalities chapter (and www.ricksteves.com, which has helpful travel tips and talks).

Make sure your travel documents are valid. If your passport is due to expire within six months of your ticketed date of return, you need to renew it. Allow up to six weeks to renew or get a passport (www.travel.state.gov).

Arrange your transportation. Book your international flights. Figure out your main form of transportation within Ireland: You can rent a car, or buy train and bus tickets (either as you go, or you can book train tickets in advance online at a discount).

Book rooms well in advance, especially if your trip falls during peak season or any major holidays or festivals.

Make reservations or buy tickets in advance for major sights. It's smart to book online for Dublin's Book of Kells, Guinness Storehouse, and Kilmainham Gaol (where reservations are required); and for Brú na Bóinne (near Dublin); Carrick-a-Rede Rope Bridge on the Antrim Coast; and the Titanic Belfast Museum. Boat trips to Skellig Michael can sell out months in advance—reserve ahead.

Consider travel insurance. Compare the cost of the insurance to the cost of your potential loss. Check whether your existing insurance (health, homeowners, or renters) covers you and your possessions overseas.

Call your bank. Alert your bank that you'll be using your debit and credit cards in Europe. Ask about transaction fees, and get the PIN number for your credit card. You don't need to bring euros or pounds for your trip; you can withdraw local currency from cash machines in Europe.

Use your smartphone smartly. Sign up for an international service plan to reduce your costs, or rely on Wi-Fi in Europe instead. Download any apps you'll want on the road, such as maps, translation, transit schedules, and Rick Steves Audio Europe.

Rip up this book! Turn chapters into mini-guidebooks: Break the book's spine and use a utility knife to slice apart chapters, keeping gummy edges intact. Reinforce the chapter spines with clear wide tape; use a heavy-duty stapler; or make or buy a cheap cover (see Travel Store at www.ricksteves.com), swapping out chapters as you travel.

Pack light. You'll walk with your luggage more than you think. I travel for weeks with a single carry-on bag and a daypack. Use the packing checklist in the appendix as a guide.

Rick's Free Video Clips and Audio Tours

Travel smarter with these free, fun resources:

Rick Steves Classroom Europe, a powerful tool for teachers, is also useful for travelers. This video library contains over 400 short clips excerpted from my public television series. Enjoy these videos as you sort through options for your trip and to better understand what you'll see in Europe. Check it out at Classroom.RickSteves.com (just enter a topic in the search bar to find everything I've filmed on a subject).

Rick Steves Audio Europe, a free app, makes it easy to download my audio tours and listen to them offline as you travel. 🎧 My two-part Dublin City Walk audio tour corresponds with this

book's chapter, covering sights in the center of town on both sides of the River Liffey. The app also offers insightful interviews from my public radio show with experts from Europe and around the globe. Find it in your app store or at RickSteves.com/AudioEurope.

Travel Smart

If you have a positive attitude, equip yourself with good information (this book), and expect to travel smart, you will.

Read—and reread—this book. To have an "A" trip, be an "A" student. Note opening hours of sights, closed days, crowd-beating tips, and whether reservations are required or advisable. Check the latest at www.ricksteves.com/update.

Be your own tour guide. As you travel, get up-to-date info on sights, reserve tickets and tours, reconfirm hotels and travel arrangements, and check transit connections. Visit local tourist information offices (TIs). Upon arrival in a new town, lay the groundwork for a smooth departure; confirm the road, train, or bus you'll take when you leave.

Outsmart thieves. Although pickpockets aren't prevalent in Ireland, it's wise to be cautious in crowded places where tourists congregate. Keep your cash, credit cards, and passport secure in a money belt tucked under your clothes; carry only a day's spending money in your front pocket. Don't set valuable items down on counters or café tabletops, where they can be quickly stolen or easily forgotten.

Minimize potential loss. Keep expensive gear to a minimum. Bring photocopies or take photos of important documents (passport and cards) to aid in replacement if they're lost or stolen. Back up photos and files frequently.

Guard your time and energy. Taking a taxi can be a good value if it saves you a long wait for a cheap bus or an exhausting walk across town. To avoid long lines, follow my crowd-beating tips, such as making advance reservations, or sightseeing early or late.

Be flexible. Even if you have a well-planned itinerary, expect changes, closures, sore feet, bad weather, and so on. Your Plan B could turn out to be even better.

Connect with the culture. Interacting with locals carbonates your experience. Enjoy the friendliness of the Irish people. Ask questions; most locals are happy to point you in their idea of the right direction. Set up your own quest for the best pub, traditional music, ruined castle, or ring fort. When an opportunity pops up, make it a habit to say "yes."

Ireland...here you come!

REPUBLIC
OF IRELAND

REPUBLIC OF IRELAND

The resilient Irish character was born of dark humor, historical reverence, and a scrappy, "We'll get 'em next time" rebel spirit. The Irish people maintain an unsinkable and optimistic belief in the future.

The modern Irish state has existed since 1922, but its inhabitants proudly claim their nation to be the only contemporary independent state to sprout from purely Celtic roots (sprinkled with a few Vikings and ship-wrecked Spanish Armada sailors to spice up the gene pool). The Romans never bothered to come over and organize the wild Irish. Through the persuasive and culturally enlightened approach of early missionaries such as St. Patrick, Ireland is one of the very few countries to have initially converted to Christianity without much bloodshed. The religious carnage came a thousand years later, with the Reformation. Irish culture absorbed the influences of Viking raiders and Norman soldiers of fortune, eventually enduring the 750-year shadow of English domination (1169-1922).

For most of the 20th century, Ireland was an isolated, agricultural economic backwater that had largely missed out on the Industrial Revolution. Things began to turn around when Ireland joined the European Community (precursor to the EU) in 1973, and really took off during the "Celtic Tiger" boom years (1995-2007), when American corporations saw big tax and labor advantages in locating here. Ireland's "Silicon Bog" became the European base for such big names as IBM, Intel, Microsoft, Apple, Facebook, and Google.

Today, the Republic of Ireland attracts both expatriates returning to their homeland and new foreign investment. As the only officially English-speaking country to have adopted the euro currency, Ireland makes an efficient base from which to access the European marketplace. About a third of the Irish population is under 25 years old, leading many high-tech and pharmaceutical firms to

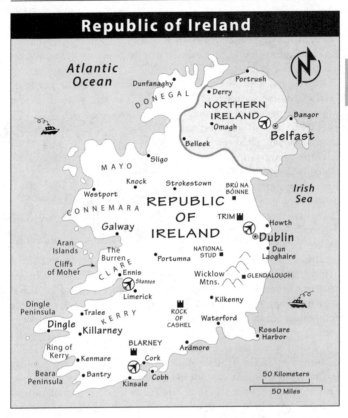

locate here, taking advantage of this young, well-educated labor force. More Viagra is made in Ireland than in any other country... though proudly virile Irish males claim it's all for export.

Other famous exports from the Republic of Ireland include rock and contemporary music (U2, Thin Lizzy, Hozier, Imelda May, the Corrs, Sinéad O'Connor, Enya), traditional Irish music (the Chieftains, Dubliners, the Clancy Brothers), opera (the Irish Tenors and John McCormack), dance (Riverdance), trivia (Guinness World Records), crystal (Waterford), beer (Guinness), iconic authors (Jonathan Swift, W. B. Yeats, James Joyce, George Bernard Shaw, Samuel Beckett, and Oscar Wilde), and a slew of memorable actors (Pierce Brosnan, Colin Farrell, Richard Harris, Michael Gambon, Colm Meaney, Saoirse Ronan, Michael Fassbender, and Maureen O'Hara).

Until recently, Ireland was one of the most ethnically homogenous nations on earth, but the Celtic Tiger economy changed all that, when the country became a destination for immigrants—mostly from the Third World and the newer EU nations. Eastern

REPUBLIC OF IRELAND

Europeans (especially Poles) came in search of higher pay...a reversal from the days when many Irish fled to start new lives abroad. A recent census found that over 10 percent of Ireland's population was born elsewhere.

Everyone here speaks English, though you'll encounter Irish Gaelic (commonly referred to as "Irish") if you venture to the western fringe of the country. The Irish love of conversation shines through wherever you go. All that conversation is helped along by the nebulous concept of Irish time, which never seems to be in short supply. Small shops post their hours as "9:00ish 'til 5:00ish." The local bus usually makes a stop at "10:30ish." A

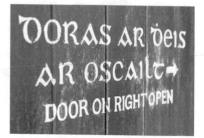

DORAS AR DEIS AR OSCAILT→ DOOR ON RIGHT OPEN

healthy disdain for being a slave to the clock seems to be part of being Irish. And the warm welcome you'll receive has its roots in ancient Celtic laws of hospitality toward stranded strangers. You'll see the phrase *"Céad míle fáilte"* in tourism brochures and postcards throughout Ireland—it translates as "a hundred thousand welcomes."

Founded in the late 1800s to preserve and promote Gaelic culture, the Gaelic Athletic Association (GAA) operates popular Irish hurling and football (not to be confused with soccer) leagues. Other sports that people closely follow in the Republic of Ireland include rugby, bike racing, horse racing, and dog racing. And it's hard to go 25 miles in Ireland without running into a golf course (there are more than 300 on the island).

Long a predominant cultural force, the influence of the Catholic Church is less apparent these days. Thirty percent of Irish weddings are now civil ceremonies, and weekly church attendance in Ireland is below the US average, having decreased dramatically over the years. (It would be even lower if not for the influx of devout Catholic Poles.) But the Church still plays a part in Irish life. Most Irish are culturally Catholic, and shrines to the Virgin Mary still grace rural roadsides. The average Irish family spends almost €500 on lavish celebrations for the First Holy Communion of each child. And the national radio and TV station, RTE, pauses for 30 seconds at noon and at 18:00 to broadcast the chimes of the Angelus bells—signaling the start of Catholic devotional prayers. The Irish say that if you're phoning heaven, it's a long-distance call from the rest of the world, but a local call from Ireland.

But modern sensibilities have come to once-traditional Ireland. In 2004, smoking was banned in all Irish workplaces (including pubs). The Irish were the first nation in the world to enact

Republic of Ireland Almanac

Official Name: The Republic of Ireland (a.k.a. "Ireland" or, in Irish, Éire).

Size: 27,000 square miles—half the size of New York State—it occupies the southern 80 percent of the island of Ireland. The country is small enough that radio broadcasts cover traffic snarls nationwide.

Population: 4.9 million people (about the same as Alabama).

Geography: The isle is mostly flat, ringed by a hilly coastline. The climate is moderate, with cloudy skies about every other day.

Latitude and Longitude: 53°N and 8°W. The latitude is equivalent to Alberta, Canada.

Biggest Cities: The capital of Dublin (556,000 people) is the only big city; about two in five Irish live in the greater Dublin area (1.4 million). Cork has about 210,000 people, Limerick 94,000, Galway 81,000, and Waterford 55,000.

Economy: The Gross Domestic Product is $382 billion, and the GDP per capita is $78,000—one of Europe's highest. Major moneymakers include tourism and exports (especially to the US and UK) of machines, medicine, Guinness, glassware, crystal ware, and software. Traditional agriculture (potatoes and other root vegetables) is fading fast, but dairy still does well.

Government: The elected president, Michael Higgins, appoints the Taoiseach (TEE-shock) or prime minister (youthful Leo Varadkar), who is nominated by Parliament. The Parliament consists of the 60-seat Senate, chosen by an electoral college, and the House of Representatives, with 166 seats apportioned after the people vote for a party. Major parties include Fianna Fáil, Fine Gael, and Sinn Féin—the political arm of the (fading) Irish Republican Army. Ireland is divided into 30 administrative counties (including Kerry, Clare, Cork, Limerick, and so on).

Flag: The Republic of Ireland's flag has three vertical bands of green, white, and orange.

The Average Irish: A typical Irish person is 5'7", 38 years old, has 1-2 kids, and will live to be 81. An Irish citizen consumes nearly 5 pounds of tea per year and spends $5 on alcohol each day. He or she speaks English, and Irish Gaelic is spoken by 40 percent (but only 5 percent of Irish people are fluent in the Irish language, mostly in pockets called Gaeltachts along the country's west coast). Nearly eight in 10 are nominally Catholic (a sharp decline in the last few years), though only one in three attends church.

RTE: The Voice of Ireland

Many a long drive or rainy evening has been saved by the engaging programs I've happened upon on RTE: Raidió Teilifís Éireann. What the BBC is to Britain, RTE is to Ireland: This government-owned company and national public broadcaster produces and broadcasts a wide range of programs on television, radio, and online. Look for it as you travel (via RTE's apps, on the radio, or on TV).

First hitting the airwaves on New Year's Eve 1961, today's RTE TV broadcasts are all digital and in English on RTE channels 1 and 2. But don't shy away from channel 4 (TG4), with Irish language TV shows subtitled in English—it's a great way to get a feel for the sound of the language. You couldn't find a richer or more accessible introduction to Irish culture.

Got a serious appetite for all things Irish? Online at www.rte.ie/archives, you'll find a treasure trove of fascinating archived RTE programs—everything from coverage of JFK's 1963 visit, to elderly recollections of the 1916 Rising, to the poetry of Seamus Heaney, to Gaelic sports.

such a comprehensive law (some pubkeepers initially grumbled about lost business, but the air has cleared). In the past decade, the Irish Department of Health has reported a 30 percent reduction in strokes and a 25 percent reduction in heart disease.

Keeping up this progressive trend, in 2015 Ireland became the first country to legalize marriage equality by popular vote. The republic in 2017 selected as its new prime minister (known as the "Taoiseach," meaning "Chieftain") the 38-year-old Leo Varadkar, a first-generation son of an Indian emigrant. A medical doctor, the openly gay Varadkar now leads a nation that, only a generation earlier, officially considered homosexuality unlawful as well as immoral. A 2018 referendum legalized abortion in limited cases, and a 2019 referendum made it easier to get a divorce, further distancing Ireland from its conservative, Catholic past.

Over time, relations between Ireland and former colonial master Britain have improved. In 2011, Queen Elizabeth II became the first British monarch to visit the Republic of Ireland since Ireland's 1921 split from the United Kingdom, which occurred during her grandfather's reign. Her four-night visit (to Dublin, Cashel, and Cork) unexpectedly charmed the Irish people and did much to repair old wounds between the two countries, establishing them, in the words of the Queen, as "firm friends and equal partners."

The big question now is how Brexit (Britain's exit from the EU) might complicate Ireland's easy trading relationship with its UK neighbors. Although the UK as a whole voted to leave the EU, the citizens of Northern Ireland voted to remain (recognizing the advantage of their soft border with the Republic). A possible "hardening" of this border is generally seen as a step backward that both countries want to avoid.

At first glance, Ireland's landscape seems unspectacular, with few mountains higher than 3,000 feet and an interior consisting of grazing pastures and peat bogs. But its seductive beauty slowly grows on you. The gentle rainfall, called "soft weather" by the locals, really does create 40 shades of green—and quite a few rainbows as well. Ancient, moss-covered ring forts crouch in lush valleys, while stone-strewn monastic ruins and lone castle turrets brave the wind on nearby hilltops. Charming fishing villages dot the coast near rugged, wave-battered cliffs.

You can't drive too far without running into road construction, as the recently affluent Irish improve their infrastructure with new motorways aimed at making travel between bigger cities faster. But the country is still laced with plenty of humble country lanes—perfect for getting lost in the wonders of Ireland. Slow down to contemplate the checkerboard patterns created by the rock walls outlining the many fields. Examine the colorful small-town shop fronts that proudly state the name of the proprietor. Embrace the laid-back tempo of Irish life.

DUBLIN

With reminders of its stirring history and rich culture on every corner, Ireland's capital and largest city is a sightseer's delight. Dublin punches above its weight in arts, entertainment, food, and fun.

Founded as a Viking trading settlement in the ninth century, Dublin grew to be a center of wealth and commerce, second only to London in the British Empire. As the seat of English rule in Ireland for over 700 years, Dublin was the heart of the "civilized" Anglo-Irish area (eastern Ireland) known as "the Pale." Anything "beyond the Pale" was considered uncultured and almost barbaric...purely Irish.

The Golden Age of English Dublin was the 18th century. The British Empire was on a roll, and the city was right there with it. Largely rebuilt during this Georgian era (1714-1830), Dublin became elegant and cultured.

But the 19th century saw Ireland endure the Great Potato Famine, and tension with the British culminated in the Easter Rising of 1916, followed by a successful guerilla war of independence and Ireland's tragic civil war that left many of its grand streets in ruins.

While bullet-pocked buildings and dramatic statues keep memories of Ireland's struggle for independence alive, today's Dublin is lively, easy, and extremely accessible. The city's economy is on the upswing, with a forest of cranes sweeping over booming construction blocks and expanding light-rail infrastructure. Dubliners are energetic and helpful, and visitors enjoy a big-town cultural scene wrapped in a small-town smile.

DUBLIN

PLANNING YOUR TIME

While you could easily spend much longer here, for most Ireland vacations, Dublin merits three nights and two days. Here's how I would fill two days in Dublin:

Day 1

9:00	Follow my "Dublin City Walk" through the center of town, with stops at City Hall (Story of the Capital exhibit) and the General Post Office (GPO Witness History exhibit)
13:00	Lunch
15:00	Visit EPIC: The Irish Emigration Museum
17:00	Enjoy an early-bird dinner deal at one of my recommended restaurants
19:30	Do the Traditional Irish Musical Pub Crawl (ends at 22:00) or another evening activity

Day 2

8:30	See the Book of Kells exhibit at Trinity College (book in advance)
10:00	Tour Trinity campus with a college student
11:00	Visit the National Museum of Archaeology
13:00	Lunch
15:00	Visit Kilmainham Gaol (book in advance)
19:00	Attend O'Sheas Pub's storytelling dinner (book in advance, finished at 21:30), the Literary Pub Crawl, or a play. Or just enjoy a free evening for dinner and traditional music in the pubs.

Orientation to Dublin

Greater Dublin sprawls with about 1.4 million people—about a third of the country's population. But the center of tourist interest is a tight triangle between O'Connell Bridge, St. Stephen's Green, and Christ Church Cathedral. Within or near this triangle, you'll find Trinity College (Book of Kells), a cluster of major museums (including the National Museum of Archaeology), touristy and pedestrianized Grafton Street, Temple Bar (touristy nightlife center), Dublin Castle, and the hub of most city tours and buses. Only two major sights are beyond easy walking distance from this central zone: Kilmainham Gaol and the Guinness Storehouse.

The River Liffey cuts the town in two, and most of your sightseeing will take place on its south bank. As you explore, be aware that many long Dublin streets change names every few blocks, including the wide main axis that cuts north/south through the tourist center. North from the O'Connell Bridge, it's called O'Connell Street; south of the bridge, it becomes Westmoreland, passes Trinity College, and becomes the pedestrian-only Grafton Street to St. Stephen's Green.

Two suburbs, Dun Laoghaire to the south and Howth to the north, offer quiet, less-expensive home-base alternatives to Dublin (with frequent and easy transit connections into town).

TOURIST INFORMATION

Dublin's busy main TI has lots of info on Dublin and all of Ireland (Mon-Sat 9:00-17:30, Sun 10:30-15:00, a block off Grafton Street at 25 Suffolk Street, tel. 01/884-7700, www.visitdublin.com). A smaller TI is just past the stainless-steel sculpture known as the Spire, on the east side of O'Connell Street (Mon-Sat 9:00-17:00, closed Sun). Beware of other shops claiming to be "Tourist Information" points, especially on O'Connell Street. Their advice is biased, aiming to sell you tours and collect commissions.

Dublin Pass: This sightseeing pass covers more than 30 sights and landmarks and hop-on, hop-off buses, and offers discounts on other attractions and the Aircoach airport bus (€69/1 day, multi-day options available, purchase online, collect at TI or use the app, www.dublinpass.ie). Skip the pass if you already have the Heritage Card (see page 562)—it covers two big Dublin sights (Kilmainham Gaol and Dublin Castle).

ARRIVAL IN DUBLIN

By Train: Dublin has two train stations, both with ATMs but no lockers.

Heuston Station, on the west end of town, serves west and southwest Ireland (nearest baggage storage is a 5-minute walk across the river at Tipperary House B&B, daily 8:00-20:00, hidden beside huge Ashcroft Hotel visible from station at 7 Parkgate Street, tel. 01/679-5317, www.tipperaryhousedublin.com).

Connolly Station is closer to the center and serves the north, northwest, and Rosslare (nearest baggage storage is directly across from station at the Internet & Call Shop, Mon-Fri 9:00-23:30, Sat-Sun from 10:00, 16 Amiens Street, tel. 01/537-7413).

If you're **changing trains** in Dublin, you may also change train stations. For example, to go from Belfast to Kilkenny you'll arrive at Connolly Station, then transfer to Heuston Station to catch a train to Kilkenny. The two stations are best connected by the red line of the LUAS tram system (20-minute ride; see "Getting Around Dublin," later). Bus #90, which runs along the river (€2.15, 4/hour), also links the train stations.

By Bus: Bus Éireann, Ireland's national bus company, uses the Busáras Central Bus Station (pronounced bu-SAUR-us), located one block south of Connolly Station.

By Car: Don't drive in downtown Dublin—traffic's terrible and parking is expensive. If you must park in central Dublin, a good option is Q-Park Christ Church, on Werburgh Street behind Jurys Inn Christ Church (€3/hour, €12/day, tel. 01/634-9805, www.ncps.ie). For more on driving, including Dublin's toll road, see "Dublin Connections" on page 129.

By Plane or Ferry: For details on Dublin's airport, UK ferries, and more, see "Dublin Connections" on page 127.

HELPFUL HINTS

Sightseeing Tips: With rising popularity and more cruise ships than ever, Dublin can be crowded. Book in advance for the Book of Kells at Trinity College, the Guinness Storehouse, and Kilmainham Gaol (reservations are mandatory for Kilmainham Gaol). And, if you are set on any evening activity, tour, or fine meal, reservations are a must.

Pickpockets: Dublin is not immune to this scourge. Be on guard— use a money belt or carefully zip things up.

Festivals: St. Patrick's Day is a four-day March extravaganza in Dublin (www.stpatricksday.ie). June 16 is **Bloomsday,** dedicated to the Irish author James Joyce and featuring the Messenger Bike Rally (www.jamesjoyce.ie). Book hotels ahead during festivals and for any weekend (see more advice in the "Sleeping in Dublin" section).

Meet a Dubliner: The free **City of a Thousand Welcomes** service brings together volunteers and first-time visitors to Dublin. You'll meet your "ambassador," head for a nearby tearoom or pub, and enjoy a drink (paid for by the city) and a friendly, informal conversation (of up to an hour). It's a great way to get oriented (sign up in advance online, meet at Little Museum

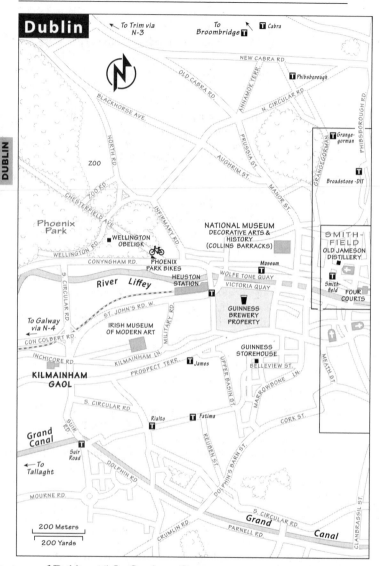

of Dublin, 15 St. Stephens Green—see map on page 74, tel. 01/661-1000, www.cityofathousandwelcomes.com).

Mass in Latin: The Roman Catholic Mass is said in Latin daily at St. Kevin's Church (Mon-Fri at 8:00, Sat at 9:00, Sun at 10:30, corner of Harrington and Synge, about 6 blocks south of St. Patrick's Cathedral, www.latinmassdublin.ie).

Bookstores: South of the Liffey, **Dubray Books** is the most central (Mon-Sat 9:00-19:00, Sun 10:00-18:00, 36 Grafton Street, tel. 01/677-5568, www.dubraybooks.ie). North of the river,

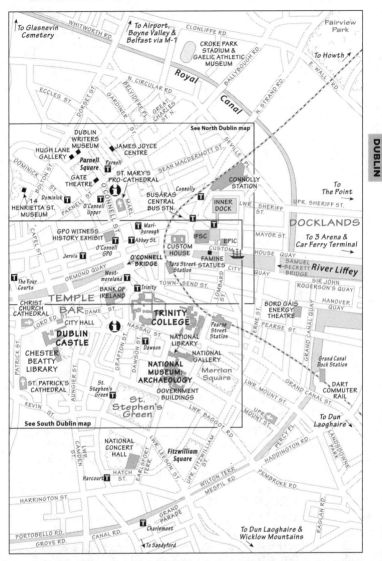

the giant granddaddy of them all is **Eason's** (Mon-Sat 8:00-19:00, Sun 12:00-18:00, 5 minutes north of the O'Connell Bridge at 40 O'Connell Street Lower, tel. 01/858-3800, www.easons.com).

Laundry: Krystal Launderette, a block southwest of Jurys Inn Christ Church on Patrick Street, offers same-day full service (Mon-Sat 8:00-20:00, Sun 12:00-17:00, tel. 01/454-6864). The **All-American Launderette** offers self- and full-service options (Mon-Sat 8:30-19:00, Sun 10:00-18:00, 40 South

DUBLIN

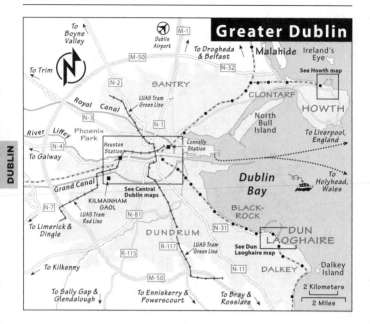

Great George's Street, tel. 01/677-2779). For locations, see the map on page 114.

Bike Rental: Phoenix Park Bikes is just inside the main entrance to Phoenix Park (north side of the Liffey, on Chesterfield Avenue)—a great place to start a low-stress ride into the huge, bike-friendly park (standard bikes—€6/1 hour, €10/3 hours, €15/day; electric bikes are double these rates; book ahead for 1-hour Segway park tours—€40/person, all rentals include helmets, Mon-Fri 10:00-19:00, Sat-Sun 9:00-19:00, "weather depending," Chesterfield Avenue, tel. 01/679-8290, www.phoenixparkbikes.com). For location, see the map on page 40.

GETTING AROUND DUBLIN

You'll do most of Dublin on foot, though when you need public transportation, you'll find it readily available and easy to use. And Dublin is a great taxi town, with reasonable, metered cabs easy to hail. With a little planning, sightseers can make excellent use of a two-day hop-on, hop-off bus ticket to link the best sights (see page 49). For cross-city travel, the expanding LUAS tram system beats bus service for reliability and ease of transporting bags.

By Public Transportation

You can buy individual tickets for the bus, tram, and commuter train, or get a transit card that can be used on all three.

Transit Cards: The **Leap Card** is good for travel on Dublin's bus, DART, and LUAS routes, and fares are lower than buying individual tickets. Leap Cards are sold at TIs, newsstands, and markets citywide—look for the leaping-frog logo—and can be topped up (€5 refundable deposit, www.leapcard.ie).

For those staying in Dun Laoghaire or Howth—or on a long-term stay in Dublin—the **Leap Visitor Card** may be a better option. It covers unlimited travel on Dublin's buses (including Airlink Express to and from the airport), DART, and LUAS trams (€10/1 day, €19.50/3 days, €40/7 days, each "day" equals 24 hours from first use, http://about.leapcard.ie/leap-visitor-card). Buy it at the airport, Dublin Bus office, or a TI.

The **Do Dublin Freedom Card** covers the Airlink Express, public buses in Dublin, and the Do Dublin hop-on, hop-off bus, and also offers some sight discounts. You can buy it in advance online, at the Do Dublin airport desk (Terminal 1), or the Dublin Bus office (€39.50/72 hours, tel. 01/844-4265, www.dodublin.ie).

Buses: Public buses are cheap and cover the city thoroughly. Most lines start at the four quays (riverfront streets) that are nearest O'Connell Bridge. If you're away from the center, nearly any bus takes you back downtown. Some bus stops are "request only": Be alert to the numbers of approaching buses, and when you see yours coming, flag it down. Tell the driver where you're going, and he'll ask for €2.15-3.30 depending on the number of stops. Bring coins, as drivers don't make change. The Dublin Bus office has free route maps and sells transit cards (Mon-Fri 9:00-17:30, Sat-Sun 9:30-14:00, 59 Upper O'Connell Street, tel. 01/873-4222, www.dublinbus.ie).

LUAS Trams: The city's street-tram system has two main lines, red and green. The **red line** is most useful for tourists, with an east-west section connecting the Heuston and Connolly train stations (a 20-minute ride apart) at opposite edges of the central zone. In between, the Busáras, Smithfield, and Museum stops are handy. Useful north-south **green line** stops are at St. Stephen's Green, Trinity College, and both ends of O'Connell Street. The lines don't intersect: The closest transfer point is a 100-yard walk between the red-line Abbey Street stop and the green-line General Post Office (GPO) stop on O'Connell Street. Monitors at boarding platforms display the time and end destination of the next tram; make sure you're on the right platform for the direction you want to go (€2.10, buy at machine, 6/hour, runs until 24:45, tel. 1-800-300-604, www.luas.ie).

DART Commuter Trains: Speedy commuter trains run along the coast, connecting Dublin with suburban Dun Laoghaire (south) and Howth (north). Think of the DART line as a giant "C" that serves coastal suburbs from Bray in the south up to Howth (€3.60, €6.75 round-trip—valid same day only, buy at machine, 4/hour, tel. 01/703-3504, www.irishrail.ie/home).

By Taxi or Uber

Taxis are everywhere and easy to hail. Cabbies are generally honest, friendly, and good sources of information (drop charge—€3.80 daytime, €4.20 nighttime, €1/each additional adult, figure about €10 for most crosstown rides, €50/hour for guided joyride).

Your Uber app will get you two choices in Dublin: "Uber" is actually a taxi (with the standard metered rate, but no tipping and billed to your account); "Uber Black" is a more expensive chauffeur-driven car.

Tours in Dublin

While Dublin's physical treasures are lackluster by European standards, the gritty city has a fine story to tell and people with a natural knack for telling it. It's a good town for walking tours, and competition is fierce. Pamphlets touting creative walks are posted all over town. Taking an evening walk is a great way to meet other travelers.

For help finding the departure points of the following recommended tours, see the map on page 74.

ON FOOT

🎧 To sightsee on your own, download my free two-part Dublin City Walk audio tour. For student-led **Trinity College campus tours,** worth ▲▲, see page 73. Unless otherwise noted, for departure points see the map on page 74.

Walking Tours
▲▲Historical Walking Tours of Dublin

This walk, led by history grads, is your best introduction to Dublin's basic historic strip (including Trinity College, Parliament House, Dublin Castle, Christ Church Cathedral, Grafton Street, and St.

Stephen's Green). You'll get the story of the city, from its Viking origins to the present, including the roots of Ireland's struggle with Britain. You'll stand in front of buildings that aren't much to look at, but give your guide lots to talk about (May-Sept daily at 11:00 and 15:00, April and Oct daily at 11:00, Nov-March Fri-Sun at 11:00). Walks last just over two hours (€14, RS%—ask when booking, free for kids under 14, can book ahead online, departs from front gate of Trinity College, private tours available, mobile 087-688-9412, www.historicalinsights.ie).

DUBLIN

1916 Rebellion Walking Tour

This two-hour walk breathes gritty life into the most turbulent year in modern Irish history, when idealistic Irish rebels launched the Easter Rising—eventually leading to independence from Britain. Lorcan Collins (author of *The Easter Rising*) and his guides are passionate about their subject (€15, RS%—ask when booking; March-Oct Mon-Sat at 11:30, Sun at 13:00; Nov-Feb Fri-Sun only; departs from International Bar at 23 Wicklow Street, mobile 086-858-3847, www.1916rising.com).

Pat Liddy's Walking Tours

Pat Liddy, a top local historian, has a crew of guides who lead an assortment of informal 2.5-hour walks of Dublin. The "Highlights and Hidden Corners" tour is a good introductory route from the General Post Office building, across the river to City Hall, through Temple Bar, to Trinity College (€14, RS%—save €2; April-Oct daily at 11:00; no tours Sun, Tue, or Thu in off-season; meet in front of Dublin Bus office at 59 Upper O'Connell Street, tel. 01/832-9406, mobile 087-905-2480, www.walkingtours.ie). While it's smart to book online, you can just show up. Pat's guides are also available for private tours (€180/half-day).

Pub Crawls
▲▲Traditional Irish Musical Pub Crawl

This entertaining tour visits the upstairs rooms of three pubs. There, you'll listen to two musicians talk about, play, and sing traditional Irish music. While having only two musi-

Dublin at a Glance

▲▲▲**Book of Kells in the Trinity Old Library** An exquisite illuminated manuscript, Ireland's most important piece of art from the Dark Ages. **Hours:** Mon-Sat 8:30-17:00, Sun from 9:30; Oct-April Mon-Sat 9:30-17:00, Sun 12:00-16:30. See page 73.

▲▲▲**National Museum of Archaeology** Excellent collection of Irish treasures from the Stone Age to today. **Hours:** Sun-Mon 13:00-17:00, Tue-Sat 10:00-17:00. See page 77.

▲▲▲**Kilmainham Gaol** Historic jail used by the British as a political prison—today a museum that tells a moving story of the suffering of the Irish people. **Hours:** Guided tours daily June-Aug 9:00-19:00, April-May and Sept until 18:00, Oct-March 9:30-17:30. See page 102.

▲▲**Historical Walking Tour of Dublin** This group tour is your best introduction to Dublin. **Hours:** May-Sept daily at 11:00 and 15:00, April and Oct daily at 11:00, Nov-March Fri-Sun at 11:00. See page 44.

▲▲**Traditional Irish Musical Pub Crawl** A fascinating, practical, and enjoyable primer on traditional Irish music. **Hours:** April-Oct daily at 19:30, Nov and Jan-March Thu-Sat only. See page 45.

▲▲**Trinity College Campus Tour** Ireland's most famous school, best visited with a 30-minute student-led tour. **Hours:** Daily 9:15-16:00, off-season weekends only, no tours Dec-Jan. See page 73.

▲▲**Chester Beatty Library** American expatriate's sumptuous collection of literary and religious treasures from Islam, Asia, and medieval Europe. **Hours:** Mon-Fri 10:00-17:00, Sat from 11:00, Sun from 13:00. See page 86.

▲▲**Temple Bar** Dublin's rowdiest neighborhood, with shops, cafés, theaters, galleries, pubs, and restaurants—a great spot for live (but touristy) traditional music. See page 92.

▲▲**O'Connell Street** Dublin's grandest promenade and main drag, packed with history and ideal for a stroll. See page 66.

▲▲**EPIC: The Irish Emigration Museum** Creative displays about the Irish diaspora highlight the impact emigrants make on their new homelands. **Hours:** Daily 10:00-18:45. See page 93.

▲▲**14 Henrietta Street** A time capsule of urban Dublin life, following the 150-year decline of an aristocratic Georgian townhouse into tenement slum. **Hours:** Guided tours Wed-Sat 10:00-16:00, Sun from 12:00, closed Mon-Tue. See page 99.

▲**National Gallery of Ireland** Fine collection of top Irish painters and European masters. **Hours:** Sun-Mon 11:00-17:30, Tue-Sat 9:15-17:30, Thu until 20:30. See page 83.

▲**Dublin Castle** Once the city's historic 700-year-old castle, now a Georgian palace, featuring ornate English state apartments. **Hours:** Daily 9:45-16:45. See page 85.

▲**Christ Church Cathedral** Neo-Gothic cathedral on the site of an 11th-century Viking church. **Hours:** Mon-Sat 9:30-17:00, Sun 12:00-14:30. See page 90.

▲**Dublinia** A fun, kid-friendly look at Dublin's Viking and medieval past with a side order of archaeology and a cool town model. **Hours:** Daily 10:00-18:30, Oct-Feb until 17:30. See page 91.

▲**St. Patrick's Cathedral** The holy site of legend where St. Patrick first baptized Irish converts. **Hours:** Mon-Fri 9:30-17:00, Sat-Sun 9:00-18:00 except during Sun services. See page 91.

▲**Jeanie Johnston Tall Ship and Famine Museum** Floating exhibit on the River Liffey explaining the Famine period that prompted desperate transatlantic crossings (by tour only). **Hours:** Daily 10:00-16:00, Oct-March 11:00-15:00. See page 95.

▲**Dublin Writers Museum** Collection of authorial bric-a-brac. **Hours:** Mon-Sat 9:45-17:00, Sun from 11:00, closed Mon Dec-March. See page 96.

▲**GPO Witness History Exhibit** Immersive presentation on the 1916 Easter Rising and its impact on Irish history, situated in the General Post Office building that served as rebel headquarters. **Hours:** Mon-Sat 10:00-17:30, Sun from 12:00. See page 99.

▲**Guinness Storehouse** The home of Ireland's national beer, with a museum of beer-making, a gallery of clever ads, and Gravity Bar with panoramic city views. **Hours:** Daily 9:30-19:00, July-Aug 9:00-20:00. See page 103.

▲**National Museum of Decorative Arts and History** Shows off Irish dress, furniture, silver, and weaponry with a special focus on the 1916 rebellion, fight for independence, and civil war. **Hours:** Tue-Sat 10:00-17:00, Sun and Mon from 13:00. See page 105.

▲**Gaelic Athletic Association Museum** High-tech museum of traditional Gaelic sports (hurling and Irish football). **Hours:** Mon-Sat 9:30-17:00, June-Aug until 18:00, Sun 10:30-17:00 year-round. On game Sundays, it's open to ticket holders only. See page 105.

cians makes the music a bit thin (Irish music aficionados will say you're better off just finding a good session), the evening—though touristy—provides a real education in traditional Irish music. The musicians clearly enjoy introducing rookies to their art and are very good at it (and really funny). In the summer, this popular 2.5-hour tour frequently sells out, but it's easy to reserve ahead online (€16, RS%—use code "RSIRISH" online, beer extra, April-Oct daily at 19:30, Nov and Jan-March Thu-Sat only, no shows in Dec, maximum 65 people, meet upstairs at Gogarty's Pub at the corner of Fleet and Anglesea in the Temple Bar area, tel. 01/475-3313, www.musicalpubcrawl.com). They also offer a dinner-show version with an earlier start that includes music and Irish dancing—it's a great primer (€48, May-Sept daily at 18:00).

Dublin Literary Pub Crawl
Two actors take 40 or so tourists on a walk, stopping at four pubs, and with clever banter introduce the high *craic* of James Joyce, Seán O'Casey, and W. B. Yeats. The two-hour tour is punctuated with 20-minute pub breaks (free time to drink and socialize). This is an easygoing excuse to drink beer in busy pubs, meet other travelers, and get a dose of witty Irish lit (€14, April-Oct daily at 19:30, Nov-March Thu-Sun only; reserve ahead in July-Aug when it can fill up, otherwise just show up; meet upstairs in the Duke Pub—off Grafton on Duke Street, tel. 01/670-5602, mobile 087-263-0270, www.dublinpubcrawl.com). Their once-a-week **morning Literary Walk** leads you on an insightful 90-minute stroll among the Dublin haunts of Irish wordsmiths (€12, Mondays at 10:30).

Food Tours
Fab Food Trails Dublin
For a 2.5-hour, six-stop edible education in Irish food, consider this food tour. With a small group (maximum 12 people), you'll visit a cheesemonger, try some fancy meats with wine, go to a bakery, hit the produce market, and maybe slurp an oyster, all with the good *craic* of your food-loving guide (€60, RS%—10 percent off with code "RSteves," April-Oct Thu-Sat at 10:00, Sat only in off-season, meeting point varies, tel. 01/497-1245, fabfoodtrails.ie).

Local Guides
With so much fascinating history and such a rich tradition of storytelling, it's no wonder there are plenty of smart and entertaining Dublin historians who work as private guides and are eager to tailor a tour to your interests. In addition to these three, the guides at **Pat Liddy's Walking Tours** can be booked privately (see earlier).

Suzanne Cole is good guide, both charming and smart (€120/2.5 hours, mobile 087-225-1262, suza.cole@gmail.com).

Witty **Dara McCarthy** will proudly show you around his hometown—when he's not leading one of my Rick Steves' Ireland tours (€120/2.5 hours, mobile 087-291-6798, dara@daramccarthy.com).

Jack Walsh is a local actor who's both high-minded and soft-spoken (€180/half-day, mobile 087-228-1570, walshjack135@gmail.com).

BY BUS
▲Hop-On, Hop-Off Bus Tours

Dublin works well for a hop-on, hop-off bus tour, which is an excellent way to orient yourself on arrival. Two companies with roofless double-deckers do similar 1.5-hour circuits of the city (up to 30 stops, buses circle every 10-15 minutes daily 9:00-17:00, usually until 19:00 in summer). With running commentaries (either live or recorded), buses run so frequently that they make  your sightseeing super-efficient. Stops include the far-flung Guinness Storehouse, Phoenix Park, and Kilmainham Gaol. Both companies offer various discounts to museums and sights in town, and two kids ride free with each adult.

Do Dublin (green buses) has drivers who provide fun and quirky narration. Your ticket includes free entry into the Little Museum of Dublin and a free walking tour from Pat Liddy's Walking Tours (€20/24 hours, €25/48 hours, tel. 01/844-4265, www.dublinsightseeing.ie).

Big Bus Tours (red buses) has a handy "blue route" that takes you as far as Glasnevin Cemetery and Croke Park (€20/24 hours, €25/48 hours, tel. 01/531-1711, www.bigbustours.com). They also offer a one-hour panoramic night tour (€15, June-Sept nightly at 19:00, 20:00, and 21:30, leaves from 13 Upper O'Connell Street, halfway between the Spire and the Gresham Hotel—see map on page 94).

BY BIKE
Dublin City Bike Tours

Pedal across this flat city on a fun, innovative 2.5-hour tour that covers five miles and visits 20 points of interest on both sides of the river (€27 includes bike and helmet; RS%—ask when booking, cash only, reserve in advance; March-Nov daily at 10:00—even in the rain, additional tours Sat-Sun at 14:00; departs Isaac's Hostel a half-block west of Busáras bus station at 2 Frenchman's Lane—see map on page 94, mobile 087-134-1866, www.dublincitybiketours. com).

Lazy Bike Tour Company
For a less strenuous option, you can grab a bright orange electric bike and matching vest, and buzz along on a guided tour that covers sights from Dublin Castle to Kilmainham Gaol. Tours start in Temple Bar and last two hours (€35; daily at 10:00, 12:30, and 15:00; book in advance in summer; meet at 4 Scarlet Row on Essex Street West in Temple Bar near Christ Church Cathedral, tel. 01/443-3671, www.lazybiketours.com).

Dublin City Walk

This two-part self-guided walk covers the basic sights in the center of town on both sides of the River Liffey. It can be done as a light, fast-paced overview in about two hours. Or you can use it to lace together many of the city's top sights. It's long but easy to do in two sections (south and north of the river).

Take this walk at the beginning of your Dublin visit to get the lay of the land—physically, culturally, and historically. As several of the stops and passageways along the route are closed after dark, this walk is best during normal business hours. (Doing it after-hours works, but you'll need to skip a few stops.)

For background on some of the historical events and personalities introduced on this walk, refer to the "Modern Ireland's Turbulent Birth" sidebar, later.

🎧 Download my free two-part Dublin City Walk audio tour.

PART 1: SOUTH DUBLIN
• *Start at the southernmost end of Grafton Street, where the city's thriving pedestrian boulevard meets its most beloved park. Stand before the big arch.*

❶ St. Stephen's Green
This city park, worth ▲, was originally a medieval commons— a space for grazing livestock. The park got its start in 1664, when the city leased some of the land as building lots—and each tenant was obligated to plant six trees.

Gradually the green was surrounded with fine Georgian buildings and access was limited to these affluent residents

("Georgian" is British for Neoclassical, named for the period from 1714 to 1830 when four consecutive King Georges occupied the British throne). Those were the glory days, when Dublin, both wealthy and powerful, was the number-two city in Britain, and squares and boulevards built in the Georgian style gave the city an air of grandeur. In 1880, the park was opened to the public, and today it provides a grassy refuge for all Dubliners.

The gateway before you is the **Fusiliers Arch.** It commemorates Irishmen who died fighting in the British Army in the Boer War (against Dutch settlers in South Africa from 1899-1902). Under the curve of the arch, see the names of those who lost their lives. In Dublin's crushingly impoverished tenements of the time, one of the few ways for a young man without means to improve his lot would be to join the army (regular meals, proper clothing, and a chance to "see the world"). You can read a little of the Irish struggle into the names: Captains were Protestant elites with English names, and grunts were Catholic with Catholic names. Many more grunts died.

Two decades later, Ireland was embroiled in its own war against Britain (the Irish War of Independence, 1919-1921), and sentiments had evolved. With Irishmen fighting to end their own centuries of English domination, locals considered the Fusiliers Arch to be a memorial to those who fought for Britain—and began referring to it as "Traitors Arch." A key Dublin battleground during that war was in and around this park. Step around to the left of the arch and look up. **Bullet marks** scarring the side of the memorial are reminders of the 1916 Easter Rising.

During that short-lived revolt, a group of passionate Irish rebels—a mishmash of romantic poets, teachers, aristocratic ladies, and slum dwellers—dug trenches in the park, believing they were creating fortified positions. They hadn't figured on veteran British troops placing snipers atop the nearby Shelbourne Hotel (with a bird's-eye view into the trenches). The park is dotted with reminders of that struggle, like the **memorial stone** honoring Irish rebel O'Donovan Rossa a few steps into the park past the arch. An oration at his funeral in 1915 was a catalyst that helped galvanize the rebels who would rise in 1916.

Take a quick walk into the park, strolling a couple hundred yards around the lake counterclockwise. (Find a park map on a post

DUBLIN

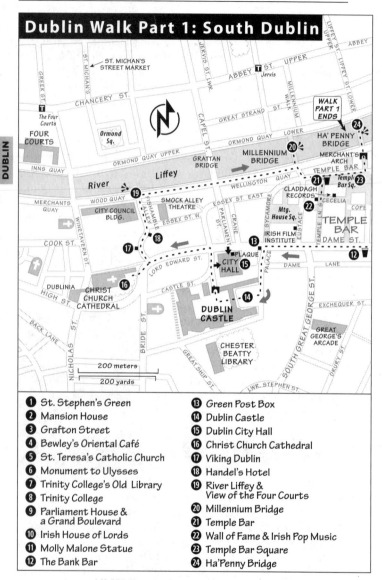

Dublin Walk Part 1: South Dublin

1 St. Stephen's Green
2 Mansion House
3 Grafton Street
4 Bewley's Oriental Café
5 St. Teresa's Catholic Church
6 Monument to Ulysses
7 Trinity College's Old Library
8 Trinity College
9 Parliament House & a Grand Boulevard
10 Irish House of Lords
11 Molly Malone Statue
12 The Bank Bar

13 Green Post Box
14 Dublin Castle
15 Dublin City Hall
16 Christ Church Cathedral
17 Viking Dublin
18 Handel's Hotel
19 River Liffey & View of the Four Courts
20 Millennium Bridge
21 Temple Bar
22 Wall of Fame & Irish Pop Music
23 Temple Bar Square
24 Ha'Penny Bridge

to orient yourself.) Walk past the palm trees (imported from chilly China, they are the only palm that can grow on the Emerald Isle).

As you round the lake, look for a rocky knoll in the trees. Hiding there is a monument to **W. B. Yeats** (by Henry Moore) and a terrace that's popular for outdoor plays and weddings. Walking across the terrace and then down, you come to the **central garden,** packed (at sunny lunchtimes) with Dublin office workers. On a pleasant afternoon, this open space is a wonderful world apart from the big

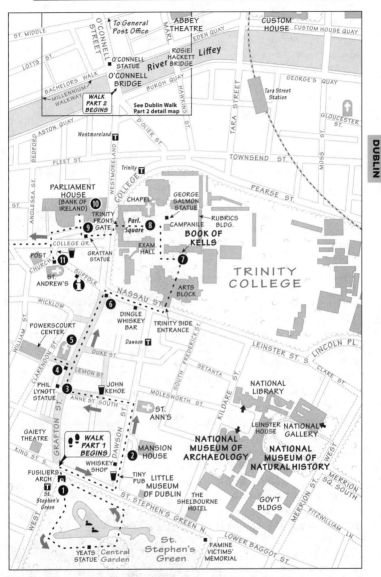

city. With romantic gazebos and carousels, duck-filled ponds, and relaxed people, today the park seems to celebrate Irish freedom.

From the central garden continue circling the **lake,** going over a bridge and back to the arch. The ducks you see are a traditional part of the scene. Generations of Dubliners treasure memories of coming here on Sundays as little kids to feed them. (Lately bully seagulls and pigeons are muscling into duck country.)

• *Exiting through the big arch, you're facing busy, pedestrianized Grafton*

Street (we'll go down it later). First we'll make a swing around the block to the right: Cross the street, dodging Dublin's new and popular tram line, and head right to the first corner, then go left, down Dawson Street.

*You can just make out the **"tiniest pub in Dublin"** (on the left at #25). Next door (#27), the **Celtic Whiskey Shop** is a reminder that in recent years Ireland has exported more whiskey than Scotland. To find out why, and maybe score a free sample, drop in. The big white Georgian building across the street is the...*

❷ Mansion House

Built in 1710, this is where Dublin's Lord Mayor lives. The building played roles in both of Ireland's wars.

In 1918 Ireland elected its representatives to the British Parliament—and chose mostly separatist members of the Sinn Féin ("Ourselves") party. The Sinn Fein parliamentarians refused to take their seats at Westminster in London. Instead, in January 1919, they created their own Irish Parliament (the Dáil Éireann) and met here, in an annex behind the Mansion House. The establishment of this rogue parliament in defiance of British rule kicked off the Irish War of Independence.

Three years later, they'd thrown off British rule, but found themselves at odds over the terms of the Anglo-Irish Treaty to end the war. Unable to agree, those opposed to ratification—led by Dáil Éireann president Éamon de Valera—marched out of parliament in protest. Within a few months, their festering disagreements ignited into the tragic Irish Civil War, eventually won by the pro-treaty forces of Michael Collins.

• *Continue down Dawson Street. The large neo-Romanesque (late 19th century) church ahead of you is the Anglican **St. Ann's Church**, where*

*Irish author Oscar Wilde was baptized and Bram Stoker (of Dracula fame) was married. Turn left onto Anne Street South and walk two blocks toward Grafton Street, past a line of busy independent retailers and a popular pub, **John Kehoe**. Customers typically spill into the street with their beloved pints in hand. (Technically, it's illegal to drink on the street, but it's only selectively enforced.)*

This legacy pub is part of the Dublin landscape: Dubliners often refer to landmark pubs rather than street names when giving directions.

Stop and enjoy the scene when you reach the busy, pedestrian boulevard.

❸ Grafton Street

Grafton Street is Dublin's most desirable retail address. It was pedestrianized in 1983, much to the consternation of local retailers—who were soon pleased to discover that business improved without all the traffic. Ireland's "Celtic Tiger" economic boom (2000-2008) gave the country Europe's hottest economy and a thriving tech sector. Business was so good that retail rents skyrocketed, which drove away small shops. Today Grafton Street is filled with mostly international retailers and a surging torrent of shoppers.

We'll stroll the boulevard to the right in a moment. But first, go directly across Grafton to Harry Street: A half-block up you'll

find a hairy rock star. This life-sized bronze statue with bass guitar, picks wedged behind the strings as fan tributes, is **Phil Lynott,** Ireland's first hard-rock star. He lived a short, fast life and is remembered for his band Thin Lizzy (of "The Boys Are Back in Town" fame). You could build an entire Dublin walk around its many popular musicians and rock stars...but I won't.

• *Return to Grafton Street, take a left, and join the river of pedestrians. Stop 50 yards down at the venerable café on the left...*

❹ Bewley's Oriental Café

Bewley's is a Dublin tradition that your Irish great-grandfather would remember for its well-priced comfort food. The facade is

done in an ornate neo-Egyptian, Art Deco style (built after the excitement of the discovery of King Tut's tomb in 1922). Approach it as if visiting an art gallery filled with people eating. Walk to the very back of the ground floor to view its famous stained-glass windows by artist Harry Clarke (1881-1931). For Clarke, famous for decorating churches with his exquisite windows, this is a rare secular subject—celebrating the four classical orders of column design. A fine Irish craftsman/artist, Clarke first learned his trade from his father, a stained-glass painter, and was part of the Irish Arts and Crafts movement. You're free to wander upstairs for more Bewley art. (For more about the restaurant, see page 121.)

• *A couple of steps farther down Grafton, turn left on the narrow lane called Johnson's Court. About 50 feet down, through the ornate archway, find a peaceful church.*

DUBLIN

❺ St. Teresa's Catholic Church

Tucked away as if hiding, St. Teresa's was built in 1792—one of the first Catholic churches allowed in Ireland after the gradual relax-

ing of the Penal Laws passed by the Protestant parliament (1691-1760) to regulate Catholics.

For a century, Catholics and their clergy were forced to practice their religion secretly, celebrating Mass at hidden rural "Mass rock" altars. But by the 1790s, the British government felt secure enough to allow some Catholic churches to be built again. They also wanted to appease the Irish—who could have been getting ideas as they observed Catholic France beheading its monarchs. Catholics were allowed to worship in actual churches as long as they kept a low profile.

Daniel O'Connell (b. 1775), an enlightened member of parliament, campaigned for Catholic equality and held political meetings at St. Teresa's. He brought down the last of those Penal Laws in 1829 by championing the Catholic right to vote. (We'll learn more about O'Connell later on this walk.)

• *Now stroll down Grafton Street. As you make your way, take a moment to enjoy a local busker (street musician) or chat at a street stall with a salt-of-the-earth woman selling flowers (these are mother-daughter hand-me-down businesses). Step out of the flow of humanity to glance up the side streets. Commercial as this street is, it has standards—notice that the arches are not golden at McDonald's. At the end of the pedestrianized section of Grafton Street, at the right corner, find a brass plaque in the pavement.*

❻ *Ulysses* Plaque

The little brass plaque on the ground, rubbed shiny by foot traffic, marks a spot mentioned in James Joyce's most famous novel, *Ulysses*. Passionate Irish-lit fans know Joyce's challenging, stream-of-consciousness work, which unfolds as a single day in the life of Leopold Bloom—June 16, 1904. The date is celebrated every year in Dublin as "Bloomsday," with scholars and enthusiasts dressing in period Edwardian garb and quoting passages from Joyce. This plaque is one of many *Ulysses* points of interest in town (there are even frequent public readings from the novel; see page 98).

• *Turn right and go a block on busy Nassau Street, passing the recommended* **Dingle Whiskey Bar** *(on the right, with 180 whiskeys on its shelves—an art form in itself). At the next corner, on the opposite (leafy) side of Nassau Street, is a side entrance to* **Trinity College.** *Follow the stream of students into the modern bunker-like Arts Building (note that on Sat-Sun after 18:00 the campus may be closed. In that case, refer to your map and walk left to the university's front door.) If you need a ticket to see the Book of Kells, two ATM-like machines in this hall can sell you one, quick and easy.*

Walk through the hall, exit the building down the ramp, and survey the grassy courtyard. The grand, gray three-story building with a line of tourists is...

❼ Trinity College's Old Library

The college's Old Library houses the **Book of Kells,** a medieval masterpiece of calligraphy and illustration. The ground floor contains the actual 1,200-year-old book (containing the gospels of Matthew, Mark, Luke, and John); the top floor is a venerable world of varnished wooden shelves giving a dignified home to a precious collection of reference books and artifacts, including  an original copy of the 1916 Proclamation of the Irish Republic, which announced Ireland's dramatic split with Britain (for more on touring the library, see page 73).

• *Go around to the left of the Old Library to enter a larger and grander square. Walk to the center, where the smooth paths intersect, and face the* **Campanile** *(bell tower).*

❽ Trinity College

You're standing on Parliament Square, in the heart of Ireland's oldest seat of learning, founded in 1592 by Queen Elizabeth to set the ill-disciplined Irish on the straight and righteous path to Protestant learning. These cobblestones were trod by Trinity graduates like Jonathan Swift, Oscar Wilde, Bram Stoker, and Samuel Beckett. (You're surrounded by dorms and administration. The actual classrooms are mostly elsewhere.)

Behind the graceful Campanile are the red-brick **Rubrics,** the oldest remaining buildings on campus (c. 1712). Their facades sport a faintly Dutch look, due to their construction soon after the reign of Dutch-born King William III of Orange. He took the British throne jointly with his English wife/cousin Mary II, bringing Dutch architecture into vogue for a generation.

Fifty feet to the left of the Campanile is a white-marble statue of a seated man, grinning down on us from his pedestal. He's **George Salmon,** a mathematician, theologian, and provost in the late 1890s, who said women would enter Trinity over his dead body. Coincidentally, days after he died in 1904, the first women were admitted to Trinity College.

Trinity remains one of the world's great universities—and would be greater if not for the financial challenges of attracting top professors. Money raised by the hordes of tourists seeing the Book of Kells goes to support the cash-strapped university. And the college has put on a charm offensive to attract wealthy students from China, as the full tuition they pay subsidizes less-wealthy Irish students.

Now turn 180 degrees to face the front gate of the college. To your right and left stand two identically majestic buildings, each with four Corinthian columns. To your right is the college chapel, and to the left is the examination hall. During final exams, there tends to be a lot of student traffic between the two buildings, nicknamed "heaven and hell."

Directly ahead, at the front gate, you'll often spot a talkative college kid wearing an academic gown staffing a small kiosk and selling tickets for the fun Trinity College campus tours (see listing on page 73).

• *Exit the campus through the front gatehouse, across hexagonal wooden pavers intended to dampen the sound of horse hooves. Before leaving the gatehouse, pretend you're a student—look at the posters to catch up on news, sports, rooms for rent, and plays and concerts.*

Exiting the college, you'll enter one of the most chaotic intersections in Dublin. Cross the street carefully to the traffic island at the bottom of the busy boulevard and stand before a statue of the guy who first cooked potatoes au Grattan (or an 18th-century member of the Irish House of Commons—you decide).

❾ Parliament House and a Grand Boulevard

The long street stretching straight in front of you is College Green, which becomes Dame Street, and then Lord Edward Street as it reaches Christ Church Cathedral, a half-mile away (and we're about to walk the entire thing). For simplicity, I'll just refer to it as "the boulevard."

Roughly 250 years ago, this spot marked the start of Dublin's version of a "Royal Mile," where the parliament, castle, university, and big banks all intersected in full glory. Logically, this spot in front of parliament was also where serious protests took place. "No taxation without representation" was a rebel rallying cry against Britain here as it was in our 13 colonies.

The grand building with a rounded colonnade is the **Parliament House** (and now home to the Bank of Ireland). The Irish

House of Commons and House of Lords met here until the 1801 Act of Union abolished the Irish parliament, moving its members to Westminster in London. Thus began Dublin's slow, century-long decay, from important British hub to largely impoverished, tenement-ridden backwater.

• *The original House of Lords survives in the bank, and it's free to visit (open Mon-Fri 10:00-16:00). Follow the signs and pop in.*

⓾ Irish House of Lords

The Irish parliament building was built in 1733 on the same model as the Houses of Parliament in London. It was the first purpose-built bicameral parliament. The House of Commons was eventually gutted, but the smaller House of Lords survived unaltered. Inside you'll see a fireplace carved of Irish oak, tapestries celebrating Protestant victories over the indigenous and Catholic Irish, and busts of British kings and admirals. The big ceremonial silver mace (in the glass case) represented the authority of the British monarch; nothing that occurred in this chamber was valid without the monarch's symbolic presence. A painting shows the appearance of the once-adjacent but now-gone House of Commons.

• *Leaving the bank, walk a block up the boulevard and take your first left (cross over at Ulster Bank), onto Church Lane. Go one block to an old church with a statue out front of a buxom maiden pushing a cart of wicker baskets.*

⓫ Molly Malone Statue

You've probably heard Dublin's unofficial theme song "Molly Malone"—now let's meet the woman commemorated in the tune. The area around the Molly Malone statue (from 1988) is a popular hangout for street musicians—and for tourists wanting a photo

with the iconic gal of Irish sing-along fame. She pauses cooperatively "in Dublin's fair city, where the girls are so pretty," to offer you "cockles and mussels, alive, alive-o" from her cart. (Tour guides created some bogus legend about good luck or good sex... and now tourists dutifully line up to help shine her breasts.)

The church was **St. Andrew's,** once a place of worship frequented by nearby members of parliament. Enjoy its 19th-century neo-Gothic stonework. Now decommissioned, its future is as a high-end food court.

Across the street is **O'Neill's,** recommended for pub grub, with a sloppy and noisy wonderland of cozy alcoves scattered over three floors. Just for fun, enter on the right and work your way through its labyrinthine interior, eventually exiting on the left. The O'Neill family has had a pub at this intersection for over 300 years and has benefited from its strategic location: It lies directly between the church and parliament, with the power brokers of the time being regular patrons.

• *Return to the main boulevard, turn left, and continue a few doors to a very fancy bank (on the left with a red sandstone facade, brass details, and showy banners) that's now a very fancy pub. Step just inside for a dazzling view.*

⓬ The Bank Bar

Built in 1894, The Bank Bar staggers visitors with its Victorian opulence. Back then, banks had to dazzle elite clients to assure them

the bank was financially solid. Today, Dublin's banks have vacated such palaces for modern offices, and many ornate former bank interiors—like this one—now dazzle diners.

Even if you're not eating here, you're welcome to stand just inside the door for a look. The stained-glass ceiling still sparkles. The many mirrors make the space seem larger, and the ornate floor tiles and crow's nest balcony catch the eye. In a case by the door, a faithful replica of the Book of Kells is under glass. A stately painting of the Custom House (surrounded by the ships so vital to Dublin's economy) fills the wall on the left. And on the right is a painting of Parliament House. The paintings face each other as pillars of society: commerce and governance. In the back-right corner are seven male busts: the seven patriot signers of the 1916 Proclamation of Irish Independence, martyrs for the Irish Republic—all executed at Kilmainham Gaol. (The basement restrooms are flanked by four old bank vaults.)

• *Exit the bar, turn left, and walk a couple of minutes (2 long blocks) until you see a green post box. Here's a fun fact while you walk: in Ireland, car license plates tell when and where a car was registered: 142-D indicates 2014, second half of the year, in Dublin.*

DUBLIN

⑬ Green Post Box

An innocent-looking, round green postal box stands sentry in a small sidewalk plaza. Like all Irish post boxes, it's Irish green. But look closely at the elaborate monogram at knee height. It's an ornate "E" for "Edward," woven with "R" for "Rex" (Latin for "king")—indicating that this box dates from just before World War I, during the reign of King Edward VII (son of Victoria)—who reigned over Ireland as part of the United Kingdom of Great Britain and Ireland. Once royal red, after Ireland won its independence it was more practical to just paint the post poxes Irish green and call it good, than replace them. In 1922, this box, with its

high-profile location at the entry to the grounds of Dublin Castle, was the first to be painted green. If a Royalist were to scratch the paint to show some underlying red, it would be repainted green before you could say Guy Fawkes.

• *Ahead is City Hall. But first we'll take a short detour, looping left and then right through the grounds of Dublin Castle before emerging just beyond City Hall.*

⑭ Dublin Castle

While Dublin Castle today shows only scant remains of its medieval architecture, it was the center of English power for 700 years, from its initial construction in 1204 (under bad King John of Magna Carta fame) until Britain handed the reins back to the Irish in 1922. Today, it's a prime example of a Georgian palace and the location for ceremonial affairs of state.

The castle's grand state rooms are open to the public (see the listing under "Sights in Dublin" for information on visiting).

• *Leave the castle grounds through the gate at the top of the courtyard. On your right, facing the busy boulevard, is the stately City Hall, worth a visit to see its interior and good history exhibit.*

ⓖ Dublin City Hall

Dublin's impressive City Hall, worth ▲, started life in 1779 as the Royal Exchange, where Irish and British currencies were ex-

changed and where merchants gathered to discuss trading affairs. It's a splendid example of the Georgian style then very popular in Britain.

It became City Hall in 1852 and was the site of the first fatalities of the 1916 Easter Rising, when Irish rebels occupied it to control the main gate to Dublin Castle. Step inside (it's free) to feel the prosperity and confidence of Dublin in her glory days. The dramatic main-floor rotunda—with its grand Caesar-like statue of the great orator Daniel O'Connell (the city's first Catholic mayor, 1841)—was inspired by the Pantheon in Rome. (They get more rain here so the oculus—the opening in the ceiling—is covered.) A cycle of heroic paintings tells the city's history in a rare example of Arts and Crafts artwork from 1919. It was here, under the rotunda, that the body of modern Irish rebel leader Michael Collins lay in state after his assassination in 1922. On the floor, a Latin inscription translates to "Obedient citizens make a happy city" (the greeter is happy to give you more information).

Downstairs, the fine and free little **Story of the Capital** exhibit does a good job of telling the city's history, including the stirring and heartbreaking events of 1916, the War of Independence, and the Irish Civil War; you'll see a few impressive artifacts, including the city seal with its seven-key lock box and an original 1916 Proclamation of Irish Independence (Mon-Sat 10:00-17:15, closed Sun, www.dublincity.ie/dublincityhall).

• *Leave City Hall through the Dame Street exit, and take the stairs on your right. Halfway down, look on the wall for a **bronze plaque** establishing the British Imperial system of inches, feet, and yards (and miles)—which, thanks to our colonial heritage, the United States is saddled with. Find the Paris Metre—Ireland now uses the metric system.*

Now, we'll turn left and continue uphill on the big boulevard to the church tower in the distance. Enter the churchyard and walk past the

downtrodden person sleeping on the bench. But wait...are those nail holes in his feet? It's a statue called **Homeless Jesus** *by the Canadian artist Timothy Schmalz.*

⓰ Christ Church Cathedral

The cathedral in front of you, worth ▲, is one of the oldest places of worship in Dublin. What you see today is an extensively renovated neo-Gothic structure dating from the 1870s, but its underground crypt goes back to 1172. An even earlier Viking-era church stood here back in the 1030s. Just beyond the *Homeless Jesus* statue, an excavation contains the low-lying ruins of a small 12th-century church building. The stones you see on the exterior of the southern transept (above the excavation site) are 12th-century Romanesque—one of the few original features not disturbed by later restorations (for more on the church, see the listing on page 90).

• *Leave the churchyard as you entered, turn left, and walk a few steps down Fishamble Street to the blocky concrete sign reading* Dublin City Council. *At your feet in the pavement is a marker celebrating some ancient history.*

⓱ Viking Dublin

You're standing on the site of Dublin's first Viking settlement, established over 1,200 years ago, with Fishamble Street as its fish

market. When the foundations for the huge bunker-like modern offices of the Dublin City Council were dug in 1978, an intact Viking settlement was exposed. A treasure trove of artifacts was uncovered, carefully excavated, and catalogued by eager archaeologists. More than a million objects were found (the best are in the National Museum of Archaeology). Even so, researchers were allowed only a short time to dig before the office building that stands here now was erected, effectively burying the rest of the settlement under the pavement. Public protests were vehement and vocal, but to no avail. In an ironic twist, Dublin's citizens must come here to get planning permission to build. Sidewalk plaques (there are 18) based on photos from the dig remind all who pass of what was found—and lost.

*• Walk farther downhill, passing **Darkey Kelly's**, a good pub with music nightly. At the end of the block, you'll see...*

⑱ Handel's Hotel

This hotel is named for the composer of the "Messiah" (with its beloved "Hallelujah Chorus"). The first public performance of this iconic oratorio took place in 1742 in a nearby music hall. Peek through the gate to the left of the hotel to see the remains of a surviving theater wall and a statue—a naked and fit Handel stands like a pillar saint atop organ pipes. Every year, on the April 13 anniversary of that premiere, this humble street fills with a full orchestra and 120 choral singers to perform the "Messiah" for the public.

• Continue walking down Fishamble all the way to the river.

⑲ River Liffey and View of the Four Courts

Look left. Across the river in the distance is a grand building with a green domed roof. This is the **Four Courts,** finished in 1802 and housing Ireland's Supreme Court. It was once the archive for irreplaceable birth and land records. When the Irish Civil War broke out in 1922, Irish nationalists opposed to British dominion occupied the building. Forces supporting the 1921 Anglo-Irish Treaty—led by Michael Collins—were left no alternative but to root them out with British-supplied artillery (the first shots of that tragic brother-against-brother conflict). The artillery onslaught resulted in the accidental detonation of rebel ammo in the Four Courts, sparking an intense fire that destroyed seven centuries of genealogical and historical records.

• Turn right and walk downstream to the second bridge, the pedestrian-only Millennium Bridge. Walk halfway out to survey the scene.

⑳ Millennium Bridge

From here the Liffey flows three miles to empty into the Irish Sea. Bordered on both sides by quays (the old English word for "wharf"), today the river is empty of vessels and contained by its concrete embankments. But it was once wider, with muddy banks, wooden piers, and sailing ships. After Vikings sailed their longboats down the Liffey in the ninth century, they built a ship harbor here, and for centuries afterward, the riverfront was the pumping heart of Dublin's commerce. The Liffey is a salty river, with high and low tides. Before the 1600s, boats could come this far upriver to the medieval port area. But with more bridges and bigger ships, the port moved farther and farther downstream. Today it's at the mouth of the river, three miles away.

Look downstream at the next bridge, the pedestrian-only **Ha' Penny Bridge,** a Dublin landmark since 1816. Its graceful cast-iron

arch is a celebration of the
emerging bridge engineer-
ing made possible by the
Industrial Revolution. It's
officially the "Wellington
Bridge," named for Arthur
Wellesley, the first duke of
Wellington, who was born
in Ireland, beat Napoleon
at Waterloo, and became a

British prime minister. (When teased in Westminster about his
Irish birth, he famously said, "Just because you're born in a stable
doesn't make you a donkey.") It got its nickname because people
paid half a penny ("Ha' penny") to cross the bridge rather than ride
a ferry across the river—the only other option in the early 1800s.

We'll cross that bridge when we get to it. But first, let's head
to the Temple Bar district, which stretches along the south bank of
the river from here past the Ha' Penny Bridge.

• *Go a block inland from the river. At East Essex Street (and the Norse-
men Pub), wander left into the heart of Dublin's infamous party district,
known as...*

㉑ Temple Bar

Inspired by thriving bohemian cultural centers such as Paris' Left
Bank and New York City's Greenwich Village, in 1991 Dublin
scuttled a plan to demolish this neighborhood (filled with drugs,
prostitutes, and decay) to build a bus station. Instead, the city imported quaint cobbles, gave tax breaks to entertainment businesses,
and created a raucous party zone. The resulting tourist crowds and
inflated beer prices drove away the locals long ago. (For more on
Temple Bar, see pages 111 and 124.)

On the first corner slouches a pub called **The Temple Bar.**
While it looks venerable, it's only 25 years old, built to cash in on
the district's rising popularity as a night spot. It encapsulates the
commercialism of the tourists' Temple Bar. Venture in and sample
the scene.

You wouldn't know it by looking at Temple Bar, but since
2001 consumption of alcohol is down almost 20 percent in Ireland.
In 2018, Guinness launched its first nonalcoholic beer—perhaps
thinking young people don't have as much time for hangovers.
Starbucks-like coffee shops are on the rise. A North Dublin pub
just opened up called The Virgin Mary—with no booze. While
Irish pubs are in vogue around the world, here on the Emerald Isle
a thousand pubs have closed in the last decade.

• *From The Temple Bar pub, side-trip right a block, up Temple Lane
South, and stop at the corner of Cecelia Street.*

DUBLIN

⓶ Wall of Fame and Irish Pop Music

The windows of the three-story, red "Wall of Fame" on your right are filled with photos of contemporary Irish musicians (Bob Geldof, Phil Lynott, Sinead O'Connor, U2, The Cranberries, and others). It marks the location of the **Irish Rock 'n' Roll Museum** (worth a visit for rock fans interested in seeing studio space and vintage mixing boards used by famous acts, visit by €16 guided tour only, daily 11:00-17:30, www.irishrocknrollmuseum. com).

Behind you, a couple doors up Cecelia Street, is **Claddagh Records,** a fine little Irish traditional music shop (closed Sun, www. claddaghrecords.com). This hole-in-the-wall shop is staffed by informed folks who love turning visitors on to Irish tunes. Above it, the modest third floor once held studios where U2 did some of its earliest recording.

• *Return to the main street and turn right into...*

⓷ Temple Bar Square

This square is the geographic heart of the Temple Bar district and a favorite haunt of street musicians. The quaint-looking pubs that front it are re-creations built in the early 2000s, when the area became so popular that pubs could sell the most expensive pints in town. Stand here on a Saturday night and you'll see how this party zone got its reputation for rowdy noise and drunken antics.

• *Walk along the square, then turn left up the narrow lane called Merchant's Arch, toward the river and* **Ha'Penny Bridge.** *Walk to the midway point of the bridge and celebrate the end of your South Dublin walk.*

You are very near the starting point of the second half of this walk, which will take us up O'Connell Street. To get there, continue across the river, turn right, and walk to the O'Connell Bridge via the wooden riverside Millennial Walkway.

PART 2: O'CONNELL STREET AND IRISH HEROES

This part of our Dublin walk features a series of sights and monuments recalling Ireland's long fight for independence. It's a straight line through the heart of North Dublin from the O'Connell Bridge up O'Connell Street to the Garden of Remembrance, a memorial park dedicated to the "terrible beauty" of this freedom-loving island.

❶ O'Connell Bridge

This bridge—actually wider than it is long—spans the River Liffey, which historically has divided the wealthy, cultivated south side

of town from the working-class north side. While there's plenty of culture on the north bank, even today the suburbs (a couple of miles north of the Liffey) are considered rougher and less safe. Dubliners joke that "north siders" are known as "the accused," while "south siders" are addressed as "your honor."

From the bridge, look downstream. Modern Dublin is developing before you. During the Celtic Tiger boom, the Irish subsidized and revitalized this formerly dreary quarter. While "the Tiger" died with the great recession of 2008-2009, Dublin's economy is booming again—as illustrated by the forest of cranes marking building sites in the east end of town and the massive redevelopment of Upper O'Connell Street (which you'll see later on this walk).

❷ O'Connell Street and Historic Highlights

Turn and look up the broad and grand O'Connell Street, leading from the O'Connell Bridge through the heart of north Dublin.

Since the 1740s, the street has been a 45-yard-wide promenade, and once the first O'Connell Bridge connected it to the Trinity College side of town in 1794, it became Dublin's main drag. It's named after Daniel O'Connell, Dublin's first Catholic mayor—we'll meet him in a moment.

These days, the city has made the street (worth ▲▲) more pedestrian-friendly, and a tram line runs alongside the median. Though filled with touristy fast-food joints and souvenir shops, O'Connell Street echoes with history. The median is dotted with statues remembering great figures from Ireland's past—particu-

DUBLIN

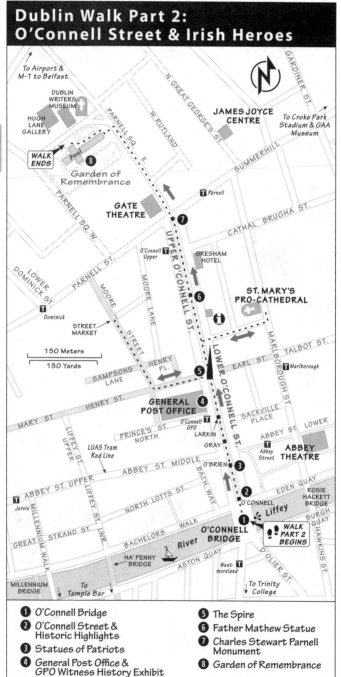

Dublin Walk Part 2:
O'Connell Street & Irish Heroes

To Airport &
M-1 to Belfast

DUBLIN WRITERS MUSEUM

HUGH LANE GALLERY

N. GREAT GEORGE'S ST.

GARDINER ST.

JAMES JOYCE CENTRE

To Croke Park Stadium & GAA Museum

PARNELL SQ. N.

WALK ENDS

Pool

8

Garden of Remembrance

W. RUTLAND

PARNELL SQ. E.

SUMMERHILL

GATE THEATRE

PARNELL SQ. W.

🚋 Parnell

CATHAL BRUGHA ST.

7

LOWER DOMINICK ST.

PARNELL ST.

🚋 Dominick

STREET MARKET

MOORE STREET

MOORE LANE

O'Connell Upper 🚋

UPPER O'CONNELL ST.

GRESHAM HOTEL

6

ST. MARY'S PRO-CATHEDRAL

ℹ️

150 Meters
150 Yards

SAMPSONS LANE

HENRY PL.

5

EARL ST.

LOWER O'CONNELL ST.

MARLBOROUGH ST.

TALBOT ST.

🚋 Marlborough

HENRY ST.

GENERAL POST OFFICE

4

O'Connell GPO 🚋

LARKIN

GRAY

SACKVILLE PLACE

ABBEY ST. LOWER

🚋 Abbey Street

ABBEY THEATRE

MARY ST.

PRINCE'S ST. NORTH

LUAS Tram Red Line

O'BRIEN

3

ABBEY ST. MIDDLE

BACH. WAY

2

O'CONNELL

EDEN QUAY

ROSIE HACKETT BRIDGE

LIFFEY ST. UPPER

ABBEY ST. UPPER

LIFFEY ST. LWR.

🚋 Jervis

NORTH LOTTS ST.

1

WALK PART 2 BEGINS

BURGH QUAY

HAWKINS ST.

GREAT STRAND ST.

MILLENNIUM WALK

BACHELORS WALK

O'CONNELL BRIDGE

Liffey

River

HA' PENNY BRIDGE

ASTON QUAY

West-moreland 🚋

D'OLIER ST.

MILLENNIUM BRIDGE

To Temple Bar

To Trinity College

1 O'Connell Bridge
2 O'Connell Street & Historic Highlights
3 Statues of Patriots
4 General Post Office & GPO Witness History Exhibit

5 The Spire
6 Father Mathew Statue
7 Charles Stewart Parnell Monument
8 Garden of Remembrance

larly the century (1830-1930) when Ireland rediscovered its roots and won its independence.

• *Now head north up O'Connell Street, walking on the wide, tree-lined median strip toward the spike in the sky. Along the way, you'll see statues honoring great Irishmen (starting with the man for whom the street is named).*

❸ Statues of Patriots

Daniel O'Connell (1775-1847) was known as the "Liberator" for founding the Catholic Association, a political group that demanded

Irish Catholic rights in the British Parliament. Having personally witnessed the violence of the French Revolution in 1789, O'Connell chose peaceful, legal means to achieve his ends. A charismatic speaker, he organized thousands of nonviolent protestors into "monster meetings," whose sheer size intimidated the British authorities. O'Connell went on to become the first Catholic mayor of Dublin (1841-1842). Below his statue (commissioned in 1880), Lady Ireland, chains broken around her feet, points to the great

emancipator (holding articles of emancipation). The many bullet holes date from the 1916 Easter Rising.

    William Smith O'Brien (1803-1864), the next statue up the street, was O'Connell's contemporary and the leader of the nationalist Young Ireland Movement. He was more willing to use force to achieve Irish self-determination. After a failed uprising in Tipperary, he was imprisoned and sentenced to death in 1848, but then exiled to Australia.

    Sir John Gray (1816-1875) was one of Daniel O'Connell's strongest supporters and advocated for the repeal of union with Britain. He was also responsible for bringing safe drinking water to Dublin, overcoming cholera and other waterborne diseases that had plagued the city.

    James Larkin (1876-1947), arms outstretched, was the founder of the Irish Transport and General Workers Union. His attempts to relieve tenement poverty through more humane work conditions earned him love from

the downtrodden and enmity from the one percent of his day. The general strike he called in 1913 is considered by many to be the first shot in the War of Independence. Larkin was arrested on this spot for trying to make a speech during the seven-month Dublin Lockout. A protest over that arrest degenerated into a riot, police brutality, and several fatalities.

• *On your left is the...*

❹ General Post Office (GPO)

This is not just any post office. It was from here that the nationalist activist Patrick Pearse read the Proclamation of Irish Independence in 1916, kicking off the

Easter Rising. On Easter Monday 1916, the building itself became the rebel headquarters and the scene of a bloody five-day siege—a kind of Irish Alamo. The post office was particularly strategic because it housed the telegraph nerve center for the entire country. Its pillars are still pockmarked with bullet holes. On the right as you enter, the engaging **GPO Witness History** exhibit brings the dramatic history of this important building to life (for details, see page 99).

• *At the intersection of O'Connell and Henry streets make like a drum major and marvel up at...*

❺ The Spire

There used to be a tall column at this intersection, crowned by a statue of the British hero of Trafalgar, Admiral Horatio Nelson.

It was blown up in 1966—the IRA's contribution to the local celebration of the Easter Rising's 50th anniversary. The spot is now occupied by a sculpture called the Spire: 398 feet of stainless steel. While it trumpets rejuvenation on its side of the river, it's a memorial to nothing and has no real meaning. Dubliners call it the tallest waste of €5 million in all of Europe. Its nickname? Take your pick: the Stiletto in the Ghetto, the Stiffy on the Liffey, the Pole in the Hole, or the Poker near the Croker (after nearby Croke Park). The "erection at the intersection" was built for the millennium, but Dub-

lin was only able to get it up in 2004. Before leaving, have fun standing close and looking way up.

• A few steps farther along is a statue of...

❻ Father Mathew

A leader of the temperance movement of the 1830s, Father Theobald Mathew was responsible, some historians claim, for enough Irish peasants staying sober to enable  Daniel O'Connell to organize them into a political force. By 1844, over half the adult population of Ireland had signed his total abstinence pledge. Then the onset of the Great Potato Famine diffused his efforts and sent thousands to their graves or onto emigration ships. Desperation drove Ireland back to whiskey.

• Over the next few years, the district ahead on the left will undergo a massive revitalization (if funding holds up). The fancy **Gresham Hotel** *(on the right), a good place for an elegant tea or beer, recalls travel to Dublin in the gilded Victorian age. Standing boldly at the top of O'Connell Street is the...*

❼ Charles Stewart Parnell Monument

Ringing the monument are the names of the four ancient provinces of Ireland and all 32 Irish counties (north and south, since this  was erected before Irish partition). The monument honors Charles Stewart Parnell (1846-1891), the member of parliament who nearly won Home Rule for Ireland in the 1880s (and who served time at Kilmainham Gaol for his nationalist activities). A Cambridge-educated Protestant of landed-gentry stock, Parnell envisioned a modern, free Irish nation of Catholics as a secular democracy. The Irish people, who remembered their grandparents' harsh evictions during the Great Potato Famine, came to love Parnell (despite his privileged birth) for his tireless work to secure fair rents and land tenure. Momentum seemed to be on his side. With the British prime minister of the time, William Gladstone, favoring a similar form of Home Rule, it looked as if Ireland was on its way toward independence as a Commonwealth nation, similar to Canada or Australia.

Then a scandal broke around Parnell and his mistress, the wife of another parliament member. The press—egged on by powerful

Catholic bishops (who didn't want a secular, free Irish state)—battered away at the scandal until finally Parnell was driven from office. Wracked with exhaustion and only in his mid-40s, Parnell died brokenhearted. (Sex scandals have a persistent way of shaping history.)

After that, Ireland became mired in the conflicts of the 20th century: an awkward independence (1921) featuring a divided island, a bloody civil war, and sectarian violence for decades afterward. Now, for just over 20 years, peace has prevailed on this troubled isle.

• *Continue uphill, straight up Parnell Square East. At the* **Gate Theatre** *(on the left), actors Orson Welles, Geraldine Fitzgerald, and James Mason had their professional stage debuts. One block up, on the left, is the...*

❽ Garden of Remembrance

Honoring the victims of the 1916 Easter Rising, this memorial garden marks the spot where the rebel leaders were held before being transferred to Kilmainham Gaol. The park was dedicated in 1966 on the 50th anniversary of the revolt that ultimately led to Irish independence. The bottom of the cross-shaped pool is a mosaic of Celtic weapons, symbolic of how the early Irish proclaimed peace by breaking their weapons and throwing them into a lake or river. In the statue (beyond the pool, under the flag), four

siblings morph into swans, referring to the "Children of Lir" of Irish mythology. W. B. Yeats' "Easter, 1916" poem describes the transformation: "a terrible beauty is born"—as independent Ireland enters a new, if uncertain, age. The Irish flag flies above: green for Catholics, orange for Protestants, and white for the hope that they can live together in peace.

One of modern Ireland's most stirring moments occurred here in May 2011, when Queen Elizabeth II made this the first stop on her historic visit to the Republic—the first by a reigning British monarch in 100 years. She laid a wreath at the statue under the Irish flag and bowed her head in silence out of respect for the Irish rebels who had fought and died trying to gain freedom from her United Kingdom. This was a hugely cathartic moment for both nations.

• *Your walk is over. The Dublin Writers Museum (see page 96) is just across the street. To get back to the center, just hop on your skateboard—it's downhill all the way to the river (or grab any tram from the Parnell Street stop—they all go to Trinity College).*

Sights in Dublin

For information on Dublin's City Hall as well as additional detail on many of the sights described below, see "Dublin City Walk," earlier, or download my free 🎧 audio tour.

SOUTH OF THE RIVER LIFFEY
Trinity College

Founded in 1592 by Queen Elizabeth I to establish a Protestant way of thinking about God, Trinity has long been Ireland's most prestigious college. Originally, the student body was limited to rich Protestant men. Women were admitted in 1903, and Catholics—though allowed entrance to the school much earlier—were given formal permission by the Catholic Church to study at Trinity in the 1970s (before that they risked mortal sin). Today, half of Trinity's 12,500 students are women, and 70 percent are culturally Catholic (although only about 20 percent of Irish youth are church-going). Notice that on campus, the official blue-and-white signs are bilingual—and the Irish comes first.

There are two worthwhile experiences here: a half-hour tour of the campus led by students, and the Book of Kells exhibit in the library.

▲▲Trinity College Campus Tour

Trinity students lead 30-minute tours of their campus (look just inside the college gate for posted departure times and students selling tickets for Authenticity Tours). You'll get a rundown of the mostly Georgian architecture, a peek at student life past and present, and the enjoyable company of your guide—a witty college kid.

Cost and Hours: €6—or €4 if you have a Book of Kells ticket, purchase tour tickets on the spot at campus gate off Dame Street; tours run daily 9:15-16:00, off-season weekends only, no tours Dec-Jan; tours depart roughly every 30 min-  utes, weather permitting, www.tcd.ie/visitors/tours.

▲▲▲Book of Kells in the Trinity Old Library

The Book of Kells—a 1,200-year-old manuscript of the four gospels—was elaborately inked and meticulously illustrated by faithful monks. Combining Christian symbols and pagan styles, it's a snapshot of medieval Ireland in transition. Arguably the finest piece of art from what is generally called the Dark Ages, the Book of Kells

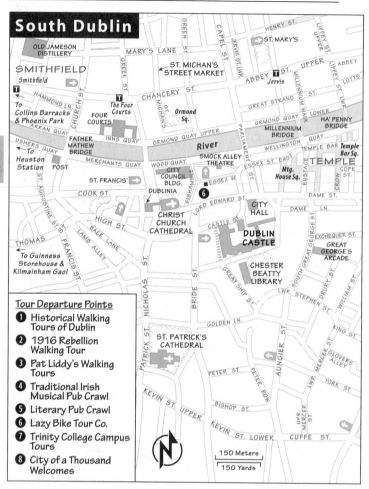

South Dublin

Tour Departure Points
1. Historical Walking Tours of Dublin
2. 1916 Rebellion Walking Tour
3. Pat Liddy's Walking Tours
4. Traditional Irish Musical Pub Crawl
5. Literary Pub Crawl
6. Lazy Bike Tour Co.
7. Trinity College Campus Tours
8. City of a Thousand Welcomes

150 Meters
150 Yards

shows that monastic life in this far fringe of Europe was far from dark.

Cost and Hours: €15, buy timed-entry ticket online in advance to avoid the line; Mon-Sat 8:30-17:00, Sun from 9:30; Oct-April Mon-Sat 9:30-17:00, Sun 12:00-16:30; audioguide—€5, tel. 01/896-2320, www.tcd.ie/visitors/book-of-kells.

Crowd Control: Without an advance ticket you'll likely wait in a long ticket-buying line (worst midday, roughly 10:00-15:00—especially when cruise ships are in). Skip it by heading to the Nassau Street/Arts Building entry to campus, where it's easy to book tickets—even same day, if available—from a pair of ticket machines in the lobby hallway.

Background: The Book of Kells was a labor of love created by dedicated Irish monks cloistered on the remote Scottish island of

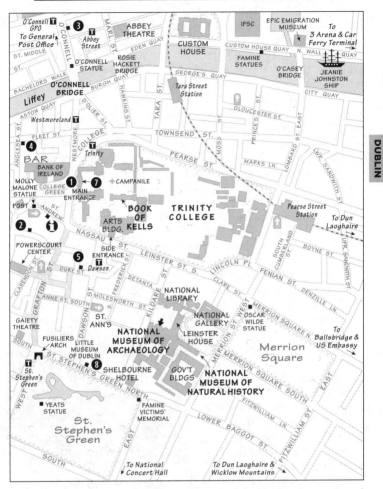

Iona. They slaughtered 185 calves, soaked the skins in lime, scraped off the hair, and dried the skins into a cream-colored writing surface called vellum. Only then could the tonsured monks pick up their swan-quill pens and get to work.

The project may have been underway in 806 when Vikings savagely pillaged and burned Iona, killing 68 monks. The survivors fled to the Abbey of Kells (near Dublin). Scholars debate exactly where the book was produced: It could have been made entirely at Iona or at Kells, or started in Iona and finished at Kells.

For eight centuries, the glorious gospel sat regally atop the high altar of the church at Kells, where the priest would read from it during special Masses. In 1654, as Cromwell's puritanical rule settled in, the book was smuggled to Dublin for safety. Here at Trinity College, it was first displayed to the public in the mid-

1800s. In 1953, the book got its current covers and was bound into four separate volumes.

Visiting the Book of Kells: Your visit has three stages: 1) an exhibit on the making of the Book of Kells, including poster-sized reproductions of its pages (your best look at the book's detail); 2) the Treasury, a darkened room containing the Book of Kells itself and other, less ornate contemporaneous volumes; and, upstairs, 3) the Old Library (called the Long Room), containing a precious collection of 16th- to 18th-century books and historical objects.

The Exhibit: The Turning Darkness into Light exhibit, with a one-way route, puts the illuminated manuscript in its historical and cultural context. This is important as it prepares you to see the original book and other precious manuscripts in the treasury. Make a point to spend some time in this exhibit before reaching the actual Book of Kells.

Especially interesting are the two continuously running video clips that show the ancient art of bookbinding and the exacting care that went into transcribing the monk-uscripts. They vividly depict the skill and patience needed for the monks' work.

The Book: The Book of Kells contains the four gospels of the Bible (two are on display at any given time). Altogether, the manuscript is 680 pages long (or 340 "folios," the equivalent of one sheet, front and back). The Latin calligraphy—all in capital letters—follows ruled lines, forming neat horizontal bars across the page. Sentences end with a "period" of three dots.

The text is elaborately decorated—of the hundreds of pages, only two are without illustration. Each gospel begins with a full-page depiction of an Evangelist and his symbol: Matthew (angel), Mark (lion), Luke (ox), and John (eagle). The apostles pose stiffly, like Byzantine-style icons, with almond-shaped eyes and symmetrically creased robes. Squint at the amazing detail. The true beauty lies in the intricate designs that surround the figures.

The colorful book employs blue, purple, red, pink, green, and yellow pigments—but no gold leaf. Letters and borders are braided together. On most pages, the initial letters are big and flowery, like in a children's fairy-tale book.

Notice how the playful monks might cross a "t" with a fish, form an "h" from a spindly-legged man, or make an "e" out of a coiled snake. Animals crouch between sentences. It's a jungle of intricate designs, inhabited by tiny creatures both real and fanciful.

Scholars think three main artists created the book: the "goldsmith" (who did the filigree-style designs), the "illustrator" (who specialized in animals and grotesques), and the "portrait painter" (who did the Evangelists and Mary).

The Old Library: The Long Room, the 200-foot-long main chamber of the Old Library (from 1732), is stacked to its towering ceiling with 200,000 books. Among the displays here, you'll find a rare first folio of Shakespeare plays and one of a dozen surviving original copies of the **1916 Proclamation of the Irish Republic.** Patrick Pearse read out its words at Dublin's General Post Office on April 24, 1916, starting the Easter Rising that led to Irish independence. Notice the inclusive opening phrase ("Irishmen and Irishwomen") and the seven signatories (each of whom was later executed).

Another national icon is nearby: the oldest surviving **Irish harp,** from the 15th century (while often called the Brian Boru harp, it was crafted 400 years after the death of this Irish king). The brass pins on its oak and willow frame once held 29 strings. In Celtic days, poets—highly influential with kings and druid priests—wandered the land, uniting the people with songs and stories. The harp's inspirational effect on Gaelic culture was so strong that Queen Elizabeth I (1558-1603) ordered Irish harpists to be hung and their instruments smashed. Even today, the love of music here is so intense that Ireland is the only country with a musical instrument as its national symbol. You'll see this harp's likeness on the back of Irish euro coins, on government documents, and on every pint of Guinness.

▲▲▲National Museum of Archaeology

Showing off the treasures of Ireland from the Stone Age to modern times, this branch of the National Museum is itself a national treasure. The soggy marshes and peat bogs of Ireland have proven perfect for preserving old objects. You'll see 4,000-year-old gold jewelry, 2,000-year-old bog mummies, 1,000-year-old Viking swords, and the collection's superstar—the exquisitely wrought Tara Brooch. Visit here to get an introduction to the rest of Ireland's historic attractions: You'll find a reconstructed passage tomb like Newgrange, Celtic art like the Book of Kells, Viking objects from Dublin, a model of the Hill of Tara, and a sacred cross from the Cong Abbey. Hit the highlights of my tour, then browse the exhibits at will, all well-described throughout. For

DUBLIN

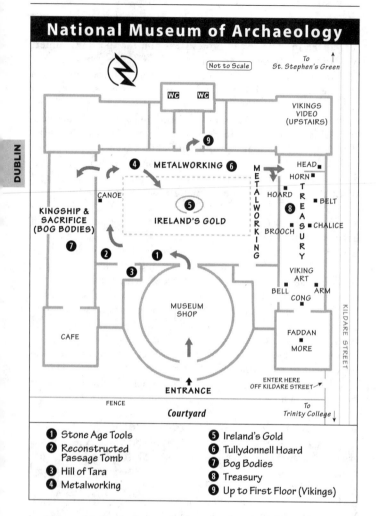

National Museum of Archaeology

To St. Stephen's Green

WC WC

VIKINGS VIDEO (UPSTAIRS)

❾

❹ METALWORKING ❻

CANOE

M E T A L W O R K I N G

HEAD
HORN
HOARD
BROOCH

T R E A S U R Y

BELT
CHALICE

KINGSHIP & SACRIFICE (BOG BODIES)

❼

❺ IRELAND'S GOLD

❽

❷ ❶

❸

MUSEUM SHOP

VIKING ART
BELL   ARM
CONG

CAFE

FADDAN MORE

KILDARE STREET

ENTER HERE OFF KILDARE STREET

ENTRANCE

FENCE   *Courtyard*   *To Trinity College*

❶ Stone Age Tools
❷ Reconstructed Passage Tomb
❸ Hill of Tara
❹ Metalworking
❺ Ireland's Gold
❻ Tullydonnell Hoard
❼ Bog Bodies
❽ Treasury
❾ Up to First Floor (Vikings)

background information on Irish art and archaeology, see the Ireland: Past & Present chapter.

Cost and Hours: Free, Sun-Mon 13:00-17:00, Tue-Sat 10:00-17:00, free audioguide download covers the Treasury room, good café, between Trinity College and St. Stephen's Green on Kildare Street, tel. 01/677-7444, www.museum.ie.

◗ Self-Guided Tour

• *Follow this tour with the help of this book's map. On the ground floor, enter the main hall and get oriented: In the center (down four steps, in the little square room) are displays of prehistoric gold jewelry. To the left are the bog bodies, to the right is the Treasury room, and upstairs is the Viking world. Let's start at the very beginning.*

❶ Stone Age Tools: Glass cases hold flint and stone ax-heads and arrowheads (7,000 BC). Ireland's first inhabitants—hunters and fishers who came from Scotland—used these tools. These early people also left behind standing stones (dolmens) and passage tombs.

❷ Reconstructed Passage Tomb: At the corner of the room, you'll see a typical tomb circa 3,000 BC—a mound-shaped, heavy stone structure, covered with smaller rocks, with a passage leading into a central burial chamber where the deceased's ashes were interred. The vast passage tombs at Newgrange and Knowth are similar but many times bigger.

• *In the smaller room to the left of the passage tomb is a gallery devoted to...*

❸ The Hill of Tara: The famous passage-tomb burial site at Tara, known as the Mound of the Hostages, was used for more than 1,500 years as a place to inter human remains. The cases in this side gallery display some of the many exceptional Neolithic and Bronze Age finds uncovered at the site.

Over the millennia, the mound became the very symbol of Irish heritage. This is where Ireland's kings claimed their power, where St. Patrick preached his deal-clinching sermon, and where, in 1843, Daniel O'Connell rallied Irish patriots to demand their independence from Britain (see illustration in the small poster on the left wall).

• *Back in the big room, walk along the length of a 50-foot-long dugout canoe, from centuries before Christ and pickled in a bog. Then turn right.*

❹ The Evolution of Metalworking: Around 2500 BC, Ireland discovered how to make metal—mining ore, smelting it in furnaces, and casting or hammering it into shapes. The rest is prehistory. You'll travel through the Bronze Age (ax-heads from 2000 BC) and Iron Age (500 BC) as you examine assorted spears, shields, swords, and war horns. The cauldrons made for everyday cooking were also used ceremonially to prepare elaborate ritual feasts for friends and symbolic offerings for the gods.

• *The most impressive metal objects are four steps down in the center of the hall. Visit the square room at the lowest level.*

❺ Ireland's Gold: Ireland had only modest gold deposits, mainly gathered by prehistoric people panning for small nuggets and dust in the rivers. But the jewelry they left, some of it more than 4,000 years old, is exquisite. The earliest fashion choice was a broad necklace hammered flat (a *lunula*, so called for its crescent-moon shape). This might

DUBLIN

be worn with accompanying earrings and sun-disc brooches. The **Gleninsheen Collar** (c. 700 BC) was found in 1932 by a farmer in one of the limestone crevices characteristic of the Burren region of County Clare. It's thought that this valuable status symbol was hidden there during a time of conflict, then forgotten (or its owner killed)—if it had been meant as an offering to a pagan god it more likely would have been left in a body of water (the portal to the underworld).

Later Bronze Age **jewelry** was cast from clay molds into bracelets and unique "dress fasteners" that you'd slip into buttonholes to secure a cloak. Some of these gold objects may have been gifts to fertility gods, offered by burying them in marshy bogs.

A small glass case shows off the ❻ **Tullydonnell Hoard,** discovered in Donegal in 2018. The four heavy gold rings, from about 1000 BC, weigh about two pounds each and are very plain. They likely were just a way to store one's wealth in the days before someone thought of coins and banks.

• *Walk past the long dugout canoe again to enter a room with...*

❼ **Bog Bodies:** When the Celts arrived in Ireland (c. 500 BC-AD 500), they brought with them a mysterious practice: They brutally murdered sacrificial slaves or prisoners and buried them in bogs. Four bodies (each in its own tiny theater with a description outside)—shriveled and leathery, but remarkably preserved—have been dug up from around the Celtic world.

Clonycavan Man is from Ireland. One summer day around 200 BC, this twenty-something man was hacked to death with an ax and disemboweled. In his time, he stood 5'9" and had a Mohawk-style haircut, poofed up with pine-resin hair product imported from France. Today you can still see traces of his hair. Only his upper body survived; the lower part may have been lost in the threshing machine that unearthed him in 2003.

Why were these people killed? It appears to have been a form of ritual human sacrifice of high-status people. Some may have been enemy chiefs or political rivals. The sacrifices could have been offerings to the gods to ensure rich harvests and good luck. Other items (now on display) were buried along with them—gold bracelets, royal cloaks, finely wrought cauldrons, and leather garments.

• *Head across the main room again, and beyond the far wall, enter the...*

❽ **Treasury:** Irish metalworking is legendary, and this room holds 1,500 years of exquisite treasures. Working from one end of the long room to the other, you'll journey from the world of the pagan Celts to the coming of Christianity, explore the stylistic impact of the Viking invasions (9th-12th century), and consider the resurgence of ecclesiastical metalworking (11th-12th century).

Pagan Era Art: The carved stone head of a mysterious pagan god greets you (#19, circa AD 100). The god's three faces express the different aspects of his stony personality. This abstract style—typical of Celtic art—would be at home in a modern art museum. A bronze horn (#17, first century BC) is the kind of curved war trumpet that Celts blasted to freak out the Roman legions on the Continent (the Romans never invaded Ireland). The fine objects of the Broighter Hoard (#15, first century BC) include a king's golden collar decorated in textbook Celtic style, with interlaced vines inhabited by stylized faces. The tiny boat was an offering to the sea god. The coconut-shell-shaped bowl symbolized a cauldron. By custom, the cauldron held food as a constant offering to Danu, the Celtic mother goddess, whose mythical palace was at Brú na Bóinne.

DUBLIN

Early Christian Objects: Christianity officially entered Ireland in the fifth century (when St. Patrick converted the pagan king), but Celtic legends and art continued well into the Christian era. You'll see various crosses, shrines (portable reliquaries containing holy relics), and chalices decorated with Celtic motifs. The Belt Shrine (#32)—a circular metal casing that held a saint's leather belt—was thought to have magical properties. When placed around someone's waist, it could heal the wearer or force him or her to tell the truth.

The Ardagh Chalice (#30) and the nearby Silver Paten (#31) were used during Communion to hold blessed wine and bread. Get close to admire the elaborate workmanship. The main bowl of the chalice is gilded bronze, with a contrasting band of intricately patterned gold filigree. It's studded with colorful glass, amber, and enamels. Mirrors below the display case show that even the underside of the chalice was decorated. When the priest grabbed the chalice by its two handles and tipped it to his lips, the base could be admired by God.

Tara Brooch: A wealthy eighth-century Celtic man fastened his cloak at the shoulder with this elaborate ring-shaped brooch (#29), its seven-inch stickpin tilted rakishly upward. Made of cast and gilded silver, it's ornamented with fine, exquisitely filigreed gold panels and studded with amber, enamel, and colored glass. The motifs include Celtic spirals, snakes, and stylized faces, but the symbolism is neither overtly pagan nor Christian—it's art for art's sake. Despite its name, the brooch probably has no connection to the Hill of Tara. In display cases nearby, you'll see other similar (but less impressive) brooches from the same period—some iron, some bronze, and one in pure gold. In the designs of this elaborate metalwork you can see the Celtic aesthetics that inspired the illuminations of the Book of Kells.

Viking Art Styles: Vikings invaded Dublin around AD 800. As Viking did, they raped and pillaged. But they also opened Ireland to a vast and cosmopolitan trading empire, from which they imported hordes of silver (see the display case of ingots). Viking influence shows up in the decorative style of reliquaries like the Lismore Crozier (#43, in the shape of a bishop's ceremonial shepherd's crook) and the Shrine of St. Lachtin's Arm (raised in an Irish-power salute). The impressive Bell of St. Patrick (#24) was supposedly owned by Ireland's patron saint. After his death, it was encased within a beautifully worked shrine (displayed above) and kept safe by a single family, who passed it down from generation to generation for 800 years.

Cross of Cong: "By this cross is covered the cross on which the Creator of the world suffered." Running along the sides of the cross (#44), a Latin inscription tells us that it once held a sacred relic, a tiny splinter of the True Cross on which Jesus was crucified. That piece of wood (now lost) had been given in 1123 to the Irish high king, who commissioned this reliquary to preserve the splinter (it would have been placed right in the center, visible through the large piece of rock crystal). Every Christmas and Easter, the cross was fitted onto a staff and paraded through the abbey at Cong, then placed on the altar for High Mass. The extraordinarily detailed decoration features gold filigree interspersed with colored glass, enamel, and (now missing) precious stones. Though fully Christian, the cross has Celtic-style filigree patterning and Viking-style animal heads (notice how they grip the cross in their jaws).

Before leaving the Treasury, enter the room behind the Cross of Cong and check out the **Faddan More Psalter**—a (pretty beat-up) manuscript of the Book of Psalms from the same era as the Book of Kells.

• *Now head up to the first floor to the Viking world. Start in the long hall directly above the Treasury, with the informative 25-minute video on the Viking influence on Irish culture.*

❾ **Viking Ireland** (c. 800-1150): Dublin was born as a Viking town. Sometime after 795, Scandinavian warriors rowed their longships up the River Liffey and made camp on the south bank, around the location of today's Dublin Castle and Christ Church Cathedral. Over the next two centuries, they built "Dubh linn" ("black pool" in Irish) into an important trading post, slave market, metalworking center, and the first true city in Ireland. (See a model of Dublin showing a recently excavated area near Kilmainham Gaol.)

The state-of-the-art Viking boats worked equally well in the open ocean and shallow rivers, and were perfect for stealth invasions and far-ranging trading. Soon, provincial Dublin was connected with the wider world—Scotland, England, northern Europe, even Asia. The museum's displays of swords and spears make it clear that, yes, the Vikings were fierce warriors. But you'll also see that they were respected merchants (standardized weights and coins), herders and craftsmen (leather shoes and bags), fashion-conscious (bone combs and jewelry), fun-loving (board games), and literate (runic alphabet). What you won't see are horned helmets, which, despite the stereotype, were not Viking. By 1050, the pagan Vikings had intermarried with the locals, become Christian, and were melting into Irish society.

• *With time and interest, you could explore the...*

Rest of the Museum: Part of the ground floor is dedicated to medieval Ireland—daily life (ploughs, cauldrons), trade (coins, pottery), and religion (crucifixes and saints). Up one more flight, the Egyptian room has coffins, *shabtis,* and canopic jars—but no mummies.

Other National Museums South of Trinity College

Adjacent to the archaeology branch are these other major museums. Also nearby is **Leinster House.** Once the Duke of Leinster's home, it now hosts the Irish Dáil (parliament) and Seanad (senate), which meet here 90 days each year.

▲National Gallery of Ireland

While not as extensive as the national gallery in London, the collections here are well worth your time. The beautifully renovated museum boasts an impressive range of works by European masters and displays the works of top Irish painters, including Jack B. Yeats (brother of the famous poet).

Cost and Hours: Free, Sun-Mon 11:00-17:30, Tue-Sat 9:15-17:30, Thu until 20:30, Merrion Square West, tel. 01/661-5133, www.nationalgallery.ie.

Tours: Take advantage of the free audioguide as well as free 45-minute guided tours (usually Sat-Sun—check online or at main information desk for times).

Visiting the Museum: Walk through the series of rooms on the ground floor devoted to Irish painting and get to know artists you may not have heard of before. Visit the National Portrait Gallery on the mezzanine level for an insight into the great personalities of Ireland. European masterworks are on the top floor, including a rare Vermeer (one of only 30-some known works by the Dutch artist), a classic Caravaggio (master of chiaroscuro and dramatic lighting), a Monet riverscape, and an early Cubist Picasso still life.

Perhaps the most iconic of all the Irish art in this museum

DUBLIN

is the melodramatic (and huge) c. 1854 depiction of the *Marriage of Strongbow and Aoife* by Daniel Maclise. It captures the chaotic union of Norman and Irish interests that signaled the start of English domination of Ireland 850 years ago. Notice how the defeated Irish writhe and lament in the bright light of the foreground, while the scheming Norman warlords skulk in the dimly lit middle ground. The ruins of conquered Waterford smolder at the back.

National Museum of Natural History

Nicknamed "the dead zoo" by Dubliners, this cramped collection of stuffed exotic animals comes across like the locker room on Noah's Ark. But if you're into beaks, bones, bugs, and boars, this Victorian relic is for you. Standing tall above a sea of taxidermy, the regal skeleton of a giant Irish elk from the last Ice Age dwarfs a modern moose.

Cost and Hours: Free, Sun-Mon 13:00-17:00, Tue-Sat 10:00-17:00, Merrion Square West, tel. 01/677-7444, www.museum.ie.

National Library of Ireland

Literature holds a lofty place in the Irish psyche. To feel the pulse of Ireland's most influential poet, visit the W. B. Yeats exhibit in the library basement. The artifacts flesh out the very human passions of this poet and playwright, with samples of his handwritten manuscripts and surprisingly interesting mini documentaries of the times he lived in. Upstairs, you can get help making use of library records to trace your genealogy. Take a moment to view the gorgeous baby-blue upstairs reading room under the expansive dome.

Cost and Hours: Free, Mon-Wed 9:30-19:30, Thu-Sat until 16:30, Sun 13:00-17:00, café, tel. 01/603-0200, 2 Kildare Street, www.nli.ie.

Merrion Square and Nearby
Merrion Square

Laid out in 1762, this square just east of the National Gallery is ringed by elegant Georgian houses decorated with fine doors—a Dublin trademark. (If you're inspired by the ornate knobs and knockers, there's a shop by that name on nearby Nassau Street.) The park, once the exclusive domain of the residents (among them, Daniel O'Connell at #58 and W. B. Yeats at #82), is now a delightful public escape and ideal for a picnic. To learn what "snogging" is, walk through the park on a sunny day, when it's full of smooching lovers. Oscar Wilde, lounging wittily on a boulder on the corner nearest the

town center and surrounded by his clever quotes, provides a fun photo op (see photo on page 98).

Little Museum of Dublin

Facing St. Stephen's Green, this pint-sized museum, just five rooms in a Georgian mansion from 1776, is a creative labor of love. Volunteers have covered its walls with historic bits and pieces of Dublin history—all donated by locals. This museum also sponsors the City of a Thousand Welcomes "Meet a Dubliner" program (see page 39).

Cost and Hours: €10 includes required 30-minute tour, daily 9:30-17:00, tours depart on the hour 10:00-17:00, 15 St. Stephen's Green, tel. 01/661-1000, www.littlemuseum.ie.

Visiting the Museum: Your visit starts with an entertaining 30-minute talk mixing modern Dublin history and pop culture as illustrated in two rooms. Then you're free to wander the remaining rooms (including one on Irish rock 'n' roll for U2 fans). Memorabilia ranges from historic letters written by Irish nationalists Éamon de Valera and Michael Collins to mementos of John F. Kennedy's 1963 Dublin visit and Muhammad Ali's 1972 fight here.

Dublin Castle and Nearby

▲Dublin Castle

Built on the spot of the first Viking fortress, this castle was the seat of English rule in Ireland for 700 years. Located where the Poddle and Liffey rivers flowed together, making a black pool (*dubh linn* in Irish), Dublin Castle was the official residence of the viceroy who implemented the will of British royalty. What you see today is the stately Georgian version, built in the late 17th and  18th centuries on top of the old medieval castle (little of which can still be recognized beyond one remaining round turret). In this stirring setting, the Brits handed power over to Michael Collins and the Irish in 1922, as stipulated by the Anglo-Irish Treaty. Today, the castle is used for fancy state and charity functions, and for presidential inaugurations.

Cost and Hours: Visiting the courtyard is free, €12 for one-hour guided tour, €8 to visit on your own (state apartments only); daily 9:45-16:45, tours depart every 30 minutes, sporadically closed for private events, tickets sold in courtyard under portico opposite clock tower, tel. 01/645-8813, www.dublincastle.ie.

Visiting the Castle: Standing in the courtyard, you can imagine the ugliness of the British-Irish situation. Notice the statue of justice above the gate—pointedly without her blindfold and admiring her sword. As Dubliners say, "There she stands, above her station, with her face to the palace and her arse to the nation."

The fancy interior offers a sedate room-by-room walk through the lavish state apartments of this most English of Irish palaces. The tour also includes a look at the foundations of the old English tower (from 1204) as well as original Viking defenses, and the best remaining chunk of the 13th-century town wall.

▲▲Chester Beatty Library

This library—located in the gardens of Dublin Castle (follow the signs)—is an exquisite, delightfully displayed collection of rare ancient manuscripts and beautifully illustrated books from around the world, plus a few odd curios. These treasures were bequeathed by Alfred Chester Beatty (1875-1968), a rich American mining magnate who traveled widely, collected 66,000 objects assiduously, and retired in Ireland.

Cost and Hours: Free; Mon-Fri 10:00-17:00, Sat from 11:00, Sun from 13:00; tel. 01/407-0750, www.cbl.ie.

◐ Self-Guided Tour: Start on the ground floor, with a 10-minute film about Beatty. Then head upstairs to the second floor to see the treasures he left to his adopted country. Note that exhibits often rotate, so they may not be on display in the order outlined here.

Sacred Traditions Gallery: This space is dedicated to sacred texts, illuminated manuscripts, and miniature paintings from around the world. The doors swing open, and you're greeted by a video highlighting a diverse array of religious rites—a Christian wedding, Muslims kneeling for prayer, whirling dervishes, and so on.

• *Tour the floor clockwise, starting with Christian texts on the left side of the room. There you'll find several glass cases containing...*

Ancient Bible Fragments: In the 1930s, Beatty acquired these 1,800-year-old manuscripts, which had recently been unearthed in Egypt. The Indiana Jones-like discovery instantly bumped scholars' knowledge of the early Bible up a notch. There were Old Testament books, New Testament books, and—rarest of all—the Letters of Paul. Written in Greek on papyrus more than a century before previously known documents, these are some of the oldest versions of these texts in existence. Unlike most early Christian texts, the manuscripts were not rolled up in a scroll but bound in a book form called a "codex." On display you may see pages from a third-century Gospel of Luke or the Gospel of John (c. AD 150-200). Jesus died around AD 33, and his words weren't recorded until decades later. Most early manuscripts date from the fourth century, so these pages are about as close to the source as you can get.

Letters (Epistles) of Paul: The Beatty has 112 pages of Saint Paul's collected letters (AD 180-200). Paul, a Roman citizen (c. AD 5-67; see Albrecht Dürer's engraving of the saint), was the apostle most responsible for spreading Christianity beyond Palestine. Originally, Paul reviled Christians. But after a mystical experience, he went on to travel the known world, preaching the Good News in sophisticated Athens and the greatest city in the world, Rome, where he died a martyr to the cause. Along the way, he kept in touch with Christian congregations in cities like Corinth, Ephesus, and Rome with these letters.

Continuing up the left side of the room, you'll find gloriously illustrated medieval Bibles and prayer books, including an intricate, colorful, gold-speckled Book of Hours (1408).

• *Turn the corner into the center of the room to find the sacred texts of...*

Islam: Muslims believe that the angel Gabriel visited Muhammad (c. 570-632), instructing him to write down his heavenly visions in a book—the Quran. You'll see Qurans with elaborate calligraphy, such as one made in Baghdad in 1001. Nearby are other sacred Islamic texts, some beautifully illustrated, where you may find the rare illuminated manuscript of the "Life of the Prophet" (c. 1595), produced in Istanbul for an Ottoman sultan.

• *On the right side of the room, you enter the world of...*

East Asian Religions: Statues of Gautama Buddha (c. 563-483 BC) and Chinese Buddhist scrolls attest to the pervasive influence of this wise man. Buddha was born in India, but his philosophy spread to China, Japan, and Tibet (see the mandalas). Continuing clockwise, you'll reach the writings from India, the land of a million gods—and the cradle of Buddhism, Hinduism, Sikhism, and Jainism.

• *Your visit continues downstairs on the first floor, in the gallery devoted to the...*

Arts of the Book: The focus here is on the many forms a "book" can take—from the earliest clay tablets and papyrus scrolls, to parchment scrolls and bound codexes, to medieval monks' wondrous illustrations, to the advent of printing and bookbinding, to the dawn of the 21st century and the digital age.

• *Tour the floor clockwise. Immediately to the left, find a glass case containing...*

Egyptian and Other Ancient Writings: A hieroglyph-covered papyrus scroll from the Book of the Dead (c. 300 BC) depicts a pharaoh on his throne (left) presiding over a soul's judgment in the afterlife. The jackal-headed god Anubis (center-right) holds a scale, weighing the heart of a dead woman to see if it's light enough for her to level up to the next phase of eternity. Nearby (in a freestanding glass case, near the bottom) are a few small cuneiform tablets and cylinder seals from as far back as 2,700 BC. These ob-

DUBLIN

Modern Ireland's Turbulent Birth

Imagine if our American patriot ancestors had fought both our Revolutionary War and our Civil War back to back—over a span of seven chaotic years—and then appreciate the remarkable resilience of the Irish people. Here's a summary of what happened when.

Easter Rising, 1916: A nationalist militia called the Volunteers (led by **Patrick Pearse**) and the socialist Irish Citizen Army (led by **James Connolly**) join forces in the Easter Rising, a week-long rebellion against British rule that is quickly defeated. The uprising is unpopular with most Irish, who are unhappy with the destruction in Dublin and preoccupied with the "Great War" on the Continent. But when 16 rebel leaders (including Pearse and Connolly) are executed, Irish public opinion reverses as sympathy grows for the martyrs and the cause of Irish independence.

Two important rebel leaders escape execution. Brooklyn-born **Éamon de Valera** is spared because of his American passport (the British don't want to anger a potential WWI ally). **Michael Collins,** a low-ranking rebel officer who fought in the Rising at the General Post Office, refines urban guerrilla-warfare strategies in prison, and then blossoms after his release as the rebels' military and intelligence leader in the power vacuum that followed the executions.

General Election, 1918: World War I ends and a general election is held in Ireland (the first in which women can vote). Promising to withdraw from the British Parliament and declare an Irish republic, the nationalist **Sinn Féin** party wins 73 out of 79 seats. Only 4 of 32 counties vote to maintain the Union with Britain (all 4 lie in today's Northern Ireland). Rather than take their seats in London, Sinn Féin representatives abstain from participating in a government they see as foreign occupiers.

War of Independence, 1919: On January 19, the abstaining Sinn Féin members set up a rebel government in Dublin called Dáil

jects from ancient Sumeria (modern-day Iraq) are older than the pyramids and represent the very birth of writing.

• *Continue up the left side of the room, perusing displays on...*

Printing, Illustrating, and Bookbinding: The printing press with movable type was perfected by Johannes Gutenberg in Germany around 1450. The printed sheets were folded, sewn together, and wrapped in a cover. With the engraving process, beautiful il-

Éireann. On the same day, the first shots of the Irish War of Independence are fired as rebels begin ambushing police barracks, which are seen as an extension of British rule. De Valera is elected by the Dáil to lead the rebels, with Collins as his deputy. Collins' web of spies infiltrates British intelligence at Dublin Castle. The Volunteers rename themselves the **Irish Republican Army;** meanwhile the British beef up their military presence in Ireland by sending in tough WWI vets, the Black and Tans. A bloody and very personal war ensues.

Anglo-Irish Treaty, 1921: Having endured the slaughter of World War I, the British tire of the extended bloodshed in Ireland and begin negotiations with the rebels. De Valera leads rebel negotiations, but then entrusts them to Collins (a clever politician, De Valera sees that whoever signs a treaty will be blamed for its compromises). Understanding the tricky position he's in, Collins signs the Anglo-Irish Treaty in December 1921, lamenting that in doing so he has signed his "own death warrant."

The Dáil narrowly ratifies the treaty, which ends the war and allows for the establishment of an independent dominion, the Irish Free State. But Collins' followers are unable to convince De Valera's supporters that the treaty's compromises are a stepping-stone to later full independence. De Valera and his anti-treaty disciples resign in protest. **Arthur Griffith,** founder of Sinn Féin, assumes the presidential post.

Irish Civil War, 1922-1923: In June 1922, the anti-treaty forces, holed up in the Four Courts building in Dublin, are fired upon by Collins and his pro-treaty forces—thus igniting the Irish Civil War. The British want the treaty to stand and even supply Collins with cannons, meanwhile threatening to reenter Ireland if the anti-treaty forces aren't put down.

In August 1922, Griffith dies of stress-induced illness, and Collins is assassinated 10 days later. Nevertheless, the pro-treaty forces prevail, as they are backed by popular opinion and better (British-supplied) military equipment. By April 1923, the remaining IRA forces dump (or stash) their arms, ending the civil war... but many bitter IRA vets vow to carry on the fight. De Valera distances himself from the IRA and becomes the dominant Irish political leader for the next 40 years.

lustrations could also be reproduced on a mass scale. Until the 20th century, it was common for a book buyer to acquire the printed sheets and then select a lavish custom-made cover.

• *Turn the corner to the center of the room.*

Islamic World: These are secular books—science textbooks and poetry—many from the rich Persian culture (modern-day Iran). Some are richly illustrated with elaborate calligraphy. While

Islam avoids representations of living things, as you can see, that restriction doesn't apply to nonreligious texts.
• *Continue to the right side of the room.*

Far East: Besides albums and scrolls, you might see eye-catching Japanese woodblock prints, ornate Chinese snuff bottles, rhino-horn cups, and the silk dragon robes of Chinese emperors of the Qing dynasty (1644-1911). The Qianlong Emperor (r. 1736-1795)—a poet and arts patron—welcomed European Jesuits to his court and commissioned a huge collection of books, including some carved from jade.

Dublin's Cathedrals Area

Because of Dublin's English past (particularly Henry VIII's Reformation, and the dissolution of the Catholic monasteries in both Ireland and England in 1539), the city's top two churches are no longer Catholic. Christ Church Cathedral and nearby St. Patrick's Cathedral are both Church of Ireland (Anglican). In the late 19th century, the cathedrals underwent extensive restoration. The rich Guinness brewery family paid to try to make St. Patrick's Cathedral outshine Christ Church—whose patrons were a rival family of wealthy whiskey barons.

▲Christ Church Cathedral

Occupying the same site as the first wooden church built on this spot by the Christianized Viking chieftan Sitric Silkenbeard (c. 1030), the present structure is a mix of peri-ods: Norman and Gothic, but mostly Victorian Neo-Gothic from the late 19th century.

Cost and Hours: €7 includes crypt exhibition, €11 adds a guided tour, €15 combo-ticket includes Dublinia (described next); Mon-Sat 9:30-17:00, Sun 12:00-14:30; guided tours Mon-Fri at 11:00, 12:00, 14:00, 15:00 and 16:00, Sat at 14:00, 15:00 and 16:00; tel. 01/677-8099, www.christchurchcathedral.ie.

Church Services and Evensong: There's a full Anglican service Sun at 11:00, and the public is welcome to a 45-minute evensong service, sung by the esteemed Christ Church choir (Wed-Thu at 18:00, Sun at 15:30).

Visiting the Cathedral: The interior is Victorian, from the 1870s. Highlights are the finely carved wooden quire (with the grand bishop's seat) and the tomb of Strongbow, the Norman warlord who helped conquer Ireland, leading to centuries of British domination. (While he was buried here in 1176, this stone is a 14th-century replacement.) From the south transept, stairs lead down into the crypt—considered the oldest structure in town. Running the entire length of the church (with a forest of stout supporting columns), it's filled with historic odds and ends (and a WC).

▲Dublinia

This exhibit, which highlights Dublin's Viking and medieval past, is a hit with youngsters. It's cheesy but meaty enough for adults as well.

Cost and Hours: €10, €15 combo-ticket includes Christ Church Cathedral; daily 10:00-18:30, Oct-Feb until 17:30, last entry one hour before closing; top-floor coffee shop, across from Christ Church Cathedral, tel. 01/679-4611, www.dublinia.ie.

Visiting the Exhibits: The displays are laid out on three floors. The ground floor focuses on Viking Dublin, explaining life aboard a Viking ship and inside a Viking house. Viking traders introduced urban life and commerce to Ireland—but kids will be most interested in their gory weaponry.

The next floor up reveals Dublin's day-to-day life in medieval times, from chivalrous knights and damsels in town fairs to the brutal ravages of the plague. Like so much of Europe at that time (1347-1349), Ireland lost one-third of its population to the Black Death. The huge scale model of medieval Dublin is well done. The top floor's "History Hunters" section is devoted to how the puzzles of modern archaeology and science shed light on Dublin's history. From this floor, you can climb a couple of flights of stairs into the tower for so-so views of Dublin, or exit across an enclosed stone bridge to adjacent Christ Church Cathedral.

▲St. Patrick's Cathedral

This Anglican cathedral is a thoughtful learning experience as well as a living church. The first church here was Catholic, supposedly built on the site where St. Patrick baptized local pagan converts. While the core of the Gothic structure you see today was built in the 13th century, most of today's stonework is 19th century. The building passed into the hands of the Anglican Church in the 16th century, after the Reformation. A century later, Oliver Cromwell's puritanical Calvinist troops—who considered the Anglicans to be little more than Catholics without a pope—stabled their horses here as a sign of disrespect.

Cost and Hours: €8 donation; Mon-Fri 9:30-17:00, Sat-Sun 9:00-18:00 except closed during Sun worship 10:30-12:30 & 14:30-16:30, last entry one hour before closing; at the intersection of Patrick Street and Upper Kevin Street, www.stpatrickscathedral.ie.

Tours: Free guided tours run several times a day in summer; check at the front desk for times.

Evensong: You'll get chills listening to the local "choir of angels" (typically Mon-Fri at 17:30 and Sun at 15:30—but schedule can vary, especially in summer, when guest choirs perform; confirm on the church website, under "Music Lists").

Visiting the Cathedral: The inside feels like an Irish Westminster Abbey, with venerable tombs and memorials to great Irish figures everywhere. The fine Victorian glass is from a Guinness-funded restoration in the 1870s. The regimental flags of the British army hang from the ceiling, colors slowly fading, in remembrance of soldiers lost. The north transept is dedicated to music. In the south transept you'll find "The Discovery Space," a delightful learning center with thousand-year-old gravestones and free brass rubbing.

Jonathan Swift (author of *Gulliver's Travels*) was dean of the cathedral from 1713 to 1745. His grave and death mask are located near the front door (on the right side of the nave), where his cutting, self-penned epitaph reads: "He lies where furious indignation can no longer rend his heart."

▲▲Temple Bar

This much-promoted area—with shops, cafés, theaters, galleries, pubs with live music, and restaurants—feels like the heart of the old city. It's Dublin's touristy "Left Bank," on the south shore of the river, filling the cobbled streets between Dame Street and the River Liffey.

Three hundred years ago, this was the city waterfront, where tall sailing ships offloaded their goods (a "bar" was a loading dock along the river, and the

Temples were a dominant merchant family). Eventually, the city grew eastward, filling in tidal mudflats, to create the docklands of modern Dublin. Once a thriving Georgian center of craftsmen and merchants, this neighborhood fell on hard times in the 20th century. Ensuing low rents attracted students and artists, giving the area a bohemian flair.

With government tax incentives and lots of development money, the Temple Bar district has now become a thriving entertainment (and beer-drinking) hot spot. It can be an absolute spectacle in the evening, when it bursts with revelers. But even if you're just gawking, don't miss the opportunity to wander through this human circus.

Temple Bar Square, just off Temple Bar Street (near Ha' Penny Bridge), hosts street musicians and a Saturday book market. On busy weekends, people-watching here is a contact sport (and pickpocketing is not). Farther west and somewhat hidden, Meeting House Square, with a lively organic-produce market (Sat 10:00-16:30), has become the neighborhood's living room.

For more on sights in Temple Bar, see page 65; for pubs and music, see page 111.

Nearby: If the rowdy Temple Bar scene gets to be too much, cross over to the north bank of the River Liffey on the Millennium Bridge (next bridge west of the Ha' Penny Bridge), where you'll find a mellower, more cosmopolitan neighborhood with one-off shops and restaurants with outdoor seating in the **Millennium Walk district.**

NORTH OF THE RIVER LIFFEY

O'Connell Street, lined with statues of leading Irishmen, is the historic core north of the river. It's covered by the second half of my Dublin Walk, "O'Connell Street and Irish Heroes" (see page 66). And there's lots more to see. After you're oriented with the walk, consider the following sights.

▲▲EPIC: The Irish Emigration Museum

Telling the story of the Irish diaspora, this museum celebrates how this little island has had an oversized impact on the world. While the museum has few actual artifacts, this is an entertaining and educational experience. "EPIC" stands for "Every Person Is Connected."

Cost and Hours: €15, daily 10:00-18:45, last entry at 17:00, audioguide—€2 (or download it for free), in the CHQ building on Custom House Quay (at the modern pedestrian bridge a few steps from the famine statues along the riverfront), tel. 01/906-0861, www.epicchq.com.

Visiting the Museum: The museum fills the wine vaults in the basement of an iron-framed warehouse from the 1820s. Its 20 themed galleries take an interactive, high-tech approach to explain the forces that propelled so many Irish around the globe. Featured illustrious emigrants include labor agitator Mother Jones, Caribbean pirate Anne Bonny, Australian bush bandit Ned Kelly, and musical Chicago police chief Francis O'Neill. Historic photos of filthy tenements and early films of bustling urban scenes document the plight of the common Irish emigrant. And all along you celebrate Irish heritage in music, literature, sports, and more.

Genealogy Help: The Irish Family History Centre on the ground floor can help you research your Celtic roots (€12.50 to access research stations; consultations—€45/30 minutes, €85/hour; Mon-Fri 10:00-17:00, Sat-Sun 12:00-17:00, tel. 01/905-9216, www.irishfamilyhistorycentre.com).

Nearby: Looking downstream, notice the modern **Samuel Beckett Bridge**—shaped like an old Irish harp and designed by Santiago Calatrava. The areas north and south of this bridge have been rejuvenated over the last 30 years with strikingly modern buildings: on the north bank, with Dublin's contemporary conven-

DUBLIN

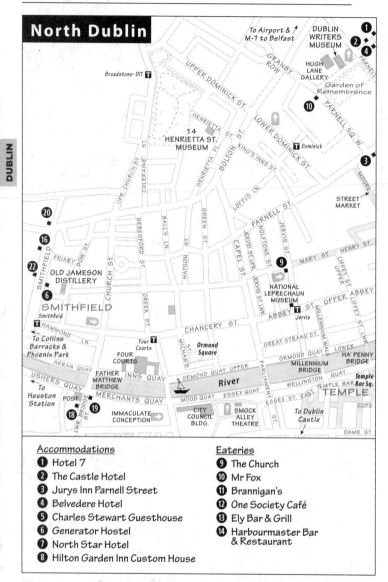

North Dublin

To Airport &
M-1 to Belfast

DUBLIN WRITERS MUSEUM

HUGH LANE GALLERY

Garden of Remembrance

Broadstone- DIT

UPPER DOMINICK ST.

GRANBY ROW

PARNELL SQ. W.

HENRIETTA PL.

LOWER DOMINICK ST.

KING'S INNS ST.

Dominick

14 HENRIETTA ST. MUSEUM

UPP. CHURCH ST.

COLERAINE ST.

BOLTON ST.

LOFTUS LN.

MOORE ST.

STREET MARKET

PARNELL ST.

WOLFETONE ST.

JERVIS ST. UPR.

GREEN ST.

BALL'S LN.

NELSON ST.

CAPEL ST.

MARY ST.

HENRY ST.

UPPER LIFFEY

OLD JAMESON DISTILLERY

FRIARY

BOW ST.

BERESFORD ST.

CHURCH ST.

GREEK ST.

SMITHFIELD

Smithfield

HAMMOND

JERVIS ST. LWR.

NATIONAL LEPRECHAUN MUSEUM

ABBEY ST.

Jervis

UPPER ABBEY

UPPER LIFFEY ST.

MILLENNIUM WK.

To Collins Barracks & Phoenix Park

FOUR COURTS

Four Courts

CHANCERY ST.

Ormond Square

MICHANS

GREAT STRAND ST.

LOWER ORMOND QUAY

HA'PENNY BRIDGE

ARRAN QUAY

FATHER MATTHEW BRIDGE

INNS QUAY

ORMOND QUAY UPPER

MILLENNIUM BRIDGE

QUAY

Temple Bar Sq.

USHERS QUAY

To Heuston Station

POST

LWR. BRIDGE ST.

MERCHANTS QUAY

River

WOOD QUAY

ESSEX QUAY

PARLIAMENT ST.

ESSEX ST. EAST

WELLINGTON QUAY

TEMPLE BAR WK.

TEMPLE

COPE

IMMACULATE CONCEPTION

CITY COUNCIL BLDG.

SMOCK ALLEY THEATRE

To Dublin Castle

DAME ST.

Accommodations
1 Hotel 7
2 The Castle Hotel
3 Jurys Inn Parnell Street
4 Belvedere Hotel
5 Charles Stewart Guesthouse
6 Generator Hostel
7 North Star Hotel
8 Hilton Garden Inn Custom House

Eateries
9 The Church
10 Mr Fox
11 Brannigan's
12 One Society Café
13 Ely Bar & Grill
14 Harbourmaster Bar & Restaurant

tion center, and just inland from the south bank, with developments such as Google's European headquarters.

Before leaving the area, wander 50 yards up the River Liffey toward the city to contemplate the skeletal sculptures of the city's evocative **Famine Memorial.** Nearby you'll spot the masts of the Jeanie Johnston Tall Ship and Famine Museum (see next). A visit here ties in well with the area's emigration theme.

DUBLIN

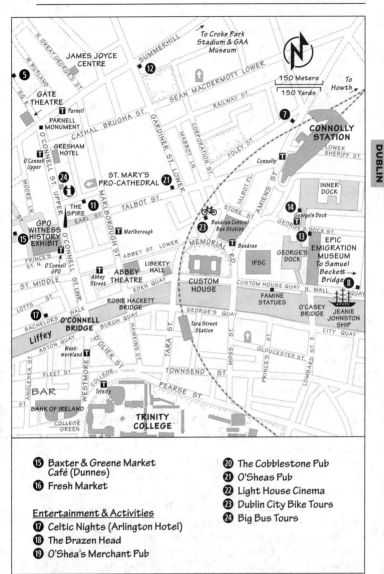

15 Baxter & Greene Market Café (Dunnes)
16 Fresh Market

Entertainment & Activities
17 Celtic Nights (Arlington Hotel)
18 The Brazen Head
19 O'Shea's Merchant Pub

20 The Cobblestone Pub
21 O'Sheas Pub
22 Light House Cinema
23 Dublin City Bike Tours
24 Big Bus Tours

▲Jeanie Johnston Tall Ship and Famine Museum

Docked on the River Liffey, this seagoing sailing ship is a replica of a legendary Irish "famine ship." The original *Jeanie Johnston* embarked on 16 eight-week transatlantic crossings, carrying more than 2,500 Irish emigrants (about 200 per voyage) to their new lives in America and Canada in the decade after the Great Potato Famine of the 1840s. While many barely seaworthy hulks were known as "coffin ships," the people who boarded the *Jeanie Johnston* were lucky: The ship was Irish owned and crewed, with a humanitarian captain and even a doctor on board, and not one life was lost. Your tour guide will introduce you to the ship's main characters and help illuminate day-to-day life aboard a cramped tall ship 160 years ago.

Note that, because this ship makes goodwill voyages to Atlantic ports, it may be away during your visit—check ahead.

Cost and Hours: €10.50, visits by 50-minute tour only, easy to book in advance online; daily 10:00-16:00, Oct-March 11:00-15:00, tours depart on the hour (except 13:00); on the north bank of the Liffey just east of Sean O'Casey Bridge, tel. 01/473-0111, jeaniejohnston.ie.

▲Dublin Writers Museum

No other country so small has produced such a wealth of literature. As interesting to those who are fans of Irish literature as it is boring to those who aren't, this three-room museum features the lives and works of Dublin's great writers. It's a low-tech museum, where you read informative plaques while perusing display cases with minor memorabilia—a document signed by Jonathan Swift, a photo of Oscar Wilde reclining thoughtfully, an early edition of Bram Stoker's *Dracula*, a George Bernard Shaw playbill, a not-so-famous author's tuxedo, and a newspaper from Easter 1916 announcing "Two More Executions Today." If unassuming attractions like that stir your blood—or if you simply want a manageable introduction to Irish lit—it's worth a visit.

Cost and Hours: €7.50, includes helpful 45-minute audio-guide; Mon-Sat 9:45-17:00, Sun from 11:00, closed Mon Dec-March, 18 Parnell Square North, tel. 01/872-2077, www.writersmuseum.com.

Visiting the Museum: The collection is chronological. While you'll follow the audioguide, here are some highlights:

Room 1 starts with Irish literature's deep roots in the roving, harp-playing bards of medieval times. By telling stories in the native language, they helped unify the island's culture. But "literature" came only with the arrival of the English language. **Jonathan Swift** (1667-1745)—Ireland's first great writer—was born in Dublin and served as dean of St. Patrick's Cathedral, though he spent much of his life in London. His stinging satire of societal hypocrisy set the tone of rebellion found in much Irish literature. The theater has been another longstanding Irish specialty, starting with the 18th-century playwright Oliver Goldsmith. In the 1890s, sophisticated Dublin (and Trinity College) was a cradle for great writers who ultimately found their fortunes in England: the playwright/poet/wit Oscar Wilde, Bram Stoker (who married Wilde's girlfriend), and the big-idea playwright George Bernard Shaw.

Poet **W. B. Yeats** stayed home, cultivating Irish folklore at soirees (hosted by the literary patron Lady Augusta Gregory).

Room 2 continues into the 20th century with Yeats' **Abbey Theatre,** the scene of premieres by great Irish playwrights (including Yeats, Shaw, and Wilde), and an important force in the developing sense of Irish national identity in the early part of the century. Dublin was also a breeding ground for bold new ideas, producing Modernist writers Samuel *(Waiting for Godot)* Beckett and James Joyce (a center devoted to him is described next). As the 20th century progressed, writers like Sean O'Casey, Brendan Behan, Seamus Heaney, John B. Keane, and Brian Friel kept Dublin at the forefront of modern theater.

Finish your visit by going **upstairs** to see an elegant Georgian library with portraits, busts, and temporary exhibits on Irish literature.

James Joyce Centre

Only aficionados of James Joyce's work will want to visit this micro-museum.

Cost and Hours: €5, Mon-Sat 10:00-17:00, Sun from 12:00, closed Mon Dec-March, two blocks east of the Dublin Writers Museum at 35 North Great George's Street, tel. 01/878-8547, www.jamesjoyce.ie. The center offers walking tours of Joyce sights several times a week.

Background: Born and raised in Dublin, James Joyce (1882-1941) wrote in great detail about his hometown and mined the local dialect for his pitch-perfect dialogue. His best-known work, *Ulysses,* chronicles one day (June 16, 1904) in the life of the fictional Leopold Bloom as he wanders through the underside of Dublin. Joyce himself left Dublin (on June 17, 1904) for Paris and lived away from the city for most of his life. He never took up the cause of Irish nationalism and rarely delved into Irish mythology. He instead wrote with a new modernist focus on linguistic invention and social frankness.

Visiting the Center: Your visit begins (top floor) with videos on Joyce's life and his enormous influence on subsequent writers. Next, a touchscreen display traces Bloom's Dublin odyssey. Photos of Joyce and quotes from his books decorate the walls. A re-creation of a messy, cramped study evokes Joyce's struggles with poverty and criticism as he forged his own path. Down one flight, see portraits of Joyce and his wife and muse, Nora Barnacle. (The first time they, um, went on a date was June 16, 1904. Joyce later set the events depicted in his masterpiece, *Ulysses,* on that date, which is commemorated annually as Bloomsday in honor of Leopold Bloom.) On the ground floor, a film version of one of Joyce's short stories,

DUBLIN

DUBLIN

Dublin's Literary Life

Dublin in the 1700s, grown rich from a lucrative cloth trade, was one of Europe's most cultured and sophisticated cities. The buildings were decorated in the Georgian style still visible today, and the city's Protestant elite shuttled between here and London, bridging the Anglo-Irish cultural gap. Jonathan Swift was the era's greatest Anglo-Irish writer—a brilliant satirist and author of *Gulliver's Travels* (1726). He

was also dean of St. Patrick's Cathedral (1713-1745) and one of the city's eminent citizens.

Around the turn of the 20th century, Dublin produced some of the world's great modern writers. Bram Stoker was the creator of *Dracula*. Oscar Wilde penned *The Picture of Dorian Gray* and a clutch of fine plays. George Bernard Shaw wrote *Pygmalion, Major Barbara, Man and Superman,* and a host of other dramas. William Butler Yeats was a prolific poet and playwright of Irish themes. And James Joyce whipped up a masterpiece called *Ulysses.*

To dip your toe into the occasionally unfathomable depths of classic Irish lit, drop by the tiny Sweny's Pharmacy for one of its daily readings from *Ulysses* or other works by Joyce. This shrine for devotees of Joyce is a time capsule, looking just as the writer described it in his novel more than a hundred years ago. The text is passed around for all to read a section aloud. Even if you don't understand its obscure local references, appreciate the rhythm of its stream-of-consciousness verbal flow...and buy a bar of lemon soap on your way out (daily, check schedule at www.sweny.ie, sometimes read in other languages...might make it easier to figure out, 1 Lincoln Place between Trinity College and Merrion Square).

The Dead, plays eternally. In a tiny back courtyard, you can see the original door from 7 Eccles Street, the address of Leopold Bloom.

Hugh Lane Gallery

This well-described exhibit of art from the 1870s onward includes a sampling of Impressionist masterpieces from the gallery's founding collection, once owned by Sir Hugh Lane, an Irish art dealer. Genteel and bite-sized, the museum holds a well-known Monet painting (*Waterloo Bridge,* 1900), the reconstructed studio of Dublin-born modern artist Francis Bacon, and a few select works by Irish artists.

Cost and Hours: Free, Tue-Thu 10:00-18:00, Fri-Sat until 17:00, Sun 11:00-17:00, closed Mon, in the Dublin City Gallery on Parnell Square North, tel. 01/222-5550, www.hughlane.ie.

▲GPO Witness History Exhibit

During the 1916 Easter Rising, Irish nationalists took over buildings in Dublin, including the General Post Office (GPO), which became the rebel headquarters. Initial euphoria led to chaotic street battles and ended with the grim realization among the insurgents that surrender was the best option—trusting that their martyrdom would inspire the country to rise more effectively. This engaging exhibit—in the working post office—is primarily focused on that pivotal Easter week. Additional exhibitions cover the related Irish War of Independence and the Irish Civil War.

Cost and Hours: €14, includes audioguide, Mon-Sat 10:00-17:30, Sun from 12:00, last entry one hour before closing, tel. 01/872-1916, www.gpowitnesshistory.ie.

Background: For European nations preoccupied with World War I, the Easter Rising was a sideshow—but it was critical to Irish nationalists. Almost every Irish generation for the preceding 125 years had launched doomed insurrections against the British. But this one had a lasting effect, although it may not have seemed so in its immediate wake—a couple of weeks later, the patriot leaders who held their ground at the post office were executed in Kilmainham Gaol. Public sympathies shifted seismically. After seven centuries of dominance, the British were on a slippery slope leading to eventual independence for its nearest and oldest colony.

Visiting the Exhibit: The hardworking exhibit has a few interesting artifacts and lots of videos, photos, and earnest ways to tell the story. It features a fairly balanced view of the rebellion, including the less popular realities (like the lack of widespread support at the beginning of the movement and the civilians who died in the crossfire). Don't miss the 15-minute widescreen depiction of events (called "The Rising") in the tiny theater. An interactive map of Dublin zooms in and out of various neighborhoods, tracking that Easter week's confrontations, with actors dramatizing the events and conversations that shaped the conflict. In video presentations, historians give their take on how the rebellion affected Irish history.

▲▲14 Henrietta Street

This four-story, 18th-century Georgian house, once an affluent mansion, had morphed into a cramped, impoverished, multifamily hovel by the 20th century. Now a museum, it explains tenement life and urban poverty in Dublin. Photos and videos telling the story of the house and its times augment the period architecture and furnishings.

Cost and Hours: €9, visit by 75-minute guided tour only, tours depart on the hour, book online in advance or take your chances; open Wed-Sat 10:00-17:00, Sun from 12:00, closed Mon-Tue; last tour one hour before closing, 14 Henrietta Street, tel. 01/524-0383, www.14henriettastreet.ie.

Visiting the House: Tours start on the top floor, where you'll learn about the aristocratic Molesworth family, who were the first occupants in the 1740s. In those days, Henrietta Street was the most exclusive enclave in Dublin, bringing balanced architectural order to this first Georgian-style lane on the rapidly expanding north side of the Liffey. Living luxuriously here, under ornate ceilings and warmed by fancy fireplaces, these privileged elite were unknowingly surrounding themselves with unhealthy choices: lead in the paint, arsenic in the wallpaper, and mercury in their makeup.

Working your way down through the building, you learn how the 1801 Act of Union pulled the plug on the good life: The Irish Parliament was dissolved, England asserted its rule, and the rich and politically well-connected moved to London. The house's once elegant rooms were subdivided, with as many 13 people (many from the famine-wracked countryside) living in one room.

By 1911, there were 110 people living in this one house, split between 17 families sharing two toilets. It's little wonder that Dublin's squalid tenements were the breeding ground for the socialist Irish Citizen Army militia of James Connolly, who fought fiercely in the 1916 Easter Rising. Rosie Hackett lived here at #14; the most famous woman in Connolly's army, she was a cofounder of the Irish Women Workers Union. Her name today adorns one of the bridges across the Liffey. The basement level is a re-creation of the meager furnishings of the Brannigans, a family of 13 who were the last residents, finally moving out in 1979.

National Leprechaun Museum

This corny, low-tech attraction is fine for kids and lighthearted adults. On this 45-minute guided meander through Irish mythology, you'll visit a wishing well, a giant's living room, and a fairy fort, listening to tales that will enchant your wee ones.

Cost and Hours: €16, daily 10:00-18:30, a block north of the River Liffey on Abbey Street across from Jervis LUAS stop, tel. 01/873-3899, www.leprechaunmuseum.ie.

Evening Visits: For adults only, a one-hour, interactive "This Dark Land" storytelling performance explores the macabre side of Irish folklore (€18, May-Sept Fri-Sat at 19:30 and 20:30).

Old Jameson Distillery

Whiskey fans enjoy visiting the old distillery. You get a 40-minute tour and a free shot in the pub. Unfortunately, the "distillery" feels corporate, overpriced, and put together for tourists. The Bushmills

DUBLIN

From Famine to Revolution

After the Great Potato Famine (1845-1849), destitute rural Irish moved to the city in droves, seeking work and causing a housing shortage. Unscrupulous landlords came up with a solution: Subdivide the city's once-grand mansions, vacated by gentry after the 1801 Act of Union transferred all power to London. The mansions' tiny rooms could then be crammed with poor renters. Dublin became one of the most densely populated cities in Europe—one of every three Dubliners lived in a slum. On Henrietta Street, once a wealthy Dublin address, these new tenements bulged with humanity. According to the 1911 census, one district counted 835 people living in 15 houses (many with a single outhouse in back or even sharing a communal chamber pot). In these cramped, neglected quarters, tuberculosis was rampant, and infant mortality skyrocketed.

Those who could get work tenaciously clung to their precious jobs. The terrible working conditions prompted many to join trade unions, but when laborers went on strike in 1913, employers locked them out (the Dublin Lockout lasted for seven months). The picket lines were brutally put down by police in the pocket of rich businessmen, led by newspaper and hotel magnate William Murphy. In response, James Larkin and James Connolly formed the Irish Citizen Army, a militia, to protect the poor trade unionists.

Murphy eventually broke the unions. Larkin headed for the US to organize workers there. Meanwhile, Connolly stayed in Ireland and brought the Irish Citizen Army into the 1916 Easter Rising as an integral part of the rebel forces. During that uprising, he slyly had a rebel flag flown over Murphy's prized hotel on O'Connell Street. The uninformed British artillery battalions took the bait—and pulverized it.

tour in Northern Ireland (in a working factory, see page 471) and the Midleton tour near Cork (in the huge original factory, page 232) are better experiences. If you do take this tour, volunteer energetically when offered the chance: This will get you a coveted seat at the whiskey taste-test table at the tour's end.

Cost and Hours: €22, Mon-Sat 9:30-18:00, Sun from 10:00, last tour at 17:15, late tours possible in summer; Bow Street, tel. 01/807-2355, www.jamesonwhiskey.com.

Nearby: The neighborhood called **Smithfield** was on the fast track to gentrification prior to the 2008-2009 economic crash. Today, it's getting back on its feet and is home not only to the Old Jameson Distillery but also the best hostel lodging in town, the Light House art-film cinema, and The Cobblestone—Dublin's most authentic traditional-music pub (see page 112). All are on the long Smithfield Square, three blocks northwest of the Four Courts

(Supreme Court building). The **Fresh Market,** near the top of the square, is a handy grocery stop for urban picnic fixings (daily until 22:00).

OUTER DUBLIN

Kilmainham Gaol (GWAY-ol) and the Guinness Storehouse are located west of the old center and can be linked by a 20-minute walk, a five-minute taxi ride, or public bus #40 or #13. (To ride the bus from the jail to the Guinness Storehouse, leave the prison and take three rights—crossing no streets—to reach the bus stop.) Another option is to take a hop-on, hop-off bus, which stops at both sights (see "Tours in Dublin" near the beginning of this chapter). For locations see the "Dublin" map on page 40.

▲▲▲Kilmainham Gaol

Opened in 1796 as Dublin's county jail and a debtors' prison, Kilmainham was considered a model in its day. In reality, the British frequently used this jail as a political prison.

Many of those who fought for Irish independence were held or executed here, including leaders of the rebellions of 1798, 1803, 1848, 1867, and 1916. James Connolly, unable to stand in front of the firing squad because of a gangrenous ankle, was tied to a chair and shot sitting down. National heroes Robert Emmett and Charles Stewart Parnell each did time here. The last prisoner to be held in the jail was Éamon de Valera, who later became president of Ireland. He was released on July 16, 1924, the day Kilmainham was finally shut down. The buildings, virtually in ruins, were restored in the 1960s. Today, it's a shrine to the Nathan Hales of Ireland.

Cost and Hours: €8, visit by one-hour guided tour only, advance booking highly recommended; daily June-Aug 9:00-19:00, last tour at 17:45; April-May and Sept until 18:00, last tour at 16:45; Oct-March 9:30-17:30, last tour at 16:15; tours run 2/hour, tel. 01/453-5984, www.kilmainhamgaolmuseum.ie.

Advance Tickets Recommended: Book online at least a few days (or up to 60 days) in advance to guarantee a spot on a tour. While you can try to buy a ticket in person, you'll likely wait in a long line, and walk-up spots go quickly.

Getting There: Hop-on, hop-off buses stop here, or take bus #69 or #79 from Aston Quay or #13 or #40 from O'Connell Street or College Green—confirm with driver. The closest LUAS tram stop is Suir Road (red line, zone 2 ticket from city center). From there, it's a 10-minute, level walk north, crossing over the Grand Canal, to the jail.

Visiting the Jail: Start your visit with a one-hour guided tour (includes 15-minute prison history slideshow in the prison chapel). It's sobering to tour the cells and places of execution—hearing tales of oppressive colonialism and heroic patriotism—alongside Irish schoolkids who know these names well. The museum has an excellent exhibit on Victorian prison life and Ireland's fight for independence.

Don't miss the dimly lit "Last Words 1916" hall upstairs, which displays the stirring final letters that patriots sent to loved ones hours before facing the firing squad. Regrettably, transcriptions of the letters are not posted, denying visitors a better understanding of the passion and patriotism of Ireland's greatest in their own last words—a lost opportunity for Americans not realizing that there are other Nathan Hales in this world who wish they had more than one life to give for their country. (Fortunately, the little bookshop for budding patriots carries the inspirational *Last Words* book.)

▲Guinness Storehouse

A visit to the Guinness Storehouse is, for many, a pilgrimage. Arthur Guinness began brewing the renowned stout here in 1759, and by 1868 it was the biggest brewery in the world. Today, the sprawling complex fills several city blocks (64 acres busy brewing 1.5 million pints a day).

Visitors (1.5 million annually) are welcomed to the towering storehouse, where the vibe is glitzy entertainment. Don't look for conveyor belts of beer bottles being stamped with bottle caps. Rather than a brewery tour, this is a Disneyland for beer lovers—huge crowds, high decibel music, and dreamy TV beer ads on big screens.

Cost and Hours: Overpriced at €19.50 or more; price depends on entry time—book ahead, admission includes a pint; daily 9:30-19:00, July-Aug 9:00-20:00, last entry two hours before closing, last beer served 45 minutes before closing; tel. 01/408-4800, www.guinness-storehouse.com.

Advance Tickets Recommended: The brewery is popular with cruise-ship excursions, making an advance ticket the only smart way to visit. Book your timed-entry slot for early or late in the day—it's cheaper, you'll minimize lines, and you'll have a better experience (a midday ticket just assures you'll be part of the mobs).

DUBLIN

DUBLIN

The Famous Record-Breaking Records Book

Look up "beer" in the *Guinness World Records,* and you'll discover that the record for removing beer bottle caps with one's teeth is 68 in one minute. But aside from listing records for amazing—or amazingly stupid—feats, this famous record book has a more subtle connection with beer.

In 1951, while hunting in Ireland's County Wexford, Sir Hugh Beaver, then the managing director at Guinness Breweries, got into a debate with his companions over which was the fastest game bird in Europe: the golden plover or the red grouse. That night at his estate, after scouring many reference books, they were disappointed not to find a definitive answer.

Beaver realized that similar questions were likely being debated nightly in pubs across Ireland and Britain. So he hired a fact-finding team in London to compile a book of answers to various questions. In 1955, the *Guinness Book of Records* (later renamed *Guinness World Records*) was published. By Christmas, it topped the British bestseller list.

In the beginning, entries mostly focused on natural phenomena and animal oddities, but grew to include a wide variety of extreme human achievements.

The iconic book is now available in more than 100 countries and 26 languages, with more than 3.5 million copies sold annually. As the bestselling copyrighted book of all time, it even earns a record-breaking entry within its own pages.

Getting There: Ride the hop-on, hop-off bus (it stops right at the site), or take bus #13, #40, or #123 from Dame Street and O'Connell Street. The James LUAS stop on the red line is a 15-minute walk west of the Storehouse.

Visiting the Brewery: Enter the brewery on Bellevue Street. The exhibit fills the old fermentation plant, used from 1902 through 1988, and reopened in 2000 as a huge shrine to the Guinness tradition. Step into the middle of the ground floor and look up. A tall, beer-glass-shaped glass atrium—14 million pints big (that's about 10 days' worth of production) soars upward past four floors of exhibitions and cafés to the skylight. Then look down at Arthur's original 9,000-year lease, enshrined under Plexiglas in the floor. At £45 per year, it was quite a bargain.

As you escalate ever higher, you'll notice that each floor has a theme. The first floor is dedicated to cooperage—the making of wooden barrels (with 1954 film clips showing master kegmakers working at their now virtually extinct trade); the second floor has the tasting rooms (described later); the third floor features advertising and a theater with classic TV ads; the fourth floor is where you can pull your own beer (at the Academy); and the fifth floor has Arthur's Bar. The top floor is the Gravity Bar, providing visitors with a commanding 360-degree view of Dublin—with vistas all the way to the sea—and an included pint of the beloved stout.

The tasting rooms (on level 2) provide a fun detour. In the "white room" you're introduced to using your five senses to appreciate the perfect porter. Then, in the "velvet chamber," you're taught how to taste it from a leprechaun-sized beer glass.

Claiming Your Beer: Your admission includes a ticket for a beer, which you can claim in one of three places. On level 4, you can pull your own pint (and then drink it). On level 5, at Arthur's Bar, you can choose among extra stout (4.2%, carbonated), Dublin Porter (3.8%, 1796 recipe), West Indies Porter (6%, toffee flavor, 1801 recipe), Hop House 13 (4.1%, a hoppy lager), and Black Velvet (half and half sparkling wine and Guinness). On the top floor (where there's the most energy and fun), drinks are limited to the basic stout or soft drinks.

DUBLIN

▲National Museum of Decorative Arts and History

This branch of the National Museum, which occupies the huge, 18th-century stone Collins Barracks in west Dublin, displays Irish dress, furniture, weapons, silver, and other domestic baubles from the past 700 years. History buffs will linger longest in the Soldiers & Chiefs exhibit, which covers the Irish at war both at home and abroad since 1500 (including the American Civil War). The sober finale is the Proclaiming a Republic room, offering Ireland's best coverage of the painful birth of this nation. Guns, flags, and personal letters help illustrate the 1916 Easter Rising, the War of Independence against Britain, and Ireland's Civil War. Also on the museum grounds is the historic *Asgard*, a 51-foot yacht used by its owner, Erskine Childers, to smuggle guns to arm Irish rebels in the 1916 Easter Rising. You'll find the boat 50 yards across a small parking lot in a well-marked separate building (free, same hours as museum).

Cost and Hours: Free, Sun-Mon 13:00-17:00, Tue-Sat from 10:00, good café; on north side of the River Liffey in Collins Barracks on Benburb Street, roughly across the river from Guinness Storehouse, LUAS red line: Museum stop; tel. 01/677-7444, www.museum.ie.

▲Gaelic Athletic Association Museum

This museum, at Croke Park Stadium in northeast Dublin, offers a high-tech, interactive introduction to Ireland's favorite games. The GAA, founded in 1884, was created to foster the development of Gaelic sports, specifically Gaelic football and hurling, and to exclude English sports such as cricket and rugby (see sidebar). An expression of the Irish cultural awakening, the GAA played an im-

DUBLIN

portant part in the fight for independence. Relive the greatest moments in hurling and Irish-football history. Then get involved: Pick up a stick and try hurling, kick a football, and test your speed and balance. A 15-minute film (played on request) gives you a "Sunday at the stadium" experience.

Cost and Hours: €7, Mon-Sat 9:30-17:00, June-Aug until 18:00, Sun 10:30-17:00 year-round—except on game Sundays, when the museum is open to ticket holders only; café, museum is located under the stands at Croke Park Stadium, enter from St. Joseph's Avenue off Clonliffe Road, tel. 01/819-2323, www. crokepark.ie/gaa-museum.

Tours: The €14, one-hour museum-plus-stadium-tour option is worth it for rabid fans who want a glimpse of the huge stadium and locker rooms. The €20 rooftop Skyline tour offers views 17 stories above the field from lofty catwalks. Both generally run daily—see the website for times.

Hurling or Gaelic Football at Croke Park Stadium

Actually seeing a match at Croke Park, surrounded by incredibly spirited Irish fans, is a fun experience. Hurling is fast and rough: like airborne hockey with no injury time-outs. Gaelic football resembles a rugged form of soccer; you can carry the ball, but must bounce or kick it every three steps. Matches are held most Saturday or Sunday afternoons in summer (May-Aug), culminating in the hugely popular all-Ireland finals on Sunday afternoons in August. Tickets are available at the stadium except during the finals. Choose a county to support, buy their colors to wear or wave, scream yourself hoarse, and you'll be a temporary local.

Cost and Hours: €20-55, box office open Mon-Fri 9:30-13:00 & 14:15-17:30, www.gaa.ie.

Getting There: Croke Park is located on the north bank of the Royal Canal, about 10 blocks north of the Connolly train station. It can be reached by bus #40 or #41, or by taxi.

Glasnevin Cemetery Museum

This is the final resting place for Ireland's most passionate patriots, writers, politicians, and assorted personalities. What Père Lachaise is to Paris, Glasnevin is to Dublin. Here you'll find the graves of Michael Collins, Charles Stewart Parnell, and teenage rebel/martyr Kevin Barry (of patriot song fame), surrounding a replica round tower atop the crypt of Daniel O'Connell. A tall wall and a half-dozen watchtowers used to deter grave robbers surround the cem-

Gaelic Athletic Association

The Gaelic Athletic Association (GAA) has long been a power-house in Ireland. The national pastimes of Gaelic football and hurling pack stadiums all over the country. When you consider that 82,000 people—paying about €25 each—stuff Dublin's Croke Park Stadium and that all the athletes are strictly amateur, you might wonder, "Where does all the money go?"

Ireland has a long tradition of using the revenue generated by these huge events to promote Gaelic athletics and Gaelic culture in a grassroots and neighborhood way. So, while the players (many of whom are schoolteachers whose jobs allow for evenings and summers free) participate only for the glory of their various counties, the money generated is funding children's leagues, school coaches, small-town athletic facilities, and traditional arts, music, and dance—as well as the building and maintenance of giant stadiums such as Croke Park.

Sports here have a deep emotional connection as a heartfelt expression of Irish identity. There was a time when membership in the GAA was denied to anyone who also attended "foreign games," defined as rugby, soccer, or cricket. If the Brits played it, it was viewed as cultural poison. So intractable was this rule that in 1938, Douglas Hyde (then president of Ireland) was kicked out of the GAA for attending an international soccer match. (The rule was abolished in 1971 with the advent of TV sports.)

In 1921, during the War of Independence, IRA leader Michael Collins orchestrated the simultaneous assassination of a dozen British intelligence agents around Dublin in a single morning. The same day, the Black and Tans retaliated. These grizzled British WWI veterans, clad in black police coats and tan surplus army pants, had been sent to Ireland to stamp out the rebels. Knowing Croke Park would be full of Irish nationalists, they entered the packed stadium during a Gaelic football match and fired into the stands, killing 13 spectators as well as a Tipperary player.

Today Croke Park's "Hill 16" grandstands are built on rubble dumped here after the 1916 Easter Rising; it's literally sacred ground. And the Hogan stands are named after the murdered player from Tipperary. Queen Elizabeth II visited the stadium during her historic visit in 2011. Her warm interest in the stadium and in the institution of the GAA did much to heal old wounds.

etery's 120 leafy acres. Guided tours of the cemetery are fascinating to those who love Irish culture and history. A wall of memorials commemorates all who were lost during the struggle for Irish independence a hundred years ago, including civilians and British soldiers. The adjacent museum offers more detail—you'll dig the graveyard superstitions.

Cost and Hours: Cemetery—free, museum—€6.75, €13.50 includes tour; daily 10:00-18:00, Oct-March until 17:00, 1.5-hour tours run hourly 10:30-15:30, more in summer; tel. 01/882-6550, www.glasnevinmuseum.ie.

Getting There: It's two miles north of the city center (get here on the hop-on, hop-off bus, or take buses #40 or #140 from O'Connell Street).

Shopping in Dublin

Shops are open roughly Monday-Saturday 9:00-18:00 and until 20:00 on Thursday. Hours are shorter on Sunday (if shops are open at all). The dominant department store in Dublin (and Ireland) is Dunnes, where you can buy everything from groceries to underwear to alcohol (branches throughout town, including on Grafton Street and near Dublin Castle, St. Stephen's Green, and the General Post Office, http://www.dunnesstores.com).

To get a good look at contemporary Irish crafts, visit the mod showrooms of the Irish Design Shop (41 Drury Lane, www.irishdesignshop.com) or Industry & Co (41 a/b Drury Street, www.industryandco.com). The Gutter Bookshop is a fine independent seller that champions Irish writers (Cow's Lane in Temple Bar, www.gutterbookshop.com). Avoca is a mini department store loaded with quality Irish crafts and food (11 Suffolk Street, www.avoca.com).

Good shopping areas include:

Grafton Street, with its neighboring streets and arcades (such as the fun Great George's Arcade between Great George's and Drury Streets), and nearby shopping centers (Powerscourt Townhouse and St. Stephen's Green). Francis Street creaks with antiques.

Henry Street, home to Dublin's top department stores (pedestrian-only, off O'Connell Street).

Nassau Street, lining Trinity College, with the popular Kilkenny Shop (Irish design, with a good cafeteria upstairs, www.kilkennyshop.com) and lots of touristy stores.

Temple Bar, worth a browse for art, jewelry, New Age paraphernalia, books, music (try Claddagh Records), and gift shops. On Saturdays, a couple of markets—one for food and another for books—set up shop. For details on this area, see pages 92 and 111.

Dublin for Kids

If the youngsters in your clan need a break from Dublin's literary sights, ancient Celtic artifacts, medieval churches, and urban rebel hideouts, try sprinkling in some of these activities.

Dublinia Kid-friendly coverage of grisly Viking history (see page 91).

Viking Splash Tours Rowdy ride through Dublin history in a WWII amphibious vehicle—driven by a Viking-costumed guide who spouts jokes and historic factoids as you ramble across town (€25, daily 10:00-17:00, www.vikingsplash.com).

National Leprechaun Museum Irish mythology for impressionable wee ones (see page 100).

Jeanie Johnston Tall Ship The experience of an Atlantic voyage of emigration told by role-playing swabbies aboard a replica sailing ship (see page 95).

Irish Rock 'n' Roll Museum The evolution of Irish rock music and studio memorabilia (see page 66).

Gaelic Athletic Association Museum High-tech Gaelic football and hurling exhibits at Croke Park Stadium—including a chance to whack the ball in the hurling equivalent of a batting cage (see page 105).

Phoenix Park Rent bikes or take a guided Segway tour in this gigantic safe-to-cycle greenbelt (includes a zoo; see page 42).

Gravedigger Ghost Tour This ghoulish bus tour is catnip for teens but too spooky for little ones (www.thegravedigger.ie).

St. Stephen's Green Kid-friendly park (feed the ducks) and secret stress reducer for mom and dad (see page 50).

Eddie Rocket's Diner This burger-and-shake franchise (there are several in central Dublin) is a step above fast food for finicky kids needing a slurp of home (www.eddierockets.ie).

Millennium Walk, a trendy lane stretching two blocks north from the River Liffey to Abbey Street. It's filled with hip restaurants, shops, and coffee bars. It's easy to miss—look for the south entry at the pedestrian Millennium Bridge, or the north entry at Jervis Street LUAS stop.

Entertainment in Dublin

Ireland has produced some of the finest writers in the English and Irish languages, and Dublin houses some of Europe's best theaters. Though the city was the site of the first performance of Handel's "Messiah" (1742), these days Dublin is famous for the rock bands that have started here: U2, Thin Lizzy, Sinéad O'Connor, and Bob Geldof's band The Boomtown Rats.

Theater

Abbey Theatre is Ireland's national theater, founded by W. B. Yeats in 1904 to preserve Irish culture during British rule (performances generally nightly at 20:00, Sat matinees at 14:30, 26 Lower Abbey Street, tel. 01/878-7222, www.abbeytheatre.ie). **Gate Theatre** does foreign plays as well as Irish classics (Cavendish Row, tel. 01/874-4045, www.gatetheatre.ie). The **Gaiety Theatre** offers a wide range of quality productions (King Street South, tel. 01/679-5622, www. gaietytheatre.ie). The **Bord Gáis Energy Theatre** (pronounced "Board-GOSH") is Dublin's newest and spiffiest venue (Grand Canal Square, tel. 01/677-7999, www.bordgaisenergytheatre.ie). Less-commercial plays can be seen at the intimate little **Smock Alley Theatre,** with seating surrounding a tiny stage, in a space on the site of the city's first theater—from 1662 (6 Lower Exchange Street—on the western fringe of Temple Bar, tel. 01/677-0014, www.smockalley.com). Browse the listings and fliers at the TI to see what's on.

Music, Dance, and Film

The 3 Arena, sited on what was once a dock railway terminus (easy LUAS red line access), is now sponsored by a hip phone company. Residents call it by its geographic nickname: The Point. It's considered one of the country's top live-music venues (East Link Bridge, tel. 01/819-8888, http://3arena.ie).

The **National Concert Hall** supports a varied performance schedule, including the National Symphony Orchestra on most Friday evenings (off St. Stephen's Green at Earlsfort Terrace, tel. 01/417-0077, www.nch.ie).

Celtic Nights combines traditional music and dancing into a big-stage, high-energy, family-friendly, Irish variety show. This touristy dinner act hits all the clichés, from *Riverdance*-style choreography to fun fiddling and comedic *craic*. It comes with a traditional three-course dinner and lots of audience participation (€38, €20 for kids 11 and under, nightly show at 20:30, on the north side of the river by the O'Connell Bridge at the Arlington Hotel, 23 Bachelors Walk—see map on page 94, tel. 01/687-5200, www. celticnights.com).

The **Irish Film Institute,** bordering Meeting House Square in Temple Bar, shows a variety of art-house flicks. A bohemian crowd relaxes in its bar/café, awaiting the next film (main entry at 6 Eustace Street, www.irishfilm.ie).

Pubs and Live Traditional Music

James Joyce once said it would be a good puzzle to try to walk across Dublin without passing a pub. For guided pub crawls (focusing on either Irish literature or music), see "Tours in Dublin," near the beginning of this chapter. Unless otherwise noted, for locations of the venues described below, see the "South Dublin Restaurants" map on page 122.

Temple Bar and Nearby

The Temple Bar area thrives with music—traditional, jazz, and rock. Pricier than the rest of Dublin and extremely touristy, it's a wild scene and—for party animals—a good place to mix beer and music. The noise, pushy crowds, and inflated prices have driven most local Dubliners away. It's craziest on summer weekend nights, holidays, and nights after big sporting events let out. Women in funky hats, part of loud "hen" (bachelorette) parties, promenade down the main drag as drunken dudes shout from pub doorways to get their attention.

In the most touristy zone around Temple Bar Square, the bars are cartoons of an Irish pub, looking like they board leprechauns upstairs. The only real Irish people you'll see are the ones playing the music, serving the beer, and keeping the rowdies at bay at the doorway. But several good pubs for traditional music are nearby—a 10-minute hike up the river west of Temple Bar takes you to a more local and less touristy scene. The pubs there have longer histories, tangled floor plans, a fun-loving energy, and a passion for trad.

Gogarty's Pub has long been the leading Temple Bar pub for trad. They have foot-tapping sessions downstairs daily at 13:00 and upstairs nightly from 21:00 (at corner of Fleet and Anglesea, tel. 01/671-1822). This is also where the **Traditional Irish Musical Pub Crawl** starts (see page 45).

Darkey Kelly's Bar is a big, fun-loving place with live music nightly. The traditional folk-music vibe here is more sing-along than hard drinking, and the pub grub is good. See their website for what's on when (daily until 23:30, west end of Temple Bar, near Christ Church Cathedral at 19 Fishamble Street, mobile 083-346-4682, www.darkykellys.ie).

The Brazen Head, which claims to be the oldest pub in Dublin, is a hit for an early dinner and late live music (good food, music nightly from 21:30), with atmospheric rooms and a courtyard perfect for balmy evenings (by south end of Father Mathew Bridge, 2 blocks west of Christ Church Cathedral at 20 Lower Bridge Street—see map on page 94; tel. 01/677-9549).

O'Shea's Merchant Pub, across the street, is encrusted with memories of County Kerry football heroes. It's popular with locals who come for the live traditional music nightly at 22:00 (the front half is a restaurant, the toe-tapping magic is in the back—enter at 12 Lower Bridge Street—see map on page 94, tel. 01/679-3797, www.themerchanttemplebar.com).

North of the River

The Cobblestone Pub offers Dublin's least glitzy and most reward-ing traditional-music scene. It's a taxi ride north from Temple Bar but worth the trouble. Stepping inside during a session is like en-tering another world—friendly and untouristy. The walls, covered with photos of honored trad musicians, set the tone. Music is re-vered here, as reflected in the understated sign: "Listening area, please respect musicians" (trad-music sessions Mon from 19:00, Tue-Thu from 17:00, Fri-Sun from 14:00; 100 yards from Old Jameson Distillery's brick chimney tower at 77 King Street North, tel. 01/872-1799, www.cobblestonepub.ie). For location, see the "North Dublin" map on page 94.

O'Sheas Pub hosts wonderful **storytelling dinners** called "Food, Folklore, and Fairies." Even at €52, it's a great value: Along with about 50 tourists, you get a hearty three-course meal that's punctuated by soulful Irish history and fascinating Irish myth-ology, delivered by Johnny—the engaging local folklorist, with occasional live tunes in between (daily 18:30-21:30, Jan-Feb Thu and Sat only; reservations required; 19 Talbot Street, show tel. 01/218-8555, www.irishfolktours.com).

Southeast of St. Stephen's Green

Down the axis of Merrion Row and Lower Baggot Street, you'll find three venerable pubs (within a block of each other) filled with businessmen and staff from nearby governmental buildings blow-ing off steam. One is great for music. All are great for beer lovers. For locations, see the "Southeast Dublin" map on page 117.

O'Donoghue's was famously the home pub of the Dubliners, for decades one of Ireland's premier traditional Irish-music groups. The pub still offers a happy scene and nightly trad sessions from 21:30 (15 Merrion Row, tel. 01/660-7194).

Doheny & Nesbitt is a photogenic choice, with wonderful woodwork and cozy conversational alcoves—and it has great pub grub. Pop in to see what the 2019 Dublin pub of the year looks like (5 Lower Baggot Street, tel. 01/676-2945).

Toner's is another well-varnished choice—it's already cele-brated its 200th anniversary. It has the added attraction of a classic snug in front and a large beer garden out back, mostly to accom-modate smokers (139 Lower Baggot Street, tel. 01/676-3090).

Sister Pubs near Trinity College

Porterhouse Central Bar has an inviting and varied menu, Dublin's best selection of microbrews, and live music (nightly from 17:00-

20:00). It's not as sloppy as Temple Bar but still loud and with a fun energy. This is a great place for dinner with music. You won't find Guinness here, just tasty homebrews. Try one of their sampler trays (45 Nassau Street, tel. 01/677-4180, check music schedule at www.theporterhouse.ie).

The Dingle Whiskey Bar boasts its namesake libation but also features 180 whiskeys from Ireland, Scotland, and North America. The ceiling is lined with staves inscribed with the names of investors who've bought a barrel and are waiting years for it to age. Tasting flights are available for novice to connoisseur palates (Mon-Thu 15:00-23:00, Fri-Sun 13:00-late, 44 Naussau Street, tel. 01/677-4180).

Sleeping in Dublin

Choosing the right neighborhood in Dublin is as important as choosing the right hotel. All of my recommended accommodations are in safe areas convenient to sightseeing.

Central Dublin is popular, loud, and expensive. You'll find big, practical, central places south of the river, near Christ Church Cathedral, Trinity College, and St. Stephen's Green. For classy, older Dublin accommodations in a quieter neighborhood, stay a bit farther out, southeast of St. Stephen's Green. North of the river are additional reliable options in an urban area well served by LUAS trams. If you're on a tight budget, get a room in outlying Dun Laoghaire or Howth (see the end of this chapter), where rooms are cheaper—and quieter (both an easy 25-minute DART train ride into the city).

I rank accommodations from $ budget to $$$$ splurge. For the best deal, contact small hotels directly by phone or email. When you book direct, the owner avoids a commission and may be able to offer a discount. Prices are often discounted on weeknights (Mon-Thu) and from November through February. For some travelers, short-term, Airbnb-type rentals can be a good alternative; search for places in my recommended hotel neighborhoods.

Book your Dublin accommodations well in advance, especially if you'll be traveling during peak season (June-August), weekends any time of year, or if your trip coincides with a major holiday or festival (see the appendix). Hotels raise their prices and are packed on rugby weekends (about four per year), during the all-Ireland Gaelic football and hurling finals (Sundays in August), and during summer rock concerts.

For more details on reservations, short-term rentals, and more, see the "Sleeping" section in the Practicalities chapter.

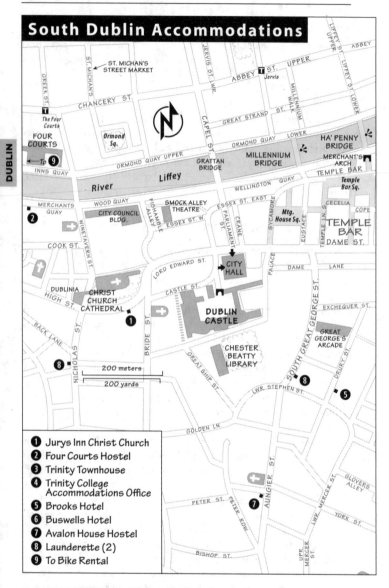

South Dublin Accommodations

1 Jurys Inn Christ Church
2 Four Courts Hostel
3 Trinity Townhouse
4 Trinity College
   Accommodations Office
5 Brooks Hotel
6 Buswells Hotel
7 Avalon House Hostel
8 Launderette (2)
9 To Bike Rental

SOUTH OF THE RIVER LIFFEY
Near Christ Church Cathedral

These lodging options cluster near Christ Church Cathedral, a 5-minute walk from the rowdy and noisy evening scene (at Temple Bar), and 10 minutes from the sightseeing center (Trinity College and Grafton Street). The cheap hostels in this neighborhood have some double rooms. If your hotel charges extra for a full Irish break-

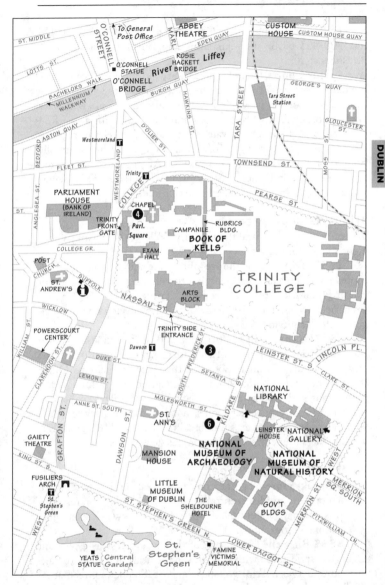

fast, you can eat for less at the many small cafés nearby; try the Queen of Tarts or Chorus Café (see listings under "Eating in Dublin," later).

$$$$ Jurys Inn Christ Church, part of a no-nonsense, American-style hotel chain, is central and offers business-class comfort in 182 identical rooms. If "ye olde" is getting old—and you don't mind big tour groups—this is a good option. Request a room far from the noisy elevator (breakfast extra, book long in advance for weekends, pay parking, Christ Church Place, tel. 01/454-0000, US tel. 800-423-6953, www.jurysinns.com, jurysinnchristchurch@ jurysinns.com).

¢ **Four Courts Hostel** is a 234-bed hostel well located immediately across the river from the Four Courts. It's within a five-minute walk of Christ Church Cathedral and Temple Bar. Bare and institutional, it's also spacious and well run, with a focus on security and efficiency (private rooms available, elevator, game room, some pay parking, 15 Merchant's Quay, from Connolly Station or Busáras Bus Station take LUAS to Four Courts stop and cross river via Father Mathew Bridge, tel. 01/672-5839, www. fourcourtshostel.com, info@fourcourtshostel.com).

Trinity College Area

You can't get more central than Trinity College; these listings offer a good value for the money.

$$$$ Trinity Townhouse offers fine, quiet lodging in 26 rooms split between two Georgian townhouses on either side of South Frederick Street, just south of Trinity College (12 South Frederick Street, tel. 01/617-0900, www.trinitytownhousehotel. com, info@trinitylodge.com).

$$$ Trinity College turns its 800 student-housing dorm rooms on campus into no-frills, affordable accommodations in the city center each summer. Look for the Accommodations Office (open Mon-Fri 8:00-18:00) on the left after going through the main front gate (rooms available late May-mid-Sept, make sure to book Trinity city center rooms, not suburban Dartry location, specify shared bath or en suite, breakfast extra, tel. 01/896-1177, www.tcd.ie/summeraccommodation, residences@tcd.ie).

Near St. Stephen's Green

$$$$ Brooks Hotel is a fine choice for great service, tending 98 plush rooms in an ideal central location. This splurge rarely disappoints (Drury Street, tel. 01/670-4000, www.brookshotel.ie, reservations@brookshotel.ie).

$$$$ Buswells Hotel, one of the city's oldest, is a pleasant Georgian-style haven with 67 rooms in the heart of the city (breakfast extra, between Trinity College and St. Stephen's Green at 23 Molesworth Street, tel. 01/614-6500, www.buswells.ie, info@ buswells.ie).

$$$ Albany House's 50 good-value rooms come with high ceilings, Georgian ambience, and some stairs. Ask for a quieter room in back, away from streetcar noise (just one block south of St. Stephen's Green at 84 Harcourt Street, tel. 01/475-1092, www. albanyhousedublin.com, info@albanyhousedublin.com).

$$$ Fitzwilliam Townhouse rents 14 renovated rooms in a

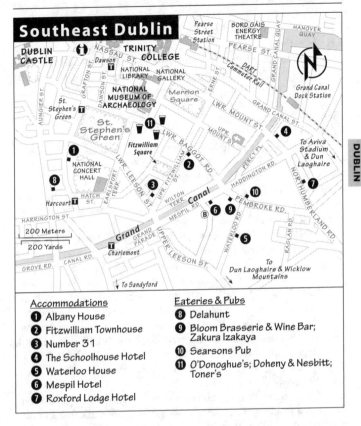

Southeast Dublin

DUBLIN CASTLE · TRINITY COLLEGE · NASSAU ST · Dawson · NATIONAL LIBRARY · NATIONAL GALLERY · Pearse Street Station · BORD GÁIS ENERGY THEATRE · GRAND CANAL QUAY · HANOVER QUAY · PEARSE ST · DART Commuter Rail · Grand Canal Dock Station

St. Stephen's Green · NATIONAL MUSEUM OF ARCHAEOLOGY · Merrion Square · LWR. MOUNT ST. · UPR. MOUNT ST. · GRAND CANAL ST.

St. Stephen's Green · Fitzwilliam Square · LWR. BAGGOT RD. · PERCY PL. · To Aviva Stadium & Dun Laoghaire · NORTHUMBERLAND RD.

AUNGIER ST. · GRAFTON ST. · NATIONAL CONCERT HALL · LWR. LEESON ST. · UPR. FITZWILLIAM ST. · WILTON TERR. · HADDINGTON RD. · RAGLAN RD.

Harcourt · EARLSFORT TERR. · HATCH ST. · MESPIL RD. · Canal · B · PEMBROKE RD. · WATERLOO RD.

HARRINGTON ST. · 200 Meters · 200 Yards · Grand · GRAND PARADE · UPPER LEESON ST. · To Dun Laoghaire & Wicklow Mountains

GROVE RD. · CANAL RD. · Charlemont · To Sandyford

Accommodations
1. Albany House
2. Fitzwilliam Townhouse
3. Number 31
4. The Schoolhouse Hotel
5. Waterloo House
6. Mespil Hotel
7. Roxford Lodge Hotel

Eateries & Pubs
8. Delahunt
9. Bloom Brasserie & Wine Bar; Zakura Izakaya
10. Searsons Pub
11. O'Donoghue's; Doheny & Nesbitt; Toner's

DUBLIN

Georgian townhouse near St. Stephen's Green (family rooms, breakfast extra, 41 Upper Fitzwilliam Street, tel. 01/662-5155, www.fitzwilliamtownhouse.com, info@fitzwilliamtownhouse.com).

¢ **Avalon House Hostel,** near Grafton Street, rents simple, clean backpacker beds (private rooms available, includes continental breakfast, elevator, a few minutes off Grafton Street at 55 Aungier Street, tel. 01/475-0001, www.avalon-house.ie, info@avalon-house.ie).

Southeast of St. Stephen's Green

The Grand Canal, Dublin's urban waterway, sports a lovely narrow greenbelt of trees and lily pads ideal for a pleasant stroll or jog. This neighborhood—stretching roughly east-west from Leeson Street to Grand Canal Street—is a perfect compromise between busy central lodging options and more sedate choices farther out. These listings are unique places (except for the business-class Mespil Hotel), and they charge accordingly. If you're going to break the bank, do it here.

$$$$ Number 31 is a hidden gem reached via gritty little

Leeson Close (a lane off Lower Leeson Street). Its understated elegance is top-notch, with six rooms in a former coach house and 15 rooms in an adjacent Georgian house; the two buildings are connected by a quiet little garden. Guests appreciate the special touches (such as a sunken living room with occasional peat fires) and outstanding breakfasts served in a classy glass atrium (family rooms, limited parking, 31 Leeson Close, tel. 01/676-5011, www.number31.ie, stay@number31.ie).

$$$$ The Schoolhouse Hotel taught as many as 300 students in its heyday (1861-1969) and was in the middle of the street fight that was the 1916 Easter Rising. Now it's a serene hideout with 31 pristine rooms and a fine restaurant (breakfast extra, book early, 2 Northumberland Road, tel. 01/667-5014, www.schoolhousehotel.com, reservations@schoolhousehotel.com).

$$$$ Waterloo House stands proudly Georgian on a quiet residential street with 19 comfortable and relaxing rooms and a pleasant back garden (family rooms, parking, 8 Waterloo Road, tel. 01/660-1888, www.waterloohouse.ie, waterloohouse@eircom.net).

$$$ Mespil Hotel is a huge, modern, business-class hotel renting 254 identical three-star rooms at a good price with all the comforts. This place is a cut above Jurys Inn (breakfast extra, elevator; small first-come, first-served free parking; 10-minute walk southeast of St. Stephen's Green or take bus #37, #38, #39, or #46A; 50 Mespil Road, tel. 01/488-4600, www.mespilhotel.com, mespil@leehotels.com).

$$$ Roxford Lodge Hotel is well managed and a great value. In a quiet residential neighborhood a 20-minute walk from Trinity College, it has 24 tastefully decorated rooms awash with hot tubs and saunas. The executive suite is honeymoon-worthy (family rooms, breakfast extra, elevator, parking, 46 Northumberland Road, tel. 01/668-8572, www.roxfordlodge.ie, reservations@roxfordlodge.ie).

NORTH OF THE RIVER LIFFEY
To locate these hotels, see the "North Dublin" map on page 94.

Near Parnell Square
A swanky neighborhood 250 years ago, this is now workaday Dublin with a steady urban hum, made accessible by LUAS trams.

$$$$ Hotel 7 spruces up an old Georgian property with 51 modern rooms that are refined and stylish. It's worth the comparatively high price for this side of town (7 Gardiner Row, tel. 01/873-7777, www.hotel7dublin.com, info@hotel7dublin.com).

$$$$ The Castle Hotel is a formerly grand but still-comfortable Georgian establishment embedded in the urban canyons of North Dublin. A half-block east of the Garden of Remembrance, it's a good value with pleasant rooms and the friendly Castle Vaults pub with live music in its basement (Great Denmark Street, tel. 01/874-6949, www.castle-hotel.ie, info@castle-hotel.ie).

$$$$ Jurys Inn Parnell Street has 253 predictably soulless but modern rooms. It's a block from the north end of O'Connell Street and the cluster of museums on Parnell Square (breakfast extra, tel. 01/878-4900, www.jurysinns.com, jurysinnparnellst@jurysinns.com).

$$$$ Belvedere Hotel has 92 plain-vanilla rooms that are short on character but long on dependable, modern comforts (Great Denmark Street, tel. 01/873-7700, www.belvederehotel.ie, reservations@belvederehotel.ie).

$$$ Charles Stewart Guesthouse, big and basic, offers 60 acceptable rooms in a good location for a fair price (breakfast extra, ask for a quieter room in the back, just beyond top end of O'Connell Street at 5 Parnell Square East, tel. 01/878-0350, www.charlesstewart.ie, info@charlesstewart.ie).

On Smithfield Square

¢ Generator Hostel provides Dublin's best hostel experience in a clean and stylishly renovated building that was once part of the Jameson Distillery property. The huge 450-bed complex leaves most other hostels looking tired and patched together, and their private double rooms are a great value (at the base of Jameson Distillery chimney observation tower, tel. 01/901-0222, www.generatorhostels.com, ask.dublin@generatorhostels.com).

Near Connolly Station and the River Liffey

$$$$ The **North Star Hotel** lies conveniently across the street from Connolly Station and is a fine splurge, with 235 lush, modern rooms. Although the rail tracks run directly behind it, the rooms are effectively soundproofed (Amiens Street, tel. 01/836-3136, www.northstarhotel.ie, reservations@northstarhotel.ie).

$$$$ Hilton Garden Inn Custom House faces the River Liffey at the edge of the rejuvenated Docklands financial district, with large, modern rooms (breakfast extra, near *Jeanie Johnston* tall ship at 1 Custom House Quay, tel. 01/854-1543, www.dublincustomhouse.hgi.com).

Eating in Dublin

While you can get decent pub grub on just about any corner, there's just no pressing reason to eat Irish in cosmopolitan Dublin. In fact, going local these days is the same as going ethnic. Eating early (17:30-19:00) saves time and money, as many top-end places offer an early-bird special at the same price as a forgettable eatery. Most restaurants serve free jugs of ice water with a smile.

I rank restaurants from **$** budget to **$$$$** splurge. For more advice on eating in Ireland, including ordering, tipping, and Irish cuisine and beverages, see the "Eating" section of the Practicalities chapter.

Dublin also offers a number of dining-plus-entertainment options, including the Celtic Nights dinner show and O'Sheas Pub's storytelling dinner (listed earlier, under "Entertainment in Dublin"), and a dinner-show version of the Traditional Irish Musical Pub Crawl (listed under "Tours in Dublin," near the beginning of this chapter).

DUBLIN

SOUTH DUBLIN EATERIES
"Bib Gourmand" Restaurants

If you want to dine well yet reasonably in Dublin without dressing up, these three restaurants are my favorites. Small, fresh, and untouristy, they've each earned the Michelin "Bib Gourmand" rating for their casual gourmet quality. Menus are creative and modern, dishes are beautifully presented, and they are cozy and romantic. Reservations are required in the evening. Delahunt, south of St. Stephen's Green, is my favorite but is a long walk or cab ride from the center. Pig's Ear and Etto are more central, between Trinity College and St. Stephen's Green, and offer early-bird dinners (three courses for around €30 weeknights before 18:30).

$$$ Delahunt is a bright star in a newly vibrant neighborhood. In a long and narrow circa-1906 grocery store, it surrounds its diners with original brass and varnished trappings. The waitstaff is friendly and the cuisine—Irish with French/Italian/Japanese flavors—is a delight. At dinner, you'll choose from a two- or three-course menu, with a selection of dishes for each course (casual lunch served Tue-Fri 12:00-14:00, dinner Tue-Sat 17:00-21:30, closed Sun-Mon, 39 Camden Street Lower, tel. 01/598-4880, www.delahunt.ie). For location, see the "Southeast Dublin" map on page 117.

$$$ The Pig's Ear fills a small and simple, dark-wood-and-candles dining hall. A steep stairway climb above Nassau Street, it overlooks the Trinity College green, and wows diners with its modern Irish menu (Mon-Sat 12:00-14:45 & 17:30-22:00, closed Sun, 4 Nassau Street, tel. 01/670-3865, www.thepigsear.ie).

$$$ Etto is a small restaurant with tight seating, high volume, and a fun energy. The enticing menu is a fusion of Italian and Irish. I enjoy the view from the bar and would consider reserving a spot there (Mon-Sat 12:00-14:30 & 17:30-22:30, closed Sun, 2 blocks off St. Stephen's Green, 18 Merrion Row, tel. 01/678-8872, www.etto.ie).

Other Restaurants in the Center

$$$ Fallon & Byrne Wine Cellar is a fun surprise. From the big, high-end grocery store on the ground floor, you hike down the stairs to a spacious and welcoming wine cellar with a casual mix of regular and barrel-top tables. The wine-friendly menu is international and modern, with €20 main dishes, meat-and-cheese boards, and a fine selection of wine by the glass. Your server can give you good wine advice (daily 12:00-22:00, tel. 01/472-1012). For a more conventional (and pricier) **restaurant** with modern Irish dishes and good pre-theater menus, climb upstairs (daily 17:30-22:00, tel. 01/472-1000, reservations smart, 11 Exchequer Street, www.fallonandbyrne.com).

$$$$ Trocadero is an old-school fixture serving beefy European and modern Irish cuisine to Dubliners interested in a slow, romantic meal. The dressy, red-velvet interior is draped with photos of local actors (daily 17:00-23:30, 4 St. Andrew Street, tel. 01/677-5545, www.trocadero.ie, Robert). Popular with theatergoers, the three-course early-bird special is a fine value at €30 (17:00-19:00, leave by 19:45).

Fast, Easy, and Cheap

For a quick and healthy lunch, you'll find chain eateries featuring nutritious fare (such as **Sprout & Co** and **Chopped**) all over town. Otherwise, try one of the places listed next.

$$ Bewley's Oriental Café is a grand, traditional eatery, centrally located on Grafton Street. Good-value breakfast, lunch, and early-evening meals are offered in a wonderful human bustle that epitomizes urban Dublin. The fine Harry Clarke stained-glass

windows (against the back wall), fun lunch theater (upstairs), and snack-worthy baked treats (inside the front door) are all great excuses to linger (Mon-Wed 7:30-19:00, Thu until 21:00, Fri until 20:00, Sat-Sun 9:00-20:00, 78 Grafton Street, tel. 01/564-0900). For the lunch theater schedule, see www. bewleyscafetheatre.com (€12, performances at 13:00, arrive at 12:45 to settle in and order before the performance begins).

$$ O'Neill's Pub is a venerable, touristy, dark, and tangled retreat offering sling-'em-out pub grub, including breakfasts and carvery lunches. While you can order from the menu, most diners grab a tray and go through their self-service cafeteria line (daily 12:00-22:30, across from the Molly Malone statue on Suffolk Street, tel. 01/679-3656).

$$ Avoca Café, on the second floor above the Avoca department store, is a cheery eatery thriving with smart local shoppers.

DUBLIN

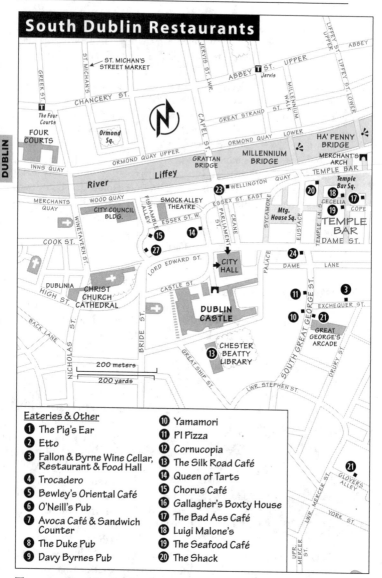

South Dublin Restaurants

Eateries & Other

1. The Pig's Ear
2. Etto
3. Fallon & Byrne Wine Cellar, Restaurant & Food Hall
4. Trocadero
5. Bewley's Oriental Café
6. O'Neill's Pub
7. Avoca Café & Sandwich Counter
8. The Duke Pub
9. Davy Byrnes Pub
10. Yamamori
11. Pl Pizza
12. Cornucopia
13. The Silk Road Café
14. Queen of Tarts
15. Chorus Café
16. Gallagher's Boxty House
17. The Bad Ass Café
18. Luigi Malone's
19. The Seafood Café
20. The Shack

They serve healthy foodie plates and great salads (daily 9:30-17:30, 11 Suffolk Street, tel. 01/672-6019). Lunching here, you feel like an in-the-know local.

$ Avoca Sandwich Counter, in the Avoca store basement, has simple seating and a cheap buffet and salad bar counter that sells food priced by weight. They also offer deli sandwiches and enticing baked goodies (good for takeaway, daily generally 10:00-18:00, 11 Suffolk Street).

DUBLIN

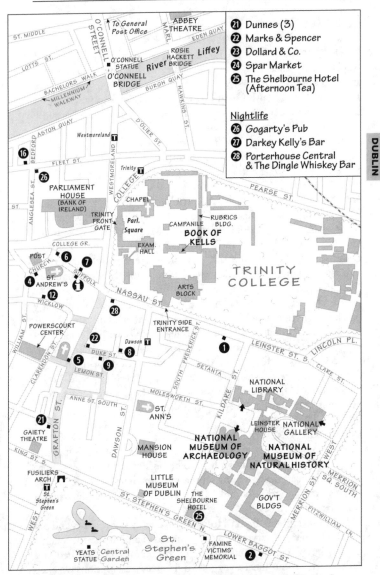

21 Dunnes (3)
22 Marks & Spencer
23 Dollard & Co.
24 Spar Market
25 The Shelbourne Hotel (Afternoon Tea)

Nightlife
26 Gogarty's Pub
27 Darkey Kelly's Bar
28 Porterhouse Central & The Dingle Whiskey Bar

$$ The Duke and **Davy Byrnes,** neighbors on Duke Street, serve reliable pub lunches. Davy Byrnes feels like pub-meets-diner (at #21, also serves dinner, tel. 01/677-5217). The Duke has a buffet lunch counter in the back from 12:00 to 16:00 (at #8, tel. 01/679-9553). Both are favorites for Irish lit fans whose heroes (James Joyce, Brendan Behan, and Patrick Kavanagh) frequented them.

$$$ Yamamori is a plain, mellow, and modern Japanese place serving seas of sushi and noodles (daily 12:00-22:30, 73 South Great George's Street, tel. 01/475-5001).

$ PI Pizza is a hit for its short list of wood-fired, thin-crust Naples-style pizza. It's mod and fun, and the chef is passionate about quality ingredients (you're welcome to split your pizza, daily 12:00-22:00, 83 South Great George's Street, www.pipizzas.it).

$$ Cornucopia is a small, earth-mama-with-class, proudly vegetarian ("98% vegan"), self-serve place two blocks off Grafton. It's friendly and youthful, with hearty breakfasts, lunches, and dinner specials (Mon-Sat 8:30-22:00, Sun 12:00-21:00, 19 Wicklow Street, tel. 01/677-7583).

Near Christ Church Cathedral

$$ The Silk Road Café at the Chester Beatty Library serves an enticing selection of Middle Eastern and Mediterranean cuisine for lunch daily (good salads and vegetarian dishes, on the grounds of Dublin Castle, tel. 01/407-0770). While you're there, be sure to pop into the amazing (free) library (see listing earlier, under "Sights in Dublin").

$ Queen of Tarts, with nice outdoor seating, does yummy breakfasts, light lunches, sandwiches, and wonderful pastries (Mon-Fri 8:00-19:00, Sat-Sun from 9:00, just off Dame Street, go 100 yards up from City Hall and left on Cow's Lane, tel. 01/670-7499).

$ Chorus Café is a friendly and plain little hole-in-the-wall diner serving breakfast, salads, panini, and pastas (daily 8:30-17:00, 7 Fishamble Street, next door to the site of the first performance of Handel's "Messiah," tel. 01/616-7088, Cyrus).

In Temple Bar

Temple Bar, while overrun with tourists, has a strange magnetism—you'll likely be drawn here to be part of the scene. It's lined with sloppy eateries charging a premium for their location. Everything's open long hours daily. If I were to eat in Temple Bar, I'd consider these places:

$$ Gallagher's Boxty House, with creaky floorboards and old Dublin ambience, serves stews and corned beef, but the specialty is boxty, the generally bland-tasting Irish potato pancake filled and rolled with various meats, veggies, and sauces (reservations wise, 20 Temple Bar, tel. 01/677-2762).

$$ The Bad Ass Café serves pizza, pasta, burgers, and salads. There's even a fun kids' menu. Their big patio fronts the Temple Bar action, and there's live music nightly from about 19:00 in the dark, sprawling, pubby interior (9 Crown Alley, tel. 01/675-3005).

$$ Luigi Malone's, with its fun atmosphere and varied menu of pizza, ribs, pasta, sandwiches, and fajitas, is just the place to take your high-school date (corner of Cecilia and Fownes streets, tel. 01/679-2723).

$$$ The Seafood Café, across from Luigi Malone's, is pricey but serves top-quality Irish oysters, lobster rolls, and more (11 Sprangers Yard, tel. 01/515-3717).

$$$ The Shack, offering traditional Irish, chicken, seafood, and steak dishes, comes with the most sanity of this bunch of Temple Bar eateries (24 East Essex Street, tel. 01/679-0043).

Near the Grand Canal

These three places are within a long block of one another in the emerging Grand Canal neighborhood. This area, southeast of St. Stephen's Green (just walk straight out Lower Baggot Street until you cross the canal), feels comfortably workaday with fewer tourists (near the intersection of Baggot Street and Mespil Road). For locations, see the "Southeast Dublin" map on page 117.

$$$ Bloom Brasserie & Wine Bar has a woody, candlelit ambience with beautifully presented dishes based on locally sourced meats (beef, lamb, duck) and seafood (Irish salmon). The menu is modern Irish meets France and changes with the seasons (daily 12:00-14:30 & 17:00-22:30, 11 Upper Baggot Street, tel. 01/668-7170).

$$ Searsons Pub, a sprawling neighborhood favorite, is a gastropub known for its roast beef, lamb, and salmon, with an open kitchen, classy-for-a-sports-bar energy, and friendly service. If there's a horse race or rugby match on, it'll be on the screens here (it's located near the rugby stadium and a betting office). You can escape the clamor out back on the patio (daily 12:00-22:00, 42 Upper Baggot Street, tel. 01/660-0330).

$$ Zakura Izakaya is a classy if noisy Japanese place—small and tight, like a sushi wine bar (daily 12:00-22:00, 7 Upper Baggot Street, tel. 01/563-8000).

HIP AND FUN IN NORTH DUBLIN

For locations, see the "North Dublin" map on page 94.

The Church is a trendy café/bar/restaurant/nightclub/beer garden housed in the former St. Mary's Church (which hosted the baptism of Irish rebel Wolfe Tone and the marriage of brewing legend Arthur Guinness). Today the **$$$ Choir Balcony** has a huge pipe organ and a refined menu (daily 17:00-22:30). The less-expensive ground floor **Nave** is dominated by a long bar and pub grub (daily 12:00-21:00). A disco thumps away in the bunker-like basement until the wee hours on Friday and Saturday. On warm summer nights, the outdoor terrace is packed. Eating here is more about the scene than the cuisine (corner of St. Mary's and Jervis Streets, tel. 01/828-0102, www.thechurch.ie).

DUBLIN

$$$ Mr Fox is an elegant and serene little basement operation serving locally sourced dishes created by chef Anthony Smith (Tue-Fri 12:00-14:00 & 17:00-21:30, Sat 17:30-22:00, closed Sun-Mon; behind the Garden of Remembrance at 38 Parnell Square West, tel. 01/874-7778, www.mrfox.ie)

$$ Brannigan's is an inviting family-run traditional pub—it's been a "beer emporium since 1909." They offer a lunch buffet (Mon-Fri 12:00-15:00). Its location—roughly halfway between the Gate and Abbey theaters—makes it convenient for theatergoers and those exploring O'Connell Street (daily 10:30-23:30, 9 Cathedral Street, 50 yards from the Spire, tel. 01/874-0137).

$ One Society Café goes for "tasty, healthy, simple" in an unpretentious little space a few blocks east of the Parnell Monument. But it surprises with inventive breakfasts and lunches as well as unique specialty pizza dinners (pizza only at night, dinner reservations required, Tue-Fri 7:30-21:00, Sat-Sun from 9:30, closed Mon, 1 Gardiner Street Lower, tel. 01/537-5261, www.onesociety.ie).

North Quay Docklands Area

This district on the north quay of the River Liffey was a derelict dockland until the late 1980s, when it was transformed into a financial and tech center.

$$$ Ely Bar & Grill offers great beef and pork dishes, made with organic meat from their County Clare farm. Choose a seat in the romantic, 200-year-old wine vault downstairs, the modern upstairs space, or the dock-view outdoor terrace (Mon-Sat 12:00-23:00, Sun until 18:00, in the CHQ Building directly behind the EPIC Emigration Museum, tel. 01/672-0010, www.elywinebar.ie).

$$$ Harbourmaster Bar and Restaurant occupies the building that once oversaw the ebb and flow of cargo on the surrounding docks. It's a fun place serving good pub grub on one end and hosting a peaceful restaurant with more varied choices on the other (Mon-Fri 12:00-23:30, Sat from 13:00, closed Sun, Custom House Dock at George's Dock, look for the little brick building with a clock tower, tel. 01/670-1688, www.harbourmaster.ie).

DELIS AND MARKETS WITH PRACTICAL EATERIES

If you want to eat fast, cheap, and healthy in the tourist center, several high-end markets offer fresh sandwiches, salad bars, and a place to sit while you eat. Department stores with fancy grocery sections also generally have what picnickers need: Try **Dunnes** (daily until 21:00, with several locations) or **Marks & Spencer** (daily until 20:00 or so, at 20 Grafton Street).

$$ **Dollard & Co.** is a gourmet grocery...and much more: pizza by the slice, meat-and-cheese boards (create yours with the cheesemonger's help), and a small inviting menu of burgers, pasta, and steaks (order at the central bar and they bring it to you). It's popular for breakfast, too. The spacious dining hall has a fun, trendy energy with views of the river (Mon-Fri 8:00-21:00, Sat 9:00-22:00, Sun 10:00-20:00; on the south bank at 2 Wellington Quay, tel. 01/616-9606).

$ **Fallon & Byrne Food Hall** is like eating at an upscale Trader Joe's. Just point to what you like (a main dish with two sides for €11) and they'll microwave it (Mon-Sat 8:00-21:00, Sun 11:00-19:00, 11 Exchequer Street, tel. 01/472-1010).

$ **Spar Market** is open 24/7; notice they actually have no front door—it's literally always open, with huge windows overlooking the Dame Street action. Shop for your groceries, then sit down right there and eat them (a block above the Temple Bar commotion at the corner of Dame Street and South Great George's Street, tel. 01/633-9070).

$ **Baxter & Greene Market Café,** north of the river behind the General Post Office, is a handy cafeteria on the third floor of the Dunnes department store in the Ilac Centre (daily 9:00-18:30, Henry Street; for location, see map on page 94).

AFTERNOON TEA

$$$$ **The Shelbourne Hotel** has been a Dublin landmark since 1824, built to attract genteel patrons and Dublin's upper-crust socialites. "Fur coat and no knickers" schlubs can sample the aristocratic good life by enjoying the tradition of afternoon tea in the hotel's Lord Mayor's Lounge (no shorts, tank tops, or T-shirts). The menu is a swirl of finger sandwiches, buttermilk scones, clotted cream, strawberry jam, ginger loaf, and fine coffee...as well as 22 varieties of tea (2-hour seatings Mon-Fri at 12:30, 15:00, and 17:30; Sat-Sun at 11:30, 14:00, 16:30, and 19:00; reservations smart, especially on weekends; live piano music, 27 St. Stephen's Green, tel. 01/663-4500, www.theshelbourne.com).

Dublin Connections

BY PLANE

Dublin Airport has two terminals located an easily walkable 100 yards apart (code: DUB, tel. 01/814-1111, www.dublinairport. com). Both have ATMs, cafés, Wi-Fi, and luggage storage (www. leftluggage.ie). There is no TI at the airport.

Getting Downtown by Bus: You have two main choices—Airlink (double-decker turquoise bus) or Aircoach (single-deck blue bus). Both pick up on the street directly in front of arrivals, at ground level, at both terminals.

DUBLIN

Airlink Express: Airlink bus #747 generally runs an east-west route that parallels the River Liffey, and includes stops at or near the Busáras Central Bus Station, Connolly Station, O'Connell Street, Temple Bar, Christ Church, and Heuston Station. Airlink bus #757 links the airport to the center along a generally north-south axis, including Trinity College, St. Stephen's Green (eastern end), and the National Concert Hall. Ask the driver which stop is closest to your destination (€7, pay driver, 3-5/hour, about 40 minutes; runs Mon-Sat 5:00-late, Sun from 7:25; tel. 01/873-4222, www.dublinbus.ie). This bus is covered by the Leap Visitor and the Do Dublin Freedom transit cards; both cards can be purchased at the airport (see page 42).

Aircoach: This bus generally runs a north-south route that follows the O'Connell and Grafton streets axis. To reach recommended hotels south of the city center, the Aircoach bus #700 works well (€8 if paying driver, discount if booked online, discount with Dublin Pass, 4/hour, fewer late night, runs 24 hours, tel. 01/844-7118, www.aircoach.ie). Aircoach also runs a bus between Dublin Airport and Belfast (see the Belfast chapter).

By Taxi: Taxis from the airport into Dublin cost about €30.

Sleeping at the Airport: A safe bet is the **$$$ Radisson Blu Dublin Airport** (tel. 01/844-6000, www.radissonblu.ie).

BY TRAIN OR BUS

The frequencies listed below are for Monday-Saturday (departures are less frequent on Sunday).

By Train from Dublin's Heuston Station to: Tralee (every two hours, most change in Mallow but one direct evening train, 4 hours), **Ennis** (10/day, 4 hours, change in Limerick, Limerick Junction, or Athenry), **Galway** (8/day, 3 hours), **Westport** (5/day, 3.25 hours). Irish Rail train info: Tel. 01/836-6222, www.irishrail.ie.

By Train from Dublin's Connolly Station to: Rosslare (3-4/day, 3 hours), Portrush (7/day, 5 hours, transfer in Belfast or Coleraine). The **Dublin-Belfast train** connects the capitals in two hours at 90 mph (8/day). Northern Ireland train info: Tel. 048/9089-9400, www.translink.co.uk.

By Bus to: Belfast (hourly, most via Dublin Airport, 3 hours), **Trim** (almost hourly, 1 hour), **Ennis** (almost hourly, 5 hours), **Galway** (hourly, 3.5 hours; faster on CityLink—hourly, 2.5 hours, tel. 091/564-164, www.citylink.ie), **Westport** (6/day, 6 hours), **Limerick** (7/day, 3.5 hours), **Tralee** (7/day, 6 hours), **Dingle** (4/day, 8.5 hours, transfer at Limerick and Tralee). Bus info: Tel. 01/836-6111, www.buseireann.ie.

BY CAR

It's best to avoid driving in hectic downtown Dublin. If you plan to drive in Ireland, save your car rental for the countryside. Consider renting a car at the airport, where you'll find all the standard car-rental agencies with longer hours than those in the city and easier access to the M-50. If you must rent in Dublin, the Hertz office on the Grand Canal in southeast Dublin is workable if you are headed south out of the city (at 2 Haddington Road, tel. 01/668-7566).

M-50 Toll Road: Drivers renting a car at Dublin Airport and heading for the countryside can bypass the worst of the big-city traffic by taking the M-50 ring road south or west. The M-50 uses an automatic tolling system called eFlow. Your rental should come with an eFlow tag installed; confirm this when you pick up your car. The €3.10 per-trip toll is automatically charged to the credit card you used to rent the car (www.eflow.ie).

Other Toll Roads: Your rental car's eFlow tag will work only for the M-50 ring road around Dublin. On any other Irish toll roads, you'll need to pay with cash (about €2/toll). These roads mostly run outward from Dublin toward Waterford, Cork, Limerick, and Galway (roads farther west are free).

CONNECTING IRELAND AND BRITAIN

It's worth spending a few minutes researching your transportation options across the Irish Sea. Most airline and ferry companies routinely offer online discounts. Before sorting out rail/ferry prices with individual companies, try www.tfwrail.wales/ticket-types/sailrail, which deals with several companies and has fares low enough to compete with cheap airlines. Ferries work for rural Wales or Scotland; for everywhere else, fly.

Flights: If you're going directly to London, flying is your best bet. Ryanair and Aer Lingus are the predominant discount carriers, but note that their London-bound flights often land at Luton or Stansted—airports some distance from the city center.

Ferries: Irish Ferries (tel. 0818-300-400, www.irishferries.com) and Stena Line (tel. 01/907-5555, www.stenaline.ie) combine to make eight daily crossings between Dublin Port (two miles east of O'Connell Bridge) and Holyhead, Wales. Most trips take 3.5 hours, but Irish Ferries offers a twice-daily fast boat that makes the trip in 2 hours. Since  these boats can fill up on summer weekends, book at least a week ahead during the peak period.

DUBLIN

Dublin Bay

Dangling from opposite ends of Dublin Bay's crescent-shaped shoreline, Dun Laoghaire (dun LEERY) and Howth (rhymes with "growth") are two peas in a pod. They offer quiet, cheaper lodging alternatives to Dublin and have easy light-rail access to the city center, just a 25-minute ride away. Dun Laoghaire is bigger and has more going on, while Howth has a sleepier vibe and a fishing fleet.

Dun Laoghaire

Dun Laoghaire is seven miles south of Dublin. This snoozy suburb, with easy connections to downtown Dublin, is a convenient small-town base for exploring the big city.

The Dun Laoghaire harbor was strategic enough to merit a line of martello towers, built in 1804 to defend against an expected Napoleonic invasion (one tower now houses the James Joyce Museum). By the mid-19th century, massive breakwaters were completed to protect the huge harbor. Ferries once sailed regularly from here to Wales (75 miles away), and the first train line in Ireland connected the terminal with Dublin. With those ferries now gone, Dun Laoghaire is much quieter.

GETTING TO DUN LAOGHAIRE

With easy DART and Aircoach options, taking a taxi is like throwing money away. But if you really need one, try ABC Taxi service (about €30 to Dublin, €40 to the airport, tel. 01/285-5444).

By DART Commuter Train: The DART commuter train connects to Dublin in 25 minutes (4/hour, runs daily until about 23:30, €3.60 one-way, €6.75 round-trip ticket is good same day only, www.irishrail.ie). If you're coming from Dublin, catch a DART train marked *Bray* or *Greystones* and get off at the Sandy-cove/Glasthule or Dun Laoghaire stop, depending on your B&B's location. Leaving Dun Laoghaire, catch a train marked *Howth* to get to Dublin. Get off at the central Tara Street Station to sightsee in Dublin, or, for train connections north, ride one stop farther to Connolly Station.

By Bus from the Airport: Aircoach bus #703 makes it easy to connect Dun Laoghaire and Dublin Airport (€10.50, runs hourly,

50 minutes, see map for stop locations, tel. 01/844-7118, www. aircoach.ie).

Parking in Dun Laoghaire: Drivers can leave their cars in Dun Laoghaire and sightsee Dublin by DART. The Pavilion Car Park under the Pavilion Theatre block has a cheap day rate (access facing bay from Queens Road, €6 online advance booking day rate, tel. 01/883-9833, www.parkrite.ie). Note that street parking is limited to three hours (except on Sundays, when it's unlimited and free).

DUBLIN

Orientation to Dun Laoghaire

Dun Laoghaire has a coastline defined by its nearly mile-long breakwaters—reaching like two muscular arms into the Irish Sea. The breakwaters are popular for strollers, bikers, birdwatchers, and fishermen.

Helpful Hints: You may find a **seasonal TI** operating from a kiosk near the Dun Laoghaire DART station. For **laundry,** try Park Laundry (full service only, Mon-Fri 8:30-17:30, Sat until 16:30, closed Sun, Upper George's Street, tel. 01/551-8977). For the **best views,** hike out to the lighthouse at the end of the East Pier or climb the tight stairs to the top of the stubby martello tower in Sandycove (see next).

Sights in Dun Laoghaire

James Joyce Tower and Museum

This squat martello tower at Sandycove was originally built to repel a possible Napoleonic invasion, but it became famous chiefly because of its association with James Joyce. The great author lived here briefly and made it the setting for the opening of his novel *Ulysses*. The museum's round exhibition space is filled with literary memorabilia, including photographs and rare first editions. For a fine view, climb the claustrophobic, two-story spiral stairwell sealed inside the thick wall to reach the rooftop cannon mount.

Cost and Hours: Free, daily 10:00-18:00, Nov-mid-March until 16:00, the museum is run by volunteers—call ahead to be sure it's open, tel. 01/280-9265, www.joycetower.ie.

National Maritime Museum of Ireland

Maritime exhibits fill a former church with model steamships, brass fittings, accounts of heroic rescue attempts, and a huge lighthouse optic (lamp lens, installed where the altar once stood). Landlubbers may find it underwhelming.

Cost and Hours: €6, daily 11:00-17:00, Haigh Terrace, tel. 01/214-3964, www.mariner.ie.

DUBLIN

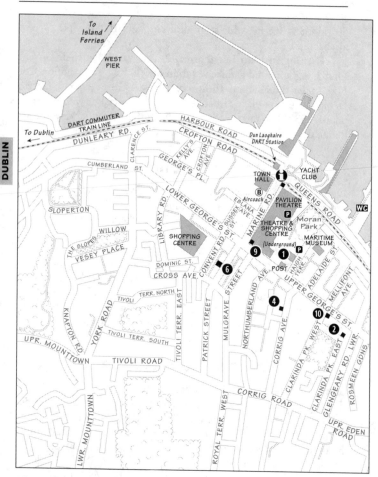

Plays and Concerts

The Pavilion Theatre offers performances in the center of town (box office open Mon-Sat 12:00-17:00, open 2 hours before performances, Marine Road, tel. 01/231-2929, www.paviliontheatre.ie).

Swimming

Kids of all ages enjoy swimming at the safe, sandy little cove bordered by rounded rocks beside the martello tower.

Sleeping in Dun Laoghaire

These places lie between the Sandycove/Glasthule and Dun Laoghaire DART stations (check the map to decide which stop to use).

$$$ The **Royal Marine Hotel** is a grand 230-room relic from the 1860s, when this town was Ireland's primary ferry port.

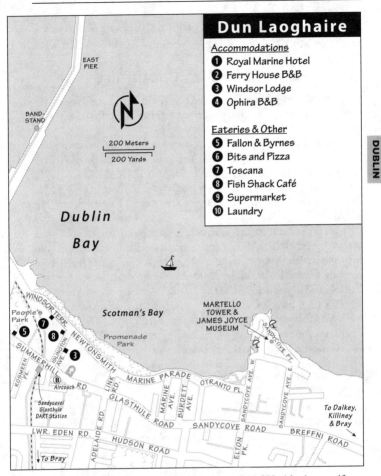

Its comfortably renovated rooms ooze Old World charm (family rooms, ground-floor pub, on Marine Road, tel. 01/230-0030, www.royalmarine.ie, reservations@royalmarine.ie).

$$ Ferry House B&B, with four high-ceilinged rooms, is a family-friendly place on a dead-end street (family room, 15 Clarinda Park North just off Clarinda Park West, tel. 01/280-8301, mobile 087-267-0511, www.ferryhousedublin.ie, ferry_house@hotmail.com, Eamon and Pauline Teehan).

$ Windsor Lodge rents four fresh, inviting rooms on a quiet street a block off the harbor (cash only, 3 Islington Avenue, tel. 01/284-6952, mobile 086-844-6646, www.windsorlodge.ie, windsorlodgedublin@gmail.com, Mary O'Farrell).

$ Ophira B&B is a historic house with four comfortably creaky rooms run by active diver-hiker-biker John O'Connor and his wife, Cathy (family room, parking, 10 Corrig Avenue, tel. 01/280-0997, www.ophira.ie, johnandcathy@ophira.ie).

Eating in Dun Laoghaire

George's Street—Dun Laoghaire's main drag, three blocks inland—has plenty of reasonably priced eateries and pubs, many with live music.

$$ Fallon & Byrnes is your best bet for fine wine and good food in a lovely glassed-in space beside the pleasant People's Park (daily 12:00-21:00, Summerhill Road, tel. 01/230-3300).

$$ Bits and Pizza is kid-friendly and a good bet for families (daily 12:00-22:00, off George's Street at 15 Patrick Street, tel. 01/284-2411).

$$ Toscana, on the seafront, is a popular little cubbyhole, serving hearty Italian dishes and pizza. Its location makes it easy to incorporate into your evening stroll. Reserve for dinner (early-bird specials before 18:30, daily 12:00-22:00, 5 Windsor Terrace, tel. 01/230-0890, www.toscana.ie).

$$ Fish Shack Café, on the stroll-worthy waterfront, serves fresh fish dishes to beachcombers (Mon-Sat 12:00-22:00, Sun until 21:00, takeout available, 1 Martello Terrace, tel. 01/284-4555).

Groceries: For picnic shopping, you'll find the **Super Valu** under the Dun Laoghaire Shopping Centre, at the corner of Marine Road and Upper George's Street (Mon-Sat 8:00-21:00, Sun 9:00-19:00).

In Glasthule: Called simply "the village" locally, Glasthule is just down the street from the Sandycove/Glasthule DART station and has an array of fun, hardworking little restaurants.

Howth

Eight miles north of Dublin, Howth rests on a teardrop-shaped peninsula that pokes the Irish Sea. Its active harbor chugs with fishing boats earnestly bringing in the daily catch, and seals trolling for scraps. Weary Dubliners come here for refreshing coastal cliff walks. Located at the north terminus of the DART commuter line, Howth makes a good place for travelers to settle in, with easy connections to Dublin for sightseeing.  But there are only a couple centrally located and worthwhile lodging options.

Howth was once an important gateway to Dublin. Near the neck of the peninsula is the suburb of Clontarf, where Irish High King Brian Boru defeated the last concerted Viking attack in 1014. Eight hundred years later, a squat martello tower was built on a bluff above Howth's harbor to defend it from a Napoleonic invasion that never came. The harbor then grew as a port for shipping from Liverpool and Wales. It was eventually eclipsed by Dun Laoghaire, which was first to gain rail access. Irish rebels smuggled German-supplied guns into Ireland via Howth in 1914, making the 1916 Easter Rising possible. Soon after, Howth became a favorite safe-house refuge for rebel mastermind Michael Collins. These days, this is a pleasant coastal hamlet.

DUBLIN

GETTING TO HOWTH

The DART light-rail system zaps travelers between Howth and the city (4/hour, 25 minutes, daily until about 23:30, €3.60 one-way, €6.75 round-trips good same day only, www.irishrail.ie). If you're coming from Dublin, catch a DART train marked *Howth* (not *Howth Junction, Malahide,* or *Drogheda*) and ride it to the end of the line—passing through Howth Junction en route. All trains departing Howth head straight to Dublin's Connolly Station, and then continue on to the Tara and Pearse stations. Get off at Connolly for sightseeing north of the River Liffey or Tara for sightseeing south of the river. Grab a morning train to minimize the jam on sunny summer weekends.

A taxi from the airport takes about 20 minutes and costs about €25. Try Executive Cabs (tel. 01/839-6020).

Orientation to Howth

Howth perches on the north shore of the peninsula and generally divides along the east-west harborfront and the north-south street that winds uphill to the village.

The quarter-mile harborfront promenade stretches from the DART station (in the west) to the martello tower on the bluff (in the east). Dominating the view are two stony piers that clutch like crab claws at the Irish Sea. The West Pier has the fishing action, while the East Pier extends to a stubby 200-year-old lighthouse and views of a rugged nearby island, Ireland's Eye. The village is reached via Abbey Street (becoming Main Street), extending uphill from the harbor near the base of the martello tower bluff. Along the street, you'll find a church, most of the shops and pubs, and a grocery store.

There are two **ATMs** in town: the tiny Ulster Bank kiosk across the street from the DART station (to the left of the Gem Market) and inside the Centra Market. The helpful **TI** is located

DUBLIN

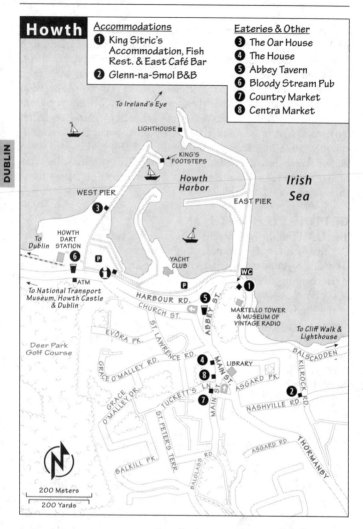

Howth

Accommodations
1. King Sitric's Accommodation, Fish Rest. & East Café Bar
2. Glenn-na-Smol B&B

Eateries & Other
3. The Oar House
4. The House
5. Abbey Tavern
6. Bloody Stream Pub
7. Country Market
8. Centra Market

on the harborfront, in a tiny wooden hut on Harbour Road, across from Howth's old courthouse (daily 9:30-17:00, shorter hours off-season, mobile 085-858-1695, www.visithowth.ie).

Sights in Howth

Other than coastal walks, sightseeing here pales in comparison to Dublin. Privately owned **Howth Castle** is a big mansion, surrounded by extensive rhododendron gardens. The castle itself can be toured only by appointment (www.howthcastle.ie).

Museum of Vintage Radio

The three-story martello tower on the bluff overlooking the East Pier is the only sight in Howth worth a glance. Curator Pat Herbert has spent decades acquiring his collection of lovingly preserved radios, gramophones, and even a hurdy-gurdy (a crank-action musical oddity)—all of which still work. Check out the radio disguised as a picture frame, which was used by the resistance in occupied France during World War II.

Before leaving the compact bluff, catch the views of the harbor and the nearby island of Ireland's Eye. Spot the distant martello tower on the island's west end and the white guano coating its eastern side, courtesy of a colony of gannets.

Cost and Hours: €5, changeable hours but generally daily 11:00-16:00, Oct-April Sat-Sun only, entry up steep driveway off Abbey Street, mobile 086-815-4189.

DUBLIN

National Transport Museum of Ireland

Housed in a large warehouse on the castle grounds, this is a dusty waste of time unless you find rapture in old trams and buses (€4, Sat-Sun 14:00-17:00, closed Mon-Fri, mobile 085-146-0499, www.nationaltransportmuseum.org).

St. Mary's Abbey

Looming above Abbey Street, the abbey ruins date from the early 1400s. Before that, a church built by Norse King Sitric in 1042 stood at this site. The entrance to the ruins is on Church Street, above the abbey grounds.

East and West Piers

Howth's piers make for mellow strolls after a meal. Poke your head into the various fishmonger shops along the West Pier to see the day's catch. At the end of the pier (on the leeward side), you'll find the footprints of King George IV carved into the stone after his 1821 visit. The East Pier is a quiet jetty barbed with a squat lighthouse and the closest views of the offshore island called Ireland's Eye.

Boat Trips

To get even closer to Ireland's Eye (and its large bird colonies), two excursion operators can either land you on the island or just sail a lap around it. Both operate daily in summer on demand (daily 10:30-17:00) from the end of the West Pier (€15 to land or €10 to sail around the island; **Island Ferries,** mobile 086-845-9154, www.islandferries.net; **Ireland's Eye Ferries,** mobile 086-077-3021, www.irelandseyeferries.com).

Dublin Bay Cruises sails the coast between Howth and Dun Laoghaire, stopping in Dublin en route (€22, daily 9:30-17:00, tel. 01/901-1757, www.dublinbaycruises.com).

Hiking Trails and Guided Hikes

Trails above the eastern cliffs of the peninsula offer enjoyable, breezy exercise. For a scenic three-hour round-trip, walk past the East Pier and martello tower, following Balscadden Road uphill. You'll soon pass Balscadden House, where writer W. B. Yeats spent part of his youth (watch for plaque on left). A 10-minute stroll beyond that, the road dead-ends, where you'll find the well-marked trailhead and easy-to-follow trail; soon you'll be walking south around the craggy coastline to grand views of the Bailey Lighthouse on the southeast rim of the peninsula. The gate to the lighthouse grounds is always locked, so enjoy the view from afar before retracing your steps back to Howth.

Guided 3.5-hour hiking excursions can be enjoyed with **Hidden Howth Experiences,** whose guides offer insights on the town's Viking history and seafood culture (mobile 087-978-1390, www.hiddenhowthexperiences.com). Another option is a four-hour coastal hike with **Howth Adventures** (mobile 086-125-0055, www.shaneshowthhikes.com).

Sleeping in Howth

$$$$ King Sitric's Accommodation is Howth's best lodging option and has a fine harborfront seafood restaurant. It fills the old harbormaster's house with eight well-kept rooms and a friendly staff (discounts for 2-night stay with dinner, East Pier below martello tower, tel. 01/832-5235, www.kingsitric.ie, reservations@kingsitric.ie, Aidan and Joan MacManus).

$ Gleann-na-Smol B&B is a homey house with six unpretentious rooms in a quiet setting, a 15-minute walk uphill along the coast behind the martello tower (family room, parking, corner of Nashville and Kilrock Road, tel. 01/832-2936, mobile 085-758-1083, gleannnasmolbandb@gmail.com, Sean and Margaret Rickard).

Eating in Howth

$$$$ King Sitric's Fish Restaurant, one of the area's most famous seafood experiences, serves Irish versions of French classics in a dining room (upstairs) with harbor views. Chef Aidan Mac-

Manus rises early each morning to select the best of the day's catch on the pier (Wed-Sat 18:00-21:30, Sun 13:00-16:00, closed Mon-Tue, reservations a good idea, tel. 01/832-5235, www.kingsitric. ie). They also operate the more economical ground-floor **East Café Bar,** serving soups, salads, steak sandwiches, and fish (daily 10:30-22:00, extra seating out front).

$$$ The Oar House sits halfway down the West Pier, serving a variety of fresh fish dishes in a bustling atmosphere (daily 12:00-"the cows come home," 8 West Pier, tel. 01/839-4568).

$$$ The House is the best value up the hill in the village. Here you'll find a comfortable local vibe, a contemporary creative menu, and a rumor that Captain Bligh once lodged here (Tue-Thu 12:00-21:30, Fri-Sat until 22:30, Mon open for lunch only, closed Sun, 4 Main Street, tel. 01/839-6388).

For standard pub grub, try the **$$ Abbey Tavern** up the hill on Abbey Street (occasional trad music and dance, call for schedule, tel. 01/839-0307). Another good choice is the **$$ Bloody Stream Pub** in front of the DART station. **The Country Market** sells picnic supplies, and its cheap and friendly upstairs tearoom offers lunch (daily 9:00-18:00, Main Street). The **Centra Market** is a block closer to the waterfront (daily until 22:00, Main Street).

DUBLIN

NEAR DUBLIN

Boyne Valley • Trim • Glendalough • Wicklow Mountains • Irish National Stud

Not far from urban Dublin, the stony skeletons of evocative ruins sprout from the lush Irish countryside. The story of Irish history is told by ancient burial mounds, early Christian monastic settlements, huge Norman castles, and pampered estate gardens. In gentler inland terrain, the Irish love of equestrian sport is nurtured in grassy pastures ruled by spirited thoroughbreds. These sights are separated into three regions: north of Dublin (the Boyne Valley, including Brú na Bóinne and the town of Trim), south of Dublin (Powerscourt Estate Gardens, Glendalough, and the Wicklow Mountains), and west of Dublin (the Irish National Stud).

Boyne Valley

The peaceful, green Boyne Valley, just 30 miles north of Dublin, has an impressive concentration of historical and spiritual sights: The enigmatic burial mounds at Brú na Bóinne are older than the Egyptian pyramids. At the Hill of Tara (seat of the high kings of Celtic Ireland), St. Patrick preached his most persuasive sermon. The valley also contains the first monastery in Ireland and several of the country's finest high crosses. You'll see Trim's 13th-century castle—Ireland's biggest—built by Norman invaders, and you can wander the site of the historic Battle of the Boyne (1690), which cemented Protestant British domination over Catholic Ireland until the 20th century.

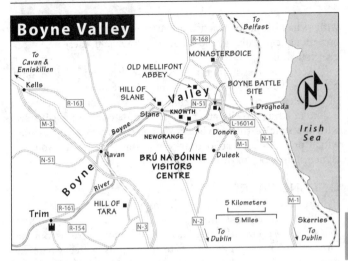

PLANNING YOUR TIME

Of these sights, only Brú na Bóinne is worth ▲▲▲ (and deserves a good three hours). The others, while relatively meager physically, are powerfully evocative to anyone interested in Irish history and culture. If you have a car, get an early start, and eat your Weetabix, you could see the entire region in a day.

If you're flying into or out of Dublin but want to avoid the intensity and expense of that big city, consider using Trim as an overnight base (45-minute drive from Dublin's airport) and tour these sights from there.

GETTING AROUND BOYNE VALLEY

The region is a joy by car: All of the described sights are within a 30-minute drive of one another. Though the sights are on tiny roads, they're well marked with brown, tourist-friendly road signs.

It's also possible to get to the Boyne Valley from Dublin with a tour. **Newgrange Tours** visits Brú na Bóinne (including inside the Newgrange tomb), the Hill of Tara, and the Hill of Slane in a seven-hour trip (€40, daily pickup from several Dublin hotels, book direct via website, mobile 086-355-1355, www.newgrangetours. com, newgrangetours@gmail.com).

Brú na Bóinne

The famous archaeological site of Brú na Bóinne—"dwelling place of the Boyne"—is also commonly called "Newgrange," after its star attraction. Here you can visit two ▲▲▲ 5,000-year-old passage tombs—**Newgrange** and **Knowth** (rhymes with "south"). These are massive grass-covered burial mounds built atop separate hills, with a chamber inside reached by a narrow stone passage. Mysterious, thought-provoking, and mind-bogglingly old, these tombs can give you chills.

Access to Newgrange and Knowth is by guided tour only. Since the Newgrange interior chamber is the most evocative part of the site, I recommend booking the Brú na Bóinne Plus ticket online in advance—the other tour is outside only. Any visit starts with the state-of-the-art visitors center with its excellent exhibit, which provides context to your tomb visits. Then catch your assigned shuttle bus to the tomb sights.

GETTING THERE

By **car,** drive 45 minutes north from Dublin on N-1 toward Drogheda, where signs direct you to the visitors center (watch for *Brú na Bóinne* signs). If you're using GPS, input "Brú na Bóinne" rather than "Newgrange" to get to the visitors center, where you must check in. Note that you can't drive up to the tombs yourself—you must take a shuttle bus from the visitors center.

Without a car, you can combine **train and taxi** service. First take a train departing Dublin Connolly station at 8:00, which puts you in the town of Drogheda around 9:00 (€12 round-trip; confirm train times at www.irishrail.ie). From here it's a short six-mile taxi ride to the Brú na Bóinne visitors center (approximately €10 one-way).

The **bus** is also an option, either with the Newgrange Tours day trip described earlier in "Getting Around Boyne Valley" or via public transit: Take bus #100x from Dublin to Drogheda, then bus #163 to the visitors center. Aim to depart the Drogheda bus station at 11:15 (return bus from the visitors center to Drogheda at 15:10, allow about 1.5 hours each way, including the connection in Drogheda).

ORIENTATION TO BRÚ NA BÓINNE

Cost: Visitors center exhibit only-€5; Brú na Bóinne Tour (outside only)-€12, Brú na Bóinne Plus (includes Newgrange chamber)-€18; visitors center is included in tour prices.

Hours: Daily 9:00-19:00, slightly shorter hours Sept-April, last bus to the tombs leaves 1.75 hours before closing, last entry to visitors center 45 minutes before closing.

Information: Tel. 041/988-0300, www.heritageireland.ie.

Tours: Both tour options visit both Newgrange and Knowth, but the Brú na Bóinne Tour does not go inside Newgrange. There is no access to Knowth's interior on either tour. Tours take about 2.75 hours including the visitors center exhibits.

Advance Tickets Recommended: If you want to see Newgrange's interior, it's essential to reserve timed-entry tickets up to three months in advance online at https://brunaboinne.admit-one. eu. Walk-up tickets are limited and can sell out. The outside-only Brú na Bóinne Tour cannot be booked ahead.

VISITING BRÚ NA BÓINNE

At the visitors center, check in and spend your waiting time in the excellent exhibition, grabbing lunch in the cheery downstairs cafeteria, and using the WCs (there are none at the tomb sites).

Brú na Bóinne Visitors Centre Exhibition

The exhibition introduces you to the Boyne River Valley and its tombs. No one knows exactly who built the 40 burial mounds found in the surrounding hills. Exhibits re-create what these pre-Celtic people might have been like—simple farmers and hunters living in huts, fishing in the Boyne, equipped with crude tools of stone, bone, or wood.

Then around 3200 BC, someone had a bold idea. They constructed a chamber of large stones, with a long stone-lined passage leading up to it. They covered it with a huge mound of dirt and rocks in successive layers. Sailing down the Boyne to the sea, they beached at Clogherhead (12.5 miles from here), where they found hundreds of five-ton stones, weathered smooth by the tides. Somehow they transported them back up the Boyne, possibly by tying a raft to the top of the stone so it was lifted free by a high tide. They then hauled these stones up the hill by rolling them atop logs and up dirt ramps, and laid them around the perimeter of the burial mound to hold everything in place. It would have taken anywhere from five years to a generation to construct a single large tomb.

Why build these vast structures? Partially, it was to bury VIPs. A dead king might be carried up the hill to be cremated on a pyre. Then they'd bring his ashes into the tomb, parading by torchlight down the passage to the central chamber. The remains were placed in a ceremonial basin, mingling with those of his illustrious ancestors.

To help bring the history to life, the exhibition displays replicas of tools and objects found at the sites, including the ceremonial basin stone and a head made from flint, which may have been carried atop a pole during the funeral procession. Marvel at the craftsmanship of the perfectly spherical stones (and the phallic one) and wonder at their purpose.

NEAR DUBLIN

The tombs also served an astronomical function; they're precisely aligned to the movements of the sun, as displays and a video illustrate. You can request a short tour and winter solstice light-show demo at a full-size replica of the Newgrange passage and interior chamber.

Since the tombs are aligned with the heavens, it begs the question: Were these structures sacred places where primal Homo sapiens gathered to ponder the deepest mysteries of existence?

▲▲▲Newgrange

This grassy mound atop a hill is 250 feet across and 40 feet high. Dating from 3200 BC, it's 500 years older than the pyramids at Giza. The base of the mound is ringed by dozens of curbstones, each about nine feet long and weighing five tons.

The entrance façade is a mosaic of white quartz and dark granite. This is a reconstruction done in the 1970s, and not every archaeologist agrees it originally looked like this. Above the doorway is a square window called the roofbox, which played a key role (as we'll see). In front of the doorway lies the most famous of the curbstones, the 10- by 4-foot entrance stone. Its left half is carved with three mysterious spirals, which have become a kind of poster child for prehistoric art.

Most of Newgrange's curbstones have designs carved into them. This was done with super-hard flint tools; the Neolithic ("New Stone Age") people had not mastered metal. The stones feature common Neolithic motifs: not people or animals, but geometric shapes—spirals, crosshatches, bull's-eyes, and chevrons. (For more information on prehistoric art, see page 540.)

Entering the tomb, you walk down a narrow 60-foot passage lined with big boulders. The passage opens into a central room—a cross-shaped central chamber with three alcoves, topped by a 20-foot-high igloo-type stone dome. Bones and ashes were placed here in a ceremonial stone basin, under 200,000 tons of stone and dirt.

While we know nothing of Newgrange's builders, it most certainly was a sacred spot—for a cult of the dead, a cult of the sun, or both. The tomb is aligned precisely east-west. As the sun rises around the shortest day of the year (winter solstice—usually on Dec 21—and two days before and after), a ray of light enters through the roofbox and creeps slowly down the passageway. For 17 minutes, it lights the center of the sacred chamber (your guide will demonstrate this). Perhaps this was the moment when the souls of the dead were transported to the afterlife, via that ray of light. Then the light passes on, and, for the next 361 days, the tomb sits again in total darkness.

▲▲▲Knowth

This site is an impressive necropolis, with one grand hill-topping mound surrounded by several smaller satellite tombs. The central mound is 220 feet wide, 40 feet high, and covers 1.5 acres.

You'll see plenty of mysteriously carved curbstones and new-feeling grassy mounds that you can look down on from atop the grand tomb.

Knowth's big tomb has two passages: one entering from the east, and one from the west. Like Newgrange, it's likely aligned so the rising and setting sun shone down the passageways to light the two interior chambers, but these are aligned to the equinox rather than the solstice. Neither passage is open to the public, but you can visit a room carved into the mound by archaeologists, where a cutaway lets you see the layers of dirt and rock used to build the mound. You also get a glimpse down one of the passages.

The Knowth site thrived from 3000 to 2000 BC. The central tomb dates from about 2000 BC. It was likely used for burial rituals and sun-tracking ceremonies to please the gods and ensure the regular progression of seasons for crops. The site then evolved into the domain of fairies and myths for the next 2,000 years and became an Iron Age fortress in the early centuries after Christ. Around AD 1000, it was an all-Ireland political center, and later, a Norman fortress was built atop the mound. Now, 4,000 years after prehistoric people built these strange tombs, you can stand atop the hill at Knowth, look out over the surrounding countryside, and contemplate the passage of time.

NEAR DUBLIN

More Boyne Valley Sights

▲▲Battle of the Boyne Site

One of Europe's lesser-known battlegrounds (but huge in Irish and British history), this is the pastoral riverside site of the pivotal 1690 battle in which the Protestant British decisively broke Catholic resistance, establishing Protestant rule over all of Ireland and Britain.

Cost and Hours: €5, daily 9:00-17:00, Oct-April until 16:00, last entry one hour before closing, tearoom/cafeteria, tel. 041/980-9950, www. battleoftheboyne.ie.

Getting There: The visitors center is on the south bank of the Boyne River, about two miles north of the village of Donore. It's well signposted for drivers from M-1, N-51, or N-2. Once you pass through the main gates, you'll find the visitors center in the mansion a quarter-mile up the driveway.

"Living History" demonstrations: The Sunday afternoon "Living History" demonstrations (March-Sept) are a treat for history buffs and photographers, with guides clad in 17th-century garb. You'll get a bang out of the musket loading and firing demo. Or catch the cavalry combat in full gallop and learn that to be an Irish watermelon is to fear the sword. Check the event program online for schedules and additional offerings such as battlefield walks.

Background: It was here in 1690 that Protestant King William III, with his English/Irish/Dutch/Danish/French Huguenot army, defeated his father-in-law—who was also his uncle—Catholic King James II and his Irish/French army. At stake was who would sit on the British throne, who would hold religious power in Ireland, and whether or not French dominance of Europe would continue.

King William's forces, on the north side of the Boyne, managed to fight their way across the river, and by the end of the day, King James was fleeing south in full retreat. He soon left Ireland, but his forces fought on until their final defeat a year later. James II (called "James da Turd" by those who scorn his lack of courage and leadership) never returned, and he died a bitter ex-monarch in France. His "Jacobite" claim to the English throne lived on among Catholics for decades, and was finally extinguished in 1745, when his grandson, Bonnie Prince Charlie, was defeated at the Battle of Culloden in Scotland.

King William of Orange's victory, on the other hand, is still celebrated in Northern Ireland every July 12, with controversial marches by Unionist "Orangemen." The battle actually took place on July 1, but was officially shifted 11 days later when the Gregorian calendar was adopted in 1752. (Even the calendar has been affected by religious strife: Protestant nations were reluctant to use a calendar developed by a Catholic—Pope Gregory in 1582. So England delayed adoption of Gregory's calendar for 170 years.)

The 60,000 soldiers who fought here made this one of the largest battles ever to take place in the British Isles. Yet it was only a side skirmish in an even larger continental confrontation pitting France's King Louis XIV against the "Grand Alliance" of nations threatened by France's mighty military and frequent incursions into neighboring lands.

Louis ruled by divine right, answerable only to God—and James modeled himself after Louis. Even the pope (who could control neither Louis nor James and was equally disturbed by Catholic France's aggressions) backed Protestant King William against Catholic King James—just one example of the pretzel logic that was the European mindset at the time.

The site of the Battle of the Boyne was bought in 1997 by the Irish Office of Public Works, part of the Republic's governmental efforts to respect a place sacred to Unionists in Northern Ireland—despite the fact that the battle's outcome ensured Catholic subordination to the Protestant minority for the next 230 years.

Visiting the Site: The **visitors center** is housed in a mansion built on the battlefield 50 years after the conflict. The exhibits do a good job of illustrating the international nature of the battle and its place in the wider context of European political power struggles. The highlight is a huge battleground model with laser lights that move troops around the terrain, showing the battle's ebb and flow on that bloody day. A separate 15-minute film (shown in the former stable house) runs continuously and does a fine job of fleshing out the battle.

As you exit the site to the north (on the L-16014 access road that connects to the main N-51 road), you'll cross the River Boyne on a **metal bridge,** locally referred to as "Old Bridge." This spot is where the most frantic action took place on the day of the battle.

Pull over and gaze at the river. Picture crack Dutch troops (from King William's homeland) marching south in formation. They were the first to cross the river here, while their comrades behind on the north bank covered their exposed position with constant protective fire. Low tides (the sea is only 7 miles downstream) allowed these soldiers to cross the river in water up to their waists. Between the gun smoke, weapon fire, and shouts filling the air, it was tough to tell friend from foe in the close, chaotic combat. Neither force had standard uniforms, so King William's troops wore sprigs of green while the troops of King James pinned white paper to their coats. Both sides bled red.

▲Hill of Tara

This site was the most important center of political and religious power in pre-Christian Ireland. While aerial views show plenty

of mystifying circles and lines, wandering with the sheep among the well-worn ditches and hills leaves you with more to feel than to see. Visits are made meaningful by an excellent 20-minute video presentation and the insightful 20-minute guided walk that usually follows (walk times unpredictable due to

frequent big bus tours; worth calling ahead to confirm availability). Wear good walking shoes—the ground is uneven and often wet.

Cost and Hours: €5, includes video and guided walk (if available when you visit), buy tickets from old church in the trees above parking lot; daily 10:00-18:00, last tour at 17:00, from mid-Sept–mid-May access is free but visitors center is closed; WCs in café next to parking lot, tel. 046/902-5903, http://hilloftara.org.

Visiting the Site: You'll see the Mound of Hostages (a Bronze Age passage grave, c. 2500 BC), a couple of ancient sacred stones, a war memorial, and vast views over the Emerald Isle. While ancient Ireland was a pig pile of minor chieftain-kings scrambling for power, the High King of Tara was king of the mountain. It was at this ancient stockade that St. Patrick directly challenged the king's authority. When confronted by the high king, Patrick convincingly explained the Holy Trinity using a shamrock: three petals with one stem. He won the right to preach Christianity throughout Ireland, and the country had a new national symbol.

This now-desolate hill was also the scene of great later events. In 1798, passionate young Irish rebels chose Tara for its defensible position, but were routed by better-organized (and more-sober) British troops. (The cunning British commander had sent three cartloads of whiskey along the nearby road earlier in the day, knowing the rebels would intercept it.) In 1843, the great orator and champion of Irish liberty Daniel O'Connell gathered 500,000 Irish peasants on this hill for his greatest "monster meeting"—a peaceful show of force demanding the repeal of the Act of Union with Britain (kind of the Woodstock of its day). In a bizarre final twist, a small group of British Israelites—who believed they were one of the lost tribes of Israel who had ended up in Britain—spent

1899 to 1901 recklessly digging up parts of the hill in a misguided search for the Ark of the Covenant.

Stand on the Hill of Tara. Think of the history it's seen, and survey Ireland. It's understandable why this "meeting place of heroes" continues to hold a powerful place in the Irish psyche.

Old Mellifont Abbey

This Cistercian abbey (the first in Ireland) was established by French monks who came to the country in 1142 to bring the Irish monks more in line with Rome. (Even the abbey's architecture was unusual, marking the first time in Ireland that a formal, European-style monastic layout was used.) Cistercians lived isolated rural lives; lay monks worked the land, allowing the more educated monks to devote all of their energy to prayer. After Henry VIII dissolved the abbey in 1539, centuries of locals used it as a handy quarry. Consequently, little survives beyond the octagonal lavabo, where the monks would ceremonially wash their hands before entering the refectory to eat. The lavabo gives a sense of the abbey's former grandeur.

The excellent 45-minute tours, available upon request and included in your admission (late May-Aug only), give meaning to what you're seeing. To get a better idea of the extent of the site, check out the model of the monastery in its heyday, located at the back of the small museum next to the ticket desk.

Cost and Hours: €5; daily 10:00-18:00, last tour at 17:30, last entry 45 minutes before closing; from Sept-late May site is free but there are no tours; tel. 041/988-0300, www.heritageireland.ie.

Monasterboice

This ruined monastery is visit-worthy for its round tower and its ornately carved high crosses—two of the best such crosses in Ireland. In the Dark Ages, these crosses, illustrated from top to bottom with Bible stories, gave monks a teaching tool as they preached to the illiterate masses. Imagine the crosses in their prime, when they were brightly painted (before years of wind and rain weathered the paint away). Today, Monasterboice is basically an old graveyard.

Cost and Hours: Free and always open.

Visiting the Site: The 18-foot-tall **Cross of Murdock** (Muiredach's Cross, c. 923, named after an abbot) is considered the best high cross in Ireland. The circle—which characterizes the Irish high cross—could represent the perfection of God. Or, to help ease pagans into Christianity, it may represent the sun, which was worshiped in pre-Christian Celtic society. Whatever its symbolic purpose, its practical function was to support the weight of the crossbeam.

Face the cross (with the round tower in the background) and study the carved sandstone. The center panel shows the Last Judg-

ment, with Christ under a dove, symbolizing the Holy Spirit. Those going to heaven are on Christ's right, and the damned are being ushered away by a pitchfork-wielding devil on his left. Working down, you'll see the Archangel Michael weighing souls, as the Devil tugs demonically at the scales; the adoration of the three—or four—Magi; Moses striking the rock to bring forth water; scenes from the life of David; and, finally, Adam, Eve, and the apple next to Cain slaying Abel. Imagine these carvings with their original, colorful paint jobs. Check out the plaque at the base of the nearby tree, which further explains the carvings on the cross.

Find the even-taller cross nearest the tower. It seems the top section was broken off and buried for a period, which protected it from weathering. The bottom part remained standing, enduring the erosive effect of Irish weather, which smeared the once-crisp features.

The door to the round tower was originally 15-20 feet above the ground (accessible by ladder). After centuries of burials, the ground level has risen.

Trim

The sleepy, workaday town of Trim, straddling the River Boyne, is marked by the towering ruins of Trim Castle. Trim feels littered with mighty ruins that seem to say, "This little town was big-time...800 years ago." The tall Yellow Steeple (over the river from the castle) is all that remains of the 14th-century Augustinian Abbey of St. Mary. Not far away, the Sheep's Gate is a humble remnant of the once-grand medieval town walls. Near the town center, the modest, 30-foot-tall Wellington Column honors native son Arthur Wellesley, the First Duke of Wellington (1769-1852), who spent his childhood in Trim, defeated Napoleon at Waterloo, and twice became prime minister.

Trim makes a great landing pad into—or launching pad out of—Ireland. If you're flying into or out of Dublin Airport and don't want to deal with big-city Dublin, this is a perfect alternative—an easy 45-minute, 30-mile drive away. You can rent a car at the airport and make Trim your first overnight base (getting used to driving on the other side of the road in easier country traffic). Or spend your last night here before returning your car at the airport. Weather permitting, my evening stroll makes for a fine first or last night on the Emerald Isle.

Orientation to Trim

Trim's main square is a traffic roundabout, and everything's within a block or two. Most of the shops and eateries are on or near Market Street, along with banks and a supermarket.

TOURIST INFORMATION

The TI is right next to the castle entrance and includes a handy coffee shop (Mon-Fri 9:30-17:30, Sat-Sun 11:00-16:00, shorter hours Sept-May, Castle Street, tel. 046/943-7227). Outside, 100 feet to the right of the TI door, you'll find a plaque with photos showing the castle dolled up for the filming of *Braveheart*.

HELPFUL HINTS

Laundry: The launderette is located close to Market Street (Mon-Sat 9:00-13:00 & 13:30-17:30, closed Sun, Watergate Street, tel. 046/943-7176).

Parking: To park on the street or in a public lot, use the pay-and-display parking system (2-hour maximum, Mon-Sat 9:00-18:00, free Sun).

Taxi: For visits to nearby Boyne sites, **Donie Quinn** can give you a lift (tel. 046/943-7777).

Adventure Tours: The menu at **Boyne Valley Activities** includes kayaking, rafting, and archery excursions (€25 for archery, €30 for "float through time river tour," €45 for kayaking; call ahead to reserve, mobile 086-734-2585, www.boynevalleyactivities.ie).

Marc O'Regan leads backcountry trout and pike fishing tours, making a splash with anglers who want to experience Ireland's bountiful lakes and rivers (tel. 046/943-1635, www.crannmor.com). O'Regan and his wife also run the recommended Crannmór Guest House.

Sights in Trim

▲▲Trim Castle

This is the biggest Norman castle in Ireland. Set in a grassy riverside park at the edge of this sleepy town, its mighty keep towers above a ruined outer wall. It replaced a wooden fortification that was destroyed in 1173 by Irish High King Rory O'Connor, who led a raid against the invad-

NEAR DUBLIN

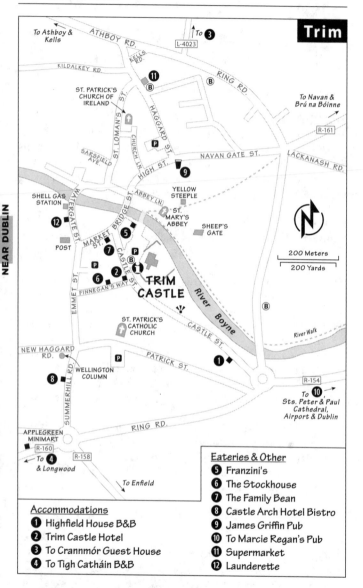

Trim

NEAR DUBLIN

To Athboy & Kells

ATHBOY RD.

To ③

L-4023

KILDALKEY RD.

KELLS RD.

RING RD.

ST. PATRICK'S CHURCH OF IRELAND

ST. LOMAN'S ST.

CHURCH LN.

HAGGARD ST.

HIGH ST.

SARSFIELD AVE.

⑪
Ⓑ

Ⓑ

To Navan & Brú na Bóinne

R-161

LACKANASH RD.

NAVAN GATE ST.

⑨

YELLOW STEEPLE

ABBEY LN.

ST. MARY'S ABBEY

SHEEP'S GATE

SHELL GAS STATION

⑫

MARKET ST.

BRIDGE ST.

POST

⑤

⑦

P

Ⓑ
①

CASTLE ST.

TRIM CASTLE

River Boyne

Ⓑ

River Walk

WATERGATE ST.

EMMET ST.

⑥

②

FINNEGAN'S WAY

ST. PATRICK'S CATHOLIC CHURCH

CASTLE ST.

NEW HAGGARD RD.

SUMMERHILL RD.

WELLINGTON COLUMN

P

PATRICK ST.

①

R-154

⑧

To ⑩

Sts. Peter & Paul Cathedral, Airport & Dublin

APPLEGREEN MINIMART

R-160

To ④ & Longwood

R-158

RING RD.

To Enfield

200 Meters

200 Yards

Accommodations

① Highfield House B&B
② Trim Castle Hotel
③ To Crannmór Guest House
④ To Tigh Catháin B&B

Eateries & Other

⑤ Franzini's
⑥ The Stockhouse
⑦ The Family Bean
⑧ Castle Arch Hotel Bistro
⑨ James Griffin Pub
⑩ To Marcie Regan's Pub
⑪ Supermarket
⑫ Launderette

ing Normans. The current castle was completed in the 1220s and served as a powerful Norman statement to the restless Irish natives. It remained a sharp barb at the fringe of "the Pale" (English-controlled territory), when English rule shrank to just the area around Dublin in the 1400s. By that time, any lands farther west were "beyond the Pale."

Cost and Hours: €5 for entrance to keep and required tour,

€2 for grounds only; daily 10:00-17:00, Nov-mid-March open Sat-Sun only 9:30-16:00, last entry one hour before closing, 45-minute tours run 2/hour but spots are limited and can fill up—so arrive early in peak season, tel. 046/943-8619, www.heritageireland.ie.

Visiting the Castle: Today the castle remains an impressive sight—so impressive that it was used in the 1994 filming of *Braveheart* (which was actually about Scotland's—not Ireland's—fight for freedom from the English). The best-preserved walls ring the castle's southern perimeter and sport a barbican gate that contained two drawbridges.

At the base of the castle walls, notice the cleverly angled "batter" wall—used by defenders who hurled down stones that banked off at great velocity into the attacking army. Notice also that the castle is built directly on bedrock, visible along the base of the walls. During sieges, while defenders of other castles feared that attackers would tunnel underground to weaken the defensive walls, that was not an issue here.

The massive 70-foot-high central keep, which is mostly a hollow shell, has 20 sides. This experimental design was not implemented elsewhere because it increased the number of defenders needed to cover all the angles. You can go inside the keep only with the included tour, where you'll start by checking out the cool ground-floor models showing the evolution of the castle. Then you'll climb a series of tightly winding original staircases and modern high catwalks, learn about life in the castle, and end at the top with great views of the walls and the countryside.

Make time to take a 15-minute walk outside, circling the castle walls and stopping at the informative plaques that show the castle from each viewpoint during its gory glory days. Night strollers are treated to views of the castle hauntingly lit in blue-green hues.

Trim Evening Stroll

Given good weather, here's my blueprint for a fine night in Trim. Start the evening by taking the pleasant **River Walk** stroll along the River Boyne from Trim Castle. Cross the wooden footbridge over the river behind the castle and turn right (east). The paved, level trail eventually leads under a modern bridge/overpass and extends a mile along fields that serfs farmed 750 years ago. During the filming of *Braveheart,* Mel Gibson's character met the French princess in her tent in these fields, with the castle looming in the background.

The trail ends in the medieval ruins of **Newtown.** This was indeed once the "new town" (mid-1200s) that sprouted as a religious satellite community to support the political power housed in the castle. Wander the sprawling, ragtag ruins of **Sts. Peter and Paul Cathedral** (1206), once the largest Gothic church in Ireland. Seek

NEAR DUBLIN

out the tomb with a carved lid depicting a medieval lord and lady; this is known locally as the tomb of the "jealous man and woman" (because they do not touch each other). Upon close inspection, you'll notice hundreds of tiny pins in the creases of the carving, left behind by superstitious visitors. Why? If you rub a pin on your stubborn wart and then leave it here...presto: wart-be-gone.

Just beyond the ruins, cross the old Norman bridge to the 13th-century scraps of the **Hospital of St. John the Baptist.** Medieval medicine couldn't have been fun, but this hospital was the best you could hope for back when life was nasty, brutish, and short. Many a knight was spent here.

Cross back over the bridge and stop for a pint at tiny, atmospheric **Marcie Regan's,** one of the oldest pubs in Ireland (an exterior sign calls it "Regan's," but most locals call it "Marcie's"). Explore its dimly lit back rooms. The pub sits beside one of the oldest bridges in Ireland (the one you just crossed).

Then walk back along the river the way you came and have dinner at the recommended **Franzini's** restaurant beside the castle. After dinner, assist your digestion by walking a lap around the castle (beautifully lit at night). End the evening a few blocks away with a pint at the recommended **James Griffin** pub. A fine night 'tis...or 'twas.

Sleeping in Trim

Because Trim is a popular spot for weddings, book as early as possible if you are visiting on a summer weekend.

$$ Highfield House B&B, across the street from the castle and a five-minute walk from town, is a stately former maternity hospital with hardwood floors and 10 spacious, high-ceilinged rooms (family rooms; above the roundabout where the road from Dublin hits Trim, Castle Street, tel. 046/943-6386, mobile 086-857-7115, www.highfieldguesthouse.com, info@highfieldguesthouse.com, Geraldine and Edward Duignan).

$$ Trim Castle Hotel is the town's modern option with 68 immaculate rooms, some with direct views of the castle, and a friendly downstairs pub (family rooms, parking, Castle Street, tel. 046/948-3000, www.trimcastlehotel.com, info@trimcastlehotel.com).

Countryside B&Bs: These two B&Bs are about a mile outside Trim (phone ahead for driving directions).

$ At ivy-draped **Crannmór Guest House,** Anne O'Regan decorates five rooms with cheery color schemes (family room; north of the Ring Road on Dunderry Road L-4023, then veer right at the first fork; tel. 046/943-1635, mobile 087-288-7390, www.crannmor.com, crannmor@eircom.net). Anne's professional-guide husband Marc knows all the best fishing holes (listed earlier, under "Helpful Hints").

$ Marie Keane's **Tigh Catháin B&B,** southwest of town, has four large, bright, lacy rooms with a comfy, rural feel and organically grown produce at breakfast (cash only, on R-160/Longwood Road, 200 yards past the Applegreen minimart, tel. 046/943-1996, mobile 086-257-7313, www.tighcathain-bnb.com, tighcathain.bnb@gmail.com).

Eating in Trim

A country market town, Trim offers basic meat-and-potatoes lunch and dinner options. My first two listings are the only full restaurants in town. Otherwise, the spots along Market Street are friendly, wholesome, and unassuming.

$$$ **Franzini's** has a fun dinner menu and an excellent location next to the castle. They serve pasta, steak, fish, and great salads in a modern, plush space (Mon-Sat 17:00-21:00, Sun 14:00-20:00, on French's Lane across from the castle parking lot, tel. 046/943-1002).

$$$ **The Stockhouse** serves hearty steaks and poultry, plus creative desserts. Sit upstairs and take in the history of Trim from the walls while you wait (Mon-Thu 17:00-21:00, Fri-Sat until 22:00, Sun 13:00-20:30, Finnegan's Way, tel. 046/943-7388).

$$ **The Family Bean** is a good local joint along Market Street for omelettes, sandwiches, and meat pies (daily 8:30-17:00, tel. 046/948-1481).

$$ The **Castle Arch Hotel,** popular with locals, serves hearty pub grub at reasonable prices in its bistro on Summerhill Road (daily 12:30-21:00, tel. 046/943-1516).

Pubs: For a fun pub experience, check out Trim's two best watering holes. The **James Griffin** (on High Street) is full of local characters with traditional Irish music sessions on Monday, Wednesday, and Thursday nights. Locals fill the tiny, low-ceilinged **Marcie Regan's,** a creaky, unpretentious pub at the north end of the old Norman bridge over the River Boyne—it's a half-mile stroll outside town, next to the ruins of Newtown.

Supermarket: The large **Super Valu** is your best bet (daily 8:00-22:00, on Haggard Street, a short walk from the town center).

Trim Connections

Trim has no train station. Buses from Trim to **Dublin** (almost hourly, 1 hour, www.buseireann.ie) pick you up at the bus shelter next to the TI and castle entrance on Castle Street.

Glendalough and the Wicklow Mountains

The Wicklow Mountains, while only 15 miles south of Dublin, feel remote—enough so to have provided a handy refuge for opponents to English rule. Rebels who took part in the 1798 Irish Rebellion hid out here. The area became more accessible in 1800, when the frustrated British built a military road to help flush out the rebels. Today, this same road—now R-115—takes you through the Wicklow area to Glendalough at its south end. While the valley is the darling of Dublin day-trip tour organizers, for the most part it doesn't live up to the hype. But two blockbuster sights—Glendalough and the Powerscourt Estate Gardens—make a visit worth considering.

GETTING AROUND THE WICKLOW AREA

By car or tour, it's easy. If you lack wheels, take a tour. It's not worth the trouble on public transport.

By Car

It's a delight. Take N-11 south from Dublin toward Bray, then R-117 to Enniskerry, the gateway to the Wicklow Mountains. Signs direct you to the gardens and on to Glendalough. From Glendalough, if you're heading west, you can leave the valley and pick up the highway over the famous but dull mountain pass called the Wicklow Gap.

By Tour from Dublin

Bus Tours: Several companies offer tours around the region. **Wild Wicklow Tours** gives you an entertaining guide who packs every minute of an all-day excursion with information and *craic* (interesting, fun conversation). With a gang of 40 packed into tight but comfortable mountain-gripping buses, the guide kicks into gear from the first pickup in Dublin. Tours cover the windy military road over scenic Sally Gap and the Glendalough monasteries (€33, RS%, runs daily year-round, stop for lunch at a pub—cost not included, several Dublin hotel pickup points, return to Dublin by 18:00, advance booking required, tel. 01/280-1899, www.wildwicklow.ie).

    Do Dublin Tours offers a shorter trip focusing on Wicklow's two main sights, Glendalough and Powerscourt Gardens, aboard bright-green, double-decker buses (€27, daily departure at 10:30, return by 17:00, tours depart from Dublin Bus head office, 59 Upper O'Connell Street, tel. 01/844-4265, www.dodublin.ie).

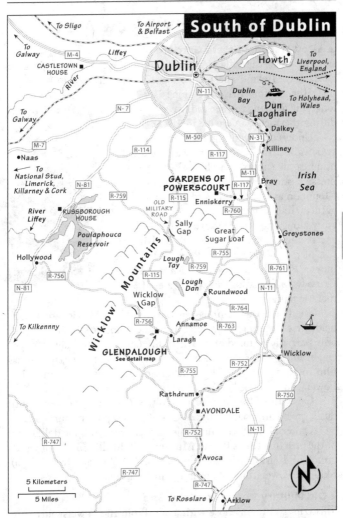

NEAR DUBLIN

Local Guide: Friendly and knowledgeable **Lisa Tully** knows the region. If you have your own car, she can meet you on location for scenic walking tours (when she's not on the road leading Rick Steves tours). Her two-hour walking tours are a bite-sized taste of the lush Wicklow countryside (€120/up to 4 people). If you're without a car, meet her by train from Dublin. Or she can arrange a full-day private driving tour from Dublin to all the best spots (from €425/up to 3 people, March-Nov, tel. 086/898-6457, www.wicklowguidedtours.ie, lisa@wicklowguidedtours.ie).

Sights in the Wicklow Area

▲▲Powerscourt Estate Gardens

A mile above the village of Enniskerry, these meticulously kept gardens are Ireland's best, covering 47 acres within a 700-acre es-

tate. The dreamy driveway alone is a mile long. The gardens you see today were created during the Victorian era (1858-1875).

Upon entry, you'll get a flier laying out two walks. The "one-hour" walk takes 30 minutes at a relaxed amble. With the impressive summit of the Great Sugar Loaf Mountain as a backdrop, and a fine Japanese garden, Italian garden, and goofy pet cemetery along the way, this attraction provides the scenic greenery I hoped to find in the rest of the Wicklow area. Parts of the lush movies *Barry Lyndon* and *The Count of Monte Cristo* were filmed in this well-watered aristocratic fantasy.

The house was commissioned in the 1730s by Richard Wingfield, first viscount of Powerscourt. The mansion's interior is still only partially restored after a 1974 fire (and only available for special events)—but spend 10 minutes checking out the easy-to-miss film room, which provides a history of the estate and a model of Powerscourt House before the fire.

Cost and Hours: €10.50, daily 9:30-17:30, Nov-Feb until dusk, great cafeteria, tel. 01/204-6000, www.powerscourt.com.

Other Sights: Kids may enjoy a peek at the antique dollhouses of the upstairs **Tara's Palace Museum of Childhood** (€5, proceeds go to children's charities, Mon-Sat 10:00-17:00, Sun from 12:00). Skip the Powerscourt Waterfall (4 miles away).

▲Old Military Road over Sally Gap

This trip is only for those with a car. From the Powerscourt Gardens and Enniskerry, go to Glencree, where you drive the tiny old military road (R-115) over Sally Gap and through the best scenery of the Wicklow Mountains (on Sundays, watch for dozens of bicycle racers). Look for the German military cemetery, built for U-boat sailors who washed ashore in World War II. Near Sally Gap, notice the peat bogs and the freshly cut peat bricks drying in the wind. Many locals are nostalgic for the "good old days," when homes were always peat-fire heated. At the Sally Gap junction, turn left, where a road winds through the vast Guinness estate. Look down on the glacial lake (Lough Tay) nicknamed "Guinness Lake," as the water looks like Ireland's favorite dark-brown stout, and the sand of the beach actually looks like the head of a Guinness

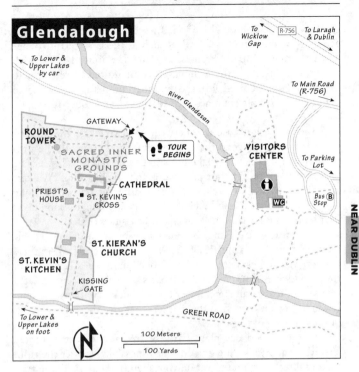

beer. The History Channel series *Vikings* was primarily filmed on a temporary set built on the shores of the lake. From here, the road meanders scenically down into the village of Roundwood and on to Glendalough.

▲▲Glendalough

The steep wooded slopes of Glendalough (GLEN-da-lock, "Valley of the Two Lakes"), at the south end of Wicklow's old military road, hide Ireland's most impressive monastic settlement. Founded by St. Kevin in the sixth century, the monastery flourished (despite repeated Viking raids) throughout the Age of Saints and Scholars until the English destroyed it in 1398. A few hardy holy men continued to live here until it was finally abandoned during the Dissolution of the Monasteries in 1539. But pilgrims kept coming, especially on St. Kevin's Day, June 3. (This might have something to do with the fact that a pope said seven visits to Glendalough had the same indulgence—or forgiveness from sins—value as one visit to Rome.) While much restoration was done in the 1870s, most of the buildings date from the 10th to 12th century.

In an Ireland without cities, these monastic communities were mainstays of civilization. At such remote outposts, ascetics (with a taste for scenic settings, but abstaining from worldly pleasures) gathered to commune with God. In the 12th century, with the arrival of grander monastic orders such as the Cistercians, Benedictines, Augustinians, Franciscans, and Dominicans, and with the growth of cities, these monastic communities were eclipsed. Today, Ireland is dotted with the reminders of this age: illuminated manuscripts, simple churches, carved crosses, and about 100 round towers.

The valley sights are split between the two lakes. The smaller, lower lake is just beyond the visitors center and nearer the best remaining ruins. The upper lake has scant ruins and feels like a state park, with a grassy lakeside picnic area and school groups. Walkers and hikers will enjoy a choice of nine different trails of varying lengths through the lush Wicklow countryside (longest loop takes four hours, hiking-trail maps available at visitors center).

Planning Your Time: Summer tour-bus crowds are terrible all day on weekends and 11:00-14:00 on weekdays. If you're there at midday, your best bet is to take the once-daily, 45-minute tour of the site (June-Aug only at 13:30, departs from visitors center). Otherwise, ask if you can tag along with a prebooked tour group's tour. If you're on your own, find the markers that give short descriptions of the ruined buildings.

Here's a good day-plan: Park for free at the visitors center. Visit the center; take the guided tour if possible; wander the ruins surrounding the round tower on your own (free); or walk the traffic-free Green Road a half-mile to the upper lake, and then walk back to the visitors center and your car along the trail that parallels the public road (an easy, roughly one-mile loop). Or you can drive to the upper lake (skippable, if you're rushed).

Cost and Hours: Free to enter site, €5 for visitors center, €4 to park at upper lake; open daily 9:30-18:00, mid-Oct-mid-March until 17:00; last entry 45 minutes before closing, tel. 0404/45352.

Visiting Glendalough: Start out at the **Glendalough Visitors Centre,** where a 15-minute video provides a good thumbnail background on monastic society in medieval Ireland. The adjacent museum room features this monastic settlement, with a model that re-creates the fortified village of the year 1050. Interactive exhibits show the contributions these monks made to intellectual life in Dark Age Europe (such as illuminated manuscripts and Irish minuscule, a more compact alphabet developed in the seventh century).

When you're ready to visit the site, head out behind the visitors center, cross the bridge over the brook, and follow the lane 100 yards to the original stone **gateway.** From here you enter the sacred inner-monastic grounds that provided sanctuary for anyone under threat. Look for the cross carved into the sanctuary stone in the gateway (at knee level). A refugee had 90 days to live safely within the walls. But on the 91st day, he would be tossed out to the waiting authorities...unless he became a monk (in which case he could live there indefinitely, no matter what his crime).

The graceful **round tower** rises from an evocative tangle of tombstones. Easily the best ruins of Glendalough gather within 100 yards of this famous 110-foot-tall tower. Towers like this (usually 60-110 feet tall with windows facing the four cardinal compass points) were standard features in such monastic settlements. They functioned as bell towers, storage lofts, beacons for pilgrims, and last-resort refuges during Viking raids. (But given enough warning, monks were safer hiding in the surrounding forest.) The towers had a high door with a pull-up ladder—both for safety and because a door at ground level would have weakened the tower's foundation. Several ruined churches (10th-12th century) lurk nearby...seek them out.

The **cathedral** is the largest and most central of all the ruins. It evolved over time with various expansions and through the reuse of stones from previous structures. The larger nave came first, and the chancel (up the couple of stairs where the altar later stood) was an addition. The east window faces toward Jerusalem and the rising sun, symbolic of Christ rising from the dead. Under the southern window is a small wall cupboard with a built-in basin. The holy vessels used during Mass were rinsed here so that the holy sacramental water would drain directly into the ground, avoiding any contamination.

Nearby is **St. Kevin's Cross.** At 10 feet tall and carved from a single block of granite, this cross was a statement of utter devotion. (Most other famous Irish high crosses were carved of softer sandstone, allowing their carvers to create more ornate depictions of biblical stories than you'll see here.) According to legend, if you hug this cross and can reach your hands around to touch your fingers on the other side, you'll have your wish granted (and your jealous friends labeling you a knuckle dragger). St. Kevin: the patron saint of dislocated shoulders.

Heading downhill, you'll pass the tiny **priests' house,** which was completely reconstructed (using the original stones) from a 1779 sketch. It might have originally acted as a kind of treasury, housing the relics of St. Kevin.

Farther down, you'll come to perhaps the prettiest structure surviving on the site: **St. Kevin's "kitchen"** (actually a church).

Its short round tower appeared to earlier visitors to be a chimney, but its function was always as a belfry. The steeply stacked stone roof conceals a croft (upper story) perhaps used as a scriptorium for copying holy manuscripts. Nearby is the less impressive stone footprint of **St. Kieran's Church,** possibly dedicated to the saint and contemporary of St. Kevin who founded Clonmacnoise Monastery (another scenic sanctuary, on the banks of the River Shannon south of the town of Athlone).

From here, pass through the kissing gate and cross the bridge over the brook. On the other side, if you're short of time, turn left to go back to the visitors center and parking lot. With more time, turn right and explore the lovely tree-shrouded **Green Road,** which leads past the **lower lake** for a half-mile to the **upper lake** as part of a pleasant one-mile loop.

The oldest ruins—scant and hard to find—lie near the upper lake. **St. Kevin's bed** is a cave where the holy hermit-founder of the monastery took shelter. It lies above the left (southern) shore and is visible and reachable only by boat. The story goes that St. Kevin's devotion was so strong that he would strip off his clothes and jump into thorn bushes rather than submit to the pleasures of the flesh. Another tale has him standing in pious stillness with arms outstretched while a bird builds its nest in his hand. If you want a scenic Wicklow walk, begin here.

Irish National Stud

Ireland's famed County Kildare—just west of Dublin—offers the perfect conditions for breeding horses. Its reputation dates all the way back to the 1300s, when Norman war horses were bred here. Kildare's grasslands lie on a bedrock table of limestone, infusing the soil with just the right mix of nutrients for grazing horses. And the nearby River Tully sparkles with high levels of calcium carbonate, essential for building strong bones in the expensive thoroughbreds (some owned by Arab sheikhs) raised and raced here.

In 1900, Colonel William Hall-Walker (Scottish heir to the Johnny Walker distilling fortune) bought a farm on the River Tully and began breeding a line of champion thoroughbreds. His amazing successes and bizarre methods were the talk of the sport. In 1916, the colonel donated his land and horse farm to the British government, which continued breeding horses here. The farm was eventually handed over to the Irish government, which in 1945 created the Irish National Stud Company to promote the thoroughbred industry.

Today, a guided tour of the grounds at the Irish National Stud

When Irish Horses Are Running

Every Irish town seems to have a betting shop for passionate locals who love to closely follow (and wager on) their favorite horses. A quick glance at the weekend sports sections of any Irish newspaper gives you an idea of this sport's high profile. Towns from Galway to Dingle host annual horse races that draw rabid fans from all over. Interestingly, Irish horse races run the track clockwise (the opposite direction from races in the US).

The five most prestigious Irish races take place at the **Curragh Racecourse,** just south of Kildare town (March-Oct, 1 hour west of Dublin, 10 minutes from the National Stud, www.curragh.ie). Horses have been raced here since 1741. The broad, open fields nearby are where the battle scenes in *Braveheart* were filmed (the neighboring Irish army base provided the blue-face-painted extras).

gives you a fuller appreciation for the amazing horses that call this place home. Animal lovers and horse-racing fans driving between Dublin and Galway can enjoy a couple of hours here, combining the tour with a stroll through the gardens.

GETTING THERE
From M-7, **drivers** take exit #13 and follow the signs five minutes south (don't take exit #12 for the Curragh Racecourse). **Trains** departing Dublin's Heuston station stop at Kildare town (1-3/hour, 45 minutes). A shuttle bus runs from Kildare's train station to the National Stud (2/hour), or you can take a taxi (about €12-15). One **bus** departs Dublin's Busáras station Monday through Saturday at 9:30 and returns from the National Stud at 15:45. On Sunday, two buses run, departing Busáras at 10:00 and 12:00, with returns at 15:00 and 17:30. Confirm this schedule at the Dublin bus station.

ORIENTATION TO IRISH NATIONAL STUD
Cost: €11.50 includes guided tour, plus entry to Japanese Gardens, St. Fiachra's Garden, and Horse Museum.

Hours: Daily 9:00-18:00, closed Nov-Jan, last entry one hour before closing; 30-minute tours depart at 10:30, 12:00, 14:00, and 16:00; tel. 045/521-617, www.irishnationalstud.ie.

Eating: There's a decent cafeteria, or bring your own food and eat at a picnic table by the parking lot.

VISITING IRISH NATIONAL STUD

The guided tour begins in the **Sun Chariot Yard** (named for the winner of the 1942 Fillies Triple Crown), surrounded by stables housing pregnant mares. A 15-minute film of a foal's birth runs continuously in a stall in the corner of the yard.

The adjacent **Foaling Unit** is where births take place, usually from February through May. The gestation period for horses is 11 months, with 90 percent of foals born at night. (In the wild, a mare and her foal born during the day would have been vulnerable to predators as the herd moved on. Instead, horses have adapted so that foals are born at night—and are able to keep up with the herd within a few hours.) Eccentric Colonel Hall-Walker noted the position of the moon and stars at the time of each foal's birth, and sold those born under inauspicious astrological signs (regardless of their parents' stellar racing records).

From here, you'll pass a working saddle-making shop and a forge where horseshoes are still hammered out on an anvil.

At the **Stallion Boxes,** you'll learn how stargazing Colonel Hall-Walker installed skylights in the stables—allowing the heavens maximum influence over the destiny of his prized animals. A brass plaque on the door of each stall proudly states the horse's name and its racing credentials. One stall bears the simple word, "Teaser." The unlucky occupant's job is to identify mares in heat... but rarely is the frustrated stallion given the opportunity to breed. Bummer.

After the tour, meander down the pleasant tree-lined **Tully Walk,** with paddocks on each side. You'll see mares and foals running free, with the occasional cow thrown in for good measure (cattle have a calming effect on rowdy horses). To ensure you come home with all your fingers, take full note of the *Horses Bite and Kick* signs. These superstar animals are bred for high spirits—and are far too feisty to pet.

Other Sights: With extra time you can explore three more attractions (all included in entry ticket). The colonel created the tranquil and photogenic **Japanese Gardens** to depict the trials of life (beware the Tunnel of Ignorance). A wander through the more extensive and natural **St. Fiachra's Garden** (the patron saint of gardening) demands more time. Equestrian buffs may want to linger among the memorabilia in the small **Horse Museum,** where you can get a grip on how many hands it takes to measure a horse.

KILKENNY &
THE ROCK OF CASHEL

Whether driving west across Ireland from Dublin to Dingle, or heading toward the southern coast, the best two stops to break up a journey across the Irish interior are Kilkenny, Ireland's finest medieval town; and the Rock of Cashel, a thought-provoking early Christian site crowning the Plain of Tipperary.

Counties Kilkenny and Tipperary ("Tipp" to locals) are friendly neighbors geographically, yet blood sporting rivals on the hurling field, with the lion's share of the GAA national championships split between them. (Kilkenny locals are quick to point out that their 34 championships top all Irish counties.) Watch for kids heading home from school, carrying hurlies (ash-wood sticks with broad, flat ends) and dressed in their local colors (black and yellow, like bumblebees, for Kilkenny; blue and gold for Tipperary).

These two counties also boast some of the finest agricultural land on this rocky and boggy island. That's why Norman invaders fought to wrestle it away and make it one of their first Irish breadbaskets, soon after they secured their County Wexford/Waterford beachhead in the 12th century. These days, farm tractors rumble the back roads where it's not a long way to Tipperary.

PLANNING YOUR TIME

With one day, drivers connecting Dublin with Kinsale can get an early start, stop in Kilkenny for lunch, and then tour the Rock of Cashel before ending up in Kinsale to spend the night. For a longer visit, Kilkenny makes a good overnight for drivers from Dublin who drive slower back roads to visit Powerscourt Gardens and Glendalough (see previous chapter).

I've listed accommodations for both Kilkenny and the Rock of

Cashel: A night in Kilkenny comes with plenty of traditional folk music in its pubs, and more to do (additional sights nearby include Jerpoint Abbey and Kells Priory). If you're driving between Dublin and Dingle (or Kenmare), the Rock of Cashel is a more direct overnight.

With a few extra days, consider worthwhile destinations along the southeast coast, such as Waterford and County Wexford (see next chapter). Travelers with more time can continue on the scenic southern coastal route west via Cobh, Kinsale, Kenmare, and the Ring of Kerry (all covered in later chapters).

Kilkenny

The country's loveliest inland city—past winner of Ireland's "Tidy Town" award—Kilkenny gives you a feel for salt-of-the-earth Ireland. The town earned its nickname, the "Marble City," because of the stone from the local quarry (actually black limestone, not marble). You can see white seashells fossilized within the black stone steps around town. While an average-size town today (around 25,000 residents), Kilkenny has a big history. It was even the capital of Ireland for a short spell in the turbulent 1640s.

Kilkenny's castle and cathedral stand like historic bookends on a higgledy-piggledy High Street of colorful shops and medieval facades. This stretch of town has been rebranded as "The Medieval Mile." Other Irish towns can't quite claim such a colorful and concentrated window into those feudal times.

Orientation to Kilkenny

TOURIST INFORMATION
The TI is a block off the bridge in the 16th-century Shee (a wealthy medieval donor family) Alms poorhouse (Mon-Sat 9:00-17:30, Sun 11:00-17:00, shorter hours and closed Sun off-season; Rose Inn Street, tel. 056/775-1500). The Kilkenny Medieval Mile Pass sold by the TI isn't worth the trouble for most travelers.

ARRIVAL IN KILKENNY
The train/bus station is four blocks from John's Bridge, which marks the center of town.

KILKENNY & CASHEL

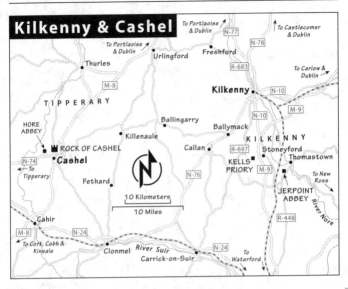

Drivers can find parking for under €2/hour at the Market Yard Car Park behind Kyteler's Inn (daily 8:00-18:00, entry off Bateman's Quay) or the pay-and-display spots on the street (enforced Mon-Sat 8:00-19:00). The multistory parking garage on Ormonde Street is the best long-term bet (3-day pass for €13.50 allows you to come and go; Sun-Thu 7:00-23:00, Fri-Sat until 24:00). If parking overnight, wait until you depart to pay, as some hotels will validate parking.

HELPFUL HINTS

Market: The square in front of Kilkenny Castle hosts a friendly produce, cheese, and crafts market on Thursday (8:00-14:30).

Bookstore: With a cheap and cheery café upstairs, **The Book Centre** is a great place to hang out on a rainy day (Mon-Sat 9:00-18:00, Sun 13:00-17:00, 10 High Street, tel. 056/776-2177).

Laundry: At the south end of town, the full-service **Laundry Basket** trumpets its existence in vivid red at 21 Patrick Street (Mon-Fri 9:00-17:00, Sat 10:00-15:00, closed Sun, tel. 056/777-0355).

Bike Rental: Kilkenny Cycling rents bikes and provides safety gear and route maps for exploring the pastoral charms of County Kilkenny (€25/day, €50 refundable deposit, office behind The Wine Centre shop at 15 John Street, mobile 086-895-4961, www.kilkennycyclingtours.com).

Tours in Kilkenny

Walking Tour

Pat Tynan and his staff offer the only regularly scheduled walking tours in town. They last one hour and depart from the TI (€10, daily at 11:00 and 14:00, Nov-mid-March by prior arrangement only, mobile 087-265-1745, www.kilkennywalkingtours.ie).

Local Guides

For more than 40 years, **Frank Kavanagh** helped visitors appreciate Kilkenny Castle. These days, he's available for custom walks of the town and castle. He also offers handy full- or half-day driving tours to destinations as far away as Cashel, Waterford, Wexford, and Cork (available Feb-Nov, book ahead, €75/half-day, €150/full day, gas and lunch cost extra, mobile 086-839-2468, http://visitkilkenny.ie/franks_medieval_tours, fkav1948@gmail.com).

Amanda Pitcairn runs scholarly tours focusing on the history of medieval Kilkenny and the daily life of its inhabitants—witchcraft and skullduggery included. Ask about her connection to mutineers from the HMS *Bounty* (€15/person, €12/person for groups of 4-6, must book ahead, mobile 087-277-6107, www.touchthepastireland.com, pitcaira@tcd.ie).

Bike Tours

At **Kilkenny Cycling,** Jason Morrissey offers a two-hour "easy-paced" guided tour (€25), which takes in a half-dozen of the town's best sights, including Kilkenny Castle, Rothe House and Garden, and St. Canice's Cathedral (usually departs at 10:00 and 14:00, also at 19:00 May-Sept). Ask about his four-hour unguided "bike-and-hike" recommended route, which includes a six-mile ride to Bennettsbridge, then a pretty hike back along the river (he'll explain where to leave the bikes). He also offers a €20 Medieval Mile cycling treasure hunt for history buffs (RS%, cash only; see "Bike Rental," earlier, for contact info).

Sights in Kilkenny

▲▲Kilkenny Castle

Dominating the town, this castle is a stony reminder that the Anglo-Norman Butler family controlled Kilkenny for 500 years. The castle once had four sides, but Oliver Cromwell's army knocked down one wall when it took the castle, leaving it as the rough "U" shape we see today.

Cost and Hours: €8; daily 9:30-17:30, June-Aug from 9:00, shorter hours in winter; tel. 056/770-4100, www.kilkennycastle.ie.

Visiting the Castle: Enter the castle gate, turn right in the courtyard, and head into the base of the turret. Here you'll find

the continuously running 12-minute video explaining how the wooden fort, built here by Strongbow in 1172, evolved into a 17th-century château. Then go into the main castle entrance, diagonally across the courtyard from the turret, to buy your entry ticket. You'll be free to walk through the castle. A pamphlet explains the exhibits, and you can also talk to stewards in the important rooms.

Now restored to its Victorian splendor, the castle's highlight is the beautiful family-portrait gallery, which puts you face-to-face with the wealthy Butler family ghosts.

Nearby: The **Kilkenny Design Centre,** across the street from the castle in some grand old stables, is full of local crafts and offers cafeteria-style lunches in its food hall (shops open Mon-Sat 10:00-19:00, Sun until 18:00; food hall open daily 9:00-18:30; tel. 056/772-2118, www.kilkennydesign.com).

▲Rothe House and Garden

This is the crown jewel of Kilkenny's medieval architecture: a well-preserved merchant's house that expanded around interior courtyards as the prosperous Rothe family grew in the early 1600s.

Cost and Hours: €7.50; Mon-Sat 10:00-17:00, Sun from 12:00; Nov-March closes at 16:30 and all day Sun; Parliament Street, tel. 056/772-2893, www.rothehouse.com.

Visiting the House and Garden: Check out the graceful top-floor timberwork supporting the roof, which uses wooden dowels (pegs) instead of nails. The museum, which also serves as the County Kilkenny genealogy center, gives a glimpse of life here in late Elizabethan and early Stuart times. The walled gardens at the far back were a real luxury in their time.

The Rothe family eventually lost the house when Oliver Cromwell banished all Catholic landowners, sending them to live on less desirable land west of the River Shannon. In the late 1800s, the building housed the Gaelic League, devoted to the rejuvenation of Irish culture through preservation of the Irish language and promotion of native Irish sports (such as hurling). One of the future leaders of the 1916 Easter Rising—Thomas McDonagh, who was executed at Dublin's Kilmainham Gaol—taught here.

▲Medieval Mile Museum

This fine museum covers Kilkenny's brutal yet pious Dark Age past and rounds out the story begun at the Rothe House (listed above).

KILKENNY & CASHEL

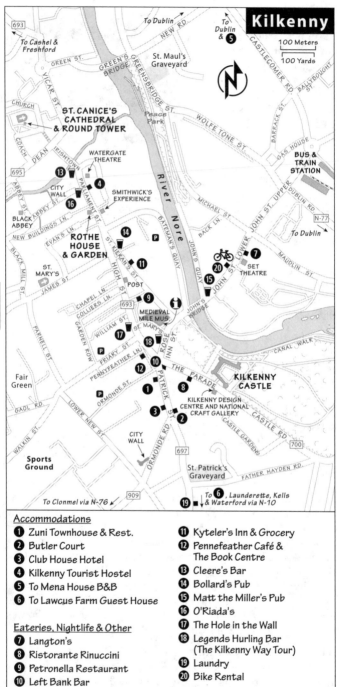

Accommodations

1 Zuni Townhouse & Rest.
2 Butler Court
3 Club House Hotel
4 Kilkenny Tourist Hostel
5 To Mena House B&B
6 To Lawcus Farm Guest House

Eateries, Nightlife & Other

7 Langton's
8 Ristorante Rinuccini
9 Petronella Restaurant
10 Left Bank Bar
11 Kyteler's Inn & Grocery
12 Pennefeather Café & The Book Centre
13 Cleere's Bar
14 Bollard's Pub
15 Matt the Miller's Pub
16 O'Riada's
17 The Hole in the Wall
18 Legends Hurling Bar (The Kilkenny Way Tour)
19 Laundry
20 Bike Rental

Cost and Hours: €8, €12 with 45-minute tour; daily 10:00-18:00, Nov-March 11:00-16:30; tours daily at 10:30, 12:30, 14:30, and 16:30; 2 Mary's Lane, tel. 056/781-7022, www.medievalmilemuseum.ie.

Visiting the Museum: Housed in the 13th-century St. Mary's Church (much of which was rebuilt in the 1700s), the museum displays medieval artifacts, including ornately carved tomb lids, ceremonial swords and scepters, and neatly penned 800-year-old civic records (with exhibits enhanced by modern touchscreen displays). You'll also find peekaboo glimpses of hidden burial vaults through Plexiglas flooring and visit the private chapel of the Rothes (the wealthy merchant family). Guided tours put flesh on the bones of this museum's stony skeleton.

The site itself also has an interesting history. This is where the famous witch trial of Alice Kyteler and her son took place in 1324. The two beat the rap with money: She paid to engineer a secret escape while her son funded the reroofing of the church. That left her destitute maid to take the heat...literally. Then, as now, the poor are at a disadvantage in court. The evocative graveyard out back whispers the righteous claims to heaven of the rich donors who built this medieval town.

▲Hurling Museum and Stadium Experience

The sport of hurling is historically and culturally important to the Irish. And Kilkenny is a hurling mecca (check out the cool statue of three players in leaping action, at the southwest end of John's Bridge). Run by PJ Lanigan, "The Kilkenny Way" is a walking tour that includes visits to a hurling pub/museum and the stadium where the Kilkenny Cats play. You'll learn about the long history and rules of this lightning-fast field game, and also get a chance to play as you figure out how to balance your *sliotar*—and how to pronounce it.

Cost and Hours: €25 for two-hour tour, includes pub meal; Mon-Sat at 14:00, reserve ahead in summer; leaves from Legends Hurling Bar, 28 Rose Inn Street, tel. 056/772-1718, www.thekilkennyway.com.

St. Canice's Cathedral

This 13th-century cathedral is early English Gothic, rich with stained glass, medieval carvings, and floors paved in history. Check out the model of the old walled town in its 1641 heyday, as well as a couple of modest audiovisuals. The 100-foot-tall **round tower,** built as part of a long-gone pre-Norman church, recalls the need for a watchtower, treasury, and refuge. The fun ladder-climb to the top affords a grand view of the countryside.

Cost and Hours: Cathedral-€4.50, tower-€4, combo-ticket-€7; Mon-Sat 9:00-18:00, Sun from 13:00; shorter hours and closed for lunch in off-season; tel. 056/776-4971, www.stcanicescathedral.com.

Smithwick's Experience Kilkenny

Smithwick's (pronounced SMIT-icks) reddish ale was born in Kilkenny...and has been my favorite Irish beer since my first visit to Ireland. Founded in 1710, it is older than Guinness (but now owned by the same parent company). No longer a working brewery, the building now houses a visitors center.

Tours focus on the historic origins of the tasty ale, first brewed by the monks of St. Francis Abbey (the 14th-century ruins of the abbey lie adjacent to the site). In the days of the monks, beer was a safer and healthier alternative to local water sources that were often contaminated. I'll drink to that.

Note that—like the Guinness Storehouse in Dublin—this is not a tour of a working brewery. It's a corporate-sponsored homage to the history of the brewery that once operated here.

Cost and Hours: €16, discount if booked online, entry includes a pint at the tour's end; daily 10:00-18:00, Nov-Feb 11:00-16:00, one-hour tours run hourly, last tour departs one hour before closing; 44 Parliament Street, tel. 056/778-6377, www.smithwicksexperience.com.

Nightlife in Kilkenny

Pubs and Traditional Music Sessions

Kilkenny has its fair share of atmospheric pubs. Visitors seeking fun traditional music sessions can try the first four places listed here. Those seeking friendly conversation in utterly unvarnished Irish surroundings should seek out the memorable duo at the end of these listings. A fun pub crawl could link all of these places with 20 minutes of walking (30 minutes crawling). Check the nightly pub trad session schedules as you explore town during the day (they may change unpredictably).

Starting at the north end of town and working south, **Cleere's Bar** is a friendly throwback with surprisingly good pub grub served until 20:00 (music Mon and Wed at 21:30, 28 Parliament Street). **Bollard's Pub,** an unpretentious landmark at the north end of St. Kieran's Street, is a good bet for lively traditional music sessions. Or sit out front under the awning and enjoy a pint as Kilkenny's humanity flows past you. Just down the same street is **Kyteler's Inn,** with a stony facade and medieval witch-haunted cellar (music nightly in summer at 18:00, 27 St. Kieran's Street). You can saunter over John's Bridge to check out the tunes at **Matt the Miller's Pub,** with its multilevel, dark-wood interior (around 18:30 most nights, next to bridge on John Street across the river from the castle).

Lacking music but high on character, **O'Riada's** is an endangered species—a wonderful, old-fashioned place that your Irish grandfather would recognize and linger in. This is an ideal place to chat with engaging locals (across from the Watergate Theatre at 25 Parliament Street).

At the other end of the conversational spectrum, **The Hole in the Wall** is a tiny, restored Elizabethan tavern (c. 1582) hidden down an alley (capacity 15-20, mostly standing). Charmingly eccentric owner Michael Conway—cardiologist by day and historian/playwright/actor/barman by night—presides over the speakeasy-like space as a labor of love. His sporadic music sessions (which mostly take place in the slightly larger, but equally creaky, timber-beamed upstairs hall) can't be pigeon-holed. But when they're on, they are usually an uninhibited, go-for-broke thump-a-thon (he plays bass drum). Spontaneous but always entertaining, Conway conducts sing-alongs of Irish classics that include helpful lyrics and explanations of Irish idioms (unpredictable hours but typically Fri-Sat from 20:00 and sometimes weeknights, confirm ahead, look for the alley beside Bourkes shop at 17 High Street, tel. 087/807-5650, www.holeinthewall.ie).

Theater
The **Watergate Theatre** houses live plays and other performances in its 300-seat space (€15-25, Parliament Street, tel. 056/776-1674, www.watergatetheatre.ie).

The **Set Theatre,** adjacent to sprawling Langton's Restaurant, is a fine, modern, 250-seat music venue attracting top-notch Irish acts in an intimate setting (€15-30, John Street, tel. 056/776-5133, www.set.ie).

Sleeping in Kilkenny

My first three listings are more central, clustered within a block of each other along Patrick Street; in general, options for smaller places in town are shrinking as they struggle to compete with bigger hotels.

Note: Kilkenny is a popular weekend destination for loud and rowdy stag and hen (bachelor and bachelorette) parties, thanks to its easy train access from Dublin (no risk of drunk driving). For quiet at night, avoid hotels with bars downstairs or nearby, and stick with smaller B&Bs, guesthouses, or rural lodging (especially Fri-Sat nights). Except for the Zuni and Club House, my recommendations should be free of these disturbances.

IN THE CENTER
$$$ Zuni Townhouse, above a fashionable restaurant, has 13 boutique-chic rooms sporting colorfully angular furnishings. Ask

about two-night weekend breaks and midweek specials that include a four-course dinner (parking in back, 26 Patrick Street, tel. 056/772-3999, www.zuni.ie, info@zuni.ie).

$$ Butler Court is Kilkenny's best lodging value. Ever-helpful Yvonne and John offer 10 modern, spacious rooms behind the beige, flag-draped archway. Bo the dog quietly patrols the courtyard (wheelchair-accessible, continental breakfast in room, will validate parking in nearby multistory garage on Ormonde Street for length of your stay, 14 Patrick Street, tel. 056/776-1178, www. butlercourt.com, info@butlercourt.com).

$$ Club House Hotel, originally a gentlemen's sporting club, comes with fading Georgian elegance; a musty, creaking ambience; a palatial, well-antlered breakfast room; and 35 comfy bedrooms (secure parking, 19 Patrick Street, tel. 056/772-1994, www. clubhousehotel.com, info@clubhousehotel.com).

¢ Kilkenny Tourist Hostel fills a fine Georgian townhouse with ramshackle fellowship at the north end of the town center, right in the action (private rooms available, cash only, pay self-serve laundry, 2 blocks from cathedral at 35 Parliament Street, tel. 056/776-3541, www.kilkennyhostel.ie, info@kilkennyhostel.ie).

FARTHER OUT

$$ Lawcus Farm Guest House is a quirky, seductive confection of rural comfort 10 miles south of Kilkenny between Kells Priory and the village of Stoneyford. Hosts Mark and Ann Marie have a passion for recycled materials and an environmental sensitivity. Mark, an inventive craftsman, renovated the original house and built the rest. A menagerie of friendly pets and farm animals shares the tasteful 20-acre property straddling the Kings River. Ask about the tiny secluded tree house (family rooms, cash only, parking, mobile 086-603-1667 or 087-291-1056, www.lawcusfarmguesthouse. com, lawcusfarm@hotmail.com). To reach the farm, go south out of Kilkenny on N-10, which becomes R-713 after crossing over the M-9 motorway. Just as you enter the village of Stoneyford, turn right onto L-1023. Go 500 yards down that lane and watch for a brown sign directing you to turn right into a 100-yard-long gravel driveway.

$ Mena House B&B is a traditional, good-value option quietly nestled a mile north of town. Behind its Tudor-style facade you'll find seven large, spotless rooms, well kept by hostess Katherine. It's about a 15-minute walk from the center and easy for drivers (family rooms, cash only, parking, located roughly across from the Newpark Hotel and just south of the Kilkenny Golf Club on Castlecomer Road, tel. 056/776-5362, www.menahousebandb. com, menahouse@eircom.net).

Eating in Kilkenny

$$$ Langton's is every local's first choice, serving high-quality Irish dishes under a labyrinthine, multichambered, Tiffany-sky-light expanse (daily 12:00-22:00, 69 John Street, tel. 056/776-5133).

$$$$ Ristorante Rinuccini serves classy, romantic, candlelit Italian meals (daily 12:00-14:30 & 17:00-22:00, reservations smart, 1 The Parade, tel. 056/776-1575, www.rinuccini.com).

$$ Petronella Restaurant warms its medieval surroundings with dependable traditional entrées and a welcoming vibe dished out by jovial Frank (Mon-Sat 12:00-15:00 & 17:00-21:00, closed Sun, Butterslip Lane off High Street, tel. 056/776-1899).

$$$$ Zuni, in one of my recommended accommodations, is a stylish splurge offering international cuisine (daily 12:30-17:00 & 18:00-20:45, weekend reservations a good idea, 26 Patrick Street, tel. 056/772-3999, www.zuni.ie).

$$$ Left Bank Bar is a dimly lit, three-story multichambered maze of creaky floored conviviality with a fun patio out back. This centrally located gastropub has better-than-average fare, but come early—its top-floor nightclub zooms with stag/hen party bedlam until late on weekends (food served Mon-Thu 12:00-21:00, Fri-Sun until 19:00, 1 Parade Gardens, tel. 056/775-0016).

$$$ Kyteler's Inn serves decent pub grub in a timber-and-stone atmosphere with a heated and covered beer garden out back. Visit their fun 14th-century cellar and ask about their witch (Mon-Sat 12:00-21:00, Sun until 20:00, 27 St. Kieran's Street, tel. 056/772-1064).

$ Pennefeather Café, above the Kilkenny Book Centre, is good for a quick, cheap, light lunch (Mon-Sat 9:00-17:30, closed Sun, 10 High Street, tel. 056/776-4063).

Grocery Store: You'll find an ample selection of picnic supplies at **Dunnes Stores** (a few doors down from Kyteler's Inn on St. Kieran's Street, Mon-Sat 8:00-21:00, Sun 10:00-20:00).

Kilkenny Connections

From Kilkenny by Train to: Dublin (6/day, 1.5 hours), **Waterford** (6/day, 35 minutes). Train info: www.irishrail.ie.

By Bus to: Dublin (8/day, 2 hours), **Waterford** (Dublin Coach every 2 hours, 40 minutes, www.dublincoach.ie), **Galway** (2/day, change in Athlone, 5 hours). Bus info: www.buseireann.ie.

KILKENNY & CASHEL

Between Kilkenny and Waterford

The fast M-9 motorway links Kilkenny and Waterford on a 45-minute drive. But drivers in no rush can savor the journey by spending a couple of enjoyable back-road hours taking in two pastoral sights: Jerpoint Abbey and Kells Priory. (You can also stitch these places into a more leisurely itinerary for an easy, triangular day trip beginning and ending in Kilkenny—about 28 miles/45 km total.) The rural roads come with old stone bridges spanning placid rivers that weave among tiny villages and abandoned mills. It's easier to visit Jerpoint Abbey first. There are no guided tours at Kells Priory; ask at the abbey for directions and pointers.

▲▲Jerpoint Abbey

Evocative abbey ruins dot the Irish landscape, but few are as well presented as Jerpoint (founded in 1180). Its claim to fame is fine stone carvings on the sides of tombs and on the columns of the cloister arcade. If you visit only one abbey in Ireland, make it this one.

Without the excellent guided tours, the site is a cold, rigid ruin. But in the hands of unusually well-versed hosts, the place truly comes alive with insights into the monastic culture that imprinted Ireland 850 years ago.

Cost and Hours: €5; daily 9:00-17:30, shorter hours Oct-Nov, Dec-March by appointment only; tel. 056/772-4623.

Getting There: It's located about 11 miles (17 km) south of Kilkenny or 2 miles (3 km) south of Thomastown, beside R-700.

Visiting the Abbey: The Cistercian monks, who came to Ireland from France in the 12th century, were devoted reformers bent on following the strict rules of St. Benedict. Their holy mission was to bring the wild Irish Christian church (which had evolved, unsupervised, for centuries on the European fringe) back in line with Rome. With an uncompromising my-way-or-the-hell-way attitude, they steamrolled their belief system across the island and stamped the landscape with a network of identical, sprawling monasteries. The preexisting form of Celtic Christianity that had thrived in the Dark Ages was no match for the organization and determination of the Cistercians.

For the next 350 years, these new monasteries held the moral high ground and were the dominant local religious authority. Monks got closer to God by immersing themselves in the hardships of manual field work, building water mills, tending kilns, and advancing the craft of metallurgy. The wealth created by this turbo-charged industriousness caused communities to form around these magnetic monastic cores.

What eventually did them in? King Henry VIII's marriage

problems, his subsequent creation of the (Protestant) Church of England, and his eventual dissolution of the (Catholic) monasteries. Walls were knocked down and roofs were torn off monasteries such as Jerpoint to make them uninhabitable. Their lands were forfeited to the king, who sold them off and enriched his treasury. It's good to be king.

▲▲Kells Priory

This place is a wonderful lonely gem. Locals claim that the massive religious complex of Kells Priory (more than 3 acres) is the largest monastic site in Europe. It's an isolated, deserted ruin that begs a curious wander (and alert side-stepping of sheep droppings).

Don't confuse this Kells with the identically named town farther north in County Meath (that's the Kells that produced the famous Book of Kells, now housed in Trinity College Library in Dublin).

Cost and Hours: Free, no set hours.

Getting There: You'll find Kells Priory about 9 miles (15 km) south of Kilkenny or 6 miles (10 km) west of Jerpoint Abbey, just off the R-697 road. From Jerpoint Abbey, turn left, then take your first right through the village of Stoneyford. At the end of the village, turn left (at the sign for Kells Priory), then continue straight.

The main parking lot lies on a slope above the south side of the ruins (a good place for a quick overview photo stop). But I prefer to park beside the Kings River on the north side of the ruins. To get there, cross the pretty stone bridge over the river, and turn right onto the L-5067 road. Drive about 100 yards past the first mill (with a craft shop in an adjacent building); when you come to the second mill (completely shuttered and abandoned), park in the gravel lot in front.

Visiting Kells Priory: From the parking lot by the abandoned mill (described above), stroll past the mill's rusty waterwheel and enjoy the wander downstream for the remaining 100 yards along the riverside path. It's a photogenic approach to the priory ruins. Once inside the complex, watch where you walk and explore at your leisure. Consider bringing a picnic to enjoy—but please respect the site and leave no trash.

Founded in 1193 by Norman soldiers of fortune with Augustinian monks in tow, this priory grew into the intimidating structure that locals call "the seven castles" today. These "castles," however, were actually Norman tower houses connected by a wall that enclosed the religious functions within. Inside the walls, the site is divided into two main areas: One is a huge interior common grazing area (larger than a football field) dominated by the encircling tower houses; the other is a tangled medieval maze of rock walls (remnants of a cloister, a church, cellars, a medieval dormitory, and a graveyard).

The most dramatic 75-year period of the site's history took place between 1252 and 1327, when it was attacked and burned three times (once by Edward the Bruce's army of Scots). The contrast between those violent times and today's pastoral decay is striking.

Rock of Cashel

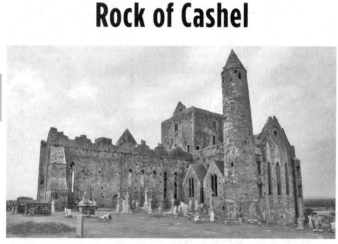

Rising high above the fertile Plain of Tipperary, the Rock of Cashel is one of Ireland's most historic and evocative sights. Seat of the ancient kings of Munster (c. AD 300-1100), this is where St. Patrick baptized King Aengus in about AD 450. Strategically located and perfect for fortification, the Rock was fought over by local clans for hundreds of years. Finally, in 1101, clever Murtagh O'Brien gave the Rock to the Church.

His seemingly benevolent donation increased his influence with the Church, while preventing his rivals, the powerful McCarthy clan, from regaining possession of the Rock. As Cashel evolved into an ecclesiastical center, Iron Age ring forts and thatch dwellings gave way to the majestic stone church buildings enjoyed by visitors today.

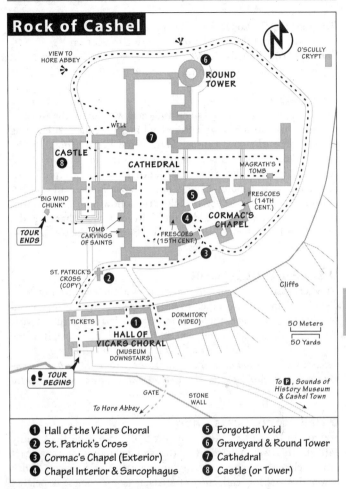

Rock of Cashel

VIEW TO
HORE ABBEY

O'SCULLY
CRYPT

⑥
ROUND
TOWER

WELL

⑦

CASTLE
⑧

CATHEDRAL

MAGRATH'S
TOMB

"BIG WIND
CHUNK"

⑤

FRESCOES
(14TH
CENT.)

CORMAC'S
CHAPEL

④

TOUR
ENDS

TOMB
CARVINGS
OF SAINTS

FRESCOES
(15TH CENT.)

③

ST. PATRICK'S
CROSS
(COPY)

②

Cliffs

DORMITORY
(VIDEO)

TICKETS

①

HALL OF
VICARS CHORAL
(MUSEUM
DOWNSTAIRS)

50 Meters

50 Yards

TOUR
BEGINS

GATE

STONE
WALL

To **P**, Sounds of
History Museum
& Cashel Town

To Hore Abbey

KILKENNY & CASHEL

❶ Hall of the Vicars Choral	❺ Forgotten Void
❷ St. Patrick's Cross	❻ Graveyard & Round Tower
❸ Cormac's Chapel (Exterior)	❼ Cathedral
❹ Chapel Interior & Sarcophagus	❽ Castle (or Tower)

ORIENTATION TO THE ROCK OF CASHEL

Cost and Hours: €8, families—€20, ticket includes guided tour—
see below; daily 9:00-17:30, summer until 19:00, winter until
16:30, last entry 45 minutes before closing; tel. 062/61437,
www.heritageireland.ie.

Crowd-Beating Tips: Summer crowds flock to the Rock (worst
June-Aug 11:00-15:00). Try to plan your visit for early or late
in the day.

Dress Warmly: Bring a coat—the Rock is exposed and often cold
and windy.

Tours: Guided walks are included with your entrance (2/hour,
about 45 minutes). Otherwise, set your own pace with my
self-guided tour.

Parking: Pay the €6 fee at the machine (under the Plexiglas shelter to the left of the exit) before returning to your car.

Services: You'll find basic WCs at the base of the Rock next to the parking lot (there are none up on the Rock).

OVERVIEW

From the parking lot, it's a steep 100-yard walk up to the Rock itself. On this 200-foot-high outcrop of limestone, the first building you'll enter is the 15th-century Hall of the Vicars Choral, housing the ticket desk, a tiny museum (with a stunted original 12th-century high cross dedicated to St. Patrick and a few replica artifacts), and a 20-minute video (2/hour, shown in the hall's former dormitory). From there you'll explore the following: a round tower, an early Christian cross, a delightful Romanesque chapel, and a ruined Gothic cathedral, all surrounded by my favorite Celtic-cross graveyard with views for miles.

➲ SELF-GUIDED TOUR

Nowhere else in Ireland can you better see the evolution of Irish devotion expressed in stone. This large lump of rock is a pedestal supporting a compact tangle of three dramatic architectural styles: early Christian (round tower and St. Patrick's high cross), Romanesque (Cormac's Chapel), and Gothic (the main cathedral).

• *Follow this tour counterclockwise around the Rock. Start by descending the indoor stairs opposite the ticket desk into the one-room, vaulted cellar museum.*

❶ Hall of the Vicars Choral

You are in the cellar of the youngest building on the Rock (early 1400s). This would have been the storage room for the vicars (minor clerics) appointed to sing during cathedral services. Today it contains a sparse collection of artifacts (some copies) associated with the religious site. Two glass cases display brooches and primitive axes, while the walls are hung with stone slab carvings. The impressively ornate shrine bell of St. Patrick is a reproduction (the bell would not have been used by him, but rather, dedicated to him, centuries later). But the star of the vault is the **original Cross of St. Patrick** at the far end. The massive stone base is hollow (see the mirror underneath it). Was it a hiding place for valuable religious objects during raids? Or just too heavy to move otherwise? The cross stood outside for centuries, but hundreds of years of wind and rain slowly buffeted away important detail, scouring it into a stub of its former glory. We'll soon see a copy outside.

• *Climb back up to the ticket desk level and continue up the indoor stairs into the living space of the vicars.*

Walk to the **great hall** with the big brown tapestry. Vicars were granted nearby lands by the archbishop and lived comfortably here, with a large fireplace and white, lime-washed walls (to reflect light and act as a natural disinfectant that discouraged bugs). Window seats gave the blessedly literate vicars the best light to read by. The furniture is original, but the colorfully ornamented oak timber roof is a reconstruction, built to medieval specifications using wooden dowels instead of nails. The large wall tapestry shows King Solomon with the Queen of Sheba.

The vicars, who formed a sort of corporate body to assist the bishop with local administration, used a special seal to authorize documents such as land leases. You can see an enlarged wooden copy of the seal (hanging above the fireplace), depicting eight vicars surrounding a seated organist. It was a good system—until some of the greedier vicars duplicated the seal for their own less holy purposes, forcing the archbishop to curtail its use.

• *Go outside the hall into the grassy space, veer left about 30 feet, and find...*

❷ St. Patrick's Cross

St. Patrick baptized King Aengus on the Rock of Cashel in about AD 450. This is a copy of the 12th-century cross carved to celebrate the handing over of the Rock to the Church 650 years after St. Patrick's visit (the original is in the museum in the Hall of the Vicars Choral, described earlier). Typical Irish high crosses use a ring around the cross' head to support its arms and to symbolize the sun (making Christianity more appealing to the sun-worshipping Celts). But instead, this cross uses the Latin design: The weight of the arms was supported by two vertical beams on each side of the main shaft, representing the two criminals who were crucified beside Christ (today only one of these supports remains).

• *Walk about 100 feet slightly uphill along the gravel path beside the cathedral. Roughly opposite the far end of the Hall of the Vicars Choral is the entry (a glass door) to the chapel.*

❸ Cormac's Chapel (Exterior)

As the wild Celtic Christian church was reined in and reorganized by Rome 850 years ago, new architectural influences from continental Europe began to emerge on the remote Irish landscape. This small chapel—Ireland's first and finest Romanesque church, constructed in 1134 by King Cormac MacCarthy—reflects this evolution. Imagine being here in the 12th century, when this chapel and the

KILKENNY & CASHEL

tall round tower were the only stone structures sprouting from the Rock (among a few long-gone, humble wooden structures).

The "new" Romanesque style reflected the ancient Roman basilica floor plan. Its columns and rounded arches created an overall effect of massiveness and strength. Romanesque churches were like dark fortresses, with thick walls, squat towers, and few windows. Irish stone churches of this period (like the one at Glendalough in the Wicklow Mountains) were simple rectangular buildings emphasizing function.

The two square towers resemble those in Regensburg, Germany, further suggesting that well-traveled medieval Irish monks brought back new ideas from the Continent.

Before stepping inside, notice the weathered tympanum above the door. The carved "hippo" is actually an ox, representing Gospel author St. Luke.

• *The modern, dark-glass chapel door is a recent addition to keep out nesting birds. Enter the chapel and let your eyes adjust to the low light.*

❹ Chapel Interior

Just inside, on your left, is an empty stone **sarcophagus.** Nobody knows for sure whose body once lay here (possibly the brother of King Cormac MacCarthy). The damaged front relief is carved in a Viking style. Vikings had been raiding Ireland for more than 200 years by the time this was carved; they had already intermarried with the Irish, and were seeping into Irish society. Some scholars interpret the relief design (a tangle of snakes and beasts) as a figure-eight lying on its side, looping back and forth forever, symbolizing the eternity of the afterlife.

You're standing in the **nave,** dimly lit by three small windows. Overhead is an arched vaulted ceiling with support ribs. The strong round arches support not only the heavy stone roof, but also the unseen second-story scriptorium chamber, where monks once carefully copied manuscripts by candlelight (their work was amazingly skillful and ornate, considering the poor light).

The big main arch overhead, studded with fist-size heads, framed the altar (now gone). Walk into the chancel and look up at the ceiling, examining the faint **frescoes,** a labor of love from 850 years ago. Frescoes are rare in Ireland because of the perpetually moist climate. (Mixing pigments into wet plaster worked better in dry climates like Italy's.) Once vividly colorful, then fading over time, these frescoes were further damaged during and after the Reformation, when Protestants piously whitewashed them. These surviving frescoes were discovered under multiple layers of whitewash during painstaking modern restoration. Take a moment to imagine the majesty of this chapel before its fine ornamentation was destroyed by those Reformation iconoclasts.

• *Walk through the other modern, dark-glass doorway, opposite the door you used to enter the chapel. You'll find yourself in a...*

❺ Forgotten Void

This enclosed little space was created when the newer cathedral was wedged between the older chapel and the round tower. Once the main entrance into the chapel, this forgotten doorway is crowned by a finely carved tympanum that decorates the arch above it. It's perfectly preserved because the huge cathedral shielded it from the wind and rain. The large lion (symbol of St. Mark's gospel) is being hunted by a centaur (half-man, half-horse) archer wearing a Norman helmet.

• *Exit the chapel, turning left, and tiptoe through the tombstones around the east end of the cathedral to the base of the round tower.*

❻ Graveyard and Round Tower

This graveyard is full. The 20-foot-tall stone shaft at the edge of the graveyard, marking the O'Scully family crypt, was once crowned by an elaborately carved Irish high cross—destroyed during a lightning storm in 1976. The fortified wall dates from the 15th century, when the riches of this outpost merited a little extra protection.

Look out over the **Plain of Tipperary.** Called the "Golden Vale," its rich soil makes it Ireland's most fertile farmland. In St. Patrick's time, it was covered with oak forests. From the corner of the church, beyond the fortified wall on the left, you can see the ruined 13th-century **Hore Abbey** dominating the fields below (free, always open and peaceful).

Gaze up at the **round tower,** the first stone structure built on the Rock after the Church took over in 1101. The shape of these towers is unique to Ireland. Though you might think towers like this were chiefly intended as a place to hide in case of invasion, they were instead used primarily as bell towers and lookout posts. The tower stands 92 feet tall, with walls more than three feet thick. The doorway, which once had a rope ladder, was built high up not only for security, but also because having it at ground level would have weakened the foundation of the top-heavy structure. The interior once contained wooden floors connected by ladders, and served as safe storage for the monks' precious sacramental treasures. The tower's stability is impressive when you consider its age, the winds it has endured, and the shallowness of its foundation (only five feet below present ground level).

KILKENNY & CASHEL

Continue walking around the cathedral's north transept, noticing the square "put-log" holes in the exterior walls. During construction, wooden scaffolding was anchored into these holes. After the structure was completed, the builders simply sawed off the scaffolding, leaving small blocks of wood embedded in the walls. With time, the blocks rotted away, and the holes became favorite spots for birds to build their nests.

On your way to the cathedral entrance find the small **well** (in the corner on the left, built into the wall). Its stone lip is groovy from ropes after centuries of use. Without this essential water source, the Rock could never have withstood a siege and would not have been as valuable to clans and clergy. In 1848, a chalice was dredged from the well, likely thrown there by fleeing medieval monks intending to survive a raid. They didn't make it. (If they had, they would have retrieved the chalice.)

• *Now enter the...*

❼ Cathedral

Traditionally, churches face east toward Jerusalem and the rising sun. Because this cathedral was squeezed between the preexisting chapel, round tower, and drinking well, to make it face east the builders were forced to improvise by giving it a cramped nave and an extra-long choir (where the clergy gathered to celebrate Mass).

Built between 1230 and 1290, the church's pointed arches and high, narrow windows proclaim the Gothic style of the period (and let in more light than earlier Romanesque churches). Walk under the central bell tower and look up at the rib-vaulted **ceiling.** The hole in the middle was for a rope used to ring the church bells. The wooden roof is long gone. When the Protestant Lord Inchiquin (who became one of Oliver Cromwell's generals) attacked the Catholic town of Cashel in 1647, hundreds of townsfolk fled to the sanctuary of this cathedral. Inchiquin packed turf around the exterior and burned the cathedral down, massacring those inside.

Ascend the terraces at the choir end of the cathedral, where the main altar once stood. Stand on the gravestones (of the 16th-century rich and famous) with your back to the east wall (where the narrow windows have crumbled away) and look back down toward the nave. The right wall of the choir is filled with graceful Gothic windows, while the solid left wall hides Cormac's Chapel (which would have blocked most sunlight). The line of stone supports on the left wall once held the long, wooden balcony where the vicars sang. Closer to the altar, high on the same wall (directly above the pointed doorway), is a small, rectangular window called the "leper's squint"—which allowed unsightly lepers to view the altar during Mass without offending the congregation.

The grand **wall tomb** on the left contains the remains of archbishop Miler Magrath, the "scoundrel of Cashel," who lived to be 100. From 1570 to 1622, Magrath was the Protestant archbishop of Cashel who simultaneously profited from his previous position as Catholic bishop of Down. He married twice, had lots of kids, confiscated the ornate tomb lid here from another bishop's grave, and converted back to Catholicism on his deathbed.

• *Walk back down the nave and turn left into the south transept.*

Peek into the modern-roofed wooden structure against the wall on your left. It's protecting 15th-century **frescoes** of the Crucifixion of Christ that were rediscovered during renovations in 2005. They're as patchy and hard to make out (and just as rare, for Ireland) as the century-older frescoes in the ceiling of Cormac's Chapel.

On the opposite side of this transept, in alcoves built into the wall, enjoy the wonderful **carvings** of early Christian saints lining the outside walls of tombs (look down at shin level).

• *Exit the cathedral opposite where you entered.*

❽ Castle (or Tower)

Back outside, stand beside the huge chunk of wall debris. (This is not "the rock" of Cashel.) Try to picture where it might have perched in the ragged puzzle of ruins above. This end of the cathedral was converted into an archbishop's castle in the 1400s (shortening the nave even more). Looking high into the castle's damaged top floors, you can see the bishop's residence chamber and the secret passageways that were once hidden inside the thick walls. Lord Inchiquin's cannons weakened the structure during the 1647 massacre, and in 1848, a massive storm (known as "Night of the Big Wind" in Irish lore) flung the huge chunk next to you from the ruins above.

In the mid-1700s, the Anglican Church transferred cathedral status to St. John's in town, and the archbishop abandoned the drafty Rock for a more comfortable residence, leaving the ruins that you see today.

NEAR THE ROCK
Sounds of History Museum

Fans of Irish music will enjoy this small museum dedicated to the story of Ireland's ancient and traditional music. (Find it in the Brú Ború Cultural Centre, below the Rock of Cashel parking lot, below the statue of the three blissed-out dancers.) The exhibit starts with a video display tracing the physical evolution of Cashel from ancient ring fort to grand religious complex. Then come displays about ancient wind instruments. At the end, a small theater shows a 15-minute film introduction to Ireland's beloved traditional music scene.

Cost and Hours: €5, Mon-Sat 9:00-17:00, closed Sun year-round, Sept-June also closed Sat, tel. 062/61122, www.bruboru.ie.

Performances: If sleeping in Cashel in the summer, consider taking in a performance of the Brú Ború musical dance troupe in the center's theater (€20-25, €50 with dinner, Tue-Sat in early July-mid-Aug, dinner at 19:00, 75-minute performance at 21:00, informal music session in the café/bar after).

Town of Cashel

The huggable town at the base of the Rock affords a good break on the long drive from Dublin to Dingle (**TI** open daily 9:30-17:30 in season, tel. 062/61333). The Heritage Centre, next door to the TI, presents a modest six-minute audio explanation of Cashel's history around a walled town model. Parking is pay-and-display (enforced Mon-Sat 9:00-18:00).

Sleeping in Cashel: If you spend the night, you'll be treated to beautifully illuminated views of the ruins. The first listing is a classy hotel in the center of town (15-minute walk from the Rock). The rest are cozy, old-fashioned, and closer to the Rock.

$$$ Bailey's Hotel is Cashel's best boutique hotel, housed in a fine Georgian townhouse (1709). Its 19 refurbished rooms are large, inviting, and well appointed, perched above a great cellar-pub restaurant (parking, 42 Main Street, tel. 062/61937, www.baileyshotelcashel.com, info@baileyshotelcashel.com).

$ Cashel Lodge is a well-kept rural oasis housed in an old stone grain warehouse, a 10-minute walk from the Rock near the Hore Abbey ruins. Its seven comfortable rooms combine unpretentious practicality with Irish country charm. Guests have a ringside seat for beautiful views of the Rock lit up at night (camping spots, parking, Dundrum Road R-505, tel. 062/61003, www.cashel-lodge.com, info@cashel-lodge.com, Tom and Brid O'Brien).

$ Rockville House, 100 yards from the Rock, is a traditional place run by gentleman owner Patrick Hayes. The house itself has six fine rooms, and its old stablehouse, lovingly converted by Patrick, has five more (family room, cash only, 10 Dominic Street, tel. 062/61760, rockvillehse@eircom.net).

$ Wattie's B&B has three rooms that feel lived-in and comfy (cash only, parking, 14 Dominic Street, tel. 062/61923, www.wattiesbandb.ie, wattiesbandbcashel@gmail.com, Maria Dunne).

Eating in Cashel: The following places are good lunch options near the Rock. **$ Granny's Kitchen** is a tiny, violet-colored place with basic soup-and-sandwich lunches (daily 11:00-16:00, just past parking lot at the base of the Rock). **$$ Café Hans** has the best lunch selection and biggest crowds (Tue-Sat 12:00-17:30, closed Sun-Mon, 75 yards down the road from the parking lot).

$$$$ Chez Hans, filling an old stone church, is good for a splurge dinner (Tue-Sat 18:00-21:30, closed Sun-Mon, a block below the Rock, tel. 062/61177, www.chezhans.net).

In town, you'll find several options. Next door to the TI, **$ Feehan's Bar** is a convenient stop for a pub grub lunch (daily 12:00-16:00, tel. 062/61929). A couple of blocks farther into town, the **$$ Cellar Pub** hides beneath Bailey's Hotel and serves satisfying dishes (daily 12:00-21:30, tel. 062/61937). **Super Valu** is the town's supermarket (Mon-Sat 7:00-22:00, Sun 8:00-21:00, 30 Main Street).

Cashel Connections: Cashel has no train station; the closest one is 10 miles away in the town of Cahir. Buses run from Cashel to **Dublin** (6/day, 2.5 hours) and **Waterford** (6/day, 2 hours; bus-train combination also possible via Cahir). Bus info: www.buseireann.ie.

KILKENNY & CASHEL

WATERFORD & COUNTY WEXFORD

If you need an overnight stop in southeast Ireland, the historic Viking port and Norman beachhead town of Waterford is your best choice. Humble Waterford town is of most interest to crystal devotees and Irish history enthusiasts, but from here, you can explore the varied sights of County Wexford, including a 12th-century lighthouse, the Kennedy homestead (now a museum), a re-creation of a famine ship, and more. Or consider staying in more-appealing Kilkenny (see the previous chapter) and sample this area via day trips (driving from Kilkenny to the County Wexford sights adds less than 30 minutes each way, making them doable in a full day).

This region has a pastoral serenity and a strong history of trading from its sheltered ports facing England. The Vikings built the ports and developed the trade routes. Their cousins, the Normans, came along 200 years later and carefully fortified the ports. In 1170, King Henry II visited his new Irish realm with a huge fleet, calling Waterford the "Gateway to Ireland." With more efficient farming techniques and advanced military technology, the Normans cranked up their dominant culture and shoved the locals aside.

But the Irish made them fight to hang on to it. Like medieval Fort Apaches, Norman-fortified tower-house castles dot the landscape. And throughout the region, you'll see evidence of Norman (French) roots in its high concentration of family names with old Norman prefixes: De Berg, De Lacy, Devereux, Fitzgilbert, Fitzsimmons, Fitzgerald, and so on. (In Norman French, "fitz" meant "son of" and "de" meant simply "of.") The first and greatest of all Norman French-speaking warlord invaders was Richard de Clare, who made his mark here and became known to history as "Strongbow."

Another local famous figure is Zorro, who was from Wexford. Or so say some historians, who claim that the inspiration for the colorful (even though he only wore black) fictitious character was none other than locally born, multilingual, 17th-century Catholic adventurer William Lamport. Lamport ran afoul of the English, fled to Spain, became a pirate, and joined a Spanish regiment fighting Swedes in the Thirty Years War. He was sent to Mexico as a spy (El Zorro means "the fox") but was executed for sympathizing with native slaves against the Mexican Inquisition.

Waterford

The oldest city in Ireland, Waterford was once more important than Dublin, and its three fine museums reflect this history. But today, while tourists associate the town's name with its famous crystal, locals are quick to remind you that the crystal is named after the town, not vice versa (come for the crystal, stay for the history). That said, Waterford is a plain, gray, workaday town of 45,000. Pubs outnumber cafés, and freighters offload cargo at the dock. Wandering the back streets, you'll get a dose of gritty Ireland, with fewer leprechauns per capita than other Irish destinations (though you'll also see some recent sprucing-up efforts as the town tries to shake its mediocre image).

PLANNING YOUR TIME
A day is enough time for Waterford's compact historic core. Visit the Waterford Crystal Visitor Centre early or late to avoid the midday big bus-tour crowds. Beyond that, your best activity is the historic walking tour (listed under "Helpful Hints," later), followed by a visit to the branch of the Waterford Museum of Treasures housed in Reginald's Tower. History buffs may want to dig deeper with visits to the other two branches of this three-museum complex: Chorister's Hall (medieval life) and Bishop's Palace (Georgian to modern age). To feel the pulse of contemporary Waterford, hang out on Barronstrand Street—the town's pedestrian artery.

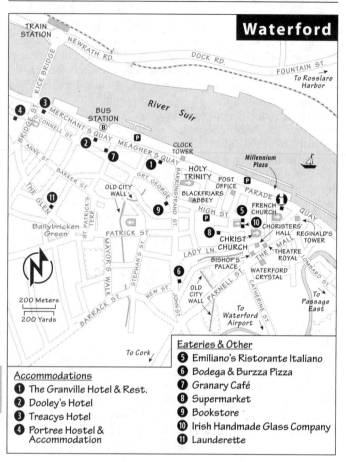

Orientation to Waterford

Waterford's main drag runs along its homely harbor; all of my recommended accommodations and sights are within a 15-minute walk from here. The sights and TI cluster within a four-block area nicknamed the "Viking Triangle." The TI and Reginald's Tower are opposite a modern, white, tent-like structure covering a raised stage called the Millennium Plaza, at the far eastern end of the harborfront from Rice Bridge. The other museums, the Waterford Crystal Visitor Centre, and the Theatre Royal are inland from Reginald's Tower, facing a street called The Mall.

A stubby three-story Victorian clock tower marks the middle of the harbor. It's also the start of Barronstrand Street, which runs two blocks inland to the town square. Also along the harbor are the bus station and easy pay parking lots (may need exact change in coins). For the best overnight parking, enter the lot next to the bus station (€5 lets you park from 17:00 to 11:00).

TOURIST INFORMATION

The TI sits on the harborfront, where Greyfriars Street meets Parade Quay, facing Millennium Plaza (Mon-Sat 9:00-17:00, usually closed Sun, shorter hours Nov-March; 120 Parade Quay, tel. 051/875-823, www.discoverireland.ie/waterford). On a pedestal on the sidewalk in front of the TI, check out the metal 3-D map of the "Viking Triangle" that defines Waterford's most historic district.

HELPFUL HINTS

Shopping: The **Irish Handmade Glass Company** features artisans trained at the old Waterford Crystal factory, who work right in front of you fashioning unique crystal creations. Their focus is to craft lovely and functional pieces that you'll actually use, rather than a decorative item to put on a shelf (Mon-Fri 9:00-17:00, Sat from 10:30, closed Sun, behind the Kite Design Studio storefront, 11 Henrietta Street, tel. 051/858-914, www.theirishhandmadeglasscompany.com).

Bookstore: The multilevel **Book Centre,** right off the main square, is a fun browse and has a cozy soup-and-sandwich café on an upstairs balcony (Mon-Sat 9:00-18:00, Fri until 21:00, Sun 13:00-17:00, 25 John Roberts Square, tel. 051/873-823).

Baggage Storage: The train station has no lockers. The bus station has a little newspaper/candy alcove in its waiting area that can store bags cheaply for the day (daily 7:00-19:00).

Laundry: Rainbow Laundry does full-service loads the same day if you drop off early (Mon-Thu 7:30-16:30, closed Fri-Sun, 28 Thomas Street).

Taxis: Try **Premiere Taxi Service** (tel. 051/373-373) or **Rapid Cabs** (tel. 051/858-585).

Historic Walking Tour: Jack Burtchaell and his partners lead entertaining, informative, hour-long, historical town walks (worth ▲▲) that go from the TI to the Waterford Crystal Visitor Centre, giving you a good handle on the story of Waterford. They meet at the TI every day at 11:45 and 13:45—or you can join the tour as it swings by the Granville Hotel at 12:00 and 14:00 (just show up, pay €8 at the end, mid-March-mid-Oct only, tel. 051/873-711, www.jackswalkingtours.com).

Theater: Waterford's small but lively **Theatre Royal** has been open since 1785. Given the dearth of other nighttime options in Waterford beyond pubs, it's worth checking out their schedule of plays, concerts, and light opera (€15-30 tickets, located on The Mall across from the Waterford Crystal Visitor Centre, tel. 051/874-402, www.theatreroyal.ie).

Waterford's History

Arriving in 819, Vikings first established Waterford as their base for piracy. Waterford was an ideal spot for launching their ships, since it's located at the gateway to one of the most extensive river networks in Ireland. From here, raiders could sail and row 50 miles into Ireland, an island with no towns, just scattered monastic settlements and small gatherings of clans—perfect for the Vikings' plan of rape, pillage, and plunder.

Later, the Vikings decided to "go legit." They turned to profiteering, setting up shop in an established trading base they named Vandrafjord, or "safe harbor." From this fully functioning Viking colony of farmers and merchants, Ireland's first permanent town eventually became known as Waterford.

In the 12th century, a deposed Irish king named Diarmuid MacMurrough opened the Irish version of Pandora's box by inviting the Normans over from England, hoping to use their advanced military technology to regain his land from a rival clan. The great warrior knight Strongbow came...and never left, beginning Ireland's long and troublesome relationship with the English. In 1170, Strongbow married the Irish princess Aoife here in Waterford (in a Gothic church where Waterford's Christ Church Cathedral stands today). One of Ireland's most famous and melodramatic paintings (hanging in the National Gallery in Dublin) depicts this event, and a copy of it covers a wall in Chorister's Hall Medieval Museum. With this marriage, Strongbow was next in line for the title of King of Leinster, which he was named after the death of his father-in-law, MacMurrough, a year later.

Strongbow's success was so rapid that King Henry II got worried about a rival kingdom blossoming on his flank. He quickly gathered his navy and sailed over from England to make sure Strongbow knew who was boss—and to intimidate Irish clan leaders into swearing loyalty to the Crown. England's first roots in Ireland had been planted.

For the English, Waterford has often proven to be a tough nut to crack. During Oliver Cromwell's brutal scorched-earth campaign of 1649-1650, he destroyed any town still loyal to King Charles I (see "The Curse of Cromwell" sidebar, later). Waterford was the only Irish city to withstand Cromwell's siege.

Sights in Waterford

▲▲WATERFORD CRYSTAL VISITOR CENTRE

With a tradition dating back to 1783 (absent about 100 years, from the late 1840s famine until the post-WWII boom), Waterford was once the largest—and is still the most respected—glassworks in the world. The economic downturn of 2008 shattered the market for luxury items like crystal, forcing the huge Waterford Crystal factory outside town to close. The company was bought by American investors who opened a new, scaled-down factory in the town center (and later sold it to a Finnish company for a handsome profit). While 70 percent of Waterford Crystal is now manufactured by cheaper labor in Poland, Slovenia, and the Czech Republic,  the finest glass craftsmen still reside here, where they create "prestige pieces" for special-order customers. The one-hour tour of this hardworking little factory is a joy. It's more intimate than the old, larger factory, and you're encouraged to interact with the craftsmen. Large tour groups descend midday, so try to visit before 10:00 or after 15:30.

Cost and Hours: Tours cost €14.50 and depart every 30 minutes (cheaper online); Mon-Sat 9:00-18:00, Sun from 9:30, last tour at 16:15; shorter hours Nov-March with last tour at 15:15; shop open longer hours; on The Mall, one block south of Reginald's Tower; tel. 051/317-000, www.waterfordvisitorcentre.com.

Visiting the Factory: The tour begins with a bit of history and a look at an impressive six-foot-tall crystal grandfather clock. It then loses momentum as you're ushered into a glitzy and pointless five-minute fireworks film montage set to a techno beat. But things pick up again as your guide takes you into the factory to meet the craftsmen in their element. Glassblowers magically spin glowing blobs of molten crystal into exquisite and recognizable shapes in minutes. If you get dizzy blowing up balloons for a kid's party, consider the lung stamina that these craftsmen display. Watch closely as the glassblower puts his thumb over the opening between breaths to keep the heat and pressure inside the blob constant.

Heavy molten crystal has an intentionally high lead content (it's what distinguishes fine crystal from common glassware). A cooling-off stage allows the crystal to set. Then glasscutters deftly cradle the fragile creations against diamond-edged cutting wheels, applying exactly enough pressure to ensure that the grooves are replicated with surgical skill. The glasscutters will be glad to demonstrate if you ask.

Watch the skilled cutters muscle rough unfinished pieces—weighing as much as bowling balls—and cut intricate patterns. The crystal vases and bowls may look light and delicate, but hold an unfinished piece (with its lead-enhanced heft) and you'll gain a new appreciation for the strength, touch, and hand-eye coordination of the glasscutters.

Afterward, visit the glittering salesroom, surrounded by hard-to-pack but easy-to-ship temptations. Take a look at the copies of famous sports trophies (they make backups of their most important commissions, just in case). If you make a significant purchase, be sure to ask about getting a VAT refund (see page 559).

MUSEUM OF TREASURES COMPLEX

Waterford presents its impressive history in a three-museum complex called the Museum of Treasures, with locations just a damsel's handkerchief-drop from each other. The museums line up along the southern flank of the "Viking Triangle," the footprint of the original Viking-fort section of town, about a two-minute walk apart (the museum's tagline is "Vikings to Victorians: 1,000 years of history in 1,000 paces").

To see the branches in historical sequence, first visit Reginald's Tower on the harborfront to understand the Viking roots of the city. Then stroll up The Mall to find Chorister's Hall Medieval Museum, a modern structure tucked behind the Theatre Royal. This branch shows Norman and Tudor artifacts above an original 13th-century vaulted wine cellar. Finally, right next door, you can visit the imposing Bishop's Palace, a fine mansion full of everything Waterford from 1700 to the present. Few Irish towns can claim a meatier bite of Irish history than Waterford.

Note: Entry to Reginald's Tower is covered by the Heritage Card (see "Passes," page 562). The Chorister's Hall and Bishop's Palace are not, but they do offer a combo-ticket for entry into both.

▲Reginald's Tower

This oldest part of the oldest town in Ireland is named after Reg-

nall, the first (Norwegian) Viking leader of Waterford, who built a fortified oaken tower here in AD 914 and later invaded Jorvik (York, England). Dating from the late 1100s, the stone Norman tower you see today replaced the wooden one and was once the most important corner of the town wall. The tower is Ireland's oldest intact building and the first made with mortar. Today, its four floors creak with Viking artifacts.

Cost and Hours: €5; includes guided tour upon request—ask for the one-hour version; daily 9:30-17:30, Jan-Feb until 17:00; tel. 051/304-220, www.waterfordtreasures.com.

Visiting the Museum: Before you enter, look for the **cannonball** embedded high above the entrance, courtesy of Cromwell's siege cannons.

Once inside, you'll find an interesting Viking town **model** opposite the ticket counter. Upstairs, a display of early coins explains how the Vikings introduced the concept of coinage to the Irish after they eventually settled down and set up trade posts. Look for the tiny **Kite Brooch** that delicately blends both Scandinavian and Irish styles. In their day, brooches were considered badges of status, and this one's owner must have been at the top of the heap. As you climb the narrow stone stairways, watch your head (people were shorter 800 years ago). And be sure to go all the way to the top floor, where an informative 10-minute animated **video** traces the evolution of the town from muddy fort to modern city.

The **statue** outside (in the middle of the street) is of Thomas Francis Meagher (see sidebar), whose short, hell-bent-for-leather life took him on precarious adventures from Waterford to Tasmania to Nicaragua to Montana and, finally, to an unknown watery grave.

Chorister's Hall Medieval Museum

This middle branch of the museum triumvirate uses its three floors to focus on life in Waterford from the Norman invasion of the late 1100s to the Williamite English triumph of the late 1600s. Your visit is enhanced by an excellent free audio/videoguide that plays automatically as you move from room to room (pay attention to the changing images it displays—they'll help you navigate among artifacts).

Cost and Hours: €10, €15 combo-ticket with Bishop's Palace; Mon-Sat 9:15-18:00, Sun from 11:00; Sept-May Mon-Sat 10:00-17:00, Sun from 11:00; last entry one hour before closing, tel. 051/304-500, www.waterfordtreasures.com.

Visiting the Museum: Begin by descending under the modern building and into an original wine-vault cellar from the 1200s (long on atmosphere but otherwise empty).

Ride the elevator to the top floor to see a grand collection of well-described Anglo-Norman artifacts. The Great Charter Roll of 1372 was compiled to reinforce Waterford's claim to a monopoly of the lucrative wine-import trade. Check out the wall-size copy of the famous painting depicting the pivotal marriage of Norman leader

Thomas Francis Meagher (1823-1867)

Waterford's favorite son had a short but amazing life. The son of the town's mayor, Meagher joined Daniel O'Connell's nonviolent movement to repeal the Act of Union with Britain. Impatient with the slow-moving political process of constant compromise, Meagher joined the radical Young Irelander movement that advocated separation from Britain by force of arms. He became an inspiring and fiery speaker nicknamed "Meagher of the Sword." He went to France in 1848 and returned with the first Irish tricolor flag—a gift from the French that represented the Catholics (green), the Protestants (orange), and peaceful coexistence between the two (white).

Involved in a failed uprising, Meagher was sentenced to hang, but his sentence was commuted to life in prison in Tasmania. In 1852, Meagher escaped Tasmania via an American whaling ship and sailed to New York, where he eventually became a lawyer and started an Irish newspaper. After a trip to Nicaragua (to study the feasibility of building a canal or railway across the isthmus), he returned to New York to fight in the American Civil War. Meagher was made a Union general, raised a regiment of Irish immigrants, and famously led them into battle at Antietam and Fredericksburg. After the war, he became the first governor of the Montana territory. At age 44, Thomas Francis Meagher fell off a riverboat one night and drowned in the Missouri River. Sheer accident, foul play, or careless drunkenness? Nobody knows for sure—but his body was never found.

To learn more about this little-known but fascinating Irish leader, read Timothy Egan's *The Immortal Irishman* (2016), which offers a vivid account of the contrasting events and locales in Meagher's life.

Strongbow to Irish princess Aoife, then bring it to life on your audioguide. Detailed town models and an informative 10-minute audiovisual presentation complete the history here.

Down one floor, you'll learn how religion played out on Waterford's historic stage. Watch this floor's audiovisual presentation first to understand the broader context of this town's role in Irish history. Then feast your eyes on "Heaven's Embroidered Cloths," a collection of priestly vestments produced in Medici Florence, decorated in affluent Bruges, and shipped to conflicted Waterford. Hidden under a flagstone in the floor of Christ Church Cathedral during a siege, they were rediscovered 123 years later during renovation.

▲Bishop's Palace

Housed in the former mansion (built 1743) of the local Protestant bishop (with his Christ Church Cathedral looming right behind it), this museum presents a grand sweep through the history of Waterford since 1700, and contains the world's largest collection of old Waterford glass.

Cost and Hours: €10, €15-combo ticket with Chorister's Hall, same hours and contact info as Chorister's Hall. Entertaining 45-minute free tours are led by actors in period dress, who inhabit the palace as servants of the bishop (hourly June-Aug 9:30-18:00, Sept-May 10:00-16:00).

Visiting the Palace: The refined interior hints at the privileged lifestyle of the holy resident. Back then, a visit with the bishop would depend on social class. The bishop would meet upper-class visitors at the top of the grand stairway, greet middle-class merchants at his office doorway, and not budge from his desk chair for anyone from the lower class. Under no circumstances would he come downstairs to greet anyone.

These days, you'll work your way through three floors spiced with characters like Waterford-born action hero Thomas Francis Meagher (see sidebar). You'll learn why the province of Newfoundland in Canada owes more than 50 percent of its population to immigrants from Waterford. And if you've ever wondered what bull baiting was, you'll be filled in on this equally cruel (and long outlawed) Irish version of a bullfight.

Particularly poignant is the top-floor coverage of local WWI loyalists (Waterford was more loyal to the British crown than most Irish towns) contrasted with the 1916 Easter Rising and flowering of Irish Republicanism.

Nearby: Outside (to the left of the palace as you face the front door), you'll see two very tall metal chair sculptures morphing into male and female figures. They're meant to be Norman warrior Strongbow and Irish princess Aoife. With Christ Church—the site of their 1170 wedding—in the background, these make for a fun photo-op.

OTHER SIGHTS IN WATERFORD

Cathedral of the Holy Trinity

The year is 1793. With Catholic France (30 million) threatening Protestant Britain (8 million) on one side, and Catholic Ireland (6 million) stirring things up on the other, English King George III was stuck between a rock and a hard place. He had just lost the American colonies a decade before and looked vulnerable. To lessen Irish resentment, the king granted Ireland the Irish Relief Act, which, among other things, allowed the Irish to build Catholic churches and worship publicly for the first time since the penal laws forbade them a hundred years earlier. Allowed new freedom, the Irish built this interesting cathedral in 1796. It's Ireland's first Catholic post-Reformation church and its only Baroque church. The building was funded by wealthy Irish wine merchants who were flourishing in Cádiz, Spain. Among its treasures are 10 Waterford Crystal chandeliers.

Cost and Hours: Free, daily 8:00-19:00.

Nearby: The cathedral faces **Barronstrand Street,** which leads from the clock tower on the harborfront through the pedestrian-friendly **town square** to Patrick Street. The street separates the medieval town (on your left with the river behind you) from the 18th-century city (on your right). A river once flowed here—part of the town's natural defenses just outside the old wall. The huge **shopping center** that dominates the old town was built right on top of the Viking town. In fact, the center is built over a church dating from 1150, whose stone foundation you can see at the bottom of the escalator (behind the glass, next to the kiddie rides).

Christ Church Cathedral

This Protestant cathedral, with 18th-century Georgian architecture, is the third church to stand here. Look for the exposed Gothic column six feet below today's floor level, a remnant from an earlier church where the Norman conqueror Strongbow was married (see "Waterford's History," earlier in this chapter).

Wander over to the macabre tomb of 15th-century mayor James Rice, which bears a famous epitaph: "I am what you will be, I was what you are, pray for me." To emphasize the point, he requested that his body be dug up one year after his death (1482) and his partially decomposed remains be used to model his likeness, now seen on the tomb's lid...complete with worms and frogs.

Cost and Hours: Free, €2 donation requested; Mon-Fri 10:00-17:00, Sat until 16:00, closed Sun except for services, tours available on request.

Sleeping in Waterford

Waterford is a working-class city. Cheap accommodations are fairly rough; fancy accommodations are venerable old places that face the water. I recommend one historic option, two modern places, and a budget choice. Many find sleepy Ardmore, an hour southwest down the coast, a smaller and more scenic home base (see page 232).

$$$ The Granville Hotel is Waterford's best and most historic hotel, grandly overlooking the center of the harborfront. The place is plush, from its Old World lounges to its 98 well-tended rooms (breakfast extra, Meagher's Quay, tel. 051/305-555, www. granvillehotel.ie, stay@granville-hotel.ie).

$$$ Dooley's Hotel, a more modern, family-run place on the harbor with 113 big rooms, can be less expensive than the Granville but is still high quality (breakfast extra, Merchant's Quay, tel. 051/873-531, www.dooleys-hotel.ie, hotel@dooleys-hotel.ie).

$$$ Treacys Hotel—family-run and modern—is on the waterfront, close to the Rice Bridge with 163 pleasant, earth-toned rooms (1 Merchants Quay, tel. 051/877-222, www. treacyshotelwaterford.com, res@thwaterford.com).

$ Portree Hostel & Accommodation is the central budget option. It's just across the bridge from the train station and combines 24 basic rooms upstairs with 15 dorm beds in its basement hostel (breakfast extra, guest kitchen in hostel section, parking, 10 Mary Street, tel. 051/874-574, www.portreehostel.ie, portreeguesthouse@gmail.com).

Eating in Waterford

For something livelier than tired pub grub, consider these good restaurants found on less-frequented back streets. They're small and popular with locals.

$$$ Emiliano's Ristorante Italiano is the most romantic place in town, hidden on a tiny lane behind Reginald's Tower. They serve a great selection of tasty pasta dishes and fine wines (Tue-Sat 17:00-22:00, also open Sat-Sun for lunch 12:30-14:30, closed Mon all day, 21 High Street, tel. 051/820-333).

$$ Bodega is my favorite wine bar, laid-back with a warm-glow Mediterranean atmosphere. Their lamb sliders get raves (Mon-Wed 17:00-21:30, Thu-Sat 12:00-22:00, closed Sun, 54 John Street, tel. 051/844-177).

$ Burzza Pizza, right next door and under the same ownership as Bodega, serves not only pizza but also "proper" hamburgers (Wed-Mon 16:30-21:30, Thu-Sun from 12:30, closed Tue, 53 John Street, tel. 051/844-969).

$ Granary Café occupies the bottom floor of an old stone warehouse facing the waterfront (café on back side, away from traffic). It's a soup/salad/sandwich cafeteria that tries harder than most (Mon-Sat 8:00-17:00, Sun from 9:00, Hanover Street, tel. 051/854-428).

On the Harborfront: With a central waterfront location, the **$ Granville Hotel**'s carvery is the traditional budget lunch option (daily 12:30-14:30, otherwise good bar food daily 10:30-21:30, Meagher's Quay).

Pub Grub and Music: Waterford's staple food seems to be pub grub. Several typical pubs serve dinner in the city center. But for some reason, the town has little live music. Ask at your hotel, or just wander around, read the notices, and follow your ears. Anything with a pulse will be found on George Street, Barronstrand Street, and Broad Street.

Supermarket: The best grocery option is **Dunnes** in the shopping center (Mon-Sat 9:00-19:00, Sun 12:00-18:00).

Waterford Connections

From Waterford by Train to: Dublin (8/day, 2.5 hours), **Kilkenny** (6/day, 45 minutes). Train info: www.irishrail.ie.

By Bus to: Cork (almost hourly, 2 hours), **Kilkenny** (2/day, 1 hour), **Rosslare** (6/day, 1.5 hours), **Wexford** (7/day, 1 hour). Waterford bus station info: Tel. 051/879-000. Bus info: www.buseireann. ie. Rapid Express offers coaches to **Dublin's airport** (€19, 12 departures between 4:40 and 18:50, 3.5 hours, tel. 051/872-149).

County Wexford

The southeast corner of Ireland, peppered with pretty views and historic sites, is easily accessible to drivers as a day trip from Kilkenny or Waterford. Five sights worth considering are within an hour's drive of Waterford and can also be done as a day loop from Kilkenny (if you get an early start).

The dramatic Hook Lighthouse—capping an intriguing and remote peninsula—comes with lots of history and a good tour. The Kennedy Homestead is a pilgrimage site for Kennedy fans. These two stops involve more back-roads navigation, but they feel more intimate.

The *Dunbrody* Famine Ship in New Ross gives a sense of what 50 days on a "coffin ship" with dreams of "Americay" must have been like. The Irish National Heritage Park near Wexford is like a Knott's Berry Farm...circa the Stone Age. And the National 1798 Centre in Enniscorthy explains the roots of the Irish struggle for liberty. These three stops, which are no strangers to tour buses, form an easy driving triangle between N-25, N-11, and N-30.

If you're driving from Waterford to Kilkenny, consider a visit to the ruins at Jerpoint Abbey and Kells Priory on the way (see the "Between Kilkenny and Waterford" section in the previous chapter.)

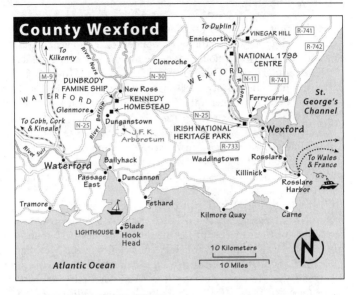

County Wexford

To Dublin ↑
VINEGAR HILL [R-741]
Enniscorthy
[R-742]
To Kilkenny
River Nore
Clonroche
W E X F O R D
[N-30]
[N-11] [R-741]
NATIONAL 1798 CENTRE
St. George's Channel
[M-9]
DUNBRODY FAMINE SHIP
W A T E R F O R D
New Ross
KENNEDY HOMESTEAD
Glenmore
River Barrow
Ferrycarrig
River Slaney
[N-25]
To Cobh, Cork & Kinsale
Dunganstown
J.F.K. Arboretum
IRISH NATIONAL HERITAGE PARK
Wexford
River Suir
[R-733]
Waterford
Ballyhack
Waddingtown
Rosslare
To Wales & France
Passage East
Duncannon
Killinick
Rosslare Harbor
Tramore
Fethard
Kilmore Quay
Carne
LIGHTHOUSE
Slade
Hook Head
10 Kilometers
N
Atlantic Ocean
10 Miles

PLANNING YOUR TIME

New Ross, Enniscorthy, and Wexford, which form a three-town triangle, are about 30 minutes apart and connected by fast roads. The Kennedy Homestead is a 15-minute drive south of New Ross, and the lighthouse is a one-hour trip from Waterford to the end of the Hook Peninsula. All are well signposted and easy to find... except for Hook Lighthouse (see details later).

Connecting Dublin with Waterford, you could visit several of these sights in a best-of-County Wexford day en route. On a quick trip, the sights are not worth the trouble by public transit. If you'll be spending the night, blue-collar Enniscorthy (with decent hotels and B&Bs) provides a good glimpse of workaday Ireland.

Sights in County Wexford

▲Hook Lighthouse

This claims to be the oldest operating lighthouse in Europe. According to legend, St. Dubhan arrived in the fifth century and discovered the bodies of shipwrecked sailors. Dismayed, he and his followers began tending a fire on the headland to warn future mariners. What you see today is essentially a structure from the 12th century, built by the Normans, who first landed five miles up the east coast (at Baginbun Head, in 1169). They established Waterford Harbor—a commercial beachhead for the rich Irish countryside they intended to conquer. This beacon assured them safe access.

Today's lighthouse is 110 feet tall and looks modern on the outside. (It was automated in 1996, and its light can be seen for 23 miles out to sea.) But, except for its modern light, it's actually 800 years old, built following a plan inspired by the lighthouse of Alexandria in Egypt—one of the seven wonders of the ancient world. Since it's a working lighthouse, it can be toured only with a guide.

Cost and Hours: Fine 45-minute tours cost €10 and depart every half-hour in peak season, every hour off-season; open daily 10:00-17:30, summer until 19:00, off-season until 17:00; tel. 051/397-055, www.hookheritage.ie.

Getting There: The lighthouse can be a bit tricky to find. But if you follow the brown *Hook Scenic Route* signs south of Ballyhack and remind yourself that you're on a gradually narrowing peninsula with the lighthouse at the southern tip, you'll be funneled straight there (more or less).

If connecting Waterford to Hook Head, use the car-ferry shortcut from Passage East to Ballyhack. Buy a round-trip and carefully save the tiny receipt for the return journey (€12 round-trip, €8 one-way, 5-minute crossing; runs continuously Mon-Sat 7:00-21:00, Sun from 9:30; Oct-March daily until 20:00, www.passageferry.ie). To reach the ferry from Waterford, take Lombard Street (near Reginald's Tower) south, and follow it all the way to Passage East (it becomes R-683).

Visiting the Lighthouse: As you view the black-stained, ribbed, vaulted ceilings and stout, 10-foot-thick walls, you can almost feel the presence of the Cistercian monks who tended this coal-burning beacon for the Normans. Climbing 115 steps through four levels rewards you with a breezy, salt-air view from the top.

Oliver Cromwell passed through here to secure the English claim to this area (see "The Curse of Cromwell" sidebar, later). He considered his two options and declared he'd take strategic Waterford "by Hook or by Crooke." Hook is the long peninsula with the lighthouse. Crooke is a little village on the other side, just south of Passage East.

There's a decent cafeteria and a shop with fliers explaining other sights on the peninsula. Kids at heart can't resist climbing out on the rugged rocky tip of the windy Hook Head.

▲Kennedy Homestead

Patrick Joseph Kennedy, President John F. Kennedy's great-grandfather, left Ireland in 1858. Distant relatives have turned the family homestead into a little museum/shrine for Kennedy pilgrims. Physically, it's not much: A barn and a wing of the modern house survive from 1858. JFK and his entourage visited here in June 1963,

JFK in Ireland

JFK arrived in Ireland for a three-day visit in late June 1963, straight from the Berlin Wall and his inspiring "Ich bin ein Berliner" speech. The Irish gave him a deliriously warm welcome in those Cold War days. Bursting with pride in his presidency (he was the first Catholic to hold the office), the Irish saw what was possible at a time when the state of the Irish economy was dire and emigration was high. Kennedy's every move was televised. Only 10 percent of Irish households had a TV at that time, so people crowded into pubs with TVs to watch. Kennedy's whirlwind itinerary included stops in Dublin, Galway, Limerick, Cork, and County Wexford, where he visited the farm of his Irish ancestors near Dunganstown.

As the third-born son, JFK's great-grandfather Patrick Joseph Kennedy had little hope of inheriting the family farm. He had learned the trade of coopering (barrel making) at a brewery in nearby New Ross and decided to emigrate to Boston in 1848 near the end of the Great Potato Famine. There he clawed out a new start from desperate poverty and started a family. But he succumbed to cholera in 1858...105 years to the day (November 22) before his great-grandson would be assassinated.

JFK's death came only five months after his triumphant Irish visit, at perhaps the peak of his popularity. After the assassination, Kennedy staffer and later New York senator Daniel Patrick Moynihan was quoted as saying, "To be Irish is to know that in the end the world will break your heart."

An old Irish superstition holds that it's bad luck to take a stone away from a "fairy fort" (the Iron Age ring forts that dot the landscape). Some say that the reason the Kennedy clan has suffered so many tragedies over the years is that an ancestor may have taken a stone from a fort, way back when.

a few months before he was assassinated. While it's now a private home, anyone interested in the Kennedys will find it worth driving the long narrow lane to see.

Cost and Hours: €7.50, daily 9:30-17:30, tel. 051/388-264, www.kennedyhomestead.ie.

Getting There: It's four miles (6 km) south of New Ross near Dunganstown (from R-733 follow brown signs with JFK's face in profile, down a long one-lane road; park behind the modern visitors center). Don't confuse the Kennedy Homestead with the nearby JFK Arboretum—a huge park with 4,500 species of trees. It's nice if you like trees and plants, but there's no Kennedy history there.

Visiting the Homestead: Inside is a fascinating exhibition on Kennedy's Irish heritage, his brief visit here, and the aftermath of his tragic death. A little barnyard houses one long shed with knickknacks and photos of his visit. Look for the old bench-style car seat (with furniture legs added by Kennedy's second cousin). This was the nicest seat in the homestead's modest home, where the eminent visitor sat to take tea. There are a couple of short videos: JFK chatting with his distant relatives, and then being whisked away by helicopter to continue his triumphant tour of the country. JFK's assassin denied him the opportunity of a promised return visit. But his widow, Jackie, made sure that his Irish relatives here got some of his precious memorabilia.

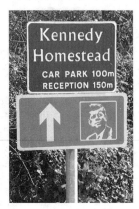

▲▲*Dunbrody* Famine Ship

Permanently moored on a river in the tiny port of New Ross, this ship was built as a re-creation of similar vessels that sailed to America full of countless hungry Irish emigrants. The *Dunbrody* is

a full-scale reconstruction of a 19th-century three-masted bark built in Quebec in 1845. It's typical of the trading vessels that originally sailed, empty, to America to pick up goods; during the famine, ship owners found that they could make a little money on the westward voyage. On board, extended families camped out for 50 days on bunk beds no bigger than a king-size mattress. Commonly, boats like this would arrive in America with only 80 percent of their original human cargo (in the worst cases, only 50 percent). Those who succumbed to "famine fever" (often typhus or cholera) were dumped overboard, and the ships gained their morbid moniker: "coffin ships."

Cost and Hours: €11; daily 9:00-18:00, Oct-March 10:00-17:00, 45-minute tours go 2/hour, last tour starts one hour before closing; upstairs café handy for lunch with nice views of the ship, tel. 051/425-239, www.dunbrody.com.

Getting There: The *Dunbrody* is in New Ross, near the Kennedy Homestead. Parking is available (pay parking during work hours).

Visiting the Ship: Your visit starts with an audiovisual presentation on the life Irish emigrants were leaving behind, followed by coverage about the building of the vessel. Then you'll follow an excellent guide on board the ship, encountering a couple of passengers (one traveling first class, the other second) who tell vivid tales about life onboard. At the end, you'll get a glimpse of the new life Irish immigrants would encounter in New York. Most arrived filthy (try skipping a shower for six weeks), illiterate, penniless, and speaking only Irish.

Roots seekers are welcome to peruse the computerized file of the names of the million immigrants who sailed on these ships from 1846 through 1865. Before you leave, check out the Irish America Hall of Fame, commemorating the contributions Irish men and women have made to US history (with short videos on Henry Ford and JFK, whose roots lie in this part of Ireland).

Ros Tapestry

Before you leave New Ross, consider a short visit to see the Ros Tapestry. Outlining the colorful Norman history of the region, it's a bit like a recently woven version of the ancient Bayeux Tapestry in Normandy. Consisting of 15 large embroidered panels, not all of which are complete yet, this is a labor of love that local women have been working on for more than 20 years. Visitors are invited upstairs to take part in its creation by doing one stitch themselves.

Cost and Hours: €8, includes audioguide; Mon-Sat 10:00-17:00, Sun 11:00-15:00; tel. 051/445-396, www.rostapestry.ie.

Getting There: It's housed on the ground floor of an old six-story stone warehouse about 100 yards north of the *Dunbrody* Famine Ship, across the street; leave your car in the *Dunbrody* parking lot.

▲Irish National Heritage Park

Since Ireland's countless ancient sights are generally unrecognizable ruins—hard to re-create in your mind—this 35-acre wooded park is intended to help out. You'll find replicas of buildings and settlements illustrating life in Ireland from the Stone Age through the 12th-century Norman Age. As a bonus, you'll see animal skin-clad characters doing their prehistoric thing—gnawing  on meat, weaving, making arrowheads, and so on. There's also an 1857 tower commemorating local boys killed in the Crimean War.

Cost and Hours: €10.50; daily 9:30-18:30, winter until 17:30, last entry 1.5 hours before closing; audioguide-€2, free guided tours leave throughout the day until about 16:00—reserve in advance, tel. 053/912-0733, www.inhp.com, info@inhp.com.

The Curse of Cromwell

The scariest bogeyman in Irish history was Oliver Cromwell. In 1649, he led Parliamentary forces to victory in the English Civil War and had King Charles I beheaded. Assuming the title of Lord Protector, he created a common-wealth (instead of a kingdom) and initiated one of the longest periods in the past 1,000 years during which England had no mon-arch. Cromwell then turned his attention to Ireland, determined to root out the last roy-alists loyal to the English monarchy and to punish the Irish for the 1641 massacre of Protestant settlers.

Driven by his Puritan Calvinist beliefs, Cromwell claimed a divine right to do God's work. To him, all Catholics were complicit in the Protestant deaths by virtue of their misguided faith. Even Protestant Anglicans (the faith founded by Henry VIII a century before) were looked on with suspicion as "Catholics without a pope." Cromwell's army of 12,000 soldiers had God on their side and Ireland in their musket-sights.

Cromwell and his army landed in Dublin on August 15, 1649, and marched north to Drogheda. In a bloody three-day siege, his soldiers massacred almost all of the town's 3,000 people. A handful of lucky survivors silently slipped into the River Boyne and played dead, floating downstream to safety. Cromwell then turned south to Wexford, where his army killed 3,000-some civilians and Irish troops. Few garrison towns re-sisted after that, and Cromwell brought most of Ireland under English control in less than a year.

Catholic landowners were forced to give up their land or face execution, and about 11 million acres of productive land was handed over to Cromwell's soldiers as payment for ser-vice. In "exchange," these Catholics got unfertile ground west of the River Shannon, a forced mass migration that essentially destroyed Ireland's Catholic landowning class. Some Catho-lics were allowed to stay on as tenants, providing labor for their new English masters.

When Cromwell died in 1658, his less-dynamic son took over, and the English began to miss their monarchy. In 1660, Charles I's son, Charles II, was invited back from exile in France and the monarchy was restored. Soon after, Cromwell's body was dug up, hung, and beheaded—his head was stuck on a pike and displayed in front of London's Parliament for 20 years. (Curiously, a heroic statue of him stands there today.) But most of Ireland's Catholics never regained their land, and for the next 250 years Ireland continued its downward cultural spiral at the hands of the English government.

Getting There: It's clearly signposted on the west end of Wexford—you'll hit it before entering town on the N-11 Enniscorthy road.

Visiting the Park: Your visit begins with a 15-minute video. From there, follow the audioguide, or better, do the hour-long guided tour. There are 16 stops, each covering a different stage of Irish civilization. The highlight is a monastic settlement from the age when Europe was dark, and Ireland was "the island of saints and scholars." While you can wander around on your own, there's hardly anything actually old here, and the visit is most worthwhile if you take the included tour.

National 1798 Centre

Located in Enniscorthy, this museum creatively tells the story of the rise of revolutionary thinking in Ireland, which led to the ill-fated rebellion of 1798 (Ireland's deadliest). Enniscorthy was the crucial Irish battleground of a populist revolution (inspired by the American and French revolutions). The town witnessed the bloodiest days of the doomed uprising. The material is compelling for anyone intrigued by the struggles for liberty, but there's little more here than video clips of reenactments and storyboards on the walls.

Cost and Hours: €7; Mon-Fri 9:00-17:00, Sat from 12:00, closed Sun, shorter hours off-season, last entry one hour before closing; tel. 053/923-7596, www.1798centre.ie.

Getting There: Enniscorthy is 12 miles (19 km) north of Wexford town. The National 1798 Centre is the town's major sight and is well signposted (follow the brown *Aras 98 Centre* signs).

Nearby: Leaving the center, look east across the River Slaney, which divides Enniscorthy, and you'll see a hill with a stumpy tower on it. This is **Vinegar Hill.** The tower is the old windmill that once flew the green rebel flag. Drive to the top for the views that the rebels had of the surrounding British forces. The doomed rebels tried desperately to hold the high ground, with no shelter from the merciless British artillery fire.

WATERFORD & COUNTY WEXFORD

KINSALE & COBH

County Cork, on Ireland's south coast, is fringed with historic port towns and scenic peninsulas. The typical tour-bus route here includes Blarney Castle and Killarney—places where most tourists wear nametags. But rather than kissing the spit-slathered Blarney Stone, spend your time in County Cork enjoying the bustling, historic maritime towns of Kinsale and Cobh. Although Cobh is a growing cruise ship port, most cruise travelers leave there on day excursions that clog iconic stops like Blarney Castle. Kinsale, meanwhile, gets all but the briefest of drive-by glimpses.

Cobh can be reached from Dublin by train (via Cork city). Meanwhile, more remote—but more charming—Kinsale lies 15 miles south of Cork's train station and makes a great home base for a visit to the coast of County Cork.

Most drivers approach the region from the northeast and visit Cobh en route to Kinsale. Drivers coming from Waterford can easily visit Ardmore and the Old Midleton Whiskey Distillery along the coastal route. Blarney Castle and Macroom make convenient stops when connecting to the Ring of Kerry or Dingle.

Avoid the mistake many travelers make—allowing destinations into their itineraries simply because they're famous from a song or as part of a relative's big-bus-tour memory. If you have the misfortune to spend the night in Killarney town (next door in County Kerry), you'll understand what I mean. The town is a

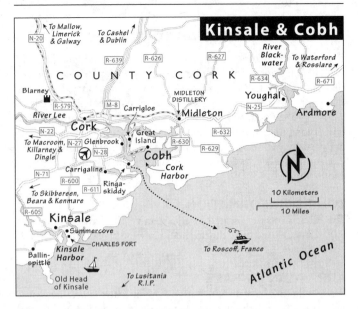

sprawling line of chain hotels and outlet malls littered with pushy shoppers looking for plastic shamrocks.

Kinsale

While Cork is the biggest city in southern Ireland, nearby Kinsale is actually more historic and certainly cuter. Pint-sized and friendly, it's delightful to visit. Thanks to the naturally sheltered bay barbed by a massive 17th-century star fort, you can submerge yourself in maritime history, from the Spanish Armada to the sailor who inspired Daniel Defoe's *Robinson Crusoe* to the *Lusitania* (torpedoed by the Germans just off the point in 1915). Apart from all the history, Kinsale has a laid-back feel with a touch of wine-sipping class.

PLANNING YOUR TIME

Kinsale is worth two nights and a day. Spend the morning checking out one or two of the town's sights, and make sure to take Don and Barry's excellent Kinsale walking tour (9:15 or 11:15 most days). After lunch, head out to Charles Fort for great bay views and insights into British military life in colonial Ireland. (You can drive, or take a taxi out and walk back.) On the way back, stop for a pint at the Bulman Bar. Finish the day with a good dinner and live music in a pub. Those blitzing Ireland can give Kinsale four hours—see the fort, wander the town, and enjoy a nice lunch—before driving on.

KINSALE & COBH

Orientation to Kinsale

Kinsale has a great natural harbor and is older than Cobh (the city of Cork's harbor town). While the town is prettier than the actual harbor, the harbor was its reason for being. Today, Kinsale is a vibrant bustle of about 5,000 residents. Its population swells to 9,000 with the many "blow-ins" who live here each summer. The town's long and skinny old center is part modern marina (attracting wealthy yachters) and part pedestrian-friendly medieval town (attracting scalawags like us). It's an easy 20-minute stroll from end to end.

TOURIST INFORMATION

The TI is centrally located at the head of the harbor (Mon-Sat 9:00-17:00, closed Sun, shorter hours in winter; tel. 021/477-2234, www.kinsale.ie).

ARRIVAL IN KINSALE

Kinsale doesn't have a train station. The **bus** stop is on Pier Road, 100 yards behind the TI, just before the gray swooping modern sculptures at the south end of town.

Drivers should park and walk. While Kinsale's windy medieval lanes are narrow and congested, parking lots ease the hassle. The most central lot is at the head of the harbor behind the TI (pay-and-display, exact change required, 2-hour maximum, enforced Mon-Sat 10:30-18:00, free on Sun). A big, safe, free parking lot is across the street from St. Multose Church at the top of town, a 5-minute walk from most recommended hotels and restaurants. An even larger free lot is east of town by the fire station (10-minute walk). Street parking is pay-and-display. Outlying streets, a 10-minute stroll from the action, have wide-open parking.

HELPFUL HINTS

Crowds: The Kinsale Rugby Sevens Tournament draws dozens of teams and hundreds of loud-and-proud, rowdy rugby fans on the first weekend in May (with its associated Bank Holiday Monday). If you're not up for the scrum, then scram.

Market: An open-air market enlivens the town square (on Market Quay) on Wednesdays in summer (9:00-14:00).

Bookstore: The **Kinsale Bookshop** is on Main Street (Mon-Sat 10:00-18:00, Sun from 12:00, 8 Main Street, tel. 021/477-4244).

Laundry: Full-service laundry is available at **Elite Laundry** (Mon-Fri 9:00-17:30, Sat 10:00-17:00, closed Sun, The Glen, tel. 021/477-7345).

Bike Rental and a Good Ride: Run by helpful Julian, **Mylie Mur-**

phy's rents bikes from a handy spot near the Centra Market (€15/day, includes lock and helmet; Mon-Sat 9:30-18:00, Sun 11:00-17:00 May-Aug only, shorter hours in winter; arrangements can be made for pickup or drop-off, 8 Pearse Street, tel. 021/477-2703, MylieMurphyShop@hotmail.com). They can recommend paths good for biking or walking that stretch around the harbor.

For a good short-and-scenic route, bike south on the Pier Road, past the marina a couple miles, and turn left across the first bridge. Turn left again at the far end of the bridge to reach the dead end of the road marked by the Dock pub. Jump off your bike and explore the great views from the grassy ruins of James Fort, uphill behind the pub (2 miles each way). Or head out to Kinsale's only beach, a couple hundred yards south of James Fort on the east side of its peninsula (over the hill, behind the Dock pub).

Taxi: Contact **Tom Canty,** whose destinations include Cork Airport for €25 or Cork city for €30 (mobile 087-237-1022).

Tours in Kinsale

▲▲Don & Barry's Kinsale Historic Stroll

To understand the important role Kinsale played in Irish, English, and Spanish history, join gentlemen Don Herlihy or Barry Moloney on a fascinating 1.5-hour walking tour (€8, daily mid-March-mid-Oct at 11:15, also Mon-Sat at 9:15 in May-Sept, no reservation necessary, by appointment only off-season, meet outside the TI, private tours possible, tel. 021/477-2873 or

087/250-0731, www.historicstrollkinsale.com). Both guides are a joy, creatively bringing to life Kinsale's past, placing its story in the wider sweep of history, and making the stony sights more than just buildings. They collect payment at the end, giving anyone disappointed in the talk an easy escape midway through. Don't get hijacked by imitation tours that pretend to be Don or Barry—ask for Don or Barry (pictured above). This walk is Kinsale's single best attraction.

Ghost Walk Tour

This is not just any ghost tour; it's more Monty Python-style slapstick comedy than horror. Two high-energy actors (Brian and David) weave funny stunts and stories into a loose history of the

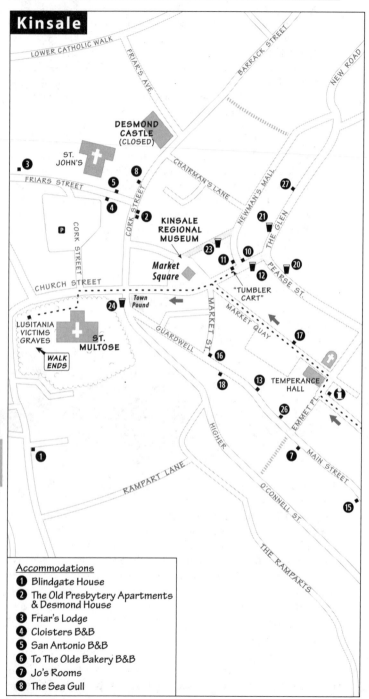

Kinsale

LOWER CATHOLIC WALK

FRIAR'S AVE.

BARRACK STREET

NEW ROAD

DESMOND CASTLE (CLOSED)

ST. JOHN'S

3

FRIARS STREET

8
5
4
2

CHAIRMAN'S LANE

27

CORK STREET

P

CHURCH STREET

KINSALE REGIONAL MUSEUM

Market Square

NEWMAN'S MALL

THE GLEN

21

23

11
10
12

20

PEARSE ST.

"TUMBLER CART"

Town Pound

24

LUSITANIA VICTIMS GRAVES

WALK ENDS

ST. MULTOSE

GUARDWELL

MARKET ST.

MARKET QUAY

17

16

18

13

TEMPERANCE HALL

EMMET PL.

26

i

7

MAIN STREET

HIGHER

O'CONNELL ST.

15

1

RAMPART LANE

THE RAMPARTS

Accommodations

1 Blindgate House

2 The Old Presbytery Apartments & Desmond House

3 Friar's Lodge

4 Cloisters B&B

5 San Antonio B&B

6 To The Olde Bakery B&B

7 Jo's Rooms

8 The Sea Gull

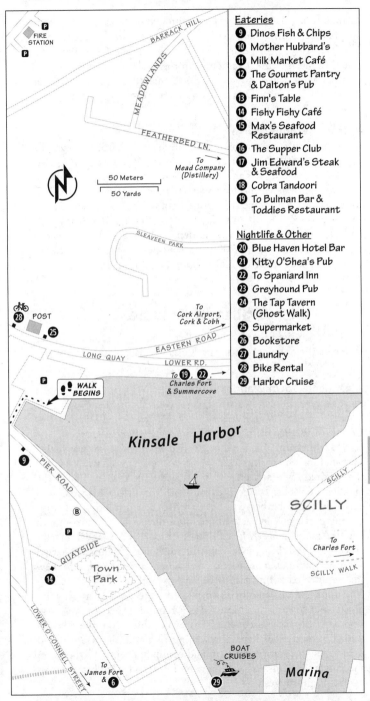

FIRE STATION

BARRACK HILL

MEADOWLANDS

FEATHERBED LN.

To Mead Company (Distillery)

50 Meters
50 Yards

SLEAVEEN PARK

POST

To Cork Airport, Cork & Cobh

EASTERN ROAD

LONG QUAY

LOWER RD.

To 19 22
Charles Fort & Summercove

WALK BEGINS

Kinsale Harbor

PIER ROAD

B

QUAYSIDE

Town Park

LOWER O'CONNELL STREET

To James Fort & 6

SCILLY

SCILLY

To Charles Fort

SCILLY WALK

BOAT CRUISES

Marina

KINSALE & COBH

Eateries
9 Dinos Fish & Chips
10 Mother Hubbard's
11 Milk Market Café
12 The Gourmet Pantry & Dalton's Pub
13 Finn's Table
14 Fishy Fishy Café
15 Max's Seafood Restaurant
16 The Supper Club
17 Jim Edward's Steak & Seafood
18 Cobra Tandoori
19 To Bulman Bar & Toddies Restaurant

Nightlife & Other
20 Blue Haven Hotel Bar
21 Kitty O'Shea's Pub
22 To Spaniard Inn
23 Greyhound Pub
24 The Tap Tavern (Ghost Walk)
25 Supermarket
26 Bookstore
27 Laundry
28 Bike Rental
29 Harbor Cruise

town, offering 75 minutes of entertainment on Kinsale's after-dark streets (€12, April-Oct Sun-Fri at 21:00, no tours Sat, leaves from The Tap Tavern, call ahead to confirm, mobile 087-948-0910). You'll spend the first 15 minutes in the back of the tavern—time to finish your drink and get to know some of the group. This tour doesn't overlap with Don and Barry's more serious historic town walk described above.

Kinsale Harbour Cruise

Enjoy a 45-minute voyage around the historic harbor aboard the nimble little 50-passenger *Spirit of Kinsale.* The voyage offers sea-level views of both Charles and James forts, as well as seal and seafowl sightings with informative commentary from captain/historian/naturalist Jerome (€13, June-Sept daily at 14:00 and 15:00, July-Aug also at 11:00 and 12:00, one sailing per day April-May and Oct, check schedule online; departs from Pier Road in front of Acton's Hotel roughly 200 yards south of the TI; not necessary to book ahead; mobile 086-250-5456, www.kinsaleharbourcruises.com).

Sights in Kinsale

Kinsale's top sight is the town walking tour with Don and Barry (listed earlier, under "Tours in Kinsale"). But with extra time, there's much more to explore.

▲▲Kinsale Town Wander

Here's a very simple town stroll to get your historic bearings.

• *Start on the harbor (just below the TI and across from Dinos Fish & Chips). To trace the route, see the "Kinsale" map in this chapter.*

Harborfront: The medieval walled town's economy was fueled by its harbor, where ships came to be stocked. The old walls defined the original town and created a fortified zone that facilitated the taxation of goods. In the 17th and 18th centuries, this small and easily defended harbor was busy with rich and hungry tall ships getting provisions and assembling into convoys for the two-month trip to America, mostly for military transport and establishing colonies. (By the 1800s, most Irish emigrants fleeing famine departed for America from Cobh instead, which had a deeper harbor for new steam-powered sailing ships.)

Look for the **memorial** shaped like the mast of a tall ship, farther out toward the marina. It's a reminder that this was also a port of military consequence. Dozens of ships from the Spanish Armada could moor here, threatening England. Since Spain and Ireland had a common religion and common enemy (Catholicism and England), Kinsale had a more prominent place in history than its size might suggest.

You're standing on reclaimed land. What seems like part of the old center was actually built later on land reclaimed from the harbor. The town sits on the floor of a natural quarry, with easy-to-cut shale hills ideal for a ready supply of fill. Notice the mudflats in the harbor at low tide.

Clear-cutting of the once-plentiful oak forest upriver (for shipbuilding and barrel-making) hastened erosion and silted up the harbor. By the early 1800s—when British ships needed lots of restocking for the Napoleonic Wars—ships were bigger, Kinsale's port was slowly dying, and nearby Cobh's deep-water port took over the lion's share of shipping. Kinsale settled into a quieter existence as a fishing port.

• *From the TI, walk inland (between the Temperance Hall and the old Methodist church) up Market Quay. Take your first right on Market Street and find an old vehicle on big wheels at the Milk Market Café, across from Dalton's Pub.*

Town Center: Parked like a big flowerbox here is a 19th-century **"tumbler cart."** This rolled through town like a garbage service collecting sewage from the townsfolk, then spread the human waste as fertilizer on the fields outside of town.

Study the green metal medieval **Kinsale model** (c. 1381) and the information panel on the wall with another map. It shows the narrow confines of the town, hiding behind its once-proud walls, before much of the bay was reclaimed. You can see how the wall lined the main street along the tidal flats. The subtle curves of Main Street trace the original coastline. (Walking this street, you'll see tiny lanes leading to today's harbor. These originated as piers—just wide enough to roll a barrel down to an awaiting ship.) Notice the town wall had three "water gates." One was called "World's End," which felt true in the 14th century.

Find **Dalton's Pub** across the street—one of 25 pubs in this small but never-thirsty town. This is one of many inviting local pubs famous for live folk and traditional music.

• *Backtrack to cross Market Square, pass the old courthouse (now the Regional Museum), and take Church Street to a vacant little lot across from The Tap Tavern.*

Town Pound: This small enclosure was where goods and livestock used to be impounded until the owner could pay the associated tax. After the James and Charles forts were built in the 1600s, the town wall became obsolete—and also boxed in the town, preventing further expansion. So the townspeople disassembled the wall and used its ready-cut stones for building projects like this.

• *Walk uphill past The Tap Tavern to the church.*

St. Multose Church: This Anglican church (open after noon) comes with a fortress-like tower. While rebuilt in recent centuries, it goes back to the Middle Ages. In its very proper Anglican interior, you'll see a list of vicars going back to 1377. The humble base of the baptismal font dates from the 6th century.

• *Leave the church and turn left, walking around the outside of it to the west end (facing most of the graves).*

Check out the **old doorway** into the church. These days, this door is always locked, but it was once the main entrance. Notice the worn lines scratched into the stone around eye level. Oliver Cromwell's soldiers garrisoned in the church in the mid-1600s and sharpened their swords on the doorway. Facing this door you can tell there were (not surprisingly) more right-handed swordsmen.

• *Walk back to the current main entrance (north side of church), then walk 20 paces, veering left and uphill to two gray, concrete-bordered, grass-covered graves (near the gate to the street).*

Lusitania Victim Graves: This remembers "Victims of the *Lusitania* Outrage 1915." Nine months into World War I, just off the coast of Kinsale, the Germans torpedoed the *Lusitania* with 128 Americans on board. It sank within 20 minutes, and more than half of the 2,000 passengers drowned. This tragedy led to the United States going "over there" and joining what was called "The Great War."

▲▲Charles Fort

Strategically set to be the gatekeeper for this critical harbor, Kinsale's star-shaped Charles Fort is a testimony to the importance of this little town in the 17th century.

Cost and Hours: €5, daily 10:00-18:00, Nov-mid-March until 17:00, last entry one hour before closing, a half-mile southeast of town, tel. 021/477-2263. Free, guided walks are included (45 minutes, generally on the hour). A little coffee-and-pastry café stands inside the walls.

Getting There: You can drive, taxi, walk (see the "Scilly Walk," next page), or take bus #253, which runs a few times daily from the bus stop on Pier Road.

Visiting the Fort: When built, Charles Fort was Britain's biggest star-shaped fort—a state-of-the-art defense when artillery made the traditional castle obsolete (low, thick walls were tougher for cannons to breach than the tall, thinner walls of older castles). The star design made defending any attack on its walls safer and more effective. Notice how the strongest walls face the sea and how the oldest buildings are crouched down below the potential cannon fire of attacking ships.

Red buoys mark the navigable lane for shipping in this shallow harbor—making any ship entering or leaving well within cannon range.

The British occupied this fort until Irish independence in 1922. Its interior buildings were torched in 1923 by anti-treaty IRA forces to keep it from being used by Free State troops during the Irish Civil War. Guided tours (free with admission) engross you in the harsh daily life of 18th-century British soldiers and the few "lucky" wives allowed to live in the fort and earn their keep doing laundry for an army.

While most of the fort is just ruined buildings with nice views, there is an important exhibit filling two floors of the Barracks Stores building (the tall intact building, just below and to the right of the entry). Climb the ramparts to enjoy the view, marvel at the cleverness of a "star-designed fort," and gaze out to Kinsale Head to see where, in 1915, the *Lusitania* was torpedoed by Germans.

After Your Visit: For a beer or meal nearby, try the recommended **Bulman Bar** in Summercove, 100 yards downhill where the road runs low near the water on the way back to town (with small parking lot). And to see how easily the forts could bottle up this key harbor, pull over at the grand harbor viewpoint at the high point on the road back into town (between Summercove and The Spaniard pub).

Scilly Walk (Kinsale to Charles Fort)

The 45-minute walk between Kinsale and Charles Fort offers a delightful chance to connect the town with its top historic attraction. Along the way you'll pass great harbor views, quaint cottages, dry-stone walls, and the recommended Bulman Bar. While the couple hundred yards at the beginning and end are along roads without sidewalks, the middle 80 percent of the walk is along a peaceful, pedestrian-only trail through lush vegetation. From Kinsale, follow the Lower Road east until you wind around onto Scilly peninsula. From the fort, look for *Scilly Walk* signs on the left when walking toward town (near top of hill, 100 yards beyond Bulman Bar).

James Fort

With its earthen formations overgrown with yellow gorse, James Fort is Kinsale's other (older) star fort, filling a forgotten peninsula and guarding the bay opposite Charles Fort. Built in the years just after the famous 1601 battle of Kinsale (when a Spanish force disembarked here—see the "Kinsale's History" sidebar, later), this fort is more ruined, less interesting, and less visited than Charles Fort. Its military usefulness ended with a bang in 1690 when the magazine containing the fort's ammunition was hit by a direct and fatal shell fired by King William's besieging army. Check out the satellite blockhouse (down a straight, 75-yard trail from the main walls), which sits below the fort at the water's edge opposite Summercove. It controlled a strong chain boom that could be raised to block ships from reaching Kinsale's docks (free, always open).

Getting There: Easily accessible by car or bike, it's two miles (3 km) south of town along Pier Road on the west shore of the bay (cross the bridge and turn left; you'll dead-end at Castle Park Marina, where you can park or leave your bike). When facing the Dock pub, the trailhead up to the fort is at the far left end of the buildings, where the parking lot ends.

Desmond Castle

This 15th-century fortified customs house (at the top of Cork Street) has had a long and varied history (may be closed to visitors). It was the Spanish armory during Spain's 1601 occupation of Kinsale. Nicknamed "Frenchman's Prison," it served as a British prison and once housed 600 cramped prisoners of the Napoleonic Wars (not to mention earlier American Revolutionary War prisoners captured at sea—who were treated as rebels, not prisoners, and chained to the outside of the building as a warning to any rebellion-minded Irish). In the late 1840s, it was a famine-relief center.

In its days as the customs house, this evocative little tower was an important cog in Ireland's little-known connection to the international wine trade. In the late Middle Ages, Kinsale was renowned for its top-quality wooden casks. Developing strong trade links with Bordeaux and Jerez, local merchants traded their dependable empty casks for casks full of wine. Later, Kinsale became a "designated wine port" for tax-collection purposes.

▲Kinsale Regional Museum

In the center of the old town, this modest museum is worth a quick visit for its fun mishmash of domestic and maritime bygones. Its Dutch architecture reflects the influence of Dutch-born King William of Orange at the end of the 1600s. Drop by at least to read the fun 1788 tax code for all Kinsale commercial transactions (outside at the front door).

Cost and Hours: Free, Tue-Sat 10:30-13:30, closed Sun-Mon, staffed by volunteers—hours can be erratic, Market Square, tel. 021/477-7930.

Visiting the Museum: Among its exhibits, the museum gives a good perspective on the controversial *Lusitania* tragedy. Kinsale had maritime jurisdiction over the waters 12 miles offshore, where the luxury liner was torpedoed in 1915. Hearings were held upstairs here in the courthouse shortly afterward to investigate the causes of the disaster—which helped propel America into World War I—and to paint the German Hun as a bloodthirsty villain. Claims by Germany that the *Lusitania* was illegally carrying munitions (and using innocent passengers as human shields) may have been inspired by the huge explosion and rapid sinking of the vessel. As the wreck slowly succumbs to a century of gravity and rust, it's collapsing on itself and the truth of its cargo may forever be lost in the ocean floor muck.

The museum displays are sparse, but include *Lusitania* flotsam such as a wicker deck chair and a US mail bag. A flickering black-and-white film shows the last happy glory days of the vessel in port. Apart from the *Lusitania* footage, you'll find a gritty little model of medieval Kinsale surrounded by its once-proud walls. Perhaps even more memorable, in the side room is the boot of the 8-foot-3-inch Kinsale giant, who lived here in the late 1700s.

Kinsale Mead Company

A tour of this working distillery in a modern warehouse on the out-skirts of Kinsale offers a rare opportunity to learn about (and taste) mead—a beverage famed in ancient times but these days mostly served at medieval castle banquets.

A wine made with honey, mead is the world's oldest alcoholic drink and the original ambrosia (or "nectar of the Gods"). Thought to bring bravery to ancient Greek warriors, mead was also part of cultures as diverse as the Egyptians, Mayans, and Vikings. The hour-long tour explains the distilling process and helps you ap-preciate honeybees and the fragile place they occupy in nature's increasingly embattled web.

Cost and Hours: €12, best to book in advance; Tue-Sun tours at 13:00, 15:00, and 17:00, closed Mon; Nov-March Fri-Sun only at 13:00 and 15:00; 15-minute walk east of town center, located at Unit 5, Barracks Lane, Troopers-Close, tel. 021/477-3538, www.kinsalemeadco.ie.

Nightlife in Kinsale

Live Folk and Traditional Music

In the Town Center: Kinsale's pubs are packed with atmosphere and live music (more likely folk, but plenty of traditional Irish, too). Rather than target a certain place, simply walk the area between Guardwell, Pearse Street, and the Market Square. Music starts up after 21:00—you'll hear it as you wander. **Dalton's Pub** hosts informal amateur sessions with locals after 21:00 (grab a seat by 20:30). The **Blue Haven Hotel Bar** and **Kitty O'Shea's** are also good bets.

Outside of Town: Irish music purists can get their trad fix at the charmingly claustrophobic **Spaniard Inn**, a 10-minute walk out to the Scilly peninsula across the harbor from town. It fills the center of a hairpin turn on the crest of the peninsula. The darkly atmospheric interior is about the size of a rail car, with the long bar

Kinsale's History

Kinsale's remarkable harbor has made this an important port since prehistoric times. The bay's 10-foot tide provided a natural shuttle service for Stone Age hunter-gatherers: They could ride it, at two miles per hour twice a day, for the eight miles up and down the River Bandon. In the Bronze Age, when people discovered that it takes tin and copper to make bronze, tin came from Cornwall (in southwest England) and copper came from this part of Ireland. From 500 BC to AD 500, Kinsale was a rich trading center. The result: Lots of Stonehenge-type monuments are nearby. The best is Drombeg Stone Circle (a one-hour drive west, just off R-597/Glandore Road).

Kinsale's importance peaked during the 16th, 17th, and 18th centuries, when sailing ships ruled the waves, turning maritime countries into global powers. Kinsale was Ireland's most perfect natural harbor and the gateway to both Spain and France—potentially providing a base for either of these two powers in cutting off English shipping. Because of this, two pivotal battles were fought here in the 17th century: in 1601 against the Spanish, and in 1690 against the army of William of Orange. Two great forts were built to combat these threats from the Continent. England couldn't rule the waves without ruling Kinsale.

To understand the small town of Kinsale, you need to understand the big picture: In about 1500, the pope divided newly discovered lands outside Europe between Spain and Portugal. With the Reformation breaking Rome's lock on Europe, maritime powers such as England were ignoring the pope's grant. This was important because trade with the New World and Asia brought huge wealth in spices (necessary for curing meat), gold, and silver.

England threatened Spain's New World piñata, and Ireland was Catholic. Spain had an economic and a religious reason to defend the pope and Catholicism. The showdown between Spain and England for mastery of the seas (and control of all that trade) was in Ireland. The excuse: to rescue the dear Catholics of Ireland from the terrible treachery of Protestant England.

So the Irish disaster unfolded. The powerful Ulster chieftains Hugh O'Neill and Red Hugh O'Donnell and their clans had been on a roll in their guerilla battles against the English on their home turf up in Ulster. With Spanish aid, they figured they could actually drive the English out of Ireland. In 1601, a Spanish fleet dropped off 3,000 soldiers, who established a beachhead in Kinsale. After the ships left, the Spaniards were pinned down in Kinsale by the English commander (who, breaking with martial etiquette, actually fought in the winter). In harsh conditions, virtually the entire Irish-clan fighting force left the north and marched to the south coast, thinking they could liberate their Spanish allies and win freedom from England.

The numbers seemed reasonable (8,000 Englishmen versus 3,000 Spaniards with 7,000 Irish clansmen approaching). The Irish attacked on Christmas Eve in 1601. But, holding the high ground around fortified and Spanish-occupied Kinsale, a relatively small English force kept the Spaniards hemmed in, leaving the bulk of the English troops to rout the fighting Irish, who were adept at ambushes but not at open-field warfare. (Today's visitors will be reminded of this crucial battle as they wander past pubs with names like "The 1601" and "The Spaniard"—see pub sign on opposite page.)

The Irish resistance was broken, and its leaders fled to Europe (the "flight of the Earls"). England made peace with Spain and began the "plantation" of mostly Scottish Protestants in Ireland (the seeds of the long-running Troubles in Ulster). England ruled the waves, and it ruled Ireland.

The lesson: Kinsale is key. England eventually built two huge, star-shaped fortresses to ensure control of the narrow waterway, a strategy it would further develop in later fortifications built at Gibraltar and Singapore.

Kinsale's maritime history continued. Daniel Defoe used the real-life experience of Scottish privateer Alexander Selkirk, who departed from Kinsale in 1703 and was later marooned alone on a desert island, as the basis for his book *Robinson Crusoe*. (Selkirk was lucky to have been marooned when he was—his ship and all aboard later perished in a hurricane off Costa Rica.)

It was just 10 miles offshore from Old Kinsale Head that the

passenger liner *Lusitania* was torpedoed by a German submarine in 1915. At the time, the liner was the fastest vessel on the seas (with a top speed of 25 knots). The primitive U-boats of the day were much slower (8 knots), giving *Lusitania*'s crew a false sense of security. Because World War I was the first conflict to employ submarine warfare, evasion tactics were largely untested. As the *Lusitania* sank, nearly 1,200 people were killed, sparking America's eventual entry into the war.

KINSALE & COBH

taking up half the space, so only about 10 seats get an actual view of the musicians (weekend nights at 21:30, arrive before 20:30 to avoid standing all night, tel. 021/477-2436).

Pubs for *Craic* Rather than Music

For conversation or an introspective pint, I like the **Greyhound** (off Newman's Mall, behind the Milk Market Café)—no live music, just a scruffy, multichambered throwback with no pretense. Another joint filled with characters who haven't changed in decades is **The Tap Tavern** (corner of Church Street and Guardwell). It's presided over by Mary O'Neill, the unofficial godmother of Kinsale, and her slyly humorous son Brian, who runs the town's recommended ghost tours. Check out the ancient holy well that came to light when they built their appealing back patio.

Sleeping in Kinsale

Kinsale is a popular place in summer for yachters and golfers (who don't flinch at paying $300 for 18 holes out on the exotic Old Head of Kinsale Golf Course). It's wise to book your room in advance. These places are all within a 15-minute walk of the town center.

$$$ Blindgate House, high up on the fringe of town behind St. Multose Church, offers 11 pristine rooms in fine modern comfort (tel. 021/477-7858, mobile 087-237-6676, www.blindgatehouse.com, info@blindgatehouse.com, Maeve Coakley).

$$$ The Old Presbytery Apartments, with a meandering floor plan and plush lounge, occupy a fine, quiet house that's been converted into four lovely apartments. Daily light breakfast is included (coffee, juice, fruit, yogurt, cheese, smoked salmon, and freshly home-baked bread). The rooms are stocking-feet cozy, and Noreen McEvoy runs the place with a passion for excellence (2-night minimum, RS%, 10 percent discount with cash, family rooms, private parking, 43 Cork Street, tel. 021/477-2027, www.oldpres.com, info@oldpres.com).

$$$ Desmond House, next door to the Old Presbytery, has four spotless, tastefully furnished rooms and tons of space to stretch out. Grainne Barnett takes pride in her homemade bread served with their fine breakfast (private parking, 42 Cork Street, tel. 021/477-3575, mobile 087-205-5566, www.desmondhousekinsale.com, desmondhouse@gmail.com).

$$$ Friar's Lodge is a slate-shingled hotel perched on the hill past St. John's Catholic Church (and frequently booked up by Rick Steves tours). What its 17 spacious rooms lack in Old World character, they make up for in dependable quality (family rooms, private parking, 5 Friar Street, tel. 021/477-7384, www.friars-lodge.com, mtierney@indigo.ie).

$$ Cloisters B&B has four snug but bright and inviting rooms with a friendly atmosphere fostered by Orla Kenneally and Aileen Healy (2 Friars Street, tel. 021/470-0680, www.cloisterskinsale. com, info@cloisterskinsale.com).

$$ San Antonio B&B is a 200-year-old house with five rooms and a funky feel, lovingly looked after by gentleman Jimmie Conron (cash only, 1 Friar Street, tel. 021/477-2341, mobile 086-878-9800, jimmiesan@yahoo.ie).

$ The Olde Bakery B&B makes you feel at home with three quilt-bedded rooms, Lilly the loveable mute mutt, and charmingly chatty hostess Chrissie Quigley. This friendly tech-free gem can only be booked by phone (cash only, 56 Lower O'Connell Street, tel. 021/477-3012).

$ Jo's Rooms is a good value, offering five fresh, practical rooms in the center of town (breakfast extra in downstairs café, cash only, small rooms with smaller double beds, 55 Main Street, mobile 087-948-1026, www.joskinsale.com, joskinsale@gmail. com).

$ The Sea Gull, perched up the hill right next to Desmond Castle, offers four retro-homey rooms. It's run by Mary O'Neill, who also runs The Tap Tavern down the hill (RS%, cash only, Cork Street, tel. 021/477-2240, mobile 087-241-6592, marytap@iol.ie).

Eating in Kinsale

Back in the 1990s, when Ireland was just getting its cuisine act together, Kinsale was the island's self-proclaimed gourmet capital. While good restaurants are common-place in Irish towns today, Kinsale still has an edge at mealtime. Local competition is fierce, and restaurants offer creative and tempting menus. Seafood is king. With so many options in the ever-changing scene, it's worth a short stroll to assess your choices. Reservations are smart, especially if eating late or on a weekend. Restaurant connoisseurs can check the menu details of Kinsale's top restaurants at www. kinsalerestaurants.com.

CHEAP AND CHEERY
$ Dinos Fish & Chips, with big windows overlooking the harbor, is a fun and family-friendly chain for budget fish-and-chips. It's modern and spacious, with a nautical theme (daily 9:00-21:30, across from the TI, tel. 021/477-4561).

$ Mother Hubbard's, tiny with six tables and packed with happy locals near Market Square, serves all-day breakfast, toasties, sandwiches, and salads (daily 8:30-15:00, 1 Market Street, tel. 021/477-2440).

$ Milk Market Café—right next door—is a hit with kids, offering burgers, pizza, and fish-and-chips (daily 10:00-18:00, 3 Market Street).

$ The Gourmet Pantry is an above-average takeout option (Mon-Sat 9:00-18:00, Sun 10:30-17:30, 4 Market Street, tel. 021/470-9215).

Groceries: You can gather picnic supplies at the **SuperValu** supermarket (Mon-Sat 8:00-21:00, Sun from 9:00, New Road, tel. 021/477-2843).

GOOD DINNERS IN THE OLD CENTER

$$$$ Finn's Table is dressy, refined, and romantic, with white tablecloths, candles, and elegant service. John Finn cooks and Julie Finn serves enticing dinner plates ranging from lamb to lobster. Meat is their passion—John comes from a long line of butchers and still gets the best cuts from his dad's butcher shop. Their three-course early-bird menu, served until 18:30, makes this pricey place more affordable (Thu-Tue 18:00-22:00, closed Wed; Nov-April Thu-Sat only, if open at all; 6 Main Street, tel. 021/470-9636, www.finnstable.com).

$$$ Fishy Fishy Café, a high-energy destination seafood restaurant with spacious seating (indoor, balcony, and terrace) and a wonderful menu, is run by Martin and Maria Shanahan. When I asked, "What's your secret?" they pointed to the portraits of fishermen on the wall and said, "Local, local, local." It's a good lunch or early dinner option. Martin's culinary prowess has led him to host a weekly cooking show on Irish TV (daily 12:00-21:00, reservations recommended, Pier Road, tel. 021/470-0415, www.fishyfishy.ie).

$$$ Max's Seafood Restaurant is a spacious and stylish—but not overly romantic—place. There's no pretense—the focus is simply on great seafood. Chef Olivier Queva from France offers a fresh and classic selection and a French flair (nice wines by the glass), while wife Anne Marie serves. While this place gets pricey, there's a good early-bird special until 19:15 (daily 18:00-21:30, 48 Main Street, tel. 021/477-2443).

$$$ The Supper Club is a linen-and-leather upmarket joint with a meat smoker, strong cocktails, and creative desserts (Tue-Sat 17:30-22:30, closed Sun-Mon, 2 Main Street, tel. 021/470-9233).

$$$ Jim Edward's Steak & Seafood Restaurant and Bar is an energetic place that's clearly a local favorite for its steaks, seafood, and vegetables. Choose between the restaurant's maritime setting or the more intimate, pub-like bar (same menu, bar open daily 12:00-22:00, restaurant from 18:00, Market Quay, tel. 021/477-2541).

$$ Cobra Tandoori is good for tasty Punjabi/Indian cuisine (daily 16:00-23:00, 69 Main Street, tel. 021/477-7911).

NEAR CHARLES FORT

$$$ Bulman Bar and Toddies Restaurant serves seafood with seasonal produce. The mussels are especially tasty; on a balmy day or evening, diners take a bucket and a beer out to the seawall. This is the only way to eat on the water in Kinsale. The **$$ pub,** strewn with fun decor and sporting a big fireplace, is also good for a coffee or beer after your visit to Charles Fort (pub open daily 12:30-21:00, restaurant open Tue-Sat from 18:30, 200 yards toward Kinsale from Charles Fort in hamlet of Summercove, tel. 021/477-2131).

Kinsale Connections

BY PUBLIC TRANSPORTATION

The closest train station is in Cork, 15 miles north. But buses run frequently between Kinsale (stop is on Pier Road, 100 yards behind TI, at south end of town) and Cork's bus station (14/day Mon-Sat, fewer on Sun, 50 minutes).

In **Cork,** the bus station and train station are a 10-minute walk apart. The bus station (corner of Merchant's Quay and Parnell Place) is on the south bank of the River Lee, just over the nearest bridge from the train station (north of the river on Lower Glanmire Road).

From Cork by Train to: Dublin (hourly, 2.5 hours, www.irishrail.ie).

From Cork by Bus to: Dublin (every 2 hours, 3.5 hours), **Galway** (hourly, 4.5 hours), **Tralee** (hourly, 2.5 hours), **Kilkenny** (7/day, 2.5 hours, www.dublincoach.ie). Bus info: Tel. 021/450-8188 or www.buseireann.ie.

BY PLANE

Cork Airport is handy for travelers starting or ending their trip in southern Ireland. Located four miles south of Cork city (on N-27/R-600 to Kinsale, a 30-minute drive away), it offers connecting flights from London Heathrow and Edinburgh on Aer Lingus, as well as from London's Stansted, Luton, and Gatwick on Ryanair. You can also fly from here directly to many European cities (code: ORK, tel. 021/431-3131, www.corkairport.com).

Bus to Kinsale: Bus #226 runs between Cork Airport and Kinsale (2/hour, 30 minutes, www.buseireann.ie).

KINSALE & COBH

Cobh

If your ancestry is Irish, there's a good chance that this was the last Irish soil your ancestors had under their feet. Cobh (pronounced "cove") was the major port of Irish emigration in the 19th century. Of the six million Irish who have emigrated to America, Canada, and Australia since 1815, nearly half left from Cobh.

The first steam-powered ship to make a transatlantic crossing departed from Cobh in 1838—cutting the journey time from 50 days to 18. When Queen Victoria came to Ireland for the first time in 1849, Cobh was the first Irish ground she set foot on. Giddy, the town renamed itself "Queenstown" in her honor. It was still going by that name in 1912, when the *Titanic* made its final fateful stop here before heading out on its maiden (and only) voyage. To celebrate their new independence from British royalty in 1922, locals changed the town's name back to its original Irish moniker. Today the town's deep harbor attracts dozens of cruise ships per year (with their large packs of eager visitors).

Orientation to Cobh

Cobh sits on a large island in Cork Harbor, connected to the mainland via a short bridge (on the north shore) and a drive-on ferry (on the west shore). The town's inviting waterfront is colorful yet salty, with a playful promenade. The butcher's advertisement reads, "Always pleased to meet you and always with meat to please you." Stroll past the shops along the water. Ponder the large and dramat-

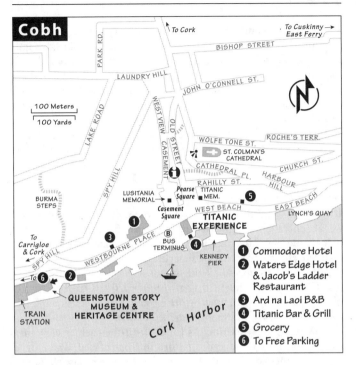

ic *Lusitania* memorial on Casement Square and the modest *Titanic* memorial nearby on Pearse Square.

A hike up the hill to the towering Neo-Gothic St. Colman's Cathedral rewards you with a fine view of the port. To get to the cathedral, walk behind the *Lusitania* memorial, go under the stone arch, and strut up steep Westview Street, passing the photogenic row of colorful houses on your right (nicknamed the "deck of cards" by locals). After panting your way to the top, turn right—you can't miss the cathedral steeple.

Tourist Information: The TI is in the old courthouse at the base of Westview Street, inside of the arch on the left wall as you head uphill (Mon-Fri 9:00-17:30, Sat-Sun 10:30-16:30, tel. 021/481-3301, www.cobhharbourchamber.ie).

Parking: If you're driving into Cobh, follow the *Heritage Centre* signs to The Queenstown Story, where you'll find some parking at the museum. There's a two-hour parking maximum anywhere in town (pay at machines on street, free overnight on street from 17:00 until 10:00 the next morning). During the busiest times and on holiday weekends, additional free parking hides behind The Queenstown Story on a long, narrow waterfront lot (car entry at farthest west end, pedestrian entry just to left when facing museum).

Walking Tours: Michael Martin and his staff lead one-hour **Titanic Trail** walking tours that give you unexpected insights into the tragic *Titanic* and *Lusitania* voyages, Spike Island, and Cobh's maritime history (€13, RS%—show this book when you pay, daily at 11:00, also 14:00 in summer with required advance booking, call ahead to confirm tour times in winter, private tours available, meet in lobby of Commodore Hotel, tel. 021/481-5211, mobile 087-276-7218, www.titanic.ie, info@titanic.ie). Seriously interested travelers should look for his book, *RMS Lusitania: It Wasn't and It Didn't*.

Sights in Cobh

▲The Titanic Experience

It's stirring to think that this modest little port town was the ship's final anchorage—and the last chance to get off. Occupying the former White Star Line building where the *Titanic*'s final passengers boarded, this compact museum packs a decent punch as it recounts the story of the ship and its final moments.

Cost and Hours: €10; daily 9:00-18:00, Oct-April until 17:30, last entry 45 minutes before closing; Casement Square, tel. 021/481-4412, www.titanicexperiencecobh.ie.

Visiting the Museum: As you look off the back balcony into the harbor, note the decayed pilings in front of you. These once supported the old pier and represent the passengers' last chance to turn back. One lucky surviving crewman with a premonition did.

Inside the museum, you travel room to room with your host, the ship's fourth mate, in audiovisual form. He meets you at the boarding dock, full of pride in the new vessel. He joins you in replicas of a posh first-class cabin and a no-frills third-class cabin before his commentary is interrupted by the sound of ice tearing at the hull. You then enter an exhibition room featuring an animation that silently depicts the ship sinking in its steel-twisting, slow-motion ballet to the bottom (settling as two crunched hulls 600 yards apart and 12,000 feet deep).

The last stop is a room highlighting the luxurious ship's innovative firsts. It was one of the first equipped with a wireless "Marconi room" to send messages from sea to shore—or to other ships. *Titanic* was the first ever to issue an SOS message by Morse code. Another wall explains in grim detail the effects of hypothermia on the human body.

Before you leave, check out the list of 123 passengers who boarded the *Titanic* in Cobh. Your entry ticket has one of these passenger's names on it. See if you survived (you've got a 30 percent chance). A passenger with the same name as one of this book's co-authors is listed among the third-class passengers lost.

▲The Queenstown Story

Filling a harborside Victorian train station, this museum is an earnest attempt to make the city's history come to life. The topics—the Famine, Irish emigration, Australia-bound prison ships, the sinking of the *Lusitania,* and the ill-fated voyage of the *Titanic*—are interesting enough to make it a worthwhile stop.

Cost and Hours: €10, includes audioguide; Mon-Sat 9:30-18:00, Sun from 11:00, Nov-April until 17:00, last entry one hour before closing; Cobh Heritage Centre, handy café, tel. 021/481-3591, www.cobhheritage.com, info@cobhheritage.com.

Visiting the Museum: Coverage of the *Titanic* and the *Lusitania* was beefed up for the centennials of these famous ships' sinking (2012 and 2015, respectively). You'll learn about one priest who got off the *Titanic* at Cobh. His photos of the early legs of the voyage are a priceless historical reference. But in general, the museum itself, while kid-friendly and engaging, is weak on actual historical artifacts. It reminds me of a big, interesting history picture book with the pages expanded and tacked on the wall.

Before departing, walk over to the Annie Moore statue next to the water, 25 yards from the front door. She emigrated from Cobh and was the first person to be processed through Ellis Island when it opened on January 1, 1892.

Nearby: Those with Irish roots to trace can use the Heritage Centre's **genealogy search service,** located right across from the Queenstown Story ticket booth. Since Cobh was the primary Irish emigration port, this can be a great place to start your search (€50/hour consultation and research assistance by appointment only, email ahead to book—genealogy@cobhheritage.com). See the sidebar for more tips on researching your Irish heritage.

Sleeping and Eating in Cobh

Sleeping: These hotels are all centrally located near the harbor, a five-minute walk from the Queenstown Story.

$$$ Commodore Hotel is a grand 170-year-old historic landmark with 40 rooms. This place was once owned by the Humbert family, wealthy Germans who opened it up to *Lusitania* refugees after the 1915 sinking. Its high-ceilinged rooms creak with Victorian character (Westbourne Place, tel. 021/481-1277, www.commodorehotel.ie, commodorehotel@eircom.net).

$$$ Waters Edge Hotel, located 50 yards from the Queenstown Story, has 19 bright, modern rooms and a pleasant harbor-view restaurant (Yacht Club Quay, tel. 021/481-5566, www.watersedgehotel.ie, info@watersedgehotel.ie).

$ Ard na Laoi B&B is a friendly place with five fresh rooms in a great central location (cash only, 15 Westbourne Place, tel.

Irish Genealogy

Lots of travelers come to the Emerald Isle intent on tracing their Irish ancestry. But too few give it enough thought before they set foot on the old sod, and instead head straight to what they think might be the right town or region to start "asking around." While this approach may bear fruit (or at least give you an opportunity to meet nice Irish people), a bit of preparation can save time and increase your chances of making a real connection to your Celtic bloodlines.

First, a common false assumption: Many novice root-searchers think their Irish ancestors were from County Cork, because Cobh is listed as their emigration departure port. But Cobh was the primary departure port for the vast majority of Irish emigrants—regardless of where they had resided in Ireland. An even earlier wave of Irish emigrants (mostly Scots-Irish from Ulster) sailed from the port of Derry (the second busiest emigration port).

If you have an idea of what town your ancestors hailed from, search for its location (www.google.com/maps is a good starting point). Correct spelling is essential: Ballyalloly is up north in County Down while Ballyally is down south in County Cork (close enough only counts in horseshoes and hand grenades). Just as there's a Springfield in almost every state in the Union, the same goes for some common Irish town names: There's a town named Kells in four different Irish counties.

Fáilte Ireland, the official government-sponsored Irish tourist board, is a safe bet for reputable genealogy sources (www.discoverireland.ie). Some fertile websites to consider browsing are www.irishgenealogy.ie or www.ancestry.com. Online access to both the 1901 and 1911 Irish censuses has been a boon (www.census.nationalarchives.ie). However, it's not a perfect science:

021/481-2742, www.ardnalaoi.ie, info@ardnalaoi.ie, Michael O'Shea).

Eating: The nicest place in town is the **$$$ Titanic Bar & Grill,** sunken under the Titanic Experience, with fun outdoor seating on fine days. I also like **$$$ Jacob's Ladder** restaurant in the Waters Edge Hotel, with another great outdoor deck option. For picnic fixings, there's the **Centra Market,** facing the water on West Beach Street (Mon-Sat 8:00-22:00, Sun 9:00-20:00).

Cobh Connections

BY TRAIN

Cork's **Kent Station** has frequent short-hop service to both Cobh and Midleton, which are on separate lines (hourly, usually de-

Many precious birth records (some dating back to the 1200s) went up in smoke when offices in the Four Courts building in Dublin burned in 1922 during the Irish Civil War.

Before you get to Ireland, make contact with the Genealogy Advisory Service at the National Library in Dublin (tel. 01/603-0213, www.nli.ie, genealogy@nli.ie). Also helpful to contact in advance: the genealogy search service in Cobh (tel. 021/481-3591, www.cobhheritage.com/genealogy, genealogy@cobhheritage.com).

If you think your heritage might be Scots-Irish, check the Discover Ulster-Scots Centre in Belfast (tel. 028/9043-6710, http://discoverulsterscots.com, discoverulsterscots@gmail.com). In Derry/Londonderry (an emigration port long before Belfast), you can find help from local genealogist Brian Mitchell (genealogy@derrystrabane.com). Also consider the Mellon Centre for Migration Studies, near Omagh in Northern Ireland (tel. 028/8225-6315, www.qub.ac.uk/cms, mcms@librariesni.org.uk).

Another option is to hire a qualified expert to assist you in drilling deeper and navigating obstacles; Fáilte Ireland may be able to give you a recommendation. This kind of help doesn't come cheap, but if you're willing to invest in an experienced researcher, you may get better results. One worth considering is Sean Quinn of My Ireland Heritage (tel. 01/689-0213, www.myirelandheritage.com, sean@myirelandheritage.com, based near Dublin in Trim, County Meath, but able to work across Ireland). Top-end services like Sean's can then drive you to the locations where your ancestors lived.

With a few emails, phone calls, and internet searches, you may just end up having a pint with someone in Ireland who looks a lot like you.

parts on the hour and returns on the half-hour, 25 minutes, www.irishrail.ie).

ROUTE TIPS FOR DRIVERS

Between Cobh and Cork or Waterford: If you're driving to Cobh from either Cork or Waterford, exit N-25 about 8 miles (13 km) east of Cork, following little R-624 over a bridge, onto the Great Island, and directly into Cobh.

Between Cobh and Kinsale: The 30-mile (50 km) drive takes 45 minutes and involves navigating Cork city traffic on well-marked roads. Driving from Cobh to Kinsale, you'll head north out of Cobh on R-624 and get on N-25 heading west, then follow the airport signs (with a little jet airplane icon) the whole way. You'll pass Cork Airport, which is conveniently located on R-600 leading south straight into Kinsale.

Between Waterford and Kinsale

If you're driving from Waterford (see previous chapter) to Cobh and Kinsale, you can easily visit these sights just off N-25 (listed from east to west).

Ardmore

This funky little beach town, with a famous ruined church and round tower, is a handy stop (just east of Youghal, 3 miles/5 km south of N-25 between Waterford and Cobh). A couple of buses run daily from Ardmore to Cork and to Waterford.

This humble little port town is just a line of pastel houses that appear frightened by the sea. Its beach claims (very modestly) to be "the most swimmable in Ireland."

The town's historic claim to fame: Christianity came to Ireland here first (thanks to St. Declan, who arrived in AD 416—15 years before St. Patrick...but with a weaker public-relations team). As if to proclaim that feat with an 800-year-old exclamation mark, one of Ireland's finest examples of a round tower stands perfectly intact, 97 feet above an evocative graveyard and a ruined church (noted for its weathered early Christian carvings on its west facade). You can't get into the tower—the entrance is 14 feet off the ground.

An easy, scenic coastal loop hike (3 miles, 1 hour) leads from the parking lot of the ritzy Cliff House Hotel along the coast, eventually cutting inland and back into town (simple to follow, ask for free rudimentary map in newsstand at end of Main Street).

Sleeping in Ardmore: $$$$ Cliff House Hotel is a died-and-gone-to-heaven splurge with 39 impeccably modern and decadently expensive rooms, all with ocean views (tel. 024/87800, www.thecliffhousehotel.com, info@thecliffhousehotel.com).

$ Duncrone B&B, run by Jeanette Dunne, has four vividly colorful rooms (half-mile outside town, up past the round tower, tel. 024/94860, www.duncronebandb.com, info@duncronebandb.com).

Eating in Ardmore: The local favorite is **$$ White Horses Restaurant** (Tue-Sun 12:30-15:30 & 18:00-22:00, closed Mon, Main Street, tel. 024/94040). For a fine lunch or dinner with cliff-perch views, check out the restaurant in the luxurious **$$$$ Cliff House Hotel** (turn right at the coastal end of Main Street and drive up narrow lane to dead end, tel. 024/87800). **An Tobar,** the only pub in town, is down near the water (but does not serve food).

▲Old Midleton Distillery

Sometime during your Ireland trip, even if you're a teetotaler, you'll want to tour a whiskey distillery. Of the three major distillery tours (this one, Jameson in Dublin, and Bushmills in Northern

Ireland), the Midleton experience is the most interesting (the "Experience" tour offers the best overview; skip the overpriced "Behind the Scenes" option). After a 10-minute video, you'll walk with a guide through a great old 18th-century plant on a 45-minute tour; see water-wheel-powered crankshafts and a 31,000-gallon copper still—the largest of its kind in the world; and learn the story of whiskey. Predictably, you finish in a tasting room and enjoy a free, not-so-wee glass. The finale is a Scotch whisky vs. Irish whiskey taste test. Your guide will take two volunteers for this. Don't be shy, and enjoy an opportunity to taste the different brands.

Cost and Hours: €22, daily 10:00-18:00, tours run regularly 10:00-16:30 in summer—4/day in winter, cafeteria, tel. 021/461-3594, www.jamesonwhiskey.com.

Getting There: It's 12 miles (19 km) east of Cork in Midleton, about a mile off N-25, the main Cork-Waterford road. There's easy parking at the distillery lot.

Between Kinsale and Killarney

If you're driving between Kinsale and the Ring of Kerry (see next chapter), you can easily visit these sights (listed from east to west).

Blarney Stone and Castle

The town of Blarney is of no importance, and the 15th-century Blarney Castle is an empty hulk (with little effort put forth to make it meaningful or interesting). It's only famous as the place of tourist pilgrimage, where busloads line up to kiss a stone on its top rampart and get "the gift of gab." The stone's origin is shrouded in myth (perhaps brought back from the Holy Land by crusaders).

The best thing about this lame sight is the opportunity to watch a cranky man lower lemming tourists over the edge—belly up and head back—to kiss the stone while a camera snaps a photo (available for purchase back by the parking lot). After a day of tour

KINSALE & COBH

groups mindlessly climbing up here to perform this ritual, the stone can be literally slathered with spit and lipstick.

The tradition goes back to the late 16th century, when Queen Elizabeth I was trying to plant loyal English settlers in Ireland to tighten her grip on the rebellious island. She demanded that the Irish clan chiefs recognize the Crown, rather than the clan chiefs, as the legitimate titleholder of all lands.

One of those chiefs was Cormac MacCarthy, Lord of Blarney Castle (who was supposedly loyal to the queen). He was smart

enough never to disagree with the queen—instead, he would cleverly avoid acquiescing to her demands by sending a never-ending stream of lengthy and deceptive excuses, disguised with liberal doses of flattery (while subtly maintaining his native Gaelic loyalties). In her frustration, the queen declared his endless words nothing but "blarney."

While the castle is a shell, the surrounding grounds are beautiful and well kept, and the fine gardens and lush forested Rock Close are photogenic.

Cost and Hours: €18, cheaper online; Mon-Sat 9:00-18:30, Sun until 18:00, later in peak season, shorter hours in winter; free parking lot, helpful TI, tel. 021/438-5252, www.blarneycastle.ie.

Getting There: It's 5 miles (8 km) northwest of Cork, the major city in south Ireland. Looking for shopping galore? Adjacent Blarney Woolen Mills has it all (right next to the castle parking lot).

Beal na Blath: Michael Collins Ambush Site

Irish history fans may want to make a brief detour en route from Kinsale to Macroom to visit nearby Beal na Blath (BALE-nuh-BLAH), where dynamic Irish rebel leader Michael Collins was assassinated on August 22, 1922, during the Irish Civil War. The site is not much more than a bend in a country road, with an Irish high cross on a raised platform to mark the spot. But it's Ireland's equivalent of Dallas' infamous "grassy knoll." (For an engrossing view of this and Collins' life, see the 1996 movie *Michael Collins*.)

Take a moment to step out of the car and climb the steps onto the fenced platform. Next to the high cross, a plaque with a photo shows the road as it appeared in 1922, with arrows approximating the position of the Collins convoy and the spots from which the ambushers fired.

Dusk was falling as the convoy carrying Collins to Cork came under attack. Collins could have ordered his driver to speed off, but chose instead to stand and fight. The identity of the anti-treaty IRA guerilla who fired the fatal shot (thought to have been an errant ricochet) remains in dispute. Following his death, Collins' body lay in state for three days at Dublin City Hall, drawing massive crowds. Although his pro-treaty Free State army later won the civil war, it's likely that modern Irish history would have been much different had Collins lived. While Éamon de Valera directed his country down the "comely maiden at the crossroads" vision, had Collins survived and taken power, Ireland likely would have been more secular and more integrated into the European economy— richer and more mainstream European.

Getting There: Beal na Blath is just off N-22, the road that runs west from Cork to Macroom, and is easiest to find if you have a detailed Ordnance Survey atlas (it covers all tiny rural lanes). About halfway between Cork and Macroom, take R-585 south off N-22 through the tiny village of Crookstown. From Crookstown, follow *Beal na Blath* signs south for about a mile to the ambush site (well-marked, but be alert in case foliage on leafy rural lanes obscures a sign at a crossroads).

Macroom

This busy, one-street market town makes a convenient coffee or lunch stop for those driving between Cork or Kinsale and Killarney. The romanticized gateway where its ruined castle once stood was owned by the father of William Penn (who founded Pennsylvania). It overlooks an entertaining main square, where you'll find limited parking. The weekly market fills the square with "casual trading" each Tuesday. The 2006 Irish Civil War saga *The Wind That Shakes the Barley* was filmed in this area.

Lynch's Coffee Shop and Bakery (the bright-yellow storefront at the far end of the square) is a welcoming place, with cheap and cheery food and drink, a WC in the back, and historic town photos on the walls. The Lynch family has run the bakery since 1869 (say "hi" to Humphrey and his wife Pat). The **Next Door Café,** in the Castle Hotel (a block from the square on the main street), serves good, fast lunches and made-to-order sandwiches.

If Macroom parking is challenging, continue driving west on N-22 another 10 miles to the little hamlet of **Ballyvourney,** where you'll find a friendly lunch at the Mills Inn (on right with easy parking behind).

KINSALE & COBH

KENMARE & THE RING OF KERRY

It's no wonder that, since Victorian times, visitors have been attracted to this dramatic chunk of Ireland. Mysterious ancient ring forts stand sentinel on mossy hillsides. Beloved Irish statesman Daniel O'Connell maintained his ancestral estate here, far from 19th-century politics. And early Christian hermit-monks left a lonely imprint of their devotion, in the form of simple stone dwellings atop an isolated rock crag far from shore...a holy retreat on the edge of the then-known world.

Today, it seems like every tour bus in Ireland makes the ritual loop around the scenic Ring of Kerry, using the bustling and famous tourist town of Killarney as a springboard. Killarney National Park is gorgeous and well worth driving through. But I prefer to skip Killarney town (useful only for its transportation connections). Instead, make the tidy town of Kenmare your home base, and use my suggestions to cleverly circle the much-loved peninsula—entirely missing the convoy of tour buses.

PLANNING YOUR TIME

All you need in compact Kenmare is one night and an early start the next day to drive the Ring of Kerry. Without a car, you can take a private tour from Kenmare, though it's not as enjoyable as driving the loop yourself. Below is my ideal plan, assuming you're coming from Kinsale. Don't attempt to depart Kinsale, drive the entire Ring, and reach Dingle all in one day.

Day 1

9:00   Depart Kinsale (the earlier you leave, the fewer
(or earlier)   bottlenecks you'll encounter). Drive the R-600 inland

route past Cork Airport, skirt Cork city on N-40, then use the N-22 road through Macroom to link onto the N-71 in Killarney town.

11:00   Reach Muckross House just south of Killarney town. Tour the house, visit the gardens, and have lunch (bring a picnic or eat in the cafeteria).

13:00   Depart Muckross House and head to Kissane Sheep
(or earlier)   Farm, driving south along the narrowest five-mile squiggly stretch of the Ring. (Warning: If you linger longer at Muckross House, you'll encounter tour-bus congestion.)

13:30   Reach Kissane Sheep Farm and watch their sheepdog demonstration (book ahead).

14:30   Leave Kissane Sheep Farm and drive south through Moll's Gap, then coast down the N-71.

15:30   Arrive in Kenmare, with a couple hours of stroll time before dinner.

Note: If you add hikes, or additional stops or activities (like Blarney Castle or Muckross Farms), skip the Muckross House tour or the sheepdog demonstration. Prioritize what's most important to you; trying to do it all leads to encountering a convoy of oncoming tour buses in the late afternoon.

Day 2

8:30   Do the Ring of Kerry loop, following my driving tour.
(or earlier)

Late   Drive to Dingle (or your next home-base destination).
afternoon

Other Options

Skipping Killarney: If you have no interest in Muckross House and Farms, Killarney National Park, or the sheep farm, just head straight to Kenmare from Kinsale, skipping the detour up to Killarney. (Instead of staying on N-22 to Killarney, you'll branch off onto R-569 a couple kilometers after you cross the border from County Cork into County Kerry.) Or if you have your heart set on a Blarney Castle visit, stop there en route from Kinsale to Kenmare.

With More Time: Hardy hikers might consider adding another day to visit the rugged island of Skellig Michael, which requires an overnight in Portmagee or St. Finian's Bay. Be aware that boats can book up months in advance, and weather can cancel boat crossings.

KENMARE & RING OF KERRY

Kenmare

Cradled in a lush valley, this charming little town (known as Nei-dín, "little nest" in Irish) hooks you right away with its rows of vividly colored shop fronts and go-for-a-stroll atmosphere. The nearby finger of the gentle sea feels more like a large lake (called the Kenmare River, just to confuse things). Far from the assembly-line tourism of Killarney town, Kenmare (rhymes with "been there") also makes a great launchpad for enjoying the sights along the road around the Iveragh (eev-er-AH) Peninsula—known to shamrock lovers everywhere as the Ring of Kerry.

Check out the Heritage Centre in the back rooms of the TI to get an overview of the region's history. Visit the Kenmare Lace and Design Centre above the TI for an up-close look at the town's famously delicate lace. A five-minute walk from the TI gives you hands-on access to a prehistoric stone circle at the edge of town. Finish up by taking a peek inside Holy Cross Church to see the fine ceiling woodwork.

Orientation to Kenmare

Carefully planned Kenmare is shaped like an "X," forming two tri-angles. The upper (northern) triangle contains the town square—where fairs and markets have been held for centuries (colorful market Wed in summer), the adjacent TI and Heritage Centre, and a cozy park. The lower (southern) triangle contains three one-way streets busy with shops, lodgings, and restaurants. Use the tall Holy Cross Church spire to get your bearings (next  to the northeast parking lot, handy public WC across the street).

Tourist Information: The helpful TI, on the town square, offers "The Trail," a brochure with a short self-guided tour; they also sporadically have €10 1.5-hour guided town walks (Mon-Sat 9:30-17:30; closed Thu in spring and fall, Sun year-round, and all of Nov-March; tel. 064/664-1233, www.kenmare.ie).

HELPFUL HINTS

Bookstore: Kenmare Bookshop is a cozy one-room cottage run by friendly John O'Connor (Mon-Sat 10:00-13:00 & 14:00-17:30, Sun 12:00-17:30, July-Aug until 21:00, on Shelbourne

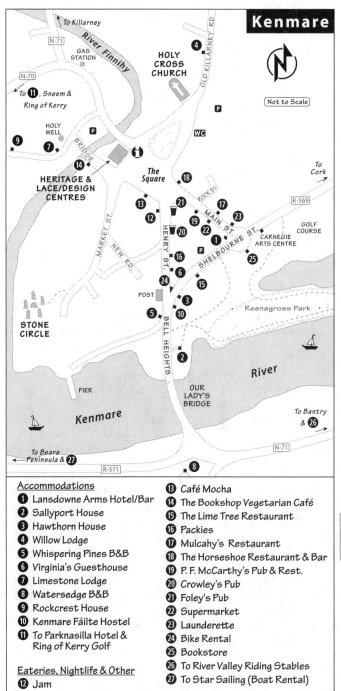

KENMARE & RING OF KERRY

Accommodations
1. Lansdowne Arms Hotel/Bar
2. Sallyport House
3. Hawthorn House
4. Willow Lodge
5. Whispering Pines B&B
6. Virginia's Guesthouse
7. Limestone Lodge
8. Watersedge B&B
9. Rockcrest House
10. Kenmare Fáilte Hostel
11. To Parknasilla Hotel & Ring of Kerry Golf

Eateries, Nightlife & Other
12. Jam
13. Café Mocha
14. The Bookshop Vegetarian Café
15. The Lime Tree Restaurant
16. Packies
17. Mulcahy's Restaurant
18. The Horseshoe Restaurant & Bar
19. P. F. McCarthy's Pub & Rest.
20. Crowley's Pub
21. Foley's Pub
22. Supermarket
23. Launderette
24. Bike Rental
25. Bookstore
26. To River Valley Riding Stables
27. To Star Sailing (Boat Rental)

Street at roundabout across from Lansdowne Arms Hotel, tel. 064/664-1578).

Laundry: O'Shea's Cleaners and Launderette offers self-service laundry, as well as Mon-Fri drop-off service (Mon-Sat 9:00-20:00, Sun 12:00-18:00; across from Lansdowne Arms Hotel on Main Street, hidden in back of O'Shea's photography shop, tel. 064/664-0808).

Bike Rental: Finnegan's Corner rents bikes and has route maps and advice on maximizing scenery and minimizing traffic (standard bike-€15/day, €20/24 hours, beefed-up road bike—€30/day; Mon-Sat 9:30-18:30, July-Aug until 19:00; Sun 12:00-18:00; leave ID for deposit, office in gift shop at 37 Henry Street, tel. 064/664-1083, www.finneganscycles.com).

Taxi: Try **Murnane Cabs** (mobile 087-236-4353) or **Kenmare Coach and Cab** (mobile 087-248-0800).

Parking: Two large public parking lots (behind the TI and across from the church, free overnight) cling to the two main roads departing town to the north. Street parking is free (2 hours).

Cultural Events: At the **Carnegie Arts Center,** you can attend concerts in its 140-seat theater (€5-20), art exhibitions, and films. In summer (June-Aug), Thursday is movie night at 20:00 for €7 (across Shelbourne Street from Lansdowne Arms Hotel, tel. 064/664-8701, www.carnegieartskenmare.ie).

Tours in Kenmare

Bus or Private Car Tours

Finnegan's Tours runs day tours with guides who provide casual, anecdotal narration. The tour—little more than a scenic joyride—generally makes three rest stops and one sightseeing stop (route depends on day: Ring of Kerry on Mon, Wed, and Fri; Beara Peninsula on Tue; Glengarriff and Garnish Island on Thu). In July and August tours leave from the TI at 10:00 and return by 17:00 (€40/person, reserve a day in advance by phone or 3 days in advance by email; for Sept-June, call to arrange tours; can also do private car tours for 4 people for €40/hour; tel. 064/664-1491, mobile 087-248-0800, www.kenmarecoachandcab.com, info@kenmarecoachandcab.com).

Kerry Experience Tours offers custom tours of the Ring of Kerry and the Beara Peninsula, as well as taxi service (generally €250/day for 1-3 passengers, €300/day for 4-7 passengers, €400 for 8-16 passengers, mobile 086-255-4098, www.kerryexperiencetours.ie, info@kerryexperiencetours.ie).

Kenmare's History:
Axes, Xs, Nuns, and Lace

Bronze Age people (2000 BC), attracted to this valley for its abundant game and fish, stashed their prized ax heads and daggers in hidden hoards. Almost 4,000 years later (in 1930), a local farmer from the O'Sullivan clan pried a bothersome boulder from one of his fields and discovered it to be a lid for a collection of rare artifacts that are now on display in the National Museum in Dublin (the "Killaha hoard"). The O'Sullivans (Irish for "descendants of the one-eyed") were for generations the dominant local clan, and you'll still see their name on many Kenmare shop fronts.

Oliver Cromwell's bloody Irish campaign (1649), which subdued most of Ireland, never reached Kenmare. However, Cromwell's chief surveyor, William Petty, knew good land when he saw it and took a quarter of what is now County Kerry as payment for his valuable services, marking the "lands down" on maps. His heirs, the Lansdownes, created Kenmare as a model 18th-century estate town and developed its distinctive "X" street plan. William Petty-Fitzmaurice, the first Marquis of Lansdowne and landlord of Kenmare, became the British prime minister who negotiated the peace that ended the American War of Independence in 1783.

Sister Margaret Cusack, a.k.a. Sister Mary Francis Clare, lived in the town from 1862 to 1881, becoming the famous Nun of Kenmare. Her controversial religious life began when she decided to become an Anglican nun after her fiancé's sudden death. Failing to be accepted as one of Florence Nightingale's nurses during the Crimean War, she converted to Catholicism, joined the Poor Clare order as Sister Mary Francis Clare, and moved with the order to Kenmare.

Sister Clare became an outspoken writer who favored women's rights and lambasted the tyranny of the landlords during the Great Potato Famine (1845-1849). She eventually took church funds and attempted to set herself up as abbess of a convent in Knock. Her renegade behavior led to her leaving the Catholic faith, converting back to Protestantism, writing an autobiography, and lecturing about the "sinister influence of the Roman Church."

After the devastation of the famine, an industrial school was founded in Kenmare to teach trades to destitute youngsters. The school, run by the Poor Clare sisters, excelled in teaching young girls the art of lacemaking. Inspired by lace created earlier in Italy, Kenmare lace caught the eye of Queen Victoria and became much coveted by Victorian society. Examples of it are now on display in the Victoria and Albert Museum (London), the Irish National Museum (Dublin), and the US National Gallery (Washington, DC).

Walking Tours

Anne-Marie Cleary gives 1.5-hour walking tours of town (€12, daily at 10:00 in summer, must book in advance, mobile 086-240-0484, www.kenmareheritagetours.com, info@kenmareheritagetours.com).

Sights in Kenmare

Heritage Centre

This humble museum, in the back rooms of the TI, consists of a series of storyboards and a model of the town. A 20-minute visit here explains the nearby ancient stone circle, the history of Kenmare's lacemaking fame, and the story of a feisty, troublemaking nun (free, same hours as TI).

Kenmare Lace and Design Centre

A single large room above the TI displays the delicate lacework that put Kenmare on the map. From the 1860s until World War I, the Poor Clare convent at Kenmare was the center of excellence for Irish lacemaking. Inspired by antique Venetian lace, nuns created their own designs and taught needlepoint lacemaking as a trade to girls in a region struggling to get back on its feet in the wake of the catastrophic famine. Queen Victoria com-  missioned five pieces of lace in 1885, and by the end of the century tourists began visiting Kenmare on their way to Killarney just for a peek at the lace. Nora Finnegan, who runs the center, usually has a work in progress to demonstrate the complexity of fine lacemaking to visitors.

Cost and Hours: Free; Mon-Sat 10:15-17:00, closed off-season and Sun year-round; mobile 087-234-6998, www.kenmarelace.ie.

Ancient Stone Circle

Of the approximately 100 stone circles that dot southwest Ireland (Counties Cork and Kerry), Kenmare's is one of the most accessible. More than 3,000 years old, the circle has a diameter of 50 feet and consists of 15 stones ringing a large center boulder (possibly a burial monument). Experts think this stone circle (like most) functioned as a celestial calendar—it tracked the position of the setting sun to determine the two solstices (in June and December). For more information on stone circles, see page 532.

Cost and Hours: €2, drop coins into honor box in hut by entry when attendant is away, always open.

Getting There: It's a 10-minute walk from the TI. From the city center, face the TI, turn left, and walk 200 yards down Market Street, passing a row of cute 18th-century houses on your right. Beyond the row of houses, veer right through an unmarked modern gate mounted in stone columns, and continue 50 yards down the paved road. You'll pass the entry hut on your right. The stone circle is behind the adjacent hedge.

Holy Cross Church

Kenmare's grand Catholic church, finished in 1864, is worth a quick visit to see the ornate wooden ceiling supported by 10 larger-than-life angels (carved in Bavaria), the fine 1914 altar carved of Italian marble, and the Victorian stained-glass windows.

Experiences near Kenmare

Horseback Riding: River Valley Riding Stables offers day treks for all levels of experience through beautiful hill scenery in the Roughty River Valley (adults-€20/hour, kids-€15/hour, group discounts, long hours, based at Sheen Falls Lodge 1.5 miles southeast of Kenmare—cross Our Lady's Bridge and turn left on N-71, mobile 087-958-5895, www.kenmare.com/rivervalleystables, rivervalleystables@hotmail.com).

Boating and Hiking: Star Sailing rents boats, gives sailing lessons, and organizes hill walks. Hop on a small two-person sailboat (€45/1 hour, €30/additional hour) or a six-person boat (€65/1 hour, €50/additional hour). Or kick around in a kayak (single-€22/hour, double-€38/hour). Phone ahead to reserve boats (daily 10:00-17:00, located 5 miles southwest of Kenmare on R-571 on Beara Peninsula, courtesy shuttle can pick you up in Kenmare, tel. 064/664-1222, www.staroutdoors.ie; adjacent Con's Restaurant is open daily 12:00-20:00).

Golfing: The Kenmare Golf Club offers a scenic day on the links, right on the edge of town (weekdays-€50, weekends-€55, on R-569 toward Cork, tel. 064/664-1291, www.kenmaregolfclub.com). Or try the Ring of Kerry Golf and Country Club (weekdays-€80, 4 miles west of town on N-70, book ahead on weekends, tel. 064/664-2000, www.ringofkerrygolf.com).

Nightlife in Kenmare

Wander the compact Kenmare town triangle and stick your head in wherever you hear something you like. Music usually starts at 21:30 (although some pubs have early 18:30 sessions—ask at the TI) and ranges from Irish traditional sessions to sing-along strummers. **Crowley's** is an atmospheric little shoebox of a pub with an

Beara: The Other Peninsula

This sleepy yet scenic wedge of land (just south of Kenmare) is worth considering if you have the luxury of two nights in Kenmare. Beara deserves honorable mention as a distant third choice after the Dingle and Ring of Kerry peninsulas, but locals rave about it like we would our home sports team. If you don't have a full day to drive the length of it, spend a memorable half-day enjoying Garnish Island and Healy Pass, skipping the western half of the peninsula.

Garnish Island is a rocky island refuge cloaked by a lush gar-

den and plopped down in the corner of Bantry Bay. Crowned by a martello tower (a stout bunker built to repel feared Napoleonic invasions, free to climb for views), the gardens were the creation of a rich landlord, who turned the barren 37 acres into a lushly vegetated fantasy in the early 1900s. You'll meander past Italian reflecting pools, a Grecian temple framing views of a placid bay, and a walled garden nursery clad in roses. Pine-forested trails, punctuated with rhododendrons, connect it all. Boats depart from the well-marked pier in Glengarriff, about 18 miles (30 km) south of Kenmare, for the scenic 15-minute cruise past seals sunning on rocks to the island (boat—€15 round-trip, 2/hour; gardens—€5, June-Aug Mon-Sat 9:30-17:30, Sun from 11:00, shorter hours off-season and closed Nov-March; tearoom, snacks, and WCs at island's pier; tel. 027/63116, www.harbourqueenferry.com).

A narrow, eight-mile mountain road (R-574) feels like a toboggan run as it squiggles over the peninsula's lumpy spine at

unpretentious clientele. **Foley's** whiskey tube collection adorns its window, inviting you in for a folksy songfest. The recommended Lansdowne Arms Hotel sponsors live traditional sessions in their **Bold Thady Quill Bar.**

Sleeping in Kenmare

$$$ Lansdowne Arms Hotel is the town's venerable grand hotel, with generous public spaces. This centrally located, 200-year-old historic landmark rents 25 large, crisp rooms (music in pub until late on Fri-Sat, parking, corner of Main and Shelbourne streets, tel. 064/664-1368, www.lansdownearms.com, info@lansdownearms.com).

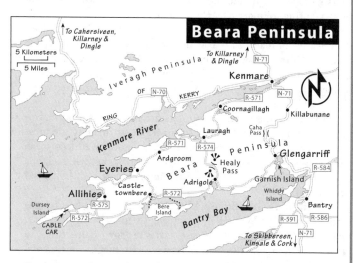

Beara Peninsula

To Cahersiveen, Killarney & Dingle

5 Kilometers
5 Miles

I v e r a g h   P e n i n s u l a

To Killarney & Dingle   N-71

Kenmare

OF   N-70   KERRY

RING

R-571   N-71

Coornagillagh

Killabunane

Kenmare River

Lauragh

Caha Pass

R-571   R-574

P e n i n s u l a

Glengarriff

R-584

Eyeries

Ardgroom

Healy Pass

B e a r a

Adrigole

Garnish Island

Castle-townbere

R-572

Whiddy Island

Bantry

Allihies

R-575

Dursey Island

R-572

Bere Island

Bantry Bay

R-591   R-586

CABLE CAR

To Skibbereen, Kinsale & Cork   N-71

Healy Pass. The road linked the north coast (County Kerry) to the south coast (County Cork) to facilitate food-relief deliveries 175 years ago. The views from the 1,000-foot summit make you marvel at the road-building skills of the famine-era workmen. The barren, rocky landscape makes it easy to spot approaching cars.

The rest of the peninsula is pastoral in the middle and edged with scenic cliffs near the tip. Ireland's only cable car connects the headland with mellow Dursey Island. The car also transports cattle one at a time. The floor is slatted so water can be sloshed over the boards to wash out the dung. Castletownbere (on the south coast) is a fishing port with plenty of pubs for lunch. Allihies and Eyeries (on the north coast) are two of the most colorfully painted towns in Ireland, splattered with pastels and vivid hues.

$$$ Sallyport House, an elegant, quiet house with five rooms filled with antique furniture, has been in Helen Arthur's family for generations. Ask her to point out the foot-worn doorstep that was salvaged from the local workhouse and built into her stone chimney (cash only, no kids, parking, closed Oct-April, 5-minute walk south of town before crossing Our Lady's Bridge, tel. 064/664-2066, www.sallyporthouse.com, port@iol.ie).

$$ Hawthorn House, a fine, modern, freestanding house with a lounge and 10 comfy rooms, is in a quiet residential location just a block from all the pub and restaurant action. Warm and friendly hostess Mary O'Brien's front parlor is an homage to her son Stephen's success on the dominant County Kerry Irish football team (family rooms, parking, Shelbourne Street, tel. 064/664-

1035, www.hawthornhousekenmare.com, hawthorn@eircom.net). Mary's modern, self-catering apartment next door works well for those wanting to linger (weekly rentals).

$$ Willow Lodge, on the main road at the edge of town, feels American-suburban, with friendly hosts and seven comfortable rooms (cash only, family rooms, parking, 100 yards beyond Holy Cross Church, tel. 064/664-2301, www.willowlodgekenmare.com, willowlodgekenmare@yahoo.com, jovial Paul and talkative Gretta Gleeson-O'Byrne).

$ Whispering Pines B&B offers five rooms with sincere, traditional Irish hospitality in a spacious house warmed by the presence of hostesses Mary Fitzgerald and daughter Kathleen (cash only, closed Oct-March, at the edge of town on Bell Heights, tel. 064/664-1194, www.whisperingpineskenmare.com, wpines@eircom.net).

$ Virginia's Guesthouse, ideally located near the best restaurants, is well kept by Neil and Noreen. Its nine rooms are fresh, roomy, and appealing (breakfast extra in downstairs café, 36 Henry Street, mobile 086-306-5291, www.virginias-kenmare.com, virginias.guesthouse@gmail.com).

$ Limestone Lodge stands rock-solid beside a holy well, with five comfy rooms in a quiet location. Friendly hosts Sinead and Siobhan Thoma are experts on Kenmare's famous lace, and Casey, their wiggly Jack Russell terrier, is an expert at being cute (family rooms, parking, tel. 064/664-2231, mobile 087-757-4411, www.limestonelodgekenmare.com, info@limestonelodgekenmare.com).

$ Watersedge B&B is a mile south of town, serenely isolated on a forested hillside and overlooking the estuary. The modern house has four clean, colorful rooms and a kid-pleasing backyard (cash only, parking, tel. 064/664-1707, mobile 087-413-4235, www.watersedgekenmare.com, watersedgekenmare@gmail.com, Noreen and Vincent O'Shea). To get here, drive south over Our Lady's Bridge, bear left, immediately look for the B&B sign, and take the first right onto the road heading uphill. Go 100 yards up the paved road, then—at the end of the white cinder-block wall (on left)—turn right onto the private lane and drive 100 yards to the dead-end. It's worth it.

$ Rockcrest House is secluded down a quiet, leafy lane, with five large rooms and a fine front-porch view (cash only; as you pass the TI heading north out of town, take the first left after crossing the bridge; tel. 064/664-1248, mobile 087-904-3788, www.visit-kenmare.com, info@visit-kenmare.com, Marian and David O'Dwyer). Ask about their two self-catering cottage rentals.

¢ Kenmare Fáilte Hostel (FAWL-chuh) maintains 34 budget beds in a well-kept, centrally located building with more charm than most hostels (private rooms available, closed mid-Oct-April,

Shelbourne Street, tel. 064/664-2333, mobile 087-711-6092, run by Finnegan's Corner bike-rental folks directly across street, www. kenmarehostel.com, info@kenmarehostel.com).

SLEEPING IN LUXURY ON THE RING OF KERRY

$$$$ Parknasilla Hotel is a 19th-century hotel with 82 rooms, lost in 500 plush acres of a subtropical park overlooking the wild Atlantic Ocean. With old-fashioned service and Victorian elegance, this luxe spot is a ritual splurge for Irish families and wedding groups. Activities include boating, archery, tennis, cycling, and walks (highest rates July-Aug, tel. 064/667-5600, www. parknasillahotel.ie, reservationsinfo@parknasillahotel.ie).

Eating in Kenmare

This friendly little town offers plenty of quality dining options. Make a reservation or have dinner early, as many finer places book up on summer evenings. Pub dinners are a good value, but pub kitchens close earlier than restaurants.

LUNCH

$ Jam, with soups, salads, and sandwiches, is an inviting place with delightful seating inside and out. They also make sandwiches or wraps to go for picnics (daily 8:00-17:00, 6 Henry Street, tel. 064/664-1591).

$ Café Mocha is a basic sandwich shop (daily 9:00-17:30, on the town square, tel. 064/664-2133).

$ The Bookshop Vegetarian Café is delightful for a healthy, peaceful lunch or some coffee, cakes, and pastries (daily 10:30-16:30, on Bridge Street just around the corner from the TI, tel. 064/667-9911).

Supermarket: Stock up for a Ring of Kerry picnic at **Murphy's Daybreak** (Mon-Sat 8:00-22:00, Sun 9:00-21:00, Main Street).

DINNER

$$$ The Lime Tree Restaurant occupies the former Lansdowne Estate office, which gave more than 4,000 people free passage to America in the 1840s. These days, it serves delicious, locally caught seafood dishes in a modern yet cozy dining hall (daily 18:30-21:30, closed Nov-March, Shelbourne Street, tel. 064/664-1225, www. limetreerestaurant.com).

$$$$ Packies, a popular bistro with a leafy, low-light interior and cottage ambience, serves traditional cuisine with French influence. Their seafood gets rave reviews (Mon-Sat 17:30-22:00, closed Sun, Henry Street, tel. 064/664-1508, www.packiesrestaurant.ie).

$$$$ **Mulcahy's Restaurant** has a jazz-mellowed, elegant vibe and creatively presented gourmet dishes with Indian, Japanese, and American influences. There's always a good vegetarian entrée available (Thu-Tue 17:00-22:00, closed Wed, Main Street, tel. 064/664-2383, www.mulcahyskenmare.ie).

$$$ **The Horseshoe Restaurant and Bar,** specializing in steak and spareribs, somehow turns rustic farm-tool decor into a romantic candlelit sanctuary (daily 17:00-22:00, 3 Main Street, tel. 064/664-1553, www.thehorseshoekenmare.com).

$$ **P. F. McCarthy's Pub and Restaurant** feels like a sloppy saloon, serving reasonable salad or sandwich lunches and filling dinner fare (daily 12:00-21:00, 14 Main Street, tel. 064/664-1516).

Kenmare Connections

Kenmare has no train station (the nearest is in Killarney, 20 miles away) and only a few bus connections. Most buses transfer in Killarney. Bus info: www.buseireann.ie.

From Kenmare by Bus to: Killarney (3/day, 45 minutes), **Tralee** (3/day, 2 hours), **Dingle** (3/day, 3-4 hours, change in Killarney and Tralee), **Kinsale** (3/day, 4 hours, 2 changes).

To reach **Dublin,** take a bus to Killarney and then transfer to a train from there.

Near Kenmare

These attractions are near Kenmare, at the eastern (inland) end of the Ring of Kerry. If you're approaching the region from Kinsale and Cobh, drive through Killarney and hop on the Ring to visit Muckross House and Muckross Traditional Farms (near the lakes), Killarney National Park, and Kissane Sheep Farm (in the mountains) en route to Kenmare. By taking a bite out of the Ring the day before you sleep in Kenmare, you'll be better situated to drive most of the remainder of the Ring of Kerry loop the next day. Get an early start from Kenmare and you should be able to avoid the worst of the bus traffic on the Ring.

Killarney

Killarney is a household word among American tourists, and it seems to be on every big-bus tour itinerary. Springing from the bus and train station of this thriving regional center are a few colorful streets lined with tourist-friendly shops and restaurants. Killarney's suburbs sprawl with vast hotels that, except for the weather, feel more like Nebraska than Ireland. Killarney's elegant Neo-Gothic church stands tall, as if to say the town existed and mattered long before tourism. But then you realize it dates from 1880...just about when Romantic Age tourism here peaked. For nonshoppers, Killarney's value is its location at the doorstep of the lush Killarney National Park. And for most tour organizers, it's the logical jumping-off point for excursions around the famous Ring of Kerry peninsula.

If you're traveling in the region without a car, you'll have to stop here. The Killarney bus and train stations flank the big, modern Killarney Outlet Centre mall. (In some touristy parts of Ireland, like this one, every other shopping center is called an "outlet"—implying factory-direct values.) If you have a layover between connections, walk five minutes straight out from the front of the mall, and check out Killarney's shop-lined High Street and New Street. The **TI** is a 15-minute walk from the train station (on Beech Street, tel. 064/663-1633).

Killarney Connections
By Bus to: Kenmare (3/day, 45 minutes), **Tralee** (hourly, 40 minutes), **Dingle** (5/day with change in Tralee, 2.5 hours), **Shannon Airport** (4/day with change in Cork, 3 hours), **Dublin** (4-5 per day, 6 hours, change in Limerick). The bus station has a left-luggage desk. For bus schedules: Tel. 01/836-6111, www.buseireann.ie.

By Train to: Tralee (8/day, 35 minutes), **Cork** (every 2 hours, 2 hours, most with change in Mallow), **Waterford** (5/day, 4-6 hours), **Dublin** (every 2 hours, fewer on Sun, 3.5 hours, 1 direct in morning, rest with change in Mallow). For train schedules, call 01/836-6222 or visit www.irishrail.ie.

To Muckross House: There's no bus service. You can hike 30 minutes (get directions from TI), rent a bike, hire a horse buggy, or catch a cab (€12).

To Ring of Kerry: Several companies offer reasonably priced private bus tours from Killarney; ask your B&B host or at the TI.

Sights near Killarney
▲Muckross House and Farms
Perhaps the best stately Victorian home you'll see in the Republic of Ireland, Muckross House (built in 1843) is magnificently set at the edge of Killarney National Park. It's adjacent to Muckross Farms, a fascinating open-air farm museum that shows rural life in the 1930s. Besides the mansion and farms, this regular stop on the tour-bus circuit also includes a fine garden idyllically set on a lake and an information center for the national park. The juxtaposition of the magnificent mansion and the humble farmhouses illustrates in a thought-provoking way the vast gap that once separated rich and poor in Ireland.

Cost and Hours: House or farms—€9.25 each, €15.50 combo-ticket includes both (Heritage Cards not accepted for farms); **house** open daily 9:00-18:00, July-Aug until 19:00, last entry one hour before closing; **farms** open daily June-Aug 10:00-18:00, May and Sept 13:00-18:00, March-April and Oct Sat-Sun only 13:00-18:00, closed Nov-Feb; better-than-average cafeteria; house tel. 064/667-0144, farms tel. 064/663-0804, www.muckross-house.ie, info@muckross-house.ie.

Tours: The only way to see the interior of the house is with the 45-minute guided tour (included with admission, offered frequently throughout the day). Book your tour as soon as you arrive (they can fill up). Then enjoy a walk in the gardens or have lunch before your tour begins.

Getting There: Muckross House is conveniently located on the long ride from Kinsale or Cashel to Dingle or Kenmare. From Killarney, follow signs to Kenmare, where you'll find Muckross House three miles (5 km) south of town. As you approach from Killarney, you'll see a small parking lot two miles before the actual parking lot. This is used by horse-and-buggy bandits to hoodwink tourists into thinking they have to pay to clip-clop to the house. Pass by to find a big, safe, and free parking lot right at the mansion.

Visiting the House and Farms: A visit to **Muckross House** takes you back to the Victorian period—the 19th-century boom time when the sun never set on the British Empire and the Industrial Revolution (born in England) was chugging the world into the modern age. Of course, Ireland was a colony back then, with big-shot English landlords. During the Great Potato Famine of 1845-1849, most English gentry lived very well—profiting off the export of their handsome crops to lands with greater buying power—while a third of Ireland's population starved.

Muckross House feels lived-in (and it was, until 1933). Its fine Victorian furniture is arranged around the fireplace under Waterford crystal chandeliers and lots of antlers. The bedroom prepared for Queen Victoria was on the ground floor—with an additional fire escape installed outside her window, since she was afraid of house fires. The owners of the house spent a couple of years preparing for the royal visit in 1861, eager to gain coveted titles and nearly bankrupting themselves in the process. The queen stayed only three nights and her beloved Prince Albert died soon after the visit. The depressed queen never granted the titles that the grand house's owners had so hoped for.

The house exit takes you through an **information center** for

Killarney National Park, with a relaxing 15-minute video explaining the park's geology, flora, and fauna (free, shown on request).

The **garden** is a hit for those with a green thumb, and a €2 booklet makes the nature trails interesting. A bright, modern cafeteria (with indoor/outdoor seating) faces the garden. The adjacent crafts shop shows weaving and potterymaking in action.

The **Muckross Traditional Farms** features six vintage farmhouses strung along a mile-long road, with an old bus shuttling those who don't want to hike (free, 4/hour).

The farm visits are a great experience—but only if you engage the attendants in conversation. Each farm is staffed by a Kerry local who enjoys talking about farm life in the old days—from the 1920s until electricity arrived in 1955. When they first got electricity, they'd pull on rubber Wellington boots for safety and nervously "switch it on." Poor farmers could afford electricity only with the help of money from relatives in America. They'd have one bulb hanging from the ceiling and, later, one plug for a hot pot. Every table had a Sacred Heart of Jesus shrine above it; the plug went directly below it. No one dreamed of actually heating the house with electricity. Children slept six to a bed, "three up and three down... feet in your face." You'll learn what happened when you had the only radio in the area, and how one flagstone on the mud floor was enough for the fiddler and dancer to set the beat. Probe with your questions...get personal.

▲Killarney National Park

This 25,000-acre park (Ireland's oldest) was established when Muckross Estate was donated to the nation in 1932. Walking trails attract hikers of all levels for views of flora and fauna. Glacially sculpted rock ridges cradle three large lakes teeming with trout and salmon, which lure sport fishermen.

Getting There: It's just south of Killarney town on N-71 toward Kenmare, on the most mountainous stretch of the Ring of Kerry.

Visiting the Park: The park information center is at Muckross House (see earlier). Take a moment to contemplate your lush surroundings. This is what the majority of Ireland looked like 8,000 years ago, before Neolithic man settled and began rudimentary slash-and-burn farming. Later English colonial harvesting of timber exacerbated the deforestation process. Today, Ireland has the smallest proportion of forested land—10.5 percent—of any EU nation. The park's old-growth oak, yew, and alder groves are the best preserved in Ireland, and rhododendrons explode beside the road in late May and June. If you visit early or late in the day, keep an eye out for Ireland's only native herd of red deer.

Enjoy an easy 10-minute stroll along a trail bordered by mossy rocks from the roadside up to **Torc Waterfall** (look for small parking lot beside N-71, 2 miles—3 km—south of Muckross House). Hikers will find more strenuous trails beyond.

Leaving the Park: Enjoy expansive lake views from **Ladies View,** right beside the N-71 road, half a mile (1 km) from the park's southern exit. Just south of the park exit, you'll pass long, thin Looscaunagh Lough (beside the road on the left). A few hundred yards farther, the Black Valley opens up beneath you on the right. This remote valley was the last chunk of Ireland to get electricity—in 1978. The highest bump on the distant ridge across the Black Valley to the west is Carrantuohill, Ireland's tallest mountain at 3,400 feet.

▲▲Kissane Sheep Farm

Call ahead to arrange an hour's visit to this hardworking 2,500-acre Irish farm, perched on a scenic slope above the Black Valley.

The Kissane family has raised sheep here for five generations. John (or his brother Noel) explains the sheep-shearing process and invites you to touch the pile of fresh wool afterward. You can feel the lanolin, which acts as natural waterproofing for the sheep and is extracted from the wool to sell to pharmaceutical firms (synthetic manufacturing has driven the price of wool so low, it's not worth selling otherwise). But the highlight of any visit is the demonstration of sheepherding by the highly alert border collies who have trained here since puppyhood. John (or Evan) commands the dogs from afar using an array of verbal calls, whistles, and hand signals. Sheep shearing takes place from mid-May to early October; spring visitors will also see newborn lambs. These days the farm makes more money from visiting tourists than it does in the traditional sheep-and-wool trade.

Cost and Hours: €8; by appointment only most afternoons April-Oct, closed Sun and Nov-March, check website for demo times, minimum 20 people—call ahead to coordinate your visit with a big bus group, farm gates open 15 minutes prior to demo; on N-71 between Ladies View and Moll's Gap, tel. 064/663-

4791, mobile 087-260-0410, www.kissanesheepfarm.com, noel@ kissanesheepfarm.com.

From Kissane Sheep Farm to Kenmare: Drive south on N-71. Going over Moll's Gap (WCs and Avoca Café beside parking lot), you'll descend into Kenmare. The rugged, bare rock on either side of the road was rounded and smoothed by the grinding action of glaciers over thousands of years. In the distance to the north (on your right) look for the Gap of Dunloe, a perfect example of a U-shaped glacial valley notch.

Ring of Kerry Loop Drive

More than twice the size of the Dingle Peninsula and backed by a muscular tourism budget that promotes every sight as a "must-see," the Ring of Kerry (Iveragh Peninsula) can seem overwhelming. Lassoed by a winding coastal road (the Ring), this mountainous, lake-splattered region comes with breathtaking scenery and the highest peak in Ireland. While a veritable fleet of big, tourist-laden buses circles it each day, they generally depart Killarney around the same time, head the same direction, and stop at the same handful of attractions. But if you avoid those places at rush hour, the Ring feels remarkably unspoiled and dramatically isolated, allowing you to enjoy one of the most rewarding days in Ireland.

You can explore the Ring by car in one satisfying day with the following plan. To see the Ring of Kerry without a car, it's easiest to take a private tour from Kenmare (see "Tours in Kenmare," earlier) or Killarney.

PLANNING YOUR DRIVE

The entire Ring of Kerry loop is 135 miles and takes 4.5 hours without stops. Factoring in time for lunch and sightseeing, the Ring is

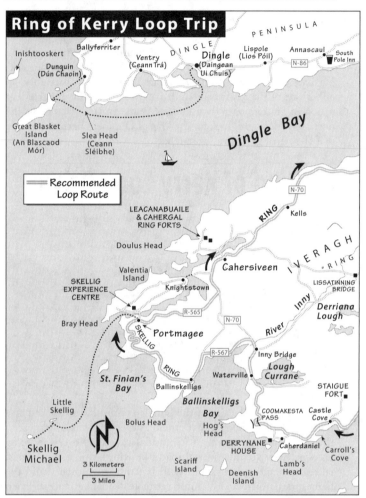

Ring of Kerry Loop Trip

PENINSULA

Inishtooskert

Ballyferriter

DINGLE

Dingle
(Daingean
Uí Chuis)

Ventry
(Ceann Trá)

Lispole
(Lios Póil)

Annascaul

N-86

South
Pole Inn

Dunquin
(Dún Chaoin)

Great Blasket
Island
(An Blascaod
Mór)

Slea Head
(Ceann
Sléibhe)

Dingle Bay

Recommended
Loop Route

LEACANABUAILE
& CAHERGAL
RING FORTS

RING

N-70

Kells

Doulus Head

Valentia
Island

Cahersiveen

IVERAGH

"RING

SKELLIG
EXPERIENCE
CENTRE

Knightstown

LISSATINNING
BRIDGE

Bray Head

R-565

N-70

Inny

Derriana
Lough

SKELLIG

Portmagee

River

R-567

Inny Bridge

Lough
Currane

RING

Waterville

St. Finian's
Bay

Ballinskelligs

STAIGUE
FORT

Little
Skellig

Ballinskelligs
Bay

COOMAKESTA
PASS

Castle
Cove

Bolus Head

Hog's
Head

Skellig
Michael

3 Kilometers

3 Miles

DERRYNANE
HOUSE

Caherdaniel

Carroll's
Cove

Scariff
Island

Lamb's
Head

Deenish
Island

KENMARE & RING OF KERRY

easily an all-day experience. Get an early start (by 8:30 at the latest) and drive clockwise around the Ring to minimize afternoon encounters with the oncoming chain of tour buses on the narrowest stretches (buses are required to drive it counterclockwise). Tank up before leaving, as gas in Kenmare is cheaper than out on the Ring. You'll pass a handy Topaz gas station on your right a half-mile north of Kenmare, just before you turn left onto the N-70 main Ring of Kerry road.

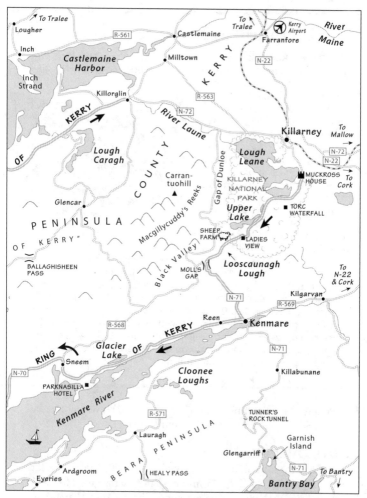

The only downside of going against the bus traffic is that, on the narrow parts of the Ring road, buses always have the right-of-way. If there's a bottleneck, you'll need to back up to the nearest wide spot in the road to let the bus through. But the road is constantly being improved, and few bottlenecks remain; the main one is the 30-foot long one-lane rock tunnel inside Killarney National Park between Muckross House and the Kissane Sheep Farm. There are also lots of scenic-view pullouts. With an early start, you can generally avoid these hassles.

Equip yourself with a good map before driving the Ring of Kerry loop, such as the *Complete Road Atlas of Ireland* by Ordnance Survey (sold in most TIs and bookstores in Ireland) or the *Fir Tree Aerial* series, with a map that covers both the Iveragh (Ring of

The Ring Forts of Kerry

The Ring of Kerry comes with three awe-inspiring prehistoric ring forts—among the largest and best preserved in all of Ireland. Stai-gue Fort (near the beginning of my recommended Ring route) is most impressive but in a desolate setting. The two others—Cahergal and Lea-canabuaile, 200 yards apart just north of Cahersiveen (closer to the end of the Ring, after Valentia Island)—are eas-ier to visit and plenty evoca-tive. Each ring fort is about a 2.5-mile (4-km) side trip off

the main drag. If you're trying to beat the tour-bus convoy, Stai-gue Fort is problematic because it eats up morning time before the buses have passed you. The Cahersiveen ring forts are your last stop in the Ring of Kerry, once bus traffic is of no concern.

All of these ring forts are roughly the same age and have the similar basic features. The circular dry-stone walls were built sometime between 500 BC and AD 300 without the aid of mortar or cement. About 80 feet across, with walls 12 feet thick at the base and up to 25 feet high, these brutish structures would have taken 100 men six months to complete. Expert opinion is divided on the reason they were built, but most believe that the people

Kerry) and Dingle peninsulas, giving you a bird's-eye feel for the terrain (sold in most bookstores in County Kerry).

ROUTE OVERVIEW

Leaving Kenmare by 8:30, head clockwise on N-70. Allow time for stops at Staigue Ring Fort (45 minutes) and Derrynane House (1 hour), and get to Waterville before noon. Shortly after Waterville, leave the main N-70 Ring for the Skellig Ring (consisting of the R-567, R-566, and R-565—roads that are too narrow for big buses). Have lunch out on the Skellig Ring, either as a picnic on the lovely beach at St. Finian's Bay, or in Portmagee. By the time you rejoin the main N-70 route, the big buses will have slunk by. On the last half of the route, there are two more hour-long stops: the Skellig Experience Centre (near Portmagee) and two additional big ring forts (near Cahersiveen).

For me, the two most photogenic coastal stretches are out near the tip of the peninsula: between Caherdaniel and Waterville (on the Ring of Kerry) and from Ballinskelligs to Portmagee (on the who built them would have retreated here at times of clan conflict. Civilization was morphing from nomadic hunter-gatherers to settled farmers, so herders used these forts to gather their valuable cattle inside and protect them from ancient rustlers. Other experts see the round design as a kind of amphitheater, where local clan chieftains would have gathered for important meetings or rituals. However, the ditch surrounding the outer walls of Staigue Fort suggests a defensive, rather than ceremonial, function. Without written records, we can only imagine the part these magnificent piles of finely stacked stones played in ancient dramas.

Because this region had copper mines, southwest Ireland has a wealth of prehistoric sights. The Bronze Age wouldn't have been the Bronze Age without copper, which was melted together with tin to make bronze for better weapons and tools (2000 to 500 BC). The many ring forts and stone circles reflect the affluence that the abundance of copper brought to the region.

Skellig Ring). The flat, inland, northeastern section of the Ring—from Killorglin to Killarney on N-72—is skippable.

Here's a kilometer by kilometer guide to my recommended clockwise route. Several of these stops are listed later, under "Sights on the Ring of Kerry."

0 km: Leave Kenmare.

17.6 km: On the right is Glacier Lake, with a long, smooth limestone "banister" carved by a glacier 10,000 years ago.

22.8 km: The recommended Parknasilla Hotel—a posh 19th-century hotel—is a great stop for tea and scones.

26 km: Visit the town of Sneem.

40.4 km: Turn off for the Staigue Ring Fort.

41.5 km: On the left, enjoy great views across the bay of the Beara Peninsula beyond a ruined hospital with IRA ties. It was funded in about 1910 by a local Englishwoman sympathetic to the Irish Republican cause. No one wants to touch these ruins today, out of fear of "kicking up a beehive."

43.5 km: Carroll's Cove has a fine beach with some of the warmest water in Ireland, grand views of Kenmare Bay, a local trailer park, and "Ireland's only beachside bar."

46.4 km: Take the turnoff for Derrynane House (home of Daniel O'Connell).

50.4 km: Enjoy brilliant views for the next two kilometers to Coomakesta Pass.

52.4 km: The Coomakesta Pass lookout point (700-foot altitude) offers grand vistas in both directions.

54.5 km: On a clear day, watch for fine views of the distant Skellig Islands with their pointy summits.

59.6 km: In the town of Waterville, you'll see a sculpture of Charlie Chaplin standing on the waterfront on the left. Waterville is also home to the Butler Arms Hotel—a fine stop for tea and scones in its Charlie Chaplin room (with lots of photos of the silent-film icon and his young wife frolicking as they lived well in Ireland).

65 km: After rejoining the main road, cross the small bridge that's locally famous for salmon fly-fishing. Take the first left (R-567) for the Skellig Ring loop (follow brown *Skellig Ring* signs through Ballinskelligs, and then scenically to Portmagee). At this point, you've left the big-bus route.

75 km: St. Finian's Bay lies about halfway around, with a pleasant little picnic-friendly beach that's recently been discovered by surfers (no WCs). Just before the bay is the small, modern Skelligs Chocolate Factory, with free, tasty samples as well as a café for coffee and muffins (Mon-Fri 10:00-17:00—but longer hours in summer, Sat-Sun from 11:00, especially fun for kids, tel. 066/947-9119, www.skelligschocolate.com).

80 km: Signs for the Kerry Cliffs lure photographers and walkers to turn left into the driveway that advertises "Best View in County Kerry." Park and pay the €4 fee at the hut. Then walk 10 minutes straight up the gravel road to get to a dramatic coastal cliff that opens up onto expansive coastal views. The beehive huts nearby are replicas but true to the originals.

83 km: You reach Portmagee, a small port town and jumping-off point for boats to the Skellig Islands.

83.2 km: Cross the bridge to the Skellig Experience Centre. You're now on Valentia Island, its name hinting at medieval trading connections with nearby Spain—which lies due south. Dinosaur hunters may want to detour and follow the signs to the modest but ancient tetrapod tracks, frozen in stone, on the north side of the island (ask for directions at the visitors center).

91.2 km: At the church in Knightstown, turn left for the Knightstown Heritage Museum.

93 km: Return to the main road and go through Knightstown to the tiny ferry (€7/car, runs constantly 8:00-21:00, 1 km trip).

95 km: Leaving the ferry, rejoin N-70 (the main Ring of Kerry route), turning left for the town of Cahersiveen. From here, you can detour a few kilometers to two impressive stone ring forts, Cahergal and Leacanabuaile.

100 km: Return to N-70 at Cahersiveen and follow signs for *Glenbeigh* and *Killorglin*. Enjoy views of the Dingle Peninsula across Dingle Bay to your left. Eagle eyes can spot stumpy Eask Tower and Inch Beach.

The rest of the loop is less scenic. At Killorglin, you've seen the best of it. From here, go either to Dingle (left) or to Kenmare/Killarney/Kinsale (right).

SIGHTS ON THE RING OF KERRY
From Kenmare to Portmagee
Sneem

Although it's inundated by tour buses daily from 14:00 to 16:00, the town of Sneem is peaceful and laid-back the rest of the day. This humble town has two entertaining squares. There's an Irish joke: "Since we're in Kerry, the square on the east side is called South Square and the one on the west is called North Square." On the first (South) square, you'll see a statue of Steve "Crusher" Casey, the local boy who reigned as world-champion heavyweight wrestler (1938-1947). A sweet little peat-toned rapid gurgles under the one-lane bridge connecting the two Sneem squares. The North Square features a memorial to former French president Charles de Gaulle's visit (Irish on his mother's side, de Gaulle came here for two weeks of R&R after his final retirement from office in 1969). Locals call it "da gallstone."

▲Staigue Fort

This impressive ring fort is worth a stop on your way around the Ring (always open, drop €1 in the little gray donation box beside the gate). While viewing the imposing pile of stone, read "The Ring Forts of Kerry" sidebar, earlier.

Getting There: The fort is 2.5 miles (4 km) off the main N-70 road up a narrow rural access lane (look for signs just after the hamlet of Castle Cove). Honk on blind corners to warn oncoming traffic as you drive up the hedge-lined lane.

▲Derrynane House

This is the home of Daniel O'Connell, Ireland's most influential 19th-century politician, whose tireless nonviolent agitation gained equality for Catholics 185 years ago. The coastal lands of the O'Connell estate that surround Derrynane (rhymes with Maryann) House are now a national historic park. A visit here is a window into the life of a man who not only liberated Ireland from the last oppressive anti-Catholic penal laws, but also first developed

The Ring of Kerry vs. the Dingle Peninsula

If I had to choose one spot to enjoy the small-town charm of traditional Ireland, it would be Dingle and its history-laden scenic peninsula. But the Ring of Kerry—a much bigger, more famous, and more touristed peninsula just to its south—is also great to visit. If you go to Ireland and don't see the famous Ring of Kerry, your uncle Pat will never forgive you. Here's a comparison to help with your itinerary planning.

Both peninsulas come with a scenic loop drive. Dingle's Slea Head Loop is 30 miles. The Ring of Kerry is 135 miles. Both loops come with lots of mega-

lithic wonder. Dingle's prehistory is more intimate, with numerous little evocative stony structures. The Ring of Kerry's prehistory shows itself in three massive ring forts—far bigger than anything on Dingle.

Dingle town is the perfect little Irish burg—alive with traditional music pubs, an active fishing harbor, and the sturdy cultural atmosphere of an Irish-speaking Gaeltacht region. You can easily spend three fun nights here. In comparison, Kenmare (the best base for the Ring of Kerry loop) is pleasant but forgettable. Those spending a night on the west end of the Ring of Kerry find a rustic atmosphere in Portmagee (the base for a cruise to magical Skellig Michael).

Near Dingle, the heather-and-moss-covered Great Blasket Island and the excellent Great Blasket Centre offer insights into the storytelling traditions and simple lives of hardy fisherfolk who—until 60 years ago—lived just off the tip of the Dingle Peninsula. Skellig Michael is a brutally rugged and remote chunk of rock in the Atlantic off the tip of the Ring of Kerry, with evocative medieval stone ruins of its long-gone hermit-monks. It's a world-class sight, but the Skellig Experience Centre near Portmagee on the mainland is less impressive than Dingle's Great Blasket Centre.

Muckross House, with its fascinating open-air farmhouse museum and beautiful lake views of Killarney National Park, is on the eastern side of the Ring of Kerry. It's also an efficient and natural stop for those driving between Kinsale and Dingle—so you can see it regardless of which scenic peninsula drive you take.

Both regions are beyond the reach of the Irish train system and require a car or spotty bus service to access. Both offer memorable scenery, great restaurants, warm B&B hospitality, and similar prices. The bottom line: With limited time, choose Dingle. If you have a day or two to spare, the Ring of Kerry is also a delight.

the idea of a grassroots movement—organizing on a massive scale to achieve political ends without bloodshed (see sidebar).

Cost and Hours: €5; daily 10:30-18:00; mid-March-April and Oct Wed-Sun 10:30-17:00, closed Mon-Tue; weekends only in Nov, closed Dec-mid-March; last entry 45 minutes before closing, tel. 066/947-5113.

Getting There: Just outside the town of Derrynane, pick up a handy free map of the area from the little private TI inside the brown Wave Crest market (TI open daily 9:00-18:00, closed in off-season, tel. 066/947-5188; market is a great place to buy picnic food). One mile after the market, take a left and follow the signs into Derrynane National Historic Park.

Visiting the House: The house has a quirky floor plan. Ask about the next scheduled 20-minute audiovisual show, which fleshes out the highlights of O'Connell's turbulent life and makes the contents of the house more interesting. Self-guided info sheets are available in the main rooms.

Downstairs in the study, look for the glass case containing the pistols used in O'Connell's famous duel. Beside them are his black gloves, one of which he always wore on his right hand when he went to Mass (out of remorse for the part it played in taking a man's life). The dining room is lined with family portraits. Upstairs in the drawing room, you'll find his ornately carved chair with tiny harp strings and wolfhound collars made of gold. And in another upstairs room is his deathbed, brought back from Genoa.

The coach house (out back) shows off the enormous grand chariot that carried O'Connell through throngs of joyous Dubliners after his release from prison in 1844. In a glass case opposite the chariot is a copy of O'Connell's celebrated speech imploring the Irish not to riot when he was arrested. He added the small chapel wing to the house in gratitude to God for his prison release.

Portmagee

Just a short row of snoozy buildings lining the bay, Portmagee is the best harbor for boat excursions out to the Skellig Islands (see "Getting There" on page 267). It's a quiet village with a handful of B&Bs, two pubs, a bakery, a market, and no ATMs—the closest ATM is 6 miles (10 km) east in Cahersiveen. On the rough harborfront, a slate memorial to sailors from here who were lost at sea reads, "In the nets of God may we be gathered."

A 100-yard-long bridge connects Portmagee to gentle Valentia Island, where you'll find the Skellig Experience Centre (on the left at the Valentia end of the bridge). A public parking lot is at the Portmagee end of the bridge, with WCs. The first permanent transatlantic cable (for telegraph communication) was laid from Valentia Island in 1866.

Daniel O'Connell (1775-1847)

Born in Cahersiveen and elected from Ennis as the first Catholic member of the British Parliament,
O'Connell was the hero of Catholic emancipation in Ireland. Educated in France at a
time when punitive anti-Catholic laws limited schooling for Irish Catholics at home,
he witnessed the carnage of the French
Revolution. Upon his return to Ireland, he
saw more bloodshed during the futile Rebellion of 1798.

Abhorring all this violence, O'Connell
dedicated himself to peacefully gaining
equal rights for Catholics in an Ireland
dominated by a wealthy Protestant minority. He formed the Catholic Association
with a one-penny-per-month membership
fee and quickly gained a huge following
(especially among the poor) with his per-
suasive speaking skills. Although Catholics weren't allowed to
hold office, he ran for election to Parliament anyway and won
a seat in 1828. His unwillingness to take the anti-Catholic Oath
of Supremacy initially kept him out of Westminster, but the
moral force of his victory caused the government to concede
Catholic emancipation the following year.

Known as "the Liberator," O'Connell began working toward his next goal—repealing the Act of Union with Britain.
When his massive "monster meeting" rallies attracted thousands, his popularity spooked the British authorities, who
threw him in jail on trumped-up charges of seditious conspir-
acy in 1844. When the Great Potato Famine hit in 1845, some
Irish protesters advocated for more violent action against the
British, which O'Connell had long opposed. He died two years
later in Genoa on his way to Rome, but his ideals lived on: His
Catholic Association was the model of grassroots organization for the Irish, both in their homeland and in America.

Sleeping in Portmagee: The first two listings are in town. The
last listing is south of Portmagee, on St. Finian's Bay. Tip: Guests
staying at any of these options have an inside track on securing
high-demand boat tickets to Skellig Michael when other sources
are booked up.

$$$ Moorings Guesthouse feels like a small hotel, with 17
rooms, a pub and a good restaurant downstairs, and the most con-
venient location in town, 50 yards from the end of the pier (fam-
ily rooms, tel. 066/947-7108, www.moorings.ie, moorings@iol.ie,
Gerard and Patricia Kennedy).

$$ Portmagee Heights B&B is a modern, solid slate home

up above town, renting eight fine rooms (cash only, family rooms, on the road into town, tel. 066/947-7251, www.portmageeheights. com, portmageeheights@gmail.com, Monica Hussey).

$ Beach Cove Lodge offers three comfortable, fresh, and lovingly decorated rooms (but no breakfasts) in splendid isolation four miles south of Portmagee, over lofty Coomanaspic ridge, beside the pretty beach at St. Finian's Bay (100 yards from the Skelligs Chocolate Factory). Bridie O'Connor's adjacent cottage out back has two double rooms, making it ideal for families (tel. 066/947-9301, mobile 087-139-0224, www.stayatbeachcove.com, beachcove@eircom.net). Bridie's husband, Jack, was the head coach of the Kerry football team until he retired in 2012...making him a very important person in this part of Ireland (Kerry has won more football titles than any other Irish county, three of them with Jack at the helm).

Eating in Portmagee: These options all line the waterfront (between the pier and the bridge to Valentia Island). **$$$ The Moorings** is a nice restaurant with great seafood caught literally just outside its front door (Tue-Sun 18:00-22:00, closed Mon and in winter, reservations smart, tel. 066/947-7108, www.moorings. ie). The **$$ Bridge Bar,** next door, does traditional pub grub. Call ahead to check on their traditional music and dance schedule (daily 12:00-22:00, live music Fri and Sun nights, tel. 066/947-7108). The **$$ Fisherman's Bar** is less flashy, with more locals and cheaper prices (daily 10:00-21:00, tel. 066/947-7103).

For picnic supplies, **O'Connell's Market** is the only grocery (Mon-Sat 9:00-19:00, Sun 9:30-12:30). **Smugglers Cafe** offers lunch options of fresh seafood dishes and salads. They can also make great sandwiches to take on Skellig boat excursions (daily 9:30-17:00, tel. 066/947-7250).

Valentia Island
These two sights are on Valentia Island, across the bridge from Portmagee.

Skellig Experience Centre
Whether or not you're actually sailing to Skellig Michael (described later), this little center (with basic exhibits and a fine 15-minute film) explains it well—both the story of the monks and the natural environment.

Cost and Hours: €5; daily 10:00-18:00, July-Aug until 19:00, off-season until 17:00, closed Dec-Feb; last entry one hour before closing, call ahead outside of peak season as hours may vary, on Valentia Island beside bridge linking it to Portmagee, tel. 066/947-6306, www.skelligexperience.com.

Boat Trips: The Skellig Experience Centre arranges two-hour

Evolution in Ireland: Tetrapods to Marconi

Evolution, literacy, communication—Ireland has played a starring role in all three.

Many Irish paleontologists believe that the fossilized tetrapod tracks preserved on Valentia Island are the oldest in Europe. It was here that some of the first fish slithered out of the water on four stubby legs 385 million years ago, onto what would become the Isle of Saints and Scholars. Over time, those tetrapods evolved into the ancestors of today's amphibians, reptiles, birds, mammals...and humans, with the desire to record their thoughts and history, and communicate with others across the miles.

Irish scribes—living in remote outposts like the Skellig Islands, just off this coast—kept literate life alive in Europe through the darkest depths of the so-called Dark Ages. In fact, in about the year 800, Charlemagne imported monks from this part of Ireland to be his scribes.

Just more than a thousand years later, in the mid-19th century, Paul Julius Reuter—who provided a financial news service in Europe—knew his pigeons couldn't fly across the Atlantic. So he relied on ships coming from America to drop a news capsule overboard as they rounded this southwest corner of Ireland. His boys would wait in their little boats with nets to "get the scoop." They say Europe learned of Lincoln's assassination (1865) from a capsule tossed out of a boat here.

The first permanent telegraph cables were laid across the Atlantic from here to Newfoundland, giving the two hemispheres instantaneous electronic communication. Queen Victoria was the first to send a message—greeting American president James Buchanan in 1858. The cable broke more than once, but it was finally permanently secured in 1866. Radio inventor Guglielmo Marconi, who was half-Irish, achieved the first wireless transatlantic communication from this corner of Ireland to America in 1901.

Today, driving under the 21st-century mobile-phone and satellite tower that crowns a hilltop above Valentia Island, while gazing out at the Skellig Islands, a traveler has to marvel at humanity's progress—and the part this remote corner of Ireland played in it.

boat trips, circling both Skellig Michael and Little Skellig (without actually bringing people ashore)—ideal for those who want a close look without the stair climb and vertigo that go with a visit to the island (€40, three sailings daily at 10:30, 13:30, and 15:00, weather permitting, depart from Valentia Island pier 50 yards below the Skellig Experience Centre).

Valentia Heritage Museum

The humble Knightstown schoolhouse, built in 1861, houses an equally humble but interesting museum highlighting the quirky things of historic interest on Valentia Island. You'll see a 19th-century schoolroom and learn about tetrapods (those first fish to climb onto land—which locals claim happened here). You'll also follow the long story of the expensive, frustrating, and heroic battle to lay telegraph cable across the Atlantic, which—after some false starts—finally succeeded in 1866, when the largest ship in the world connected the tiny island of Valentia with Newfoundland. This project was the initiative of the Atlantic Telegraph Company, which later became Western Union. These stories and more are told with intimate black-and-white photos and typewritten pages.

Cost and Hours: €3.50, daily 10:30-17:30, closed Oct-April, tel. 066/947-6985, www.valentiaisland.ie.

Getting There: Coming from Portmagee, take a hairpin left as you enter the village (at the lighthouse sign) and find it on your right past the church.

Nearby: If you're interested in those tetrapods, the actual "first footprints" are a 15-minute drive from the museum, on a rugged bit of rocky shoreline, a 10-minute hike below a parking lot (free, always viewable, get details locally).

Rest of the Ring

Cahergal and Leacanabuaile Ring Forts

Crowning bluffs in farm country, 2.5 miles (4 km) off the main road at Cahersiveen, these two windy and desolate forts are each different and worth a look. Just beyond the Cahersiveen town church at the tourist office, turn left, cross the narrow bridge, turn left again, and follow signs to the ancient forts—you'll see the huge stone structures in the distance. You'll hike 10 minutes from the tiny parking lot (free, always open, no museum). Both forts are roughly 100 yards off the road (uphill on the right) and are 200 yards from each other. For details, see "The Ring Forts of Kerry" sidebar, earlier.

KENMARE & RING OF KERRY

Skellig Michael

A trip to this jagged, isolated pyramid—the Holy Grail of Irish monastic island settlements—rates as a truly memorable ▲▲▲ experience. After visiting Skellig Michael a hundred years ago, Nobel Prize-winning Irish playwright George Bernard Shaw called it "the most fantastic and impossible rock in the world."

Rising seven miles offshore, the Skelligs (Irish for "splinter") are two gigantic slate-and-sandstone rocks crouched aggressively on the ocean horizon. The larger of the two, Skellig Michael, is more than 700 feet tall and a mile around, with a tiny cluster of abandoned beehive huts clinging near its summit like stubborn barnacles. The smaller island, Little Skellig, is home to a huge colony of gannet birds (like large, graceful seagulls with six-foot wingspans), protected by law from visitors setting foot onshore.

Skellig Michael (dedicated to the archangel) was first inhabited by sixth-century Christian monks. Inspired by earlier hermit-monks in the Egyptian desert, they sought the purity of isolation to get closer to God. Neither Viking raids nor winter storms could dislodge them, as they patiently built a half-dozen small, stone, igloo-like dwellings and a couple of tiny oratories. Their remote cliff-terrace perch is still connected to the sea 600 feet below by an amazing series of rock stairs. Viking Olav Trygvasson, who later became king of Norway and introduced Christianity to his country, was baptized here in 993.

Chiseling the most rudimentary life from solid rock, the monks lived a harsh, lonely, disciplined existence here, their colony surviving for more than 500 years. They collected rainwater in cisterns and lived off fish and birds. To supplement their meager existence, they traded bird eggs and feathers with passing boats for cereals, candles, and animal hides (used for clothing and for copying scripture). They finally moved their holy community ashore to Ballinskelligs in the early 1100s. But Christian pilgrims continued to visit Skellig Michael for centuries as penance...edging out onto a ledge to kiss a stone cross that has since toppled into the ocean.

In 2014, the ruggedly exotic Skellig Michael was used as a filming location for the final scenes of *Star Wars: The Force Awakens*. To keep the filming top-secret, the Irish Navy was called in to enforce a two-mile exclusionary zone around the island. But controversy soon arose: Environmental groups voiced concerns about the impact on the island's fragile ecosystem, especially native seabirds who are sensitive to disturbances in the Force and might be spooked into seeking other nesting grounds. Disney scrapped plans for filming the next installment, *Star Wars VIII*, on the island. Instead it built its own version of the location at Sybil Head on the Dingle Peninsula. Expect a constant stream of *Star Wars* tourists at both filming locations. *Go mbeidh an Fórsa leat!* (May the Force be with you!)

GETTING THERE

Boat trips sail to Skellig Michael daily from mid-May through September, but the schedule is heavily dependent on weather conditions. If the seas are too choppy, the boats cannot safely drop people at the concrete island pier (it's a bit like jumping off a trampoline onto an ice rink). Experienced boat captains say they are able to bring visitors ashore roughly five days out of seven in an average summer week.

In addition to weather constraints, the number of daily visitors to the island is limited due to its fragile ecosystem as a puffin breeding ground. Just 15 boats carrying 12 passengers each are licensed to land on the island once a day. Additional boats circle the island without landing, with multiple departure times each day.

Booking a Trip: Tickets sell out months in advance. The best first step is to ask the host at your accommodations as soon as you know your travel dates; many know of a limited number of sailing slots through their local connections. You can also email skelligadventure@gmail.com. Otherwise, you can try contacting boat captains individually: **Paul Devane** (mobile 087-617-8114; www.skelligmichaelcruises.com), **Patrick Murphy** (mobile 087-234-2168), or **Brendan Casey** (tel. 066/947-2437, mobile 087-450-1211). For a list of everyone that runs trips to the island, see www.skelligexperience.com/other-sea-tours.

Boats that land on the island cost €125, and generally depart Portmagee between 9:30 and 10:30 (depending on tides), sail for an hour, leave you on the island, and get you back into Portmagee between 14:30 and 16:30 (with time to drive on to Dingle). Boat trips that circle the island without landing cost €40.

Planning Tips: Your best bet is to reserve a room near Portmagee or St. Finian's Bay. It's possible to sleep in Kenmare and get up early to drive two hours straight to Portmagee—but you'll be frustrated by not having time to enjoy the Ring's attractions along the way. Contact the boat operator on the morning of departure to get the final word about whether the weather is favorable for sailing.

Bring your camera, lunch (easy to buy at the recommended Smugglers Cafe in Portmagee), water, sunscreen, rain gear, hiking shoes, and your sense of wonder.

VISITING SKELLIG MICHAEL

Since you'll have only about 2.5 hours to explore the island, begin by climbing the seemingly unending series of stone stairs to the monastic ruins (600 vertical feet of uneven steps with no handrails). Save most of your photographing for the way down. Those who linger too long below risk missing the enlightening 20-minute free talk among the beehive huts, given by guides who camp on the island from May through September. Afterward, poke your head into some of the huts and try to imagine the dark, damp, and devoted life of a monk here more than 1,000 years ago. After rambling through the ruins, you can give in to the puffin-spotting photo frenzy as you wander back down the stairs.

The two lighthouses on the far side of the island are now automated, and access to them has been blocked off. There are

no WCs or modern shelters of any kind on Skellig Michael.

If you visit between May and early August, you'll be surrounded by fearless rainbow-beaked puffins, which nest here in underground burrows. Their bizarre swallowed cooing sounds like a distant chainsaw. These portly little birds live off fish, and divers have reported seeing them 20 feet underwater in pursuit of their prey.

Your return boat journey usually includes a pass near Little Skellig, which looms like an iceberg with a white coat of guano—courtesy of the 20,000 gannets that circle overhead like feathered confetti. These large birds suddenly morph into sleek darts when pursuing a fish, piercing the water from more than 100 feet above. You're also likely to get a glimpse of gray seals lazing on rocks near the water's edge.

DINGLE PENINSULA

Dingle Town • Slea Head Loop Drive • Blasket Islands • Tralee

The Dingle Peninsula, the westernmost tip of Ireland (and Europe, for that matter), offers just the right mix of far-and-away beauty, isolated walks and bike rides, and ancient archaeological wonders—all within convenient reach of its main town. Dingle town is just large enough to have all the necessary tourist services and the steady nocturnal beat of Ireland's best traditional music scene.

For almost 40 years, my Irish dreams have been set here on this sparse but lush peninsula, where locals are fond of saying, "The next parish over is Boston." There's a feeling of closeness to the land in Dingle. When I asked a local if he was born here, he thought for a second and said, "No, it was about six miles down the road." I asked his friend if he'd lived here all his life. He said, "Not yet."

Dingle feels so traditionally Irish because it's part of the Gaeltacht, a region where the government subsidizes the survival of the Irish language and culture. While English is always there, the signs, chitchat, and songs come in Irish Gaelic. Children carry Gaelic footballs to class, and the local preschool brags "ALL Gaelic." And although Dingle is crowded in summer, it still feels like the fish and the farm really matter. A half-dozen fishing boats sail from here, tractors leave tracks down the main drag, and a faint whiff of peat fills the nighttime streets.

But Dingle is a destination in transition—more travelers discover it each year, and big-bus crowds crush in at midday after touring the peninsula. Small cruise ships eye the harbor from a distance with the hope of docking here a few years down the road (if infrastructure and dredging plans go through). And weekend stag and hen (bachelor and bachelorette) parties are starting to appear,

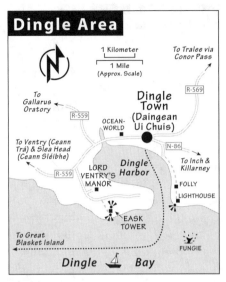

Dingle Area

1 Kilometer

1 Mile
(Approx. Scale)

To Tralee via
Conor Pass

R-569

To
Gallarus
Oratory

R-559

**Dingle
Town
(Daingean
Ui Chuis)**

OCEAN-
WORLD

N-86

To Ventry (Ceann
Trá) & Slea Head
(Ceann Sléibhe)

R-559

LORD
VENTRY'S
MANOR

*Dingle
Harbor*

To Inch &
Killarney

FOLLY

LIGHTHOUSE

EASK
TOWER

To Great
Blasket Island

FUNGIE

Dingle   Bay

attracted by Dingle's growing reputation as "a drinking town with a fishing problem." The filming of a recent *Star Wars* movie at the tip of the peninsula has once again put this Irish paradise on the big screen (it was previously featured in *Ryan's Daughter* and *Far and Away*).

Despite growing more touristy, Dingle's charms are resilient. As the older generation slows down and fades away, a new generation of entrepreneurs—either local kids or "blow ins" from out of town—is giving Dingle fresh vitality. While residents hold a "goodbye to Dingle" party with the start of each tourist season in the spring and a "no more tourists" party at the end of the season, their welcome is warm and genuine.

PLANNING YOUR TIME

For the shortest visit, give **Dingle** two nights and a day. By car, it takes five hours to get here from Dublin, four hours from Galway, and three hours from Cork. By spending two nights, you'll feel more like a local on your second evening in the pubs. You'll need the better part of a day to explore the 30-mile loop from Dingle around the peninsula and back by bike or car (following my **"Slea Head Loop Drive"** on page 304). To do any serious walking or relaxing, you'll need three nights and two days. It's not uncommon to find Americans slowing way, way down in Dingle.

In good weather, **Great Blasket Island** (off the western tip of the Dingle Peninsula, with the best ferry options from Dingle town) is a rewarding and easy-to-navigate hiking option (see page 315).

Dingle Peninsula

The Seven Hogs

Rough Point

Atlantic Ocean

3 Kilometers

3 Miles

Brandon Head

Brandon Bay

Mt. Brandon

Castlegregory

See Slea Head Loop Drive map

Tiduff

Cloghane • Ballyduff

Three Sisters

GALLARUS ORATORY

CONOR PASS

Sybil Head

Ballyferriter (Baile an Fheirtearaigh)

DINGLE PENINSULA (AN DAINGEAN)

Clogher Head

See Dingle Area map

Dingle (Daingean Ui Chuis)

Lispole (Lios Póil)

Annascaul

South Pole Inn

N-86

Ventry (Ceann Trá)

Inishtooskert

Dunquin (Dún Chaoin)

PUICIN WEDGE TOMB

MINARD CASTLE

Slea Head (Ceann Sléibhe)

Dingle Bay

Great Blasket Island (An Blascaod Mór)

Dingle's activity level ramps up in late April, peaks through July and August, and slows by late September. It's smart to book your lodging as soon as you know what dates you'll be in town. I've generally listed hours for the tourist season (April-Sept). Hours may be longer in July and August, and many places cut back or shut down entirely from October to March.

Dingle Town

Of the peninsula's 10,000 residents, about 2,000 live in Dingle town (Daingean Ui Chuis). Its few streets, lined with ramshackle but gaily painted shops and pubs, run up from a rain-stung harbor always sheltering fishing boats and leisure sailboats. Traditionally, the buildings were drab gray or whitewashed, but Ireland's "Tidy Town" competition a few decades back prompted everyone to paint their buildings in playful pastels.

The courthouse (1832) is open one day per month. The judge does his best to wrap up business within a few hours. During the day, you'll see teenagers—already working on ruddy, beer-glow cheeks—roll kegs up the streets and into the pubs in preparation

for another night of music and *craic* (fun conversation and atmosphere). It's a friendly town.

Orientation to Dingle

Dingle—extremely comfortable on foot—hangs on a medieval grid of streets between the harbor (where the bus to Tralee, with the nearest train station, stops) and Main Street (three blocks inland). Nothing in town is more than a 10-minute walk away. Street numbers are rarely used. Everyone knows each other, and people on the street are fine sources of information. Locals love their soda bread, and they understand that tourism provides the butter.

TOURIST INFORMATION

The TI has a great town map (free) and staff who know the town, but less about the rest of the peninsula (Mon-Sat 9:00-13:00 & 13:30-17:00, generally closed Sun, shorter hours off-season, on Strand Street by the water, tel. 066/915-1188). For advice on outdoor activities, drop by the Mountain Man shop on Strand Street (see "Helpful Hints," later), or talk to your B&B host.

ARRIVAL IN DINGLE

By Bus: Dingle has no bus station and only one bus stop, on the waterfront behind the SuperValu supermarket (look for the bus shelter with the roof made from an overturned traditional black-tarred boat).

By Car: Drivers choose two roads into town: the easy southern route on N-86 or the much more dramatic, scenic, and treacherous Conor Pass on the R-560 leading into the R-569 (see "Route Tips for Drivers" at the end of this chapter). It's 30 miles (48 km) from Tralee either way. If you're not staying overnight, use the waterfront parking lot extending west from the TI, or the lot four blocks inland on Spa Road (€1/hour, pay-and-display, daily 8:00-18:00).

By Plane: Kerry Airport, halfway between Tralee and Killarney, is a one-hour drive from Dingle. Short puddle-jumper flights connect the region to Dublin and make a visit to Dingle possible even for travelers with limited time. For more on Kerry Airport, see the end of this chapter.

HELPFUL HINTS

Before You Go: Check the local website for a list of festivals and events (www.dingle-peninsula.ie).

Crowds: Crowds trample Dingle's charm throughout July and August. The craziest times are during the Dingle Races (early Aug), Dingle Regatta (early to mid-Aug), Blessing of the Boats (end of Aug or beginning of Sept), and Dingle Food Festival (first weekend in October). Easter week brings Irish families. The first Mondays in May, June, and August are Bank Holidays—three-day weekends when Dingle fills up. The town's metabolism (prices, schedules, activities) rises and falls with the tourist crowds, so late October through March is sleepy, windy, and chilly.

Farmers Market: From mid-April to mid-October on Fridays from 9:00 to 15:00, farmers sell fresh produce, homemade marmalade, and homespun crafts in a small parking lot across the street from SuperValu grocery store.

Money: Expect to use cash (rather than credit cards) to pay for most peninsula activities. Two banks with ATMs are staggered across from each other on Main Street.

Bookstore: An Café Liteartha is a perfect rainy-day hideout, with stacks of books and a backroom café. It lurks across the lane from Paddy's Bike Hire (daily 10:00-18:00, closed Sun Oct-May, Dykegate Street—see map on page 302, tel. 066/915-2204).

Laundry: Dingle Cleaners is convenient (Mon-Sat 9:00-18:00, closed Sun, up Spa Road—see map on page 297, tel. 066/915-

0680, mobile 087-793-5621, run by Ciarán—pronounced key-a-RAWN). There's no self-service laundry in Dingle.

Bike Rental: Try **Paddy's Bike Hire,** with reliably maintained 21-speed hybrids (€15/day, includes helmet and lock, daily 9:00-19:00, must leave driver's license, directly across Dykegate from An Café Liteartha—see map on page 297, tel. 066/915-2311). **Dingle Electric Bike Experience** rents less-tiring electric bikes as well as 24-speed hybrid bikes, and can deliver them to your hotel and pick them up later (electric—€45/day, hybrid—€20/day, mobile 086-084-8378, www.dinglebikes.com, info@dinglebikes.com).

To bike the peninsula, get a bike with skinny street tires, not slow and fat mountain-bike tires. Be aware that Dingle and the Dingle Peninsula have no bike lanes and increasing traffic volume.

Taxi: Try **Diarmuid Begley** (mobile 087-250-4767), Sean with **Dingle Cabs** in Dingle (mobile 087-660-2323), or **Kathleen Curran** (mobile 087-254-9649).

Travel Agency: Maurice O'Connor at **Galvin's Travel Agency** can book plane tickets, as well as ferry rides to Britain (Mon-Fri 9:30-18:00, Sat 10:00-14:00, closed Sun, John Street, tel. 066/915-1409).

Activities: The **Mountain Man,** a hiking shop run by local guide Adrian Curran, is a clearinghouse for information on hiking, horseback riding, sea kayaking, climbing, and peninsula tours. Call a few days ahead to see which guided, scenic, mountain day-hikes are scheduled (daily 9:00-18:00, June-mid-Sept until 21:00, just off harbor at Strand Street—see map on page 297, tel. 066/915-2400, www.themountainmanshop.com, info@themountainmanshop.com).

The **Dingle Hillwalking Club** is an informal, visitor-friendly hiking group and a great way to connect with fun, active locals. But you must have serious footwear for the rugged terrain (free, every other Sun at 10:00, meet in front of SuperValu, www.dinglehillwalkingclub.com).

At the **Dingle Falconry Experience,** master falconer Eric leads encounters with hawks, falcons, owls, and eagles (€15, reserve in advance, most days at 17:00 at Milltown House, just over the bridge west of town; private falconry experience-€150/5 people, "hawk walk" (hawks only) at nearby beach or forest-€100/2 people; mobile 087-055-2313, www.dinglefalconry.com).

Tours in Dingle

Minibus Tours

Sciúird Archaeology Tours, worth ▲▲▲, are offered by a father-son team with a passion for sharing the long history of the Dingle Peninsula. Tim Collins (the retired Dingle police chief) and his archaeologist son Michael give informative three-hour-plus tours in their 16-passenger minivan with running commentary that basically follows the self-guided route in this book (Tim helped me write it). The four main stops include beehive

huts, the Reasc Monastery, the Gallarus Oratory, and Kilmalkedar Church with its ancient ogham stone—but not the Great Blasket Centre (€30, departs daily at 10:00 from the Fungie statue at the TI or at your B&B by request, book by email as soon as you know your dates, mobile 087-419-8617, www.ancientdingle.com, info@ancientdingle.com). Off-season, you may have to call back to see if a minimum of six people have signed up.

Dingle Slea Head Tours is a small company (just Rory, Eibhlis, and Colm) that does single- and multi-day private driving tours of the region from their Dingle home base. They also run Slea Head tours daily at 9:30 and 13:30 (4 hours, €30, minimum 4 people, www.dinglesleaheadtours.com).

Walking Tours

Celtic Nature Walking Tours, run by Claire Galvin and Kevin O'Shea, takes fit hikers (with proper footwear) into the scenic backcountry of the Dingle Peninsula, ranging from climbing Mount Brandon to hiking Great Blasket Island. Routes can be tailored to your interests (mobile 087-624-7230 or 087-790-3950, www.celticnature.com).

The **Dingle Historical Town Walk** introduces you, on a 1.5-hour stroll led by knowledgeable locals, to the surprisingly important role this little town has played over the centuries (€5, Sat at 10:00, meet at Fungie statue next to TI).

Boat Tours

When hard times fell on the local fishing industry, hardworking captains converted to sightseeing operators. From April to September, a guerilla flotilla of former fishing boats load up with tourists and crisscross Dingle harbor. Most churn around the sheltered bay to spot Fungie the friendly dolphin. Others offer three-hour "eco-voyages" beyond the mouth of the harbor to spy puffins, dolphins,

Dingle at a Glance

▲▲▲**Slea Head Loop Drive** Scenic 30-mile loop from Dingle, featuring the Gallarus Oratory (impressive early Christian church), Iron Age stone huts and "fairy forts," Norman ruins, and spectacular coastal views. See page 304.

▲▲▲**Sciúird Archaeology Tours** Fascinating three-hour minibus tours offer an up-close look into the peninsula's ancient history. **Hours:** Tours generally depart at 10:00 in peak season. See page 276.

▲▲▲**Dingle Town Walk** This short stroll introduces you to the town, its finest craft shops, and its characteristic pubs. See page 278.

▲▲▲**Traditional Music** Best enjoyed at one of Dingle's many pubs; early birds can take in early-evening folk concerts at St. James' Church or the Siopa Ceoil music shop. See page 292.

▲▲**Harry Clarke Windows** Imaginative stained-glass Bible scenes inside a lovely Neo-Gothic chapel in the middle of Dingle town. **Hours:** Mon-Fri 9:00-17:00, Sat-Sun 10:00-15:00. See page 285.

▲▲**Great Blasket Island** Until quite recently home to one of Ireland's most traditional communities; best appreciated after a visit to the excellent Great Blasket Centre on the mainland. **Hours:** Great Blasket Centre open daily 10:00-18:00, closed Nov-Easter. See page 315.

▲**Fungie** Dingle Harbor's resident dolphin (and town mascot), who makes regular appearances in the bay. See page 286.

▲**Oceanworld** Aquarium with penguin exhibit, petting pools, and no shortage of Fungie lore. **Hours:** Daily 10:00-18:00, shorter hours off-season. See page 287.

▲**Short Hikes** Bike ride-plus-hike to nearby Eask Tower for great town and peninsula views, or mellow waterside stroll out to the town's lighthouse. See page 288.

and seals, and dependable transport to Great Blasket Island off the tip of the peninsula.

Amid the confusing smattering of options, it mostly boils down to these major operators:

Dingle Dolphin Boat Tours, with a fleet of six boats, offers the widest variety of sailing options. These include a one-hour bay cruise with a guarantee to see Fungie or get your money back (€16, at least 4 times daily in summer), a 2.5-hour "Sea Safari" focus-

ing on coastal wildlife (€50, daily at 12:30), and a day trip to Great Blasket Island (six-hour round-trip voyage puts you on the island for about 3.5 hours). In good weather, it departs at 11:00, arrives on the island by 12:30, departs at 16:00, and returns to Dingle by 17:30 (€55, must book ahead, schedules vary with weather and tides, office in back corner of TI beside Fungie sculpture, tel. 066/915-2626, www.dingledolphin.com).

Dingle Boat Tours covers a similar lineup at competitive prices. Their office is at the base of the large Dingle Marina jetty— not to be confused with the shorter commercial fishing pier. They also offer a long eco-cruise that circles Skellig Michael off the tip of the Ring of Kerry (€100/person, tel. 066/915-1344, mobile 087-672-6100, www.dingleboattours.com, info@dinglebaycharters.com).

Blasket Island Ferry shuttles visitors from Dunquin Pier at the far west end of the peninsula to Great Blasket Island (€30, kids—€15, hourly starting at 10:00, weather permitting, advanced booking recommended, tel. 066/915-6422, mobile 085-775-1045, www.blasketisland.com, blasketislandferries@hotmail.com).

Dingle Town Walk

This quick, self-guided circle through town, worth ▲▲▲, gives you a once-over-lightly historical overview and good orientation.

• *Start just beyond the "old roundabout" and beside the playground at the...*

❶ **Tiny Bridge:** This pedestrian bridge, with its black-and-gold wrought-iron railing, was part of the original train line coming into Dingle (the westernmost train station in all of Europe from 1891 to 1953). The train once picked up fish in Dingle; its operators boasted that the cargo would be in London markets within 24 hours. The narrow-gauge tracks ran right along the harborfront.

All the land beyond the old buildings you see today has been reclaimed from the sea. Look inland and find the building on the left with the slate siding (the back wall of O'Flaherty's pub), facing the worst storms coming in from the sea. This was the typical design for 19th-century weatherproofing. The radio tower marks the sky-blue police station.

• *From here, cross the roundabout and walk up the big street called...*

❷ **The Mall:** After about 20 yards, two stubby red-brick pillars mark the entry to the police station. These pillars are all that

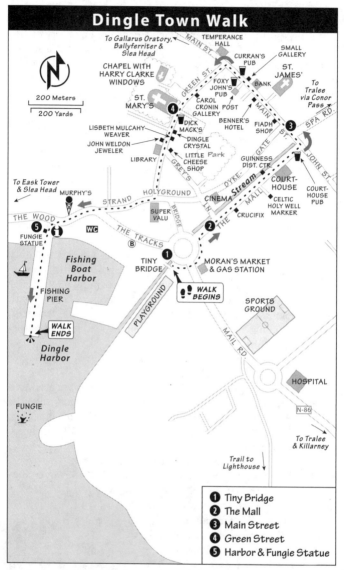

Dingle Town Walk

To Gallarus Oratory,
Ballyferriter &
Slea Head

TEMPERANCE HALL

MAIN ST.

CURRAN'S PUB

SMALL GALLERY

CHAPEL WITH HARRY CLARKE WINDOWS

GREEN ST.

ST. JAMES'

BANK

FOXY JOHN'S PUB

To Tralee via Conor Pass

200 Meters

200 Yards

ST. MARY'S

CAROL CRONIN GALLERY

POST OFFICE

MAIN ST.

❹

DICK MACK'S

BENNER'S HOTEL

FIADH SHOP

❸

SPA RD.

LISBETH MULCAHY WEAVER

JOHN WELDON JEWELER

DINGLE CRYSTAL

Park

GATE ST.

JOHN ST.

LIBRARY

LITTLE CHEESE SHOP

GUINNESS DIST. CTR.

To Eask Tower & Slea Head

MURPHY'S

HOLYGROUND

GRET'S LN.

DYKE LN.

Stream

COURTHOUSE

COURT-HOUSE PUB

STRAND

CINEMA

THE MALL

CELTIC HOLY WELL MARKER

THE WOOD

SUPER VALU

BRIDGE

CRUCIFIX

❺

THE TRACKS

❷

FUNGIE STATUE

WC

❶

B

Fishing Boat Harbor

TINY BRIDGE

MORAN'S MARKET & GAS STATION

WALK BEGINS

FISHING PIER

PLAYGROUND

SPORTS GROUND

WALK ENDS

Dingle Harbor

MAIL RD.

HOSPITAL

FUNGIE

N-86

To Tralee & Killarney

Trail to Lighthouse

❶ Tiny Bridge
❷ The Mall
❸ Main Street
❹ Green Street
❺ Harbor & Fungie Statue

remain of the 19th-century British Constabulary, which afforded a kind of Green Zone for British troops when they tried to subdue the local insurgents here. It was burned down in 1922, during the Civil War; the present building dates from 1938. Today, in a small, peaceful town like Dingle, the police department is virtually unarmed.

The big white **crucifix** across the street and 50 yards up The

Mall is a memorial to heroes who died in the 1916 Rising. Note that it says in the people's language, "For honor and glory of Ireland, 1916 to 19__." The date is unfinished until Ireland is united and free. The names listed are of local patriots who died fighting the British, and one (Thomas Ashe) who died while on a hunger strike.

• *Just past the Russel's B&B sign, take 15 paces up the B&B's driveway to see an old stone etched with a cross sitting atop the wall (on the right).*

This marks the site of a former **Celtic holy well,** a sacred spot for people here 2,000 years ago. Now, cross over the street, and continue walking uphill along the delightful gurgling stream.

Fifty yards farther up is another much-honored spot: the distribution center for **Guinness.** From this warehouse with its rusty, red, corrugated second floor, pubs throughout the peninsula are stocked with beer. The wooden kegs have been replaced by what locals fondly call "iron lungs."

Across the street is the blocky, riot-resistant 19th-century **courthouse,** made of gray stone. Once a symbol of British oppression, today it's a laid-back place where the roving County Kerry judge drops by to adjudicate cases on the last Friday of each month (mostly domestic disputes and drunken disorderliness). Next door, the blue building is the popular (and recommended for trad music) **Courthouse Pub.**

• *Continue to the big intersection and pause at the small bridge over a little stream. Notice the colors.*

A century ago, all these buildings were just shades of black and white. Their exteriors were originally exposed stonework (like the houses upstream). Then in the 1920s came the plaster (notice the bumps on the yellow Small Bridge Pub), and in the 1970s, cheery pastels (along with modern tourism).

• *Now head left into the commercial heart of the town on...*

❸ **Main Street:** First, find the little **Fiadh Handwoven Design Shop,** on the left just past the first little corner, across from Ashes Bar. Fiadh (pronounced Fia) Durham creates locally inspired contemporary designs with local wool at her loom and welcomes curious visitors (check out her fine scarves).

A few steps farther up on the left is **Benner's Hotel.** This was Dingle's first hotel, where the old Tralee stagecoach route ended. Note the surviving Georgian facade and door.

Across the street, up a short gravel alley, is **St. James' Church.** Since the 13th century, a church has stood here (just inside the

What's in a Name?

Linguistic politics have stirred up a controversy over the name of this town and peninsula. As a Gaeltacht, the entire region gets subsidies from the government (which supports the survival of the traditional Irish culture and language). A precondition of this financial support is that towns use their Irish Gaelic name. In 2005, well-meaning government officials in Dublin dictated that Dingle convert its name to the Irish Gaelic "An Daingean" (on DANG-un). But as it turns out, four separate Irish towns are named Daingean ("fortress"), so in 2012 Dingle's name was changed again—to Daingean Ui Chuis (DANG-un e koosh, "Fortress of the Husseys," a Norman founding family back in the late Middle Ages).

The town has resisted these dictates from Dublin. Dingle has become so wealthy from the tourist trade that it sees its famous name as a trademark, and doesn't want to become "the cute tourist town with the unpronounceable name, formerly known as Dingle." Until recently, official road signs identified the town only as *Daingean Ui Chuis;* however, so many were modified by stubborn locals, who stenciled in a crude *DINGLE,* the government eventually gave up and changed the signs back to *Dingle.* In town, most businesses, all tourist information, and nearly all people—locals and tourists alike—refer to it as Dingle.

For the sake of clarity, in this book I follow the predominant convention: Dingle instead of An Daingean or Daingean Ui Chuis, Great Blasket Island instead of An Blascaod Mór, and so on. But for ease of navigation, I've also generally included the place's Irish name in parentheses. For a list of these bilingual place names, see the sidebar on page 303.

medieval wall, closed to public during the day). Today, it's Anglican on Sundays and filled with great traditional music several nights a week. In 2003, a midwinter concert series sprang up at the church, featuring internationally known artists seeking an intimate venue. It became known as the "Other Voices" series and grew to become an annual event. (Amy Winehouse filmed her "One Shining Moment" TV concert here in 2006.)

• *Farther uphill on the same side is a co-op gallery.*

The Small Gallery (An Gailearai Beagg) is the cute little showroom of the West Kerry Craft Guild, a collective of 14 local artists and artisans who each man the shop two days a month to show off their work. Drop in and see who's working today and learn about their work.

Facing each other just uphill are two of Dingle's most unapologetically **traditional drinking holes,** Curran's and Foxy John's. You're welcome to pop in and look around, though you'll feel a

DINGLE PENINSULA

little more welcome if you order a drink (a small beer is "a glass" or half-pint). The publicans are happy to reminisce about old Dingle. These pubs are throwbacks to the humble day when a single hole-in-the-wall address would do double duty: commercial shop by day, pub by night.

James Curran runs **Curran's Pub** out of what was once his grandma's general store. On the last Saturday of every month—when farm families were in town for the market—the wives would pick up their basics here, ordering butter, tea, sugar, jams, and salted meat through the little window. (Just about everything else they consumed was homegrown.) The same shelves grandma used for jams and socks today stock beer and whiskey. Notice the "snug" in front. Until the 1950s, women weren't really welcome to drink in Irish pubs, but they could discreetly nurse a sherry in the "snug" while their men enjoyed the main room. The great photos all around give you a sense for the old days. This was one of American actor Robert Mitchum's favorite pubs while here to film *Ryan's Daughter* in 1969. Buy a beer and chat with Mr. Curran.

Foxy John's Pub, across the street, is still a working hardware store. Any time of day, you can order a bag of nails with your pint. Notice the back room; while pubs historically have had a legal "last call" at 11:30, the action would often migrate to the back room after the front door was locked.

• *Walk uphill to the Green Street intersection.*

On your right, notice the big **Temperance Hall,** which dates back to a 19th-century church-promoted movement that attempted to cut down the consumption of alcohol. To this day Ireland has a serious alcohol problem behind the happy veneer of all this pub fun. You'll see pickled old-timers who spend every morning of their last years on the same barstool. Today the Temperance Hall is a meeting place for AA groups, youth clubs, scouts, and other various social and support groups.

Directly across the street, you'll find a small **plaque** on the wall. This marked a safe house prepared during the French Revolution for the French Queen, Marie Antoinette. But the queen refused to leave France and was beheaded in 1789.

• *Now head downhill opposite the Temperance Hall to discover...*

❹ **Green Street:** Green Street is a reminder that 16th-century Dingle traded with Spain and was a port of embarkation for pilgrims on their way to Santiago de Compostela. A few steps down Green Street on the left, look above Kanon's Korner Fish shop to find a stone carved with the year "1586"—perhaps a remnant of that Spanish influence.

Farther along on the left, look for the **Carol Cronin Gallery,** an art gallery that clearly loves the sea. Popping in, you're likely to meet Carol at work. Many find her seascape paintings absolutely mesmerizing.

Down the street on the right, pop into the beautiful, modern **St. Mary's Church.** The former convent behind it shows off its
delightful **Harry Clarke stained-glass windows**— the single most important cultural sight in Dingle. Don't miss them (described later, under "Sights in Dingle"). Then, wander in the backyard to check out the tranquil nuns' cemetery, with its white-painted iron crosses huddling peacefully together under a big copper beech tree.

Across from St. Mary's (hence the nickname "the last pew") is **Dick Mack's Pub,** another traditional pub well worth a peek, even for nondrinkers. This was once a tiny leather shop that expanded into a pub at night. The pub was established in 1899 by great-grandpa Mack (master of the westernmost train station in Europe), whose mission was to provide "liquid replenishment" to travelers. Today, Dick Mack retains its old leather-shop ambience. In fact it's popular for handcrafted belts. (Their motto: "Step up and get waisted.") The latest Mack, Finn, has changed the focus to whiskey—very trendy in Ireland—and is also starting up a microbrewing operation in the back lot. Finn has no menu—guests just ask him for their options. Exploring the pub, you'll see a classic snug by the window, wonderful photos of generations past, and Hollywood-style stars on the sidewalk outside that recall famous visitors.

Green Street continues downhill past inviting boutiques, cafés, and estate agents. Many fine Dingle shops show off work by local artisans.

Dingle Crystal features Sean Daly and his Waterford-trained crystal-cutting skills. Sean prides himself on the deep, sharp cuts in his designs—see the video of him at work. The shop is run by his daughter Bella.

A few steps farther on is the shop of **Lisbeth Mulcahy Weaver,** filled with traditional but stylish woven woolen wear. It's also the Dingle sales outlet of her husband, a well-known potter from Slea Head. Across the street is **John Weldon Jewellers**—ideal for those interested in handcrafted gold and silver with Celtic designs.

• *At the corner, take a left on Grey's Lane and follow your nose.*

The **little cheese shop** is a foodie shrine playfully governed by Maja Binder, a German who trained in Switzerland. Poke your

Dingle's History

The wet sod of Dingle is soaked with medieval history. In the dimmest depths of the Dark Ages, peace-loving, bookish monks fled the chaos of the Continent and its barbarian raids. They sailed to the drizzly fringe of the known world—to places like Dingle. These monks kept literacy alive in Europe, and later provided scribes to Charlemagne, who ruled much of central Europe in the year 800.

It was from this peninsula that the semi-mythical explorer-monk St. Brendan is said to have set sail in the sixth century in search of a legendary western paradise. Some think he beat Columbus to North America by almost a thousand years (see sidebar on page 329).

Dingle was a busy seaport in the late Middle Ages. Dingle and Tralee (covered later in this chapter) were the only walled towns in Kerry. Castles stood at the low and high ends of Dingle's Main Street, protecting the Normans from the angry and dispossessed Irish outside. Dingle was a gateway to northern Spain—a three-day sail due south. Many 14th- and 15th-century pilgrims left from Dingle for the revered Spanish church in Santiago de Compostela, thought to house the bones of St. James.

In Dingle's medieval heyday, locals traded cowhides for wine. When Dingle's position as a trading center waned, the town faded in importance. In the 19th century, it was a linen-weaving center. Through most of the 20th century, fishing dominated, and the only visitors were scholars and students of old Irish ways. Then, in 1970, the movie *Ryan's Daughter* introduced the world to Dingle. The trickle of Dingle fans has grown to a flood as word of its musical, historical, gastronomical, and scenic charms—not to mention its friendly dolphin—has spread.

head inside, even if only for a whiff of her various traditional hand-made cheeses.

Back on Green Street you'll see **Dingle's library,** a gift from the Carnegie Foundation, with a small exhibit about local patriot Thomas Ashe and the Blasket Island writers. The best historic photos you'll find in town decorate the library's walls with images of 19th-century Dingle.

• *At the bottom of Green Street, take a right and head (past the best ice cream in town—at the recommended Murphy's) to...*

❺ **The Harbor and the Fungie Statue:** The harbor was built in 1992 on reclaimed land. The string of old stone shops facing the harbor was the loading station for the railway that hauled the fish from Dingle until 1953. Dingle's fishing industry survives, but it's an international endeavor. Most fishing boats that now ply these waters are Spanish, French, and Basque. Rather than going home with their catch, they offload their fish (mackerel, tuna, cod, herring, and prawns) onto trucks that lumber directly to their homelands. (European Union member countries can fish in other countries' waters, which can leave a little country like Ireland at the mercy of other nations that have many times the people, appetite, and purchasing power.)

In the old days, sailors would hang out at the Marina Inn Pub. But today they barely get off their boats. The trucks that haul their catch home return to Ireland loaded with provisions for their fishermen, a situation that does very little to bolster Dingle's economy. But don't be too sad for Dingle. The parking lot to the right is often filled with tour buses, as Dingle is on the big-bus route from Killarney to Slea Head (in season, thousands stop here daily for a few hours).

Enjoy the kid-friendly scene around the **bronze statue** of Dingle's beloved dolphin, Fungie (described later). From the Fungie statue, look straight out. Dead ahead on the distant hill is the Eask Tower. While it serves the useful purpose of marking this hidden harbor for those far out at sea, it was built primarily as a famine-era make-work project. A bit to the right, the big, yellow 18th-century manor house across the harbor was owned by Lord Ventry, the dominant English landlord of the time, and is now a school. The pyramid in the distance is Mount Eagle, marking Slea Head at the end of Dingle Peninsula. The building to the left with two big basement doors is a boathouse. At high tide, boats would float in, and be dry-docked at low tide for repairs. Beyond the boathouse and the harbor wall is the mouth of Dingle Harbor, playful Fungie, and the open sea. The booking office for harbor and Fungie boat tours (which leave from here; see "Tours in Dingle," earlier) faces the statue.

• *Your walk is over. For a little extra charm, stroll straight ahead to the end of the dock for a salty view, a look at the fishing boats, and a chat with a fisherman or two.*

Sights in Dingle

▲▲Harry Clarke Windows
Just behind Dingle's St. Mary's Church stands the former Presentation Sisters' convent, now home to the Díseart (dee-SHIRT) Institute of Education and Celtic Culture. The sisters of this order, who came to Dingle in 1829 to educate local girls, worked heroically during the famine. The convent contains the beautiful Neo-Gothic Chapel of the Sacred Heart, built in 1884. During Mass in the chapel, the Mother Superior would sit in the covered stall in

the rear, while the sisters—filling the carved stalls—chanted in response.

The chapel was graced in 1922 with 12 windows—the work of Ireland's top stained-glass man, Harry Clarke. Long appreciated only by the sisters, these special windows—showing scenes from the life of Christ—are now open to the public. The convent has become a center for sharing Christian Celtic culture and spirituality.

Cost and Hours: €3, Mon-Fri 9:00-17:00, Sat-Sun 10:00-15:00, tel. 066/915-2476, www.diseart.ie.

Visiting the Chapel: Stop at the reception room to pick up a loaner description with a self-guided walk. While Harry Clarke's windows are the big draw, it's also worth noting the recently painted, charming art of Coloradan Eleanor Yates, especially her *Last Supper* that pictures Dingle Harbor out the window. Upstairs is the chapel with the beloved stained glass of Harry Clark. While the windows behind the altar are Victorian, Clark's early-20th-century windows ring the chapel with six easy-to-read scenes. Clockwise from the back entrance, they are the visit of the Magi, the Baptism of Jesus, "Let the little children come to me," the Sermon on the Mount, the Agony in the Garden, and Jesus appearing to Mary Magdalene. Each face is lively and animated in the imaginative, devout, neo-medieval, and fun-loving style of Harry Clarke.

▲Fungie

In 1983, a bottlenose dolphin moved into Dingle Harbor and became a local celebrity. Fungie (FOON-ghee) is now the darling of

the town's tourist trade and one reason you'll find so many tour buses parked along the harbor. A recent study theorizes that he may be one of a half-dozen dolphins released from "Dolphinariums" (under pressure from animal-rights activists) on the southern coast of Britain. This would account for Fungie's loner ways and comfort around humans.

Hardy little tour boats thrive by baiting passengers with the chance of an up-close Fungie encounter, then motoring out to the mouth of the harbor, where they troll around looking for him (see "Tours in Dingle," earlier). You don't pay unless you see the dolphin. Fungie is slowing down a bit as he ages and locals are gearing up for a day when tour boats will have to settle for puffins. Still, if there's a group of boats at the mouth of the harbor, Fungie always comes out to play.

▲Oceanworld

This aquarium offers a little peninsula history, 300 different species of fish in thoughtfully described tanks, and the easiest way to see Fungie the dolphin: on video. Walk through the tunnel while fish swim overhead. You'll see local fish as well as a colorful Amazon collection. The penguin exhibit has a dozen of the little tuxedo torpedoes darting underwater and splashing up onto their fake Arctic ice block. Newer additions include young otters, tiny crocodiles, and a steamy "butterfly oasis" chamber. The aquarium's mission is to teach, and you're welcome to ask questions. The petting pool is fun. Splashing attracts the rays, which are unplugged.

Cost and Hours: €15.50, €47-53 for families with children (4-6 people), daily 10:00-18:00, shorter hours off-season, cafeteria, just past harbor on west edge of town, tel. 066/915-2111, www. dingle-oceanworld.ie.

Dingle Distillery Tour

Whiskey is as trendy as Dingle, and the hometown distillery would love to give you a sample. The one-hour tour includes earnest explanations and two hard drinks—a whiskey and a gin or vodka. The distillery is a 20-minute walk from town, just over the bridge on Slea Head Drive (€15, tours run daily in season at 12:00, 14:00, and 16:00—more with demand, see map on page 297, tel. 066/402-9011, www.dingledistillery.ie).

Music Shops

Danlann Gallery sells violins made by the owner, tin whistles, woodcrafts, and traditional toys, with a tiny vegetarian café upstairs (Mon-Fri 10:00-18:00 in summer, "flexible hours" on weekends and off-season, Dykegate Street).

Siopa Ceoil (literally "The Music Shop") is an inviting little music shop worth seeking out. It's enthusiastically run by Michael Herlihy, who plays a mean accordion and offers free quick-and-dirty *bodhrán* (traditional drum) lessons. Michael, his son Dara, and omni-pleasant Caitriona are virtual encyclopedias of Irish music knowledge (Mon-Sat 9:30-20:00, Sun 14:00-19:00, shorter hours off-season, near the waterfront on a short dead-end lane called The Colony, tel. 066/915-2618, mobile 087-914-5826). The shop hosts "unplugged" traditional music concerts several nights a week, and sells advance discounted tickets for concerts at St. James' Church (see "Folk Concerts," later).

DINGLE PENINSULA

ACTIVITIES

▲Short Harbor Walk from Dingle

This easy stroll along the harbor out of town—to the lighthouse and back—gives you a chance to see Fungie and takes about 1.5 hours round-trip. Head east from the old roundabout (just past O'Flaherty's pub) and walk uphill past the Texaco station. Just after Bambury's B&B, take a right, then immediately bear left (toward the cell-phone tower). The road curls downhill and dead-ends at a tiny Irish Coast Guard station beside the bay. Turn left at the station, climbing the steps over the low wall and following the seashore path to the mouth of Dingle Harbor (passing Hussey's folly, an empty two-story shell of a tower built by a 19th-century fat cat). Ten minutes beyond that is a two-story (white with red trim) lighthouse. This is Fungie's neighborhood. If you see tourist boats out, you're likely to see the dolphin. The trail continues another half-mile to dramatic cliff views and an intimate little beach.

▲Bike and Hike to Eask Tower

The bike-and-hike trek to Eask Tower, totaling about 10 miles round-trip, is a good compromise for those wanting more exercise than the mellow harbor walk to the lighthouse, but less sweat than biking the entire 30-mile Slea Head Loop. The lazy option: Skip the bike, drive to the trailhead, and walk up from there.

Rent a bike in town and pedal west past the aquarium, going left at the roundabout that takes you over the bridge onto R-559 toward Slea Head. After almost two miles, turn left at the brown sign to *Holden's Leather Workshop*. A narrow leafy lane leads another two miles or so to a hut on the right marked *Eask Tower* (the tower looms on the bare hill above).

Pay the €2 trail fee at the hut (if unattended, feed the honor box) and hike about a mile straight up the hill. It's a steep trail. You'll zigzag around sheep and tiptoe over their droppings. You'll also need to navigate through (possibly climb) a couple of waist-high, metal-rung gates. After 45 minutes, you'll reach the stone signal tower on the crown of the hill. Enjoy fantastic views of Dingle town (to the north) and Dingle Bay with the Iveragh Peninsula (home of the Ring of Kerry to the south). Spot the two jagged Skellig Islands off the distant tip of the Iveragh Peninsula.

Horseback Riding

Dingle Horse Riding takes beginners out for a 1.5-hour (€60) trail ride (pony rides for kids available, €25/30 minutes). More experienced riders can choose between two-hour (€75-100 depending on pace), half-day (€195), and full-day (€300) excursions (book online or call; to find it, follow Main Street out of Dingle, and turn right at the sign; tel. 066/915-2199, www.

dinglehorseriding.com). **Long's Horseriding Centre** is farther out on the peninsula just past Ventry (sign on right)—an easy stop for drivers doing the Slea Head Loop (one-hour beach ride-€45, two-hour beach and mountain trail ride—€80; open Mon-Sat, closed Sun; book online or call, mobile 087-225-0286, www.longsriding.com). In either case, mountain rides are only for advanced riders, and all horses come with English-style saddles (no horns to hang on to—anyone with only Western saddle experience is considered a beginner).

Dingle Pitch & Putt

This course's scenic 18 holes (ranging from 30 to 95 yards in length) offer a relaxing diversion for average duffers on a green headland overlooking the harbor. They also have a "crazy course" (miniature golf).

Cost and Hours: €7.50, includes gear, daily 10:00-19:00, closed Nov-March; located behind Milltown House about a 25-minute walk out of town—after crossing over the bridge, take the first left and then the first right; tel. 066/915-2020.

Golf

Located out west, near the wildly scenic tip of the Dingle Peninsula and the town of Ballyferriter, Ceann Sibéal/Dingle Links offers a round of golf in a hard-to-beat setting.

Cost and Hours: €90 July-Aug, €75 April-June and Sept, €40-50 Oct-March, open daily till dusk, Baile an Fheirtearaigh, 9 miles west of Dingle town, tel. 066/915-6255, www.dinglelinks.com.

EAST OF DINGLE TOWN
▲Minard Castle

Three miles southwest of the town of Annascaul (Abhainn an Scáil), off the Lispole (Lios Póil) Road, is the largest fortress on the peninsula. Built by the Knights of Kerry in 1551, Minard Castle was destroyed by Cromwell's troops in about 1650. With its corners

DINGLE PENINSULA

Tom Crean, Unsung Antarctic Explorer

Kerrymen are known as a hardy lot, and probably none more so than Antarctic explorer and Annascaul native Thomas Crean. As a 15-year-old lad looking for steady employment and a chance to see the world, Crean left these shores in 1893 to join the British Royal Navy, and in 1901 volunteered to join the crew of the RSS *Discovery*. Onboard were Captain Robert Falcon Scott and other soon-to-be famous explorers, including Ernest Shackleton. Their mission: to be the first men to reach the South Pole.

It was the world's first serious attempt to reach the pole, an effort that required pulling sleds laden with tons of supplies across miles and miles of ice in extreme conditions. One of the team's most able man-haulers, Crean quickly gained his mates' trust and respect for his hard work, calm presence, and cheerful (if tuneless) singing. The *Discovery* Expedition pushed the boundaries of Antarctic exploration, but didn't reach the pole (Britain's second attempt, in 1909 under Shackleton, got much closer before also turning back).

Determined to try again, Scott chose Crean among the first of his handpicked crew for the *Terra Nova* Expedition (1910-1913). Early on, Crean saved some expedition members stranded on a drifting ice floe—encircled by orcas (who can tip ice to make vulnerable seals slide off)—by leaping between floating chunks of ice, then scaling an ice wall to get help. Later, Crean and two others were the last support team ordered to turn back as Scott made the final push to the pole (having come so close, the unshakable Crean wept at the news). Near the end of the 730-mile

undermined by Cromwellian explosives, it looks ready to split—it's no longer safe to enter this teetering ruin.

From the outside, look for the faint scallop in the doorway, the symbol of St. James. Medieval pilgrims would stop here before making a seafaring pilgrimage from Dingle to St. James' tomb at Santiago de Compostela in northern Spain. Imagine the floor plan of the castle: ground floor for animals

return trip, Crean's two mates, sick and freezing, could go no far- ther. Exhausted and provisioned with only three cookies and two sticks of chocolate, Crean made a nonstop, solo, 35-mile march through a blizzard to reach help, saving his mates' lives. (Though Scott's party did reach the pole, a Norwegian team led by Roald Amundsen beat them to it—by a month; Scott and his men didn't survive the trip back.)

Crean's most famous act of heroism took place on his third and final polar expedition (1914-1917), led by Shackleton. Their ship, the *Endurance,* was crushed by ice, marooning the crew on Elephant Island. Hoping to find help at a whaling station, Shack- leton, Crean, and four others sailed a modified open lifeboat 800 miles in 17 days to South Georgia Island. There they were forced to hike across the rugged, unexplored interior to reach the station on the other side. A ship was sent to rescue the exhausted and malnourished crew, all of whom had miraculously survived the 18- month ordeal.

Crean never did reach the South Pole himself, turning down Shackleton's request to join him on his next (and last) trek. But Crean distinguished himself as a hero among explorers—who named both a mountain and a glacier after him in Antarctica—and was honored by King George V. In 1920, he retired from the navy, returned to County Kerry, and stashed his medals away, never again speaking of his experiences—partly out of modesty, and partly because his service in the (British) navy could have made him a target for Irish nationalists. An uneducated farmer's son, Crean left few records of his exploits and didn't achieve the fame of his lauded (and more well-to-do) contemporaries. Crean mar- ried, bought a pub (South Pole Inn—see "East of Dingle Town"), and raised three daughters. After bravely escaping many near- deaths in the Antarctic, he finally died in 1938 of a burst appendix.

and storage, main-floor living room with fireplace, then a floor with sleeping quarters, and, on top, the defensive level.

The setting is dramatic, with the Ring of Kerry across the way and Storm Beach below. The beach is notable for its sandstone boulders that fell from the nearby cliffs. Grinding against each other in the wave and tidal action, the boulders eroded into cigar- shaped rocks. Pre-Christian Celts would carry them off and carve them into ogham stones to mark clan boundaries.

Next to the fortress, look for the "fairy fort," an Iron Age fort from about 500 BC. Locals thought it unlucky to pluck stones from these ring forts, so they remain undisturbed, overgrown with greenery, all across Ireland.

Puicin Wedge Tomb

While pretty obscure, this is worth the trouble for its evocative setting. Above the hamlet of Lispole (Lios Póil) in Doonties, park your car and hike 10 minutes up the ridge. At the summit is a pile of rocks made into a little room with one of the finest views on the peninsula. Beyond the Ring of Kerry you may just make out the jagged Skellig Michael, noted for its sixth-century monastic settlement (see previous chapter).

South Pole Inn

This pub, once owned by modest-yet-heroic Antarctic explorer Tom Crean, is still open for business. You'll see it as you pass through Annascaul on N-86 (at the bottom of a hill, on the left if you're heading east). Consider dropping in to have a pint and peruse the walls of lovingly maintained photos devoted to Crean's incredible adventures (see sidebar).

Inch Strand

This four-mile sandy beach was made famous by the movie *Ryan's Daughter*. It's rated a "Blue Flag" beach for its clean water and safe swimming (usually has a lifeguard in summer).

Nightlife in Dingle

▲▲▲Music in Dingle Pubs

Traditional pub music is Dingle town's best experience. Even if you're not into pubs, take an afternoon nap and then give these an evening whirl. Dingle is renowned among traditional musicians as an ideal place to perform. The town has piles of pubs that feature music most nights, and there's never a cover charge—just buy a beer. The scene is a decent mix of locals, Americans, Brits, and Germans. Music normally starts at 21:30ish, and the last call for drinks is at "half eleven" (23:30), sometimes later on weekends. For a seat near the music, arrive early. If the place is chockablock with people, power in and find breathing room in the back. By midnight, the door is usually closed and the chairs are stacked.

Make a point to wander the town and follow your ear. Smaller pubs may feel a bit foreboding to a tourist, but rest assured that people—locals as well as travelers—are out for the *craic*. Irish culture is very accessible in the pubs; they're like highly interactive museums waiting to be explored. If you sit at a table, you'll be left alone. But stand or sit at the bar and you'll be engulfed in conversation with new friends.

DINGLE PENINSULA

Have a glass in an empty, no-name pub and chat up the publican. Pubs are no longer smoky, but can be stuffy and hot, so leave your coat at home. I know it's going to be a great trad music session when my eyeglasses steam up as I enter.

For some background, see "Traditional Irish Music" on page 7. For locations of the following pubs, see the "Dingle Center Restaurants & Pubs" map, later.

Dingle Pub Crawl

The best place to start a pub crawl is at **O'Flaherty's,** the first music pub in Dingle, located on Holyground street. Quietly intense owner Fergus O'Flaherty, a fixture since my first visit to Dingle, can belt out a song as he joins a varying lineup of loyal local musicians. Talented Fergus sings and plays a half-dozen different instruments during almost nightly traditional-music sessions. His domain has a high ceiling and is dripping in old-time photos and town memorabilia—it's unpretentious, cluttered fun.

Moving up Strand Street, find **John Benny's.** Its dependably good traditional-music sessions come with John himself joining in on accordion when he's not pouring pints or explaining his extensive whiskey choices. **Paddy Bawn Brosnan's Pub** (also on the Strand) brags no music and no food—just beer and sports. If a game is on TV—especially Gaelic football or hurling—you can watch it here with the locals.

Then head up Green Street. **Dick Mack's,** across from the church, is nicknamed "the last pew." Once a leather shop, today the pub sells only drinks, with several rooms, a fine snug, ample beer choices, and a fascinating ambience. The latest Mack, Finn, focuses on whiskey and craft beers.

Green Street climbs to Main Street, where two more Dick Mack-type places are filled with locals deep in conversation (but no music): **Foxy John's** (a hardware shop by day) and **Curran's** (across the street, a small clothing shop by day). For more on each of these (and Dick Mack), see the town walk, earlier.

Wander down Main Street. The **Dingle Pub** seems designed for John Denver and Irish Rovers fans. It's well established as *the* place for folk-ballad singing rather than the churning traditional beat of an Irish folk session. Just downhill, **Neligan's** is another lively traditional music session option with fun dance lessons for beginners on summer Thursday nights. At the bottom of Main Street, **Small Bridge Bar** offers live music nightly. These days, its dimly lit confines are popular with a younger, late-night crowd.

I'd finish my night at the **Courthouse Pub** (on The Mall, next to the old gray courthouse). This is a steamy little hideaway with low ceilings and high-caliber musicians who perform nightly at 21:00, and my favorite men's room in Ireland—with kegs for

DINGLE PENINSULA

urinals. Owner Tommy O'Sullivan is a guitar-strumming fixture on the trad-music scene. His wife, Saundra, is from Houston and also sings.

Off-Season: From October through April, the music hibernates. On weekends, your best bets are the Small Bridge Bar, O'Flaherty's, the Courthouse Pub, and John Benny's. Check for winter performances of the "Other Voices" series at St. James Church (see next).

▲▲Folk Concerts

If you're not a night owl, these are your best opportunities to hear Irish traditional music in a more controlled, early evening environment.

St. James' Church: Top local musicians offer a quality evening of live, acoustic, traditional Irish music in the fine little St. James' Church (100 seats), just off Main Street. If you prefer not to be packed into a pub with the distractions of conversation, these concerts are a good option. They are organized by local piper Eoin Duignan, whose command of the melodic *uileann* bagpipes is a highlight most nights. Surprisingly, this humble church is the home venue of the acclaimed "Other Voices" winter concert TV series that has drawn the likes of Amy Winehouse, Sinéad O'Connor, and Donovan, among others (€13 in advance, €15 at the door; Mon, Wed, and Fri at 19:30, May-Oct only; mobile 087-284-9656, www.duigo.com; see sign on church gate or, for more details or to book a ticket, drop by Paul Geaneys Pub, Leac a Ré craft shop, or Siopa Ceoil music shop).

The Siopa Ceoil Trad Concert: The Siopa Ceoil music shop hosts intimate traditional Irish music sessions in its cozily cramped, 45-seat space. The show is casual and run by the family, with a running commentary to explain the local music culture. It generally features two musicians playing two 45-minute sets with a 20-minute break (€20, includes a tasty Irish decaf between sets; May-Sept Tue, Thu, and Sat at 19:00, plus Sun July-Sept; 2 The Colony, mobile 086-080-8448, www.siopaceoil.ie).

Cinema

Dingle's little theater is The Phoenix on Dykegate. Its film club (50-60 locals) meets here Tuesdays year-round at 20:45 for coffee and cookies, followed by a film at 21:00 (€8 for film, anyone is welcome). The leader runs it almost like a religion, with a sermon on the film before he rolls it. The regular film schedule for the week is posted on the door.

DINGLE PENINSULA

Sleeping in Dingle

Prices vary with the season, with winter cheap, and July and August tops.

IN OR NEAR THE TOWN CENTER

$$$$ Benners Hotel was the only hotel in town a hundred years ago. It stands bewildered by the modern world on Main Street, with sprawling public spaces and 52 abundant, overpriced rooms (tel. 066/915-1638, www.dinglebenners.com, info@dinglebenners. com).

$$$ Greenmount House sits among chilly palm trees at the top of town. A five-minute hike up from the town center, this guesthouse commands a fine view of the bay and mountains. Gary Curran runs one of Ireland's best B&Bs, with two fine rooms, three superb rooms, and nine sprawling suites in a modern building with lavish public areas and wonderful breakfasts (parking, top of John Street, tel. 066/915-1414, www.greenmounthouse.ie, info@ greenmounthouse.ie). Seek out the hot tub in their back-garden cabin.

$$$ Barr Na Sráide Inn, central and hotel-like, has 29 nicely refurbished rooms (huge family room sleeps 5, self-service laundry, bar, parking, past McCarthy's pub on Upper Main Street, tel. 066/915-1331, www.barrnasraide.ie, barrnasraide@eircom.net).

$$ Bambury's Guesthouse, hosted by cheerful Bernie Bambury, is big and modern with views of grazing sheep and the harbor. The 12 rooms are airy and comfy (coming in from Tralee it's on your left on Mail Road, 2 blocks before the Texaco station; tel. 066/915-1244, mobile 086-324-4281, www.bamburysguesthouse. com, bamburysguesthouse@gmail.com).

$$ Alpine Guesthouse looks like a Monopoly hotel, and is fittingly comfortable and efficient. Its 14 bright and fresh rooms come with pastoral views, a cozy lounge, and friendly owner Paul O'Shea (RS%, family rooms, easy parking, Mail Road, tel. 066/915-1250, www.alpineguesthouse.com, alpinedingle@gmail.com). Driving into town from Tralee, it's the first lodging on your right, next to the sports field and a block uphill from the Texaco station.

$$ Sraíd Eoin House offers five pleasant, top-floor rooms above Galvin's Travel Agency (RS%, family rooms, John Street, tel. 066/915-1409, www.sraideoinbnb.com, sraideoinhouse@ hotmail.com, friendly Kathleen and Maurice O'Connor).

$$ O'Neill's B&B is homey and friendly, with six nifty rooms on a quiet street at the top of town (cash only, parking, John Street, tel. 066/915-1639, www.oneillsbedandbreakfast.com, info@ oneillsbedandbreakfast.com, Mary and Stephen O'Neill).

$ Eileen Collins Kirrary B&B, which takes up a quiet cor-

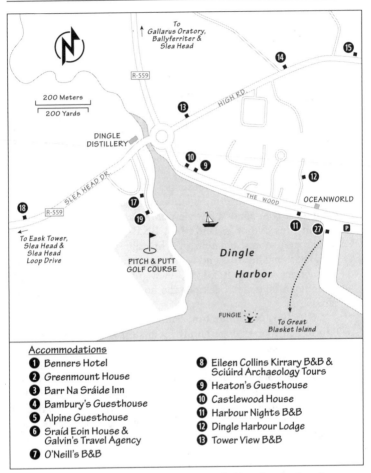

Accommodations

1. Benners Hotel
2. Greenmount House
3. Barr Na Sráide Inn
4. Bambury's Guesthouse
5. Alpine Guesthouse
6. Sraíd Eoin House & Galvin's Travel Agency
7. O'Neill's B&B
8. Eileen Collins Kirrary B&B & Sciúird Archaeology Tours
9. Heaton's Guesthouse
10. Castlewood House
11. Harbour Nights B&B
12. Dingle Harbour Lodge
13. Tower View B&B

ner in the town center, is run by the same Collins family that does archaeological tours of the peninsula (see page 276). They offer five pleasant rooms, great prices, a large garden, and a homey friend-liness (cash only, Kirrary House, just off The Mall on Avondale at Dykegate and Grey's Lane, tel. 066/915-1606 or mobile 087-150-0017, www.collinskirrary.com, collinskirrary@eircom.net, Eileen Collins). They also rent a cozy, family-friendly, self-catering cottage a couple hundred yards up behind town with great views (sleeps 5, 3-night minimum, contact their son Hugh to reserve, hughocoileain@gmail.com).

BEYOND THE PIER

These accommodations are a 10- to 15-minute walk from Dingle's town center. They tend to be quieter, since they are farther from the late-night pub scene.

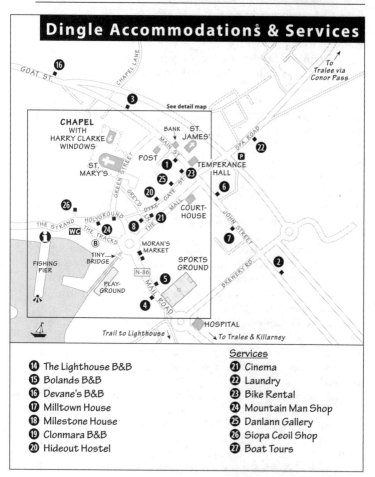

Dingle Accommodations & Services

⑭ The Lighthouse B&B
⑮ Bolands B&B
⑯ Devane's B&B
⑰ Milltown House
⑱ Milestone House
⑲ Clonmara B&B
⑳ Hideout Hostel

Services
㉑ Cinema
㉒ Laundry
㉓ Bike Rental
㉔ Mountain Man Shop
㉕ Danlann Gallery
㉖ Siopa Ceoil Shop
㉗ Boat Tours

$$$ Heaton's Guesthouse, big, peaceful, and comfortable, is on the water just west of town at the end of Dingle Bay—a five-minute walk past Oceanworld on The Wood. The 16 thoughtfully appointed rooms come with all the amenities (creative breakfasts, parking, The Wood, tel. 066/915-2288, www.heatonsdingle.com, info@heatonsdingle.com, David Heaton).

$$$ Castlewood House is a palatial refuge with 12 tasteful rooms, classy furnishings, and delicious breakfasts. The breakfast room and patio have a wonderful view of Dingle Harbor (parking, The Wood, tel. 066/915-2788, www.castlewooddingle.com, info@castlewooddingle.com, Brian and Helen Heaton).

$$ Harbour Nights B&B weaves together a line of old row houses to create a 17-room guesthouse facing the harbor (parking, just past the aquarium on The Wood, tel. 066/915-2499, mobile

DINGLE PENINSULA

087-686-8190, www.dinglebandb.com, info@dinglebandb.com, Seán and Kathleen Lynch).

$$ Dingle Harbour Lodge is a former hostel, pleasantly refurbished and morphed into a comfy hotel hybrid with 29 rooms. You'll feel like a fancy hotel guest without the fancy prices (family rooms, up a long driveway off The Wood past the aquarium, tel. 066/915-1577, www.dingleharbourlodge.com, info@ dingleharbourlodge.com).

ABOVE TOWN

Arcing inland above the town's western slope are four good lodging choices on a road that changes names three times in a half mile. Starting from the corner of Green Street and Main Street (headed uphill) you'll be on Goat Street, then Ashmount Terrace, then High Road.

$$ Tower View B&B is a big, modern home just outside of town on a lovely quiet lot. This kid-friendly mini farm rents eight fine rooms (family rooms, High Road, tel. 066/915-2990, www. towerviewdingle.com, info@towerviewdingle.com, Aidan & Helen Murphy).

$$ The Lighthouse B&B is a cozy place with six prim rooms, wonderful views near the crest of the hill, and Lucky the fluffball mutt (family rooms, High Road, tel. 066/915-1829, www. lighthousedingle.com, info@lighthousedingle.com, Denis & Mary Murphy).

$$ Bolands B&B is family-run with a traditional, welcoming atmosphere and eight comfortable rooms (family rooms, Goat Street, tel. 066/915-1426, mobile 085-714-2297, www. bolandsdingle.ie, info@bolandsdingle.ie, Breda & Michael Boland).

$ Devane's B&B caters to the active bike-and-hike crowd, with six clean and practical rooms that are a good value given their close proximity to town (cash only, Goat Street, tel. 066/915-1193, www.devanesdingle.com, devanesdingle@eircom.net, Kevin & Geraldine Devane).

OVER THE BRIDGE, WEST OF TOWN

These options are a 25- to 30-minute level walk along the Dingle Bay shore from town. They suffer from being located on the far side of a 50-yard-long unlit stone bridge with no sidewalks (making a walk back at night a bit dodgy). A taxi from town should only cost about €6. All three have parking and are in comfortable, modern buildings with attentive ownership adopting a "we try harder" attitude. Be aware that Milltown House and Clonmara are frequently booked up by Rick Steves tours.

$$$ Milltown House hosted Robert Mitchum during the

filming of *Ryan's Daughter*. Its 10 rooms are nicely refurbished, and some enjoy bay views. The casual vibe comes with a cozy in-house bar and two gentle-giant Irish wolfhounds dozing nearby. In warmer months, Dingle Falconry shows off birds of prey in the huge front yard. With room to run, unusual animals, and its proximity to Dingle Pitch & Putt, kids love this place (family rooms, The Wood, first left after crossing the bridge, tel. 066-915-1372, www.milltownhouse.com, info@milltownhouse.com, Stephen McPhilemy).

$$$ Milestone House is farthest out, but an ideal option for longer stays. Friendly hosts Barbara and Michael Carroll converted a fine guesthouse into two separate self-catering apartments (upstairs apartment has 3 double rooms, ground-floor apartment has 2 doubles). The front yard sports a 3,500-year-old standing stone as an ancient territorial marker (3-night minimum, on road R-559, tel. 066/915-1831, www.milestonedingle.com, milestonehousedingle@gmail.com).

$$ Clonmara B&B's host Blandina O'Connor grew up next door to Milltown House and knows the area well. You'll find five homey rooms in a peaceful setting with grand views across Dingle Bay (cash only, tel. 066/915-1656, mobile 087-204-2243, www.clonmara.com, clonmara@hotmail.com).

HOSTEL

¢ Hideout Hostel is friendly and central, just across the lane from the movie theater. Michael (ME-hall) grew up on this street and manages a relaxed, fun atmosphere (private rooms available, Dykegate Street, tel. 066/915-0559, www.hideouthostel.ie, info@hideouthostel.ie).

ON GREAT BLASKET ISLAND

You can really get away from it all on Great Blasket Island, a couple of miles off the tip of the peninsula (described later in this chapter). No phone, no lights, no cars. Not a single luxury. Like Robinson Crusoe (or Gilligan), it's primitive as can be. Book your boat crossing in advance (see page 278).

$$ Great Blasket Accommodation is the only lodging or modern amenity on the otherwise uninhabited island. This very basic seasonal crash pad, in an unforgettable setting at the top of the fishing-village ghost town on the east end of the island, consists of three cottages, each with two bedrooms, kitchen with a gas stove, living room, and bathroom (no electricity or Wi-Fi, bring your own food, closed off-season, mobile 086-057-2626 or 086-313-5098, www.greatblasketisland.net, info@greatblasketisland.net, Billy O'Connor).

Eating in Dingle

DINING IN DINGLE

All of these restaurants are good, but I've listed them in order of my personal preference. The top-end places generally offer good-value, multicourse, early-bird specials from about 17:30 to 19:00. Remember that while seafood is a treat here, so is the lamb.

$$$$ Out of the Blue Seafood-Only Restaurant is the locals' choice for great fresh fish. The interior is bright and elegantly simple. The chalkboard menu is dictated by what the fishermen caught that morning. If they're closed, there's been a storm and the fishermen couldn't go out. Dinners are artfully presented, with a touch of nouvelle cuisine and certainly no chips (Mon-Sat 17:00-21:30, Sun 12:30-15:00, reservations smart, some outdoor picnic-table seating, just past the TI, facing the harbor on The Waterside, tel. 066/915-0811, www.outoftheblue.ie).

$$$ James G. Ashe Pub and Restaurant, an old-fashioned joint, is popular with locals for its nicely presented, top-quality, traditional Irish food and seafood at good prices. Check out the photos of Gregory Peck, who was related to the Ashe family and visited the pub often. I like their beef-and-Guinness stew (daily 12:00-15:00 & 17:30-21:30, Main Street, tel. 066/915-0989).

$$$$ Global Village Restaurant is where Nuala Cassidy and Martin Bealin concoct their favorite dishes. Martin has a passion for making things from scratch and giving dishes a creative twist with inspiration gleaned from his world travels. No chips, no deep-fat-fried anything. It's an eclectic, healthy, fresh seafood-eaters' place (daily 17:30-22:00, Nov-Feb Fri-Sun only, good salads, top of Main Street, tel. 066/915-2325, mobile 087-917-5920).

$$$$ Chart House Restaurant serves contemporary cuisine in a sleek, well-varnished dining room. Settle back into the ship-shape, lantern-lit space. The menu is shaped by what's fresh and seasonal, and the chef is committed to always offering a good veg-etarian entrée (daily 18:00-22:00 except closed Mon Oct-May, reservations wise, at roundabout at base of town, tel. 066/915-2255, www.thecharthousedingle.com, Jim McCarthy).

$$$$ Lord Baker's is the venerable elder among fine Dingle dining options. John Moriarty and his family concoct quality dish-es served in a friendly yet refined atmosphere. The seafood soup is a memorable specialty (Fri-Wed 18:00-21:30, closed Thu, reservations smart, Main Street, tel. 066/915-1277 or 066/915-1141, www.lordbakers.ie).

$$$$ Fenton's is good for seafood meals with a memorable apple-and-berry-crumble dessert (Tue-Sun 18:00-21:30, closed Mon, reservations smart, on Green Street down the hill below the church, tel. 066/915-2172, mobile 087-248-2487).

DINGLE PENINSULA

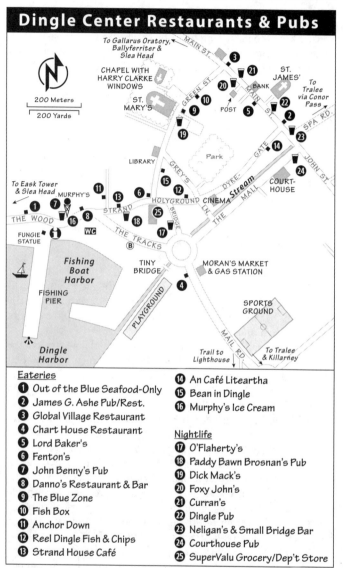

Dingle Center Restaurants & Pubs

Eateries
1. Out of the Blue Seafood-Only
2. James G. Ashe Pub/Rest.
3. Global Village Restaurant
4. Chart House Restaurant
5. Lord Baker's
6. Fenton's
7. John Benny's Pub
8. Danno's Restaurant & Bar
9. The Blue Zone
10. Fish Box
11. Anchor Down
12. Reel Dingle Fish & Chips
13. Strand House Café
14. An Café Liteartha
15. Bean in Dingle
16. Murphy's Ice Cream

Nightlife
17. O'Flaherty's
18. Paddy Bawn Brosnan's Pub
19. Dick Mack's
20. Foxy John's
21. Curran's
22. Dingle Pub
23. Neligan's & Small Bridge Bar
24. Courthouse Pub
25. SuperValu Grocery/Dep't Store

LESS EXPENSIVE DINGLE MEALS

While the top-end restaurants charge on average €25-35, you can eat well for €15-20 in Dingle's pubs and international eateries. Many cheap and cheery lunch places close at 18:00. Most pubs stop serving food at about 21:00 (to make room for their beer drinkers and musicians). Anyone will serve tap water for free.

$$ John Benny's Pub dishes up traditional Irish fare on the waterfront. John, the proprietor and a Dingle fixture since my first visits, takes his outstanding selection of whiskeys as seriously as his choice of quality local musicians. Come here for dinner, and stay for a drink and great nightly live music (food daily 12:30-21:30, music after 21:30, The Pier, tel. 066/915-1215).

$$ Danno's Restaurant and Bar is a sprawling and fun-loving eatery popular with tourists and locals for inexpensive burgers, fish-and-chips, and pub grub. Danno's interior is a mix of railroad and rugby memorabilia. He offers some of the best outdoor seating in town with a heated and leafy patio out back (closed Mon, Strand Street, mobile 086-236-4404).

$$ The Blue Zone is a hip jazz wine bar offering pizza, salad, and an international cosmopolitan vibe. Tight, busy, and family-friendly, it's a tasty alternative to Dingle's pub grub and fish-dominated fare. Or just kick back and enjoy a late-night conversation over a glass of wine set to eclectic background music (Thu-Tue 17:30-11:30, closed Wed, Green Street across from St. Mary's Church, tel. 066/915-0303).

$$ Fish Box connects generations of Flannery family fishing to this pleasant little brightly white-tiled fish restaurant (daily 12:00-21:00, takeout available, Green Street just up from St. Mary's Church, mobile 087-052-6896).

$$ Anchor Down is a fresh fish option that's easy on the wallet. The Sheehy family, who are local fishermen, supply their simple little cottage with a variety of fresh fish—and chips if you want them (daily 11:30-21:30, closed Dec-Feb, up a lane off Strand Street, 3 The Colony, tel. 066/915-1545).

$ Reel Dingle Fish & Chips is the best chippy in town, serving mostly takeout, but with a few stools. It's not fast, because they cook the fish fresh to order. They serve generous portions—consider splitting—and are also good for burgers (daily 13:00-22:00, near SuperValu grocery store on Holyground, tel. 066/915-1713).

$ Strand House Café is a cozy spot where their fresh-made pastry tempts you to hang out with an extra cup of coffee (daily 10:00-17:00, Sun from 11:00, perched above the centrally located Strand House on Strand Street, tel. 066/915-2703).

$ An Café Liteartha, a simple refuge hidden behind a wonderfully cluttered bookstore, serves soup and sandwiches to a good-natured crowd of Irish speakers (daily 10:00-18:00, Oct-April until 17:00 and closed Sun, Dykegate Street, tel. 066/915-2204).

$ Bean in Dingle is an inviting and hip coffee shop run by Justin and Luke Burgess. They serve baked goodies and fresh sandwiches along with good coffee drinks (daily 8:30-18:00, Green Street).

Ice Cream: For two decades **Murphy's** ice cream has been a Dingle favorite. Their famously adventurous "handmade" flavors

All Roads Lead to Daingean Ui Chuis

The western half of the Dingle Peninsula is part of the Gael-tacht, where locals speak the Irish Gaelic language. In an effort to ward off English-language encroachment, all place names on road signs were controversially changed to Irish-only, though some are now back in English. As you travel along Slea Head Drive (known as Ceann Sléibhe in Irish), refer to this cheat sheet of the most useful destination names. A complete translation of all Irish place names is included in the Gazetteer section at the back of the *Complete Road Atlas of Ireland* by Ordnance Survey.

English Name	Irish Gaelic Name
Dingle	*Daingean Ui Chuis* (DANG-un e koosh)
Ventry	*Ceann Trá* (k'yown—rhymes with "crown" traw)
Slea Head	*Ceann Sléibhe* (k'yown SHLAY-veh)
Dunquin	*Dún Chaoin* (doon qween)
Blasket Islands	*Na Blascaodaí* (nuh BLAS-kud-ee)
Great Blasket Island	*An Blascaod Mór* (on BLAS-kade moor)
Ballyferriter	*Baile an Fheirtearaigh* (BALL-yuh on ERR-ter-ee)
Reasc Monastery	*Mainistir Riaisc* (MON-ish-ter REE-isk)
Gallarus	*Gallaras* (GAHL-russ)
Kilmalkedar	*Cill Mhaoil-cheadair* (kill moyle-KAY-dir)
Annascaul	*Abhainn an Scáil* (ow'en on skahl)
Lispole	*Lios Póil* (leesh pohl)
Tralee	*Trá Lí* (tra-LEE)

include lavender, candied chili pepper, rosewater, clove, and even gin (daily 11:00-22:00, shorter hours off-season, on Strand Street).

ON SLEA HEAD DRIVE

$$ The Stone House is an appealing lunch or dinner option about seven miles (12 km) west of Dingle on Slea Head Drive. Serving local specialties, from scones to fresh seafood and steak dishes, David and Michelle Foran nurture a cozy atmosphere. Their front-porch outdoor tables are popular seaview perches on warm summer evenings, and the fresh Dingle Bay crab salad is a favorite

DINGLE PENINSULA

(daily 10:00-18:00, June-Aug until 20:00, reservations smart, tel. 066/915-9970, www.stonehouseventry.com).

THE ONLY CHEAP MEAL IN DINGLE: PICNIC

The **SuperValu** supermarket/department store, at the base of town, has everything and stays open late (Mon-Sat 8:00-21:00, Sun until 19:00, daily until 22:00 July-Aug). Smaller groceries, such as **Centra** on Main Street (daily 8:00-21:00), are scattered throughout the town. Consider a grand-view picnic out on the end of the newer pier (as you face the harbor, it's the pleasure-boat pier on your right). You'll find picnic tables on the harbor side of the roundabout and benches along the busy harborfront.

Dingle Connections

Tralee (Trá Lí), 30 miles from Dingle, is the region's transportation hub (with the nearest train station). Most bus trips make connections in Tralee.

From Dingle by Bus to: Galway (5/day, 6 hours, transfer in Tralee and Limerick), **Dublin** (3/day, 7 hours, transfer in Tralee and Limerick), **Rosslare** (2/day, 9 hours), **Tralee** (5/day, fewer off-season and Sun, 1.5 hours). Most bus trips out of Dingle require at least one or two (easy) transfers. Remember, buses stop on the waterfront behind the SuperValu (bus info Tel. 01/836-6111, www.buseireann.ie, or Tralee station at 066/712-3566; Tralee train info tel. 066/712-3522). For more information, see "Tralee Connections" at the end of this chapter.

Slea Head Loop Drive

The gloriously green Dingle Peninsula is 10 miles wide and runs 40 miles from Tralee to Slea Head. The top of its mountainous spine is Mount Brandon—at 3,130 feet, it's the second-tallest mountain in Ireland. While only a few tiny villages lie west of Dingle town, the peninsula is home to 50,000 sheep.

The Slea Head Loop, worth ▲▲▲, is a scenic road that lassoes the peninsula in about 30 miles (45 km). It must be driven (or biked) in a clockwise direction. It's easy by car, or a demanding five hours by bike. Remember that minibus tours are offered, too (see "Tours in Dingle" on page 276).

As you navigate the loop, you'll see lots of grass-fed Friesian (or Holstein) cows and the belted Galloway breed from Scotland (looking like they have a white blanket tossed over them). The only wild animal you'll encounter is a rabbit. In spring or summer, you'll

likely enjoy a festival of flowers as you follow the blue signs with white squiggles—a stylized "WAW"—reminding you that this is "The Wild Atlantic Way" (part of a marketing campaign by the Irish Tourist Board).

PLANNING YOUR DRIVE

This route is littered with similar minor sights. I've recommended my favorites to help reduce sightseeing redundancy. Ideally, pull off the road at or near each stop to read the next section and familiarize yourself with what's coming up.

If you'll be visiting Great Blasket Island later, allow time for a stop at the Great Blasket Centre, with interesting exhibits and views across to the island (about half-way around the loop).

Tips for Drivers: To help locate points of interest, I've given distances in kilometers so you can follow along with your odometer. To match my listed distances, set your odometer to zero at Oceanworld as you leave Dingle. You'll stay on R-559 the entire way, following brown *Slea Head Drive* signs for most of the route (through kilometer 37). The road is narrow and can be congested from mid-July to late August.

Tips for Cyclists: Bikers often find this route dangerous and stressful (the road is narrow with high hedges and cliffs crowding the traffic). If biking, try to leave early (consider renting your bike the night before) to avoid the heavy bus and car traffic on busy summer afternoons.

From Dingle Town to Ventry

Leave Dingle town west along the waterfront (0.0 km at Oceanworld). Driving out of town, on the left you'll see a row of humble "two up and two down" cottages from a 1908 affordable-housing government initiative.

0.5 km: Dingle Harbor has an eight-foot tide. The seaweed

DINGLE PENINSULA

Slea Head Loop Drive

To Tiduff

Three Sisters

Smerwick Harbor

KILMALKEDAR CHURCH

Sybil Head

GALLARUS ORATORY (See detail map)

Ballyferriter (Baile an Fheirtearaigh)

To Tralee via Conor Pass

Clogher Head

R-559

REASC MONASTERY

R-559

Dingle (Daingean Uí Chúis)

LONG'S HORSERIDING CENTRE

GREAT BLASKET CENTRE (Ionad An Blascaod Mór)

Mt. Eagle

Ventry (Ceann Trá)

To Killarney

Dingle Harbor

PUB

Dunquin (Dún Chaoin)

FOLLY

ABANDONED VILLAGE

STONE HOUSE

BEEHIVE HUTS

Ventry Bay

LORD VENTRY'S MANOR

EASK TOWER

BULL'S LIGHT-HOUSE

R-559

DUNBEG FORT

Slea Head (Ceann Sléibhe)

Great Blasket Island (An Blascaod Mór)

Dingle Bay

N

Note: Driving route width exaggerated for clarity

2 Kilometers

2 Miles

- - - - Recommended Driving Loop

was used to make formerly worthless land arable. (Seaweed is a natural source of potash—organic farming, before it was trendy.) Across the River Milltown estuary, the recommended **Milltown House** was Robert Mitchum's home during the 1969 filming of the Academy Award-winning movie *Ryan's Daughter*. (Behind that is Dingle's pitch-and-putt golf course.) Look for the narrow mouth of this blind harbor (behind you, in the distance at the opposite end of the harbor, where Fungie the dolphin frolics) and the Ring of Kerry beyond that. Dingle Harbor is so hidden that ships needed the hilltop Eask Tower to find its mouth. If a group of small boats are gathered at the mouth of the harbor, Fungie has come out to play.

0.7 km: At the roundabout, turn left over the bridge. On the far side, the blue building on the right was the site of a corn-grinding mill in the 18th century (with a ghostly black waterwheel hiding behind it). Today it's a modern warehouse that shelters the **Dingle Distillery** (tours daily—see "Sights in Dingle," earlier). Just beyond that on the right, you'll pass the junction where you'll complete this loop 30 miles from now. The gas station on your left is the westernmost on the peninsula (you won't see another on this drive, so consider topping up the tank).

1.3 km: The recommended Milestone House is named for the stone **pillar** (*gallaun* in Irish) in its front yard. This pillar may have been a prehistoric grave or a boundary marker between two tribes. Half of the stone's length is buried underground. This peninsula, literally an open-air archaeological museum, is dotted with more than 2,000 such monuments dating from the Neolithic Age (roughly 3000 BC) through early Christian times. Another stone pillar stands in the field across the road (100 yards away, on the left). The pillar's function today: cow scratcher.

The land ahead on the left holds the estate and mansion of Lord Ventry, whose family came to Dingle as post-Cromwellian War landlords in 1666. Today his mansion (built in 1750, out of view and closed to the public) houses an all-Irish-language girls boarding school.

As you drive past the **Ventry estate** (at 2.8 km, on the right, is Ventry's slate-roofed blacksmith shop), you'll pass palms, magnolias, and exotic flora, which were introduced to Dingle by Lord Ventry. The Gulf Stream is the source of the mild climate, which supports subtropical plants (it rarely snows here). Fuchsias—imported from Chile and spreading like weeds—line the roads all over the peninsula and redden the countryside from June through September. About 75 inches of rain a year gives this area its "40 shades of green."

4.6 km: Stay off the "soft margin" as you enjoy views of Ventry Harbor, its long beach (to your right as you face the water), and distant Skellig Michael, which you'll see all along this part of the route. **Skellig Michael**—the pyramid-shaped island in the distance—holds the rocky remains of a sixth-century monastic settlement (described in previous chapter). It's popular these days because the last scene of *Star Wars: The Force Awakens* (2015) was filmed on its dramatic crags.

In 1866, the first transatlantic cable was laid from nearby Valentia Island to Canada's Newfoundland (see sidebar on page 264). Mount Eagle (1,660 feet), rising across the bay, marks the end of Ireland—and that's where you're heading.

From Ventry to Slea Head

6.6 km: In the town of **Ventry**—a.k.a. Ceann Trá (translated roughly as "beach head")—Irish is the first language. Ventry is little more than a bungalow holiday village today. Urban Irish families love to come here in the summer to immerse their kids in the traditional culture and wild nature. A large hall at the edge of the village is used as a classroom where big-city students come to learn the Irish language.

Just past town, a lane leads left to a fine beach and mobile-home vacation community. An information board explains the history, geology, and bird life of the harbor. The humble trailer park has no running water or electricity. Locals like it for its economy

DINGLE PENINSULA

and proximity to the beach. From here, a lane leads inland to **Long's Horseriding Centre** (described earlier, under "Sights in Dingle").

At the start of World War II (1939), a German U-boat churned into this bay and put 28 Greek sailors ashore (depositing them on neutral Irish soil). The Greeks were survivors from a merchant ship that the sub had sunk...not the kind of humanitarian gesture that German U-boat captains were known for making.

7.3 km: The bamboo-like **rushes** on either side of the road are the kind used to make the local thatched roofs. Thatching, which nearly died out because of fire danger, is more popular now that anti-flame treatments are available. It's expensive, as few qualified thatchers remain in Ireland. Black-and-white magpies fly overhead.

8.5 km: This intersection has the "Three Gs"—God (a church), groceries, and Guinness. The pub just past the church is **Paddy O'Shea's.** The Irish football star Páidí Ó Sé (Paddy O'Shea) was a household name in Ireland. He won eight all-Ireland football titles for Kerry as a player from 1970 to 1988. He then trained the Kerry team for many years before further endearing himself to his fans by running this pub. A heroic **statue** remembers Paddy, who died in 2012.

10.7 km: *Taisteal go Mall* means "go slowly"; the building on the right, surrounded by a tall net to keep the balls in, is the **village schoolhouse.** In summer  it's used for Irish Gaelic courses for kids from the big cities. On the left is the small Celtic and Prehistoric Museum, a quirky private collection of prehistoric artifacts, including arrowheads and ancient jewelry, collected by a retired busker (musician) named Harris (€5, daily 10:00-17:00).

11.1 km: The circular mound (which looks like a big round hedge) on the right is a late Stone Age **ring fort**. It was a petty Celtic chieftain's headquarters—a stone-and-earth stockade filled with little thatched dwellings. Such mysterious sites survived untouched through the centuries because of superstitious beliefs that they were "fairy forts." While this site is unexcavated, archaeologists have found evidence that people have lived on this peninsula since about 4000 BC (There must be a dozen such minor sights along this route. I'll recommend my favorites.)

11.7 km: Look ahead up Mount Eagle at the patchwork of stone-fenced fields. In the distance on the left is another view of Skellig Michael.

12.5 km: Dunbeg Fort (50 yards downhill on the left) is made

DINGLE PENINSULA

up of a series of defensive ramparts and ditches around a central *clochan* (€3, May-Sept 9:00-18:00, July-Aug until 19:00). A third of the fort fell into the sea during a violent storm in 2014. Forts like this are the most important relics left from Ireland's Iron Age (500 BC-AD 500).

The modern stone-roofed dwelling across the street was built to blend in with the landscape and the region's ancient rock-slab architecture (AD 2000). It's the welcoming and recommended **Stone House Restaurant,** with an adjacent visitors center, where you can check out a 10-minute video (€2.50) that gives a bigger picture of the prehistory of the peninsula (included with Dunberg Fort ticket). A traditional *currach* boat is permanently dry-docked in the parking lot.

Roughly 50 yards up the road and 100 yards off the road to the right is a thatched **cottage** abandoned by a family named Kavanaugh during the famine (around 1848). With a few rusty and chipped old artifacts and good descriptions, it offers an evocative peek into the simple lifestyles of the area in the 19th century (€3, daily 10:00-18:00, closed Nov-April). The owner, Gabriel, also runs working sheepdog demonstrations (in Irish for the dogs, English for tourists; €5, €7 combo-ticket covers cottage and dog demo, must book ahead by phone, mobile 087-762-2617, www.dinglesheepdogs.com).

13.2 km: A group of **beehive huts** *(clochans)* is a short walk uphill (€3, daily 9:00-19:00, WC). While reconstructed, these mysterious stone igloos, which cluster together within a circular wall, are a better sight than the similar group of beehive huts down the road.

Farther on (at 14.0 km), you'll ford a stream. There's never been a bridge here; this bit of road—

nicknamed the "upside-down bridge"—was designed as a ford.

14.7 km: Pull off to the left at this second group of beehive huts. (Aedan runs this family enterprise where you can see more *clochan*s, hold a baby lamb, and use the WC for €3.) Look downhill at the rocky field. In the movie *Far and Away,* that's where Lord Ventry evicted (read: torched) peasants from their cottages. Even without Hollywood, this is a bleak and godforsaken land. Look across the bay at the Ring of Kerry in the distance and ahead at the Blasket Islands.

From Slea Head to Ballyferriter

16.0 km: At **Slea Head** (Ceann Sléibhe)—marked by a crucifix, a pullout, and great views of the Blasket Islands (described later)—you turn the corner on this tour. On stormy days, the waves are "racing in like white horses."

16.7 km: Pull into the little parking lot (at *Dún Chaoin* sign) for views of **Great Blasket Island** and **Dunmore Head** (the westernmost point in Europe) and to review the roadside map (which traces your route) posted in the parking lot.

Great Blasket Island is an icon of traditional Irish culture. Because the islanders subsisted off the sea, rather than on potatoes, they survived the famine. The most traditional of Irish communities, about 100 people lived there until 1953, when the government evacuated the island. While the island is uninhabited today, small tour boats shuttle visitors from Dingle and from Dunquin Harbor (just ahead). To read more about this fascinating island, see the next section of this chapter. And to learn more, visit the Great Blasket Centre (a few miles farther down the road).

As you drive on, notice the ruined stone houses (and the sheep oblivious to the amazing views). The scattered village just down the road was abandoned during the famine. Some homes are now fixed up, as this is a popular place these days for summer vacationers. You can see more good examples of land reclamation, patch by patch, climbing up the hillside. Mount Eagle was the first bit of land that Charles Lindbergh saw after crossing the Atlantic on his way to Paris in 1927. Villagers here were as excited as he was—they had never seen anything so big in the air.

Look above, at the patches of land slowly made into farmland by the inhabitants of this westernmost piece of Europe. Rocks were cleared and piled into fences. Sand and seaweed were laid on the clay, and in time it was good for grass. The created land, if at all tillable, was generally used for growing potatoes; otherwise, it was only good for grazing. Much of this farmland has now fallen out of use.

About a kilometer down a road on the left, a plaque celebrates the 30th anniversary of the filming of *Ryan's Daughter*. From here, a trail leads down to a wild beach.

19.0 km: The Blasket Islands' residents had no church or cemetery on the island. On the left stretches their **cemetery.** The famous Blascaod storyteller Peig Sayers (1873-1958) is buried at its center. Just off this coast is the 1588 shipwreck of the *Santa María de la Rosa* of the Spanish Armada. And ahead is the often-tempestuous Dunquin Harbor. Blasket Island farmers—who on a calm day could row across in 30 minutes—would dock here and hike over the saddle and 12 miles into Dingle to sell their produce.

Hey! There's a dead man floating out at sea. Oh, it's just an island. (While its official name is The Sleeping Giant, that island has always been known to Blasket Islanders as "The Dead Man.")

21.3 km: From here a lane leads a kilometer to the **Great Blasket Centre,** worth ▲▲. This excellent modern cultural museum is an essential stop if you plan to visit the islands— or a good place to learn about them if you won't be making the crossing (€5, daily 10:00-18:00, closed Nov-Easter, fine cafeteria run by friendly Christy, tel. 066/915-6444, www. blasket.ie).

The state-of-the-art Blascaod and Gaelic heritage center gives visitors the best look possible at the language, literature, and way of life of Blasket Islanders. The building's award-winning design mixes interpretation and the surrounding countryside. Its spine, a sloping village lane, leads to an almost sacred view of the actual island. Don't miss the exceptional 20-minute video, a virtual visit to the island back when it was inhabited (shows on the half-hour), then hear the sounds, read the poems, browse through old photos, and gaze out the big windows at those rugged islands...and imagine. Even if you never got past limericks, the poetry of these people—so pure and close to each other and nature—will have you dipping your pen into the cry of the birds.

23.1 km: Grab the scenic **Clogher Head pullout.** The view from here is spectacular. Ahead is Mount Brandon, Ireland's second highest peak (at 3,130 feet). Working to the left you'll see Butter Harbor (the name believed to originate from times when Vikings stopped here to grease up their hulls). Then spot the three swoopy peaks—the Three Sisters. Left of that is Sybil Head (where scenes from *Star Wars: The Force Awakens* were shot). On the summit of Sybil Head, the tiny black square is a watchtower from the days when Britain feared an invasion from Napoleon. The entire coast was lined with these, all within sight of each other to relay

Building a Rock Fence

The Emerald Isle is as rocky as it is green. When the English took the best land, they told the Irish to "go to hell or go to Connaught" (the rugged western part of Ireland where the soil was particularly poor and rocky). Every spring, farmers "harvest" rocks driven up by the winter frost in order to plant more edible fare. Over generations, Irish farmers stacked these rocks into fences, which still divide so much of the land.

The fences generally have no visible gates. But upon closer look, you'll see a "V" built into the wall by larger rocks, which are then filled in with smaller rocks. When a farmer needs to move some cattle, he slowly unstacks the smaller rocks, moves the cattle through, and then restacks them. Flying low over western Ireland, the fields—alligatored by these rock fences—seem to stretch forever. And nearly all have these labor-intensive V-shaped gates built in.

a warning signal if under attack by the bloody French. And under the Three Sisters is the popular Dingle Links golf course.

Ahead, on the right, study the top fields, untouched since the planting of 1845, when the potatoes didn't grow, but rotted in the ground. The faint vertical ridges of the potato beds can still be seen—a reminder of the famine. Before the famine, 40,000 people inhabited this peninsula. After the famine, the population was so small that there was never again a need to farm so high up. Today, only 10,000 people live on the peninsula.

From this pullout, a breezy 15-minute walk leads out to **Clogher Head.** The dirt road stretches off to the left and peters out after 200 yards. But it's all open ground and easy to navigate. Just step carefully over bog puddles and head uphill through the rocky heather to the lumpy summit. There you'll be rewarded with postcard-worthy panoramic views.

From Ballyferriter to Dingle

28.0 km: The town of **Ballyferriter,** established by a Norman family in the 12th century, is the largest on this side of Dingle Peninsula. The pubs serve grub, the fine old church dates to the 1860s, and the old schoolhouse (on the left) is a museum with modest exhibits that provide the best coverage of this very historic peninsula (€3, generally daily 10:00-17:00, closed Oct-May, tel. 066/915-6333, www.westkerrymuseum.com). The early Christian slab cross in front of the schoolhouse looks real. Tap it...it's fiberglass—a prop from the *Ryan's Daughter* bus-stop scenes. Across the street, next to the church, is the handy Your Stop market.

Keep on Slea Head Drive (R-559), following signs to *Dingle.*

30.0 km: The road bends over a tiny yellow bridge, past a pub and microbrewery (on the right); 50 yards after that watch for a tiny unmarked paved road going uphill on the right. Detour right up this lane, where you'll find the scant remains of **Reasc Monastery** about 300 yards up (no sign).

This is the stony footprint of a monastic settlement dating from the 6th to 12th century (free, always open). The inner wall divided the community into sections for prayer and business (cottage industries helped support the monastery). In 1975, only the stone pillar was visible, as the entire site was buried. The layer of black tar paper (near the base of the walls) marks where the original rocks stop and the excavators' reconstruction begins. The stone pillar is Celtic (c. 500 BC).

When Christians arrived in the fifth century, they didn't throw out the Celtic society. Instead, they carved a Maltese-type cross over the Celtic scrollwork. The square building was an oratory (church, which is facing east—you'll see an intact oratory at the next stop). The round buildings would have been *clochans*—those stone igloo-type dwellings.

One of the cottage industries operated by the monastery was a double-duty kiln. Just outside the wall (opposite the oratory, past the duplex *clochan*, at the bottom end), find a stone hole with a passage facing the southwest wind. This was the kiln—fanned by the wind, it was used for cooking and drying grain. Locals would bring their grain to be dried and ground, and the monks would keep a tithe (their 10 percent cut). With the arrival of the Normans in the 12th century, these small religious communities were pushed aside by a militaristic feudal system.

Return to the main road and continue on.

32.0 km: Go left at the big Dingle Peninsula Hotel, following *Gallarus* signs and staying on Slea Head Drive.

33.0 km: Turn right up the narrow lane. The "free" car park is a private enterprise on private land (with a short video, WC, and shop), where you'll be charged €3 to see the site. To park for free, go farther up the lane (at 33.4 km) to a tiny five-car pullout on the left, where a path leads through a gate 200 yards to the amazing **Gallarus Oratory** (free, always open).

Built about 1,300 years ago, the Gallarus Oratory is one of Ireland's best-preserved early Christian churches. Shaped like an upturned boat, its finely fitted dry-stone walls are still waterproof. As you step in, notice how thick the walls are. A simple, small arched window offers scant daylight over where the altar would have stood. Picture the interior lit by candles during medieval monastic services. It would have been tough to fit more than about a dozen monks inside. Notice the holes once used to secure covering at the door, and the fine alternating stonework on the corners.

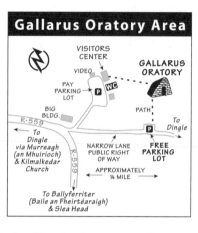

Gallarus Oratory Area

VISITORS CENTER

VIDEO

GALLARUS ORATORY

PAY PARKING LOT

WC

BIG BLDG.

PATH

R-559

To Dingle

P

To Dingle via Murreagh (an Mhuiríoch) & Kilmalkedar Church

NARROW LANE PUBLIC RIGHT OF WAY

FREE PARKING LOT

APPROXIMATELY ¼ MILE

To Ballyferriter (Baile an Fheirtéaraigh) & Slea Head

From the oratory, return to the main road and continue, following the brown *Slea Head Drive* signs. (To skip the Kilmalkedar Church—last stop on this tour—and go directly back to Dingle, continue up the narrow lane and turn right when you hit the bigger road.)

35.5 km: At the junction in the center of the next village, leave Slea Head Drive by taking a right on R-559 (signed with *Dingle, 10 km*). For an optional stop (your own private mini Gallarus Oratory), pull off at 37.1 km at the cemetery, cross the road, and hike 200 yards to St. Brandon's Oratory, which dates to the sixth century (even older than Gallarus).

37.3 km: The **ruined church of Kilmalkedar** (Cill Mhaoil-cheadair, on the left at the yellow hiker sign) was the Norman center of worship for this end of the peninsula. It was built when England replaced the old monastic settlements in an attempt to centralize their rule. The 12th-century church has a classic Romanesque arch and a well-worn cross atop its roof. It's surrounded by a densely populated graveyard (which has risen noticeably above the surrounding fields over the centuries). In front of the church, you'll find the oldest (late medieval) tombs, a stately early Christian cross (substantially buried by the rising graveyard and therefore oddly proportioned), and a much older ogham stone. This stone, which had already stood here 900 years when the church was built, is notched with the mysterious Morse code-type ogham script used from the third to seventh century. It may have marked a grave or a clan border, indicating that this was an important pre-Christian gathering place. The hole was drilled through the top of the stone centuries ago as a place where people would come to seal a deal by touching thumbs through this stone. The church fell into ruin during the Reformation.

38.0 km: Continue uphill, overlooking the water. You'll pass another ancient **"fairy fort"** on the right. The bay stretched out below you is Smerwick Harbor. In 1580 a force of 600 Italian and Spanish troops (sent by the pope to aid a rebellion against the Protestant English) surrendered at this bay to the English. All 600 were beheaded by the English forces, which included Sir Walter Raleigh.

41.7 km: At the crest of the hill you may see the belted Galloway beef cattle with their white blankets. The spruce forest on the right was planted with government supplements (to meet EU forest standards for minimizing Ireland's carbon footprint). From here, enjoy a long coast back into Dingle town (sighting, as old-time mariners did, the Eask Tower).

44.0 km: Take a left past the Dingle Distillery, go over the bridge, and head back into Dingle. At 45 km, you're back at the Oceanarium where you started. Well done!

Blasket Islands

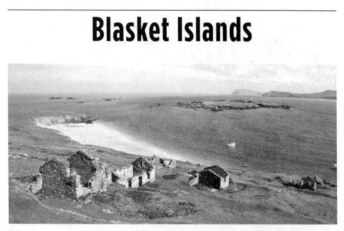

This rugged group of six islands off the tip of Dingle Peninsula seems particularly close to the soul of Ireland. The only one you can visit, Great Blasket Island, worth ▲▲, was once home to as many as 160 people. Life here was hard, but the sea provided for all, and no one went hungry. Each family had a cow, a few sheep, and a plot of potatoes. They cut their peat from the high ridge and harvested fish from the sea. To these folk, World War I provided a bonus, as occasionally valuable cargo washed ashore from merchant ships sunk by U-boats. There was no priest, pub, or doctor. Because they were not entirely dependent upon the potato, island inhabitants survived the famine relatively unscathed. These people formed the most traditional Irish community of the 20th century—the symbol of ancient Gaelic culture.

DINGLE PENINSULA

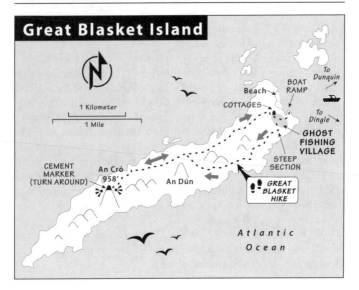

A special closeness to an island—combined with a knack for vivid storytelling—is inspirational. From this simple but proud fishing/farming community came three writers of international repute whose Gaelic works—basically tales of life on Great Blasket Island—have been translated into many languages. You'll find *Peig* (by Peig Sayers) and *The Islandman* (Thomas O'Crohan) in shops everywhere. But the most readable and upbeat is *Twenty Years A-Growing* (Maurice O'Sullivan), a somewhat-true, Huck Finn-esque account of the author's childhood and adolescence and of island life as it was a hundred years ago.

The population dwindled until the government moved the last handful of elderly residents to the mainland in 1953. Today Great Blasket is little more than a ghost town overrun with rabbits on a peaceful, grassy, three-mile-long poem.

GETTING THERE

In summer, various boats run between **Dingle town** and the Blasket Islands, with anywhere from a 3.5- to 6-hour stop to explore Great Blasket. The ride (which may include a quick look at Fungie the dolphin) traces the spectacular coastline all the way to Slea Head. Competing boats offer similar services from Dingle town and operate when there's enough demand. The tricky landing at Great Blasket Island's primitive and slippery little boat ramp makes getting off a challenge and landing virtually impossible in wet weather. Boats generally depart from the marina pier in Dingle at 9:00 or 11:00 and return from Great Blasket at 15:00 or 17:30.

For details, see the boat tour listings under "Tours in Dingle," earlier.

Schedules are soft—reconfirm the day before. Hikers (bringing their own picnic) should take the early boat out and a late boat back. With a bit of planning, you can spend a half-day and really do the island justice. Nonhikers can put ashore for an hour or two just to explore the ghost-town ruins.

Boats also go from **Dunquin Harbor** to the Blasket Islands (book ahead; see Blasket Island Ferry listing under "Tours in Dingle," earlier).

VISITING GREAT BLASKET ISLAND

Boats bring visitors ashore at the abandoned village, next to the beach, at the east end of the island (the only landing on the island). Be sure to reconfirm the return boat schedule with the crew before you disembark. Those arriving on early boats may be treated to the sight of dozens of gray seals lounging on the beach (dangerous to approach).

Upon dropping anchor, you'll be ferried from the boat to the boat ramp in a six-person RIB/zodiac. (Be especially careful of the slippery tidal muck as you get off the RIB boat.) Then ask the Office of Public Works guide on shore when the next guided walk of the abandoned village starts; those here to hike can start their trek immediately if it's a long wait. There are no eateries (bring a picnic), but you can stay here in a simple rental cottage (see "Sleeping in Dingle," earlier).

Tourist Information: Before you go, visit the **Great Blasket Centre** on the mainland near Dunquin (see page 311) and spend some time on the excellent **website** of the Office of Public Works, devoted to both the island and the visitors center (www.blasket.ie).

Great Blasket Hike: Given decent weather, this is one of my favorite hiking destinations in Ireland. The long (roughly 3.5 miles), thin island is flanked by easy-to-follow hiking trails across blankets of moss on a treeless terrain, making it simple to wander on your own. You can also book a guided tour led by Claire Galvin or Kevin O'Shea of Celtic Nature Walking Tours, based in Dingle (see "Tours in Dingle," earlier).

If it rained the day before, the moss will retain the moisture and you'll be stomping on wet sponges (wear good shoes either way). But given dry weather, it's an ideal experience with intoxicating views in all directions. Know that there are no modern WCs or dependable shelter (unless you've booked one of the three cottages at the top of the ghost town).

Think of the island as a giant hog's back running generally northeast to southwest, with parallel trails running along the south-facing and north-facing slopes. Successively taller summits

DINGLE PENINSULA

(the tallest, An Cró, is 950 feet) can be hiked up. An easy loop circles the lowest and closest ridge, linking the south- and north-flank trails (do this if you're short on time). Beyond that junction, the trail becomes a single heather-clumped path that heads right up the ridge to the two taller summits.

The only steep section of the hike is the first hundred-yard slope behind the abandoned village that you'll take to reach the flanks of the ridge, which the rest of the trail follows. I like to take the south-facing trail outbound with the morning light and save the north side for the return, when parts of the trail are brought out of the shade by the afternoon sun.

You could simply hike out for an hour and then hike back (or split whatever amount of time you have between your start time and your village-ruins tour or boat departure). You'll know you've reached the third summit when you encounter a stubby hip-high concrete pylon marker (there's no need to go farther as the views are best from here).

Tralee

While Killarney is the tour-bus capital of County Kerry, Tralee  (Trá Lí in Irish, both pronounced Tra-LEE) is its work-aday market and transit hub. For drivers zipping between Dingle and Galway, this amiable town near the base of the Dingle Peninsula is worth an hour's stop.

The town comes alive for the famous Rose of Tralee International Festival, usually held in mid-August. It's a celebration of arts and music, culminating in the election of the Rose of Tralee—the most beautiful woman at the festival (no matter which country she was born in, as long as she has Irish heritage).

Sights in Tralee

▲Kerry County Museum

Easily the best place to learn about life in Kerry, this museum (located in Ashe Memorial Hall in the center of town) has three parts: Kerry slide show, museum, and medieval-town walk.

Cost and Hours: €5; daily 9:30-17:30, Oct-May until 17:00 and closed Sun-Mon; tel. 066/712-7777, www.kerrymuseum.ie.

Visiting the Museum: Get in the mood by relaxing for 10 minutes through the continuous slide show of Kerry's spectacular scenery. Then wander through 7,000 years of Kerry history in the museum. The Irish joke that when a particularly stupid guy moved from Cork to Kerry, he raised the average IQ in both counties—but this museum is pretty well done. It starts with good background info on the archaeological sites of Dingle, progresses through Viking artifacts found in the area, and goes right up to a video showing highlights of the Kerry football team (a fun look at Irish football, which is more like rugby than soccer). Good coverage is given to adventurous Kerryman Tom Crean, who survived three Antarctic expeditions with Scott and Shackleton (see sidebar on page 290). Also covered is the tragic life of humanitarian Roger Casement, a 1916 Easter Rising gentleman rebel, who was captured on a nearby beach and later executed. The lame finale is a stroll back in time on a re-creation of Tralee's circa-1450 Main Street. Before leaving, horticulture enthusiasts will want to ramble through the rose garden in the adjacent park.

Blennerville Windmill

On the western edge of Tralee, just off the N-86 Dingle road, spins a restored mill originally built in 1780. Its eight-minute video tells the story of the windmill, which ground grain to feed Britain as that country steamed into the Industrial Age. In the 19th century, Blennerville was a major port for America-bound emigrants. It was also the home port where the *Jeanie Johnston* was built. This modern-day replica of a 19th-century ship occasionally tours Atlantic ports, explaining the Irish emigrant experience. Most of the time, it's docked and available to tour in Dublin, on the north shore of the River Liffey (see page 95).

Cost and Hours: €7 gets you a one-room emigration exhibit, the video, and a peek at the spartan interior of the working windmill; daily 9:00-18:00, April-May and Sept-Oct 9:30-17:30, closed Nov-March, last entry 45 minutes before closing, tel. 066/712-1064, www.blennerville-windmill.ie.

Tralee Connections

Travelers headed for Dingle using public transportation will likely find themselves passing through Tralee.

From Tralee by Train to: Dublin (every 2 hours, 6/day on Sun, 1 direct in morning, otherwise change in mellow Mallow, 4 hours, arrives at Heuston Station), **Killarney** (8/day, 35 minutes). Train info: Tel. 066/712-3522, www.irishrail.ie.

By Bus to: Dingle (6/day, fewer off-season and on Sun, 1 hour), **Galway** (8/day, 4 hours), **Limerick** (7/day, 2 hours), **Doolin/Cliffs of Moher** (5/day, 5 hours), **Ennis** (6/day, 3.5 hours, change in Limerick), **Rosslare** (3/day, 7 hours with changes), **Shannon** (7/day, 3 hours), **Dublin** (5/day, 6 hours). Tralee's bus station is across the parking lot from the train station. Bus info: Tel. 066/716-4700, www.buseireann.ie.

By Plane: Kerry Airport is a 20-minute drive from Tralee and a one-hour drive from Dingle (code: KIR, tel. 066/976-4644, www.kerryairport.ie).

It's just off the main N-22 road, halfway between Killarney and Tralee. It has a half-dozen handy rental-car outlets and an ATM. Dingle Shuttle Bus is your best connection to Dingle town, but you must reserve in advance (about €30-40/person one-way depending on number of passengers, minimum 3 passengers, mobile 087-250-4767, www.dingleshuttlebus.com). You can also connect to the airport via taxi (€35 from Tralee, €90 from Dingle) or bus (3/day to Dingle via Tralee). The Kerry Airport offers two flights per day to **Dublin.** International destinations served from this tiny airport include London's Stanstead and Luton airports as well as Frankfurt Hahn airport (about 75 miles from Frankfurt).

Route Tips for Drivers: If you're **driving to Dingle,** you have two choices as you enter the neck of the Dingle Peninsula:

the narrow, but very exciting, Conor Pass road; or the faster, easier N-86 through Lougher and Annascaul (Abhainn an Scáil). On a clear day, Conor Pass comes with incredible views over Tralee Bay and Brandon Bay. On the north slope approaching the pass, pull out at the waterfall. From here, there's a fun five-minute scramble to a dramatic little glacier-created lake. Pause also at the summit viewpoint to look down on Dingle town and harbor.

If you're **driving from Dingle,** heading north straight to Galway, the inland Limerick route is fastest and cheapest (roughly €2 in tolls). But if you're going to the Cliffs of Moher and the

Burren, the 20-minute Killimer-Tarbert ferry connection allows you to avoid the 80-mile detour around the River Shannon and is more scenic (€20/carload, departs hourly, June-Sept every 30 minutes; generally departs at :30 past the hour going north and on the hour going south—check timetables online; no need to reserve, tel. 065/905-3124, www.shannonferries.com).

COUNTY CLARE & THE BURREN

Ennis • Cliffs of Moher • Doolin • Lisdoonvarna • Irish Workhouse Centre

Those connecting Dingle in the south with Galway up the coast to the north can entertain themselves along the way by joyriding through the fascinating landscape and tidy villages of County Clare. Ennis, the county's major city, is a workaday Irish place with a medieval history, a great traditional Irish music scene, and a market bustle—ideal for anyone tired of the tourist crowds. Overlooking the Atlantic, the dramatic Cliffs of Moher offer tenderfeet a thrilling hike. The Burren is a unique, windblown limestone moonscape that hides an abundance of flora, fauna, caves, and history. The sobering Irish Workhouse Centre in Portumna offers an opportunity to contemplate the country's harsh Victorian-era options for the destitute. And at the other end of the spectrum, for your evening entertainment, join a tour-bus group for a medieval banquet in a castle in Kinvarra or meet up with trad-music enthusiasts from around Europe for tin whistling in Doolin.

PLANNING YOUR TIME

By Car: A car is the best way to experience County Clare and the Burren. The region can be an enjoyable daylong drive-through or a destination itself. None of the sights take much time. But do get out and walk a bit.

If you're driving from Dingle to Galway, I'd recommend the following day plan: Rather than taking the main N-21 road via Limerick, drive north from Tralee on N-69 via Listowel to catch the Tarbert-Killimer car ferry (avoiding Limerick traffic). Even though the ferry is slower and more expensive, it's more direct to the Burren (see the end of the previous chapter). From Killimer, drive north on N-67 via Kilkee and Milltown Malbay. The little

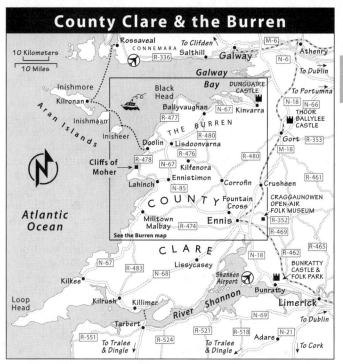

surfer-and-golfer village of Lahinch makes a good lunch stop. Then drive the coastal route to the Cliffs of Moher for an hour-long break. (You could wait to eat at the cafeteria at the cliffs, but big-bus tour groups can smother it at midday in summer.) The scenic drive from the cliffs through the Burren, with a couple of stops, takes about two hours. Consider partaking in the 17:30 medieval banquet at Dunguaire Castle, near Kinvarra (one hour south of Galway).

By Train or Bus: Using public transportation, your gateways to this region are Ennis from the south and Galway from the north; Limerick (via Ennis) and Galway are connected by rail—a big plus for those staying in Ennis without a car. Linking the smaller sights within County Clare and the Burren by bus is difficult: Book a tour instead (see "Tours in the Burren," later in this chapter).

Tip: Skip the crowded **Bunratty Castle and Folk Park**—I'd leave this to the jet-lagged, big-bus tour groups.

County Clare

Ennis

This bustling market town (pop. 25,000), the main town of County Clare, provides those relying on public transit with a handy transportation hub (good rail connections to Limerick, Dublin, and Galway). Ennis is 15 miles from Shannon Airport and makes a good first- or last-night base in Ireland for travelers not locked into Dublin flights. It also offers a chance to wander around an Irish town that is not reliant upon the tourist dollar (though not shunning it either). Muhammad Ali visited the town in 2008 after discovering that one of his great-grandfathers had been born in Ennis. Locals credit his success to his fightin' Irish side.

The center of Ennis is a tangle of contorted streets (often one-way). Use the steeple of Saints Peter and Paul Cathedral and the Daniel O'Connell monument column (at either end of the main shopping drag, O'Connell Street) as landmarks.

Orientation to Ennis

TOURIST INFORMATION

The TI is just off O'Connell Square (Mon-Sat 9:30-17:30, closed Sun year-round and Mon Oct-May; some lunchtime closures, tel. 065/682-8366).

ARRIVAL IN ENNIS

By Car: Day-trippers can park in one of several pay-and-display lots (€1/hour, enforced Mon-Sat 9:30-17:30, free on Sun, usually 3-hour maximum). The centrally located multistory lot on Market Place Square charges €5 per day (Mon-Sat 7:30-19:30, closed Sun).

By Train or Bus: The train and bus station is located southeast of town, a 15-minute walk from the center. To reach town, exit the station parking lot and turn left on Station Road, passing through a roundabout and past the recommended Grey Gables B&B. Turn right after the recommended Old Ground Hotel onto O'Connell Street.

By Plane: Shannon Airport is about 15 miles south of Ennis (see "Ennis Connections," later).

HELPFUL HINTS

Festival: Crowds flock to the **Fleadh Nua** (*fleadh*, pronounced "flah") to celebrate Irish culture at the end of May, making it a challenge to find accommodations (www.fleadhnua.com).

Bookstore: The **Ennis Bookshop** has a good selection (Mon-Fri 9:30-18:30, Sat until 18:00, closed Sun, 13 Abbey Street, tel. 065/682-9000).

Laundry: Fergus launderette is opposite the Harvey's Quay parking lot (Mon-Sat 8:30-18:00, closed Sun, tel. 065/682-3122).

Supermarket: Dunnes Stores has a location in the shopping center on O'Connell Street (Mon-Sat 8:00-21:00, Sun from 9:00).

Taxi: A good local bet is **Burren Taxis** (tel. 065/682-3456).

Walking Tours: Jane O'Brien leads 1.5-hour walking tours of Ennis departing from the TI (€10, mid-May-mid-Sept Mon-Tue and Thu-Sat at 11:00; no regularly scheduled tours Wed, Sun, or off-season; available for private tours, mobile 087-648-3714, www.enniswalkingtours.com). **Ollie's Tours** operates 1.5-hour walking tours, departing from the O'Connell Monument (€10, May-Sept daily at 10:45, mobile 086-202-3534, www.olliestours.com). They also offer 2.5-hour evening food tours (€65, May-Sept Wed-Sun at 17:30, same meeting point).

Sights in Ennis

Clare Museum

This small but worthwhile museum, housed in the large TI building, has eclectic displays about ancient ax heads, submarine development, and local boys who made good—from 10th-century High King Brian Ború to 20th-century statesman Éamon de Valera. Coverage includes the Battle of Dysert O'Dea in 1318. One of the few Irish victories over the invading Normans, it delayed English domination of most of County Clare for another 200 years.

Cost and Hours: Free, Mon-Sat 9:30-13:00 & 14:00-17:30, closed Sun year-round and Mon Oct-May, tel. 065/682-3382, www.clarelibrary.ie.

Ennis Friary

The Franciscan monks arrived here in the 13th century, and the town grew up around their friary (which is like a monastery). Today, it's still worth a look for its 15th-century limestone carvings (now protected by a modern roof to keep their details from further deterioration).

Cost and Hours: €5, sometimes includes tour—depends on staffing, daily 10:00-18:00, closed Nov-March, tel. 065/682-9100.

Visiting the Friary: If more than one guide is on duty, ask for a brief introduction to the five carvings taken from the McMahon family tomb. The last one, of Christ rising on the third day, has a banner with a tiny swastika. But look closely: It's reversed so that it rotates as the rising sun would. Despite the swastika's later Nazi association, it's actually a centuries-old symbol of good luck (the word "swastika" comes from Sanskrit and means "well-being").

COUNTY CLARE & THE BURREN

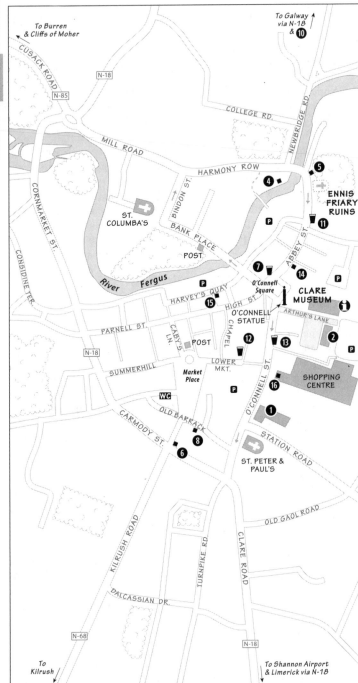

To Burren
& Cliffs of Moher

To Galway
via N-18
& 10

CUSACK ROAD

N-18

N-85

COLLEGE RD.

NEWBRIDGE RD.

MILL ROAD

HARMONY ROW

4

5

BINDON ST.

ENNIS
FRIARY
RUINS

CORNMARKET ST.

ST.
COLUMBA'S

BANK PLACE

P

11

CONSIDINE TER.

POST

ABBEY ST.

14

River Fergus

7

HARVEY'S QUAY

15

O'Connell
Square

CLARE
MUSEUM

HIGH ST.

CHAPEL LN.

O'CONNELL
STATUE

ARTHUR'S LANE

2

PARNELL ST.

N-18

CABY'S LN.

POST

12

13

P

SUMMERHILL

Market
Place

LOWER
MKT.

O'CONNELL ST.

SHOPPING
CENTRE

WC

P

16

OLD BARRACK

CARMODY ST.

8

1

6

STATION ROAD

ST. PETER &
PAUL'S

KILRUSH ROAD

TURNPIKE RD.

OLD GAOL ROAD

CLARE ROAD

DALCASSIAN DR.

N-68

N-18

To
Kilrush

To Shannon Airport
& Limerick via N-18

Ennis

Accommodations
1. Old Ground Hotel & Poet's Corner Pub
2. Temple Gate Hotel
3. Grey Gables B&B
4. Rowan Tree Hostel

Eateries
5. The Cloisters Restaurant & Pub
6. Henry's Bistro & Wine Bar
7. Knox's Pub
8. Numero Uno Pizzeria

Nightlife & Other
9. Glór Irish Music Centre
10. To Cois na hAbhna Show
11. Cruise's Pub
12. Quinn's Pub
13. Brogan's Pub
14. Ennis Bookshop
15. Launderette
16. Supermarket

One-way streets

100 Meters
100 Yards

Postwar visitors, unaware of the symbol's older meaning, misunderstood it and tried to rub it out of the carving, thus its very faint presence today.

The guides can also fully explain the crucifixion symbolism in the 15th-century *Ecce Homo* carving on a nearby pillar. Every item surrounding Christ on the cross has its own purposeful meaning (nothing on this carving is done just for the sake of decoration). It's a fascinating glimpse into how illiterate worshippers 600 years ago could understand icons even though they couldn't read.

NEAR ENNIS
▲Craggaunowen

This open-air folk museum nestles in a pretty forest, an easy 20-minute drive east of Ennis. All the structures are replicas, except for the small 16th-century castle (tower house), which the park was built around. A friendly weaver, spinning her wool on the castle's ground floor, is glad to tell you the tricks of her trade. A highlight is the Crannog, a fortified Iron Age thatch-roofed dwelling built on a small manmade island, which gives you a  grubby idea of how clans lived 2,000 years ago. A modern surprise hides in a corner of the park under a large glass teepee: the *Brendan,* the original humble boat that scholar Tim Severin sailed from Ireland to North America in 1976 (via frosty stepping stones like Iceland and Greenland). He built this boat out of tanned hides, sewn together using primitive methods, to prove that Ireland's St. Brendan may indeed have been the first European to visit America on his legendary voyage, 900 years before Columbus and 500 years before the Vikings.

Cost and Hours: €11, daily 10:00-17:00, shorter hours off-season, last entry one hour before closing, tel. 061/711-222, www.shannonheritage.com.

Getting There: The park is well signposted nine miles (15 km) east of Ennis off R-469, which leads out of town past the train station.

Nightlife in Ennis

Glór Irish Music Centre

The town's modern theater center (*glór* is Irish for "sound") connects you with Irish culture. It's worth considering for traditional music, dance, or storytelling performances (€10-25, year-round

The Voyage of St. Brendan

It has long been part of Irish lore that St. Brendan the Naviga-tor (AD 484-577) and 12 followers sailed from the southwest of Ireland to the "Land of Promise" (what is now North Ameri-ca) in a *currach*—a wood-frame boat covered with ox hide and tar. According to a 10th-century monk who poetically wrote of the journey, St. Brendan and his crew encountered a paradise of birds, were attacked by a whale, and suffered the smoke of a smelly island in the north before finally reaching their Land of Promise.

The legend and its precisely described locations still fas-cinate modern readers. Parts of the tale hold up: The smelly island could well be the sulfuric volcanoes of Iceland. Other parts seem like devoted delirium: The holy monks claimed to have come upon Judas, chained to a rock in the middle of the ocean for all eternity.

A British scholar of navigation, Tim Severin, re-created the entire journey in 1976-1977. He and his crew set out from Brendan Creek in County Kerry in a *currach*. The prevailing winds blew them to the Hebrides, the Faroe Islands, Iceland, and finally to Newfoundland. While this didn't successfully prove that St. Brendan sailed to North America, it did prove that he could have. (You can visit Tim Severin's boat at the Craggaunowen open-air folk museum.)

According to his 10th-century biographer, "St. Brendan sailed from the Land of Promise home to Ireland. And from that time on, Brendan acted as if he did not belong to this world at all. His mind and his joy were in the delight of heaven."

usually at 20:00, 5-minute walk behind TI on Friar's Walk, ticket office open Mon-Sat 10:00-17:00, closed Sun, tel. 065/684-3103, www.glor.ie).

Cois na hAbhna

This original stage show, housed in the local Cois na hAbhna (COSH-na-HOW-na) Hall, is a fine way to spend an evening. Sponsored by Comhaltas, a nonprofit focused on Irish traditional music, it's a celebration of Irish performing arts presented in two parts. The first features great Irish music, song, and dance. After the break, you're invited to kick up your heels and take the floor as the dancers teach some famous Irish set dances. Phone ahead to see if a *ceilidh* is scheduled on off nights (€10-15, sporadically May-Sept Wed and Fri at 20:30, call ahead to confirm, at edge of town on N-18 Galway road, tel. 065/682-4276, www.coisnahabhna.ie).

Traditional Music

Live music begins in pubs at about 21:30. The best is **Cruise's** on Abbey Street, with music nightly year-round and good food (bar is cheaper than restaurant, tel. 065/682-8963). Other pubs offering weekly traditional music nights (generally on weekends, but schedules vary) are **Quinn's** on Lower Market Street (tel. 065/682-8148), **Knox's** on Abbey Street (tel. 065/682-287), and **Brogan's** on O'Connell Street (tel. 065/682-9480). The **Old Ground Hotel** hosts live music year-round in its pub (Tue-Sun, open to anyone); although tour groups stay at the hotel, the pub is low-key and feels real, not staged.

Sleeping in Ennis

My first two listings are fancy hotels that you'll share with tour groups.

$$$$ Old Ground Hotel is a stately, ivy-covered 18th-century manse (minister's residence) with 105 rooms and a family feel. Pan Am clipper pilots stayed here during the early days of transatlantic seaplane flights (four blocks from station at intersection of Station Road and O'Connell Street, tel. 065/682-8127, www.oldgroundhotelennis.com, reservations@oldgroundhotel.ie).

$$$$ Temple Gate Hotel's 70 rooms are more modern and less personal (breakfast extra, just off O'Connell Street, in courtyard with TI, tel. 065/682-3300, www.templegatehotel.com, info@templegatehotel.com).

$ Grey Gables B&B has 12 tastefully decorated rooms (cash only, wheelchair access, family rooms, parking, on Station Road 5 minutes from train station toward town center, tel. 065/682-4487, mobile 085-739-3793, www.greygables.ie, info@greygables.ie, Mary Keane).

¢ Rowan Tree Hostel is a well-run budget option, centrally located beside the gurgling River Fergus. It incorporates a grand old gentleman's club into its modern additions with better-than-expected private rooms and tidy dorm rooms. A pleasant café/bar rounds out the complex (on Harmony Row next to the bridge, tel. 065/686-8687, www.rowantreehostel.ie, info@rowantreehostel.ie).

Eating in Ennis

The Cloisters, next door to Ennis Friary, inhabits equally historic 800-year-old walls. Its steak, lamb, and fish dishes are the best in town and are served in a tasteful atmosphere, either in the upstairs **$$$$ restaurant** (Tue-Sun 17:30-21:00) or the downstairs **$$$ pub** (Tue-Sun 12:00-17:30, both sections closed Mon, Abbey Street, tel. 065/686-8198).

$$$ Henry's Bistro & Wine Bar is run by friendly Dermot with attention on quality entrées, including ribeye steaks, lamb shanks, and salmon fillets. A great wine selection is hard to find in rural Ireland, but he's got one (Wed-Sat 12:00-14:30 & 17:30-21:00, Sun 12:30-20:00, closed Mon-Tue, Upper Market Street, tel. 065/689-9393).

$$$ Poet's Corner pub, at the recommended Old Ground Hotel, serves up hearty meals (Mon-Sat 12:00-21:00, Sun from 16:00).

For better-than-average pub grub, I like **$ Knox's Pub** on Abbey Street (daily 12:00-21:00, tel. 065/682-287). Or try one of the other places mentioned under "Nightlife in Ennis," earlier.

The simple **$ Numero Uno Pizzeria** is good for an easy pub-free dinner (Mon-Sat 12:00-23:00, Sun from 15:00, on Old Barrack Street off Market Place, tel. 065/684-1740).

Ennis Connections

From Ennis by Train to: Galway (5/day, 1.5 hours), **Limerick** (9/day, 40 minutes), **Dublin** (10/day, 4 hours, change in Limerick, Limerick Junction, or Athenry). Train info: Tel. 065/684-0444, www.irishrail.ie.

By Bus to: Galway (hourly, 1.5 hours), **Dublin** (almost hourly, 5 hours), **Rosslare** (4/day, 6.5 hours), **Limerick** (hourly, 1 hour), **Lisdoonvarna** (5/day, 2 hours), **Ballyvaughan** (1/day, 2.5 hours), **Tralee** (6/day, 3.5 hours, change in Limerick), **Doolin** (5/day, 2 hours). Bus info: Tel. 065/682-4177, www.buseireann.ie.

SHANNON AIRPORT

The major airport in western Ireland comes with far less stress than Dublin's overcrowded airport (airport code: SNN, www.shannonairport.ie). It has a TI (daily 6:30-19:30, Oct-May until 17:30, tel. 061/471-664), ATMs, Wi-Fi, and baggage storage. A taxi between the airport and Ennis should run about €35.

From Shannon Airport by Bus to: Ennis (bus #51 runs between the airport and the Ennis train station hourly, 20 minutes after the hour starting at 8:20, 30 minutes), **Galway** (bus #51, hourly, 2 hours), **Limerick** (at least 2/hour, 1 hour, can continue to Tralee—2 hours more, and Dingle—4/day, another 2 hours; bus tel. 061/313-333, www.buseireann.ie).

Sleeping near Shannon Airport: Consider **$$ Park Inn by Radisson Shannon Airport** (tel. 061/471-122, www.parkinn.com).

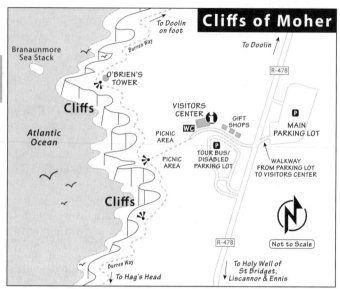

Cliffs of Moher

A visit to the Cliffs of Moher (pronounced "MO-hur")—a ▲▲▲ sight—is one of Ireland's great natural thrills. For five miles, the dramatic cliffs soar as high as 650 feet above the Atlantic.

GETTING THERE
By Car
The Cliffs of Moher are located on R-478, south of Doolin. The parking lot across the road from the visitors center is for the general public; pay the attendant as you drive in. The lot next to the visitors center is for tour buses and visitors with disabilities.

Without a Car
From Galway: Galway Tour Company offers direct shuttle service (not a tour) to and from the Cliffs of Moher (€25, includes cliffs admission; see listing on page 354 for contact details). If the weather cooperates, you can add a Cliffs of Moher cruise (€15). They also offer a tour that includes the Burren (see "Tours in the Burren," later in this chapter).

You can also get here by public bus from Galway (8/day in summer, some with change in Ennis, 2 hours, www.buseireann.ie).

From Doolin: The Cliffs of Moher are reachable by coastal hike or shuttle bus, or you can take a cruise from Doolin to see (but not visit) the cliffs. For details on these options, see "Activities in Doolin," later.

ORIENTATION TO THE CLIFFS OF MOHER

Cost: €8, €4 if you book online and visit before 11:00 or after 16:00, includes parking and admission to the visitors center and its exhibit. It's not worth the €2 to climb O'Brien's Tower.

Hours: Daily 8:00-19:00, gradually later closing times toward midsummer (as late as 21:00 May-Aug), Nov-Feb 9:00-17:00.

Information: Tel. 065/708-6141, www.cliffsofmoher.ie.

Services: You'll find an information desk and ATM in the visitors center—the Tolkienesque labyrinth tucked under the grassy hillside—flanked by six hobbit garages housing gift shops (across the street from the parking lot). **Cliffs View Café,** upstairs in the visitors center, serves coffee and substantial cafeteria-style hot meals until 16:30. There's also the **Puffin's Nest,** a small sandwich café downstairs.

VISITING THE CLIFFS OF MOHER

The visitors center is designed smartly to orient you to the cliffs experience, spiraling up and finally out onto the cliffs themselves in this order: entry (TI, shop, café); nature exhibit; short film in theater; main restaurant and WC; and outside to the cliffs. (While this is ideal, if the weather seems iffy and you see a sun break, you could do the cliff walk first.)

Visitors Center: The Atlantic Edge exhibit, downstairs, focuses mainly on natural and geological history, native bird and marine life, and virtual interactive exhibits aimed at children. You may even learn why the cliffs are always windy. A small theater shows *The Ledge Experience,* a film following a gannet as he flies along the cliffs and then dives underwater, encountering puffins, seals, and even a humpback whale along the way. (The film is on a five-minute loop with the start-time clock ticking down above the theater door.)

The Cliffs: After leaving the visitors center, walk 200 yards to the **cliff** edge. A protective wall of the local Liscannor slate (notice the squiggles made by worms, eels, and snails long ago when the slate was still mud on the seafloor) keeps visitors safely back from the cliff. You can walk behind the protective wall in either direction. The trail to the right (north, uphill toward the castle-like tower) is the most rewarding.

For years, the Irish didn't believe in safety fences, just natural selection. Anyone could walk right up to the cliffs, until numerous fatal accidents (and suicides) prompted the hiring of "rangers"—

ostensibly there to answer questions, but mainly there to keep you from getting too close to the edge (wind gusts can be sudden, strong, and deadly).

As you gaze down at the waves crashing far, far below you, consider this: Surfing in wet suits is popular in Ireland. Most sane Irish surfers stick to the predictable waves at Lahinch (5 miles south of here). But the monster waves that rear up beneath the Cliffs of Moher on stormy days are coveted by extreme surfers, who work in tandem with tow/rescue helpers skimming the waves on Jet Skis. (You can check it out on YouTube.)

O'Brien's Tower, built in 1835, marks the highest point of the cliffs (but isn't worth the fee to climb...30 feet up doesn't improve the views much). To reach it from the main viewpoint, closest to the visitors center, turn right and hike five minutes up the stairs to the tower. In the distance, on windy days, you can see the Aran Islands wearing their white necklace of surf.

Hike to Hag's Head: From the main viewpoint, look left (south) and spot the tiny tower in the far distance. It's farther than it looks because of the gaping alcoves hidden behind each cliff headland, but fit hikers can spend 2.5 hours (5 miles round-trip) following the up-and-down trail along the lip of the cliffs the whole way. Initially, you'll be slowed down by idle crowds on the too-narrow trail (flagstones on one side, barbed and electric fencing on the other side). But after 500 yards, you'll leave them behind and can pick up the pace.

Eventually, you'll have nothing between you and the abyss. Be extremely careful on the uneven trail (next to unsupported overhangs) and mindful of the sudden wind gusts. Although the cliffs become less spectacular the farther you go, this hike is a great excuse to stretch your legs. Alternatively, you can book the longer Doolin Cliff Walk, with local guide Pat Sweeny, which covers the northern end of the cliffs (see "Activities in Doolin," later).

Nearby: Before leaving the area, drivers can take 10 minutes to check out the **Holy Well of St. Bridget,** located beside the tall column about a half-mile (1 km) south of the cliffs on the main road to Liscannor. In the short hall leading into the hillside spring, you'll find a treasure of ex-votos (religious offerings)  left behind by devoted visitors seeking cures and blessings. A trickle of water springs from the hillside at the far end. To the right of the simple hall entrance is a stairway heading up into a peaceful graveyard. Be sure to check out the wishing tree (sometimes called a fairy bush or rag tree) halfway up the left side of the stairway. It's usually draped in ribbons tied to branches. These were offerings to saints as part of a healing ritual. The simple gray column outside was a folly erected over 150 years ago by a local landlord with money and ego to burn.

Doolin

This town was once a strange phenomenon: It had long been a mecca for Irish musicians, who came together here to play before a few lucky aficionados. Many music lovers would come here directly from Paris or Munich, as the town was on the tourist map for its traditional music. But now crowds have overwhelmed the musicians, and I prefer Dingle's richer music scene. Still, as Irish and European fans crowd the pubs, the *bodhrán* beat goes on.

Orientation to Doolin

Doolin has plenty of accommodations and a Greek-island-without-the-sun ambience. The "town" is just a few homes and shops strung out along a valley road from the tiny harbor. Residents generally divide the town into an Upper Village and Lower Village. The Lower Village is the closest thing to a commercial center (it has a couple of pubs and a couple of music shops).

Doolin is without an official and unbiased **TI.** The Upper Village has two privately owned TIs that generally exist to book lodging and Aran Islands boat trips, one for each company (daily 8:30-19:00, closed in off-season, tel. 065/707-5642). You'll find a similar boat-booking outfit in the Lower Village.

The Lodge Doolin offers **laundry** service (drop-off only, pick up clothes in 8 hours, daily 8:00-20:00). **Alamo Cabs** is handy for folks without wheels wanting to link a night of fun in Doolin with a bed in Lisdoonvarna (mobile 086-235-3100).

Activities in Doolin

Traditional Music

Doolin is famous for three pubs, all featuring Irish folk music: Nearest the harbor, in the Lower Village, is **Gus O'Connor's Pub** (tel. 065/707-4168). A mile farther up the road, the Upper Village—straddling a bridge—is home to two other destination pubs: **McGann's** (tel. 065/707-4133) and **McDermott's** (tel. 065/707-4328). Music starts between 21:30 and 22:00, finishing at about midnight. Get there before 21:00 if you want a place to sit, or pop in later and plan on standing. The *craic* is great regardless. Pubs serve decent dinners before the music starts.

At **Doolin Music House,** you can enjoy live trad music and folklore by accomplished flute-and-whistle player Christy Barry in his home. It's a wonderfully cozy and intimate small-group experience (€25, advance booking required; Mon, Wed and Fri 19:00-20:30, tel. 065/707-4584, mobile 086-824-1085, www.doolinmusichouse.com).

Hike, Bus, or Cruise to the Cliffs of Moher

From Doolin, you can hike up the Burren Way along the coast to the Cliffs of Moher. Local guide and farmer Pat Sweeny operates **Doolin Cliff Walk,** leading walking tours that depart daily at 10:00 from O'Connor's Pub. The five-mile walk to the cliffs takes three hours and is not safe for kids under age 10; you catch the 13:30 bus back to Doolin (€10, May-Sept, tel. 065/707-4170, mobile 086-822-9913, www.doolincliffwalk.com, phone ahead to reserve and check weather/trail conditions).

Alternatively, the **Hop-on, Hop-off Coastal Shuttle Bus** (16 seats) stops throughout Doolin, along the Cliffs of Moher coastal walk, and in the town of Liscannor (€6, departs every 90 minutes starting at 9:00 from Doolin Park & Ride lot—next to R-478, down the hill halfway between N-67 and Doolin Pier, tel. 065/707-5599, mobile 087-775-5098, www.cliffsofmohercoastalwalk.ie). Serious hikers could make a day of it by catching the 9:00 bus southbound, arriving at Liscannor at 10:00, and hiking 7.5 miles (about three hours) back to Doolin. Wear solid footwear for the rugged terrain. Local guide Pat Sweeny can be hired to join you (see above, contact him for cost) or just follow the coastal trail yourself. You can't get lost, unless you take a few too many steps to the left.

To get a different perspective of the cliffs, take a boat cruise along their base. Try for an afternoon cruise, when the sun is coming from the west, illuminating the detail on the dramatic cliffs. Two companies—**Doolin2Aran Ferries** (tel. 065/707-5949, mobile 087-245-3239, www.doolin2aranferries.com) and **Doolin Ferry/O'Brien Line** (tel. 065/707-5618, www.obrienline.com)—offer almost identical cruises. Both make the one-hour voyage past sea stacks and crag-perching birds. Boats depart from the pier in Doolin (same dock as Aran Islands boat, €20, runs daily April-Oct, 3/day, weather and tides permitting, call or go online for sailing schedule and to reserve). They also operate day-trip cruises from Doolin to Inisheer (the closest Aran Island), then along the base of the Cliffs of Moher and back to Doolin (for details, see page 369).

Sleeping in Doolin

$$ Harbour View B&B offers six rooms in a fine modern house overlooking the coast a mile from the Doolin fiddles. Amy Lindner keeps the place immaculate (on main road halfway between Lisdoonvarna and Cliffs of Moher, next to Aran View Market and gas station, tel. 065/707-4154, www.harbourviewdoolin.com, clarebb@eircom.net).

$$ Oar Restaurant & Rooms has five fine rooms, upstairs from the best fine-dining option in town (in the Upper Village, tel. 065/704-7990, www.oardoolin.ie, oardoolin@gmail.com).

$$ Half Door B&B is the coziest place around, with five woody rooms (thin walls) and a pleasant sun porch. It's just a short walk from the pubs in the Upper Village (cash only, family rooms, a keg's roll from McDermott's pub, tel. 085/864-2388, www. halfdoordoolin.com, ann@halfdoordoolin.com, Anne Hughes).

$ The Lodge Doolin is a modern compound of four stone buildings with 21 bright, airy, good-value rooms (located halfway between Upper and Lower Villages, tel. 065/707-4888, www. doolinlodge.com, info@doolinlodge.com). The lodge offers laundry service.

¢ Doolin Inn & Hostel, right in Doolin's Lower Village, caters creatively to the needs of backpackers in town for the music. Friendly Anthony and Dierdre are on top of the local scene. The upper house has the Inn, which offers good-value double rooms and a café. The lower house across the road is the hostel (tel. 065/707-4421, www.doolininn.ie, reservations@doolininn.ie).

Eating in Doolin

The only dinner option above pub grub or café fare is **$$$ Oar Restaurant & Rooms,** in the Upper Village, 50 yards behind Half Door B&B. Reservations are smart (good-value early-bird special, lamb and fish dishes, Wed-Sun 17:30-21:30, closed Mon-Tue, tel. 065/704-7990, https://oardoolin.ie/oar-restaurant/).

The **$$ Ivy Cottage,** in the Lower Village just past the bridge, has a pleasant, leafy tea garden out front. They do a dish of the day as well as simple sandwiches, quiche, or chowder (daily 10:00-18:00, mobile 089-977-1873). You can order fish-and-chips to take away.

$$ The Cliff Coast Café, across the bridge in the Doolin Inn, serves dependable dishes (daily 11:00-21:00, shorter hours off-season, mobile 087-282-0587).

Doolin has earned a reputation for consistently good pub grub. In the Lower Village, try **$$ Gus O'Connor's Pub,** and in the Upper Village, give **$$ McGann's** a spin. **Mac's Daybreak** is the town market and gas station (daily 7:00-20:00, on R-478 above town next to the Harbour View B&B).

Doolin Connections

From Doolin by Bus to: Galway (5/day, 1.5 hours), **Ennis** (5/day, 2 hours). Buses depart from Doolin's hostel.

By Ferry to the Aran Islands: Doolin2Aran Ferries or Doolin Ferry/O'Brien Line both take you to the closest island, Inisheer (with time to explore), then back along the Cliffs of Moher (they also go to Inishmore, the farthest island; if doing that, it's best to spend the night on the island). For details, see the Aran Islands chapter.

Lisdoonvarna

Treated almost like an inland extension of Doolin, this town of 1,000 (4.3 miles/7 km from Doolin) is a bit bigger, with a few more amenities but no coastal charm. It was known for centuries for its spa, its matchmakers, and its traditional folk-music festivals. Today, it's pretty sleepy, except for a few weeks in September, during its Matchmaking Festival (www.matchmakerireland.com), which partially inspired the 1997 film *The Matchmaker*. It's more of a town than Doolin and, apart from festival time, less touristy.

Sleeping in Lisdoonvarna: $$ Ballinsheen House & Gardens is the best value in town. It's perched on a hill with five tastefully decorated rooms and a pleasant, glassed-in breakfast terrace looking out on their inviting back garden (parking, 5-minute walk north of town on N-67 Galway Road, tel. 065/707-4806, mobile 087-124-1872, www.ballinsheen.com, ballinsheenhouse@hotmail.com, Mary Gardiner). Almost directly across the road is **$$ Greenlawn Lodge,** set back from N-67 behind its expansive grounds with modern, quiet rooms in a fine house (tel. 065/707-4861, mobile 086-880-8777, patriciamcmahon0@gmail.com).

Eating in Lisdoonvarna: The **$$ Roadside Tavern** is a favorite local hangout with filling pub grub, great atmosphere, and occasional traditional-music sessions most summer evenings at 21:00 (daily, tel. 065/707-4084, on N-67 in town tucked behind the Royal Spa Hotel in hard-to-miss bright red). **$$$ The Burren Storehouse** is the tavern's modern addition next door, serving chargrilled steaks and seafood, along with pizza and salad options

(Mon-Thu 18:00-22:00, Fri-Sat from 14:00, closed Sun, tel. 087-830-0069).

The Burren

Literally the "rocky place," the Burren is just that. This 10-square-mile limestone plateau, a ▲▲ sight, is so barren that a disappointed Cromwellian surveyor of the 1650s described it as "a savage land, yielding neither water enough to drown a man, nor a tree to hang him, nor soil enough to bury him." But he wasn't much of a botanist, because the Burren is in fact a unique ecosystem, with flora that has managed to adapt since the last Ice Age, 10,000 years ago. It's also rich in prehistoric and early Christian sites. This limestone land is littered with hundreds of historic stone structures, including dozens of Iron Age stone forts. When the first human inhabitants of the Burren came about 6,000 years ago, they cut down its trees with shortsighted slash-and-burn methods, which accelerated erosion of the topsoil (already scoured to a thin layer by glaciers)—making those ancient people partially responsible for the stark landscape we see today.

You can either get a quick overview using my self-guided driving tour, or take your time and really get a feel for the land with one of the walking tours next. Travelers without a car can see the Burren with a bus tour.

Tours in the Burren

Walking Tours
Most travelers zip through the seemingly barren Burren without stopping, grateful for the soft soil they garden back home. But healthy hikers and armchair naturalists may want to slow down and take a closer look. Be sure to wear comfortable shoes for the

wet, uneven, rocky bedrock. These guides can bring the harsh landscape to life.

From Ballyvaughan (at the northern entrance to the Burren): **Shane Connolly** leads in-depth, three-hour guided walking tours, explaining the region's history, geology, and diverse flora, and the role humans have played in shaping this landscape. This proud farmer really knows his stuff (€15, daily at 10:00 and 15:00, call to book and confirm meeting place in Ballyvaughan, tel. 065/707-7168, mobile 086/265-4810, www.burrenhillwalks.ie).

From Carran (in the center of the Burren): **Tony Kirby** leads regularly scheduled 2.5-hour "Heart of Burren Walks" during the summer, and the rest of the year by appointment. His expertise peels back the rocky surface to reveal the surprisingly fascinating natural and human history that created this unique region (€30, June-Aug Tue-Thu at 10:30, Fri at 14:15; meet opposite Cassidy's Pub in village of Carran, about seven miles east of Kilfenora; tel. 065/682-7707, mobile 087-292-5487, www.heartofburrenwalks.com, info@heartofburrenwalks.com).

Bus Tours

From Galway: Galway Tour Company's standard all-day bus tour of the Burren covers Kinvarra, Aillwee Cave, Poulnabrone Dolmen, and the Cliffs of Moher (€35, discounts if you book online, departs at 10:00, returns about 18:00, confirm schedule ahead). For €15 more, you can add a boat ride out from nearby Doolin to the Aran Island of Inisheer. **Lally Tours** and **Healy Tours** run similar day trips (see page 354 for contact information for all three companies).

Burren Drive

KILFENORA TO KINVARRA

This drive offers the best quick swing through the historic Burren (and easily can be done on the way to Galway). Covering about 30 miles from start to finish, it packs in a lot of interesting sights and will give you a feel for the unique geology, history, and culture of the region. Music lovers with more time might want to loop back to Kilfenora to join the locals on their set-dancing nights.

• *Begin in the town of Kilfenora, 8 kilometers (5 miles) southeast of Lisdoonvarna, at the T-intersection where R-476 meets R-481.*

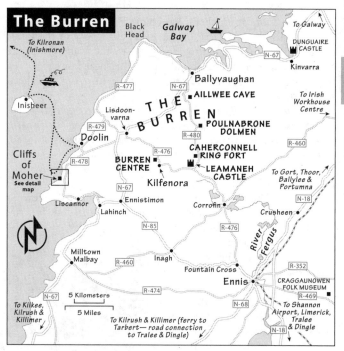

Kilfenora

This town's hardworking, community-run **Burren Centre** shows an informative 10-minute video explaining the geology and botany of the region, and then ushers you into its enlightening museum exhibits (€6, daily June-Aug 9:30-17:30, mid-March-May and Sept-Oct 10:00-17:00, closed in winter, tel. 065/708-8030, www.theburrencentre.ie). You'll also see copies of a fine eighth-century golden collar and ninth-century silver brooch (originals in Dublin's National Museum). Brief coverage of the Kilfenora Ceili Band (a national fixture since 1909) primes the set-dancing pumps for what to expect in the town's Barn Pub dance hall (see next page). Ceili bands play a form of Irish traditional music embellished with piano and snare drums to create the driving beat popular for set dancing, something County Clare excels in.

The ruined **church** next door has a couple of 12th-century crosses, but there isn't much to see. Mass is still held in the church, which claims the pope as its bishop by papal dictate. As the smallest and poorest diocese in Ireland, Kilfenora was almost unable to function after the famine, so in 1866 Pope Pius IX supported the town as best he could—by personally declaring himself its bishop.

For lunch in Kilfenora, consider the cheap and cheery **Burren Centre Tea Room** (daily 9:30-17:30, located at far back of building) or the more atmospheric **Vaughan's Pub.** If you're spending the night in County Clare, make a real effort to join the locals at the fun set-dancing get-togethers run by the Vaughans in the **Barn Pub,** adjacent to their regular pub. This local dance scene is a memorable treat (€5, Sun at 21:30, also Thu in July-Aug, call ahead to confirm schedule, tel. 065/708-8004).

• *To continue from Kilfenora into the heart of the Burren, head east out of town on R-476. After about 5 kilometers (3 miles), you'll come to the junction with northbound R-480. Take the sharp left turn onto R-480, and slow down to gaze up (on the left) at the ruins of...*

Leamaneh Castle

This ruined shell of a fortified house is closed to everyone except the female ghost that supposedly haunts it. From the outside, you

can see how the 15th-century fortified tower house (the right quarter of the remaining ruin) was expanded 150 years later (the left three-quarters of the ruin). The castle evolved from a refuge into a manor, and windows were widened to allow for better views as defense became less of a priority.

• *From the castle, continue north on R-480 (direction: Ballyvaughan). After about 8 kilometers (5 miles), you'll hit the start of the real barren Burren. Keep an eye out for the next stop.*

Caherconnell (Cahercommaun) Ring Fort

Of many ring forts in the area, this one is the most accessible. You can see the low stone profile of Caherconnell to the left on the crest of a hill just off the road. You can park in the gravel lot and walk up to the small visitors center and handy café for an informative 20-minute film followed by a quick wander through the small fort. The fort sometimes features a sheepherding demo with dogs (generally at 12:00 and 15:00—call to confirm).

Cost and Hours: €6, €10 with sheepherding demo, daily 10:00-18:00, Easter-June and Sept-Oct 10:30-17:30, closed in winter, tel. 065/708-9999, www.caherconnell.com.

• *The stretch from the ring fort north to Ballyvaughan offers the starkest scenery. Soon you'll see a 10-foot-high stone structure a hundred yards off the road to the right (east, toward an ugly gray metal barn). Pull over for a closer look.*

Poulnabrone Dolmen

While it looks like a stone table, this is a portal tomb. Two hundred years ago, locals called this a "druids' altar." Five thousand years ago, it was a grave chamber in a cairn of stacked stones. Amble over for a look. (It's crowded with tour buses at midday, but it's all yours early or late.)

Wander about for some quiet time with the wildflowers and try to think like a geologist. You're walking across a former seabed, dating from 250 million years ago when Ireland was at the equator (before continental drift nudged it north). Look for white smudges of fossils. Stones embedded in the belly of an advancing glacier ground the scratches you see in the rocks. The rounded boulders came south from Connemara, carried on a giant conveyor belt of ice and then left behind when the melting glaciers retreated north.

• *As you drive away from the dolmen (continuing north), look for the 30-foot-deep sinkhole beside the road on the right (a collapsed cave). From here, R-480 winds slowly downhill for about 6 kilometers (4 miles), eventually leaving the rocky landscape behind and entering a comparatively lush green valley. Eventually, on the right, you'll find the turn up to...*

Aillwee Cave

As this is touted as "Ireland's premier show cave," I couldn't resist a look. While fairly touristy and not worth the time or money if you've seen a lot of caves, it's the easiest way to sample the massive system of caves that underlies the Burren. Your guide walks you 300 yards into the plain but impressive cave, giving a serious 40-minute geology lesson. During the Ice Age, underground rivers carved countless caves such as this one. Brown bears, which became extinct in Ireland a thousand years ago, found them great for hibernating. If you take the tour, you'll need a sweater: The cave is a constant 50°F.

Just below the cave (and on the same property) is the **Burren Birds of Prey Centre,** which houses owls, eagles, hawks, and falcons. During the demo talks, you'll see raptors in action and may be able to briefly hold one as the leather glove is passed around the crowd (bird demonstrations May-Aug at 12:00, 14:00, and 16:00, Sept-April at 12:00 and 15:00—but call for daily schedule).

Adjacent to the cave, the **Hawk Walk** gets visitors face-to-beak with a Harris hawk, "the world's only social raptor." After a brief training session, an instructor leads a small group on a one-hour hike up a nearby mountain trail. Those paying the stiff €95 fee

Botany of the Burren in Brief

The Burren is a story of water, rock, geological force, and time. It supports the greatest diversity of plants in Ireland. Like no-where else, Mediterranean and Arctic wildflowers bloom side by side in the Burren. It's an orgy of cross-pollination that attracts more insects than Doolin does music lovers—even beetles help out. Lime-stone, created from layers of coral, seashells, and mud, is the bedrock of the Burren. (The same formation resurfac-es 10 miles or so out to sea to form the Aran Islands.)

Geologic forces in the earth's crust heaved up the land, and the glaciers swept it bare and shattered it like glass under their weight—dropping boulders as they receded. Rain, react-ing naturally with the limestone to create a mild but deter-mined acid, slowly drilled potholes into the surface. Rainwater cut through the limestone's weak zones, leaving crevices on the surface and one of Europe's most extensive systems of caves below. Algae grew in the puddles, dried into a pow-der, and combined with bug parts and rabbit turds (bunnies abound in the Burren) to create a very special soil. Plants and flowers fill the cracks in the limestone. Grasses and shrubs don't do well here, and wild goats eat any trees that try to grow, giving tender little blossoms a chance to enjoy the sun. Different blooms appear throughout the months, sharing space rather than competing. The flowers are best in June and July.

get to launch and call the bird back to perch on their arm (€22 for a nonparticipating companion; limited slots, must reserve).

Cost and Hours: Cave—€15, bird center—€15, €22 combo-ticket includes both sights but not Hawk Walk; open daily at 10:00, last tour at 18:30 July-Aug, otherwise 17:30, Dec-Feb call ahead for limited tours; clearly signposted just south of Ballyvaughan, tel. 065/707-7036, www.aillweecave.ie.

• *Continuing on, our final destination is...*

Kinvarra

This tiny town, between Ballyvaughan and Galway, is waiting for something to happen in its minuscule harbor. It faces Dunguaire Castle, a four-story tower house from 1520 that stands a few yards out in the bay.

The touristy but fun **Dunguaire Castle medieval banquet** is Kinvarra's most worthy attraction (€63, cheaper if you book online, most evenings at 17:30 and sometimes at 20:30, mid-April–mid-Oct, reservations required, tel. 061/360-788, castle tel.  091/637-108, www.shannonheritage.com). **Warning:** This company also operates banquets at two other castles in the region, so be sure that you make your reservation for the correct castle.

The evening is as intimate as a gathering of 55 tourists under one time-stained, barrel-vaulted ceiling can be. You get a decent four-course meal with wine (or mead if you ask sweetly), served amid an entertaining evening of Irish tales and folk songs. Remember that in medieval times, it was considered polite to flirt with wenches. It's a small and multitalented cast: one harpist and three singer/actors who serve the "lords and ladies" between tunes. The highlight is the 40-minute stage show, which features songs and poems by local writers, and comes with dessert.

You can visit the castle itself by day without taking in an evening banquet (€8, daily 10:00-16:30).

Irish Workhouse Centre

For those who want to see the Victorian "cure" for poverty, the Irish Workhouse Centre in Portumna is a memorable side trip from Ennis. It's a sad story, of most interest to history buffs or those with Irish heritage, but it sets the stage for Ireland's most cataclysmic tragedy (the Great Potato Famine).

This is one of the few remaining intact workhouses in Ireland. There were once 163; most were either knocked down or repurposed after Ireland's first step toward independence in 1922. Portumna's workhouse has been restored but not renovated; it stands, grim and foreboding, in much the same condition as when it was closed.

GETTING THERE

The workhouse is about an hour east of Ennis or Kinvarra, located just over the border in County Galway (and best fits into a jaunt from neighboring County Clare). From Ennis, it's a rural, winding one-hour drive—stay on R-352 the entire way. As you enter

Portumna, turn left at Bank of Ireland, continue on, and the Irish Workhouse Centre is on your right.

ORIENTATION TO THE CENTER

Cost and Hours: €7, daily 9:30-17:00, closed Nov-Feb, St. Brigid's Road, Portumna, tel. 090/975-9200, www.irishworkhousecentre.ie.

Tours: Helpful guides give 45-minute tours that add a human angle to the spartan buildings.

VISITING THE CENTER

Workhouses were British institutions, set up by the government in the 1830s (unaware that Ireland's Great Potato Famine was less than a decade away) to provide vagrants with an alternative to starvation and death. However, as the government didn't want the "poorhouse" alternative to be too "tempting," punitive Poor Laws made them a gruesome alternative. To enter the poorhouse, you had to give up any assets you still had, and while you  were allowed to enter with your family, you'd likely never see them again once you arrived. Men and women were housed separately; children were also separated by gender. Children over age three were expected to work. There were no common areas for mingling.

Imagine these soul-sapping surroundings during the famine. Since their alternative was starvation, people flooded into these packed quarters—but since workhouses were often not funded properly, the inhabitants were also malnourished. Like cramped emigration "coffin ships," workhouses became transmission points for disease.

Law dictated that workhouses not compete with any local trades or businesses, and therefore they offered the dregs of labor, such as rock-breaking for men and corn-grinding for women. Unraveling old, worn rope and reweaving the salvageable strands into new rope was a task for anyone too weak to do heavy labor.

Life was bleak, food was scarce and of poor quality, and conditions were notoriously inhumane, especially for children. Ironically, it was cheaper for landlords to pay for the boat passage of their paupers to North America than it was to keep them in poorhouses (workhouses were financed by a property tax). Another way to escape was to commit a crime: The food was better in prison, and the regimen was less strict.

GALWAY

Galway offers the most easily accessible slice of Ireland's west coast. It's also Ireland's most international city: One out of every four residents was born outside of Ireland. With 80,000 people, this is Galway County's main city, a lively university town, and the region's industrial and administrative center. As it's near the traditional regions of Connemara and the Aran Islands, it's also a gateway to these Gaelic cultural preserves. And in 2020, Galway was named as one of the European Capitals of Culture, shining brighter with a celebration of everything that makes this city unique.

While Galway has a long and interesting history, precious little from old Galway survives. What does remain has the interesting disadvantage of being built in the local limestone, which, even if medieval, looks like modern stone construction. Galway's reason for being was its ideal position on a large, placid bay, centrally located for trade with all other points on the west coast, as well as beyond to continental Europe.

What Galway lacks in sights it makes up for in ambience. Spend an afternoon just wandering its medieval streets, with their delightful mix of colorful facades, labyrinthine pubs, weather-resistant street musicians, and steamy eateries. Galway also offers tourists plenty of traditional music, easy train connections to Dublin, and a convenient jumping-off point for a visit to the Aran Islands. After dark, blustery Galway heats up, with a fine theater and a pub scene that attracts even Dubliners. Visitors mix with old-timers and students as the traditional music goes round and round.

Galway's History

In 1234, the medieval fishing village of Galway went big time, when the Normans captured the territory from the O'Flaherty family. Making the town a base, the Normans invited in their Anglo friends, built a wall (1270), and kicked out the Irish. Galway's Celtic name (Gaillimh) comes from an old Irish word, *gall,* which means "foreigner." Except for a small section in the Eyre Square Shopping Centre and a chunk at the Spanish Arch, that Norman wall is gone.

In the 14th century, 14 merchant families, or "tribes," controlled Galway's commercial traffic, including the lucrative wine trade with Spain and France. These English families constantly clashed with the local Irish. Although the wall was built to "keep out the O's and the Macs," it didn't always work. A common prayer at the time was, "From the fury of the O'Flahertys, good Lord deliver us."

Galway's support of the English king helped it prosper. But with the rise of Oliver Cromwell in the 1640s (see sidebar on page 206), Galway paid for that prosperity. After sieges by Cromwell's troops (in 1651) and those of Protestant King William of Orange (in 1691), Galway declined. It wasn't until the last half of the 20th century that it regained some of its importance and wealth.

PLANNING YOUR TIME

Galway merits two nights and a day. The city's sights are little more than pins upon which to hang the old town, and can be seen in just a couple of hours. The real joy of Galway is in its street- and traditional-music scene. On your first night, stroll from Eyre Square through old Galway, seeking out a pub with music. On the next day, visit the Aran Island of Inishmore, or consider day trips to the Burren and Cliffs of Moher, or the Connemara region, all doable by car or with a bus tour (these destinations are covered in other chapters). At night, return to Galway to enjoy another music-filled evening.

Note for Drivers: Instead of day-tripping, you can visit a number of these sights on the way into or out of Galway. If you're driving north from Dingle to Galway, you can visit the Cliffs of Moher and the Burren en route (see page 322 for route tips). If heading to Northern Ireland from Galway, you can tour Connemara on the way (see page 390 for a plan).

Orientation to Galway

The center of Galway is Eyre (pronounced "air") Square. Within three blocks of the square, you'll find the TI, Aran boat offices, a tour pickup point, accommodations (from the best cheap hostel beds to fancy hotels), and the train station. The train and public bus station butt up against The Hardiman hotel, a huge gray railroad hotel that overlooks and dominates Eyre Square. The lively old town lies between Eyre Square and the river. From Eyre Square, Williams Gate leads a pedestrian parade right through the old town (changing street names several times) to Wolfe Tone Bridge. Nearly everything you'll see and do is within a few minutes' walk of this spine.

TOURIST INFORMATION

The well-organized TI, located a block from the bus/train station, has regional as well as local information (Mon-Sat 9:00-17:00, closed Sun, Forster Street, tel. 091/537-700, www.discoverireland. ie). Pick up the TI's free city guide with its simplified town map.

ARRIVAL IN GALWAY

Trains and most buses share the same station, virtually on Eyre Square (which has the nearest ATMs). The train station can store your bag (Mon-Fri 8:00-18:00, closed Sat-Sun). To get from the station to the TI, go left on Station Road as you exit the station (toward Eyre Square), and then turn right on Forster Street.

Don't confuse the public bus station (in same building as the train station) with the coach station (a block away, just beyond the TI), which handles privately owned coaches. Citylink buses from Dublin and Dublin's airport, as well as regional day-tour buses, use the coach station.

Drivers staying overnight at a College Road B&B can park there for free (each has a small lot in front). For daytime parking, the handiest and most central parking garage is under the recommended Jurys Inn Galway in the town center (€2.20/hour, €30/24 hours, Mon-Sat 8:00-1:00 in the morning, Sun 9:00-18:00). Otherwise, you buy a pay-and-display ticket and put it on your dashboard (€2, 2-hour maximum).

HELPFUL HINTS

Crowd Control: Expect huge crowds—and much higher prices—during the **Galway Arts Festival** (mid-late July, www. galwayartsfestival.com) and **Galway Oyster Festival** (late Sept, www.galwayoysterfest.com). The **Galway Races** are heaven for lovers of horse racing and hell for everyone else (summer races in late July-early Aug, fall races in mid-Sept

GALWAY

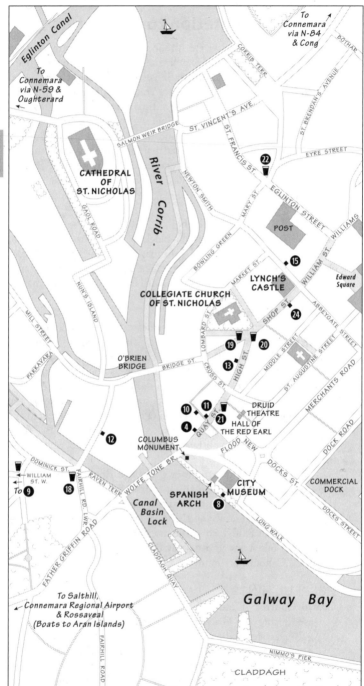

Eglinton Canal

To
Connemara
via N-84
& Cong

To
Connemara
via N-59 &
Oughterard

SALMON WEIR BRIDGE
ST. VINCENT'S AVE.
ST. BRENDAN'S AVENUE
BOTHAR

CORRIB TERR.
EYRE STREET
22

GAOL ROAD
EGLINTON STREET

CATHEDRAL
OF
ST. NICHOLAS

River
Corrib

NEWTON SMITH
ST. FRANCIS ST.
MARY ST.

POST
WILLIAM ST.

BOWLING GREEN
MARKET ST.
15
Edward
Square

NUN'S ISLAND
MILL STREET
PARKAVARA

COLLEGIATE CHURCH
OF ST. NICHOLAS
LYNCH'S
CASTLE
WILLIAMSGATE STREET

SHOP ST.
24

ABBEYGATE STREET

O'BRIEN
BRIDGE
BRIDGE ST.
LOMBARD ST.
CROSS ST.
HIGH ST.
19   20
13
MIDDLE STREET
ST. AUGUSTINE STREET
MERCHANTS ROAD

10   11
QUAY ST.
21
DRUID
THEATRE
DOCK ROAD

4
HALL OF
THE RED EARL

12
COLUMBUS
MONUMENT
FLOOD
NEW DOCKS ST.
DOCKS STREET

DOMINICK ST.
FAIRHILL RD.
RAVEN TERR.
WOLFE TONE BR.
CITY
MUSEUM
COMMERCIAL
DOCK

WILLIAM
ST. W.
18
SPANISH
ARCH
8
LONG WALK

To
9
Canal
Basin
Lock
FATHER GRIFFEIN ROAD
CLADDAGH QUAY

To Salthill,
Connemara Regional Airport
& Rossaveal
(Boats to Aran Islands)

Galway Bay

FAIRHILL ROAD
NIMMO'S PIER

CLADDAGH

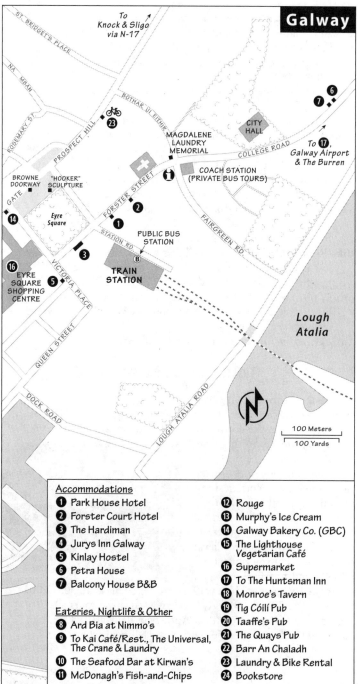

Galway

To Knock & Sligo via N-17

CITY HALL

To 🔟, Galway Airport & The Burren

MAGDALENE LAUNDRY MEMORIAL

COACH STATION (PRIVATE BUS TOURS)

BROWNE DOORWAY

"HOOKER" SCULPTURE

Eyre Square

PUBLIC BUS STATION

TRAIN STATION

EYRE SQUARE SHOPPING CENTRE

Lough Atalia

ST. BRIDGET'S PLACE
NA MBAN
ROSEMARY ST.
BÓTHAR UÍ EITHIR
PROSPECT HILL
FORSTER STREET
STATION RD.
COLLEGE ROAD
FAIRGREEN RD.
GATE
VICTORIA PLACE
QUEEN STREET
DOCK ROAD
LOUGH ATALIA ROAD

100 Meters
100 Yards

GALWAY

Accommodations

1 Park House Hotel
2 Forster Court Hotel
3 The Hardiman
4 Jurys Inn Galway
5 Kinlay Hostel
6 Petra House
7 Balcony House B&B

Eateries, Nightlife & Other

8 Ard Bia at Nimmo's
9 To Kai Café/Rest., The Universal, The Crane & Laundry
10 The Seafood Bar at Kirwan's
11 McDonagh's Fish-and-Chips
12 Rouge
13 Murphy's Ice Cream
14 Galway Bakery Co. (GBC)
15 The Lighthouse Vegetarian Café
16 Supermarket
17 To The Huntsman Inn
18 Monroe's Tavern
19 Tig Cóilí Pub
20 Taaffe's Pub
21 The Quays Pub
22 Barr An Chaladh
23 Laundry & Bike Rental
24 Bookstore

and late Oct, www.galwayraces.com); prices double for food and lodging, and simple evening strolls feel like punt returns.

Markets: On Saturdays year-round and Sundays in summer, a fun market clusters around St. Nicholas' Church (all day, best 9:00-14:00).

Bookstore: Dubray Books is directly across the pedestrian drag from Lynch's Castle (Mon-Sat 9:00-18:00, Thu-Fri until 21:00, Sun 12:00-18:00, 4 Shop Street, tel. 091/569-070).

Laundry: You have two full-service drop-off options. The first is more central (but closed Sat-Sun) while the second is on the west end of town (closed Sun). **Prospect Hill Launderette** is beside the bike-rental shop a block north of Eyre Square (Mon-Fri 8:30-18:30, closed Sat-Sun, Prospect Hill Road, tel. 087/313-7715). **Sea Road Launderette** is three blocks west of the Wolfe Tone Bridge (Mon-Sat 8:30-18:30, closed Sun, 4 Sea Road, tel. 091/584-524).

Bike Rental: On Yer Bike rents bikes to tool around flat Galway town. Consider a pleasant ride out to the end of Salthill's beachfront promenade and back (€15-20/day, Mon-Sat 9:00-19:00, Sun 12:00-18:00, shorter hours off-season, 42 Prospect Hill, tel. 091/563-393, mobile 087-942-5479, www.onyourbikecycles.com).

Taxi: Give **Big-O-Taxis** a try (tel. 091/585-858).

Tours in Galway

▲Hop-On, Hop-Off City Bus Tours

Guided, one-hour double-decker bus tours compete for your euros. They depart from the northwest end of Eyre Square (opposite end of the square from the huge Hardiman hotel), have similar schedules and prices, and make the dozen most important stops, including the cathedral, Salthill, and the Spanish Arch. These large coaches can't penetrate some of the winding medieval back streets, but you can get off, explore, and hop back on later.

Galway City buses are blue (€10, April-Sept daily at 10:30, 12:00, 14:00, and 15:30, tel. 091/770-066, www.galwaybustours.ie). **City Sightseeing** buses are red (€12, April-Sept daily at 10:30, 12:00, 13:30, and 15:00, tel. 091/562-905, www.lallytours.com).

Walking Tours

There are many walking tours in this town. Most are flexible in their start time and location (call ahead to confirm).

Galway Walking Tours are led by Fiona Brennan, who takes her guests on leisurely 1.5-hour explorations of the city (€10, mobile 087-290-3499, www.galwaywalkingtours.com, feebrenn@iol.ie).

Liam Silke comes from one of Galway's oldest families and leads 1.5-hour tours (€10, departs from Brown's Doorway by flags on north side of Eyre Square, tel. 091/588-897, mobile 086-348-0958, www.walkingtoursgalway.com, info@walkingtoursgalway.com).

Galway Walk and Talk Tours operates with the motto that "a walker has plenty of stories to tell" (€10, departs at 10:30 from TI, mobile 087-690-1452).

Great Guides of Galway offers historical walking tours in the early evening (€10, departs from steps of The Hardiman hotel on Mon, Wed, and Fri at 17:00, Sat at 14:00, mobile 086-727-4888, greatguidesofgalway@hotmail.com).

Food Tours

Galway Food Tours take you on 2.5-hour strolls that introduce you to eight "culinary hotspots," including the marketplace. You're encouraged to graze along the way (as a replacement for lunch). Stops run the gamut from sushi to doughnuts, with traditional yet creative options in between (€60, reserve in advance; Mon-Sat at 10:30, meet in front of Griffin's Bakery, 21 Shop Street, mobile 086-733-2885, www.galwayfoodtours.com).

Excursions from Galway

Good day-trip options from Galway include the Aran Islands, the Burren and Cliffs of Moher, and the Connemara region. Multiple Galway-based companies offer day tours.

Faherty Tours makes it easy to visit Inishmore, the largest of the three Aran Islands, as part of a group tour led by a guide native to the island. If you don't mind paying more than doing it yourself, this saves you the headache of figuring out transportation from Galway to the island and back, and planning your time there. Tours depart daily at 9:00 from the coach station and have you back in Galway by 18:45 (€50, tel. 091/442-913, mobile 087/611-0913, www.fahertytours.com, fahertytours@gmail.com).

High King Tours takes a bite-sized chunk of Connemara focused on Cong and the last Irish King, Rory O'Connor. The tour follows a relaxed itinerary that includes Cong Abbey's ruins, the grounds of Ashford Castle, and a two-hour cruise on the River Corrib. Tours depart from the coach station at 9:00 and return by 18:00 (€70, tel. 091/398-116, www.highkingtours.ie, info@ highkingtours.ie).

Galway Tour Company runs bus tours all over the region, including to the Burren, Cliffs of Moher, and Connemara (office located just a few doors down Forster Street from TI, toward Eyre Square, tours depart from private coach station on Fairgreen Road— across from TI, tel. 091/566-566, www.galwaytourcompany.com, info@galwaytourcompany.com). If Galway Tour Company is booked, try similar **Lally Tours** (tel. 091/562-905, www.lallytours. com) or **Healy Tours** (tel. 091/770-066, mobile 087-259-0160, www.healytours.ie). All three companies offer discounts if you book two separate tours. Drivers take cash only; to pay with a credit card, book in advance. For details on what these tours cover, see page 340 for the Burren and Cliffs of Moher and page 387 for Connemara.

For details on the ferry to the Aran Island of Inishmore from Rossaveal (20 miles from Galway), see page 369.

Sights in Galway

EYRE SQUARE AND THE MEDIEVAL "LATIN QUARTER"

Walking from Eyre Square down the pedestrian (and tourist) spine of old Galway to the River Corrib takes you past the essential sights in town. I've connected these sights in an easy downhill stroll.

▲Eyre Square

Galway is dominated by its main, parklike square. On a sunny day, Eyre Square is filled with people just hanging out. In the Middle Ages, it was a field right outside the town wall. The square is named for the mayor who gave the land to the city in 1710. While still called Eyre Square, it now contains John F. Kennedy Park—established in memory of the Irish American president's visit in 1963 when he filled this space with adoring Irish for one

of his speeches, a few months before he was assassinated (a JFK bust near the kids' play area commemorates his visit). Though Kennedy is celebrated as America's first Irish-Catholic president, several US presidents were descended from Protestant Ulster stock (even Barack Obama is part Irish).

Walk to the rust-colored "Hooker" sculpture, built in 1984 to celebrate the 500th anniversary of the incorporation of the city.

The sails represent Galway's square-rigged fishing ships ("hookers") and the vessels that made Galway a trading center so long ago. The Browne Doorway, from a 1627 fortified townhouse, is a reminder of the 14 family tribes that once ruled the town (Lynch's Castle, nearby, gives you a feel for an intact townhouse). Each family tribe had a town castle—much like the towers that characterize the towns of Italy, with their feuding noble families. So little survives of medieval Galway that the town makes a huge deal of any remaining window or crest. Each of the 14 colorful flags lining the west end of the square represents a different original Norman founding tribe.

GALWAY

• *From the top of Eyre Square, walk down Williams Gate—a street named for the old main gate of the Norman town wall that once stood here. The spine of medieval Galway, the road changes names several times (to William, Shop, High, and Quay streets) as it leads downhill to the River Corrib. (As you stroll, remember that this is Galway's tourist slalom—with about 80 percent of its tourists and tourist traps.) After about three blocks you'll see a bold limestone "town castle" on your right.*

Lynch's Castle

Now a bank, this limestone tower, Galway's best late 15th-century fortified townhouse, was the home of the Lynch family—the most powerful of the town's 14 tribes—and the only one of their mansions to survive. More than 80 of the mayors who ruled Galway in the 16th and 17th centuries were from the Lynch family.

• *Continuing another block downhill, you'll veer half a block to the right off the main pedestrian flow, to the big church.*

Collegiate Church of St. Nicholas

This church, the finest medieval building in town (1320), is dedicated to St. Nicholas of Myra, the patron saint of sailors. Columbus is said to have worshipped here in 1477, undoubtedly contemplating a scary voyage. Its interior is littered with obscure bits of town history—fine windows, historic tombs, lots of limestone—all described in a handy 23-point flier (€2 suggested donation). Consider attending an evening concert of traditional Irish music in this atmospheric venue (see "Nightlife in Galway," later).

An **open-air market** surrounds the church most Saturdays year-round and also on Sundays in summer.

• *Returning to the pedestrian mall, carry on another block and a half downhill. Look for The Quays pub on your left.*

The Quays

This pub was once owned by "Humanity Dick," an 18th-century Member of Parliament who was the original animal-rights activist. His efforts led to the world's first conviction for cruelty to animals in 1822. It's worth a peek inside for its lively interior.

• *Head down the lane just before the pub, about 50 yards, to the big glass windows on the right.*

Hall of the Red Earl

A big glass wall shows the excavation site of the Hall of the Red Earl. Wall diagrams and storyboards explain that these are the dusty foundations of Galway's oldest building, once the 13th-century hall of the Norman lord Richard de Burgo (free, closed Sun).

Across the lane is the **Druid Theatre.** This 100-seat venue offers top-notch contemporary Irish theater. Although the theater company is away on tour more often than not, it's worth checking their schedule online or dropping by to see if anything's playing tonight (€20-30 tickets, Chapel Lane, tel. 091/568-660, www.druid. ie).

• *Finally, walk to the end of the pedestrian mall, cross the busy street, and follow it to the Wolfe Tone Bridge, where you'll find two gray stone monuments (each about as tall as you are). Above the bridge, a sign says* Welcome to Galway's West End. *You just walked the tourist gauntlet. (Across the river and to the right is a trendy foodie zone.) Stand between the two stone monuments.*

Columbus Monument

The monument (closest to the bridge) was given to Galway by the people of Genoa, Italy, to celebrate the 1477 visit here of Christopher Columbus—Cristoforo Colombo in Italian. (That acknowledgment, from an Italian town so proud and protective of its favorite son, helps to substantiate the famous explorer's legendary visit.) The other memorial is dedicated to sailors lost at sea.

• *Don't cross the bridge. Instead, stroll left downstream to the old fortified arch.*

Spanish Arch

Overlooking the River Corrib, this makes up the best remaining chunk of the old city wall. A reminder of Galway's former importance in trade, the arch (c. 1584) is the place where Spanish ships would unload their cargo (primarily wine).

• *Walk through the arch and take an immediate right. Go past the stone steps to the far corner of the embankment over the river.*

River Corrib Sights

Enjoy this river scene. On either side is a park—a constant party on sunny days. (It's ideal for a picnic of fish-and-chips from the recommended McDonagh's chipper, near the end of the pedestrian mall.) Across the river is the modern housing project that replaced the original Claddagh in the 1930s. **Claddagh** was a picturesque, Irish-speaking fishing village with a strong tradition of independence—and open sewers. This gaggle of thatched cottages functioned as an independent community with its own "king" until the early 1900s, when it was torn down for health reasons.

The old Claddagh village is gone, but the tradition of its popular ring (sold all over town) lives on. The **Claddagh ring** shows two hands holding a heart that wears a crown. The heart represents love, the crown is loyalty, and the hands are friendship. If the ring is worn with the tip of the heart pointing in, it signifies that the wearer is taken. However, if the tip of the heart points out, it means the wearer is available.

Survey the harbor. A few of Galway's famous square-rigged "hooker" fishing ships are often tied up and on display. Called "hookers" for their method of fishing with multiple hooks on a single line, these sturdy yet graceful boats were later used to transport turf from Connemara, until improved roads and electric heat made them obsolete. Beyond that, a huge park of reclaimed land is popular with the local kids for Irish football and hurling. From there, the promenade leads to the resort town of Salthill.

• *Your town intro walk is finished. Just behind the Spanish Arch is a stony riverside warehouse called Nimmo's that contains Ard Bia, one of the best restaurants in town. And just beyond that (see the name towering overhead) is the...*

City Museum

Fragments of old Galway are kept in this modern museum. Check out the intact Galway "hooker" fishing boat hanging from the ceiling. The ground floor houses the archaeological exhibits: prehistoric and ancient Galway-related treasures such as medieval pottery, Iron Age ax heads, and Bronze Age thingamajigs. The first floor sheds light on Galway's role in the Irish struggle for independence in the early 1900s. The top floor is devoted to "sea science" (oceanography).

Cost and Hours: Free, Tue-Sat 10:00-17:00, Sun from 12:00, closed Sun Oct-March and Mon year-round, handy café with cheap lunches, tel. 091/532-460, www.galwaycitymuseum.ie.

GALWAY

Galway Legends and Factoids

Because of the dearth of physical old stuff, the town milks its legends. Here are a few that you'll encounter repeatedly:

- In the 15th century, the mayor, one of the Lynch tribe, condemned his son to death for the murder of a Spaniard. When no one in town could be found to hang the popular boy, the dad—who loved justice more than he loved his son—did it himself.
- Columbus is said to have stopped in Galway in 1477. He may have been inspired by tales of the voyage of St. Brendan, the Irish monk who is thought by some (mostly Irish) to have beaten Columbus to the New World by almost a thousand years.
- On the main drag, you'll find a pub called The King's Head. It was originally given to the man who chopped off the head of King Charles I in 1649. For his safety, he settled in Galway—about as far from London as an Englishman could get back then.
- William Joyce, born in America, spent most of his childhood in Galway and later was seduced by fascist ideology in the 1930s. He moved to Germany and became "Lord Haw-Haw," infamous as the radio voice of Nazi propaganda during World War II. After the war, he was hanged in London for treason. His daughter had him buried in Galway.

MORE SIGHTS IN GALWAY

▲Cathedral of St. Nicholas

Opened by American Cardinal Cushing in 1965, this is one of the last great stone churches built in Europe. The interior is a treat and is worth a peek.

Cost and Hours: Free, open to visitors daily 8:30-18:30 as long as you don't interrupt Mass, church bulletins at doorway list upcoming Masses and concerts, located across Salmon Weir Bridge on outskirts of town, tel. 091/563-577.

Visiting the Cathedral: Inside, you'll see mahogany pews set on green Connemara marble floors under a Canadian cedar ceiling. The acoustically correct cedar enhances the church's fine pipe organ. Two thousand worshippers sit on three sides facing the central altar. A Dublin woman carved the 14 larger-than-life stations of the cross. The carving above the chapel (left of entry) is from the old St. Nicholas church. Explore the modern stained glass. Find the Irish Holy Family—with Mary knitting and Jesus offering Joseph a cup of tea. The window depicting the Last Supper is particularly creative—find the 12 apostles.

Next, poke your head into the side chapel with a mosaic of Christ's resurrection (if you're standing in the nave facing the main altar, it's on the left and closest to the front). Take a closer look at the profiled face in a circular frame, below and to the right of Christ—the one looking up while praying with clasped hands. It's JFK, nearly a saint in Irish eyes at the time this cathedral was built.

Salmon Weir Bridge

This bridge was the local "bridge of sighs." It led from the courthouse (opposite the church) to the prison (torn down to build the cathedral). Today, the bridge provides a fun view of the fishing action. Salmon run up this river most of the summer (look for them). Fishermen, who wear waders and carry walking sticks to withstand the strong current, book long in advance to get half-day appointments for a casting spot.

Canals multiplied in this city (once called the "Venice of Ireland") to power more water mills.

OUTER GALWAY

▲Salthill

This small resort town packs pubs, nightclubs, a splashy water park, amusement centers, and a fairground up against a fine, mile-long beach promenade (Ireland's longest). Watch for local power walkers "kicking the wall" when they reach the western end of the promenade to emphasize that they've gone the entire distance.

At the **Atlantaquaria Aquarium,** which features native Irish aquatic life and some Amazonian species, kids can help feed the fish at 13:00 (freshwater), 15:00 (big fish), 16:00 (small fish), and 17:00 (naughty kids fed to piranhas). They can cuddle the crustaceans anytime (€13, kids-€8.50, Mon-Fri 10:00-17:00, Sat-Sun until 18:00, touch tanks, The Promenade, tel. 091/585-100, www.nationalaquarium.ie).

For beach time, a relaxing sunset stroll, late-night traditional music, or later-night nightclub action, Salthill hops.

Getting There: To get to Salthill, catch bus #401 from Eyre Square in front of the AIB bank, next to The Hardiman (3/hour, €2).

GALWAY

Magdalene Laundries Memorial

Documentaries and films such as *The Magdalene Sisters* and *Philomena* have highlighted the 20th-century plight of unmarried, pregnant Irish women who were incarcerated and put to work doing laundry as virtual slaves. Viewing premarital pregnancy as one step short of prostitution, various Catholic orders operated these infamous "Magdalene laundries." (No such stigma applied to the men involved.) Across from the TI (at 47 Forster Street), a modest and easy-to-miss statue stands on the site of one such facility, operated by the Sisters of Mercy, which opened in 1824 with a capacity of 110 young women, and closed in 1984 with 18 inmates remaining. It's estimated that upwards of 10,000 women passed through the Magdalene laundry system. Magdalene survivors claim that they were held against their will, forced to work without pay, and physically abused...and their children were sold for adoption. The Irish government apologized in 2013 for turning a blind eye to the mistreatment of these "fallen women," who were imprisoned out of sight, often with the consent of their shamed families.

Nightlife in Galway

▲TRADITIONAL IRISH MUSIC

Galway, like Dingle and Doolin, is a mecca for good Irish music (nightly 21:30-23:30). But unlike Dingle and Doolin, this is a university town (enrollment: 12,000), and many pubs are often overrun with noisy students. Still, your chances of landing a seat close to a churning band surrounded by new Irish friends are good any evening of the year.

Pubs

Touristy and student pubs are found and filled along the main drag down from Eyre Square to the Spanish Arch, and across Wolfe Tone Bridge (along William Street West and Dominick Street).

Across the Bridge: A good place to start is at **Monroe's Tavern,** with its vast, music-filled interior (check website for trad-music schedule, Dominick Street, tel. 091/583-397, www.monroes. ie). Several other pubs within earshot frequently feature traditional music. **The Crane,** a couple blocks west of Monroe's, has trad sessions nightly at 21:30 downstairs, a variety of other music upstairs, and Celtic Tales storytelling sessions on Thursdays from April to

October (€10 for storytelling at 20:00, other sessions free, 2 Sea Road, tel. 091/587-419, www.thecranebar.com).

On the Main Drag: Pubs known for Irish music include **Tig Cóilí,** featuring Galway's best trad sessions (Mon-Sat at 18:00 and 22:00, Sun at 14:00 and 21:00, intersection of Main Guard Street and High Street, tel. 091/561-294); **Taaffe's** (nightly music sessions at 17:30 and 21:30, Shop Street, across from St. Nicholas Church, tel. 091/564-066); and **The Quays** (trad music most nights at 21:30, sporadic schedule, young scene, Quay Street, tel. 091/568-347). A bit off the main drag, **Barr An Chaladh** is a scruffy little place offering nightly trad or ballad sessions and more locals (3 Daly's Place, tel. 091/895-762).

Performances

Instead of a pub, you can also attend a concert or performance.

Trad on the Prom: This fine, traditional, music-and-dance troupe was started by Galway-born performers, who returned home after years of touring with *Riverdance* and the Chieftains. Their show—so popular that it's lasted for more than a decade—is a great way to enjoy live step dancing and accomplished musicians in a fairly intimate venue (€32-59, mid-May-mid-Oct only, shows at 20:30 on Tue, Thu, and Sun—call to confirm, and best to reserve ahead online; at Leisureland Theatre beside Salthill Park, 30-minute walk west of town along the Salthill promenade or short ride on bus #401 from Eyre Square; tel. 091/582-860, mobile 087-674-1877, www.tradontheprom.com).

Celtic Dream is an Irish music-and-dance show hosted by Monroe's Tavern with an option to grab a pub-grub dinner before the performance (€30, €5 discount off pub meal if booked for performance, May-Sept Mon-Wed at 20:00, 14 Dominick Street Upper, tel. 085/842-9912, www.monroes.ie/events).

Tunes in the Church: The Collegiate Church of St. Nicholas is a mellow, medieval venue with great acoustics, hosting a rotating lineup of accomplished trad musicians. The 1.5-hour concerts are fun for early birds who don't want to stay up to catch the same great players in a local pub later that night (€15; June-Aug Mon-Fri at 20:00, where High Street and Shop Street intersect, mobile 087-962-5425, www.tunesinthechurch.com).

Sleeping in Galway

There are three price tiers for most beds in Galway: off-season, high season (Easter-Oct), and charge-what-you-like festival and race weekends (see "Crowd Control" on page 349).

Note: With easy train access from Dublin, Galway is a popular weekend destination for rambunctious stag and hen parties. If you want a good night's sleep on a Friday or Saturday, steer clear of hotels with bars downstairs or nearby; instead, opt for a smaller B&B or guesthouse (I list a few, including a couple outside of town—B&Bs are becoming harder to find as they struggle to compete with bigger hotels).

GALWAY

HOTELS

$$$$ Park House Hotel, a plush, business-class hotel, offers the best value for a fancy place. Ideally located a block from the train station and Eyre Square, it has 84 spacious rooms and all the comforts you'd expect (expensive full Irish breakfast, elevator, pay parking, great restaurant, helpful staff, Forster Street, tel. 091/564-924, www.parkhousehotel.ie, reservations@parkhousehotel.ie).

$$$$ Forster Court Hotel has a quiet and professional vibe with 50 uncluttered and refined rooms a half-block from Eyre Square (elevator, Forster Street, tel. 091/564-111, www.theforstercourt.ie, reservations@theforstercourt.ie).

$$$$ The Hardiman, filled with palatial Old World elegance and 97 rooms, marks the end of the Dublin-Galway train line and the beginning of Galway. Since 1845, it has been Galway's landmark hotel...JFK stayed here in 1963 when it was the Great Southern (elevator, at the head of Eyre Square, tel. 091/564-041, www.thehardiman.ie, info@thehardiman.ie).

$$$$ Jurys Inn Galway has 130 American-style rooms in a modern hotel, centrally located where the old town hits the river. The big, bright rooms have double beds and huge modern bathrooms (breakfast extra, elevator, lots of tour groups, pay parking, Quay Street, tel. 091/566-444, US tel. 800-423-6953, www.jurysinns.com, jurysinngalway@jurysinns.com).

¢ Kinlay Hostel is a no-nonsense place just 100 yards from the train station, with 224 beds in bare, clean, and simple rooms, including 15 doubles/twins. Easygoing people of any age feel welcome here, but if you want a double, book well ahead—several months in advance for weekends (private rooms available, elevator, baggage storage, laundry service, on Merchants Road just off Eyre Square, tel. 091/565-244, www.kinlaygalway.ie, info@kinlaygalway.ie).

even a small cup, it's worth it for flavors like Dingle sea salt (hand harvested) and caramelized brown bread (daily 12:00-22:30, 12 High Street).

NEAR EYRE SQUARE
$$ Galway Bakery Company (GBC) is a popular, basic place for a quick Irish meal with a self-serve buffet line (daily 8:00-18:00, later in summer, 7 Williams Gate, near Eyre Square, tel. 091/563-087). They have a simple, good-value restaurant upstairs (open later).

$$ The Lighthouse Vegetarian Café is a calm and cozy little vegetarian haven (lunch only) with creative, well-presented plates and fresh-baked goods, just steps behind Lynch's Castle (Mon-Sat 10:00-17:30, Sun 11:00-16:00, 8 Abbeygate Street Upper, mobile 087-352-0198).

Supermarket: Dunnes is tucked in the Eyre Square Shopping Centre (Mon-Sat 9:00-19:00, Thu-Fri until 21:00, Sun 11:00-19:00, supermarket in basement). Lots of smaller grocery shops are scattered throughout town.

NORTH END OF COLLEGE ROAD
$$ The Huntsman Inn is an easy 10-minute walk north of my College Road B&Bs. It's modern, friendly, and far from the tourist action, with dependable dishes that draw mostly locals (daily 12:00-21:00, 164 College Road, tel. 091/562-849).

OUTSIDE GALWAY
If you have a car, consider a Dunguaire Castle medieval banquet in Kinvarra, a 30-minute drive south of Galway (for details, see page 345). You can fit the banquet in very efficiently when you're driving into Galway (B&Bs can accommodate late arrivals if you call ahead).

Galway Connections

From Galway by Train to: Dublin (nearly hourly, 2.5 hours), **Limerick** (6/day, 2 hours), **Ennis** (5/day, 1.5 hours). For **Belfast, Tralee,** and **Rosslare,** you'll change in or near Dublin. Train info: Tel. 091/561-444, www.irishrail.ie.

By Bus to: Dublin (hourly, 3.5 hours; also see Citylink, later), **Kilkenny** (3/day, 5 hours), **Cork** (hourly, 4.5 hours), **Ennis** (hourly, 1.5 hours), **Shannon Airport** (hourly, 2 hours), **Cliffs of Moher** (8/day in summer, some with change in Ennis, 2 hours), **Doolin** (5/day, 1.5 hours), **Limerick** (hourly, 2 hours), **Dingle** (5/day, 6 hours), **Tralee** (8/day, 4 hours), **Westport** (6/day, 2-4 hours), **Rosslare** (2/day, 8 hours), **Belfast** (every 2 hours, 6 hours, change in Dublin), **Derry** (6/day, 5.5 hours). Bus info: Tel. 091/562-000, www.buseireann.ie.

Citylink runs cheap and fast bus service from the coach station near the TI to **Dublin** (arriving at Bachelor's Walk, a block from Tara Street DART station; hourly, 2.5 hours), **Dublin Airport** (hourly, 3 hours), and **Cork Airport** (6/day, 4 hours). Bus info: Tel. 091/564-164, www.citylink.ie.

By Car: For ideas on driving from Galway to Derry in Northern Ireland, see the Westport & Connemara chapter for a suggested sightseeing route through Connemara, and the Donegal & the Northwest chapter for some worthwhile stops farther north (near and in Donegal).

ARAN ISLANDS

Inishmore • Inisheer

Strewn like limestone chips hammered off the jagged west coast, the three Aran Islands—Inishmore, Inishmaan, and Inisheer—confront the wild Atlantic with stubborn grit ("Inish" is Irish for "island"). The largest, Inishmore ("big island," 9 miles by 2 miles), is by far the most populated, interesting, and visited. Easily reached from Galway, it's my island of choice (try to spend a night here). Inisheer ("east island") is the smallest at 1.5 miles square. Best reached from Doolin, it's worth considering for travelers with less time. Snoozing between them is Inishmaan ("middle island," 3.5 miles square), with little tourism infrastructure and not covered in this chapter.

The landscape of all three islands is harsh. Craggy, vertical cliffs fortify their southern flanks (particularly Inishmore). Windswept rocky fields, stitched together by stone walls, blanket the interiors. And the islands' precious few sandy beaches hide in coves that dimple their northern shores. During the winter, severe gales sweep through; because of this, most of the settlements on the islands are found on the more sheltered northeastern side.

There's a stark beauty about the Aran Islands and the simple lives their inhabitants eke out of a mean sea and less than six inches of topsoil. Precious little of the land is productive. In the past, people made a precarious living here from fishing and farming. The scoured bedrock offered little in the way of soil, so over centuries the islanders created it, layering seaweed with limestone sand and animal dung. Fields are small, divided by several thousand miles of "dry stone" wall (made without mortar). Most of these are built in the Aran "gap" style, in which spaces between angled upright stones are filled with smaller stones. This allows a farmer who

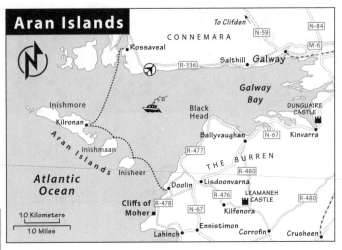

Aran Islands

wants to move livestock to dismantle a short section of wall as a temporary gate, and then rebuild that section afterward. It also allows the harsh winter winds to blow through without knocking down the wall.

Nowadays, tourism boosts the islands' economy. The islands are a Gaeltacht area. While the islanders speak Irish among themselves, they happily speak English for their visitors. Many islanders have direct, personal connections with close relatives in America.

Today, the 800 people of Inishmore greet as many as 2,000 visitors a day. The vast majority of these are day-trippers, who hop on a minivan at the dock for a 2.5-hour visit to Dun Aengus (the must-see Iron Age fort), grab lunch, and then spend an hour or two browsing through the few shops or sitting at a picnic table outside a pub with a pint of Guinness. Inisheer and Inishmaan are smaller, much less populated, and less touristy, but they do have B&Bs, daily flights, and ferry service. For most, Inishmore is quiet enough—though Inisheer is gaining steam as an alternative to the big island. An overnight on either Inishmore or Inisheer is a memorable low-stress treat.

PLANNING YOUR VISIT

On Your Own: Consider these factors as you plan your island trip. Rossaveal is the best port for reaching Inishmore, and Doolin is the best departure point for Inisheer. Although boats sail to all three islands from both ports, you'll maximize your island time by taking the ferry from the closest port (it's a two-hour drive between Rossaveal and Doolin).

If day-tripping, consider a flight from Connemara Regional airport to maximize your island time. Flying costs about twice as much as a ferry. But it takes only 10 minutes, comes with wonderful island views, and allows you to arrive before the day-tripping ferry crowds do, then linger a few hours more after they sail back.

With a Tour: Group tours take you from Galway to Inishmore and back, and include transportation and the services of a guide the whole day. While convenient, this is more expensive than figuring it out yourself and limits you to a set itinerary (for details, see page 353 of the Galway chapter).

GETTING TO THE ISLANDS

For an overview map of the region, see previous page.

By Ferry from Rossaveal (near Galway)

Island Ferries sails to Inishmore from the port of Rossaveal, 20 miles west of Galway. In peak season (mid-April-Sept), ferries depart from Rossaveal at 10:30, 13:00, and 18:30; from Inishmore at 8:15 (9:00 on Sun), 12:00, and 17:00 (also at 16:00 in June and 18:30 in July-Aug; confirm schedule online). They also run a shuttle bus from Galway to the Rossaveal dock (3/day in peak season, bus ride and ferry crossing each take 45 minutes; coming from Galway, allow 2 hours total; €25 round-trip boat crossing plus €9 round-trip for shuttle bus, 10 percent discount if you book online). Catch shuttle buses from Galway on Queen Street, a block behind the Kinlay Hostel (check-in 1.5 hours before sailing); shuttles return to Galway immediately after each boat arrives. Island Ferries has two offices in Galway: on Forster Street across from the TI and at 19 Eyre Square (tel. 091/568-903, after-hours tel. 091/572-273, www. aranislandferries.com).

Note: The boat you take out to the islands may not be the same as the one you come back on. And sometimes you'll board by walking up the gangplank of one boat and walking across its deck to another boat docked beside or behind it.

Parking in Rossaveal: Drivers should go straight to the ferry landing in Rossaveal, passing several ticket agencies and pay parking lots. At the boat dock, you'll find a convenient €8/day lot and an office that sells tickets for Island Ferries (with better WCs than on the ferry).

By Ferry from Doolin

Boats from Doolin sail to all three Aran Islands but make the most sense if you're day-tripping to Inisheer or overnighting on Inishmore. (While it's possible to travel from Doolin to Inishmore and back in one day, it's a 75-minute trip each way, leaving less time ashore; sail from Rossaveal instead).

Buying Tickets: The scene at the Doolin ferry dock is a confusing mosh pit of competition. Two ferry companies operate from three ticket huts with one thing in mind: snaring your business. They have similar schedules and prices. No matter which company you choose, it's smart to check online for discounts (as much as 30 percent). It's also important to double-check schedules and arrive at least 15 minutes early. Be patient: Boats can be 30 minutes late... or 10 minutes early. You're on Irish time.

Doolin2Aran Ferries is run by the Garrihy family (to Inisheer: €20 same-day round-trip, 30 minutes, departs Doolin at 10:00, 11:00, 16:00, and 17:30, departs Inisheer at 8:30, 10:20, 11:20, 12:15, 13:45, and 16:45; to Inishmore: €25 round-trip, 75 minutes, generally departs Doolin at 10:00, 11:00, and 13:00, departs Inishmore at 11:30 and 16:00). They also offer a fun €30 triangular day trip that takes you from Doolin to Inisheer, drops you off on Inisheer for about 3.5 hours, then sails along the base of the Cliffs of Moher before docking back in Doolin (departs at 10:00 and 11:00, returns to Doolin by 16:45, runs March-Oct, tel. 065/707-5949, mobile 087-245-3239, www.doolin2aranferries.com).

Doolin Ferry/O'Brien Line, run by Bill O'Brien, has been at it the longest, with similar schedules and occasionally cheaper prices. They also offer a cruise along the base of the Cliffs of Moher that includes a stop at Inisheer (tel. 065/707-5618, mobile 087-958-1465, www.obrienline.com).

Parking in Doolin: With a car, Doolin is easy to reach; without one, it's better to go to Inishmore from Rossaveal. Parking at the Doolin dock is pay-and-display (€1/2 hours, €5 overnight). Give yourself enough time to deal with parking and the line of visitors waiting to pay at the single machine. For details on staying in Doolin, see page 337.

By Plane

Aer Arann Islands, a friendly and flexible little airline, flies daily from Connemara Regional Airport, serving all three islands (3/day, up to 11/day in peak season, €25 one-way, €49 round-trip, 10-minute flight, tel. 091/593-034, www.aerarannislands.ie, info@aerarannislands.ie). The eight-seat planes get booked up—reserve as soon as you are sure of your dates (by email, with a credit card). Note that your baggage weight limit is 50

pounds total, so if you're overnighting, pack a bag with just what you need and leave your remaining clothes (but not your valuables) locked in the trunk of your car or stored in your Galway hotel.

Chartered sightseeing-only Aer Arann flights leave from the same airport (by reservation only). Cruising at 500 feet, you'll fly above all three Aran Islands with an extra swoop past the Cliffs of Moher (€960 for seven-passenger aircraft, 35 minutes).

Getting to and from the Airports: Connemara Regional Airport is 20 slow miles west of Galway—allow 45 minutes for the drive, plus 30 minutes to check in before the scheduled departure. A minibus shuttle—€5 one-way—runs from Victoria Hotel off Eyre Square in Galway an hour before each flight. Be sure to reserve a space on the shuttle bus at the same time you book your flight. The Kilronan airport on Inishmore is minuscule. A minibus shuttle (€3 one-way, €5 round-trip) travels the two miles between the airport and Kilronan (stop is behind the Aran Sweater Market).

Inishmore

The largest of the Aran Islands has a blockbuster sight: the striking Dun Aengus fort, set on a sheer cliff. Everyone arrives at Kilronan, the Aran Islands' biggest town, though it's just a village. Groups of backpackers wash ashore with the docking of each ferry. Minivans, bike shops, and a few men in pony carts sop up the tourists.

PLANNING YOUR TIME

Most travelers visit Inishmore (Inis Mór) as a day trip by boat from Rossaveal, near Galway (it's possible from Doolin, but farther—see "Getting to the Islands," earlier). Here's a good framework for a day trip: Leave Galway at 9:00 by car or shuttle bus to Rossaveal, where you'll catch the 10:30 boat. Arriving in Kilronan about 11:15, arrange minivan transport or rent a bike. Visit Dun Aengus, and grab a bite at a simple café near the base of the Dun Aengus fort trail (or bring a picnic). Explore the island during low tide, and depart on the boat when high tides return between 16:00 and 18:00. Return to Galway by car or shuttle bus.

Staying Overnight: If you're spending the night, plan your time around the crush of day-trippers, who make a beeline straight off the boat to Dun Aengus. Upon arrival, head first in the opposite direction to check out the subtle charms of the less-visited eastern end of the island. Buy a picnic at the supermarket in Kilronan. Then walk to either the ruins of tiny St. Benen's Church (an easy 45-minute hike one-way from Kilronan) or the rugged Black Fort ruins (a rocky one-hour scramble one-way from Kilronan). Save

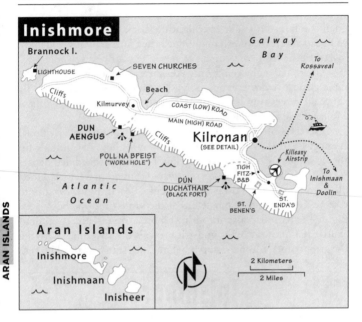

Dun Aengus for later in the afternoon, after the midday crowds have subsided. Enjoy an evening in the pubs and take a no-rush midmorning boat trip or flight back to the mainland the next day.

Orientation to Inishmore

Your first stop on Inishmore is the town of Kilronan, huddling around the pier. There are half a dozen shops, a scattering of B&Bs, a few restaurants, and a couple of bike-rental huts. A few blocks inland up the high road, you'll find the best folk-music pub (Joe Watty's), a post office, and a tiny bank (open one day a week) across from the roofless Anglican church ruins.

The friendly Man of Aran café/shop lurks on the back side of the stony Aran Sweater Market building, across from the high cross (sells hiking maps, offers Irish lessons, and shows *Man of Aran* film; see listing later for details). Public WCs are 100 yards beyond the TI on the harbor road.

The huge Spar supermarket, two blocks inland from the harbor, seems too big for the tiny community and has the island's only ATM. If you don't have plenty of cash on you, get some here—most B&Bs and quite a few other businesses don't accept credit cards.

TOURIST INFORMATION

Facing the harbor, Kilronan's TI is helpful (daily 10:00-17:00, may close during lunch, shorter hours in winter, tel. 099/20862). The

Currach and *Navogue* Boats

These are the traditional fishing boats of the west coast of Ireland—lightweight and easy to haul. In your coastal travels, you'll see a few actual *currach* or *navogue* boats—generally retired and stacked where visitors can touch them and ponder the simpler age when they were a key part of the economy.

The *currach* is native to the Aran Islands, while the *navogue* is native to the Dingle Peninsula. It's primarily a case of semantics and, to us, they look almost the same. But a fisherman would build a boat to suit his needs: a higher bow to deal with more surf, higher sides to lean over when pulling up lobster pots, a flat stern, etc. Few raw materials were needed to make the boats: a wooden frame with canvas (originally cowhide) and paint with tar. But the skill in making them came from generations of fine-tuning by fishermen who knew their environment intimately. The advantage of both boats was maneuverability on the sea and ease in getting them in and out of the water (the seamanship of these skilled sailors is too often underestimated). Their disadvantage was their fragility when hauling anything other than men or fish. When transporting sheep, farmers would lash each sheep's pointy little hooves together and place it carefully upside-down in the *currach*—so it wouldn't kick a hole in the little craft's thin canvas skin.

free map given out by the TI or ferry operator is all the average day-tripper or leisure biker will need. But serious hikers who plan on scampering out to the island's craggy fringes will want to invest in the detailed Ordnance Survey map (€13.50, sold at the Man of Aran shop).

Audioguides: Mobile phone-size audioguides are rented by the day. Clear and informative commentary covers the island's major sights, and the guide comes with a numbered, color-coded map. While no substitute for fun and colorful ad-libbing by a minivan driver or pony-cart handler, the scholarly, bite-size info is particularly useful for bikers and hikers, who are not being driven around the island by a local (€8/day, rent from recommended Rustic Rock Restaurant facing harbor).

Events: The three-day **Patrún** celebration during the last weekend of June includes *currach* boat races, Galway "hooker" boat races, and a fun run. June 23 is **St. John's Eve Bonfire Night,** a Christian/pagan tradition held the night before St. John's Day, close to (but not on) the summer solstice. Each community stokes a raging fire around dusk, and dozens are visible not only on the island but also on the distant shore of Connemara.

GETTING AROUND INISHMORE

By Minivan or Pony Cart: Just about anything on wheels functions as a taxi here. A trip from Kilronan to Dun Aengus to the Seven Churches and back to Kilronan costs €15 per person in a shared minivan. Pony carts cost about €25 per person for a trip to Dun Aengus and back. For details, see the next section.

By Bike: Biking here is great. You can rent a bike at huts near the pier (daily 9:00-17:00, regular 21-speed bikes about €10/day plus €10 deposit, electric bikes €25/day plus €20 deposit).

Figure 30 minutes to ride from Kilronan to the start of the trailhead up to Dun Aengus. Cyclists should take the high road over and the low road back—you'll encounter fewer hills, scenic shoreline, and at low tide, a dozen seals basking in the sun. Novice bikers should be aware that the terrain is hilly and there are occasional headwinds and unpredictable showers.

Keep a sharp lookout along the roadside for handy, modern limestone signposts (with distances in kilometers) that point the way to important sights. They're in Irish, but you'll be clued in by the small metal depictions of the sights embedded within them.

Tours on Inishmore

▲▲Island Minivan Tours

Fewer than 100 vehicles roam the island, and most of them seem to be minivans. A line of vans (seating 8-18 passengers) awaits the arrival of each ferry, offering €15 island tours. They're basically a

shared taxi service that will take you to the various sights, drop you off, and return at an agreed time to take you to the next attraction.

The tour zips you to the end of the island for a quick stroll in the desolate

ARAN ISLANDS

fields, gives you 15 minutes to wander through the historic but visually unimpressive Seven Churches, and then drops you off for two hours at Dun Aengus (30 minutes to hike up, 30 minutes at the fort, 20-minute hike back down, 40 minutes in café for lunch or shopping at drop-off point) before running you back to Kilronan. These sights can be linked together in various sequences, but the trailhead crossroads below Dun Aengus—with two cafés—makes the best lunch stop. Ask your driver to take you back along the smaller coastal road (scenic beaches and well-camouflaged sunbathing seals at low tide).

Chat with a few drivers to find one who likes to talk. On a recent tour, I learned that 800 islanders live in 14 villages (actually just crossroads), with three elementary schools and three churches. Most islanders own a small detached field where they keep a couple of cows (sheep are too much trouble). When pressed for more information, my guide explained that there are 400 types of flowers and 19 types of bees on the island. Then he pointed to the 2,000-year-old ring fort on the hilltop and grinned, saying, "It's so popular with visitors that we plan to build another 2,000-year-old ring fort next year."

▲Walking & Bike Tours
Cyril O'Flaherty leads tours (on foot or by bike) that take the navigational hassle out of reaching natural wonders like the Worm Hole, the Black Fort, or St. Benen's Church while adding rich insights on local history, wildlife, language, and culture (mobile 087-688-0688, www.aranwalkingtours.com, info@aranwalkingtours.com).

Sights and Activities on Inishmore

IN KILRONAN
Man of Aran Film
This Oscar-winning 1934 movie (1.25 hours) is a documentary, partly staged, about traditional island life. It's basically a silent movie, with an all-local cast and the sounds of surf, seagull, and sailor (muttering in barely audible Irish) dubbed in. It's a strangely fascinating glimpse of the past and was groundbreaking in its time. The movie tries to re-create life in the early 1900s—when you couldn't rent bikes—and features *currach*s (canoe-like boats) in a storm, shark fishing with handheld harpoons, kids fishing off cliffs, and farmers creating soil and cultivating the patches from bare rock. But make this film a rainy-day option: Don't waste time indoors when the real thing is right outside.

Cost and Hours: €5, 3 showings/day—usually on request,

plays in Man of Aran Coffee & Craft Shop (upstairs) behind Aran Sweater Market; open daily 10:00-20:00, shorter hours off-season.

Irish Lessons: Gearóid (pronounced gair-OH-id), who runs the café, also teaches one-hour Irish lessons to tourists for €5. Learn how to say "please" and "thank you," order a beer, and more in this unusual language. Don't worry, he writes everything down phonetically (mobile 085-710-5254, gearoid.browne@gmail.com).

Music
Kilronan's pubs offer music sporadically on summer evenings. Expect guitar-strumming folk songs rather than traditional Irish sessions (lacking the variety of instrumentation that the term "sessions" implies). Ask at your B&B or look for posted notices in front of the supermarket or post office. **Joe Watty's Bar,** on the high road 100 yards past the post office, is worth the 10-minute walk from the dock. Its appealing front porch goes great with a pint, and live music warms the interior most nights. The more central **Joe Mac's Pub** (next to the hostel) and **The Bar** (next to the high cross at the base of the high road) are also possibilities.

Fishing Excursions
Tim Murray at **Calypso Sea Angling** offers charter fishing trips for beginners, experts, and families lasting anywhere from 2-10 hours (mobile 086-819-4500, timmurray@eircom.net).

BEYOND THE TOWN
▲▲▲Dun Aengus (Dún Aonghasa)
This is the island's blockbuster sight. The stone fortress hangs spectacularly and precariously on the edge of a cliff 200 feet above the Atlantic. The crashing waves seem to say, "You've come to the end of the world." Gaze out to sea and consider this: Off this coast, Hy-Brasil—a phantom island cloaked in mist—was said to pop into view once every seven years. This mythical place appeared on maps as late as the mid-1800s.

Little is known about this 2,000-year-old Iron Age fort. Its concentric walls are 13 feet thick and 10 feet high. As an added defense, the fort is ringed with a commotion of spiky stones, sticking up like lances, called *chevaux-de-frise* (literally, "Frisian horses," named for the Frisian soldiers who used pikes to stop charging cavalry). Slowly, as the cliff erodes, hunks of the fort fall into the sea.

Dun Aengus gets crowded after 11:00. If you can, get there early or late. A small visitors center (housing the ticket office and controlling access to the trail) displays aerial views of the fort and tells the story of its inhabitants. Trail access to the fort is open and free when the visitors center is closed.

Cost and Hours: €5; daily 9:30-18:00, off-season until 16:00, closed Mon-Tue in Jan-Feb; last entry one hour before closing, during June-Aug guides at the trailhead answer questions and can sometimes give free tours up at the fort if you call ahead, 5.5 miles from Kilronan, tel. 099/61008.

Warnings: Like the Burren (its nearby mainland limestone cousin), this is rocky, irregular ground with primitive steps of varying heights and some smooth surfaces that can get slippery when wet. The trail is gravel for the first half of the hike and lined with rock walls. But watch your step on bare rock—some stable-looking rocks can be surprisingly shaky. Rangers advise visitors to wear sturdy walking shoes and watch kids closely; there's no fence between you and a crumbling 200-foot cliff overlooking the sea. Also, be wary of unexpected gusts of wind and uncertain footing near the edge. The Irish don't believe in litigation, just natural selection.

ARAN ISLANDS

Seven Churches (Na Seacht Teampaill)

Close to the western tip of the island, this gathering of ruined chapels, monastic houses, and fragments of a high cross dates from the 8th to 11th century. Inishmore is dotted with reminders that Christianity was brought to the islands in the fifth century by St. Enda, who established a monastery here. Many great monks studied under Enda. Among these "Irish apostles" who started Ireland's "Age of Saints and Scholars" (AD 500-900) was Columba (Colmcille in Irish), the founder of a monastery on the island of Iona in Scotland—home of the Irish monks who produced the Book of Kells. Check out the ornate gravestones (best detail on sunny days) of the "seven Romans," located in the slightly elevated back corner of the graveyard, farthest from the road. These pilgrims came here from Rome in the ninth century, long after the fall of the Roman Empire.

Kilmurvey

The island's second-largest village nestles below Dun Aengus. More a simple crossroads than a village, it sports two soup-and-sandwich cafés, a gaggle of homes, and a great sheltered swimming beach with a blue flag. Throughout Ireland, "blue flag" beaches proclaim clean water, safe currents, and the color of your toes when you shiver back to your towel. This is the place for peaceful solitude. Located on the narrowest section of the island, it also has the best grazing land, a fact not lost on the local landlord who claimed it for himself.

The Worm Hole (Poll na bPeist)

Off the beaten path and accessible only by hiking, this site (also called the "Serpent's Lair") takes the "logic" out of geo-*logic*. It's a large, perfectly rectangular, 40-by-100-foot seawater-filled pool (60 feet deep) that was cut by nature into the flat coastal bedrock. You'd swear that God used a cake knife to cut out this massive slab—just to mess with us. But limestone often fractures at right angles. So, the Worm Hole was formed when the roof of the hidden cave underneath (cut by tidal action) collapsed just so. To add to the surreal scene, Red Bull has featured this site several times in its annual cliff-diving competition from the 90-foot cliff above it (search YouTube for thrilling video clips).

Boulder-hopping your way across the narrowest section of the island, you'll find the Worm Hole beneath the island's southern cliffs, one mile straight south of Kilmurvey's fine beach. Consult your map and start with the primitive gravel lane leading in the direction of the tiny inland community of Gort na gCapall. From there you'll be using dead reckoning. It's signposted from the Main Road as *Pol na bPeist,* but the detailed Ordnance Survey map (available at the Man of Aran Coffee & Craft Shop) is handy for navigating here.

Aran Artisan Garden

This private residence and garden should be viewed from the road only (please respect their privacy...they're not trying to get famous). It's a "back to basics" family homestead, fronted by a creative garden (spelling out "LOVE" in block letters), and inspired by an appreciation of a holistic lifestyle. It's a refreshing addition to the island landscape that blends in beautifully. The garden is located about halfway between Kilronan and Kilmurvey, downhill on the right side if you are heading west on the High Road.

Ancient Sites near Killeany

The quiet eastern end of Inishmore offers ancient sites in evocative settings for overnight visitors with more time, or for those seeking rocky hikes devoid of crowds. First, get the detailed Ordnance Survey map (available at the Man of Aran Coffee & Craft Shop). Then consider assembling a picnic, to fuel up either before or after you spend a couple of hours exploring these sights on foot. Ask the folks in town for directions (almost always a memorable experience in Ireland).

Closest to the road, amid the dunes one mile past the Tigh Fitz B&B and just south of the airport, is the eighth-century **St. Enda's Church** (Teaghlach Einne). Protected from wave erosion by a stubborn breakwater, it sits half-submerged in a sandy graveyard, surrounded by a sea of sawgrass and peppered with tombstones.

St. Enda is said to be buried here, along with 125 other saints who flocked to Inishmore in the fifth century to learn from him.

St. Benen's Church (Teampall Bheanáin) perches high on a desolate ridge opposite the Tigh Fitz B&B. Walk up the stone-walled lane, passing a holy well and the stubby remains of a round tower. Then take another visual fix on the church's silhouette on the horizon, and zigzag up the stone terraces to the top. The 30-minute hike up from the B&B pays off with a

great view. Dedicated to St. Benen, a young disciple of St. Patrick himself, this tiny (12-by-6-foot) 10th-century oratory is aligned north-south (instead of the usual east-west) to protect the doorway from prevailing winds. It's thought that this structure was built, not as a place to say Mass, but primarily to house holy relics (a splinter from Christ's cross, a thorn from his crown, etc.), which at the time were highly sought after. Also, its prominent location served as something like a beacon to those many pilgrims who had made the arduous journey to this remote holy island on the edge of the then-known world.

About a five-minute walk past the Tigh Fitz B&B (on your left as you head toward the airport), you'll notice an abandoned stone pier and an adjacent, modest medieval ruin. This was **Arkin Fort,** built by Cromwell's soldiers in 1652 using cut stones taken from the round tower and the monastic ruins that once stood below St. Benen's Church. The fort was used as a prison for outlawed priests before English authorities sent them to the West Indies to be sold into slavery.

Hidden on a remote, ragged headland an hour's walk from Kilronan to the south side of the island, you'll find the **Black Fort** (Dún Duchathair). After Dun Aengus, this is Inishmore's most dramatic fortification, built on a promontory with cliffs on three sides. Its defenders would have held out behind dry-stone ramparts, facing the island's interior attackers. The Ordnance Survey map is essential to navigate here. Watch your step on the uneven ground and be ready to course-correct as you go, and chances are you'll have this windswept ruin all to yourself. Imagine the planning and cooperative effort that went into building these life-saving structures 2,000 years ago.

Sleeping on Inishmore

All of the following places are in Kilronan. Remember, this is a rustic island. Many rooms are plain, with simple plumbing. Luxury didn't make the leap from the mainland.

$$$ The Aran Islands (Ostan Aran) Hotel is the most modern option on the island. Its 20 rooms (four with large harbor-facing porches) have the comforts you'd expect. An additional dozen boxy "chalets" (freestanding studios with queen-size beds) cascade down the slope beside the hotel—the island's first "glamping" option. Beware of loud weekend stag/hen parties drawn to their downstairs pub (tel. 099/61104, 10-minute walk east of the dock on the coast road heading toward Killeany, www.aranislandshotel.com, info@aranislandshotel.com,).

$$ The Pier House stands solidly 50 yards from the pier, offering 12 decent rooms, a good restaurant downstairs, and harbor views from many of its rooms (tel. 099/61417, www.pierhousearan.com, pierhousearan@gmail.com).

$$ Clai Ban, the only really cheery place in town, is run by friendly Marion and Bartley Hernon. Their six rooms and warm hospitality are worth the 10-minute uphill walk from the pier. The place is energized by their affectionate adolescent hound, Porter (cash only, family rooms, walk past bank out of town and up the 50-yard-long lane on left, tel. 099/61111, claibanhouse@gmail.com).

$ Tigh Catherine is a well-kept B&B with four homey rooms overlooking the harbor (cash only, on Church Road up behind the Halla Ronain community center, tel. 099/61464, mobile 087-980-9748, catherineandstiofain@gmail.com, Catherine Mulkerrin).

$ Seacrest B&B offers six uncluttered rooms in a central location behind the Aran Sweater Market (cash only, tel. 099/61292, mobile 087-161-6507, seacrestaran@gmail.com, Geraldine and Tom Faherty).

$ Dormer House has eight centrally located rooms and has been run by Alice Joyce for over 30 years. It's on par with the neat, no-frills vibe of the other B&Bs in town (cash only, next to Spar Market, tel. 099/61125, dormerhouse@mail.com).

¢ Kilronan Hostel, overlooking the harbor near the TI, is cheap but noisy above Joe Mac's Pub (tel. 099/61255, www.kilronanhostel.com, kilronanhostel@gmail.com).

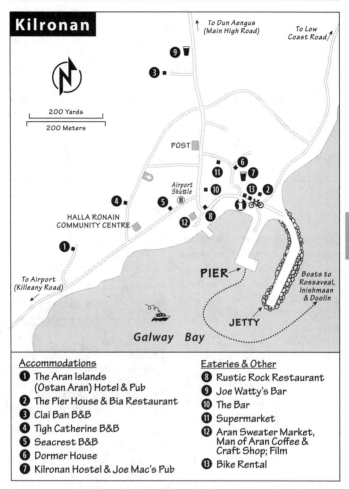

Accommodations
1 The Aran Islands
  (Ostan Aran) Hotel & Pub
2 The Pier House & Bia Restaurant
3 Clai Ban B&B
4 Tigh Catherine B&B
5 Seacrest B&B
6 Dormer House
7 Kilronan Hostel & Joe Mac's Pub

Eateries & Other
8 Rustic Rock Restaurant
9 Joe Watty's Bar
10 The Bar
11 Supermarket
12 Aran Sweater Market,
   Man of Aran Coffee &
   Craft Shop; Film
13 Bike Rental

Eating on Inishmore

There are few restaurants in Kilronan and none are fancy. Expect comfort food at reasonable prices. Beyond the places listed here, Kilronan's modest cafés dish up hearty soup, soda bread, sandwiches, and tea.

$$ Rustic Rock Restaurant, standing proudly beside the high cross, is the island's most central and stylish (a relative term) option. Soup, salads, burgers, and pizza fuel up tired bikers and hikers (daily 12:00-21:00, mobile 086-792-9925). This is also where you can rent island audioguides (see "Tourist Information," earlier).

$$ Joe Watty's Bar, up the hill, has a friendly vibe and tasty grub. Try the chicken goulash with a pint and stick around for the music (daily April-Oct 12:30-15:30 & 17:00-21:00, tel. 099/20892, pleasant front-porch seating).

$$ The Aran Islands Hotel pub is a modern place serving simple soup-and-sandwich lunches and hot dinners (daily 12:00-21:00, tel. 099/61104).

$$$ Bia Restaurant, on the ground floor of The Pier House guesthouse, is dependable (daily May-Sept 11:00-21:30, tel. 099/61811).

Supermarket: The **Spar** has all the groceries you'll need (Mon-Sat 9:00-18:00, July-Aug until 19:00, Sun 10:00-17:00).

Inisheer

The roughly circular little island of Inisheer (Inis Oírr) has less than a quarter of the land area and population of Inishmore. But Inisheer's close proximity to the mainland makes it an easy 35-minute boat journey from Doolin and a good option for those with limited time who aren't going north to Galway.

Inisheer offers a vivid glimpse of Aran Island culture and has an engaging smorgasbord of salty but modest sights. It's also slowly gaining in popularity as an alternative to Inishmore. Inisheer is now being combined with the Cliffs of Moher on some Galway-based bus/boat/bus day tours. Also, boat service from the mainland is becoming more dependable following completion of a second pier at Doolin, allowing Inisheer to siphon off some of the summer crowds from Inishmore.

Planning Your Time: Take an early boat from Doolin to maximize your time on Inisheer. For more details, see "Getting to the Islands" at the beginning of this chapter.

Orientation to Inisheer

You'll dock on the north side of the island in its only settlement. Facing inland with your back to the pier, you'll be able to spot nearly all of the island's landmarks (except for the *An Plassy* shipwreck and the lighthouse on the southern shore). Although some pony carts and minivan drivers meet you at the pier, I'd rely on them only on a rainy day (€10).

For me, the joy of compact Inisheer is seeing it on a bike ride or

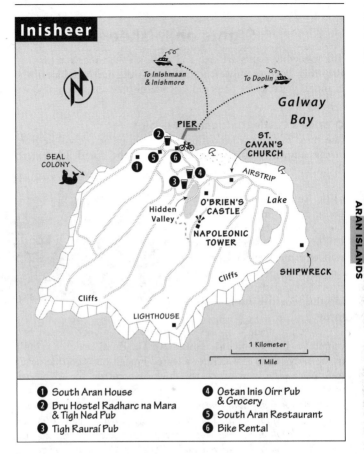

Inisheer

To Inishmaan & Inishmore

To Doolin

Galway Bay

PIER

SEAL COLONY

ST. CAVAN'S CHURCH

AIRSTRIP

Hidden Valley

O'BRIEN'S CASTLE

Lake

NAPOLEONIC TOWER

SHIPWRECK

Cliffs

Cliffs

LIGHTHOUSE

1 Kilometer

1 Mile

ARAN ISLANDS

❶ South Aran House
❷ Bru Hostel Radharc na Mara & Tigh Ned Pub
❸ Tigh Rauraí Pub

❹ Ostan Inis Oírr Pub & Grocery
❺ South Aran Restaurant
❻ Bike Rental

a long breezy walk. The bike-rental outfit is right at the base of the pier (€10/2 hours, €12/day, tel. 099/75049, www.rothai-inisoirr. com, no deposit necessary "unless you look suspicious"). Any of the boat operators can give you a free map of the island showing Inisheer's primitive road network. That's all you'll need to navigate.

There are three pubs on the island, one small grocery store, and no ATMs. All the sights, with the exception of the lonely lighthouse on the southern coast, are concentrated on the northern half.

Inisheer lacks the dramatic (and much higher) coastal cliffs of Inishmore but has its own unique photogenic charms. Fans of the 1990s British sitcom *Father Ted* may recognize parts of the island, which were featured in the show's intro depicting its fictional Craggy Island location.

Sights on Inisheer

The following sights are free and open all the time. See them in the order listed, from west to east, across the northern half of the island. If you bike, be prepared to walk the bike up (or down) short, steep hills.

O'Brien's Castle (Caislean Ui Bhriain)

The ruins of this castle dominate the hilltop and are visible from almost anywhere on the northern half of the island. It's a steep

20-minute walk from the pier up to the castle ruins. The small castle was built as a tower-house refuge around 1400 by the O'Brien clan from nearby County Clare. It sits inside a low wall of a much older Iron Age ring fort. Cromwell's troops destroyed the castle in 1652, leaving the evocative ruins you see today.

If you've made it up to O'Brien's Castle, go another easy five minutes to the **Napoleonic Tower** (An Tur Faire), which was built in the early 1800s to watch for a feared French invasion that never took place. The views from this highest point on the island are worth it.

• *Consult your map and continue walking (south) on the paved road into the heart of the island. Take your first right turn, roughly 100 yards after the Napoleonic Tower, onto a rocky, grassy cow lane that zigzags downhill into a lush* **hidden valley,** *displaying the prettiest mosaic of ivy-tangled rock walls and small green fields I've seen anywhere on the Aran Islands.*

Once you've wound your way back down to the main north-shore road again, turn right and continue east with the airstrip on your left. On your right, you'll soon see a time-passed graveyard up atop a sandy hill. Hike the 50 yards up into the graveyard to find...

St. Cavan's Church (Teampall Chaomhain)

St. Cavan was the brother of St. Kevin, who founded the monastery at Glendalough in the Wicklow Mountains. In the middle of the graveyard is a sunken sandpit holding the rugged, roofless remains of an 11th-century church. The shifting sand dunes almost buried it before sawgrass stabilized the hill. St. Cavan's reputed gravesite is protected by a tiny modern structure worth poking your head into for its candlelit atmosphere. Local folklore held that if you spent a night sleeping on the tomb lid, your particular illness would be cured.

• *Walk back down to the north-shore road and head out on the coast road (to the southeast) 30 minutes to the remote...*

Shipwreck of the *An Plassy*

This freighter was wrecked offshore on Finn's Rock in 1960. But islanders worked with the coastal patrol to rescue the crew with no loss of life. A couple of weeks later the unmanned ship was washed high up onto the rocky shore, where it still sits today, a rusty but fairly intact ghost ship with a broken back. The fierce winter winds and record-breaking waves of 2013 shifted the wreck, further weakening it, and discussions are under way to remove it as it deteriorates. A local told me, "We may have to go out some night with lanterns to bring in a new shipwreck."

Beware of unstable footing on the rounded cobbles thrown up by the surf near the wreck. It's extremely dangerous to touch the wreck, and those trying to climb it are begging for a rusty puncture wound...or worse.

• *With more time, consult your map and seek out the remaining intimate little church ruins and holy wells that the island has to offer. Or head back to town for a beverage while you await the return ferry.*

Sleeping on Inisheer

A scattering of B&Bs dots the northern half of the island. Here are two good options:

$ South Aran House is a quiet, well-run place with five spic-and-span, black-and-white rooms. Humorous Enda and friendly Maria Conneely are generous with local tips and also run the nearby South Aran Restaurant, where you'll have breakfast (easy 10-minute walk west of pier on north-shore road, call ahead with your ferry arrival time so they can meet you with keys, tel. 099/75073, mobile 087-340-5687, www.southaran.com, info@southaran.com). Their small rental cottage sleeps two.

¢ Bru Hostel Radharc na Mara is a simple 40-bed option just 100 yards west of the pier, next to Tigh Ned Pub. They also offer five basic doubles in their adjacent B&B directly behind (includes continental breakfast, open mid-March-Oct, tel. 099/75024, radharcnamara@hotmail.com).

Eating on Inisheer

Inisheer's three main pubs offer decent pub grub (usually 12:30-20:30). There's also a good restaurant if you overnight here.

$$ Tigh Rauraí Pub (House of Rory) is the epicenter of island social life (from the pier, head east to the edge of the beach and turn right—inland—up a narrow lane for 100 yards).

$$ Ostan Inis Oírr Pub (Hotel Inisheer), closer to the beach, sports a colorful collage of international flags draping the pub's ceiling and stag/hen parties on weekends.

$$$ Tigh Ned Pub (House of Ned) is right next door to the hostel, near the pier on the north-shore road. Sit outside at their appealing front tables on a summer evening, enjoying a pint in the salt air.

$$ South Aran Restaurant, a five-minute walk west of the pier on the north-shore road, is a good choice for a mellow evening meal (daily 18:00-21:00, tel. 099/75073, mobile 087-340-5687).

Grocery Store: Picnic lovers flock to the small Siopa XL grocery, behind Ostan Inis Oírr Pub and below Tigh Rauraí Pub (Mon-Sat 9:00-18:00, Sun 10:00-14:00).

ARAN ISLANDS

WESTPORT & CONNEMARA

If you have a car, consider spending a day exploring the wild western Irish fringe known as Connemara. The best home base in this area is the prim and charming town of Westport (home to a pub owned by a member of the traditional Irish music group The Chieftains). From here, you can easily reach the highlights of Connemara. Hike the peak of Croagh Patrick, the mountain from which St. Patrick supposedly banished the snakes from Ireland. Pass through the desolate Doo Lough Valley on a road stained with tragic famine history. Bounce on a springy peat bog.

This beautiful area also claims a couple of towns—Cong and Leenane—where classic Irish movies were filmed, as well as the photogenic Kylemore Abbey. At the end of the chapter, I've also described a few interesting stops east of Westport, including a Virgin Mary shrine and the thoughtful Irish National Famine Museum.

PLANNING YOUR TIME

By Car: The Connemara area makes a satisfying day trip by car from Galway. I've listed the region's prime towns and sights in a loop that starts and ends in Galway (driving north, then back south). But drivers who are aiming for Northern Ireland from Galway can easily modify the loop route and still see the main sights. Both routes are described next.

Without a Car: It's most efficient to take a **day tour** from Galway. Three Galway-based companies—Galway Tour Company, Lally Tours, and Healy Tours—run all-day **bus tours** of nearby regions. Most tours of Connemara include the Quiet Man Museum in Cong, Kylemore Abbey, Clifden, and a "famine village" (or some

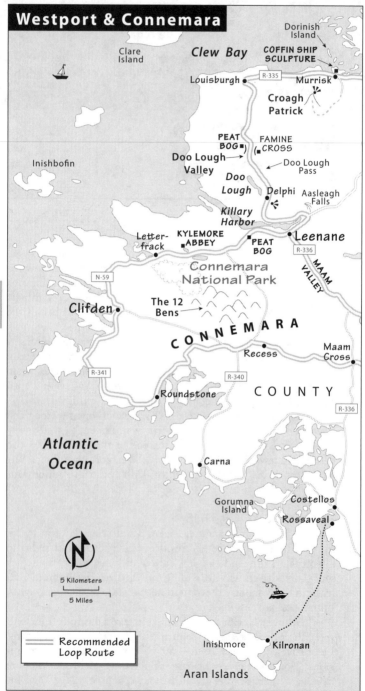

Westport & Connemara

WESTPORT & CONNEMARA

Dorinish Island

Clare Island

Clew Bay

COFFIN SHIP SCULPTURE

Louisburgh   R-335   Murrisk

Croagh Patrick

Inishbofin

PEAT BOG   FAMINE CROSS

Doo Lough Valley   Doo Lough Pass

Doo Lough   Delphi   Aasleagh Falls

Killary Harbor

Letterfrack   KYLEMORE ABBEY   PEAT BOG   Leenane   R-336   MAAM VALLEY

N-59   Connemara National Park

Clifden   The 12 Bens   CONNEMARA

Recess   Maam Cross

R-341   R-340   COUNTY

Roundstone   R-336

Atlantic Ocean

Carna

Gorumna Island   Costellos

Rossaveal

5 Kilometers
5 Miles

Recommended Loop Route

Inishmore   Kilronan

Aran Islands

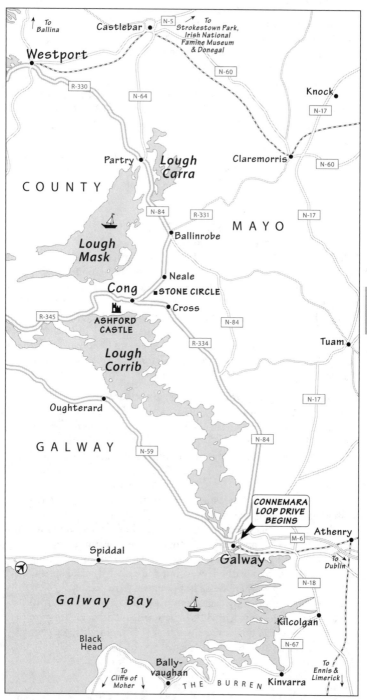

To Ballina

Castlebar

N-5

To Strokestown Park, Irish National Famine Museum & Donegal

Westport

R-330

N-60

Knock

N-64

N-17

Partry

Lough Carra

Claremorris

N-60

C O U N T Y

N-84

R-331

M A Y O

N-17

Lough Mask

Ballinrobe

Neale

Cong

STONE CIRCLE

Cross

N-84

R-345

ASHFORD CASTLE

R-334

Tuam

Lough Corrib

Oughterard

N-17

G A L W A Y

N-59

N-84

CONNEMARA LOOP DRIVE BEGINS

Athenry

M-6

Spiddal

Galway

To Dublin

N-18

Galway Bay

Kilcolgan

Black Head

N-67

Bally-vaughan

To Cliffs of Moher

T H E   B U R R E N

Kinvarra

To Ennis & Limerick

combination of these places). Tours go most days, heading out at 10:00 and returning at 17:30 (€30, call or go online to confirm details, see page 353 for contact information).

For a more intimate experience, consider a private **driver/ guide.** Neal Doherty knows this corner of Ireland well and can take up to six people from Westport to anywhere in County Mayo or County Galway in his Land Rover (€300/half-day, €500/full day, mobile 086-259-6887, www.alchemytours.ie, info@alchemy-tours.ie).

Public transportation in this region (except to and from Westport) is patchy, and some areas are not served at all. Buses run between Galway and Westport, but by train you must connect through Dublin.

CONNEMARA DRIVING ROUTES
Connemara Loop Drive (from Galway)

With a long and well-organized day, you can loop around from Galway and enjoy the most important sights of Connemara (5 hours of driving and 200 miles). Pick up a good map before departing. For maximum coverage, lace together the sights described in this chapter in a route that goes in this order: Cong, Westport, Murrisk, Louisburgh, through the Doo Lough Valley to Leenane, then on to Clifden (passing Kylemore Abbey and Connemara National Park), along the coast to Roundstone, and finally back to Galway.

Galway to Northern Ireland Drive (via Westport)

If heading from Galway to Northern Ireland (Derry or Portrush), visit the described sights in this order: Cong, then across the Maam Valley to Leenane, up to Louisburgh and Murrisk on the way to Westport (consider spending the night). From there you'll head northeast to Sligo, Donegal, and across the border into Northern Ireland.

One of the most interesting parts of this route is the stretch from Cong through the remote **Maam Valley** to Leenane. The brooding and desolate valley feels like a land of ghosts, as the region, once densely populated with potato-eating peasants, was depopulated in the famine and remains that way to this day. The old sod cottages are long washed away, but you can still make out the sad corduroy ridges where those last potatoes were planted.

The direct route between Westport and Derry (or Portrush) comes with a series of worthwhile little stops and detours. They are all fast and easy, and don't take much time. For highlights, see page 409 of the Donegal & the Northwest chapter.

Cong

The town of Cong offers a fascinating mix of attractions: a medieval ruined abbey, a modern church with exquisite stained-glass windows, a museum about a John Ford film *(The Quiet Man),* and a falconry experience on the grounds of the extravagant Ashford Castle. Everything is within a short walk of the parking lot in front of the abbey.

The **TI,** where you can pick up a handy map, is across from the entrance to Cong Abbey (Tue-Sat 9:15-17:00, closed Sun-Mon and Nov-March, tel. 094/954-5050). There are no banks or ATMs in Cong. Public WCs are 50 yards down the street from the TI.

Cong (from *conga,* Irish for "isthmus") lies between two large lakes. On the way in or out of town, you may see a dry 19th-century canal as you pass over a scenic bridge. Built between 1848 and 1854, the canal was a Great Potato Famine work project that stoked only appetites. The canal, complete with locks, was intended to link Lough Mask to the north with Lough Corrib to the south, providing boat access much deeper into Connemara. But the limestone bedrock proved too porous, making the canal an expensive idea that just wouldn't hold water. The project was abandoned. The unfinished canal sits there, dry to this day, as an embarrassment to English Victorian Age engineering.

Sights in Cong

Cong Abbey

The ruins of Cong Abbey (free and always open) are the main attraction in town. Construction on the abbey began in the early 1100s in Romanesque style and continued into the Gothic age. You'll notice a mix of styles—with both round Romanesque and pointed Gothic arches (especially around the doorway). The famous Cross of Cong, which was believed to have held a splinter of the True Cross (now on display in Dublin's National Museum), was hoisted aloft at the front of processions of Augustinian monks during High Masses in this church. Rory O'Connor, the last Irish high king, died in this abbey in 1198. After O'Connor realized he could never outfight the superior Norman armies, he retreated to Cong and spent his last years here in monastic isolation.

Nearby: Take a walk through the cloister and down the gravel path behind the abbey. The forested grounds are lush, and

the stream water is clear. Cong's salmon hatchery contributes to western Ireland's reputation for great fishing. From a little bridge you'll see the **monks' stone house.** It was designed so part of the stream would flow directly under it. The monks simply lowered a net through the floor and attached a bell to the rope; whenever a fish was netted, the bell would ring.

Next to the abbey's cemetery is the modern, concrete, bunker-like **Church of St. Mary of the Rosary** (free, daily 8:00-22:00). Drop in to marvel at its three exquisite windows, made by Irish artist Harry Clarke in 1933. Step behind the altar to get up close.

Quiet Man Museum

This cottage-museum is interesting (only) for fans of the 1951 movie. This town (but not this cottage) is where John Wayne and Maureen O'Hara made the famous John Ford film *The Quiet Man.* You'll see modest historical exhibits and film props.

Cost and Hours: €5, daily 10:00-16:00, closed Nov-mid-March, tel. 094/954-6089, www.quietman-cong.com.

Ashford Castle

This massive stone palace (now a hotel) sits on a vast, exclusive estate that's a lush and peaceful 15-minute walk from town. Its river serves as a modern-day moat: To cross the bridge you'll need to pay €10 (unless you're a hotel guest or have a falconry appointment—see next listing). The building is not open to tourists (guests pay big money to sleep there and don't want their serenity disturbed by casual tourists). But the grounds are a gardener's  delight, creating a lakeside paradise of greenery. Many scenes from *The Quiet Man* were filmed on these grounds.

▲▲Ireland School of Falconry

If you've never experienced falconry, this is a great chance. Animal lovers, aviation engineers, and wannabe medieval hunters will thrill to the Ireland School of Falconry, hidden on the Ashford Castle grounds. You must have an appointment to visit the school, but if you're walking the castle grounds you may see a group and their guide, strolling around as a hawk flies to and from a tourist's well-padded arm.

Cost and Hours: You must reserve ahead for the hour-long falconry experience. It's €95 for one person, €75/person for two, €65/person for three, or €55/person for 4-10 people. All walks are private—you are not grouped with strangers. Ask about convenient

parking (tel. 094/954-6820, mobile 087-297-6092, www.falconry.
ie, info@falconry.ie).

Getting There: The falconry school is about a 10-minute walk
from the castle: Cross the bridge onto the castle grounds, circle
right through the parking lot, and go around the right end of the
castle into the lake-fronted back garden. Then follow "falconry"
signs until you reach a gate with a buzzer (deep in the forest).

Falconry Experience: You'll start in the courtyard surrounded by pens housing hawks. After a brief Hawks 101 lesson, you're
led on a "hawk walk" through the forest with an expert handler,
sporting on his forearm a Harris hawk—a breed the school's brochure says is "renowned for its easygoing temperament and unusually sociable nature." The handler teaches you the fascinating intri-
cacies of falconry, and then you have an opportunity to launch and
land a bird from your own arm...a unique opportunity you didn't
realize you had on your bucket list.

You'll spend a half-hour or so on the castle grounds as your
hawk flies away in search of his prey and returns for the tasty re-
ward the trainer has tucked into your protective mitt. You'll do
this again and again, all the while shooting lots of amazing photographs and getting into the food-centric mind of your graceful and
majestic bird.

Eating in Cong

Fuel up with a pub grub lunch at **$$ The Crowe's Nest** (daily
12:00-21:00, in Ryan's Hotel on Main Street, tel. 094/954-6243).
The **Spar Market** meets the town's grocery needs (Mon-Sat 7:00-
20:00, Sun 8:00-19:00, Main Street).

Westport

Westport, with just 9,000 people, is "the big city" in this part of
Ireland. While other villages seem organic and grown out of the
Middle Ages, this is a
planned town. It was built
in the late 1700s with a
trendy-back-then   Geor-
gian flair by celebrated ar-
chitect James Wyatt, who
designed it to support the
adjacent estate of the Eng-
lish Lord Browne. The
town thrived in its early
days on linen created on local Irish handlooms. But, after the Act
of Union with Britain in 1801, Westport was unable to compete

with the industrialized British linenmakers and fell into decline. With the famine, things got even worse. The town is still pretty (famously "tidy") and well worth a stop. If in need of an overnight between Galway and Derry or Portrush, this would be my choice.

Orientation to Westport

Westport's main street, Bridge Street, stretches from the clock tower up to the river. A block from the clock tower is the eight-sided main "square" called the Octagon. The **TI** (called the "Discover Ireland Centre") is on Bridge Street (Mon-Sat 9:00-17:45, closed Sun, tel. 098/25711). To get oriented, follow my "Westport Walk" or join the guided walk (both described below).

HELPFUL HINTS

Parking: It's free to park on the street for one hour. Otherwise, there are several handy, inexpensive pay-and-display lots in the center.

Laundry: You can get same-day service if you drop off early at **Gills** (Mon-Sat 9:00-18:00, closed Sun, James Street, tel. 098/25819).

Bookstore: Run by friendly Seamus, **The Bookshop** is a delightful place (Mon-Sat 9:30-18:30, Sun 11:00-18:00, later in summer, Bridge Street, tel. 098/26816).

Theater: The **Town Hall Theatre** is worth checking out for music concerts or stage plays (€15-20, in Town Hall facing the Octagon, tel. 098/28459, www.westporttheatre.com).

Town Walk: For a lighthearted and entertaining hour, join Stephen Clarke on his guided walk around town with a tea-and-scones stop at the end. You'll feel like you've made friends with a local and get a sense for the town's pride and personality. No need to reserve—just show up at the Octagon and look for a sprightly man in a yellow jacket (€5, Mon-Fri at 10:00 and 12:00, May-Sept only, mobile 087-410-1363, www.westportwalkingtours.ie).

Westport Walk

This little self-guided walk—almost a complete loop—will acquaint you with Westport's charms, beginning at the Octagon and ending at the clock tower on Bridge Street.

Octagon: This is Westport's main square, but as it's eight-sided, it's called the "Octagon." Surrounded by 30 townhouses, it was the centerpiece of the planned town back in the 1760s. The big limestone structure with the clock was the old **market house,** where trade was organized, and taxes and customs paid.

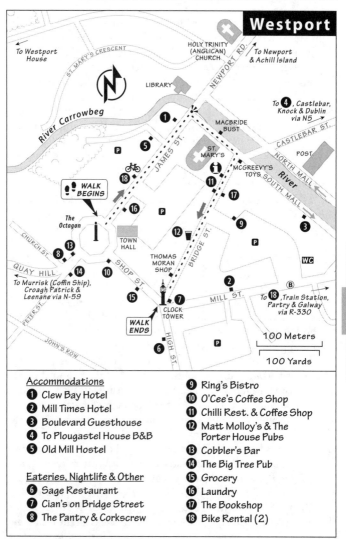

Accommodations
1 Clew Bay Hotel
2 Mill Times Hotel
3 Boulevard Guesthouse
4 To Plougastel House B&B
5 Old Mill Hostel

Eateries, Nightlife & Other
6 Sage Restaurant
7 Cian's on Bridge Street
8 The Pantry & Corkscrew
9 Ring's Bistro
10 O'Cee's Coffee Shop
11 Chilli Rest. & Coffee Shop
12 Matt Molloy's & The Porter House Pubs
13 Cobbler's Bar
14 The Big Tree Pub
15 Grocery
16 Laundry
17 The Bookshop
18 Bike Rental (2)

The **monument** in the center of the Octagon was built in 1843 (just before the famine) to honor Lord Browne's banker, George Glendenning. But the statue of the English banker was shot to pieces by Irish patriots in 1922, during the civil war (notice the gunfire-pocked column). Today, St. Patrick perches on top, garbed in Roman clothes (recalling his kidnapping from Britain's corner of the crumbling Roman Empire).

As you wander around town, you'll see Westport is a proud little place with a strong community spirit. It's competitive, too. In

2012 Westport got the award for "best Irish town to live in." The skinny **bronze statue** just up the hill from the Octagon celebrates Westport's claim to be the most livable town in Ireland.

• *Stroll downhill from the Octagon along James Street.*

James Street: Notice a few things. First, there are no stop signs. That's because traffic is supposed to be so friendly that drivers yield to anyone in a crosswalk without being reminded. Second, there are no chain stores. The town council has allowed no big chains to open in the town center. Finally, note how locals seem to have almost no expressions on their faces. (I'm told that's because the biggest employer here is Allergan Pharmaceuticals, and about a thousand people in Westport earn their living making Botox.)

Halfway down the street, on the left, you'll see a **bike-rental shop** (Westport Bikes for Hire), one of several in town. They're all busy because of the Great Western Greenway bike path (see page 397). Photos in the window show the popular 26-mile route, which runs from Westport to Achill Island over the abandoned right-of-way of a narrow-gauge railway that operated from 1895 to 1937.

• *At the bottom of James Street, stand at the bridge.*

Along the River: Look over at the fancy Anglican church across the river (wealthy English Protestants). Rather than crossing the bridge, we'll head right, to the more humble Catholic church (poor indigenous Catholics, not much inside).

In front of the church, by the water, is a bust of Westport-born **Major John MacBride,** one of the more colorful rebels of the 1916 Easter Rising. MacBride joined a band of insurgents marching into position in Dublin at the start of the rebellion, and was among the 14 men executed at Kilmainham Gaol after its failure.

The river feels like a canal here. Lord Browne, inspired by the embankments he saw in Paris, decided to show off by having this promenade built here, at the western fringe of Western civilization. The flowers along the embankment and on the bridges sure are tidy.

• *At the next bridge, turn right and go uphill on Westport's main street.*

Bridge Street to the Clock Tower: McGreevy's Toy Store (on the corner) gets heat from townsfolk for its tacky **giant ice cream cones,** which the owner insists on posting on the sidewalk (not tidy). Bridge Street is, nevertheless, lined by some of the finest old storefronts in Ireland.

Farther up the street, **Matt Molloy's Pub** is the biggest draw in town—famous because its namesake owner is the flutist for the trad group The Chieftains. You can hear music here nightly (see "Entertainment in Westport," later). Explore the pub during the day when it's quiet and empty. The back room is a small theater with photos of celebrated guests on the wall.

At the top of Bridge Street you'll reach the classic storefront of **Thomas Moran**—so classic it's on an Irish stamp. Try out a hurling stick. Tidy flower patches (tended by an army of volunteers) surround the **clock tower,** which dates to 1947. Back when people needed a reliable timekeeper to set their watches to, this tower had a practical function. The tower marks the town's second square—and the end of our walk.

Activities in Westport

▲▲▲Biking the Great Western Greenway

For an easy way to enjoy Ireland's great and scenic natural beauty, consider the popular 26-mile ride along the Great Western Greenway. From 1895 to 1937, a narrow-gauge railway operated from Westport to Achill Island. In 2010, the rails were replaced by a level, paved path, creating an ideal rural route dedicated to bikers and walkers—no vehicles allowed (www.greenway.ie).

Bike rental places will shuttle you by bus to Achill Island (connected to the mainland by bridge); you then bike scenically for three hours (with the wind generally at your back) along the old train bed back to Westport. You'll cross stone bridges, wind through forested and open bog stretches, and usually have the sea in sight as you hug the coastline. About midway, you'll pass Mulranny village (with a pub and old station renovated into an inviting café). At Newport village you'll bike over an old viaduct.

Westport has several good bike rental places (smart to reserve in advance). **Westport Bikes for Hire** runs daily shuttles at 10:00 and 12:00 to Achill, included in the price of a bike (€30/day for 21-speed bike, €50/day for electric bike, includes yellow vest and helmet, daily 9:00-18:00, James Street, mobile 086-088-0882, www.westportbikehire.com, Jerry). **Clew Bay Bike Hire** also rents bikes and has shuttle-bus options to Newport, Mulranny, or Achill, plus they offer kayaking trips (€30/day for bike, €50/day for electric bike, daily 9:00-18:00, Distillery Road, tel. 098/24818 or 098/37675, www.clewbaybikehire.ie).

Entertainment in Westport

Westport has plenty of live traditional music nightly in its pubs.

On Bridge Street: The most popular place in town is **Matt Molloy's Pub,** whose owner plays with The Chieftains, the group credited with much of the worldwide resurgence of interest in Irish music over the past 50 years. They have traditional music nightly at 21:30 (be there early or stand all night, no food, tel. 098/26655).

The Porter House (next door to Matt Molloy's) is a popular pub for traditional music and also has nightly sessions at 21:30. You'll find more room and fewer crowds here. Larry, the head barman, is proud of his craft beers.

On or near the Octagon: Two pubs have live trad music most evenings in summer: **Cobbler's Bar** and **The Big Tree Pub** (on Lower Peter Street, marked by a big tree a couple of steps up the hill from the Octagon).

Sleeping in Westport

$$$ Clew Bay Hotel has 54 large, modern rooms decked out in cherry-wood furniture (free use of adjacent pool and fitness center, James Street, tel. 098/28088, www.clewbayhotel.com, info@clewbayhotel.com).

$$$ Mill Times Hotel has a fresh, woody feel, with 34 comfortable rooms and convenient, free underground parking (Mill Street, tel. 098/29200, www.milltimeshotel.ie, info@milltimeshotel.ie).

$ Boulevard Guesthouse is the best value in town. Located right on the leafy South Mall, it has six large, quiet, tasteful rooms and a cushy lounge with an interesting guest library under the stairs. Sadie and John Moran make you feel welcome (family rooms, cash only, RS%—discount with multiple-night stay, light continental breakfast, parking, South Mall, tel. 098/25138, mobile 087-284-4018, www.boulevard-guesthouse.com, boulevardguesthouse@gmail.com).

$ Plougastel House B&B, named after Westport's sister town in Brittany, has eight inviting, smartly furnished earth-tone rooms with marble-floored bathrooms (cash only, Distillery Road, tel. 098/25198, www.plougastel-house.com, info@plougastel-house.com, Sandra Corcoran).

¢ Old Mill Hostel is a thick-walled stone structure that could stop a tank. Like many hostels, it's an inexpensive ramshackle bunkhouse for an international mix of youthful vagabonds (James Street, tel. 098/27045, www.oldmillhostel.com, info@oldmillhostell.com).

Eating in Westport

CONTEMPORARY IRISH

Each of these places serves contemporary Irish cuisine in a cozy and inviting space, and generally offer a three-course early-bird special for about €25 if you order before 18:30. All are popular enough to merit making reservations.

$$$ Sage Restaurant is filled with a happy energy. Shteryo (a talented Bulgarian chef) cooks while his wife Eva serves (daily from 17:30, 10 High Street, tel. 098/56700, www.sagewestport.ie).

$$$ Cian's on Bridge Street, serving beautifully presented dishes and always a good vegetarian plate, is the current choice of foodies, so reservations are a must (Mon-Sat 17:00-22:00, closed Sun, top of Bridge Street at #1, tel. 098/25914, www.ciansonbridgestreet.com).

$$$ The Pantry & Corkscrew is another local favorite, serving modern Irish with a dash of Asian in a woody, welcoming atmosphere (Tue-Sun 17:00-22:00, closed Mon, The Octagon, tel. 098/26977, www.thepantryandcorkscrew.com).

BUDGET EATING

You'll find plenty of options along Bridge Street; for pub grub, consider J. J. O'Malley's.

$ Ring's Bistro, presided over by hardworking Joe and Eithne Ring, is a friendly and filling locals' hangout for breakfast or lunch (Mon-Sat 8:00-17:30, closed Sun, hidden up Market Lane off Bridge Street, tel. 098/29100).

$ O'Cee's Coffee Shop serves good, basic cafeteria-style lunches (Mon-Sat 8:30-18:30, Sun 9:00-16:00, on the Octagon, tel. 098/27000).

$ Chilli Restaurant & Coffee Shop is another reliable local diner (daily 9:30-17:00, Bridge Street, tel. 098/27007).

Groceries: The **SuperValu** market has picnic fare; it's just off the Octagon on Shop Street (daily 8:00-22:00).

Westport Connections

By Bus to: Galway (6/day, 2-4 hours), **Derry** (3/day, 6 hours, bus #440 to Knock Airport or Charleston then #64 to Derry), **Dublin** (6/day, 6 hours with transfer in Galway, train is better). For details, see www.buseireann.ie.

By Train to: Dublin (5/day, 3.25 hours, www.irishrail.ie).

Connemara Loop Drive Sights

The towns and sights below are arranged in the order you will reach them on my "Connemara Loop Drive" as you leave Westport and circle back to Galway (for route details, see "Planning Your Time" at the beginning of this chapter). The first two stops on the drive—Cong and Westport—are covered earlier.

Murrisk, Croagh Patrick, and a Coffin-Ship Sculpture

In the tiny town of Murrisk you'll find the trailhead for the long hike up Croagh Patrick and a monument remembering the famine.

Croagh Patrick: This fabled mountain-pilgrimage destination rises 2,500 feet above the bay from Murrisk. St. Patrick is said to have fasted on its summit for the 40 days of Lent in the fifth centu-

ry. It's from here that he supposedly rang his bell, driving all the snakes from Ireland. As there were actually no snakes in Ireland, the story represents the pagan beliefs that Patrick's newly arrived Christianity replaced. Every year on the last Sunday of July, "Reek Sunday" (a "reek" is a mountain peak), as many as 30,000 pilgrims hike three hours up the rocky trail to the summit in honor of St. Patrick. The most penitent attempt the hike barefoot (some come down on a stretcher). On that Sunday, Mass is celebrated throughout the day in a modest cinderblock chapel at the summit.

A few years ago, valuable gold deposits were discovered within Croagh Patrick. Luckily, public sentiment has kept the sacred mountain free of any commercial mining activity.

Hiking Croagh Patrick: From the trailhead at Murrisk (where you'll find a big pay-and-display parking lot and a visitors center), you can see the ruddy trail worn down by a thousand years of pilgrims heading up the hill and along the northeast ridge to the summit. Fit hikers should allow three hours to reach the top and two hours to get back down (wear good shoes—solid boots if you have them, and bring rain gear, sunscreen, and plenty of water). The first half of the trail is easy to follow. But once you're on the upper half of the mountain, it's a steep slope of loose, shifting scree. I highly advise buying or renting a walking stick in nearby Westport (most important for unexpected gravel skids on the way down). There's a primitive WC near the summit.

Coffin-Ship Sculpture: Across the street from the Croagh Patrick trailhead is a modern bronze ship sculpture. A memorial

to the famine, it depicts a "coffin ship," like those of the late 1840s that carried the sick and starving famine survivors across the ocean in hope of a new life. Weak from starvation, the desperate emigrants were vulnerable to "famine fever," which they spread to others in the barely seaworthy ships' putrid, cramped holds. Many who lived through the six- to eight-week journey died shortly after reaching their new country. Pause a moment to look at the silent skeletons swirling around the ship's masts.

Now contemplate the fact that famine still exists in the

world—in virtually every country—even though there's enough food grown worldwide to feed the hungry. The challenge is distribution and buying power. If my cat has more buying power than your child, my cat gets the tuna. That's simply the free market system.

Clew Bay

Stretching west on R-335 from Murrisk is Clew Bay, peppered with more than 300 humpbacked islands of glacial gravel dumped by retreating glaciers at the end of the last Ice Age. A notorious 16th-century local named Grace O'Malley (dubbed the "Pirate Queen") once ruled this bay, even earning the grudging respect of Queen Elizabeth I with her clever exploits.

Doo Lough Valley and a Famine Cross

The Doo Lough Valley, unfolding between Louisburgh and Delphi (on R-335), is some of the most desolate country in Ireland. Signs of human habitation vanish from the bog land, and it seems ghosts might appear beside the road. Stop at the summit (north end of the valley, about 13 kilometers south of Louisburgh) when you see a simple gray stone cross. The lake below is Doo Lough (Irish for "Black Lake"). This is the site of one of the saddest famine tales.

County Mayo's rural folk depended almost exclusively on the potato for food and were the hardest hit when the Great Potato Famine came in 1845. In the winter of 1849, about 600 starving Irish walked 19 kilometers (12 miles) from Louisburgh over this summit and south to Delphi Lodge, hoping to get food from their landlord. But they were turned away. On the walk back,  almost 200 of them died along the side of this road. Today, the road still seems to echo with the despair of those hungry souls, and it inspires an annual walk that commemorates the tragedy. Archbishop Desmond Tutu made the walk in 1991, shortly before South Africa ended its apartheid system.

Killary Harbor and Aasleagh Falls

As you drive toward the town of Leenane, you'll skirt along Killary Harbor, an Irish example of a fjord. This long, narrow body of water was carved by an advancing glacier. The rows of blue floats in the harbor mark mussel farms, with the mollusks growing on hanging nets in the cold seawater.

At the east end of Killary Harbor, stop to enjoy the scenic Aasleagh Falls. In late May, the banks below the falls explode with lush, wild, purple rhododendron blossoms.

Leenane

The "town" of Leenane (just a crossroads) is a good place for a break. The 1990 movie *The Field,* starring Limerick-born Richard Harris, was filmed here. Glance at the photos of the making of the movie on the wall of Hamilton's Pub. While you're there, find the old photo of the British dreadnought battleships that filled Killary Harbor when King Edward VII visited a century ago. Drop into the Leenane Sheep and Wool Centre (across the street) to see interesting wool-spinning and weaving demonstrations (€7, daily 9:30-18:00, closed Nov-March; demos run June-Aug at 10:00, 11:30, 14:00, and 15:30; café, tel. 095/42323, www.sheepandwoolcentre.com).

Bog Fun

About eight kilometers west of Leenane, you'll spot areas on the south side of the road that offer a good, close look at a turf cut in a peat bog. Be sure to get out and frolic in the peat fields...with decent footwear and an eagle eye for mushy spots.

Walk a few yards onto the spongy green carpet. (Watch your step on wet days to avoid squishing into a couple of inches of water.) Find a dry spot and jump up and down to get a feel for it. Have your companion jump; you'll feel the vibrations 30 feet away. Rip off a piece of turf and squeeze the water out of it. It's almost all water.

These bogs once covered almost 20 percent of Ireland. As the climate got warmer at the end of the last Ice Age, plants began growing along the sides of the many shallow lakes and ponds. When the plants died in these waterlogged areas, there wasn't enough oxygen for them to fully decompose. Over the centuries, the moss built up, layer after dead layer, helping to slowly fill in the lakes. During World War I, this sphagnum moss was collected to use in bandages to soak up blood (it absorbs many times its weight in fluids).

It's this wet, oxygen-starved ecosystem that has preserved ancient artifacts so well, many of which can be seen in Dublin's National Museum. Even forgotten containers of butter, churned centuries ago and buried to keep cool, have been discovered. But most bizarre are the wrinkled bog mummies that are occasionally

Ireland's Misunderstood Nomads

When you see a small cluster of trailers at the side of an Irish road, you're looking at a dying way of life. These are the Trav-

ellers, a nomadic throwback to the days when wandering craftsmen, musicians, and evicted unfortunates crowded rural Ireland. Often mislabeled as "gypsies," they have no ethnic ties to those Eastern European nomads, but rather have an Irish heritage going back centuries.

There were once many more Travellers, who lived in tents and used horse-drawn carts as they wandered the countryside in search of work. Before the Great Potato Famine, when Irish hospitality was a given, Travellers filled a niche in Irish society. They would do odd jobs, such as repairing furniture, sweeping chimneys, and selling horses. Skilled tinsmiths, they mended pots, pans, and stills for *poitín*—Irish moonshine. (Travellers used to be called "tinkers," but this label is now considered derogatory.) Settled-down farm folk, who rarely ventured more than 20 miles from home their entire lives, depended on the roaming Travellers for news and gossip from farther-flung regions. But post-famine rural depopulation and the gradual urbanization of the countryside forced this nomadic group to adapt to an almost sedentary existence on the fringes of towns.

Today, the 30,000 remaining Travellers are outsiders, usually treated with suspicion by other Irish. Locals often complain that petty thefts go up when Travellers set up camp in a nearby "halting site," and that they leave garbage behind when they depart.

Travellers tend to keep to themselves, marry young, have large families, and speak their own Irish Gaelic-based language (called Shelta, Gammon, or Cant). They are very religious and often camp near the pilgrimage town of Knock. Attempts to settle Travellers in government housing and integrate their children into schools are controversial, as portrayed poignantly in the 1992 movie *Into the West*.

WESTPORT & CONNEMARA

unearthed. These human remains (many over 2,000 years old) are so incredibly intact that their eyelashes, hairstyles, and the last meal in their stomachs can be identified. They were likely sacrificial offerings to the pagan gods of Celtic times.

Since these acidic bogs contain few nutrients, unique species of carnivorous plants have adapted to life here by trapping and digesting insects. The tiny pink sundew (less than an inch tall) has delicate spikes glistening with insect-attracting fluid. Find a mossy area and look closely at the variety of tiny plants. In summer, you'll see white tufts of bog cotton growing in marshy areas.

People have been cutting, drying, and burning peat as a fuel source for more than a thousand years. The cutting usually begins in April or May, when drier weather approaches. You'll probably see stacks of "turf" piled up to dry along recent cuts. Pick up a brick and fondle it. Dried peat is surprisingly light and stiff. In central Ireland, there are even industrial peat cuts that were begun after World War II to fuel power stations. But in the past few decades, bogs have been recognized as a rare habitat, and conservation efforts have been encouraged. These days, the sweet, nostalgic smell of burning peat is becoming increasingly rare.

Kylemore Abbey

This Neo-Gothic country house was built by the wealthy English businessman Mitchell Henry in the 1860s, after he and his wife

had honeymooned in the area. Now they are both buried on the grounds. After World War I, refugee Benedictine nuns from Ypres, Belgium, took it over and ran it as an exclusive girls' boarding school—which peaked at 200 students—until it closed in 2010. In 2015 the Indiana-based University of Notre Dame signed a 30-year lease to use part of the facility for summer classes and student housing. The nuns still live upstairs, but you can visit the half-dozen open rooms downstairs that display the Henry family's cushy lifestyle.

For me, the best thing about the abbey is the view of it from the lakeshore. But garden enthusiasts will seek out the extensive walled Victorian gardens. From the abbey, the gardens are a one-mile, level walk or quick shuttle bus ride (runs every 15 minutes). Hourly tours of the abbey and gardens are so-so; it's best just to enjoy the setting.

Cost and Hours: Overpriced €14 combo-ticket for abbey and gardens; daily 9:00-18:00, July-Aug until 19:00, shorter hours off-season; WCs in gift shop next to parking lot, cafeteria can be overwhelmed by multiple big-bus tour groups, tel. 095/52001, www.kylemoreabbeytourism.ie.

Connemara National Park

This park encompasses almost 5,000 acres of wild bog and mountain scenery. The visitors center (just outside Letterfrack) displays worthwhile exhibits of local flora and fauna, which are well explained in the 15-minute *Man and the Landscape* film that runs every half-hour (free; park open daily year-round; visitors center open daily 9:00-17:30, closed Nov-Feb; tel. 095/41054, www.connemaranationalpark.ie). For a quick visit, take a nature walk along the boardwalk raised above the bog. Nature lovers may want to join a two-hour walking tour with a park naturalist (July-Aug, Wed and Fri at 11:00, departs from visitors center). Call ahead to confirm walking-tour schedules, and bring rain gear and hiking shoes.

Coastal Connemara

If you're short on time, you can connect Clifden and Galway with the fast main road (N-59). But the slower coastal loop along R-341 rewards drivers with great scenery. The essence of scenic Connemara—rocky yet seductive—is captured in this neat little 38-kilometer stretch. The 12 Bens (peaks) of Connemara loom deeper inland. In the foreground, broad shelves of bare bedrock are netted with stone walls, which interlock through the landscape. The ocean slaps the hardscrabble shore. Fishermen cast into their favorite little lakes, and ponies trot in windswept fields. Abandoned, roofless stone cottages stand mute. While the loop is pretty desolate, Roundstone is a perfect place to stop for a cup of coffee to fuel your ride back to Galway.

WESTPORT & CONNEMARA

East of Connemara

The following sights are due east of Westport (about 45 minutes to the shrine and 1.5 hours to the museum).

Knock Shrine

In 1879, locals in the little town of Knock reported a miracle—an apparition of the Virgin Mary, St. Joseph, and St. John in the south gable of their humble church. Pilgrims started coming. Word of miraculous healings on that spot turned the trickle of pilgrims into a flood and put Knock solidly on the pilgrimage map. And the pilgrims keep coming, even precipitating construction  of a commercial airport (Ireland West Airport, about 12.5 miles northeast of Knock). Today, you can visit the shrine. At the edge

Virgin Mary Shrines

During your time in Ireland, you'll frequently see pretty little roadside shrines and grottoes honoring the Virgin Mary. The older ones were built in 1929 to celebrate 100 years of Catholic emancipation (the Roman Catholic Relief Act of 1829, spearheaded by Daniel O'Connell—see page 262). The majority were constructed in the "Marian Year" (devoted to Mary) of 1954. This was the 100th anniversary of Pope Pius IX's 1854 proclamation of the dogma of the Immaculate Conception (God kept the Virgin Mary "from the stain of original sin" from the moment she was conceived). A record number of devout Catholics flocked to the holy pilgrimage village of Knock to pray during the centenary, and many Irish girls born that year were named Marian.

A more recent, related event happened in 1985 at a shrine devoted to the Virgin Mary on the other side of the country, outside the tiny hamlet of Ballinspittle (4 miles southwest of Kinsale in County Cork). Several locals claimed they had witnessed the statue of Mary moving spontaneously, and thousands of pilgrims flocked there that summer. Some pilgrims said they also witnessed the statue moving. But the Catholic Church remained neutral on the Ballinspittle event, and interest in it eventually subsided.

of the site, a small but earnest folk museum shows Knock's knick-knacks, photos of a papal visit, and sturdy slices of traditional life.

Cost and Hours: Shrine—free, museum—€4, daily 10:00-18:00, Aug until 19:30, tel. 094/937-5034, www.knockshrine.ie.

Getting There: The shrine is located on N-17, midway between Galway and Sligo (about 45 kilometers east of Westport).

▲▲Strokestown Park and Irish National Famine Museum

The Irish National Famine Museum, on the former estate of the British Mahon family, offers a solid introduction to the Great Potato Famine of 1845-1849 (the bleakest period in Irish history), a tour of the Mahon mansion, and access to six acres of Georgian walled gardens. You'll come away with a greater understanding of the class divide and traumatic events that led to the great Irish diaspora (which sent desperate, hungry peasants across the globe) and crystallized Irish nationalist hatred of British rule.

Cost and Hours: €14 includes the museum, 45-minute "Big

House" tour, and gardens; open daily 10:30-17:30, Nov-mid-March until 16:00; house tours run daily in high season at 12:00, 14:30, and 16:00; good café in museum.

Information: The museum is in the market town of Strokestown, 90 kilometers northeast of Galway and 110 kilometers east of Westport (about 1.5 hours from either). Tel. 071/963-3013, www.strokestownpark.ie.

Visiting the Museum: Thoughtful exhibits explain how before the famine, three million Irish peasants survived on a surprisingly nutritious diet of buttermilk and potatoes (12 pounds per day per average male laborer...potatoes are 80 percent water). When a fungus destroyed the potato crop, it sparked the Great Potato Famine, and as many as a million Irish people died of starvation.

Major Mahon, the ill-fated landlord here during the famine, found it cheaper to fill three "coffin ships" bound for America with his evicted, starving tenants than pay the taxes for their upkeep in the local workhouse. When almost half died at sea of "famine fever," he was assassinated.

Tours of the musty Big House showcase the gulf that divided the Protestant ascendancy and their Catholic house staff. Afterward, find the servants' tunnel—connecting the kitchen to the stable—built to avoid cluttering the Mahon family's views with unsightly common laborers.

WESTPORT & CONNEMARA

DONEGAL & THE NORTHWEST

County Donegal, the northernmost part of the island (and west of Derry), is about as far-flung as Ireland gets. It's not on the way to anywhere, and it wears its isolation well. With more native Irish speakers than in any other county, the old ways are better preserved here.

Donegal is connected to the Republic by a slim, five-mile-wide umbilical cord of land on its southern coast. A forgotten economic backwater (part of the Republic but riding piggyback on the North), it lacks blockbuster museums or sights. But it's also Ireland's second-biggest county, with a wide-open "big sky" interior and a shattered-glass, 200-mile, jagged coastline of islands and inlets. A visit here is about the journey, and adventurous drivers—a car is a must—will be rewarded with a time-capsule peek into old Irish ways and starkly beautiful scenery.

For drivers who want to explore the region fully, I've laid out a day-trip loop through the northernmost reaches of County Donegal (starting and ending in the Northern Ireland town of Derry, and best for people home-basing there). Drivers connecting the Republic (Galway or Westport) and Northern Ireland without time for a Donegal deep dive can easily hit several interesting sights en route, including a swing through a swath of County Donegal and the town of the same name (with a worthwhile reconstructed castle).

PLANNING YOUR TIME

To drive in a single day between the Republic (Galway or Westport) and Northern Ireland (Derry or Portrush), get an early start so you have time to stop at your pick of several worthwhile sights lined up along the N-15 road between Sligo and Derry (listed under the "Between Westport and Derry" section). Donegal town makes a good lunch stop. From there, you can continue straight to the border and into Derry, or on to Portrush (both covered in later chapters).

If coming from Galway, consider breaking the drive into two days (sleeping in Westport) so you can follow my suggested route for touring the Connemara area first (see page 390).

To see more of Donegal, consider sleeping two nights in Derry, with one day spent crossing back into the Republic for a scenic driving loop through a remote part of this county (covered at the end of this chapter). For details on Derry, see the Derry chapter later in this book.

Between Westport and Derry

Each of these stops is either on N-15 (the route between Sligo and Derry) or within a few kilometers of it. I've listed these sights in the order you'll reach them driving north from the Republic to Northern Ireland. (Heading north on N-15, navigation is easy as, after Sligo, Derry is signposted the whole way.) To see more of County Donegal, consider adding in a few sights from my "County Donegal Driving Tour" (later in this chapter).

Drumcliff Village

For a classic medieval high cross, the nub of a round tower, and the grave of the poet W. B. Yeats, pull off N-15 just north of Sligo at Drumcliff (easy parking). Look for the brown signs for Yeats' grave and the stout stone church spire peeking above the trees just off the road. Walking from the car park you'll see, in this order, the following: church, grave, café/gift shop/WC, high cross, trail to the river, and round tower.

The stately little **church** has a delightful and stony interior (with an interesting video playing in the entryway). To the left of the church (as you face it, about 10 paces) is the simple **grave** of the beloved Irish poet, William Butler Yeats (1865-1939) and his wife, George. The tombstone reads: "Cast a cold eye on life, on death. Horsemen pass by."

Benbulben, the mountain that inspired Yeats, looms behind the graveyard, looking like a sphinx.

Just past the café/gift shop, find the highest cross in the graveyard. This classic **high cross**—along with the stub of a **round tower** (with its defensive door high above ground level) across the busy highway—were part of a monastic settlement a thousand years ago. These symbols of medieval Ireland once dotted the countryside.

The cross (once colorfully painted) is carved with reliefs designed to help teach the people Bible lessons. Find Adam and Eve,

Cain clubbing Abel, and Christ in Majesty on one side and a camel (trying to get through the eye of a needle) on the other.

This is a historic spot, the site of a monastery founded in AD 574 by St. Columba. He and another saint had a quarrel over the rights to a book, which actually led to a battle here in which 3,000 people were killed. Columba was so distraught by the bloodshed that he eventually banished himself from Ireland and sailed to Iona (in Scotland), where he founded another monastery (famous as the original home of the magnificent Book of Kells).

Across from the high cross, a small path leads to a river path with dramatic views of Benbulben, ideal for getting into the spirit of Yeats for a moment.

Mullaghmore Head Loop

A few kilometers north of Drumcliff, leave N-15 at Cliffoney for a 10-kilometer (6-mile) loop side trip around Mullaghmore Head.

It was just off this scenic bluff that, on August 27, 1979, the IRA detonated a radio-controlled bomb on the vacation yacht of Lord Louis Mountbatten (79-year-old second cousin of Queen Elizabeth II), killing him and members of his family.

As you drive around this scenic loop, you'll see a rugged coastline and desolate beaches with the lonely castle retreat of the royal Mountbatten family crowning the horizon. Drive past beech-tree forests (from which Lord Mountbatten constructed his boat) and a rough little stone harbor (from where he and his family sailed that fateful day), and stop at the peninsula's far end (just 12 miles south of the border of Northern Ireland). Check out the views across Donegal Bay to where the bomb went off, just a few hundred yards offshore. Continue circling the bluff as the road brings you back to N-15.

Belleek Pottery Visitors Centre

If you're interested in pottery, consider a slight detour, about 10 kilometers (6 miles) off N-15, over the border into Northern Ireland to the sleepy town of Belleek. The Belleek Parian China factory welcomes visitors with a small gallery and museum, a 20-min-

ute video, a cheery cafeteria, and 30-minute guided tours of its working factory.

Cost and Hours: Free, tours-£6; Mon-Fri 9:00-17:30, Sat from 10:00, Sun from 14:00; longer hours in July-Sept, shorter hours in Oct-Feb and possibly closed weekends; call to confirm tour schedule and reserve a spot (Sat tours June-Sept only, none on Sun), tel. 028/6865-9300, www.belleekpottery.ie, takethetour@belleek.ie.

Donegal Town

The main town (Donegal) in the Republic of Ireland's northern-most county (Donegal) has a striking reconstructed castle. Donegal means "Fort of Foreigners"—a reminder that the Vikings invaded here in the 9th century. Detour 5 kilometers (3 miles) off N-15 for a quick visit.

The charming town's main square ("The Diamond") is lined by inviting shops and eateries. Try the comfy café above Magee's tweed shop (Mon-Sat 10:00-18:00, Sun from 14:00). The monument in the center honors four friars who created a record of early Irish history. The small but historic Donegal Castle is half a block beyond that (look for the pointy church spire).

Donegal Castle: This was originally the fortified base of the mighty O'Donnell clan (originally built by Hugh O'Donnell in about 1500). Around 1600, the Eng-lish defeated the O'Donnells and made the castle closer to what exists today. This castle offers a fine chance to see a reconstructed version of the fortified towers so common in Ireland. Your €5 entry includes an info sheet or a half-hour guided tour (at least hourly with demand, open daily 10:00-18:00, off-season 9:30-16:30).

Wandering through the castle, you'll see the original stone floor and 10-foot-thick walls on the ground floor, a spiral "trip staircase" winding clockwise to give the right-handed defender the advantage, the banqueting hall with its finely carved fireplace, and a top floor with historical exhibits under 40 tons of Irish oak beams—a 17th-century design with only wooden pegs holding it all together. The extension outside the tower dates from the time of the English lord's manor house (c. 1620).

Most of these fortified towers date from the 15th century and were built initially by the English to assert their control over the Irish. But Irish clan leaders were quick studies and began building their own. This particular castle reminds locals of the devastating Nine Years' War (1594-1603). It started well for the Irish, here on their home turf. But when the powerful Ulster clans marched south to engage the English at Kinsale, they were crushed. Soon after, the clan royalty of Ireland (including the O'Donnells) fled the island, and English rule was firmly and brutally established.

Border Crossing

When you cross the border between the Republic of Ireland and Northern Ireland you'll notice lots of changes. If traveling north along N-15, you'll cross the border in the town of Lifford (in the Republic) into the town of Strabane (in Northern Ireland). As you cross the River Foyle you enter the "United Kingdom of Great Britain and North Ireland" (as of now, you don't need to show a passport, though Brexit could change that). Kilometers become miles, euros become British pounds (actually, Ulster pounds, which are the same as English pound sterling and legal tender in England), the farmland becomes richer and more productive, and Derry is now signposted as "Londonderry"—although, even today, many of the signs will have the "London" spray-painted out. On the south side of the river the sign reads: "Derry, 24 km." On the other side of the bridge, suddenly it reads: "Londonderry, 14 miles." As you drive deeper into Northern Ireland, you'll see lots of Union Jack flags and even towns with their curbs painted red, white, and blue.

County Donegal Drive

DONEGAL LOOP FROM DERRY

Donegal is the most remote (and perhaps the most ruggedly beautiful) county in Ireland. Here's my choice for a scenic mix of Donegal highlands and coastal views, organized as a daylong circuit for drivers based across the border in Derry. If you're coming north from Galway or Westport, you could incorporate parts of this drive into your itinerary. Remember, Derry is part of the UK (pounds, miles); Donegal is the Republic (euros, kilometers).

PLANNING YOUR DRIVE

The total drive is about 240 km (150 miles). Allow about four hours without stops, up to a full day if you stop at many sights.

You'll start by driving west out of Derry, and into Letterkenny, which is where the loop around County Donegal begins and ends. From Letterkenny you'll head northwest, passing Glenveagh National Park, the coastal hamlet of Bunbeg, and the Bloody Foreland headland. From here you head east through the town of Dunfanaghy. At Dunfanaghy you can detour around Horn Head (adding

Donegal: Saints to Singers

Donegal is the home turf of St. Columba (Colmeille, "dove of the church" in Irish), who was born here in 521. In the hierarchy of revered Irish saints, he's second only to St. Patrick. A proud Gaelic culture held out in Donegal to the bitter end, when the O'Donnells and the O'Dohertys, the two most famous local clans, were finally defeated by the English in the early 1600s. After their defeat, the region became known as Dun na nGall ("the fort of the foreigner"), which was eventually anglicized to Donegal.

As the English moved in, four Donegal-dwelling friars (certain that Gaelic ways would be lost forever) painstakingly wrote down Irish history from Noah's Ark to their present. This labor of love became known as the Annals of the Four Masters, and without it, much of our knowledge of early Irish history and myth would have been lost. An obelisk stands in their honor in the main square of Donegal town.

The hardy people of County Donegal were once famous for their quality tweed weaving, a cottage industry that gradually gave way to modern industrial production in far-off cities. A small but energetic Irish fishing fleet still churns offshore—in the wake of larger EU factory ships. Today, emigration has taken its toll, and the region's economy relies on a trickle of tourism spilling over from Northern Ireland.

Culturally, the county shines. Capturing the feel of County Donegal on screen, *The Secret of Roan Inish* was filmed here. The traditional Irish musicians of Donegal play a driving style of music with a distinctively fast and forceful rhythm. Meanwhile, Enya (local Gweedore gal made good) has crafted languid, ethereal tunes that evoke the wild and remote Donegal landscape as they glide from mood to mood.

DONEGAL & THE NORTHWEST

about an hour) or head south back to Letterkenny and then along the same road back to Derry.

An early start is essential, and the sights along this route are well marked. Don't underestimate the time it takes to get around here, as the narrow roads are full of curves and bumps. Dogs, bred to herd sheep, dart from side lanes to practice their bluffing techniques. You'll be lucky to average 65 kilometers per hour (about 40 mph) over the course of the day. Those wanting to linger at more than a few sights should consider an overnight in Dunfanaghy.

A few tips: It's cheapest to top off your gas tank in Letterkenny. Consider bringing a picnic lunch to enjoy from a scenic roadside pullout along the Bloody Foreland, or out on Horn Head.

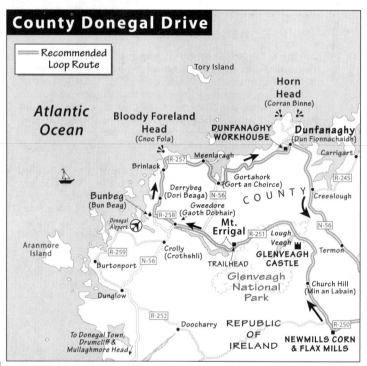

County Donegal Drive

Recommended Loop Route

Tory Island

Atlantic Ocean

Horn Head (Corran Binne)

Bloody Foreland Head (Cnoc Fola)

DUNFANAGHY WORKHOUSE

Dunfanaghy (Dun Fionnachaidh)

Carrigart

R-257 Meenlaragh

Brinlack

Gortahork (Gort an Choirce)

R-245

Derrybeg (Dori Beaga) N-56

COUNTY

Creeslough

Bunbeg (Bun Beag)

R-258 Gweedore (Gaoth Dobhair)

Mt. Errigal R-251 Lough Veagh

N-56

Donegal Airport

GLENVEAGH CASTLE

Termon

Aranmore Island

R-259 Crolly (Crothshli)

N-56 Burtonport

TRAILHEAD

Glenveagh National Park

Church Hill (Min an Labain)

Dunglow

R-252 Doocharry

REPUBLIC OF IRELAND

R-250

To Donegal Town, Drumcliff & Mullaghmore Head

NEWMILLS CORN & FLAX MILLS

DONEGAL & THE NORTHWEST

DERRY TO GLENVEAGH

• *Drive west out of Derry (direction: Letterkenny) on Buncrana Road, which becomes A-2. This becomes N-13 across the border in the Republic, near the town of Bridge End. You'll see a sign for the* Grianan Aileach Ring Fort *posted on N-13, not far from the junction with R-239. Turn up the steep hill at the modern church with the round roof, and follow signs three kilometers (2 miles) to find...*

▲Grianan Aileach Ring Fort

This dramatic, ancient ring fort perches on an 800-foot hill just inside the Republic, a stone's throw from Derry. It's an Iron Age fortification, built about the time of Christ, and was once the royal stronghold of the O'Neill clan, which dominated Ulster for centuries. Its stout dry-stone walls (no mortar) are 12 feet thick and 18 feet high, creating an interior sanctuary 80 feet in diameter (entry is free and unattended).

Once inside, you can scramble up the stairs, which are built into the walls, to enjoy

panoramic views in all directions. Murtagh O'Brien, King of Desmond (roughly, today's Limerick, Clare, and Tipperary counties), destroyed the fort in 1101...the same power-play year in which he gave the Rock of Cashel to the Church. Legend says he had each of his soldiers carry away one stone, attempting to make it tougher for the O'Neill clan to find the raw materials to rebuild. What you see today is mostly a reconstruction from the 1870s.

Skip the nearby well-signposted Old Church Visitors Center beside the N-13 road. Accessed through a modern hotel, it contains a couple of earnest models, costume props, and an uninterested staff.

• *Return to N–13 and follow signs into Letterkenny, continuing out the other (west) end of town on R–250. Eight kilometers (5 miles) west of Letterkenny on this road, you'll reach the...*

Newmills Corn and Flax Mills

Come here for a glimpse of long-gone rural industry (the oldest building in the compact complex is close to 400 years old).

Linen, which comes from flax, was king in this region. The 15-minute film does a nifty job of explaining the process, showing how the common flax plant ends up as cloth. Working in a mill sounds like a mellow job, but conditions were noisy, unhealthy, and exhausting. Veteran mill workers often braved respiratory disease, deafness, lost fingers, and extreme fire danger. For their trouble, they usually got to keep about 10 percent of what they milled.

The corn mill is still in working condition but requires a skilled miller to operate it. This mill ground oats—"corn" meant oats in Ireland. (What we call corn, they called maize.) The huge waterwheel, powered by the River Swilly, made five revolutions per minute and generated eight horsepower.

The entire operation could be handled by one miller, who knew every cog, lever, and flume in the joint. Call ahead to see when working mill demonstrations are scheduled; otherwise, tours last 45 minutes and are available on request.

Cost and Hours: Free, daily 10:00-18:00, closed mid-Sept-mid-May, last entry 45 minutes before closing, Churchill Road, Letterkenny, tel. 074/912-5115.

• *Continue on R-250, staying right (north) at Driminaught onto R-251. Stay on R-251, passing through Church Hill. Watch for* Glenveagh Castle *and* National Park *signs, and park in the visitors center lot (on the left).*

▲▲Glenveagh Castle and National Park

One of Ireland's six national parks, Glenveagh's jewel is pristine Lough Veagh (Loch Ghleann Bheatha in Irish). The lake is three miles long, occupying a U-shaped valley scoured out of the Derryveagh Mountains by powerful glaciers during the last Ice Age.

In the 1850s, this scenic area attracted the wealthy land speculator John George Adair, who bought the valley in 1857. Right away, Adair clashed with local tenants, whom he accused of stealing his sheep. After his managing agent was found murdered, he evicted all 244 of his bitter tenants to great controversy, and set about creating a hunting estate in grand Victorian style.

His pride and joy was his country mansion, Glenveagh Castle, finished in 1873 on the shore of Lough Veagh. After his death, his widow added to the castle and introduced rhododendrons and rare red deer to the estate. After her death, Harvard art professor Kingsley Porter bought the estate and promptly disappeared on the Donegal coast. (He's thought to have drowned.) The last owner was Philadelphia millionaire Henry McIlhenny, who filled the mansion with fine art and furniture while perfecting the lush surrounding gardens. He donated the castle to the Irish nation in 1981.

Cost and Hours: Park entry-free, guided castle tour-€7, garden tour-€5, daily 9:00-18:00, Nov-Feb until 17:00, tel. 076/1002-537, www.glenveaghnationalpark.ie, glenveaghbookings@chg.gov.ie. Without a car, you can reach Glenveagh Castle and National Park by bus tour from Derry (see page 437 of the Derry chapter).

Getting Around the Park: From the visitors center to the castle is a 30-minute/2.5-mile **walk,** a 10-minute **shuttle-bus ride** (€3 round-trip, 4/hour, departs from visitors center, last shuttle 75 minutes before closing), or a pleasant **bike ride** on the same traffic-free path (rental kiosk in the parking lot, June-Sept daily 10:00-17:00, electric bike—€18/3 hours, 21-speed—€12/3 hours, tel. 074/911-9988, mobile 087-665-5599, www.grassroutes.ie). The bike-rental place also offers a €32 **guided bike tour** connecting the visitors center to the castle (reservations smart).

Visiting the Castle and National Park: Start at the park **visitors center,** which explains the region's natural history. Hiking trails in the park are scenic and tempting, but beware of the tiny midges that seem to want to nest in your nostrils.

Once at the castle, take the 45-minute **castle tour,** letting your Jane Austen and Agatha Christie fantasies go wild. Antlers abound on walls, in chandeliers, and in paintings by Victorian hunting artists. A table crafted from rare bog oak (from ancient trees hundreds of years old, found buried in the muck) stands at attention in one room, while Venetian glass chandeliers illuminate a bathroom. A round pink bedroom at the top of a tower is decorated in Oriental style, with inlaid mother-of-pearl furnishings. The library, which displays paintings by George Russell, has the castle's best lake views.

Afterward, stroll through the **gardens** and enjoy the lovely setting. A lakeside swimming pool had boilers underneath it to keep it heated. It's no wonder that Greta Garbo was an occasional guest, coming to visit whenever she "vanted" to be alone.

GLENVEAGH TO DUNFANAGHY

• *Leave the national park and follow R-251 west, watching for the Mount Errigal trailhead. It's southeast of the mountain, and starts at the small parking lot beside R-251 on the mountain's lower slope (easy to spot, with a low surrounding stone wall in the middle of open bog land).*

Mount Errigal (An Eargail)

The mountain (2,400 feet) dominates the horizon for miles around. Rising from the relatively flat interior bog land, it looks taller from a distance than it is. Beautifully cone-shaped (but not a volcano), it offers a hearty, nontechnical climb with panoramic views (four hours round-trip, covering five miles). Hikers should get a weather

Donegal or Bust

Part of western County Donegal is in the Gaeltacht, where locals speak the Irish Gaelic language. In the spring of 2005, a controversial law was passed that erased all English place names from local road signs in Gaeltacht areas. Signs now have only the Irish-language equivalent, an attempt to protect the region from the further (and inevitable) encroachment of the English language.

Here's a cheat sheet to help you decipher the signs as you drive the Donegal loop (parts of which are in the Gaeltacht). There's also a complete translation of all Irish place names in the recommended *Complete Road Atlas of Ireland* by Ordnance Survey, in the Gazetteer section in the back.

Irish	English
Leitir Ceanainn (*LET-ir CAN-ning*)	Letterkenny
Min an Labain (*MEEN on law-BAWN*)	Churchill
Loch Ghleann (*LOCKH thown*)	Lough (Lake)
Bheatha (*eh-VEH-heh*)	Veagh
An Earagail (*on AIR-i-gul*)	Mt. Errigal
Gaoth Dobhair (*GWEE door*)	Gweedore
Crothshli (*CROTH-lee*)	Crolly
Bun Beag (*bun bee-OWG*)	Bunbeg
Dori Beaga (*DOR-uh bee-OWG-uh*)	Derrybeg
Cnoc Fola (*NOK FAW-luh*)	Bloody Foreland
Gort an Choirce (*gurt on HER-kuh*)	Gortahork
Dun Fionnachaidh (*doon on-AH-keh*)	Dunfanaghy
Corran Binne (*COR-on BIN-eh*)	Horn Head

report before setting out (frequent mists squat on the summit). Ask the TI in Letterkenny or Donegal town for more detailed hiking directions.

• *Continue on R-251 as it merges into N-56 headed west; at Gweedore, stay west on R-258. After 6 kilometers (4 miles), you'll reach R-257, where you'll turn right and pass through the seaside hamlet of Bunbeg (Bun Beag).*

Depart Bunbeg going north on R-257. The 8 kilometers (5 miles) of road heading north—as Bunbeg blends into Derrybeg (Dori Beaga) and a bit beyond—are some of the most densely populated sections of this loop tour. Modern holiday cottages pepper the landscape in what the Irish have come to call "Bungalow Bliss" (or "Bungalow Blight" to nature lovers). Next you'll come to the...

Bloody Foreland (Cnoc Fola)

Named for the shade of red that heather turns at sunset, this scenic headland is laced with rock walls and forgotten cottage ruins. If you brought a picnic, this is a great place to pull off at a lofty roadside viewpoint and savor a meal with rugged coastal views.

• *Continue on R-257, and then rejoin N-56 near Gortahork. Follow N-56 east to the Dunfanaghy Workhouse, about a kilometer south of Dunfanaghy town.*

Dunfanaghy Workhouse

Opened in 1845, this structure was part of an extensive workhouse compound (separating families by gender and age)—a dreaded last resort for the utterly destitute of coastal Donegal. There were once many identical compounds built across Ireland (serious history buffs should seek out the most intact and evocative example in Portumna—see page 345). It was a rigid Victorian solution to the spiraling problem of Ireland's rapidly multiplying poor. Authorities at the time thought that poverty stemmed from laziness and should be punished. So, to motivate those lodging at the workhouse to pull themselves up by their bootstraps, conditions were made hard. But the system was unable to cope with the starving, homeless multitudes who were victims of the famine.

The harsh workhouse experience is told through the true-life narrative of Wee Hannah Herrity, a wandering orphan and former resident of this workhouse. During the famine, more than 4,000 young orphan workhouse girls from across Ireland were shipped to Australia as indentured servants in an attempt to offset the mostly male former convict population there. But Hannah's fate was different. She survived the famine by taking meager refuge here, dying at age 90 in 1926. With the audioguide, you'll visit three upstairs rooms where stiff papier-mâché figures relate the powerful episodes in her life.

Cost and Hours: €5, includes audioguide; daily 10:00-17:00, Oct-April until 16:00, call to confirm winter hours; good book/coffee/craft shop and helpful TI desk—pick up map for Horn Head loop here, tel. 074/913-6540, www.dunfanaghyworkhouse.com.

• *Now continue a few minutes more into the town of...*

Dunfanaghy (Dun Fionnachaidh)

This planned town, founded by the English in the early 1600s for local markets and fairs, has a prim and proper appearance. Dunfanaghy (dun-FAN-ah-hee) is a good place to grab a pub lunch or some picnic fixings from the town market. Enjoy them from a scenic viewpoint on the nearby Horn Head loop drive (described later). The modest town square, mostly a parking lot, marks the center of

Dunfanaghy. Helpful local info can be found on the town's website (www.dunfanaghy.info).

Tours from Dunfanaghy: Seas the Bay Charters operates 1.5-hour wildlife-spotting cruises that show off dramatic Horn Head, plus 3-hour (€35) and 6-hour (€60) deep-sea fishing excursions (tel. 087/613-6400, www.seasthebay.ie, james@seasthebay.ie).

Sleeping in Dunfanaghy: $$$ The Mill Accommodation is a diamond in the Donegal rough. Susan Alcorn nurtures seven wonderful rooms with classy decor, in a quiet setting ideal for a romantic weekend (one mile out of town past the Dunfanaghy Workhouse on the right, parking, tel. 074/913-6985, www.themillrestaurant.com, info@themillrestaurant.com).

$$$ Shandon Hotel is a comfortable modern spa option with 68 large rooms, many looking down on lush Marble Hill Bay. You'll find every amenity, a professional staff, outdoor hot tub, big tour groups, and a ground-floor pub (family rooms, parking, 3 miles east of town off N-56 at the end of Faugher Heights Road, tel. 074/913-6137, www.shandonhotelspa.com, info@shandonhotelspa.com).

$$$ Arnold's Hotel is a comfortable, old-fashioned place that's been in the Arnold family since 1922. In the center of town, it has 30 cozy rooms that are well kept by a helpful staff (family rooms, parking, tel. 074/913-6208, www.arnoldshotel.com, enquiries@arnoldshotel.com).

$$ Anseo B&B is set back from the road. Its traditional whitewashed cottage walls hide four inviting rooms where Lisa McGrath has deftly assembled a homey vibe with understated decor and curl-your-toes comfort (cash only, family room, parking, 5-minute walk east of town off N-56, tel. 074/913-6609, mobile 087-366-1839, www.tatuanseo.com, lisa@tatuanseo.com).

Eating in Dunfanaghy: Groceries are sold in the **Centra Market** (daily 7:30-21:00) on the main road opposite the town square.

Your other choices are simple sandwich joints and pub grub. **$ Arnold's Hotel** (in town) and the **$ Shandon Hotel** (east of town) both have ground-floor pubs serving decent grub. **$ Muck & Muffin** is a simple sandwich café above the pottery shop in the stone warehouse on the town square (daily 9:30-17:00, until 18:00 in summer, tel. 074/913-6780). **$ The Great Wall** is a hole-in-the-wall Chinese takeaway place (daily 16:30-23:00, tel. 074/910-0111, next door to Centra Market). A few doors down, **$$ The Oyster Bar** does pub grub and live music on Friday and Saturday nights.

Irish Fishermen Feel the Squeeze

The biggest fishing port in Ireland is Killybegs, about 30 kilometers (19 miles) west of Donegal town. But today, fishing is a

sadly withering lifestyle. When Ireland joined the EU in 1973, Irish farmers and infrastructure benefited most from generous subsidies that helped transform the country a generation later into the "Celtic Tiger." But as the country reaped over €35 billion from the EU in its first 25 years of membership, the Irish fishing industry suffered. With the

Mediterranean overfished, other EU nations set sail for rich Irish waters that were newly opened to them. Some estimate that 40 percent of the fish caught each year in Europe—valued at €175 billion—comes from Irish territorial seas. Huge factory ships from Spain are far more efficient at hauling in a catch than the 1,500 remaining Irish boats (most of which are less than 40 feet long). Irish fishermen lament that for every €1 accepted in EU subsidies, €5 have gone out in foreign nets. And the irony is that much of the fish sold in Irish grocery stores and restaurants is now imported from other EU nations...who caught the fish off the Irish coast.

My vote for most atmospheric pub in town is **Patsy Dan's,** with trad tunes Monday and Friday nights (18:00-21:00). Pub grub is served only in summer, when their pizza-porch out back becomes a local favorite (daily 17:00-22:00, Main Street, tel. 074/910-0604).
• *From Dunfanaghy, you can return to Derry by driving south on N-56 back to Letterkenny and then onward to Derry via N-13 and A-2.*

But if you have extra time (about an hour), before heading back to Letterkenny, consider a lost-world plateau drive around Horn Head.

HORN HEAD LOOP (CORRAN BINNE)

This heaving headland with few trees has memorable coastal

views that make it popular with hikers.

Consult your map and get off N-56, following the *Horn Head* signs all the way around the eastern lobe of the peninsula. There are fewer than eight kilometers (5 miles) of narrow, single-lane road out here, with very little traffic. But be alert and willing to pull over at wide spots to cooperate with other cars.

This stone-studded peninsula was once an island. Then, shortly after the last Ice Age ended, ocean currents deposited a sandy spit in the calm water behind the island. A hundred years ago, locals harvested its stabilizing dune grass, using it for roof thatching and sending it abroad to Flanders, where soldiers used it to create beds for horses during World War I. With the grass gone, the sandy spit was free to migrate again. It promptly silted up the harbor, created a true peninsula, and ruined Dunfanaghy as a port town.

A short spur road leads to the summit of the headland, where you can park your car and walk another 50 yards up to the abandoned WWII lookout shelter. The views from here are dramatic, looking west toward Tory Island and south to Mount Errigal. Some may choose to hike an additional 30 minutes across the heather, to the ruins of the distant signal tower (not a castle, but instead a lookout for a feared Napoleonic invasion), clearly visible near the cliffs. But from here, it's still easy to bushwhack your way through (in sturdy footwear) to the rewarding cliff views at the base of the old signal tower. Navigate back to your car, using the lookout shelter on the summit as a landmark.

NORTHERN IRELAND

NORTHERN IRELAND

Northern Ireland is a different country than the Republic—both politically (it's part of the United Kingdom) and culturally (a combination of Irish, Scottish, and English influences). Occupying the northern one-sixth of the island of Ireland, it's only about 13 miles from Scotland at the narrowest point of the North Channel, and bordered on the south and west by the Republic.

When you leave the Republic of Ireland and enter Northern Ireland, you are crossing an international border. For years, the border has been almost invisible, without passport checks, though Brexit, the UK's withdrawal from the EU, could potentially change the way the border is handled in the future (see "The Brexit Effect" sidebar, later).

You won't use euros here; Northern Ireland issues its own Ulster pound, which, like the Scottish pound, is interchangeable with the English pound (€1=about £0.90; £1=about $1.30). Price differences create a lively daily shopping trade for those living near the border. Some establishments near the border may take euros, but at a lousy exchange rate. Keep any euros for your return to the Republic, and get pounds from an ATM inside Northern Ireland instead. And if you're heading to Britain next, it's best to change your Ulster pounds into English ones (free at any bank in Northern Ireland, England, Wales, or Scotland).

But some differences between Northern Ireland and the Republic are disappearing: Following the Republic's lead, Northern Ireland legalized same-sex marriage and decriminalized abortion in 2019 (also bringing its legislation more in line with rest of the United Kingdom).

A generation ago, Northern Ireland was a sadly contorted corner of the world. On my first visit, I remember thinking that even the name of this region sounded painful ("Ulster" seemed to me like a combination of "ulcer" and "blister"). But today, Northern Ireland has emerged from the dark shadow of the decades-long political strife and violence known as the Troubles. While not as popular among tourists as its neighbor to the south, Northern Ireland offers plenty to see and do...and learn.

Northern Ireland Almanac

Official Name: Northern Ireland (pronounced "Norn Iron" by locals). Some call it Ulster (although historically that term included three counties that today lie on the Republic's side of the border), while others label it the Six Counties.

Size: 5,400 square miles (about the size of Connecticut), constituting a sixth of the island. With 1.8 million people, it's the smallest of the four United Kingdom countries (the others are England, Wales, and Scotland).

Geography: Northern Ireland is shaped roughly like a doughnut, with the UK's largest lake in the middle (Lough Neagh, 150 square miles and a prime eel fishery). Gently rolling hills of green grass rise to the 2,800-foot Slieve Donard. The weather is temperate, cloudy, moist, windy, and hard to predict.

Latitude and Longitude: 54°N and 5°W (as far north as parts of the Alaskan panhandle).

Biggest Cities: Belfast, the capital, has 300,000 residents. Half a million people—nearly one in three Northern Irish—inhabit the greater Belfast area. Derry (called Londonderry by Unionists) has 95,000 people.

Economy: Northern Ireland's economy is more closely tied to the UK than to the Republic of Ireland, and is subsidized by the UK. Traditional agriculture (potatoes and grain) is fading fast, but Northern Ireland remains a major producer of sheep, cows, and grass seed. Modern software and communications companies are replacing traditional manufacturing. Once-proud shipyards are rusty relics, and the linen industry is now threadbare.

Government: Northern Ireland is not a self-governing nation, but is part of the UK, ruled from London by Queen Elizabeth II

and Prime Minister Boris Johnson, and represented by 18 elected Members of Parliament. For 50 years (1922-1972), Northern Ireland was granted a great deal of autonomy and self-governance, known as "Home Rule." Today some decisions are delegated to a National Assembly (90-seat Parliament), but political logjams often render it ineffective.

Flag: The official flag of Northern Ireland is the Union flag of the UK. But you'll also see the green, white, and orange Irish tricolor (waved by Nationalists) and the Northern Irish flag (white with a red cross and a red hand at its center), which is used by Unionists (see "The Red Hand of Ulster" sidebar on page 512).

NORTHERN IRELAND

It's important for visitors to Northern Ireland to understand the ways in which its population is segregated along political, religious, and cultural lines. Roughly speaking, the eastern seaboard is more Unionist, Protestant, and of English-Scottish heritage, while the south and west (bordering the Republic of Ireland) are Nationalist, Catholic, and of indigenous Irish descent. Cities are often clearly divided between neighborhoods of one group or the other. Early in life, locals learn to identify the highly symbolic (and highly charged) colors, jewelry, sports jerseys, music, names, accents, and vocabulary that distinguish the cultural groups.

The roots of Protestant and Catholic differences date back to the time when Ireland was a colony of Great Britain. Four hundred years ago, Protestant settlers from England and Scotland were strategically "planted" in Catholic Ireland to help assimilate the island into the British economy. In 1620, the dominant English powerbase in London felt entitled to call both islands—Ireland as well as Britain—the "British Isles" on maps (a geographic label that irritates Irish Nationalists to this day). These Protestant settlers established their own cultural toehold on the island, laying claim to the most fertile land. Might made right, and God was on their side. Meanwhile, the underdog Catholic Irish held strong to their Gaelic culture on their ever-diminishing, boggy, rocky farms.

Over the last century, the conflict between these two groups has not been solely about faith. Heated debates today are usually about politics: Will Northern Ireland stay part of the United Kingdom (Unionists), or become part of the Republic of Ireland (Nationalists)?

By the beginning of the 20th century, the sparse Protestant population could no longer control the entire island. When Ireland won its independence in 1921 (after a bloody guerrilla war against British rule), 26 of the island's 32 counties became the Irish Free State, ruled from Dublin with dominion status in the British Commonwealth—similar to Canada's level of sovereignty. In 1949, these 26 counties left the Commonwealth altogether and became the Republic of Ireland, severing all political ties with Britain. Meanwhile, the six remaining northeastern counties—the only ones with a Protestant majority who considered themselves British—chose not to join the Irish Free State and remained part of the UK.

But within these six counties—now joined as the political entity called Northern Ireland—was a large, disaffected Irish (mostly Catholic) minority who felt marginalized by the drawing of the new international border. This sentiment was represented by the Irish Republican Army (IRA), who wanted all 32 of Ireland's counties to be united in one Irish nation—their political goals were "Nationalist." Their political opponents were the "Union-

Northern Ireland

Atlantic Ocean

See Antrim Coast map

Rathlin Island

Antrim Coast

Bushmills • Giant's Causeway

Portrush •

Coleraine

Cushendall

To Cairnryan, Scotland

Glens of Antrim

GLENARIFF FOREST PARK

Letterkenny •

• Derry

NORTHERN

Ballymena

To Cairnryan, Scotland & Liverpool, England

COUNTY DONEGAL

IRELAND

• Strabane

Larne •

THE GOBBINS CLIFF PATH

Carrickfergus •

Donegal •

• ULSTER-AMERICAN FOLK PARK

Lough Neagh

• Antrim

Bangor

George Best City Airport

Lower Lough Erne

• Omagh

Belfast

MOUNT STEWART HOUSE

• Belleek

Belfast International Airport

Strangford Lough

• Enniskillen

Upper Lough Erne

• Armagh

Mourne Mtns.

Downpatrick

To Galway

Newry •

REPUBLIC OF IRELAND

Dundalk •

Irish Sea

20 Kilometers

20 Miles

To Dublin

ists"—Protestant British eager to defend the union with Britain, who were primarily led by two groups: the long-established Orange Order, and the military muscle of the newly mobilized Ulster Volunteer Force (UVF).

In World War II, the Republic stayed neutral while the North enthusiastically supported the Allied cause—winning a spot close to London's heart. Derry (a.k.a. Londonderry) became an essential Allied convoy port, while Belfast lost more than 900 civilians during four Luftwaffe bombing raids in 1941. After the war, the split between North and South seemed permanent, and Britain invested heavily in Northern Ireland to bring it solidly into the UK fold.

In the Republic of Ireland where the population was 94 percent Catholic and only 6 percent Protestant, there was a clearly dominant majority. But in the Northern Ireland, Catholics were a sizable 35 percent of the population—enough to demand attention when they exposed anti-Catholic discrimination on the part of the Protestant government. It was this discrimination that led to the Troubles, the conflict that filled headlines from the late 1960s to the late 1990s.

Partly inspired by Martin Luther King, Jr. and the civil rights movement in America, in the 1960s the Catholic minority in Northern Ireland began a nonviolent struggle to end discrimination, advocating for better jobs and housing. Extremists polarized issues, and once-peaceful demonstrations became violent.

Unionists were afraid that if the island became one nation, the relatively poor Republic of Ireland would drag down the comparatively affluent North, and feared losing political power to a Catholic majority. As the two sides clashed in 1969, the British Army entered the fray. Their role, initially a peacekeeping one, gradually evolved into acting as muscle for the Unionist government. In 1972, more than 500 people died as combatants moved from petrol bombs to guns, and a new, more violent IRA emerged. In the 30-year (1968-1998) chapter of the struggle for an independent and united Ireland, more than 3,000 people died.

In the 1990s—with the UK (and Ireland's) membership in the EU, the growth of its economy, and the weakening of the Catholic Church's authority—the Republic of Ireland's influence became less threatening to the Unionists. Optimists hailed the signing of a breakthrough peace plan in 1998, called the "Good Friday Peace Accord" by Nationalists, or the "Belfast Agreement" by Unionists. This led to the release of political prisoners on both sides in 2000—a highly emotional event.

British Army surveillance towers in Northern Ireland's cities were dismantled in 2006, and the army formally ended its 38-year-long Operation Banner campaign in 2007. In 2010, the peace process was jolted forward by a surprisingly forthright apology offered by then-British Prime Minister David Cameron. The apology was prompted by the Saville Report—the results of an investigation conducted by the UK government as part of the Good Friday Peace Accord. It found that the 1972 shootings of Nationalist civil-rights marchers—known as Bloody Sunday—by British soldiers was "unjustified" and the victims innocent (vindication for the victims' families, who had fought since 1972 to clear their loved ones' names).

Major hurdles to a lasting peace persist. Occasionally backward-thinking extremists ape the brutality of their grandparents' generation. And as the UK leaves the European Union, many worry that tensions between the Republic and Northern Ireland will flare up. But the downtown checkpoints are long gone, replaced by a forest of construction cranes, especially in rejuvenated Belfast.

When locals spot you with a map and a lost look on your face, they're likely to ask, "Wot yer lookin fer?" in their distinctive Northern accent. They're not suspicious of you, but trying to help you find your way. They may even "giggle" (Google) it for you. You're safer in Belfast than in many UK cities—and far safer, statistically, than in most major US cities. Just don't seek out spit-and-

Northern Ireland Terminology

You may hear Northern Ireland referred to as **Ulster**—the traditional name of Ireland's ancient northernmost province. When the Republic of Ireland became independent in 1922, six of the nine counties of Ulster elected to form Northern Ireland, while three counties joined the Republic.

The mostly Protestant **Unionist** majority—and the more hardline, working-class **Loyalists**—want the North to remain in the UK. The **Ulster Unionist Party** (UUP) is the political party representing moderate Unionist views (Nobel Peace Prize co-winner David Trimble led the UUP from 1995 to 2005). The **Democratic Unionist Party** (DUP) takes a harder stance in defense of Unionism. The **Ulster Volunteer Force** (UVF), the **Ulster Freedom Fighters** (UFF), and the **Ulster Defense Association** (UDA) are Loyalist paramilitary organizations: All three are labeled "proscribed groups" by the UK's 2000 Terrorism Act.

The mostly Catholic **Nationalist** minority—and the more hardline, working-class **Republicans**—want a united and independent Ireland ruled by Dublin. The **Social Democratic Labor Party** (SDLP), founded by Nobel Peace Prize co-winner John Hume, is the moderate political party representing Nationalist views. **Sinn Féin** takes a harder stance in defense of Nationalism. The **Irish Republican Army** (IRA) is the now-disarmed Nationalist paramilitary organization historically linked with Sinn Féin. The **Alliance Party** wants to bridge the gap between Unionists and Nationalists.

The long-simmering struggle to settle Northern Ireland's national identity precipitated the **Troubles,** the violent, 30-year conflict (1968-1998) between Unionist and Nationalist factions. To gain more insight into the complexity of the Troubles, the 90-minute documentary *Voices from the Grave* provides an excellent overview (easy to find on YouTube). Also check out the University of Ulster's informative and evenhanded Conflict Archive at https://cain.ulster.ac.uk.

Northern Ireland Politics

NATIONALISTS
(MOSTLY CATHOLICS)
"Feel Irish"

UNIONISTS
(MOSTLY PROTESTANTS)
"Feel British"

SINN FEIN   ALLIANCE   DUP

SDLP   UUP
John Hume   *David Trimble*
(retired)   *(retired)*

REPUBLICANS   MODERATES   LOYALISTS

GREEN   ORANGE

Not to scale &
not all opinions shown

sawdust pubs in working-class neighborhoods and spew simplistic opinions about sensitive local topics. Tourists notice lingering tension mainly during the "marching season" (Easter-Aug, peaking in early July). July 12—"the Twelfth"—is traditionally the most confrontational day of the year in the North, when proud Protestant Unionist Orangemen march to celebrate their Britishness (often through staunchly Nationalist Catholic neighborhoods—it's still good advice to lie low if you stumble onto any big Orange parades).

As the less-fractured Northern Ireland enters the 21st century, one of its most valuable assets is its industrious people (the "Protestant work ethic"). When they emigrated to the US, they became known as the Scots-Irish and played a crucial role in our nation's founding. They were signers of our Declaration of Independence, a dozen of our presidents (think tough-as-nails "Old Hickory" Andrew Jackson as a classic example), and the ancestors of Davy Crockett and Mark Twain.

Northern Irish workers have a proclivity for making things that go. They've produced far-reaching inventions like Dunlop's first inflatable tire. The Shorts aircraft factory (in Belfast) built the Wright Brothers' first aircraft for commercial sale and the world's first vertical takeoff jet. The *Titanic* was the only flop of Northern Ireland's otherwise successful shipbuilding industry. The once-futuristic DeLorean sports car was made in Belfast.

Notable people from Northern Ireland include musicians Van Morrison and James Galway, and actors Liam Neeson, Roma Downey, Ciarán Hinds, and Kenneth Branagh. The North also produced Christian intellectual and writer C. S. Lewis, Victorian physicist Lord Kelvin, engineer Harry Ferguson (inventor of the modern farm tractor and first four-wheel-drive Formula One car), and soccer-star playboy George Best—who once famously remarked, "I spent most of my money on liquor and women...and the rest I wasted."

As in the Republic, sports are big in the North. Northern-born golfers Rory McIlroy, Graeme McDowell, and Darren Clarke have won a fistful of majors, filling local hearts with pride. With close ties to Scotland, many Northern Irish fans follow the exploits of Glasgow soccer teams—but which team you root for betrays which side of the tracks you come from. Those who cheer for Glasgow Celtic (green and white) are Nationalist and Catholic; those waving banners for the Glasgow Rangers (blue with red trim) are Unionist and Protestant. To maintain peace, some pubs post signs on their doors banning patrons from wearing sports jerseys. Luckily, sports with no sectarian history are now being introduced, such as the Belfast Giants ice hockey team—a hit with both communities.

NORTHERN IRELAND

The Brexit Effect

A hundred years ago, the British Isles were ruled from one place: London. Today, parts of this geographic area (Ireland, Scotland, and England/Wales) drift in separate directions. And Northern Ireland, with strong cultural, geographic, and economic connections to all three, is being stretched uncomfortably.

In 2016, the people of the United Kingdom narrowly approved a referendum to leave the European Union ("Brexit"). But in Northern Ireland (as in Scotland), a majority of people voted to remain.

To the east, Scotland is flirting with independence: Separating from the UK would allow it to stay in the EU. (And many among the North's Unionist community trace their ancestry to Scotland.) To the south, the Republic of Ireland (an EU member) fills 80 percent of the island of Ireland; a growing minority in the North would like to see the island come together as a single Irish nation—inside the EU.

Which direction will the North lean? Special status within the UK? Reunification with the Republic?

The Good Friday agreement that ended the Troubles assumed there'd be open borders between Northern Ireland and the Republic. As the UK leaves the EU, one of the largest questions is what form the new border will take. Few want a "hard border," with trade tariffs and border controls between EU and UK zones. For example, the Northern Ireland border city of Derry has a struggling economy that relies on easy access to rural County Donegal, next door in the Republic. Making that market harder to reach would cause further hardship to a vulnerable community.

Beyond the economics, a hard border could add fuel to "them and us" perceptions, rekindling tension between dormant Republican and Loyalist extremists. No one wants to go back to the days when the border between Northern Ireland and the Republic was a closely patrolled line in a war zone.

Some Northern Irelanders are hedging their bets: Anyone born in Northern Ireland is eligible for a British passport, an Irish one, or both. Traditionally, Nationalist Catholics chose an Irish one and Unionist Protestants went for a British one. But with Brexit looming, many staunchly loyal Unionists are quietly applying to get an Irish passport as well to keep their options open.

Stay tuned to see how the swirling currents of Brexit, the Scottish independence movement, and the Irish reunification dream will affect this unique corner of the world...perched precariously between diverging cultural and economic powers: Ireland, Scotland, and England.

NORTHERN IRELAND

The North is affordable, the roads are great, and it's small enough to get a real feel for the place on a short visit. Fishers flock to the labyrinth of lakes in County Fermanagh, hikers seek out County Antrim coastal crags, and those of Scots-Irish descent explore their ancestral farmlands (some of the best agricultural land on the island). Today, more tourists than ever are venturing north to Belfast and Derry, and cruise-ship crowds disembark in Belfast to board charter buses that fan out to visit the Giant's Causeway and Old Bushmills Distillery.

As you travel through Northern Ireland today, you'll encounter a fascinating country with a complicated, often tragic history—and a brightening future.

DERRY

No city in Ireland connects the kaleidoscope of historical dots more colorfully than Derry. From a leafy monastic hamlet to a Viking-pillaged port, from a cannonball-battered siege survivor to an Industrial Revolution sweatshop, from an essential WWII naval base to a wrenching flashpoint of sectarian Troubles... Derry has seen it all.

Though Belfast is the capital of Northern Ireland, this pivotal city has a more diverse history and a prettier setting. Derry was a vibrant city back when Belfast was just a mudflat. With roughly a third of Belfast's population (95,000), Derry feels more welcoming and manageable to visitors.

The town is the mecca of Ulster Unionism. When Ireland was being divvied up, the River Foyle was the logical border between the North and the Republic. But, for sentimental and economic reasons, the North kept Derry, which is otherwise on the Republic's side of the river. Consequently, this predominantly Catholic-Nationalist city was much contested throughout the Troubles.

While most of its population and its city council call it "Derry," some maps, road signs, and all UK train schedules use "Londonderry," the name on its 1662 royal charter and the one favored by Unionists. I once asked a Northern Ireland rail employee for a ticket to "Derry"; he replied that there was no such place, but he would sell me one to "Londonderry." I'll call it Derry in this book since that's what the majority of the city's inhabitants do.

The past 15 years have brought some refreshing changes. Manned British Army surveillance towers were taken down in 2006, and most British troops finally departed in mid-2007, after 38 years in Northern Ireland. In 2011, a curvy pedestrian bridge across the River Foyle was completed. Locals dubbed it the Peace Bridge because it links the predominantly Protestant Waterside (east bank) with the predominantly Catholic Cityside (west bank). Today, you can feel comfortable wandering the streets and enjoying this underrated city.

PLANNING YOUR TIME

If just passing through (say, on your way to Portrush—see the next chapter), it takes a few hours to see the essential Derry sights: Visit the Tower Museum and catch some views from the town wall.

With more time, spend a night in Derry, so you can see the powerful Bogside murals and take a walking tour around the town walls. With two nights in Derry, consider crossing back into the Republic for a scenic driving loop through part of remote County Donegal (see page 412).

Orientation to Derry

The River Foyle flows north, slicing Derry into eastern and western chunks. The old town walls and almost all worthwhile sights are on the west side. (The tiny train station and Ebrington Square—at the end of the Peace Bridge—are the main reasons to spend time on the east side.) Waterloo Place and the adjacent Guildhall Square, just outside the north corner of the old city walls, are the pedestrian hubs of city activity. The Strand Road area extending north from Waterloo Place makes a comfortable home base, with lodging and restaurant suggestions within a block or two. The Diamond (main square) and its War Memorial statue mark the heart of the old city within the walls.

TOURIST INFORMATION

The TI sits on the riverfront and rents bikes (£5/2 hours, £8/4 hours, £12/8 hours), and can book bus and walking tours (Mon-Fri 9:00-17:30, Sat-Sun 10:00-17:00, closes earlier in off-season; 44 Foyle Street, tel. 028/7126-7284, www.visitderry.com).

ARRIVAL IN DERRY

By Train: Next to the river on the east side of town, Derry's little end-of-the-line train station (no storage lockers) has service to Portrush, Belfast, and Dublin. Each arriving train is greeted by free shuttle buses to Ulsterbus Station on the west side of town, a couple of minutes' walk south of Guildhall Square on Foyle Street (luggage storage at post office around corner in same building, Mon-Fri 9:30-17:30—beware of lunch closure, closed Sat-Sun). Otherwise, it's a £5 taxi ride to Guildhall Square. The same free shuttle service leaves Ulsterbus Station 15 minutes before each departing train.

DERRY

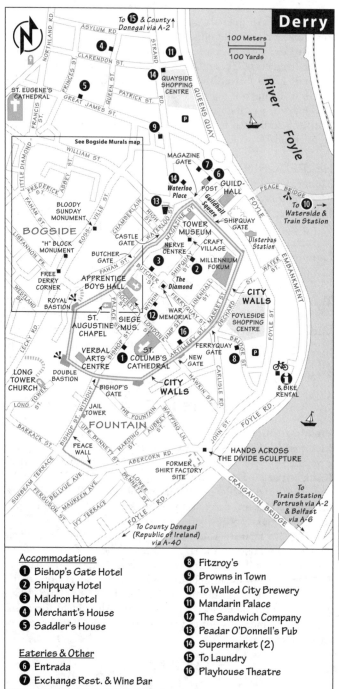

Derry

100 Meters
100 Yards

To ⑮ & County
Donegal via A-2

River Foyle

QUAYSIDE
SHOPPING
CENTRE

ST. EUGENE'S
CATHEDRAL

See Bogside Murals map

MAGAZINE
GATE

Waterloo
Place

POST

GUILD-
HALL

PEACE BRIDGE

To ⑩
Waterside &
Train Station

BLOODY
SUNDAY
MONUMENT

BOGSIDE

"H" BLOCK
MONUMENT

FREE
DERRY
CORNER

ROYAL
BASTION

CASTLE
GATE

BUTCHER
GATE

APPRENTICE
BOYS HALL

Guildhall
Square

TOWER
MUSEUM

NERVE
CENTRE

CRAFT
VILLAGE

MILLENNIUM
FORUM

The
Diamond

WAR
MEMORIAL

SHIPQUAY
GATE

Ulsterbus
Station

CITY
WALLS

FOYLESIDE
SHOPPING
CENTRE

WATER
EMBANKMENT

ST.
AUGUSTINE
CHAPEL

SIEGE
MUS.

VERBAL
ARTS
CENTRE

ST.
COLUMB'S
CATHEDRAL

FERRYQUAY
GATE

NEW
GATE

CITY
WALLS

LONG
TOWER
CHURCH

DOUBLE
BASTION

BISHOP'S
GATE

JAIL
TOWER

THE FOUNTAIN

WAPPING LN.

& BIKE
RENTAL

FOUNTAIN

PEACE
WALL

FORMER
SHIRT FACTORY
SITE

HANDS ACROSS
THE DIVIDE SCULPTURE

To County Donegal
(Republic of Ireland)
via A-40

CRAIGAVON BRIDGE

To
Train Station,
Portrush via A-2
& Belfast
via A-6

DERRY

<u>Accommodations</u>
❶ Bishop's Gate Hotel
❷ Shipquay Hotel
❸ Maldron Hotel
❹ Merchant's House
❺ Saddler's House

<u>Eateries & Other</u>
❻ Entrada
❼ Exchange Rest. & Wine Bar

❽ Fitzroy's
❾ Browns in Town
❿ To Walled City Brewery
⓫ Mandarin Palace
⓬ The Sandwich Company
⓭ Peadar O'Donnell's Pub
⓮ Supermarket (2)
⓯ To Laundry
⓰ Playhouse Theatre

By Bus: All intercity buses stop at the Ulsterbus Station, on Foyle Street close to Guildhall Square.

By Car: Foyleside parking garage across from the TI is handy for day-trippers (£1/hour, £3/4 hours, Mon-Tue 8:00-19:00, Wed-Fri until 22:00, Sat until 20:00, Sun 12:00-17:00, tel. 028/7137-7323). If staying overnight, ask about parking at your B&B, or try the Quayside parking garage behind the Travelodge (£1/hour, £3/4 hours, £8 additional for overnight, daily 7:30-21:00, closes earlier on weekends).

HELPFUL HINTS

Money: Danske Bank is on Guildhall Square and the Bank of Ireland is on Strand Road.

Bookstore: Foyle Books is a dusty little pleasure for browsing (Mon-Fri 11:00-17:00, Sat 10:00-17:00, closed Sun, 12 Magazine Street at entrance to Craft Village, tel. 028/7137-2530).

Laundry: Bubbles has drop-off service—bring it in the morning, pick up later that day (Mon-Fri 9:00-17:00, Sat from 10:00, closed Sun, 141 Strand Road, tel. 028/7136-3366).

Taxi: Try **City Cabs** (tel. 028/7126-4466), **The Taxi Company** (tel. 028/7126-2626), or **Foyle Taxis** (tel. 028/7127-9999).

Car Rental: Enterprise is handy (70 Clooney Road, tel. 028/7186-1699, www.enterprise.co.uk). Another option is **Desmond Motors** (173 Strand Road, tel. 028/7136-7136, www.desmondmotors.co.uk).

Tours in Derry

Walking Tours

McCrossan's City Tours leads insightful hour-long walks, giving a rounded view of the city's history. Tours depart from 11 Carlisle Road, just below Ferryquay Gate (£4; daily at 10:00, 12:00, 14:00, and 16:00; tel. 028/7127-1996, mobile 077-1293-7997, www.derrycitytours.com, derrycitytours@aol.com). They also offer private group tours (£60).

Bogside History Tours offers walks led by Bogside residents who lost loved ones in the tragic events of Bloody Sunday (£6, £9 combo-ticket with Museum of Free Derry; April-Sept daily at 11:00 and 13:00, in summer also Mon-Fri also at 15:00; departs from in front of the Guildhall, mobile 077-3145-0088 or 078-0056-7165, www.bogsidehistorytours.com, paul@bogsidehistorytours.com). Tour guides also offer various taxi tours (£25/hour, call or email for options).

Bus Tours

Game of Thrones Tours brings you to the beautiful North Antrim Coast, focusing on locations used in the *Game of Thrones* TV series (see sidebar on page 470). Stops included on the all-day tour are Dunluce Castle (photo stop), Carrick-a-Rede Rope Bridge, Giant's Causeway, and the Dark Hedges (photo stop), with a lunch stop in Ballintoy (£40, bus departs Derry TI daily at 8:00, returns by 17:30, no kids under 12, some walking, tel. 028/9568-0023, www.gameofthronestours.com).

City Sightseeing's hop-on, hop-off double-decker buses are a good option for a general overview of Derry. The one-hour loop covers both sides of the river (seven stops overall), including the Guildhall, the old city walls, political wall murals, cathedrals, and former shirt factories. Your ticket is good for 24 hours (£12.50, pay driver, bus departs April-Sept daily on the hour 10:00-16:00 from in front of TI and Guildhall Square, tel. 028/7137-0067, www.citysightseeingderry.com).

City Sightseeing also offers trips from Derry to the Giant's Causeway, Old Bushmills Distillery, and Carrick-a-Rede Rope Bridge in County Antrim (£40, does not include entry fees, runs daily May-Sept, depart TI at 10:00, return by 16:00, minimum 10 people).

Walks in Derry

Though calm today, Derry is stamped by years of tumultuous conflict. These two self-guided walks (less than an hour each) explore the town's history. "Walk the Walls," starting on the old city walls and ending at the Anglican Cathedral, focuses on Derry's early days. My "Bogside Murals Walk" guides you to the city's compelling murals, which document the time of the Troubles. These walks, each worth ▲▲, can be done separately or linked, depending on your time.

WALK THE WALLS

Squatting determinedly in the city center, the old city walls of Derry (built 1613-1618 and still intact, except for wider gates to handle modern vehicles) hold an almost mythic place in Irish history.

It was here in 1688 that a group of brave apprentice boys, some of whom had been shipped to Derry as orphans after the great fire of London in 1666, made their stand. They slammed the city gates shut in the face of the approaching Catholic forces of deposed King

James II. With this act, the boys galvanized the city's indecisive Protestant defenders inside the walls.

Months of negotiations and a grinding 105-day siege followed, during which a third of the 20,000 refugees and defenders crammed into the city perished.

The siege was finally broken in 1689, when supply ships broke through a boom stretched across the River Foyle. The sacrifice and defiant survival of the city turned the tide in favor of newly crowned Protestant King William of Orange, who arrived in Ireland soon after and defeated James at the pivotal Battle of the Boyne.

To fully appreciate the walls, take a walk on top of them (free, open from dawn to dusk). Almost 20 feet high and at least as thick, the walls form a mile-long oval loop. The most interesting section is the half-circuit facing the Bogside, starting at Magazine Gate (stairs face the Tower Museum Derry inside the walls) and finishing at Bishop's Gate.

• *Enter the walls at Magazine Gate and find the stairs opposite the Tower Museum. Once atop the walls, head left.*

Walk the wall as it heads uphill, snaking along the earth's contours. In the row of buildings on the left (just before crossing over Castle Gate), you'll see an arch entry into the **Craft Village,** an alley lined with a cluster of cute shops and cafés that showcase the economic rejuvenation of Derry (Mon-Sat 9:30-17:30, closed Sun).

• *After crossing over Butcher Gate, stop in front of the grand building with the four columns to view the...*

First Derry Presbyterian Church: This impressive-looking building is the second church to occupy this site. The first was built by Queen Mary in the 1690s to thank the Presbyterian community for standing by their Anglican brethren during the dark days of the famous siege. That church was later torn down to make room for today's stately Neoclassical, red-sandstone church finished in 1780. Over the next 200 years, time took its toll on the structure, which was eventually closed due to dry rot and Republican firebombings. But in 2011, the renovated church reopened to a chorus of cross-community approval (yet one more sign of the slow reconciliation taking place in Derry). The **Blue Coat School** exhibit behind the church highlights the important role of Presbyterians in local history (free but donation encouraged, Wed-Fri 11:00-16:00, closed Sat-Tue in summer and all of Oct-April, tel. 028/7126-1550).

• *Just up the block is the...*

Apprentice Boys Memorial Hall: Built in 1873, this houses the private lodge and meeting rooms of an all-male Protestant organization. The group is dedicated to the memory of the original 13 apprentice boys who saved the day during the 1688 siege. Each year, on the Saturday closest to the August 12 anniversary date, the modern-day Apprentice Boys Society celebrates the end of the siege with a controversial march atop the walls. These walls are considered sacred ground for devout Unionists, who claim that many who died during the famous siege were buried within the battered walls because of lack of space. The **Siege Museum** stands behind the hall, giving a narrow-focus Unionist view of the siege (£4, Mon-Sat 10:00-16:30, closed Sun, 18 Society Street, tel. 028/7126-1219).

Next, you'll pass a large, square pedestal on the right atop Royal Bastion. It once supported a column in honor of Governor George Walker, the commander of the defenders during the siege. In 1972, the IRA blew up the column, which had 105 steps to the top (one for each day of the siege). An adjacent plaque shows a photo of the column before it was destroyed.

• *Opposite the empty pedestal is the small Anglican...*

St. Augustine Chapel: Set in a pretty graveyard, this Anglican chapel is where some believe the original sixth-century monastery of St. Columba stood. The quaint grounds are open to visitors (Mon-Sat 10:30-16:30, closed Sun except for worship). In Victorian times, this stretch of the walls was a fashionable promenade walk.

As you walk, you'll pass a long wall (on the left)—all that's left of a former **British Army base,** which stood here until 2006. Two 50-foot towers used to loom out of it, bristling with cameras and listening devices. Soldiers built them here for a bird's-eye view of the once-turbulent Catholic Bogside district below. The towers' dismantlement—as well as the removal of most of the British Army from Northern Ireland—is another positive sign in cautiously optimistic Derry. The walls of this former army base now contain a parking lot.

Stop at the **Double Bastion** fortified platform that occupies this corner of the city walls. The old cannon is nicknamed "Roaring Meg" for the fury of its firing during the siege.

From here, you can see across the Bogside to the not-so-faraway hills of County Donegal in the Republic. Derry was once an island, but as the River Foyle gradually changed its course, the area you see below the wall began to drain. Over time, and especially after the Great Potato Famine, Catholic peasants from rural Donegal began to move into Derry to find work during the Industrial Revolution. They settled on this least desirable land...on the soggy bog side of the city. From this vantage point, survey the Bogside with its political murals and Palestinian flags.

Derry's History

Once an island in the River Foyle, Derry (from *doire,* Irish for "oak grove") was chosen by St. Columba (St. Colmcille) around AD 546 for a monastic settlement. He later banished himself to the island of Iona in Scotland out of remorse for sparking a bloody battle over the rights to a holy manuscript that he had secretly copied.

A thousand years later, the English defeated the last Ulster-based Gaelic chieftains in the Battle of Kinsale (1601). With victory at hand, the English took advantage of the power vacuum. They began the "plantation" of Ulster with loyal Protestant subjects imported from Scotland and England. The native Irish were displaced to less desirable rocky or boggy lands, sowing the seeds of resentment that eventually fueled the Troubles.

A dozen wealthy London guilds (grocers, haberdashers, tailors, and others) took on Derry as an investment and changed its name to "Londonderry." They built the last great walled city in Ireland to protect their investment from the surrounding—and hostile—Irish locals. The walls proved their worth in 1688-1689, when the town's Protestant defenders, loyal to King William of Orange, withstood a prolonged siege by the forces of Catholic King James II. "No surrender" is still a passionate rallying cry among Ulster Unionists determined to remain part of the United Kingdom.

The town became a major port of emigration to the New World in the early 1800s. Then, when the Industrial Revolution provided a steam-powered sewing factory, the city developed a thriving shirtmaking industry. The factories here employed mostly Catholic women who flocked in from rural County Donegal. Although Belfast grew larger and wealthier, Unionists tightened their grip on "Londonderry" and the walls that they regarded with almost holy reverence. In 1921, they insisted that the city be included in Northern Ireland when the province was partitioned from the new Irish Free State (later to become the Republic of Ireland). A bit of gerrymandering (with three lightly populated Unionist districts outvoting two densely populated Nationalist

DERRY

Directly below and to the right are Free Derry Corner and Rossville Street, where the tragic events of Bloody Sunday took place. Down on the left is the 18th-century Long Tower Catholic church, named after the monk-built round tower that once stood in the area (see page 452).

• *Head to the grand brick building behind you. This is the...*

districts) ensured that the Protestant minority maintained control of the city, despite its Catholic majority.

Derry was a key escort base for US convoys headed for Britain during World War II, and 60 surviving German U-boats were instructed to surrender here at the  end of the war. After the war, poor Catholics—unable to find housing—took over the abandoned military barracks, with multiple families living in each dwelling. Only homeowners were allowed to vote, and the Unionist minority, which controlled city government, was not eager to build more housing that would tip the voting balance away from them. Over the years, sectarian pressures gradually built—until they reached the boiling point. The ugly events of Bloody Sunday on January 30, 1972, brought worldwide attention to the Troubles (see the "Bloody Sunday" sidebar on page 444).

Today, life has stabilized in Derry, and the population has increased by 25 percent in the last 30 years. The 1998 Good Friday Peace Accord made significant progress toward peace, and the British Army withdrew 90 percent of its troops in mid-2007. With a population that is over 70 percent Catholic, the city has agreed to alternate Nationalist and Unionist mayors. There is a feeling of cautious optimism as Derry—the epicenter of bombs and bloody conflicts in the 1960s and 1970s—now boasts a history museum that airs all viewpoints.

The city continues to work on building a happier image. The wall—with all its troubled imagery and once nicknamed "the noose"—is now called "the necklace." With its complicated history, you're damned-if-you-do and damned-if-you-don't when it comes to calling it Derry (pro-Catholic, Nationalist) or Londonderry (pro-Protestant, Unionist). Some call it Derry/Londonderry or Londonderry/Derry. Others just say "Slashtown." And the tourist board calls it "legend-Derry."

DERRY

Verbal Arts Centre: A former Presbyterian school, this center promotes the development of local literary arts in the form of poetry, drama, writing, and storytelling. Drop in to check the events schedule (Mon-Fri 9:00-17:00, Sat 12:00-14:00, closed Sun, tel. 028/7126-6946, www.verbalartscentre.co.uk).

• *Go another 50 yards around the corner to reach...*

Bishop's Gate: From here, look up Bishop Street Within (inside the walls). This was the site of another British Army surveillance tower. Placed just inside the town walls, it overlooked the neighborhood until 2006. Now look in the other direction to see Bishop Street Without (outside the walls). You'll spot a modern wall topped by a high mesh fence, running along the left side of Bishop Street Without.

This is a so-called **"peace wall,"** built to ensure the security of the Protestant enclave living behind it in Derry's Fountain neighborhood. When the Troubles reignited over 50 years ago, 20,000 Protestants lived on this side of the river. This small housing development of 1,000 people is all that remains of that proud community today. The rest have chosen to move across the river to the mostly Protestant Waterside district. The stone tower halfway down the peace wall is all that remains of the old jail that briefly held doomed rebels after a 1798 revolt against the British.

• *From Bishop's Gate, those short on time can descend from the walls and walk 15 minutes directly back through the heart of the old city, along Bishop Street Within and Shipquay Street to Guildhall Square. With more time, consider visiting St. Columb's Cathedral, the Long Tower Church, and the murals of the Bogside.*

BOGSIDE MURALS WALK

The Catholic Bogside area was the tinderbox of the modern Troubles in Northern Ireland. Bloody Sunday, a terrible confrontation during a march that occurred nearly 50 years ago, sparked a sectarian inferno, and the ashes have not yet fully cooled. Today, the murals of the Bogside give visitors an accessible glimpse of this community's passionate perception of those events.

Getting There: The events are memorialized in 12 murals painted on the ends of residential flats along a 200-yard stretch of Rossville Street and Lecky Road, where the march took place. For the purposes of this walk, you can reach them from Waterloo Place via William Street. They are also accessible from the old city walls at Butcher Gate via the long set of stairs extending below Fahan Street on the grassy hillside, or by the stairs leading down from the Long Tower Church. These days, this neighborhood is gritty but quiet and safe.

The Artists: Two brothers, Tom and William Kelly, and their childhood friend Kevin Hasson are known as the Bogside Artists. They grew up in the Bogside and witnessed the tragic events that

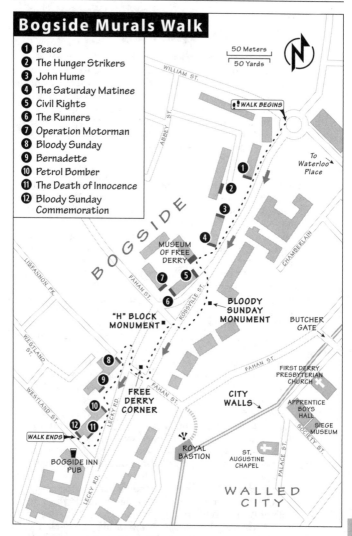

Bogside Murals Walk

1 Peace
2 The Hunger Strikers
3 John Hume
4 The Saturday Matinee
5 Civil Rights
6 The Runners
7 Operation Motorman
8 Bloody Sunday
9 Bernadette
10 Petrol Bomber
11 The Death of Innocence
12 Bloody Sunday Commemoration

took place there, which led them to begin painting the murals in 1994. One of the brothers, Tom, gained a reputation as a "heritage mural" painter, specializing in scenes of life in the old days. In a surprising and hopeful development, Tom was later invited into Derry's Protestant Fountain neighborhood to work with a youth club there on three proud heritage murals that were painted over paramilitary graffiti.

The Murals: Start out at the roundabout intersection of Rossville and William streets.

The Bogside murals face different directions (and some are

Bloody Sunday

Inspired by civil rights marches in America in the mid-1960s, and the Prague Spring uprising and Paris student strikes of 1968, civil rights groups began to protest in Northern Ireland around this time. Initially, their goals were to gain better housing, secure fair voting rights, and end employment discrimination for Catholics in the North. Tensions mounted, and clashes with the predominantly Protestant Royal Ulster Constabulary police force became frequent. Eventually, the British Army was called in to keep the peace.

On January 30, 1972, about 10,000 people protesting internment without trial held an illegal march sponsored by the Northern Ireland Civil Rights Association. British Army barricades kept them from the center of Derry, so they marched through the Bogside neighborhood.

That afternoon, some youths rioted on the fringe of the march. An elite parachute regiment had orders to move in and make arrests in the Rossville Street area. Shooting broke out, and after 25 minutes, 13 marchers were dead and 13 were wounded (one of the wounded later died). The soldiers claimed they came under attack from gunfire and nail-bombs. The marchers said the army shot indiscriminately at unarmed civilians.

The clash, called "Bloody Sunday," uncorked pent-up frustration as moderate Nationalists morphed into staunch Republicans overnight and released a flood of fresh IRA volunteers. An investigation at the time exonerated the soldiers, but the relatives of the victims called it a whitewash and insisted on their innocence.

In 1998, then-British Prime Minister Tony Blair promised a new inquiry, which became the longest and most expensive in British legal history. In 2010, a 12-year investigation—the Saville Report—determined that the Bloody Sunday civil rights protesters were innocent and called the deaths of 14 protesters unjustified.

In a dramatic 2010 speech in the House of Commons, then-British Prime Minister David Cameron apologized to the people of Derry. "What happened on Bloody Sunday was both unjustified and unjustifiable. It was wrong," he declared. Cheers rang out in Derry's Guildhall Square, where thousands had gathered to watch the televised speech. After 38 years, Northern Ireland's bloodiest wound started healing.

DERRY

partially hidden by buildings), so they're not all visible from a single viewpoint. Plan on walking three long blocks along Rossville Street (which becomes Lecky Road) to see them all. Residents are used to visitors and don't mind if you photograph the murals. Local motorists are uncommonly courteous with allowing visitors to cross the busy street.

From William Street, walk south along the right side of Ross-ville Street toward Free Derry Corner. The murals will all be on your right.

The first mural you'll walk past is the colorful ❶ *Peace*, showing the silhouette of a dove in flight (left side of mural) and an oak leaf (right side of mural), both created from a single ribbon. A peace campaign asked Derry city schoolchildren to write sugges-tions for positive peacetime images; their words inspired this artwork. The dove is a traditional symbol of peace, and the oak leaf is a traditional symbol of Derry—recognized by both communities. The dove flies from the sad blue of the past toward the warm yel-low of the future.

❷ *The Hunger Strikers,* repainted during the summer of 2015, features two Derry-born participants of the 1981 Maze Prison hunger strike, as well as their mothers, who sacrificed and sup-ported them in their fatal decision (10 strikers died). The prison was closed after the release of all prisoners (both Unionist and Na-tionalist) in 2000.

Smaller and easy to miss (above a ramp with banisters) is ❸ *John Hume.* It's actually a collection of four faces (clockwise from upper left): Nationalist leader John Hume, Martin Luther King, Jr., Nelson Mandela, and Mother Teresa. The Brooklyn Bridge in the middle symbolizes the long-term bridges of understanding that the work of these four Nobel Peace Prize-winning activists created. Born in the Bogside, Hume still maintains a home here.

Now look for ❹ *The Saturday Matinee,* which depicts an out-gunned but undaunted local youth be-hind a screen shield. He holds a stone, ready to throw, while a British ar-mored vehicle approaches (echoing the famous Tiananmen Square photo of the lone Chinese man facing the tank). Why *Saturday Matinee?* It's because the weekend was the best time for lo-cals to engage in a little "recreational rioting" and "have a go at" the army; people were off work and youths were out of school. The "MOFD" at the bot-tom of this mural stands for the nearby Museum of Free Derry.

Nearby is ❺ *Civil Rights,* showing a marching Derry crowd carrying an anti-sectarian banner. It dates from the days when

Martin Luther King, Jr.'s successful nonviolent marches were being seen worldwide on TV, creating a dramatic, global ripple effect. Civil rights marches, inspired by King and using the same methods to combat a similar set of grievances, gave this long-suffering community a powerful new voice.

All along this walk you'll notice lots of flags, including the red, black, white, and green Palestinian flag. Palestinians and Catholic residents of Northern Ireland have a special empathy for each other—both are indigenous people dealing with the persistent realities of sharing what they consider their rightful homeland with more powerful settlers planted there for political reasons.

In the building behind this mural, you'll find the intense **Museum of Free Derry** (£6, £9 combo-ticket with Bogside History Tours, open Mon-Fri 9:30-16:00 year-round, also open April-Sept Sat-Sun 13:00-16:00, 55 Glenfada Park, tel. 028/7136-0880, www.museumoffreederry.org). Photos, shirts with bullet holes, and a video documentary convey Bogside residents' experiences during the worst of the Troubles. At the far end of the museum's outdoor wall (high up on the second floor of an adjacent residential building) is a copy of a famous painting by Francisco Goya depicting another massacre—this one in Spain—called the *Third of May 1808*. This reproduction draws a stark parallel to the local events that occurred here. Below and to the left of the painting (next to a gated alley) are two large bullet holes in the wall, inflicted on Bloody Sunday and preserved behind glass.

Cross over to the other side of Rossville Street to see the **Bloody Sunday Monument.** This small, fenced-off stone obelisk lists the names of those who died that day, most within 50 yards of this spot. Take a look at the map pedestal by the monument, which shows how a rubble barricade was erected to block the street. A 10-story housing project called Rossville Flats stood here in those days. After peaceful protests failed (with Bloody Sunday being the watershed event), Nationalist youths became more aggressive. British troops were wary of being hit by Molotov cocktails thrown from the rooftop of the housing project.

Cross back again, this time over to the grassy median strip that runs down the middle of Rossville Street. At this end stands a granite letter *H* inscribed with the names of the IRA hunger strikers who died (and how many days they starved) in the H-block of Maze Prison (see *"The Hunger Strikers,"* earlier in the walk).

Political Murals

The dramatic and emotional murals you'll encounter in Northern Ireland will likely be one of your trip's most enduring travel memories. During the 19th century, Protestant neighborhoods hung flags and streamers each July to commemorate the victory of King William of Orange at the Battle of the Boyne in 1690. Modern murals evolved from these colorful annual displays. With the advent of industrial paints, temporary seasonal displays became permanent territorial statements.

Unionist murals were created during the extended Home Rule political debate that eventually led to the partitioning of the island in 1921 and the creation of Northern Ireland. Murals that expressed opposing views in Nationalist Catholic neighborhoods were outlawed. The ban remained until the eruption of the modern Troubles, when staunchly Nationalist Catholic communities isolated themselves behind barricades, eluding state control and gaining freedom to express their pent-up passions. In Derry, this form of symbolic, cultural, and ideological resistance first appeared in 1969 with the simple "You are now entering Free Derry" message that you'll still see painted on the surviving gable wall at Free Derry Corner.

Found mostly in working-class neighborhoods of Belfast and Derry, today's political murals have become a dynamic form of popular culture. They blur the line between art and propaganda, giving visitors a striking glimpse of each community's history, identity, and values.

From here, as you look across at the corner of Fahan Street, you get a good view of two murals. In ❻ *The Runners* (right), four rioting youths flee tear gas from canisters used by the British Army to disperse hostile crowds. More than 1,000 canisters were used during the Battle of the Bogside; "nonlethal" rubber bullets killed 17 people over the course of the Troubles. Meanwhile, in ❼ *Operation Motorman* (left), a soldier wields a sledgehammer to break through a house door, depicting the massive push by the British Army to open up the Bogside's barricaded "no-go" areas that the IRA had controlled for three years (1969-1972).

Walk down to the other end of the median strip where the white wall of **Free Derry Corner** announces "You are now entering Free Derry" (imitating a similarly defiant slogan of the time in once-isolated West Berlin). This was the gabled end of a string of

DERRY

houses that stood here almost 50 years ago. During the Troubles, it became a traditional meeting place for speakers to address crowds. A portion of this mural changes from time to time, calling attention to injustice suffered by kindred spirits around the world (the plight of Palestinians and Basques are common themes).

Cross back to the right side of the street (now Lecky Road) to see ❽ *Bloody Sunday,* in which a small group of men carry a body from that ill-fated march. It's based on a famous photo of Father Edward Daly that was taken that day. Hunched over, he waves a white handkerchief to request safe passage in order to evacuate a mortally wounded protester. The bloodstained civil rights banner was inserted under the soldier's feet for extra emphasis. After Bloody Sunday, the previously marginal IRA suddenly found itself swamped with bitterly determined young recruits.

Near it is a mural called ❾ *Bernadette.* The woman with the megaphone is Bernadette Devlin McAliskey, an outspoken civil rights leader, who, at age 21, became the youngest elected member of British Parliament. Behind her kneels a female supporter, banging a trash-can lid against the street in a traditional expression of protest in Nationalist neighborhoods. Trash-can lids were also used to warn neighbors of the approach of British patrols.

❿ *Petrol Bomber,* showing a teen wearing an army-surplus gas mask, captures the Battle of the Bogside, when locals barricaded their community, effectively shutting out British rule. Though the main figure's face is obscured by the mask, his body clearly communicates the resolve of an oppressed people. In the background, the long-gone Rossville Flats housing project still looms, with an Irish tricolor flag flying from its top.

In ⓫ *The Death of Innocence,* a young girl stands in front of bomb wreckage. She is Annette McGavigan, a 14-year-old who was killed on this corner by crossfire in 1971. She was the 100th fatality of the Troubles, which eventually took more than 3,000 lives (and she was also a cousin of one of the artists). The broken gun beside

her points to the ground, signifying that it's no longer being wielded. The large butterfly above her shoulder symbolizes the hope for peace. For years, the artists left the butterfly an empty silhouette until they felt confident that the peace process had succeeded. They finally filled in the butterfly with optimistic colors in the summer of 2006.

Finally, around the corner, you'll see a circle of male faces. This mural, painted in 1997 to observe the 25th anniversary of the tragedy, is called ⓬ *Bloody Sunday Commemoration* and shows the 14 victims. They are surrounded by a ring of 14 oak leaves—the symbol of Derry. When relatives of the dead learned that the three Bogside Artists were beginning to paint this mural, many came forward to loan the artists precious photos of their loved ones, so they could be more accurately depicted.

Across the street, drop into the **Bogside Inn** for a beverage and check out the black-and-white photos of events in the area during the Troubles. This pub has been here through it all, and lives on to tell the tale.

While these murals preserve the struggles of the late 20th century, today sectarian violence has given way to negotiations and a settlement that seems to be working in fits and starts. The British apology for the Bloody Sunday shootings was a huge step forward. Former Nationalist leader John Hume (who shared the 1998 Nobel Peace Prize with then-Unionist leader David Trimble) once borrowed a quote from Gandhi to explain his nonviolent approach to the peace process: "An eye for an eye leaves everyone blind."

Sights in Derry

▲▲Tower Museum Derry

This well-organized museum combines modern audiovisual displays with historical artifacts to tell Derry's story from a skillfully unbiased viewpoint, sorting out some of the tangled history of Northern Ireland's Troubles. Occupying a modern reconstruction of a fortified medieval tower house that belonged to the local O'Doherty clan, it provides an excellent introduction to the city.

Cost and Hours: £4, includes audioguide for Armada exhib-

DERRY

its, daily 10:00-17:30, last entry at 16:00, Union Hall Place, tel. 028/7137-2411, www.derrystrabane.com/towermuseum.

Visiting the Museum: The museum is divided into two sections: the Story of Derry (on the ground floor) and the Spanish Armada (on the four floors of the tower).

Start with the **Story of Derry,** which explains the city's monastic origins 1,500 years ago. The exhibit moves through pivotal events, such as the 1688-1689 siege, as well as unexpected blips, like Amelia Earhart's emergency landing. Don't miss the thought-provoking 15-minute film in the small theater—it offers an evenhanded local perspective on the tragic events of the modern sectarian conflict, giving you a better handle on what makes this unique city tick. Scan the displays of paramilitary paraphernalia in the hallway lined with colored curbstones—red, white, and blue Union Jack colors for Unionists; and the green, white, and orange Irish tricolor for Nationalists.

The tower section holds the **Spanish Armada** exhibits, filled with items taken from the wreck of *La Trinidad Valencera.* The ship sank off the coast of Donegal in 1588 in fierce storms nicknamed the "Protestant Winds." A third of the Armada's ships were lost in storms off the coasts of Ireland and Scotland. Survivors who made it ashore were hunted and killed by English soldiers. But a small number made it to Dunluce Castle (see page 473), where the sympathetic lord, who was no friend of the English, smuggled them to Scotland and eventual freedom in France.

Guildhall

This Neo-Gothic building, complete with clock tower, is the ceremonial seat of city government. Inside the hall are the Council Chamber, party offices, and an assembly hall featuring stained-glass windows showing scenes from Derry history.

Cost and Hours: Free, daily 10:00-17:30, free and clean WCs on ground floor, tel. 028/7137-6510, www.derrystrabane.com/guildhall.

Background: The Guildhall first opened in 1890 on reclaimed lands that were once the mudflats of the River Foyle. Destroyed by fire and rebuilt in 1913, it was massively damaged by IRA bombs in 1972. In an ironic twist, Gerry Doherty, one of those convicted of the bombings, was elected as a member of the Derry City Council a dozen years later. (When I first visited Derry with tour groups back in the 1990s, a bus of curious Americans was such a rarity that the mayor actually invited our entire group into his office here for tea and a friendly Q&A session.)

Visiting the Hall: Take an informational pamphlet from the front window and explore, if civic and cultural events are not taking place inside. Rotating exhibits fill a ground-floor hall just to the right of the front reception desk. The Ulster Plantation exhibition is worth a visit. A mighty pipe organ fills much of a wall in the grand hall. It's lonely and loves to be played (if you would like to give it a go, just ask a guard).

On the back terrace, facing the river, you'll find locals lunching at the pleasant Guild Café (daily 9:30-17:00). And across the street is the modest but heartfelt Peace Park, with hopeful, nonsectarian children's quotes on tiles that line the path.

Peace Bridge Stroll

Stroll across the architecturally fetching Peace Bridge for great views over the river toward the city center (best at sunset). The €14 million pedestrian Peace Bridge opened in 2011, linking neighborhoods long divided by the river (Catholic Nationalists on the west bank and Protestant Unionists on the east bank). On the far side from the old city walls, the former Ebrington Barracks British Army base (1841-2003) sits on prime real estate and surrounds a huge square that was once the military parade ground. This area features a fun gastropub, and serves as an outdoor concert venue and community gathering spot. Plans are in progress to develop this area further with a hotel and museum complex.

Hands Across the Divide

Designed by local teacher Maurice Harron, this powerful metal sculpture of two figures extending their hands to each other was inspired by the growing hope for peace and reconciliation in Northern Ireland (located at roundabout at west end of Craigavon Bridge).

The Tillie and Henderson's shirt factory (opened in 1857 and burned down in 2003) once stood on the banks of the river beside the bridge, looming over the figures. In its heyday, Derry's shirt industry employed more than 15,000 workers (90 percent of whom were women) in sweathouses typical of the human toll of the Industrial Revolution. Karl Marx mentioned this factory in *Das Kapital* as an example of women's transition from domestic to industrial work lives.

St. Columb's Cathedral

Marked by the tall spire inside the walls, this was the first Protestant cathedral built in Britain after the Reformation. St. Columb's played an important part in the defense of the city during the siege. During that time, cannons were mounted on its roof, and the original spire was scavenged for lead to melt into cannon shot. This Anglican cathedral was built from 1628 to 1633 in a style called "Planter's Gothic," financed by the same London companies that backed the Protestant plantation of Londonderry.

Cost and Hours: £2 donation, Mon-Sat 9:00-17:00, closed Sun, tel. 028/7126-7313, www.stcolumbscathedral.org.

Visiting the Cathedral: Before you enter, walk over to the "Heroes' Mound" at the end of the churchyard closest to the town wall. Underneath this grassy dome is a mass grave of some of those who died during the 1689 siege.

In the cathedral entryway, you'll find a hollow cannonball that was lobbed into the city—it contained the besiegers' surrender terms. Inside, along the nave, hangs a musty collection of battle flags and Union Jacks that once inspired troops during the siege, the Crimean War, and World War II.

An American flag hung among them until a few years ago when its gradual deterioration prompted its current storage under glass (viewable in wooden case to right of front altar—fourth drawer from top). It's from the time when the first GIs to enter the European theater in World War II were based in Northern Ireland.

To the left of the front altar is a seven-minute video covering the cathedral's history. Check out the small chapter-house museum in the back of the church to see the huge original locks of the gates of Derry and more relics of the siege.

Long Tower Church

Built below the walls on the hillside above the Bogside, this modest-looking church is worth a visit for its stunning high altar. The name comes from a stone monastic round tower that stood here for centuries but was dismantled and used for building materials in the 1600s.

Cost and Hours: Free, generally open Mon-Sat 8:30-20:30, Sun 7:30-18:00, tel. 028/7126-2301, www.longtowerchurch.org.

Visiting the Church: Long Tower Church, the oldest Catholic church in Derry, was finished in 1786, during a time of enlightened relations between the city's two religious communities. Protestant Bishop Hervey gave a generous-for-the-time £200 donation and had the four Corinthian columns shipped in from Naples to frame the Neo-Renaissance altar.

Outside, walk behind the church and face the Bogside to find a simple shrine hidden beneath a hawthorn tree. It marks the spot where outlawed Masses were secretly held before this church was built, during the Penal Law period of the early 1700s. Through the Penal Laws, the English attempted to weaken Catholicism's influence by banishing priests and forbidding Catholics from buying land, attending school, voting, and holding office.

Nearby: The adjacent **St. Columba Heritage Centre** fleshes out the life of Derry's patron saint and founding father (£3, Mon-Fri 10:00-16:00, Sat-Sun from 13:00, closed Mon Oct-April, tel. 028/7136-8491, www.stcolumbscathedral.org).

Nightlife in Derry

The **Millennium Forum** is a modern venue that reflects the city's revived investment in local culture, concerts, and plays (box office open Mon-Sat 9:30-17:00, inside city walls on Newmarket Street near Ferryquay Gate, tel. 028/7126-4455, www.millenniumforum. co.uk, boxoffice@millenniumforum.co.uk).

The **Nerve Centre** hosts a wide variety of art-house films and live concerts (inside city walls at 7 Magazine Street, near Butcher Gate, tel. 028/7126-0562, www.nervecentre.org).

The **Playhouse Theatre** is an intimate venue for plays (£9-20 tickets, inside walls on Artillery Street, between New Gate and Ferryquay Gate, tel. 028/7126-8027, www.derryplayhouse.co.uk).

To mingle with Derry's friendly conversational residents, try **Peadar O'Donnell's** pub on Waterloo Street for the city's best nightly traditional music sessions (often start late, at 23:00; 53 Waterloo Street, tel. 028/7137-2318).

Sleeping in Derry

The first three options are located inside the city's walls and feature all the modern comforts. The others are in historic buildings with creaky charm and friendly hosts.

$$$$ Bishop's Gate Hotel is Derry's top lodging option and priced that way. A former gentlemen's club once frequented by Winston Churchill, it has 30 rooms that ooze with cushy refinement (fine bar, 24 Bishop Street, tel. 028/7114-0300, www. bishopsgatehotelderry.com, sales@bishopsgatehotelderry.com). They also rent one apartment (sleeps 4).

$$$$ The **Shipquay Hotel** rents 21 rooms with stylish minimalist comfort above its ground-floor Lock & Quay cocktail bar (15 Shipquay Street, tel. 028/7126-7266, www.shipquayhotel.com, info@shipquayhotel.com).

$$ Maldron Hotel features 93 modern and large rooms, a bistro restaurant, and 20 private basement parking spaces (Butcher

454 Rick Steves Ireland

Street, tel. 028/7137-1000, www.maldronhotelderry.com, info.derry@maldronhotels.com).

$ Merchant's House, on a quiet street a 10-minute stroll from Waterloo Place, is a fine Georgian townhouse with a grand, colorful drawing room and nine rooms sporting marble fireplaces and ornate plasterwork (family rooms, 16 Queen Street, tel. 028/7126-9691, www.thesaddlershouse.com, saddlershouse@btinternet.com). Joan and Peter Pyne also run the Saddler's House (see below), and offer appealing self-catering townhouse rentals inside the walls (great for families or anyone needing extra space, 3-night minimum).

$ Saddler's House is a charming Victorian townhouse with seven rooms located a couple of blocks closer to the old town walls. Their muscular bulldog Bruno provides lovable comic relief (36 Great James Street, tel. 028/7126-9691, www.thesaddlershouse.com, saddlershouse@btinternet.com).

Eating in Derry

$$$ Entrada is a crisp, modern restaurant with a faintly Spanish theme, serving great meals and fine wines in a posh, calm space. It faces the river a block from the Guildhall (Wed-Sat 12:00-21:30, Sun until 20:00, closed Mon-Tue, Queens Quay, tel. 028/7137-3366).

The hip, trendy **$$$ Exchange Restaurant and Wine Bar** offers lunches and quality dinners with flair, in a central location near the river behind Waterloo Place (Mon-Fri 12:00-14:30 & 17:30-22:00, Sat 17:00-22:00, Sun 14:00-20:00, Queen's Quay, tel. 028/7127-3990).

$$$ Fitzroy's, tucked below Ferryquay Gate and stacked with locals, serves good lunches and dinners (Mon-Sat 12:00-22:00, Sun 13:00-20:00, 2 Bridge Street, tel. 028/7126-6211).

$$ Browns in Town is a casual, friendly lunch or dinner option near most of my recommended lodgings (Mon-Sat 12:00-15:00 & 17:30-21:00, Sun 17:00-20:30, 21 Strand Road, tel. 028/7136-2889).

$$ Walled City Brewery, across the Peace Bridge, is a fun change of pace. The brewpub ambience and dependable comfort food can be washed down with a local fave: Derry chocolate milk stout (Wed-Thu 17:00-23:30, Fri-Sun from 14:00, closed Mon-Tue, 70 Ebrington Square, tel. 028/7134-3336).

$ Mandarin Palace is crowded with loyal locals eating filling Chinese fare; easy takeout is available (Mon-Sat 16:00-23:00, Sun from 13:00, Queens Quay, tel. 028/7137-3656).

$ The Sandwich Company is a cheap and easy lunch counter and coffee shop in the center of the old town walls (Mon-Wed and

Sat 8:00-17:30, Thu-Fri until 19:00, Sun 10:00-17:00 (6 Bishop Street Within, tel. 028/7137-2500).

Supermarkets: You'll find everything you need for picnics at **Tesco** (Mon-Fri 8:00-21:00, Sat until 19:00, Sun 13:00-18:00, corner of Strand Road and Clarendon Street) or **SuperValu** (Mon-Sat 8:30-19:00, Sun 12:30-17:30, Waterloo Place).

Derry Connections

From Derry, it's an hour's drive to Portrush. If you're using public transportation, consider a Zone 4 iLink smartcard, good for all-day train and bus use in Northern Ireland (see page 483). Keep in mind that some bus and train schedules, road signs, and maps may say "Londonderry" or "L'Derry" instead of "Derry."

From Derry by Train to: Portrush (16/day, 1.5 hours, usually change in Coleraine), **Belfast** (16/day, 2 hours), **Dublin** (6/day, 4 hours, change in Belfast).

By Bus to: Galway (6/day, 5.5 hours), **Westport** (3/day, 6 hours, bus #64 to Knock Airport or Charleston then bus #440 to Derry), **Portrush** (5/day, 1.5 hours, change in Coleraine), **Belfast** (hourly, 2 hours), **Dublin** (12/day, 4 hours).

Near Derry

▲Ulster American Folk Park

This combination museum and folk park (in a wonderfully scenic and walkable rural forest) commemorates the many Irish who left their homeland during the hard times of the 18th century. Your visit progresses through four sections. You'll start by walking through the excellent museum, then head outdoors to visit the remaining three sections in chronological order: life in

DERRY

Ulster before emigration, passage on the boat, and the adjustment to life in unfamiliar America. You'll gain insight into the origins of the tough Scots-Irish stock—think Davy Crockett (his people were from Derry) and Andrew Jackson (Carrickfergus roots)—who later shaped America's westward migration. You'll also find good coverage of the *Titanic* tragedy, and its effect on the Ulster folk who built the ship and the loved ones it left behind.

Cost and Hours: £9; Tue-Sun 10:00-17:00; Oct-Feb Tue-Fri

10:00-16:00, Sat-Sun from 11:00; closed Mon year-round; cafeteria, 2 Mellon Road, tel. 028/8224-3292, www.nmni.com.

Getting There: The folk park is 48 kilometers (30 miles) south of Derry on A-5—about a 45-minute drive.

Nearby: The adjacent **Mellon Centre for Migration Studies** is handy for genealogy searches (Tue-Fri 10:00-16:00, Sat from 11:00, closed Sun-Mon, tel. 028/8225-6315, www.qub.ac.uk/cms).

PORTRUSH &
THE ANTRIM COAST

The Antrim Coast—the north of Northern Ireland—is one of the most interesting and scenic coastlines in Ireland. Portrush, at the end of the train line, is an ideal base for exploring the highlights of the Antrim Coast. Within a few miles of the train terminal, you can visit evocative castle ruins, tour the world's oldest whiskey distillery, catch a thrill on a bouncy rope bridge, and hike along the famous Giant's Causeway.

PLANNING YOUR TIME

You need a full day to explore the Antrim Coast, so allow two nights in Portrush. The main sights on the coast are the Giant's Causeway, Old Bushmills Distillery, Carrick-a-Rede Rope Bridge, and Dunluce Castle (all doable with a car in one busy day). Add a third night if you plan to take longer hikes and visit Rathlin Island (book ahead for summer ferries).

Advance planning is important here. Book a timed-entry ticket online to cross the Carrick-a-Rede Rope Bridge. Arrive early for the Giant's Causeway (a guided hike can be booked a day in advance; can also be done on your own with no reservation). For sights that can't be reserved, pick the one that most interests you and visit it first, then take your chances with the rest. Visit Dunluce Castle last; it's the least crowded of these four main choices.

Getting an early start is essential. My ideal day would start with the Giant's Causeway, arriving by 9:00, when crowds are lightest—choose between a quickie visit or longer hike (options described on page 467). Early birds will find that the trails are always open.

Follow this with a tour of Old Bushmills Distillery. For lunch, you can bring a picnic, or eat cheaply in either the visitors center at the causeway or the Old Bushmills hospitality room.

After lunch, drive to Carrick-a-Rede (about 20 minutes from the distillery). Without a ticket, you can still enjoy the scenic cliff-top trail hike all the way to the bridge, as well as the nearby view-point for dramatic views of the bridge.

From here, hop in your car and double back west all the way to dramatically cliff-perched Dunluce Castle for a late-afternoon tour. The castle is only a five-minute drive from Portrush.

If driving on to Belfast from Portrush, consider the slower but scenic coastal route via the Glens of Antrim.

GETTING AROUND THE ANTRIM COAST

By Car: A car is the best way to explore the charms of the Antrim Coast. Distances are short and parking is easy.

By Bus: In peak season, an all-day bus pass helps you get around the region economically. The **Causeway Rambler** links Portrush to Old Bushmills Distillery, the Giant's Causeway, and the Carrick-a-Rede Rope Bridge (stopping at the nearby town of Ballintoy). The bus journey from Portrush to Carrick-a-Rede takes 45 minutes (£8/day, runs roughly 10:00-18:00, hourly May-Sept, fewer off-season). Pick up a Rambler bus schedule at the TI, and buy the ticket from the driver (in Portrush, the Rambler stops at Dunluce Avenue, next to public WC, a 2-minute walk from TI; operated by Translink, tel. 028/9066-6630, www.translink.co.uk).

By Bus Tour: If you're based in Belfast, you can visit most of the sights on the Antrim Coast with a **McComb's** tour (see page 485). Those based in Derry can get to the Giant's Causeway and Carrick-a-Rede Rope Bridge with City Sightseeing (see page 437).

By Taxi: Groups (up to four) can reasonably visit most sights by taxi (except the more distant Carrick-a-Rede and Rathlin Island sailings from Ballycastle). Approximate one-way prices from Portrush: £12 (Dunluce Castle), £15 (Old Bushmills Distillery), £23 (Giant's Causeway). Try **Andy Brown's Taxi** (tel. 028/7082-2223), **Hugh's Taxi** (mobile 077-0298-6110), or **North West Taxi** (tel. 028/7082-4446).

Portrush

Homey Portrush used to be known as "the Brighton of the North." It first became a resort in the late 1800s, as railroads expanded to offer the new middle class a weekend by the shore. Victorians believed that swimming in saltwater would cure many common ailments.

This is County Antrim, the Bible Belt of Northern Ireland. When a large supermarket chain decided to stay open on Sundays, a local reverend called for a boycott of the store for not honoring the Sabbath. And in 2012, when the Giant's Causeway Visitor Centre opened, local Creationists demanded that, alongside modern geologic explanations about the age of the unique rock formations, an exhibit be added explaining their viewpoint (that, according to the Bible, the earth here was only 6,000 years old, not 60 million—carbon dating be damned).

While it's seen its best days, Portrush retains the atmosphere and architecture of a genteel seaside resort. Its peninsula is filled with lowbrow, family-oriented amusements, fun eateries, and B&Bs. Summertime fun seekers promenade along the tiny harbor and tumble down to the sandy beaches, which extend in sweeping white crescents on either side.

Superficially, Portrush has the appearance of any small British seaside resort (and Union Jacks fly with a little extra gusto around here), but its history and large population of young people (students from nearby University of Ulster at Coleraine) give the town a little more personality. Along with the usual arcade amusements, there are nightclubs, restaurants, summer theater productions in the Town Hall, and convivial pubs that attract customers all the way from Belfast.

Orientation to Portrush

Portrush's pleasant and easily walkable town center features sea views in every direction. On one side are the harbor and most of the restaurants, and on the other are Victorian townhouses and vast, salty vistas. The tip of the peninsula is filled with tennis courts, lawn-bowling greens, putting greens, and a park.

The town is busy with students during the school year. July and August are beach-resort boom time. June and September are laid-back and lazy. There's a brief but intense spike in visitors in mid-May for a huge annual motorcycle race and on Easter weekend (see "Crowd Alert" later). Families pack Portrush on Saturdays, and revelers from Belfast crowd its hotels on Saturday nights.

Tourist Information: The TI is located underneath the very central, red-brick Town Hall (Mon-Sat 9:00-17:00, Sun 11:00-16:00, shorter hours off-season and closed Oct-March; Kerr Street, tel. 028/7082-3333). Consider the Collins Ireland Visitors Map (£9), the free *Visitor Guide* brochure, and, if needed, a free Belfast map.

Arrival in Portrush: The train tracks stop at the base of the tiny peninsula that Portrush fills (no baggage storage at station). Most of my listed B&Bs are within a 10-minute walk of the train station. The bus stop is two blocks from the train station.

Crowd Alert: Over a four-day weekend in mid-May, thousands of die-hard motorcycle fans converge on Portrush, Port Stewart, and Coleraine to watch the **Northwest 200 Race.** Fearless racers scorch the roads at 200 miles per hour on the longest straightaway in motorsports. Accommodations fill up a year ahead, and traffic is the pits (dates and details at www.northwest200.org). Avoid visiting during crowded **Easter weekend.**

Laundry: Full service is available at **Causeway Laundry** (Mon-Tue and Thu-Fri 9:00-16:30, Wed and Sat until 13:00, closed Sun, 68 Causeway Street, tel. 028/7082-2060).

Sights in Portrush

Barry's Old-Time Amusement Arcade

This fun arcade is bigger than it looks and offers a chance to see Northern Ireland at play. Older locals visit for the nostalgia, as many of the rides and amusements go back 50 years. Ride prices are listed at the door. Everything runs with tokens (£0.50 each or £10/24, buy from coin-op machines). Located just below the train station on the harbor, Barry's is filled with "candy floss" (cotton candy) and crazy "scoop treats" (daily 12:30-22:00 in summer, weekends only Easter-May, closed Sept-Easter, www.barrysamusements.com).

Royal Portrush Golf Club

Irish courses, like those in Scotland, are highly sought after for their lush greens in glorious settings. Serious golfers can get a tee time at the Royal Portrush, a links course that hosted the British Open in 1951 and then again in 2019. Check out the trophy case and historic photos in the clubhouse (green fees generally £220, less most days in off-season). The adjacent, slightly shorter Valley Course is more budget-friendly (green fees £50, 10-minute walk from station, tel. 028/7082-2311, www.royalportrushgolfclub.com).

Portrush Recreation Grounds

For some easygoing exercise right in town, this well-organized park offers lawn-bowling greens (£6/hour with gear), putting greens, tennis courts, and a great kids' play park. You can rent tennis shoes, balls, and rackets, all for £10/hour (Mon-Sat 10:00-dusk, Sun from 12:00, closed mid-Sept-May, tel. 028/7082-4441).

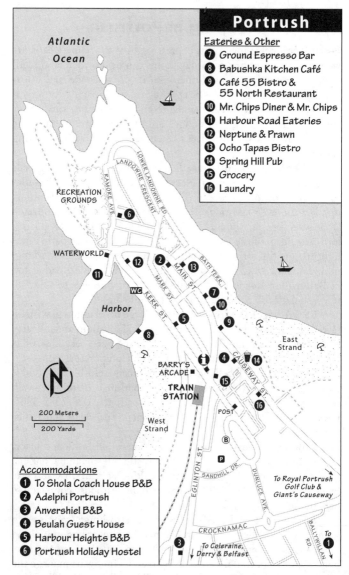

Portrush

Eateries & Other
7 Ground Espresso Bar
8 Babushka Kitchen Café
9 Café 55 Bistro &
   55 North Restaurant
10 Mr. Chips Diner & Mr. Chips
11 Harbour Road Eateries
12 Neptune & Prawn
13 Ocho Tapas Bistro
14 Spring Hill Pub
15 Grocery
16 Laundry

Atlantic Ocean

RECREATION GROUNDS

LANDONNE RD.
LOWER LANDONNE RD.
LANDONNE CRESCENT
RAMORE AVE.

WATERWORLD

BATH TERR.
MAIN ST.
MARK ST.
KERR ST.
WC

Harbor

East Strand

BARRY'S ARCADE

TRAIN STATION

CAUSEWAY ST.

POST

West Strand

200 Meters
200 Yards

EGLINTON ST.
SANDHILL DR.
DUNLUCE AVE.

B
P

To Royal Portrush
Golf Club &
Giant's Causeway

CROCKNAMAC

BALLYWILLAN RD.

To Coleraine,
Derry & Belfast

Accommodations
1 To Shola Coach House B&B
2 Adelphi Portrush
3 Anvershiel B&B
4 Beulah Guest House
5 Harbour Heights B&B
6 Portrush Holiday Hostel

Waterworld

For more fun, consider Waterworld, with pools, waterslides, and bowling (£5, Mon-Sat 10:30-18:00, Sun from 12:00, closed Sept-June; wedged between Harbour Bistro and Ramore Wine Bar overlooking the harbor, tel. 028/7082-2001).

Sleeping in Portrush

Portrush's hotels range from depressing to ritzy. Some B&Bs are well worn. August and Saturday nights can be crowded (and loud) with young party groups. Otherwise, it's a "you take half a loaf when you can get it" town. Sea views are worth paying for only if you get a bay window. Ask for a big room (some doubles can be very small; twins are bigger). Lounges are invariably grand and have bay-window views. Most places listed have lots of stairs. Parking is easy.

$$$ Shola Coach House is a memorable treat that exceeds other B&B experiences in Northern Ireland. About 1.5 miles south of town, it's easiest for drivers (otherwise it's a 30-minute uphill walk or £5 taxi ride). The secluded, 170-year-old, renovated stone structure once housed the coaches and horses for a local landlord. The decor of the four rooms is tasteful, the garden patio is delightful, and Sharon and David Schindler keep it spotless (parking, no kids under 18, 2-night minimum, 110A Gateside Road at top of Ballywillan Road, tel. 028/7082-5925, mobile 075-6542-7738, www.sholabandb.com, sholabandb@gmail.com).

$$$ Adelphi Portrush is the best large hotel in town, with 28 tastefully furnished modern rooms, an ideal location, and a hearty bistro downstairs (family rooms, 67 Main Street, tel. 028/7082-5544, www.adelphiportrush.com, stay@adelphiportrush.com).

$ Anvershiel B&B, with seven nicely refurbished rooms, is a great value (RS%, family rooms, parking, 10-minute walk south of train station, 16 Coleraine Road, tel. 028/7082-3861, www.anvershiel.com, enquiries@anvershiel.com, Alan and Janice Thompson).

$ Beulah Guest House is a traditional, old-fashioned place. It's centrally located and run by cheerful Helen and Charlene McLaughlin, with 11 prim rooms (parking at rear, 16 Causeway Street, tel. 028/7082-2413, www.beulahguesthouse.com, stay@beulahguesthouse.com).

$ Harbour Heights B&B rents nine retro-homey rooms, each named after a different town in County Antrim. It has an inviting guest lounge, supervised by two tabby cats, overlooking the harbor. Friendly South African hosts Sam and Tim Swart manage the place with a light hand (family rooms, 17 Kerr Street, tel. 028/7082-2765, mobile 078-9586-6534, www.harbourheightsportrush.com, info@harbourheightsportrush.com).

¢ Portrush Holiday Hostel offers clean, well-organized, economical lodging (private rooms available, tel. 028/7082-1288, mobile 078-5037-7367, 24 Princess Street, www.portrushholidayhostel.com, portrushholidayhostel@gmail.com).

Eating in Portrush

As a family getaway from Belfast and a beach escape for students from the nearby university in Coleraine, Portrush has more than enough fish-and-chips joints. And in recent years, the refined tastes of affluent golfers and urban professionals out for a weekend has prompted the town to up its culinary game.

LUNCH SPOTS

$ Ground Espresso Bar makes fresh sandwiches and panini, soup, and great coffee (daily 9:00-17:00, July-Aug until 22:00, 52 Main Street, tel. 028/7082-5979).

$ Babushka Kitchen Café serves fresh sandwiches and creative desserts with an unbeatable view—actually out on the pier (daily 9:15-17:00, West Strand Promenade, tel. 077-8750-2012).

$$ Café 55 Bistro serves basic sandwiches with a great patio view (daily 9:00-17:00, longer hours in summer, shorter hours off-season, 1 Causeway Street, beneath fancier 55 North restaurant, tel. 028/7082-2811).

$ Mr. Chips Diner and **Mr. Chips** are the local favorites for cheap, quality fish-and-chips (daily 12:00-22:00, 12 and 20 Main Street). Both are mostly takeout, while the diner also has tables. The smaller Mr. Chips cooks with lard (less healthy, more traditional). The bigger Mr. Chips cooks with vegetable oil (healthier) and hangs the stars and bars of the Confederate flag on the wall (when it comes to the Catholic/Protestant issue, this is a conservative town with some redneck tendencies).

Groceries: For picnic supplies, try **Spar Market** (daily 7:00-20:00, summer until 23:00, across from Barry's Arcade on Main Street, tel. 028/7082-5447).

HARBOUR ROAD EATERIES

A creative, diverse, and lively cluster of restaurants overlooks the harbor. With the same owner, they all have a creative and fun energy, are often jammed with diners, and are basically open from about 17:00 to 22:00. All are described at RamoreRestaurant.com. Only Basalt and Mermaid Kitchen & Bar take reservations.

$$ Ramore Wine Bar is a salty, modern place, with an inviting menu ranging from steaks to vegetarian items. It's very casual but with serious cuisine. Order at the bar and take a table (open daily for lunch and dinner, tel. 028/7082-4313).

$$ The Tourist is a hit for its pizza, tacos, burritos, and burgers. It's noisy and youthful with tight seating (daily, tel. 028/7082-3311).

$$$ Harbour Bistro is dark, noisy, and sprawling with a sloppy crowd enjoying chargrilled meat and fish (daily, no kids after 20:00, tel. 028/7082-2430).

$$ Mermaid Kitchen & Bar is all about fresh fish dishes with a Spanish twist and great harbor views. Those at the bar get a bird's-eye view of the fun banter and precision teamwork of the kitchen staff (closed Mon-Tue, no kids under 18, tel. 028/7082-6969).

$$ Basalt has Spanish-influenced small plates and an outdoor terrace (closed Wed-Thu, no kids under 18, tel. 028/7082-6969).

$$$ Neptune & Prawn (just across the inlet from the others) is the most yacht-clubby of the bunch. Serving Asian and other international food, with a fancy presentation and many plates designed to be shared, this place is noisy and high-energy, with rock music playing (daily, no kids under 18, tel. 028/7082-2448).

OTHER DINING OPTIONS OFF THE HARBOR

$$$ 55 North (named for the local latitude) has the best sea views in town, with windows on three sides. The filling pasta-and-fish dishes, along with some Asian plates, are a joy. Their lunch and early-bird special (order by 18:45) is three courses at the cost of the entrée (daily 12:30-14:00 & 17:00-21:00, 1 Causeway Street, tel. 028/7082-2811).

$$ Ocho Tapas Bistro brings sunny Spanish cuisine to the chilly north, featuring a great early-bird menu—choose any three tapas from a varied list (Tue-Fri 17:00-21:30, Sat-Sun 12:30-14:30 & 17:00-22:00, closed Mon, 92 Main Street, tel. 028/7082-4110).

PUBS

Harbour Bar is an old-fashioned pub next to the Harbour Bistro (see above). **Harbour Gin Bar** (above Harbour Bar) is romantic and classy—a rustic, spacious, and inviting place with live acoustic folk music from 20:30 (almost nightly) and a fun selection of 45 gins.

Neptune & Prawn Cocktail Bar (above the restaurant by the same name; see listing above) has great views over the harbor and is the most classy-yet-inviting place in town for a drink.

Spring Hill Pub is a good bet for its friendly vibe and occasional live music, including traditional sessions Thursdays at 21:30 (17 Causeway Street, tel. 028/7082-3361).

Portrush Connections

Consider a £17.50 Zone 4 iLink smartcard, good for all-day Translink train and bus use in Northern Ireland (£16.50 top-up for each additional day). Translink's website has the latest schedules and prices for both trains and buses in Northern Ireland (tel. 028/9066-6630, www.translink.co.uk).

From Portrush by Train to: Coleraine (hourly, 12 minutes), **Belfast** (15/day, 2 hours, transfer in Coleraine), **Dublin** (7/day, 5 hours, transfer in Belfast). Note that on Sundays, service is greatly reduced.

By Bus to: Belfast (12/day, 2 hours; scenic coastal route, 2.5 hours), **Dublin** (4/day, 5.5 hours).

Antrim Coast

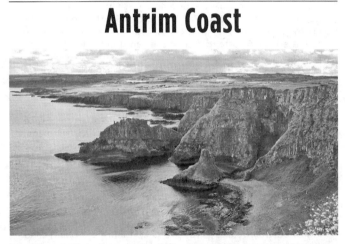

The craggy 20-mile stretch of the Antrim Coast extending eastward from Portrush to Ballycastle rates second only to the tip of the Dingle Peninsula as the prettiest chunk of coastal Ireland. From your base in Portrush, you have a grab bag of sightseeing choices: Giant's Causeway, Old Bushmills Distillery, Dunluce Castle, Carrick-a-Rede Rope Bridge, and Rathlin Island.

It's easy to weave these sights together by car, but connections are patchy by public transportation. Bus service is viable only in summer, and taxi fares are reasonable only for the sights closest to Portrush (Dunluce Castle, Old Bushmills Distillery, and the Giant's Causeway). For details on how to plan your day on the Antrim Coast, and for more on your transportation options, see "Planning Your Time" and "Getting Around the Antrim Coast," at the beginning of this chapter.

The Scottish Connection

The Romans called the Irish the "Scoti" (meaning pirates). When the Scoti crossed the narrow Irish Sea and invaded the land of the Picts 1,500 years ago, that region became known as Scoti-land. Ireland and Scotland were never conquered by the Romans, and they retained similar clannish Celtic traits. Both share the same Gaelic branch of the linguistic tree.

On clear summer days from Carrick-a-Rede, the island of Mull in Scotland—only 17 miles away—is visible. Much closer on the horizon is the boomerang-shaped Rathlin Island, part of Northern Ireland. Rathlin is where Scottish leader Robert the Bruce (a compatriot of William "Braveheart" Wallace) retreated in 1307 after defeat at the hands of the English. Legend has it that he hid in a cave on the island, where he observed a spider patiently rebuilding its web each time a breeze knocked it down. Inspired by the spider's perseverance, Robert gathered his Scottish forces once more and finally defeated the English at the decisive Battle of Bannockburn.

Flush with confidence from his victory, Robert the Bruce decided to open a second front against the English...in Ireland. In 1315, he sent his brother Edward over to enlist their Celtic Irish cousins in an effort to thwart the English. After securing Ireland, Edward hoped to move on and enlist the Welsh, thus cornering England with their pan-Celtic nation. But Edward's timing was bad—Ireland was in the midst of famine. His Scottish troops had to live off the land and began to take food and supplies from the starving Irish. He might also have been trying to destroy Ireland's crops to keep them from being used as a colonial "breadbasket" to feed English troops. The Scots quickly wore out their welcome, and Edward the Bruce was eventually killed in battle near Dundalk in 1318.

This was the first time in history that Ireland was used as a pawn by England's enemies. Spain and France saw Ireland as the English Achilles' heel, and both countries later attempted invasions of the island. The English Tudor and Stuart royalty countered these threats in the 16th and 17th centuries by starting the "plantation" of loyal subjects in Ireland. The only successful long-term settlement by the English was here in Northern Ireland, which remains part of the United Kingdom today.

It's interesting to imagine how things might be different today if Ireland and Scotland had been permanently welded together as a nation 700 years ago. You'll notice the strong Scottish influence in this part of Ireland when you ask a local a question and he answers, "Aye, a wee bit." The Irish joke that the Scots are just Irish people who couldn't swim home.

Sights on the Antrim Coast

▲▲Giant's Causeway

This five-mile-long stretch of coastline is famous for its bizarre basalt columns. The shore is covered with largely hexagonal pillars that stick up at various heights. It's as if the earth were offering God a choice of 37,000 six-sided cigarettes.

Geologists claim the Giant's Causeway was formed by volcanic eruptions more than 60 million years ago. As the surface of the lava flow quickly cooled, it contracted and crystallized into columns (resembling the caked mud at the bottom of a dried-up lakebed, but with far deeper cracks). As the rock later settled and eroded, the columns broke off into the many stair-like steps that now honeycomb the Antrim Coast.

Of course, in actuality, the Giant's Causeway was made by a giant Ulster warrior named Finn MacCool who knew of a rival giant living across the water in Scotland. Finn built a stone bridge over to Scotland to spy on his rival, and found out that the Scottish giant was much bigger. Finn retreated to Ireland and had his wife dress him as a sleeping infant, just in time for the rival giant to come across the causeway to spy on Finn. The rival, shocked at the infant's size, fled back to Scotland in terror of whoever had sired this giant baby. Breathing a sigh of relief, Finn tore off the baby clothes and prudently knocked down the bridge. Today, proof of this encounter exists in the geologic formation that still extends undersea and surfaces in Scotland (at the island of Staffa).

Cost and Hours: The Giant's Causeway is free and always open. But in practice, anyone parking there needs to pay £12.50/adult. This includes an audioguide (or one-hour guided walk; leaves regularly with demand), a map, and entrance to the visitors center (daily 9:00-18:00, June-Sept until 19:00, Nov-March until 17:00, tel. 028/2073-1855, www.nationaltrust.org.uk/giantscauseway). A gift shop and café are in the visitors center.

Visiting the Causeway: For cute variations on the Finn story, as well as details on the ridiculous theories of modern geologists, start in the **Giant's Causeway Visitor Centre.** It's filled with kid-friendly interactive exhibits giving a worthwhile history of the Giant's Causeway, with a regional overview. On the far wall opposite the entrance, check out the interesting three-minute video showing the evolution of the causeway from molten lava to the geometric,

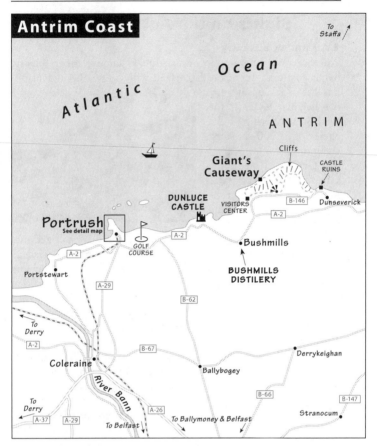

geologic wonderland of today. The large 3-D model of the causeway offers a bird's-eye view of the region. There's also an exhibit about the history of tourism here from the 18th century.

The **causeway** itself is the highlight of the entire coast. The audioguide highlights 15 stops along the causeway, each with a photo of the formation being described; all stops are shown on the map you'll receive with your ticket.

From the visitors center, you have several options for visiting the causeway:

Short and Easy: A **shuttle bus** (4/hour from 9:00, £1 each way) zips tourists a half-mile from the visitors center down a paved road to the causeway. This standard route (the blue dashed line on your map) offers the easiest access and follows the stops on your audioguide. Many choose to walk down and then take the shuttle back up.

Mid-Level Hike: For a longer hike and a more varied dose of causeway views, consider the cliff-top trail (red dashed line on

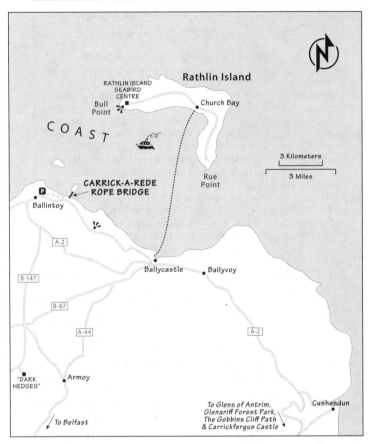

N

Rathlin Island

RATHLIN ISLAND
SEABIRD
CENTRE

Bull
Point

Church Bay

C O A S T

3 Kilometers

3 Miles

Rue
Point

**CARRICK-A-REDE
ROPE BRIDGE**

P

Ballintoy

A-2

B-147

B-67

Ballycastle

Ballyvoy

A-44

A-2

"DARK
HEDGES"

Armoy

Cushendun

To Glens of Antrim,
Glenariff Forest Park,
The Gobbins Cliff Path
& Carrickfergus Castle

To Belfast

your map). Take the easy-to-follow trail uphill from the visitors center 10 minutes to Weir's Snout, the great fence-protected precipice viewpoint. Then hike 15 minutes farther (level) to reach the Shepherd's Steps. Then grab the banister on the steep (and slippery-when-wet) stairs that zigzag down the switchbacks toward the water. At the T-junction, go 100 yards right, to the tower-

ing rock pipes of "the Organ." (You can detour another 500 yards east around the headland, but the trail dead-ends there.) Now retrace your steps west on the trail (don't go up the steps again), continuing down to the tidal zone, where the "Giant's Boot" (6-foot boulder, on the right) provides some photo fun. Another 100 yards

For *Game of Thrones* Fans

Even if you don't give a bloody Stark about the *Game of Thrones* TV saga, you'll notice references to it as you travel around Northern Ireland. Much of the series was filmed here, both on location and in the Titanic Quarter studio in Belfast. An average visit to the Antrim Coast is a traipse through the set: Dragonstone, the Stormlands, and the Iron Islands were brought to life along the same route that travelers use to see Dunluce Castle and Carrick-a-Rede Rope Bridge. For those who are truly interested in the approach of a very long winter, there are several options: both McComb's (www.mccombscoaches.com; see page 485) and Game of Thrones Tours (www.gameofthronestours.com) run day tours from Belfast or Derry to various spots in the seven kingdoms.

With a car, use the map at www.discovernorthernireland.com/GameofThrones to find filming locations. Without leaving County Antrim, you can visit Ballintoy Harbour (Stormlands), Larrybane (Iron Islands), Murlough Bay (Storm's End), and the Dark Hedges (King's Road) with no more than an hour's driving time. Just avoid any reenactments, as the nearest major hospital that treats dragon burns is in Belfast.

farther is the dramatic point where the causeway meets the sea. Just beyond that, at the asphalt turnaround, is the shuttle bus stop.

Just below the bus stop is a fine place to explore the uneven, wave-splashed rock terraces, watching your every easy-to-trip step. Look for "wishing coins"—rusted and bent—that have been jammed into the cracks of rock just behind the turnaround (where the trail passes through a notch in the 20-foot-high rock wall).

Return to the visitors center by hiking up the paved lane (listening to the audioguide at stops along the way). Or, from the turnaround, you can catch the shuttle bus back to the visitors center (just line up and pay the driver).

Longer Hike: Hardy hikers and avid photographers can join the guided **Clifftop Experience** trek exploring the trail that runs along a five-mile section of the Causeway Coast, starting at the meager ruins of Dunseverick Castle—east of Giant's Causeway on B-146 (yellow dashed line on your map). The hike is led by a naturalist, who ventures beyond the usual big-bus tourist crowds to explore the rugged rim of this most-scenic section of the Antrim Coast. Expect undulating grass and gravel paths with no WC options and no shelter whatsoever from bad weather (£35, includes parking; daily at 12:15, Nov-Feb at 10:15, must book online by 16:00 a day ahead; allow 3.5 hours, no kids under 12, hikers meet at visitors center and bus to Dunseverick trailhead, tel. 028/2073-

3419, www.giantscausewaytickets.com, northcoastbookings@ nationaltrust.org.uk).

The Clifftop Experience hike route is a public right-of-way and can also be done on your own. If going independently, a good plan is to take the Causeway Rambler bus (see "Getting Around the Antrim Coast," earlier) or a taxi from Portrush to Dunseverick Castle and hike to the visitors center (there's also limited parking at the Dunseverick Castle trailhead). From the castle, hike west, following the cliff-hugging contours of Benbane Head back to the visitors center. You'll generally have a fence on your left and the cliff on the right, so there's little doubt about the route. When you reach the visitors center, it's easy to arrange travel back to Portrush by taxi or Rambler bus (check bus schedules ahead of time at Portrush TI or at www.translink.co.uk). For more info on hiking the route without a naturalist, see www.visitcausewaycoastandglens.com and search for "North Antrim Cliff Path." Note that occasional rock falls and slides can close this trail (ask first at Portrush TI, or call ahead to visitors center).

▲▲Old Bushmills Distillery

Bushmills claims to be the world's oldest distillery. Though King James I (of Bible translation fame) only granted Bushmills its li-

cense to distill "Aqua Vitae" in 1608, whiskey has been made here since the 13th century. Distillery tours waft you through the process, making it clear that Irish whiskey is triple distilled—and therefore smoother than Scotch whisky (distilled merely twice).

Cost and Hours: £9 for 45-minute tour followed by a tasting; tours go on the half-hour Mon-Sat 9:30-16:00 (last tour), Sun from 12:00; Nov-March tours run Mon-Sat 10:00-15:30 (last tour), Sun from 12:00; tours are limited to 18 people and can fill up (only groups of 15 or more can reserve ahead); note that in July, you can still tour, but the distillery machinery is shut down for annual maintenance; tel. 028/2073-3218, www.bushmills.com.

Visiting the Distillery: Tours start with the mash pit, which is filled with a porridge that eventually becomes whiskey. (The leftovers of that porridge are fed to the county's particularly happy cows.) Bushmills is made of only three ingredients: malted barley, water, and yeast. You'll see a huge room full of whiskey aging in oak casks—casks already used to make bourbon, sherry, and port.

Whiskey picks up its color and personality from this wood (which breathes and has an effective life of 30 years). Bushmills shapes the flavor of its whiskey by carefully finessing the aging process—often in a mix of these casks.

To see the distillery at its lively best, visit when the 100 workers are staffing the machinery—Monday morning through Friday noon. (The still is still on weekends and in July.) The finale, of course, is the opportunity for a sip in the 1608 Bar—the former malt barn. Visitors get a single glass of their choice. Hot-drink enthusiasts might enjoy a cinnamon-and-cloves hot toddy. Teetotalers can just order tea. After the tour, you can get a decent lunch in the hospitality room.

Shoppers: The distillery cannot ship purchases. See page 560 for details on bringing alcohol back home in your luggage.

Nearby: The distillery is just outside of **Bushmills town,** which is a Unionist festival of red, white, and blue flags and bunting. Banners posted throughout the town celebrate illustrious Ulster men and women and people far and wide with Ulster heritage (like Mark Twain and Dolly Parton).

▲▲Carrick-a-Rede Rope Bridge

For 200 years, fishermen hung a narrow, 90-foot-high bridge (planks strung between wires) across a 65-foot-wide chasm between the mainland and a tiny island. Today, the bridge (while not the original version) gives access to the sea stack where salmon nets were set (until 2002) during summer months to catch the fish turning and hugging the coast's corner. (The complicated system is described at the gateway.) A pleasant, 30-minute, one-mile  walk from the parking lot takes you down to the rope bridge. Cross over to the island for fine views and great seabird-watching, especially during nesting season. A coffee shop and WCs are near the parking lot.

Cost and Hours: £9 trail and bridge fee, book online in advance; daily 9:30-18:00, June-Aug until 20:00, Nov-Feb until 15:30, last entry 45 minutes before closing; tel. 028/2076-9839, www.nationaltrust.org.uk.

Advance Tickets Recommended: Tickets sell out and lines can be long. Buying a timed-entry ticket in advance will save you time and possibly the frustration of not getting a ticket at all (available at http://carrickaredetickets.com; can sell out up to 4 months in advance). Without an advance ticket, arrive as early as possible.

Nearby Viewpoint: If you have a car and a picnic lunch, don't miss the terrific coastal scenic rest area one mile steeply uphill and east of Carrick-a-Rede (on B-15 to Ballycastle). This grassy area offers one of the best picnic views in Northern Ireland (tables but no WCs). Feast on bird's-eye views of the rope bridge, nearby Rathlin Island, and the not-so-distant Island of Mull in Scotland.

▲Dunluce Castle

These romantic ruins, perched dramatically on the edge of a rocky headland, are a testimony to this region's turbulent past. Dur-

ing the Middle Ages, the castle was a prized fortification. But on a stormy night in 1639, dinner was interrupted as half of the kitchen fell into the sea, taking the servants with it. That was the last straw for the lady of the castle. The countess of Antrim packed up and moved inland, and the castle "began its slow submission to the forces of nature."

Cost and Hours: £5.50, daily 10:00-17:00, winter until 16:00, tel. 028/2073-1938.

Visiting the Castle: While it's one of the largest castles in Northern Ireland and is beautifully situated, there's precious little left to see among Dunluce's broken walls. Look for distinctively hexagonal stones embedded in the castle walls, plucked straight from the unique pillars of rock making up the nearby Giant's Causeway.

Before entering, catch the eight-minute video about the history of the castle (across from the ticket desk). The ruins themselves are dotted with plaques that show interesting artists' renditions of how the place would have looked 400 years ago.

There were primitive fortifications here hundreds of years before the castle was built. Your guide will point out the underground hiding place where locals would try to wait out Viking raiders. But the 16th century saw the biggest expansion of the castle, financed by treasure salvaged from a shipwreck. In 1588, the Spanish Armada's *Girona*—overloaded with sailors and the valuables of three abandoned sister ships—sank on her way home after the aborted mission against England. More than 1,300 drowned, and only five survivors washed ashore. The shipwreck was more fully excavated in 1967, and a bounty of golden odds and silver ends wound up in Belfast's Ulster Museum.

Rathlin Island

The only inhabited island off the coast of Northern Ireland, Rathlin is a quiet haven for hikers, birdwatchers, and seal spotters. Less than seven miles from end to end, this "L"-shaped island is reachable by ferry from the town of Ballycastle.

Getting There: The Rathlin Island passenger-only ferry departs from Ballycastle, just east of Carrick-a-Rede. There are 11 trips per day in summer: seven fast 30-minute trips, and four slower one-hour trips (£12 round-trip per passenger, smart to book ahead, as the ferry can sell out on summer days; tel. 028/2076-9299, www.rathlinballycastleferry.com).

Drivers can park in Ballycastle (only special-permit holders can take a car onto the ferry). A taxi from Portrush to Ballycastle runs £30 one-way. Bus service from Portrush to Ballycastle is spotty (check with the TI in Portrush, or contact Translink—tel. 028/9066-6630, www.translink.co.uk).

Visiting Rathlin Island: Rathlin's population of 110 islanders clusters around the ferry dock at Church Bay. Here you'll find the **Rathlin Boathouse Visitor Centre,** which operates as the island's TI (daily 10:00-12:30 & 13:00-17:00, closed in winter, on the bay 100 yards east of the ferry dock, tel. 028/2076-0054).

In summer, a shuttle bus (£5 round-trip) meets arriving ferries and drives visitors to the **Rathlin Island Seabird Centre** at the west end of the island. Entry to the Seabird Centre includes a tour of its unique lighthouse, extending down the cliff with its beacon at the bottom (£5, daily 10:00-16:00, May-Aug until 17:00, closed Oct-Feb). It's upside-down because the coast guard wants the light visible only from a certain distance out to sea. The bird observation terrace at the center (next to the lighthouse) overlooks one of the most dramatic coastal views in Ireland—a sheer drop of more than 300 feet to craggy sea stacks just offshore that are draped in thousands of seabirds. Bring your most powerful zoom lens for photos.

Rathlin has seen its fair share of history. Flint ax heads were quarried here in Neolithic times. The island was one of the first in Ireland to be raided by Vikings, in 795. Robert the Bruce hid out from English pursuers on Rathlin in the early 1300s (see "The Scottish Connection" sidebar, earlier). In the late 1500s, local warlord Sorely Boy MacDonnell stashed his extended family on Rathlin and waited on the mainland at Dunluce Castle to face his English enemies...only to watch in horror as they headed for the island instead to massacre his loved ones. And in 1917, a WWI U-boat sank the British cruiser HMS *Drake* in Church Bay. The wreck is now a popular scuba-dive destination, 60 feet below the surface.

▲Antrim Mountains and Glens

Not particularly high (never more than 1,500 feet), the Antrim Mountains are cut by a series of large glens running northeast to the sea. Glenariff, with its waterfalls—especially the Mare's Tail—is the most beautiful of the nine glens (described next). Travelers going by car can take a pleasant drive from Portrush to Belfast, sticking to the (more scenic but less direct) A-2 road that stays near the coast and takes in parts of all the Glens of Antrim.

▲Glenariff Forest Park

Glenariff Forest Park offers scenic picnic spots and lush hiking trails as well as a cozy tea shop. The parking lot alone has a lovely view down the glen to the sea. You'll find more spectacular scenery on the three-mile waterfall walkway trail along the river gorge, while an easygoing half-mile stroll on the viewpoint trail via the ornamental gardens also provides lovely views (£5 parking fee, daily 10:00-dusk, trail map available at café onsite, tel. 028/7034-0870, www.nidirect.gov.uk).

Getting There: The entry is off A-43 (via A-26; eight miles south of Cushendall, follow signs).

Nearby: Continue along the A-2 scenic coastal route and take a short jog up to Cushendall, where there's a nice beach for a picnic, or just head south on A-2 toward the Gobbins Cliff Path and the castle at Carrickfergus (see listings in the Belfast chapter).

BELFAST

Northern Ireland's capital city is best known for its role in the Troubles, and as the birthplace of the *Titanic* (and many other ships that didn't sink).

Today the historic Titanic Quarter symbolizes the rise of Belfast. The city is bristling with cranes and busy with tourists. It's hard to believe that the bright and bustling pedestrian center was once a subdued, traffic-free security zone. These days, while Catholics and Protestants still generally live and study in segregated zones, they are totally integrated where they work—and they all root for the Belfast Giants ice hockey team. Aggressive sectarian murals are slowly being repainted with scenes celebrating heritage pride... less carnage, more culture. It feels like a new morning in Belfast.

PLANNING YOUR TIME

If you're staying in Dublin and not planning on visiting Belfast, reconsider. A long day trip from Dublin to Belfast is one of the most interesting days you could have anywhere in Ireland. It's just a two-hour train ride away—about €40 for "day return" tickets, and much less if bought online in advance.

Day Trip from Dublin

Here's how I'd do it (any day but Sun when trains don't run as early or late):

7:35	Catch the train from Dublin's Connolly Station
9:45	Arrive at Belfast's Lanyon Place/Central Station
11:00	Take the free City Hall tour, browse the pedestrian zone, have lunch

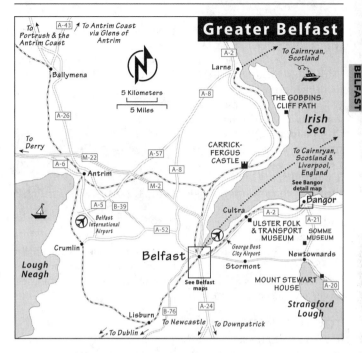

Greater Belfast

13:00 Take a taxi tour of the sectarian neighborhoods in West Belfast

15:00 Visit the Titanic Belfast Museum (after midday crowds subside)

17:00 Dinner in the Titanic Quarter or Cathedral Quarter

20:00 Catch the train back to Dublin

With More Time

If you're circling Ireland by car, Belfast can easily fill two days of sightseeing. On the first day, follow my day-trip itinerary. On the second day, consider side-tripping to sights outside of town, such as the Ulster Folk Park and Transport Museum or Carrickfergus Castle.

Orientation to Belfast

Belfast is flat and spread out. Restaurants and live music venues are all within walking distance of the town center. When planning, think of Belfast as having four sightseeing zones:

Central Belfast: The perfectly walkable city center has a dozen or so mostly minor sights that are never crowded and often free. Review the options and lace together your own plan (keeping opening days and times in mind). Sights include Donegall Square,

City Hall, pedestrian shopping areas, and the Cathedral Quarter with its lively night scene.

West Belfast: The working-class, sectarian neighborhoods along Falls Road and Shankill Road, while walkable, are much more interesting with a taxi tour (90 minutes, inexpensive, and almost as easy as hailing a taxi).

Titanic Quarter: The northeast bank of the River Lagan is dominated by the Titanic Belfast Museum, but there's much more here, including a wonderful riverside stroll with a string of sightseeing stops along the way.

South Belfast: This neighborhood is really just a strategic hit on the great Ulster Museum or Botanic Gardens, depending on your interest. This is where you'll find more cozy B&B guesthouses, rather than just chain hotels.

TOURIST INFORMATION

The modern TI (look for *Visit Belfast* sign) faces City Hall and has a courteous staff and baggage storage (£4/bag for 4 hours, £6/bag for 8 hours; Mon-Sat 9:00-17:30, June-Sept until 19:00, Sun 11:00-16:00 year-round; 9 Donegall Square North, tel. 028/9024-6609, http://visitbelfast.com). City walking tours depart from the TI (see "Tours in Belfast," later). Pick up a free copy of *Visit Belfast*, which lists all the sightseeing and evening entertainment options.

ARRIVAL IN BELFAST

By Train: Arriving at Belfast's Lanyon Place/Central Station, take the Centrelink bus, which loops to Donegall Square, where you'll find City Hall and the TI (4/hour, free with any train or bus ticket, the stop is out the station and 50 yards to the right). Allow £6 for a taxi to Donegall Square or the Titanic Belfast Museum; £10 to my accommodation listings south of the university.

Slower trains arc through the city, stopping at several downtown stations, including Great Victoria Street Station (most central, near Donegall Square and most hotels) and Botanic Station (close to the university, Botanic Gardens, and some recommended lodgings). It's easy and cheap to connect stations by train (£1.50).

If day-tripping into Belfast from Bangor, use the station closest to your targeted sights. Note that trains cost the same from Bangor to all three Belfast stations (Lanyon Place/Central, Great Victoria Street, and Botanic).

Belfast's Troubled History

Seventeenth-century Belfast was just a village. With the influx, or "plantation," of mostly Scottish settlers—and the subjugation of the native Irish—Belfast blossomed, spurred by the success of local industries. The city built many of the world's biggest and finest ships. And when the American Civil War shut down the US cotton industry, the linen mills of Belfast were beneficiaries. In fact Belfast became known as "Linen-opolis."

The Industrial Revolution took root in Belfast with a vengeance. While the rest of Ireland remained rural and agricultural, Belfast earned another nickname, "Old Smoke," during the time when many of the brick buildings that you'll see today were built.

The year 1888 marked the birth of modern Belfast. After Queen Victoria granted Belfast city status, it boomed. The population (only 20,000 in 1800) reached 350,000 by 1900. And its citizens built Belfast's centerpiece—its grand City Hall.

Belfast was also busy building ships, from transoceanic liners like the ill-fated *Titanic* to naval vessels during the world wars. (Belfast's famous shipyards were strategic enough to be the target of four German Luftwaffe bombing raids in World War II.) Two huge, mustard-colored, rectangular gantry cranes (built in the 1970s, and once the biggest in the world, nicknamed Samson and Goliath) stand like idle giants over the shipyards—a reminder of Belfast's shipbuilding might.

Of course, the sectarian Troubles ravaged Belfast along with the rest of Northern Ireland from 1969 to 1998—a time when downtown Belfast was ringed with security checks and nearly shut down at night. There was almost no tourism for two decades (and only a few pubs downtown). Thankfully, at the beginning of the 21st century, the peace process began to take root, and investments from south of the border—the Republic of Ireland—injected new life into the dejected shipyards where the *Titanic* was built.

Still, it's a fragile peace. Hateful bonfires, built a month before they're set ablaze, still scorch the pavement in working-class Protestant neighborhoods each July. Pubs with security gates are reminders that the island is still split—and 900,000 Protestant Unionists in the North prefer it that way.

By Car: Driving in Belfast is a pain. Avoid it if possible. Street parking in the city center is geared for short stops (use pay-and-display machines, £0.30/15 minutes, one-hour maximum, Mon-Sat 8:00-18:00, free in evenings and on Sun).

By Plane: For information on Belfast's airports, see the "Belfast Connections" section on page 522.

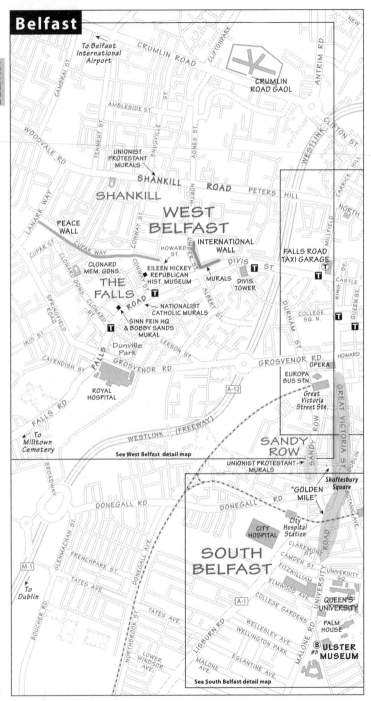

Belfast

To Belfast International Airport

CRUMLIN ROAD

CAMBRAI ST.

CRUMLIN ROAD GAOL

CLIFTONPARK

WESTLINK

CLIFTON ST.

ANTRIM RD.

NEW

AMBLESIDE ST.

WOODVALE RD.

TENNENT ST.

SNUGVILLE ST.

AGNES ST.

SHANKILL

UNIONIST PROTESTANT MURALS

SHANKILL ROAD

PETERS HILL

NORTH

CARRICK

MILLFIELD

WEST BELFAST

LANARK WAY

PEACE WALL

CONWAY ST.

NORTH ST.

HOWARD ST.

INTERNATIONAL WALL

DIVIS ST.

FALLS ROAD TAXI GARAGE

KING ST.

CASTLE ST.

QUEEN ST.

CUPAR ST.

CUPAR WAY

CLONARD GDNS.

CLONARD MEM. GDNS.

CONWAY ST.

EILEEN HICKEY REPUBLICAN HIST. MUSEUM

MURALS

DIVIS TOWER

COLLEGE SQ. N.

DURHAM ST.

THE FALLS

SPRINGFIELD ROAD

CLONARD ST.

IRIS ST.

FALLS ROAD

NATIONALIST CATHOLIC MURALS

SINN FEIN HQ & BOBBY SANDS MURAL

ALBERT ST.

HOWARD

LEESON ST.

GROSVENOR RD.

OPERA

CAVENDISH ST.

Dunville Park

GROSVENOR RD.

FALLS RD.

ROYAL HOSPITAL

EUROPA BUS STN.

Great Victoria Street Stn.

GREAT VICTORIA ST.

DUBLIN RD.

To Milltown Cemetery

WESTLINK (FREEWAY)

A-12

SANDY ROW

SANDY ROW

See West Belfast detail map

UNIONIST PROTESTANT MURALS

Shaftesbury Square

BROADWAY

M-1

DONEGALL RD.

DONEGALL RD.

"GOLDEN MILE"

BOTANIC AVE.

GLENMACHAN ST.

FRENCHPARK ST.

DONEGALL AVE.

CITY HOSPITAL

City Hospital Station

CLAREMONT ST.

CAMDEN ST.

FITZWILLIAM

UNIVERSITY SQ.

To Dublin

TATES AVE.

A-1

SOUTH BELFAST

ELMWOOD AVE.

COLLEGE GARDENS

UNIVERSITY RD.

QUEEN'S UNIVERSITY

BOUCHER RD.

NORTHBROOK ST.

TATES AVE.

LISBURN RD.

COLLEGE GARDENS

WELLESLEY AVE.

WELLINGTON PARK

MALONE RD.

PALM HOUSE

ULSTER MUSEUM

B #8

LOWER WINDSOR AVE.

MALONE AVE.

EGLANTINE AVE.

See South Belfast detail map

BELFAST

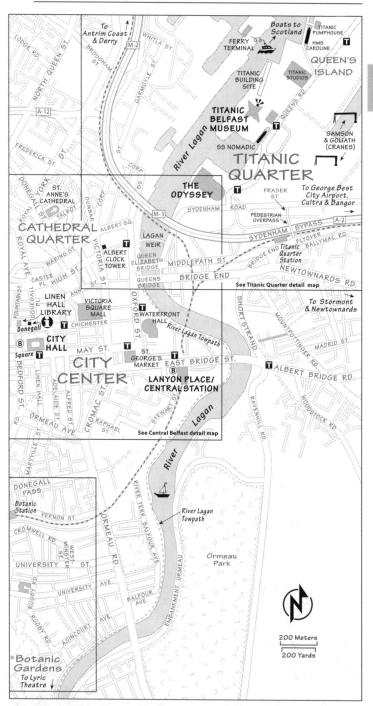

To Antrim Coast & Derry

M-2

Boats to Scotland

FERRY TERMINAL

TITANIC PUMPHOUSE

HMS CAROLINE

QUEEN'S ISLAND

TITANIC BUILDING SITE

TITANIC STUDIOS

TITANIC BELFAST MUSEUM

SS NOMADIC

SAMSON & GOLIATH (CRANES)

TITANIC QUARTER

THE ODYSSEY

FRASER ST.

To George Best City Airport, Cultra & Bangor

SYDENHAM ROAD

PEDESTRIAN OVERPASS

SYDENHAM BYPASS

A-2

M-3

ST. ANNE'S CATHEDRAL

CATHEDRAL QUARTER

LAGAN WEIR

ALBERT SQ.

ALBERT CLOCK TOWER

QUEEN ELIZABETH BRIDGE

QUEENS BRIDGE

MIDDLEPATH ST.

BRIDGE END

Titanic Quarter Station

NEWTOWNARDS RD.

BALLYMAC RD.

See Titanic Quarter detail map

To Stormont & Newtownards

LINEN HALL LIBRARY

VICTORIA SQUARE MALL

WATERFRONT HALL

River Lagan Towpath

SHORT STRAND

MOUNT POTTINGER RD.

MADRID ST.

Donegall

CITY HALL

Square

CITY CENTER

ST. GEORGE'S MARKET

LANYON PLACE/ CENTRAL STATION

EAST BRIDGE ST.

ALBERT BRIDGE RD.

RAVENHILL RD.

WOODSTOCK RD.

See Central Belfast detail map

River Lagan

DONEGALL PASS

Botanic Station

VERNON ST.

CROMWELL RD.

WESTMINSTER ST.

UNIVERSITY ST.

UNIVERSITY

RUGBY RD.

RUGBY AVE.

AGINCOURT AVE.

ORMEAU RD.

BALFOUR AVE.

River Lagan Towpath

ORMEAU

Ormeau Park

Botanic Gardens

To Lyric Theatre

N

200 Meters

200 Yards

HELPFUL HINTS

Belfast Visitor Pass: This pass combines sightseeing discounts with iLink smartcards for free bus, rail, and tram rides within the Belfast Visitor Pass Zone (downtown Belfast as far out as the Ulster Folk Park and Transport Museum in Cultra, but not as far as Carrickfergus or Bangor). You'll save money with the one-day pass if you visit the Titanic Belfast Museum (£3 discount) and the Ulster Folk Park and Transport Museum (30 percent discount) and connect them by train or bus (free with pass). Buy it at the TI, any train station, either airport, Europa Bus station, or online (1-day pass-£6, 2 consecutive days-£11, 3 days-£14.50, tel. 028/9066-6630, www.translink.co.uk).

Place Names: Place names in Belfast can be confusing. The main train station, long called "Central Station," is now called "Lanyon Place" (many old maps have yet to get the memo). The key reference point in the center is Donegall Square, which is right in front of City Hall. The biggest attraction in town, the museum about the *Titanic,* is branded as "Titanic Belfast." For clarity in this chapter, I'll call it the "Titanic Belfast Museum."

Market: On Friday, Saturday, and Sunday, the Victorian confines of **St. George's Market** are a commotion of commerce and a people-watching delight (see page 495).

Shopping Mall: Victoria Square is a glitzy American-style mall where you can find whatever you need (3 blocks east of City Hall—bordered by Chichester, Victoria, Ann, and Montgomery streets; www.victoriasquare.com).

Phone Tips: For details on making calls between the Republic of Ireland and Northern Ireland, see page 584.

Laundry: Globe Launderers has both self-serve and drop-off service (Mon-Fri 8:00-21:00, Sat until 18:00, Sun 12:00-18:00, 37 Botanic Avenue, tel. 028/9024-3956). **Whistle Cleaners** is handy to hotels south of the university (drop-off service, Mon-Fri 8:30-18:00, Sat 9:00-17:30, closed Sun, 160 Lisburn Road, at intersection with Eglantine Avenue, tel. 028/9038-1297). For locations, see the map on page 511.

Bike Rental: Belfast City Bikes rents bikes of all types, from fancy electric (£50/day) down to Dorothy-and-Toto style (£10/day). It's located at Norm's Bikes, near the Cathedral Quarter (Unit 12 Smithfield Marketplace, Winetavern Street, mobile 079-8081-6057, www.belfastcitybiketours.com). They also offer bike tours (see "Tours in Belfast," later).

GETTING AROUND BELFAST

If you line up your sightseeing logically, you can do most of this flat city on foot. But for more far-flung sights, the train, bus, or tram can be useful. If you plan to use public transit, consider the Belfast Visitor Pass (see "Helpful Hints," earlier).

By Train, Bus, or Tram: Translink operates Belfast's system of trains, buses, and trams (tel. 028/9066-6630, www.translink.co.uk).

At any **train** station, ask about iLink smartcards, which cover one day of unlimited train, tram, and bus travel. The Zone 1 card (£6) covers the city center, Cultra (Ulster Folk Park and Transport Museum), and George Best Belfast City Airport. The handy Zone 2 card (£11) adds Bangor and Carrickfergus Castle. The Zone 3 card (£14.50) is only useful for reaching Belfast's distant international airport. Zone 4 (£17.50) gets you anywhere in Northern Ireland, including Portrush and Derry. For those lingering in the North, one-week cards offer even better deals. Without a pass, if you're traveling from Belfast to only one destination—Carrickfergus Castle, Cultra, or Bangor—a "day return" ticket is cheaper than two one-way tickets.

Pink-and-white city **buses** go from Donegall Square East to Malone Road and my recommended accommodations (any #8 bus, 3/hour, covered by iLink smartcards, otherwise £2.40, £4.20 all-day pass, cheaper after 9:30 and on Sun). Sunday service is less frequent.

The slick two-line Glider **tram** system opened in 2018 and connects East and West Belfast (line #G1) and downtown with the Titanic Quarter (line #G2). Rides on these "trams on wheels" cost £2 (6/hour, ticket machines at each stop, covered by iLink smartcards). The #G2 is particularly handy for travelers connecting City Hall with all the Titanic area sights.

By Taxi: Taxis are reasonable (£3 drop charge plus £1.60/mile) and a good option—but they can be hard to flag down. Locals routinely call for a cab, as do restaurants and hotels for their guests. Try **Valu Cabs** (tel. 028/9080-9080). If you're going up Falls Road, ride a shared cab (explained later, under "Touring the Sectarian Neighborhoods"). Uber is nicknamed "Uber Expensive" here—it doesn't work well.

Tours in Belfast

Beyond the tours listed below, I highly recommend visiting the **sectarian neighborhoods** in West Belfast on a taxi or walking tour (see "Touring the Sectarian Neighborhoods" on page 497).

ON FOOT

Belfast's history is more interesting than its actual sights (and its people are really fun to get to know). A guided walk makes a lot of sense here. In fact, you could take several guided walks, as each one would be filled with entertaining insights on different angles of the city (and tours are relatively cheap).

Walking Tours

Free tours are actually "pay what you think it's worth" tours, led by locals who spin a good yarn while sharing the basics of the city. These tours take a couple hours and leave from in front of City Hall and the TI (daily in season at 11:00 and 14:30, just show up, www.belfastfreewalkingtour.com).

Experience Belfast Tours, a step up, introduces you to the city's 300-year history. Their "Hidden Belfast" tour includes City Hall, the Cathedral Quarter, and the Linen Hall Library (£10, 1 hour, daily at 11:00 and 13:00). Their "Troubles" tour covers everything on the "Hidden" tour plus the River Lagan and Belfast's political murals (£15, 2.5 hours, daily at 10:00). Both meet in front of the City Hall main gate facing Donegall Square North (mobile 077-7164-0746, https://experiencebelfast.com).

Belfast Hidden Tours focuses on the culture of North Belfast, going heavy on trade and industry with a sprinkling of rebel sedition and Luftwaffe destruction, while leading visitors to less obvious corners of the city (£10, 1 hour; March-Oct daily at 10:00, 12:00, and 14:00; meet at TI, mobile 079-7189-5746, www.belfasthiddentours.com).

Street Art Tours

Belfast is gaining notoriety for its colorful and edgy **street art.** Rather than sectarian political murals, this is pure urban art with a statement that is hard to understand without a local guide. Ask at the TI or search the web for companies offering these walks.

Food Tours

Taste & Tour offers a palate-pleasing array of food, beer, and whiskey tours, generally in small groups with six stops and lots of fun. Their basic food tour runs Friday and Saturday only and books up well in advance (£60, 3-4 hours, departure points vary, tel. 028/9045-7723, www.tasteandtour.co.uk).

Local Guides

Dee Morgan is smart and delightful. She grew up on Falls Road and can tailor your tour to history, food, politics, or music (£180/half-day, info@deetoursireland.com).

Susie Millar is a sharp former BBC TV reporter with family connections to the *Titanic* tragedy. She can also take you farther afield by car (yours or hers, 3-hour tour-£30/person, mobile 078-5271-6655, www.titanictours-belfast.co.uk).

Lynn Corken is another knowledgeable and flexible Jill-of-all-guiding trades, with a passion for her hometown, politics, history, and Van Morrison (on foot or with her car, £100/half-day, £200/day, mobile 077-7910-2448, lynncorken@hotmail.co.uk).

ON WHEELS
▲Hop-On, Hop-Off Bus Tours

City Sightseeing offers the best quick introduction to the city's political and social history. Their open-top, double-decker buses

link major sights and landmarks, including the Catholic and Protestant working-class neighborhoods, the Stormont Parliament building, Titanic Belfast Museum, and City Hall, with commentary on political murals and places of interest. The route has convenient stops near several recommended hotels: Fisherwick Place (Jurys Inn), Shaftsbury Square (Benedicts Hotel and Belfast International City Hostel), and Malone Road (Malone Lodge and Wellington Park Hotel). Pay cash on the bus (£14/24 hours, £15/48 hours, 2/hour, fewer in winter, daily 10:00-16:00, 20 stops, 1.5-hour loop; departs from Castle Place on High Street, 2 blocks west of Albert Memorial Clock Tower; tel. 028/9032-1321, http://belfastcitysightseeing.com).

City Tours offers a route with more than 20 stops. It starts on High Street (near Albert Clock), then veers westward to take in Falls and Shankill roads (£11/24 hours, £12.50/72 hours, pay cash on bus or book in advance, 2/hour, daily 9:45-16:45, tel. 028/9032-1912, www.citytoursbelfast.com).

Countryside Bus Tours

McComb's offers several big-bus tours, day-tripping out of Belfast to distant points. Their "Giant's Causeway Tour" visits Carrickfergus Castle (photo stop), the Giant's Causeway, Dunluce Castle (photo stop), and Carrick-a-Rede Rope Bridge (£25, daily depending on demand, book through and depart from recommended Belfast International City Hostel, pickup around 9:00, back to Belfast by 19:00). Their *"Game of Thrones* Tour" visits many of the sites where the hit TV series was filmed (£35, pickup at 8:30, return by 19:00, tel. 028/9031-5333, www.mccombscoaches.com).

Bike Tours

Belfast City Bikes offers two tours—one in the city and one in the countryside. The "City Bike Tour" stays urban for nine miles and rides thorough the Titanic Quarter, St. Georges Market, and Queen's University (£30, 3 hours). The "Bike and Brew Tour" goes into the countryside for 12 miles along the River Lagan Towpath, ending at the Hilden Brewery (£50 plus £4 train trip back to Belfast, lunch included, 4 hours). Both depart Thu-Sun at 10:00 (helmets included, reserve ahead—for contact info see "Bike Rental" under "Helpful Hints," earlier).

BY BOAT
Harbor Tours

The **Lagan Boat Company** offers a one-hour tour with an entertaining guide showing the shipyards, the fruits of the city's £800 million investment in its harbor, and the rusty *Titanic* heritage (£12; April-Oct daily sailings at 12:30, 14:00, and 15:30; fewer off-season, tel. 028/9024-0124, www.laganboatcompany.com, Joyce). Tours depart from near the Lagan Weir just past the Albert Clock Tower.

Sights in Belfast

Belfast breaks down into four sightseeing zones: Central Belfast (government center, shopping and restaurant district, trendy nightlife), West Belfast (both Republican and Loyalist sectarian neighborhoods), the Titanic Quarter (superstar museum and riverside walk), and South Belfast (college vibe, good hotels and B&Bs, gardens and history museum).

CENTRAL BELFAST

The sights of central Belfast are mostly minor but fun to check out. Nearly all are within a ten-minute walk of City Hall.

Donegall Square and Nearby
▲▲City Hall

This grand structure's 173-foot-tall copper dome dominates Donegall Square at the center of town. Built between 1898 and 1906, with its statue of Queen Victoria scowling down Belfast's main drag and the Neoclassical dome looming behind her, City Hall is a stirring sight. Free tours of the building run daily, and the worthwhile 16-room Belfast History and Culture exhibit fills the ground floor. It covers the history of the city, culture, industry, the World War II bombings, and the Troubles.

Cost and Hours: City Hall—free, daily 8:00-17:00; Belfast History and Culture exhibit—free, daily 9:00-17:00; audioguide-£3.50; Bobbin coffee shop on ground floor, tel. 028/9032-0202, www.belfastcity.gov.uk/cityhall.

Tours: Free 45-minute tours run Mon-Fri at 10:00, 11:00, 14:00, 15:00, and 16:00; Sat-Sun at 12:00, 14:00, 15:00, and 16:00 (fewer off-season); drop by, call, or check online to confirm schedule and book a spot.

Linen Hall Library

Across the street from City Hall, the 200-year-old Linen Hall Library welcomes guests (notice the red hand above the front door facing Donegall Square North; for more on its meaning, see the sidebar on page 512). Described as "Ulster's attic," the library takes pride in being a neutral space where anyone trying to make sense of the sectarian conflict can view the "Troubled Images," a historical collection of engrossing political posters. The library has a fine hardbound ambience and a royal newspaper reading room. Climb to the top floor and then go down the back staircase, where the walls are lined with fascinating original posters from those tough times.

Cost and Hours: Free, Mon-Fri 9:30-17:30, closed Sat-Sun, 45-minute tours (£5) run daily at 10:30, 17 Donegall Square North, tel. 028/9032-1707, www.linenhall.com.

Donegall Square to the Cathedral Quarter

This little stroll through Belfast's shopping district takes you from City Hall to the Cathedral Quarter in 10 minutes or less.

Donegall Square: The front yard of City Hall is littered with statues of historic figures. Take a close look at the **Queen Victoria** monument. It celebrates the industrial might of Belfast: shipping, linen (the woman with the bobbin), and education (the student). At her right is a reminder of how Belfast was a springboard for the European battlefront in World War II—a **monument** dedicated by General Dwight D. Eisenhower in 1945 to the more than 100,000 US troops who were stationed in Northern Ireland. And around to the left (as you face the building), you'll find the thought-provoking **Titanic Memorial Garden.**

Donegall Place: City Hall faces the commercial heart of Belfast. With your back to City Hall, follow Queen Victoria's gaze across the square and down the shopping street called Donegall Place (note the **TI** on the left). Victoria would recognize the fine 19th-century brick buildings—built in the Scottish Baronial style when the Scots dominated Belfast. But she'd be amazed by the changes since then. As a key shipbuilding and industrial port, Belfast was bombed by the Germans in World War II. (On the worst night of bombing more than 900 died.) And, with the Troubles killing the economy in the last decades of the 20th century, little

Belfast at a Glance

▲▲▲**Titanic Belfast Museum** Excellent high-tech exhibit covering the famously infamous ship and local shipbuilding, in a stunning structure on the site where the *Titanic* was built. **Hours:** Daily June-Aug 8:30-19:00, April-May and Sept 9:00-18:00; Oct-March 10:00-17:00. See page 508.

▲▲▲**Sectarian Neighborhoods Taxi Tours** Local cabbies drive visitors through West Belfast's Falls Road and Shankill Road neighborhoods, offering personal perspectives on the slowly fading Troubles. See page 496.

▲▲**City Hall** Central Belfast's polished and majestic celebration of Victorian-era pride built with industrial wealth. **Hours:** Daily 8:00-17:00. See page 486.

▲▲**Live Music** For the cost of a beer, connect with Belfast's culture, people, and music in a pub. **Hours:** Nightly after 21:30. See page 516.

▲**HMS *Caroline*** WWI battleship that looks just like it did at the Battle of Jutland in 1916. **Hours:** Daily 10:00-17:00. See page 509.

▲**St. George's Market** Thriving scene filling a huge Victorian market hall with artisans, junk dealers, street food, and fun. **Hours:** Fri-Sun 9:00-15:00. See page 495.

▲**Ulster Museum** Mixed bag of local artifacts, natural history, and coverage of political events; a good rainy-day option near Queen's University. **Hours:** Tue-Sun 10:00-17:00, closed Mon. See page 510.

was built. With peace in 1998—and government investing to subsidize that peace—the 21st century has been one big building boom.

Ahead of you, look for a **stained-glass window.** While the *Titanic* connection is still strong, the latest craze here is *Game of Thrones* tourism (much of the show was filmed in Northern Ireland). To recognize the show's importance to Ireland's film industry, and please countless fans, Belfast erected six stained-glass windows around town (one for each episode of the final season).

Walk down Donegal Place

▲**Botanic Gardens** Belfast's best green space, featuring the Palm House loaded with delicate tropical vegetation. **Hours:** Gardens daily 7:30 until dusk; Palm House daily 10:00-17:00, Oct-March until 16:00. See page 511.

Near Belfast
▲▲**Ulster Folk Park and Transport Museum** A glimpse into Northern Ireland's hardworking heritage, split between a charming re-creation of past rural life and halls of vehicular innovation (8 miles east of Belfast). **Hours:** March-Sept Tue-Sun 10:00-17:00; Oct-Feb Tue-Fri 10:00-16:00, Sat-Sun from 11:00; closed Mon year-round. See page 513.

▲**Carrickfergus Castle** Northern Ireland's first and most important fortified refuge for invading 12th-century Normans (14 miles northeast of Belfast). **Hours:** Daily 9:00-17:00, Oct-March until 16:00. See page 514.

▲**The Gobbins** Rugged, unique, wave-splashed hiking trail cut into coastal rock, accessible by guided tour (34 miles northeast of Belfast). **Hours:** Visitors center daily 9:30-17:30, guided hikes about hourly in good weather. See page 514.

Near Bangor
▲**Mount Stewart House** Fine 18th-century manor house displaying ruling-class affluence, surrounded by lush and calming gardens (18 miles east of Belfast). **Hours:** Daily 11:00-17:00, closed Nov-Feb. See page 526.

past the **eight stylized sails** celebrating the great ships built here for the White Star Line (their names all end in "ic").

Shopping Streets: At the sail for the *Celtic,* cruise to the right down Castle Lane. This is the busker zone, alive with street music on nice days. Ahead is the striking, modern **"Spirit of Belfast" statue** (a.k.a. the "Onion Rings"). That "spirit" is the spirit of industry—specifically linen and shipbuilding (light and strong, like the statue). The spirit could also be the resilience of this city with its complicated history and the oversized impact it's had in a broader sense (for example, at least 17 US presidents have some Ulster roots).

To the right of the statue (down William Street) is the sleek and modern **Victoria Square Shopping Center,** worth a visit for its free elevator to the top of its glass dome offering grand city

BELFAST

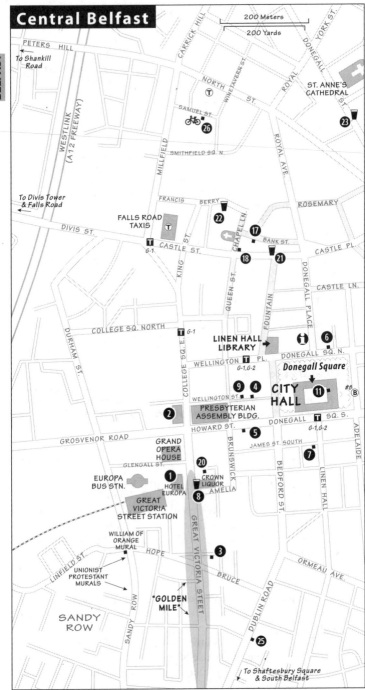

Central Belfast

200 Meters
200 Yards

PETERS HILL

To Shankill Road

WESTLINK (A12 FREEWAY)

CARRICK HILL

NORTH ST.

WHITEHAVEN ST.

ROYAL

DONEGALL

YORK ST.

ST. ANNE'S CATHEDRAL

(T)

SAMUEL ST.

🚲 26

23

SMITHFIELD SQ. N.

MILLFIELD

To Divis Tower & Falls Road

FRANCIS

BERRY

ROYAL AVE.

ROSEMARY

FALLS ROAD TAXIS

DIVIS ST.

(T)

22

CHAPELIN

17

BANK ST.

CASTLE PL.

T G-1

CASTLE ST.

18

21

CASTLE LN.

KING ST.

QUEEN ST.

FOUNTAIN

DONEGALL PLACE

COLLEGE SQ. NORTH

T G-1

DURHAM ST.

COLLEGE SQ. E.

LINEN HALL LIBRARY

ⓘ

6

DONEGALL SQ. N.

WELLINGTON PL.
T G-1, G-2

Donegall Square

2

9 4

WELLINGTON ST.

CITY HALL

11

#8
(B)

PRESBYTERIAN ASSEMBLY BLDG.

GROSVENOR ROAD

HOWARD ST.

5

DONEGALL SQ. S.
T G-1, G-2

BRUNSWICK

JAMES ST. SOUTH

ADELAIDE

GRAND OPERA HOUSE

GLENGALL ST.

20

BEDFORD ST.

7

LINEN HALL ST.

EUROPA BUS STN.

1

HOTEL EUROPA

CROWN LIQUOR

8

AMELIA

GREAT VICTORIA STREET STATION

GREAT VICTORIA STREET

WILLIAM OF ORANGE MURAL

LINFIELD ST.

HOPE

3

BRUCE

ORMEAU AVE.

UNIONIST PROTESTANT MURALS

SANDY ROW

"GOLDEN MILE"

SANDY ROW

DUBLIN ROAD

25

To Shaftesbury Square & South Belfast

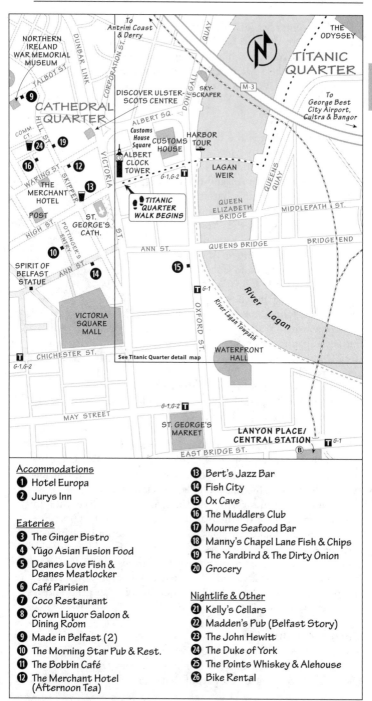

Accommodations
1 Hotel Europa
2 Jurys Inn

Eateries
3 The Ginger Bistro
4 Yūgo Asian Fusion Food
5 Deanes Love Fish & Deanes Meatlocker
6 Café Parisien
7 Coco Restaurant
8 Crown Liquor Saloon & Dining Room
9 Made in Belfast (2)
10 The Morning Star Pub & Rest.
11 The Bobbin Café
12 The Merchant Hotel (Afternoon Tea)
13 Bert's Jazz Bar
14 Fish City
15 Ox Cave
16 The Muddlers Club
17 Mourne Seafood Bar
18 Manny's Chapel Lane Fish & Chips
19 The Yardbird & The Dirty Onion
20 Grocery

Nightlife & Other
21 Kelly's Cellars
22 Madden's Pub (Belfast Story)
23 The John Hewitt
24 The Duke of York
25 The Points Whiskey & Alehouse
26 Bike Rental

views. The center has lots of movies, restaurants, and shops (Mon-Sat 9:30-18:00, Wed-Fri until 21:00, Sun 13:00-18:00).

Victoria Street: Exiting the mall, it's a short walk up Victoria Street to the Albert Memorial Clock Tower (and the start of my "Titanic Quarter Walk") and the Cathedral Quarter, described later in this section.

The Golden Mile

The "Golden Mile" is the overstated nickname of a Belfast entertainment zone with a few interesting sights on Great Victoria Street, just southwest of City Hall.

The **Presbyterian Assembly Building,** a fine example of Scottish Baronial architecture, has a welcoming little visitor exhibition that tells the story of the Presbyterians in Northern Ireland. They were discriminated against (like the Roman Catholics) because they also refused to embrace the High Church approach to Christianity as dictated by the Anglican Church. You'll learn about the founder, John Knox, and find out why a pitch pipe, which made singing hymns without accompaniment possible, was necessary (free, Mon-Fri 9:30-17:00, closed Sat-Sun, across from Jury's Inn at 2 Fisherwick Place).

The **Grand Opera House,** originally built in 1895, bombed and rebuilt in 1991, and bombed and rebuilt again in 1993, is extravagantly Victorian and *the* place to take in a concert, play, or opera (ticket office open Mon-Sat 10:00-17:00, closed Sun; ticket office to right of main front door on Great Victoria Street, tel. 028/9024-1919, www.goh.co.uk). The nearby **Hotel Europa,** considered to be the most-bombed hotel in the world (33 times during the Troubles), actually feels pretty laid-back today.

The **Crown Liquor Saloon** is the ultimate gin palace. Built in 1849 (when Catholic Ireland was suffering through the Great Potato Famine), its mahogany, glass, and marble interior is a trip back into the days of Queen Victoria. Wander through and imagine the snugs (booths designed to provide a little privacy for un-Victorian behavior) before the invasion of selfie-snapping tourists. Upstairs, the recommended Crown Dining Room serves pub grub and is decorated with historic photos.

Cathedral Quarter

Tucked between St. Anne's Cathedral and the River Lagan, this rejuvenating district is busy with shoppers by day and clubbers by night. And, being the oldest part of Belfast, it's full of history. Be-

fore World War I, this was the whiskey warehouse district—at time when the Belfast region produced about half of all Irish whiskey.

While today's Cathedral District has a few minor sights, the big attraction is its night-life—restaurants, clubs, and pubs. For the epicenter of this zone, head for the intersection of **Hill Street and Commercial Court** and peek into nearby breezeways. As you explore, you'll find a maze of narrow streets, pubs named for the colorful characters that gave the city its many legends, and creative street-art murals that hint at the artistic spirit and still-feisty edginess of Belfast.

The Cathedral Quarter extends to the old merchant district, with its Victorian-era **Customs House** backed up to the river.

Nearby, at the intersection of High Street and Victoria Street, is Belfast's "Little Big Ben," the **Albert Memorial Clock Tower.** The tower was built in 1870 to honor to Queen Victoria's beloved Prince Albert, nine years after he died. It sits on the birthplace of the city, where Belfast was founded over a thousand years ago on a little river that later became High Street. (The little river still runs under the street.) The tower famously leans (as it was built on an unstable riverbank), and locals say Albert looks like he's ready to leap to safety when the tower finally falls.

About 50 yards in front of Albert is **St. George's Church** (with an interesting history posted at its gate). A church has stood here for over a millenium.

The clock tower is the start of my "Titanic Quarter Walk" (see page 503).

St. Anne's Cathedral

Also known as Belfast Cathedral, this Anglican church was built in the early 1900s, at the peak of Belfast's industrial power. Its mosaics and stained glass are colorful and modern. Lord Edward Carson, the fervent Unionist attorney who put Oscar Wilde behind bars—and whose Machiavellian political maneuverings ensured the creation of Northern Ireland in 1921—is buried here. The structure was nearly destroyed by a Luftwaffe bomb in 1941.

1916

This pivotal year means vastly different things to Northern Ireland's two communities. When you say "1776" to most Americans, it means revolution and independence from tyranny. But when you say "1916" to someone in Northern Ireland, the response depends on who's talking.

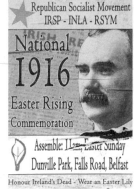

To Nationalists (who are usually Catholic), "1916" brings to mind the Easter Rising—which took place in Dublin in April of that year and was the beginning of the end of 750 years of British rule for most of Ireland. Some Nationalist murals still use images of Dublin's rebel headquarters or martyred leaders like Patrick Pearse and James Connolly. To this community, 1916 emphasizes their proud Gaelic identity, their willingness to fight to preserve it, and their stubborn anti-British attitude.

To Unionists (who are usually Protestant), "1916" means the brutal WWI Battle of the Somme in France, which began that July. (For more on the Somme, visit the Somme Museum in Bangor.) Although both Catholic and Protestant soldiers died in this long and costly battle, the first wave of young men who went over the top were the sons of proud Ulster Unionists. The Unionists hoped this blood sacrifice would prove their loyalty to the Crown—and assure that the British would never let them be gobbled up by an Irish Nationalist state (a possible scenario just before the Great War's outbreak). You'll see Tommies heroically climbing

out of their trenches in some of Belfast's Unionist murals. For the Unionists, 1916 is synonymous with devout, almost righteously divine, Britishness.

Today, the sleek "Spire of Hope" (added in 2007) is a 130-foot-tall witness to God's love of Belfast—in the form of a spike like the Spire in Dublin—but much shorter. Goofy nicknames are an Irish passion: This one's dubbed "The Rod to God."

Cost and Hours: £5, Mon-Sat 9:00-17:00, evensong Mon-Fri at 17:30 (Sept-June) and Sun at 15:30, Donegall Street, tel. 028/9032-8332.

Northern Ireland War Memorial

Across the street from St. Anne's, this one-room sanctuary is dedicated to the lives lived and lost in this corner of the UK during World War II. Coverage includes the American troops based here during the war and the damage done by multiple German bombing raids during the Blitz.

Cost and Hours: Free, Mon-Fri 10:00-16:30, closed Sat-Sun, 21 Talbot Street, tel. 028/9032-0392, www.niwarmemorial.org.

Discover Ulster-Scots Centre

This bright and inviting gallery is designed to promote the Ulster-Scots heritage. Ulster and Scotland are 13 miles apart, and this exhibit feels almost like propaganda, asserting that prehistoric Scots migrated from northeastern Ireland—thus, the cultures are rightfully intertwined. If your heritage is Scots-Irish (as they became known in America) this drills home the impact Ulstermen and women had in building America and is a good place to begin your genealogy research.

Cost and Hours: Free, Mon-Fri 10:00-16:00, closed Sat-Sun, one block from clock tower at 1 Victoria Street, tel. 028/9043-6710, http://discoverulsterscots.com.

The Merchant Hotel

One of the finest buildings in town (34 Waring Street), this was once the headquarters of the Ulster Bank. Back when this was built (mid-1800s) most people didn't have  access to real banking, so banks were designed with over-the-top extravagance to give their aristocratic clientele confidence. In modern times, banking has changed, and all over Britain such dazzling mansions of finance have been vacated and often turned into fancy restaurants. Its recommended Bert's Jazz Bar is famous for its cocktails and in the Great Room, under a grand dome and the largest chandelier in Ireland, people dress up for the ritual of afternoon tea (see "Eating in Belfast," later). You're welcome to poke around.

East of Donegall Square
▲St. George's Market

This was once the largest covered produce market in Ireland. Today the farmers are gone and everyone else, it seems, has moved in. Three days a week (Fri-Sun, about 9:00-15:00) St. George's Market becomes a thriving arts, crafts, and flea market with a few fish and produce stalls to round things out. With a diverse array of street food and homemade goodies added to the mix, it's a fun place for lunch (five blocks east of City Hall, at the corner of Oxford and East Bridge streets, tel. 028/9043-5704).

SECTARIAN NEIGHBORHOODS IN WEST BELFAST

This slowly rejuvenating section of gritty West Belfast is home to two sectarian communities, living along the main roads to either side of the Peace Wall: Unionist/Loyalists/Protestants along Shankill Road and Republicans/Nationalists/Catholics along Falls Road.

There's plenty to see in the sectarian hoods—especially murals. While you could simply (and safely) walk through these districts on your own, you'd be missing an easy opportunity to employ working-class locals who'd love to give you their firsthand, personal take on the Troubles from the perspective of their communities.

Here I list my recommendations for touring the sectarian neighborhoods, then describe the sights you'll see along the way. Before you go, make sure to read the "Understanding Belfast's Sectarian Neighborhoods" sidebar to give context to your visit.

Touring the Sectarian Neighborhoods

You can visit with a shared taxi, a private taxi tour, or on foot (with a guide, or your own—using cabs as you go). Hop-on, hop-off bus tours also drive these roads, but are impersonal and keep you at a distance. Skip them in favor of one of these options.

▲▲▲Sectarian Neighborhood Taxi Tours

Taxi tours are easy, inexpensive, and, for me, the most interesting 90 minutes you can have in Belfast. Quiz the cabbie (who grew up here) and pull over for photos. You'll get honest (if biased) viewpoints on the Troubles and local culture, see the political murals, and visit the many Troubles-related sights.

Falls Road Shared Taxi Service: The **West Belfast Taxi Association** (WBTA), run by a group of local Falls Road men, is located in the Castle Junction Car Park at the intersection of Castle and King streets. On the ground floor of this nine-story parking garage, a passenger terminal (entrance on King Street) connects travelers with old black cabs—and the only Irish-language signs in downtown Belfast.

These shared black cabs efficiently shuttle residents from out-

Understanding Belfast's Sectarian Neighborhoods

For centuries, Ireland has lived with tensions between Loyalists (also called Unionists, generally Protestants, who want to remain part of the United Kingdom, ruled from London) and Republicans (also called Nationalists, generally Roman Catholics, who want to be part of a united Ireland, independent from Great Britain). The Catholic Irish are the indigenous Irish and the Protestant loyalists are later arrivals, mostly "Scotch Irish," planted by London from Scotland in the north of Ireland.

A flare-up of violence in 1969 between these two communities led to a spontaneous mass reshuffling of working-class people in Belfast. Those who were minorities decided it was too dangerous to stay in the "wrong" sectarian neighborhood and moved into districts where they would be among their "tribe." Protestants left the Falls Road area for the Shankill Road area and Catholics left the Shankill Road area for the Falls Road area.

It's said that in these neighborhoods, the Catholics became more Irish than the Irish and the Protestants became more British than the British. Fighting between the two districts led the British army to build a "Peace Wall" to keep them apart. Paramilitary organizations on each side incited violence, and what came to be known as the Troubles began.

With two newly created ghettos dug in, it was a sad and bloody time that lasted until the Good Friday peace agreement in 1998. Since then, the bombings, assassinations, and burnings have stopped and peace has had the upper hand.

But Belfast is still segregated. Most working-class Protestants live and go to school with only Protestants. And the same is true in the Catholic community. The two groups have no trouble working or even socializing together downtown, but at night they retreat back to their separate enclaves.

The Peace Wall no longer stops projectiles and its gates are mostly open. There is peace. But there is no forgiveness: Murderers still cross paths with their victims' loved ones. Locals say it'll take another generation to be truly over the Troubles.

lying neighborhoods up and down Falls Road and to the city center. All shared cabs go up Falls Road, past Sinn Féin headquarters and lots of murals, to the Milltown Cemetery (sit in front and talk to the cabbie). Shared taxi cars have their roof sign removed and no meters. You'll pay £2/ride. You can get a cab at the Castle Junction Car Park, or anywhere along Falls Road, where easy-to-flag-down cabs run every minute or so in each direction. Just flag one down to stop it, and rap on the window to exit. Hop in and out.

This service originated almost 50 years ago at the beginning

BELFAST

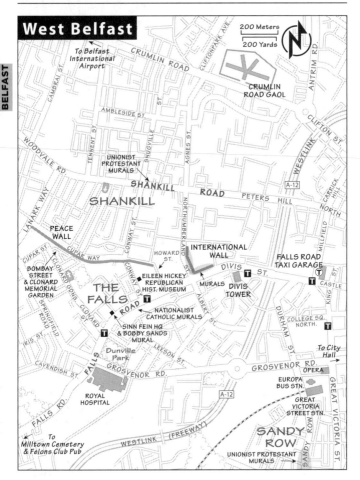

West Belfast

of the Troubles, when locals would hijack city buses and use them as barricades in the street fighting. Because of this, city bus service was discontinued, and local sectarian groups established a shared taxi service. Although the buses are now running again, these cab rides are still a great value for their drivers' commentaries. You can also hire a cab for a private 90-minute tour (see next).

Black Taxi Tours of Falls Road: Nearly any of the WBTA cabs described above are ready and able to give private tours (£45 for 3 people, more for up to 6, 90 minutes). While the drivers are Republican, these days they venture into the Loyalist zone as well. Taxi tours work great in the rain, as the cabbie just parks and talks while you look out the window. Three is comfortable in a cab. More than that and you'll have a hard time seeing. Just drop into the WBTA Passenger Terminal and they'll set you up (Taxi Trax

Black Taxi Tours, tel. 028/9031-5777, mobile 078-9271-6660, www.taxitrax.com).

Cab Tours Belfast: This group of driver/guides from both communities (Catholic and Protestant) has teamed up and is committed to giving unbiased dual-narrative tours. Their "Belfast Murals Tour" covers both neighborhoods and is a fascinating 90 minutes. As their £35 price covers two people and includes free pick up and drop-off within central Belfast, this can work  very efficiently with your sightseeing day (mobile 077-1364-0647, www.cabtoursbelfast.com).

Sectarian Neighborhood Walking Tours

On your own, get a map and lace together the sights along Falls Road by walking the street. Walking mixes well with hopping into shared taxis (described earlier) that go up and down constantly. They are generally big black cabs without a *Taxi* sign on top and without meters. Wave and they'll stop. Rap the window and they'll let you out. Riding in one of these cabs, you'll certainly get to talk with local people.

Or consider one of the following **walking-tour companies.**

Coiste Irish Political Tours offers the Republican/Catholic community perspective on an extended, two-hour "Falls Road Murals" walking tour. Led by former IRA prisoners, you'll visit murals, gardens of remembrance, and peace walls, and get to know the community. Tours meet beside the Divis Tower (the solitary, purple 20-story apartment building at the east end of Divis Road) and end at Milltown Cemetery. Afterwards, you're invited for a complimentary glass of Guinness at the Felons Club Pub—run by former IRA prisoners (£10; Tue, Thu, and Sat at 10:00; Sun at 14:00; best to book in advance, tel. 028/9020-0770, www.coiste.ie).

Belfast Political Tours runs a unique tour called "Conflicting Stories" in which former combatants from each side show and tell their story: a Republican for Falls Road sights and then a Unionist for Shankill Road sights (£18, 3 hours, most days at 9:30 and 14:30, departs from Divis Tower, mobile 073-9358-5531, www.belfastpoliticaltour.com).

Sandy Row Walking Tours provides the Unionist/Loyalist point of view during 90-minute walks centering on Sandy Row, Belfast's oldest residential neighborhood. Tours go beyond the

Troubles to cover the city's industrial heritage, the Orange Order, both world wars, and historic local churches. They depart from the William of Orange mural at the intersection of Sandy Row and Linfield Road (£7.50; most days at 10:00, 12:00, and 14:00; call to book, mobile 079-0925-4849, www.historicsandyrow.co.uk).

Sights in the Sectarian Neighborhoods

The sectarian neighborhoods are known for their murals. People here are working class and most live in row houses. The end of a row house is ready made for a big political mural—and there are lots of them.

It's a land where one community's freedom fighter is another community's terrorist. Although fighters didn't actually wear military uniforms, they're often portrayed in uniform in proud murals. (On Shankill Road there are still murals that celebrate "Top Gun" patriots who killed lots of Roman Catholics.)

But with more peaceful times, the character of these murals is slowly changing. The government is helping fund programs that replace aggressive murals with positive ones. Paramilitary themes are gradually being covered over with images of pride in each neighborhood's culture. The *Titanic* was built primarily by proud Protestant Ulster stock and is often seen in their neighborhood murals—reflecting their industrious work ethic. And in the Catholic neighborhoods, you'll see more murals depicting mythological heroes from the days before the English came.

Shankill Road

In the Loyalist Shankill Road area there are plenty of vivid murals and lots of red, white, and blue. You'll see fields where bonfires are built, with piles of wood awaiting the next Orange Day, July 12—when Protestants march and burn huge fires (and when Catholics choose to leave town on vacation). There is a particularly interesting series of murals at Lower Shankill Estate. And at the edge of the area is the Crumlin Road Gaol, a prison where combatants (mostly Republicans) did time (described next).

Crumlin Road Gaol

This Victorian-era jail a half-mile to the north of Shankill Road was kept busy from 1846 to 1996 incarcerating people—men, women, and even children. Its purpose: to control the angry indigenous Irish. One-hour guided tours show how the prison was run, who was held here, and what was life like for the prisoners. You'll trace the jail's history from opening to closing, climb the tunnel to the derelict courthouse across the street, and visit actual cells where inmates lived (£12, open daily 10:00-16:30, tours at least hourly, book and confirm tours by phone, 53 Crumlin Road, tel. 028/9074-1500, www.crumlinroadgaol.com).

BELFAST

Peace Wall

The sad, corrugated structure called the Peace Wall runs a block or so north of Falls Road (along Cupar Way) separating the Catholics from the Protestants in the Shankill Road area. The wall has five gates that open each day from about 8:00 to 18:00. On the Protestant side there is a long stretch where tour groups stop to write peaceful and hopeful messages.

The first cement wall was 20 feet high—it was later extended another 10 feet by a solid metal addition, and then another 15 feet with a metal screen. Seemingly high enough now to deter a projectile being lobbed over, this is one of many such walls erected in Belfast during the Troubles. Meant to be temporary, these barriers stay up because of old fears among the communities on both sides.

International Wall

Just past the gate on Townsend Street on the Republican side stretches the colorful, so-called "International Wall"—an L-shaped, two-block-long series of political murals that shows solidarity with other oppressed groups. (For example, Catholics in Ulster have a natural affinity with Basques in Spain and Palestinians in Israel). Along the Falls Road section of the International Wall are "current events" murals as up-to-date as last month.

Falls Road and Nearby

In the Catholic Falls Road area, you'll notice that the road signs are in two languages (Irish first). Sights include the many political murals, neighborhood memorial gardens, and Bombay Street, which the Protestants burned in 1969, igniting the Troubles. Next to the well-fortified Sinn Féin Press Office is a political gift-and-book shop. The powerful local Republican museum is two blocks away. Farther down Falls Road is the Milltown Cemetery where the hunger strikers are buried and revered as martyrs (all described next).

Sinn Féin Press Office: Near the bottom of Falls Road, at #51, is the press center for the hardline Republican party, Sinn Féin. While the press office is not open to the public, the adjacent **book-**

Bobby Sands MP
POET, GAEILGEOIR, REVOLUTIONARY, IRA VOLUNTEER.

EVERYONE
REPUBLICAN
OR OTHERWISE
HAS THEIR OWN
PARTICULAR
ROLE TO PLAY

OUR
REVENGE
WILL BE THE
LAUGHTER
OF OUR
CHILDREN

store (with an intriguing gift shop) is welcoming and worth a look. Page through books featuring color photos of the political murals that decorated these buildings. Money raised here supports the families of deceased IRA members. Around the corner is a big and bright mural remembering **Bobby Sands,** a member of parliament who led a hunger strike in prison with fellow inmates and starved himself to death to very effectively raise awareness of the Republican concerns.

Eileen Hickey Republican History Museum: This volunteer-run museum, tucked away in a residential complex, has a clear mission: "For Republican history to be told by Republicans. To educate our youth so they may understand why Republicans fought, died, and spent many years in prison for their beliefs." This is an unforgettable museum, with real (if totally biased) history shown and told by people who played a part in it (free, Tue-Sat 10:00-14:00, closed Sun-Mon, two blocks from Sinn Féin Press Office at 5 Conway Place, tel. 028/9024-0504, www.eileenhickeymuseum.com).

Bombay Street and Clonard Memorial Garden: About a 10-minute walk from the Sinn Féin Press Office is Bombay Street and the Clonard Memorial Garden. On August 15, 1969, Loyalists set fire to the Catholic homes and a monastery on this street. In the violence, a Republican teenager was killed. The burning of this Catholic street led to the "sorting out" of the communities and the building of the Peace Wall. Today you'll see Bombay Street nicely rebuilt, photos of the terrible event, and a peaceful memorial garden against the wall.

Milltown Cemetery: To reach the cemetery, take a taxi or the #G1 Glider tram to the Falls Park stop; it's too far to walk (cemetery open daily 9:00-16:00, 546 Falls Road, tel. 028/9061-3972). This burial site for Republican martyrs can be a pilgrimage for some. You'll walk past all the Gaelic crosses down to the far right-hand corner (closest to the highway), where little green railings set apart the IRA Roll of Honor from the thousands of other graves. These martyrs are treated like fallen soldiers. Notice the memorial to Bobby Sands and nine other hunger strikers. They starved themselves to death in the nearby Maze Prison in 1981, protesting for political prisoner status as opposed to terrorist criminal treatment (the prison closed in the fall of 2000).

Sandy Row

To the southwest of City Hall, Sandy Row is a smaller Unionist, Protestant working-class street just behind Hotel Europa that offers a cheap and easy way to get a dose of a sectarian neighborhood. From Hotel Europa, walk a block down Glengall Street, then turn left and walk for 10 minutes. A stop in a Unionist memorabilia shop, a pub, or one of the many cheap eateries here may give you an opportunity to talk to a local. Along the way you'll see murals filled with Unionist symbolism. The mural of William of Orange's victory over the Catholic King James II (Battle of the Boyne, 1690)

thrills Unionist hearts. You'll find that one at the northern end of Sandy Row at the corner with Linfield Road.

TITANIC QUARTER

At its height, the Belfast shipyards employed more than 30,000 people. But after World War II, with the advent of air travel and the rise of cheaper labor at shipyards located in Asia, shipbuilding declined here and moved to other parts of the world. The last ocean liner was built here in 1961 and the very last ship of any kind built here sailed away in 2003. The shipyards continually downsized; some were abandoned while others morphed into repair yards for other maritime endeavors like oil-rig and oceanic wind-turbine repair.

By the mid-1990s, the proud former shipbuilding district along the River Lagan was a barren industrial wasteland. But during the Celtic Tiger boom years (which spilled over into the North), shrewd investors saw the real-estate potential and began building posh, high-rise condos.

The first landmark project to be completed was the Odyssey entertainment complex (in 2000). To draw more visitors and commemorate the proud shipbuilding industry of the Victorian and Edwardian ages, another flagship attraction was needed. The 100th anniversary of the *Titanic* disaster in 2012 provided the perfect opportunity, and the result was the Titanic Belfast Museum, a phenomenally popular exhibition about the ill-fated ship. Today, the entire eastern bank of the Lagan is a riverfront promenade nicknamed "the Maritime Mile" and is a delightful walk (described later).

While you can just go the Titanic Belfast Museum, if you have time, see the museum as part of my walk. The slick new Glider tram #G2 from City Hall makes stops all along the way, including at the Titanic Belfast Museum and the HMS *Caroline*.

▲▲Titanic Quarter Walk

This self-guided walk takes about an hour, not including its two major stops: the Titanic Belfast Museum and the HMS *Caroline* (both described later).

• *Belfast's leaning* ❶ **Albert Memorial Clock Tower** *marks the start of this walk (for more about the clock tower, see page 493). From there, head for the River Lagan, where you'll find the...*

❷ Lagan Weir

The first step in rejuvenating a derelict riverfront is to tame the river, get rid of the tides, and build modern embankments. The star of that major investment is the Lagan Weir, the people-friendly gateway to the Titanic Quarter. Built in 1994, the weir is made up of four large pier houses and five giant gates that divide freshwater from saltwater and control the river's flow—no more flooding. You can walk across the weir on a curving pedestrian footbridge (added in 2015). Notice how much lower the water is on the saltwater side of the weir (depending on the tide). Looking downstream, on the left stands a glassy high-rise apartment building—the tallest in all of Ireland. Moored below that is the funky harbor tour boat (described earlier, under "Tours in Belfast"). On the other side, a popular riverside walk goes scenically inland from here 14 miles along the old tow path.

• *Cross the weir and turn left.*

❸ Maritime Mile Walk

This parklike promenade laces together several sights along the riverbank. It's lined with historic photo plaques that tell the story of this industrial river. The far side of the river was busy with trade (importing and exporting) and this side was all about shipbuilding. All along the way you'll get glimpses (to the right) of the city's iconic and giant yellow cranes. The big *H&W* stands for Harland and Wolff, Belfast's once mighty shipyard, but locals

just call them Samson and Goliath. (In 2019, the last 130 employees of Harland and Wolf saw their once proud company file for bankruptcy.)

Today, shipbuilding is the stuff of museums; this riverbank is all about entertainment and tourism. Find a *Game of Thrones* stained-glass window. You'll see a couple of these on this walk. (Belfast has six, commemorating the TV series filmed here that gave tourism in Northern Ireland a nice bump.)

• *Continue walking until you reach the Odyssey arena complex.*

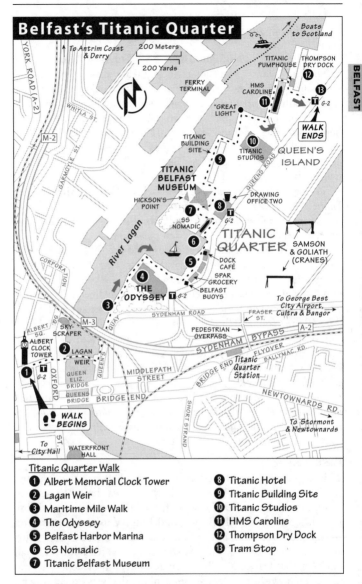

Belfast's Titanic Quarter

Titanic Quarter Walk

1. Albert Memorial Clock Tower
2. Lagan Weir
3. Maritime Mile Walk
4. The Odyssey
5. Belfast Harbor Marina
6. SS Nomadic
7. Titanic Belfast Museum
8. Titanic Hotel
9. Titanic Building Site
10. Titanic Studios
11. HMS Caroline
12. Thompson Dry Dock
13. Tram Stop

❹ The Odyssey

This huge millennium-project complex offers a food pavilion, bowling alley, 12-screen cinema, and the **W5 science center** with interactive, educational exhibits for youngsters. Where else can a kid play a harp with laser-light strings? The "W5" stands for "who, what, when, where, and why" (£10, Mon-Sat 10:00-18:00, Sun from 12:00, 2 Queen's Quay, tel. 028/9046-7790, www.w5online.co.uk).

There's also the 12,000-seat **SSE Odyssey Arena,** where the Belfast Giants professional hockey team skates. The arena is all about boosting nonsectarian sports (like hockey) rather than traditionally Loyalist (cricket, rugby, soccer) or Republican (hurling, Gaelic football) sports that amp up anger between the tribes here. Under one giant roof, the entire city gets together—Loyalists and Republicans alike—and roots for the same team (hockey tickets from £20, Fri-Sat evenings Sept-March, tel. 028/9073-9074, www.belfastgiants.com).

• *Turning inland, you come to the* ❺ **Belfast Harbor Marina** *with an arc of shops and condos. On the corner are three huge buoys (buoy is pronounced "boy" in Britain). "The Belfast Buoys" (fondly called Tom, Dick, and Harry here) are described on info boards.*

At the far end of the arc of shops, find the **Dock Café,** a welcoming, convivial, and homey spot. Volunteer-run by local churches, its mission is to celebrate tolerance and "love your neighbor"—even if they practice a different religion. The coffee and cakes are wonderful, and you famously pay whatever you like at the "honesty box." There's soup and bread at lunch time (Mon-Sat 11:00-17:00, closed Sun). You're welcome to bring in a picnic from the adjacent SPAR grocery. Browsing the café's exhibits and displays and talking with its volunteers just makes you feel good here in a city with such a difficult story.

• *Ahead looms the superstar of the Titanic Quarter, the Titanic Belfast Museum with its striking white-and-gray building—as tall as the mighty ship itself. As you approach, you'll pass a big ship that was just the tender (the shuttle dinghy) for the* Titanic.

❻ SS *Nomadic*

This ship once ferried first-class passengers between the dock and the *Titanic.* Sitting in the dry dock where it was built, it's restored to appear as it was in 1912 when it ferried Benjamin Guggenheim, John Jacob Astor, Molly Brown, and Kate Winslet to that fateful voyage (50 yards south of the Titanic Belfast Museum, same hours and ticket as the museum). Nearby is **Hickson's Point,** a small building that was originally a chapel, built to provide a space for reflection for visitors to the *Titanic* exhibit. That was expecting a bit much from the tourists—no one used it, and now it's a pub.

• *Now is a good time to tour the* ❼ **Titanic Belfast Museum** *(see listing later in this section). Afterwards walk across the plaza to the...*

❽ Titanic Hotel

Housed in the former Harland and Wolff shipyard headquarters (known as the Drawing Office), this new hotel was permitted on condition that the public would be allowed to wander through its historic spaces. For 150 years, many of the largest and finest ships in the world were designed here. Now it's a classy hotel. Pick up an info sheet at the reception and treat the place like a free museum. *Titanic* aficionados and maritime design geeks love the place. The well-lit central space, now the Drawing Office Two pub, is where the plans for the *Titanic* were drawn.

BELFAST

• *Head for the river to see the place where the* Titanic *was actually built.*

❾ *Titanic* Building Site

A big, stylized **map** in the pavement shows the route of the *Titanic's* one and only voyage. The brown benches are long and short—set up in dots and dashes to represent the Morse code distress transmissions sent on that fateful day. Just beyond two dashes, a few steps to the left, find the symbolic steel tip of the ship in the pavement and stand there looking out. This was where the bow was; the lampposts (stretching 300 yards before you) mark the size of the ship built here. Fifty yards ahead is a memorial with the names of all who perished.

• *Walk to what would have been the stern of the* Titanic.

❿ Titanic Studios

The *Game of Thrones* stained-glass window here features the Iron Throne. (You've just got to get a selfie.) The giant warehouse-like building to your right was once the shipyard's Paint Hall, and is now Titanic Studios (not open to public)—the soundstage where much of *Game of Thrones* was filmed. Farther along is the gracefully revolving "Great Light" from a 1920s lighthouse.

It was moved here from a nearby island. (The info board enthralls lighthouse fans.)

• *Continue walking up the promenade to the...*

⓫ HMS *Caroline*

A WWI battleship that fought in the 1916 Battle of Jutland, the HMS *Caroline* is one of only three surviving Royal Navy ships from that war, and well worth exploring (tour described later). During World War II and later, the *Caroline* served as a headquarters and training ship until being decommissioned in 2011—the second-oldest ship in the Royal Navy's service.

• *Walking from the HMS Caroline away from the river toward the tram stop you'll pass the...*

🕧 Thompson Dry Dock

This is the massive dry dock where the *Titanic* last rested on dry land. The Edwardian pump house filled the dry dock with water—and emptied it—in record time (26 million gallons in one hour). Slipways rolled new hulls down a slope into the water, where they were then towed to a dry dock. It's here that the final outfitting was completed, adding extra weight before the final watertight launch. You can pay to go inside the pump room and descend into the dry dock to walk in the *Titanic*'s massive footprint (£5, daily 10:00-17:00, café, tel. 028/9073-7813, www.titanicsdock.com).

• *Across the street is a* 🕭 *tram stop. From here you can catch the Glider tram #G2 back to City Hall, retracing much of what you just walked past with nice views of cranes and harbor action as you glide.*

Titanic Quarter Sights
▲▲▲Titanic Belfast Museum

This £97 million attraction stands right next to the original slipways where the *Titanic* was built. Creative displays tell the tale of

the famous ocean liner, proudly heralded as the largest man-made moving object of its time. The sight has no actual artifacts from the underwater wreck (out of respect for the fact that it's a mass grave). The artifacts on display are from local shipbuilding offices and personal collections.

Cost and Hours: £19, £11.50 Late Saver Ticket sold one hour before closing; daily June-Aug 8:30-19:00, April-May and Sept 9:00-18:00, Oct-March 10:00-17:00; audioguide-£4, but you get plenty of info without it; tel. 028/9076-6399, www.titanicbelfast.com. Early Riser Tickets for some morning slots (book online) can save up to 30 percent.

Crowd-Beating Tips: Book ahead online to get the entry time you want and avoid ticket lines. For fewer crowds, go early or late as big bus tours and cruise-ship excursions can clog the exhibits from 9:30-15:00.

Getting There: From the Albert Memorial Clock Tower at the edge of the Cathedral Quarter, it's a 10-minute walk: Follow my "Titanic Quarter Walk" (described earlier). From Donegall Square, take the Glider tram (#G2, 6/hour) or go by taxi (about £6).

Tours: The **Discovery Tour** explains the striking architecture of the Titanic Belfast Museum building and the adjacent slipways where the ship was built (£9, 1 hour, call ahead for tour times).

Eating: The ground floor includes a **$ Galley Express** (sandwich café) as well as **$$ Bistro 401** (a carvery-style restaurant). Choices nearby include the upscale **$$$ Drawing Office Two** pub, occupying the rooms where the ill-fated vessel was designed (across the lane in the Titanic Hotel), and the **$ Dock Café,** a church-run community center serving pay-what-you-like soup, bread, cake, and coffee (described in the walk).

Visiting the Museum: The spacey architecture of the Titanic Belfast Museum building is a landmark on the city's skyline. Six stories tall, it's clad in more than 3,000 sun-reflecting aluminum panels. Its four corners represent the bows of the many ships (most of which didn't sink) that were built in these yards during the industrial Golden Age of Belfast.

You'll follow a one-way route through the exhibit's nine galleries on six floors. Helpful "crew" (museum staff) are posted throughout to answer questions.

The "shipyard ride" near the beginning is a fun (if cheesy) five-minute experience. Six people share a gondola as you glide through a series of vignettes that attempt to capture what it was like to be a worker building the ship. (There can be a 20-minute wait—if short on time, I'd skip it and use my time more productively in the fascinating displays that follow.)

Continuing on, you'll find a big window overlooking the actual construction site (which you can visit after leaving the building). Next, you'll see exhibits on the construction, historic photographs, proud displays of the opulence on board, a recounting of the disaster (with Morse code transmissions sent after the ship hit the iceberg) and, in the 200-seat Discovery Theatre, the seven-minute *Titanic Beneath* video, with eerie footage of the actual wreckage sprouting countless "rusticles" 12,000 feet down on the ocean floor. Don't miss the see-through floor panels at the foot of the movie screen where the wreck passes slowly under your feet. The last escalator leaves you on the ground floor facing the back door of the center.

And what do the people of Belfast have to say about the ship they built that sank on her first voyage? "She was OK when she left."

▲HMS *Caroline*

Launched in 1914, the HMS *Caroline* is the sole surviving ship of the greatest naval battle of World War I—the Battle of Jutland in the North Sea. Despite being the bloodiest day in British naval

history, it's regarded as a victory over the German Navy, which never challenged Britain again. Follow the one-way route with the included audioguide. You'll start with a fascinating exhibit about the ship, which includes a 10-minute *Jutland Experience* video. Then you'll enter the actual ship, restored as if time stopped in 1916 (dinner is still on the table), and are free to explore from the torpedo exhibit to the thunderous engine room. Locals nicknamed the *Caroline* the "HMS *Never Budge*" because she's been moored here for decades—she finally was converted into a museum in 2016.

Cost and Hours: £13.50, daily 10:00-17:00; walk around the ship to the adjacent building—the old pump house for the Thompson Dry Dock—for tickets; Alexandra Dock, Queen's Road, www.nmrn.org.uk.

SOUTH BELFAST
▲Ulster Museum

This is Belfast's most venerable museum. It offers an earnest and occasionally thought-provoking look at the region's history, with a cross-section of local artifacts.

Cost and Hours: £5 suggested donation; Tue-Sun 10:00-17:00, closed Mon; south of downtown, in the Botanic Gardens on Stranmillis Road, tel. 028/9044-0000, www.nmni.com.

Visiting the Museum: The five-floor museum is pretty painless. Ride the elevator to the top floor and follow the spiraling exhibits downhill through various zones. The top two floors are dedicated to rotating art exhibits, the next floor down covers local nature, and the two below that focus on history. The ground floor covers the Troubles, and has a coffee shop and gift shop.

The Art Zone displays beautifully crafted fine crystal and china. In the Nature Zone, audiovisuals trace how the Ice Age affected the local landscape. Dinosaur skeletons lurk, stuffed wildlife play possum, and geology rocks. Kids will enjoy the interactive Discover History room.

After a peek at a pretty good mummy, check out the *Girona* treasure. Soggy bits of gold, silver, leather, and wood were salvaged from the Spanish Armada's shipwrecked *Girona,* lost off the Antrim Coast north of Belfast in 1588.

In the delicately worded History Zone, a highlight is the wall covered with antique text. On the left is the Ulster Covenant

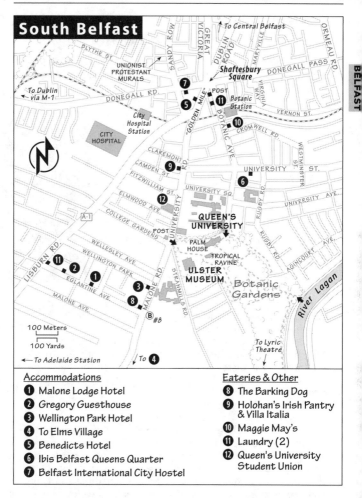

South Belfast

BELFAST

To Central Belfast
Shaftesbury Square
To Dublin via M-1
City Hospital Station
CITY HOSPITAL
UNIONIST PROTESTANT MURALS
POST
Botanic Station
QUEEN'S UNIVERSITY
PALM HOUSE
TROPICAL RAVINE
ULSTER MUSEUM
Botanic Gardens
River Lagan
To Lyric Theatre
To Adelaide Station
To ❹
100 Meters
100 Yards

Accommodations
❶ Malone Lodge Hotel
❷ Gregory Guesthouse
❸ Wellington Park Hotel
❹ To Elms Village
❺ Benedicts Hotel
❻ Ibis Belfast Queens Quarter
❼ Belfast International City Hostel

Eateries & Other
❽ The Barking Dog
❾ Holohan's Irish Pantry & Villa Italia
❿ Maggie May's
⓫ Laundry (2)
⓬ Queen's University Student Union

(1912), signed in blood by Unionist Protestants to resist incorporation into an independent Irish state. On the right is the Irish Proclamation of the Republic (1916), dear to Nationalist Catholic hearts as the moral compass of the Easter Uprising. Compare the passion of these polar opposite points of view.

Then continue through the coverage of the modern-day Troubles as this museum strives for balanced and thought-provoking reflections. It's encouraging to see: When I first came to the North over 40 years ago, institutions like this would have only presented one point of view.

▲Botanic Gardens

This is the backyard of Queen's University, and on a sunny day, you couldn't imagine a more relaxing park setting. On a cold day, step

The Red Hand of Ulster

All over Belfast, you'll notice a curious symbol: a red hand facing you as if swearing a pledge or telling you to halt. You'll spot it, faded, above the Linen Hall Library door, in the wrought-iron fences of the Merchant Hotel, on old-fashioned clothes wringers (in the Ulster Folk Park and Transport Museum at Cultra), above the front door of a bank in Bangor, in the shape of a flowerbed at Mount Stewart House, in Loyalist paramilitary murals, on shield emblems in the gates of Republican memorials, and even on the flag of Northern Ireland (the white flag with the red cross of St. George). It's known as the Red Hand of Ulster—and it is one of the few emblems used by both communities in Northern Ireland.

Nationalists display a red hand on a yellow shield as a symbol of the ancient province of Ulster. It was the official crest of the once-dominant O'Neill clan (who fought tooth and nail against English rule) and today signifies resistance to British rule in these communities.

But you'll more often see the red hand in Unionist areas. They see it as a potent symbol of the political entity of Northern Ireland. The Ulster Volunteer Force chose it for their symbol in 1913 and embedded it in the center of the Northern Irish flag upon partition of the island in 1921. You may see the red hand clenched as a fist in Loyalist murals. One Loyalist paramilitary group even named itself the Red Hand Commandos.

The origin of the red hand comes from a mythological tale of two rival clans that raced by boat to claim a far shore. The first clan leader to touch the shore would win it for his people. Everyone aboard both vessels strained mightily at their oars, near exhaustion as they approached the shore. Finally, in desperation, the chieftain leader of the slower boat whipped out his sword and lopped off his right hand...which he then flung onto the shore, thus winning the coveted land. Moral of the story? The fearless folk of Ulster will do *whatever it takes* to get the job done.

into the Tropical Ravine for a jungle of heat and humidity. Take a quick walk through the Palm House, reminiscent of the one in London's Kew Gardens, but smaller. The Ulster Museum is on the garden's grounds.

Cost and Hours: Free; gardens daily 7:30 until dusk; Palm House daily 10:00-17:00, Oct-March until 16:00; tel. 028/9031-4762, www.belfastcity.gov.uk/parks.

Nearby: Just south of the gardens is the **Lyric Theatre,** an architecturally innovative building rebuilt in 2011 (no tours, but there are performances; see "Nightlife in Belfast," later).

BEYOND BELFAST
▲▲Ulster Folk Park and Transport Museum
This sprawling 180-acre, two-museum complex straddles the road and rail line at Cultra, midway between Bangor and Belfast (8 miles east of town).

Cost and Hours: £9 for each museum, £11 combo-ticket for both, £29 for families; March-Sept Tue-Sun 10:00-17:00; Oct-Feb Tue-Fri 10:00-16:00, Sat-Sun 11:00-16:00; closed Mon year-round; check the schedule for the day's special events, tel. 028/9042-8428, www.nmni.com.

Getting There: From Belfast, you can reach Cultra by taxi (£15), bus #502 (2/hour, 30 minutes, from Laganside Bus Centre), or train (2/hour, 15 minutes, from any Belfast train station or from Bangor). Buses stop right in the park, but schedules are skimpy on Saturday and Sunday. Train service is more dependable (and more frequent on the weekend): Get off at the Cultra stop.

Planning Your Time: Allow three hours, and expect lots of walking. Most people will spend an hour in the Transport Museum and a couple of hours at the Folk Park. You'll arrive (by rail or car) between the two museums a bit closer to the Transport Museum. From here, you have a choice of going downhill to the Transport Museum or 200 panting yards uphill into the Folk Park. Assess your energy level and plan accordingly. Those with a car can drive between the Transport Museum and the Folk Park (each has a parking lot), but as it is only 300 yards, it's simpler just to walk between them than to look for an open space on a busy day. Note that the Transport Museum is all indoors. The Folk Park involves more walking exposed to the elements between buildings spread across the upper hillside.

Visiting the Museums: The **Transport Museum** consists of three buildings. Start at the bottom and trace the evolution of transportation from 7,500 years ago—when people first decided to load an ox—to the first vertical takeoff jet. In 1909, the Belfast-based Shorts Aviation Company partnered with the Wright brothers to manufacture the first commercially available  aircraft. The middle building holds an intriguing section on the sinking of the *Titanic*. The top building covers the history of bikes, cars, and trains. The car section rumbles from the first car in Ireland (an 1898 Benz), through the "Cortina Culture" of the 1960s, to the local adventures of controversial automobile designer John DeLorean and a 1981 model of his sleek sports car.

The **Folk Park,** an open-air collection of 34 reconstructed buildings from all over the nine counties of Ulster, showcases the region's traditional lifestyles. After wandering through the old-town site (church, print shop, schoolhouse, humble Belfast row house, silent movie theater, and so on), you'll head off into the country to nip into cottages, farmhouses, and mills. Some houses are warmed by a wonderful peat fire and a friendly attendant. Your visit can be dull or vibrant, depending upon whether attendants are available to chat. Drop a peat brick on the fire.

▲Carrickfergus Castle

Built during the Norman invasion of the late 1100s, this historic castle stands sentry on the shore of Belfast Lough. William of

Orange landed here in 1690, when he began his Irish campaign against deposed King James II. In 1778, the American privateer ship *Ranger* (the first ever to fly the Stars and Stripes), under the command of John Paul Jones, defeated the HMS *Drake* just up the coast. These days the castle feels a bit sanitized and geared for kids, but it's an easy excursion if you're seeking a castle experience near the city.

Cost and Hours: £5.50; daily 9:00-17:00, Oct-March until 16:00; tel. 028/9335-1273.

Getting There: It's a 20-minute train ride from Belfast (on the line to Larne). Turn left as you exit the train station and walk straight downhill for five minutes—all the way to the waterfront—passing under the arch of the old town wall en route. You'll find the castle on your right.

▲The Gobbins Cliff Path

Reopened in 2016, the Gobbins Cliff Path is an Edwardian adventure with birds, beautiful scenery, and occasional rogue waves. Located 20 miles northeast of Belfast, beyond Carrickfergus, this complex path—a mix of tunnel bridges, railings, and steps carved, hammered, or fastened to the cliff—was first opened in 1902, designed to boost tourism. Once popular, it fell into disrepair during World War II and was closed for decades. The newly reinforced path (which, to spoil all the turn-of-the-century fun, now requires helmets and guides) takes two to three hours to hike, and is awkward and steep in places, but not terribly strenuous. You'll spot puffins, cormorants, and kittiwakes in nesting areas along the way.

Cost and Hours: £10, visitors center open daily 9:30-17:30, required guided hikes generally hourly (weather permitting), book in advance as tours can fill up, tel. 028/9337-2318, 68 Middle Road, Islandmagee, www.thegobbinscliffpath.com.

Getting There: By car, take the A-2 from Belfast to Larne, turn right on B-90, and follow signs to *Islandmagee* and *The Gobbins.* Without a car, take a train to Ballycarry (on the Larne line) and either walk a mile to the visitors center, or take a taxi (Ballycarry Cabs, tel. 028/9303-8131). McCombs Coach Tours may offer summer excursions here from Belfast, which will be the best connection for those without wheels—check their offerings by phone or online (tel. 028/9031-5333, www.mccombscoaches.com, info@mccombscoaches.com).

Nightlife in Belfast

Theater

Located beside the River Lagan (near Queen's University), the **Lyric Theatre** is a Belfast institution. Rebuilt in 2011, it represents the cultural rejuvenation of the city—the building was partially funded by donations from actors such as Liam Neeson, Kenneth Branagh, and Meryl Streep. While there are no public tours, it's a good place to see quality local productions (tickets £15-25, box office open daily 10:00-17:00, 55 Ridgeway Street, tel. 028/9038-1081, www.lyrictheatre.co.uk).

Traditional Music and Dance

Belfast Story features former *Riverdance* musicians and dancers in an energetic hour-long performance celebrating the people, poetry, and music of Belfast. It's held in a characteristic and recommended pub—with the local crowd on the ground floor and tourists packed into a tiny performance room upstairs (£25; May-Oct Fri-Sat at 20:00, upstairs in Madden's Pub at 74 Berry Street, mobile 079-7189-5746, www.belfasthiddentours.com, Conner Owens).

Musical Pub Crawl

Belfast Trad Trail Tours is led by two local musicians. You'll walk to three fun drinking establishments in the Cathedral Quarter, where they play and explain traditional Irish music. It's a great intro to Irish music and Belfast's pulsing evening scene (£15, 2.5 hours, mid-May-Aug Sat at 16:00, meet at Dirty Onion Pub, 3 Hill Street, tel. 028/9028-8818, www.tradtrail.com).

▲▲Live Music

A great way to connect with the people and culture of Belfast is over a beer in a pub. The first five pubs listed here have music—mostly traditional Irish (a.k.a. trad)—nearly every night. Four are near each other in the Cathedral Quarter. The Points Whiskey and Alehouse is farther south near the "Golden Mile"/Great Victoria Street. Bert's, also in the Cathedral Quarter, is a slinky lounge for live jazz and cocktails. Check pub websites to see what's on when you're in town.

Kelly's Cellars, once a rebel hangout (see plaque above door), still has a very gritty Irish feel. It's 300 years old, has a great fun-loving energy inside, and a lively  terrace (Mon-Sat 11:30-24:00, Sun 13:00-23:30; live music nightly at 21:30, trad music Tue-Thu and Sat-Sun at 21:30; 32 Bank Street, 100 yards behind Tesco supermarket, access via alley on left side when facing Tesco, tel. 028/9024-6058, www.facebook.com/kellys. cellars). They only serve traditional Irish stew until 16:00 but you can bring in fish-and-chips from the corner joint (the recommended Manny's) any time.

Madden's Pub is wonderfully characteristic, with a local crowd and trad music every night from 21:00 (no food, also hosts the "Belfast Story" described earlier, 2 blocks from Kelly's Cellars at 74 Berry Street, tel. 028/9024-4114).

The John Hewitt is committed to the local arts scene—giving both musicians and artists a platform. They don't serve food but they do dish up live music almost nightly from 21:30 (trad music Tue and Sat-Sun, rock on Fri, folk and acoustic on Mon and Thu, closed Wed, 51 Donegall Street, tel. 028/9023-3768, www. thejohnhewitt.com).

The Duke of York is noisy for both eyes and ears—jammed with vintage mirrors and memorabilia, it feels like a drunken lamps-and-lighting store. They have live music nightly (from 21:30, often just one guitarist hollering above the din) to crank up the volume even more. It's on Commercial Court, the noisiest and most trendy/touristy street for nightlife in Belfast (7 Commercial Court, tel. 028/9024-1062, www.dukeofyorkbelfast.com).

The Points Whiskey and Alehouse is an authentic Belfast pub, famed for its music—trad and Irish rock on two stages nightly after 22:00. It's near Hotel Europa at 44 Dublin Road. They offer more music in the quieter and adjacent **An Síbín pub** (tel. 028/9099-4124, www.thepointsbelfast.com).

Bert's Jazz Bar, at the Merchant Hotel, is good if you're in the mood for a cocktail in a plush, velvety Art Deco lounge with live jazz (from 21:00 nightly, 16 Skipper Street, tel. 028/9026-2713).

Sleeping in Belfast

Belfast is more of a convention town than a tourist town, so business-class room rates are lower or soft on weekends. For cozy B&Bs, check out the Queen's University area or the nearby seaside town of Bangor.

CENTRAL BELFAST
To locate these hotels, see the "Central Belfast" map on page 490.

$$$$ Hotel Europa is Belfast's landmark hotel—fancy, comfortable, and central—with four stars and lower weekend rates. Modern yet elegant, this place is the choice of visiting diplomats (breakfast extra, Great Victoria Street, tel. 028/9027-1066, www. hastingshotels.com, res@eur.hastingshotels.com).

$$$ Jurys Inn, an American-style hotel that rents 190 identical modern rooms, is perfectly located two blocks from City Hall (breakfast extra, Fisherwick Place, tel. 028/9053-3500, www. jurysinns.com, jurysinnbelfast@jurysinns.com).

SOUTH BELFAST
To locate these hotels, see the "South Belfast" map on page 511.

South of Queen's University
Many of Belfast's best budget beds cluster in a comfortable, leafy neighborhood just south of Queen's University (near the Ulster Museum). The Botanic, Adelaide, and City Hospital **train stations** are nearby (I find Botanic the most convenient), and buses zip down Malone Road every 20 minutes. Any **bus** on Malone Road goes to Donegall Square East. **Taxis** take you downtown for about £6 (your host can call one).

Located directly across University Road from the red-brick university building, **Queen's University Student Union** is just as handy for tourists as it is for college students. Inside you'll find an ATM, WCs, a minimarket, and Wi-Fi. Grab a quick and cheap sandwich and coffee at **Clement's Coffee Shop** (closed Sun).

$$$$ Malone Lodge Hotel, by far the classiest listing in this neighborhood, provides slick, business-class comfort in 119 spacious rooms on a quiet street (elevator, restaurant, parking, 60 Eglantine Avenue, tel. 028/9038-8000, www.malonelodgehotel.com, info@malonelodgehotel.com).

$$$$ Gregory Guesthouse, with its stately red brick, ages gracefully behind a green lawn with 15 large, fresh rooms. Prices are soft, so it can be a good value with its subtle charm on a quiet street (family room, parking, 32 Eglantine Ave, tel. 028/9066-3454, www.thegregorybelfast.com, info@thegregorybelfast.com).

$$ Wellington Park Hotel is a dependable, if unimaginative, chain-style hotel with 75 rooms. It's predictable but in a good location (pay parking, 21 Malone Road, tel. 028/9038-1111, www.wellingtonparkhotel.com, info@wellingtonparkhotel.com).

¢ Elms Village, a huge Queen's University dorm complex, rents 100 basic, institutional rooms (all singles) to travelers during summer break (July and Aug only, coin-op laundry, self-serve kitchen; reception building is 50 yards down entry street, marked *Elms Village* on low brick wall, 78 Malone Road; tel. 028/9097-4525, www.stayatqueens.com, accommodation@qub.ac.uk).

Between Queen's University and Shaftesbury Square

$$$ Benedicts Hotel has 32 rooms in a good location at the northern fringe of the Queen's University district. Its popular bar is a maze of polished wood and can be loud on weekend nights (elevator, 7 Bradbury Place, tel. 028/9059-1999, www.benedictshotel.co.uk, info@benedictshotel.co.uk).

$$ Ibis Belfast Queens Quarter, part of a major European hotel chain, has 56 practical rooms in a convenient location. It's a great deal if you're not looking for cozy character (breakfast extra, elevator, a block north of Queen's University at 75 University Street, tel. 028/9033-3366, https://ibis.accorhotels.com, h7288@accor.com).

¢ Belfast International City Hostel, big and creatively run, provides the best value among Belfast's hostels. It's near Botanic Station, in the heart of the lively university district, and has 24-hour reception. Paul, the manager, is a veritable TI, with a passion for his work (private rooms available, 22 Donegall Road, tel. 028/9031-5435, www.hini.org.uk, info@hini.org.uk).

Eating in Belfast

CENTRAL BELFAST
For locations, see the "Central Belfast" map on page 490.

Fine Dining Near City Hall
$$$ The Ginger Bistro serves a smart local crowd Irish/Asian cuisine with special attention to vegetarian and fish dishes. The casual front is for walk-ins, and the quieter, more romantic back is for those with reservations (Tue-Sat 12:00-22:00, closed Sun-Mon, early-bird specials Tue-Fri until 18:45, 68 Great Victoria Street, tel. 028/9024-4421, www.gingerbistro.com).

$$$ Yügo Asian Fusion Food is a foodie fave, trendy but with no pretense and lots of booze. The small dining room is tight with a dozen tables; eating at the bar gets you a fun view of the open kitchen. While they have main courses, their small plates—£5-10 each—are designed to be eaten tapas style (vegetarian-friendly, Tue-Sat 12:00-15:00 & 17:00-22:00, closed Sun-Mon, reservations smart, 3 Wellington Street, tel. 028/9031-9715, www.yugobelfast. com).

$$$ Deanes Love Fish and **Deanes Meatlocker** are side-by-side sister places run by the powerhouse restaurateur of Deanes Eipic, a Michelin-star place next door. Each has a confident, impersonal vibe with good-value meals in a classy atmosphere; the lunch and pre-theater specials are especially economic. I prefer the Loves Fish place with its minimalist, nautical feel. The Meatlocker is more for red meat and romance (Mon-Sat 12:00-15:00 & 17:00-22:00, closed Sun, one block from City Hall at 28 Howard Street, tel. 028/9033-1134, www.michaeldeane.co.uk).

$$$ Café Parisien serves French dishes with a classy *Titanic* (and peaceful blues) ambience. It's in a great central location with a terrace looking directly at City Hall—especially nice when dining outdoors (Mon-Fri 11:30-16:00 & 17:00-22:30, Sat-Sun 12:00-22:30, evening reservations smart; a few doors east of the TI on Donegall Square North, tel. 028/9590-4338, www. cafeparisienbelfast.com).

Other Options Near City Hall

$$$ Coco Restaurant is a spacious place with a quirky sense of style, serving reliably tasty modern Irish and Continental dishes (nightly from 17:30, good early-bird specials until 19:00, a couple of blocks behind City Hall at 7 Linen Hall Street, tel. 028/9031-1150, Tim).

$$ Crown Liquor Saloon and Dining Room is a dazzling gin palace on every sightseers list. The ground floor pub is a mesmerizing mishmash of mosaics and shareable snugs (booths—best to reserve), topped with a smoky tin ceiling. The dining room upstairs is similarly elegant but much quieter. Both serve the same pub grub but upstairs seating comes with

table service (downstairs 11:30-20:00, upstairs 12:30-22:00, across from Hotel Europa at 46 Great Victoria Street, tel. 028/9024-3187, www.nicholsonspubs.co.uk).

$$ Made in Belfast has a crazy, fake-bohemian dining room with a creative and fun-loving menu. While exciting a decade ago, it's a bit tired now, but I find the food inviting, the spacious seating enjoyable, and the lunch/early-bird specials (until 18:00) a good value (daily, on Wellington Street a block from City Hall, tel. 028/9024-6712). A second location with similar vibes and menu is in the Cathedral Quarter (facing the cathedral at 23 Talbot Street, tel. 028/9545-8120).

$$ The Morning Star is a well-worn, once-elegant eatery with a characteristic pub on the ground floor (serving a hearty £6 lunch buffet) and a low-energy dining hall upstairs. It has a good reputation for solid food in a historic pub (same pub-grub menu throughout, daily 12:00-22:00; down an alley just off High Street at 17 Pottinger's Entry, alley entry is roughly opposite the post office, tel. 028/9023-5986).

Cheap Lunches in City Hall: $ The **Bobbin Café** at City Hall is a good, cheap, and cheery little cafeteria serving soups, sandwiches, and hot dishes (daily 9:00-17:00, tel. 028/9050-2068). A nonprofit, they employ young people with learning disabilities.

Groceries: Small late-night corner grocery stores are all over town. The **Tesco Express** across from Hotel Europa is open very late and seems equipped for the hungry traveler.

Cathedral Quarter

In addition to the eateries listed here, there's a second location of Made in Belfast (see above).

$$$$ The Merchant Hotel presents its afternoon tea in an expensive ritual. You'll enjoy velvety Victorian splendor under an opulent dome with a piano accompaniment. Sit under the biggest chandelier in Northern Ireland as you dine in the great hall of a former bank headquarters. If you've got a little money to burn, consider dressing up the best you can and indulging. You'll go home with a fancy box of leftovers (£30/person, daily 12:30-16:30, reservations smart, 35 Waring Street, tel. 028/9023-4888, www.themerchanthotel.com). Dinner is less expensive (daily 17:30-21:45, mod Irish/French cuisine).

$$$ Bert's Jazz Bar, also at the Merchant Hotel, is a fine option if you're looking for French cuisine served with jazz. Their early-bird special is a good value (daily generally 17:00-22:00, 16 Skipper Street, tel. 028/9026-2713).

$$ Fish City is a simple, peaceful dining room with an open kitchen, attentive service, spacious seating with nautical decor, and a focus on quality. Their seafood is caught under high environmental standards (daily 12:00-21:00, 33 Ann Street, tel. 028/9023-1000, Grace).

$$$ Ox Cave is a sleek and mod place with aproned French elegance. It was designed by the owners of the adjacent Michelin-starred Ox restaurant to entertain diners with wine and cheese as they wait for their table. But with charming Alain as your host, you could settle in here to make a meal from their charcuterie and cheese plates and exciting wines. Have fun with their wine matrix—lots of vintages by the glass at the same price (Tue-Sat 16:00 until late, closed Sun-Mon, 3 Oxford Street, tel. 028/9023-2567).

$$$$ The Muddlers Club, a loud, trendy, spacious, industrial-mod place, has an open kitchen and a fun format: a single, six-course, £55 fixed-price meal of international-style dishes that changes daily. Their wine-pairing option makes the tasting menu even better. Eating here is expensive, but it's a memorable slice of Belfast (Tue-Sat 17:30-22:00, closed Sun-Mon, Warehouse Lane off Waring Street, tel. 028/9031-3199).

$$$ Mourne Seafood Bar is my choice for seafood in an elegant setting with a fun staff and smart clientele. It's run by a marine biologist and a great chef—no gimmicks, just top-quality seafood (daily 12:00-21:30, reservations smart, 34 Bank Street, tel. 028/9024-8544, www.mourneseafood.com). As it's next to Kelly's Cellars (described earlier, under "Nightlife in Belfast"), consider dining here and then enjoying the music next door.

$ Manny's Chapel Lane Fish & Chips is a classic, cheap, neighborhood chippie. You're welcome to bring your fish down the block to Kelly's Cellars for a beer and to enjoy the music (closed Sun, 11 Chapel Lane, tel. 028/9031-9165).

$ The Yardbird, rough and spacious, is housed in an open-beam attic and serves a down-and-dirty menu of ribs and wings. It's known for its cheap and tasty rotisserie chicken (daily 12:00-22:00, 3 Hill Street, tel. 028/9024-3712). The **Dirty Onion** (downstairs) is a popular pub that spills suds and live music into its packed outer courtyard on summer nights.

NEAR QUEEN'S UNIVERSITY

For locations, see the "South Belfast" map on page 511.

$$$ The Barking Dog, elegant and inviting, serves small plates to be enjoyed family style, along with pastas and burgers. It's closest to my cluster of accommodations south of the university (daily 12:00-14:30 & 17:00-22:00, near corner of Eglantine Avenue at 33 Malone Road, tel. 028/9066-1885).

$$$ Holohan's Irish Pantry is like eating in a wealthy grandma's dining room. It's small with an inviting and nostalgic menu of Irish dishes—both classic and modern. The chef has a passion for seasonal ingredients (Tue-Sat 17:00-23:30, Sun 12:00-21:00, closed Mon, reservations smart, 43 University Road, tel. 028/9029-1103, www.holohanspantry.co.uk).

$$ Villa Italia packs in crowds hungry for linguini and *bistecca*. Huge and family-friendly, with checkered tablecloths and a wood-beamed ceiling draped with grape leaves, it's a little bit of Italy in Belfast (Mon-Sat 17:00-23:00, Sun 12:30-21:30, three long blocks south of Shaftesbury Square, at intersection with University Street, 39 University Road, tel. 028/9032-8356).

$$ Maggie May's serves hearty, simple, affordable meals in a tight and cheery little bistro room (Sun-Thu 8:00-22:00, Fri-Sat until 23:00, one block south of Botanic Station at 50 Botanic Avenue, tel. 028/9032-2662).

Belfast Connections

BY TRAIN OR BUS

For schedules and prices for trains and buses in Northern Ireland, check with Translink (tel. 028/9066-6630, www.translink.co.uk). Note that service is less frequent on Sundays.

From Belfast by Train to: Dublin (8/day, 2 hours), **Derry** (10/day, 2.5 hours), **Larne** (hourly, 1 hour), **Portrush** (15/day, 2 hours, transfer in Coleraine), **Bangor** (2/hour, 30 minutes).

By Bus to: Portrush (12/day, 2 hours; scenic-coast route, 2.5 hours), **Derry** (hourly, 2 hours), **Dublin** (hourly, most via Dublin Airport, 3 hours), **Galway** (every 2 hours, 5 hours, change in Dublin), **Glasgow** (3/day, 6 hours), **Edinburgh** (1/day direct, 2/day with change in Glasgow, 7-8 hours). The Europa Bus Centre is behind Hotel Europa (Ulsterbus tel. 028/9033-7003 for destinations in Scotland and England).

BY PLANE

Belfast has two airports. **George Best Belfast City Airport** (airport code: BHD, tel. 028/9093-9093, www.belfastcityairport.com) is a five-minute, £8 taxi ride from town (near the docks) or a £2.60 ride on the Airport Express bus #600 (hourly from Europa Bus Centre). Meanwhile, **Belfast International Airport** (airport code: BFS, tel. 028/9448-4848, www.belfastairport.com) is 18 miles west of town—an £8 ride on the Airport Express bus #300 (hourly from Europa Bus Centre next to Hotel Europa).

If you're headed for Edinburgh or Glasgow, flying is generally better than taking the ferry (slow and not that scenic), as it's a fairly cheap, short trip.

It's also fast, cheap, and easy to get to Belfast directly from **Dublin Airport.** The **Aircoach** express bus runs through the night in each direction (hourly, 2 hours). It stops at both Dublin Airport terminals and in downtown Belfast on Glengall Street (next to the Europa Hotel and Great Victoria Street station). With this service you can spend your last night in Belfast and fly out of Dublin in the morning (£14 from Belfast, €17 from Dublin, tel. 028/9033-0655, www.aircoach.ie). For Dublin Airport details, see page 127.

BY FERRY

To Scotland: You can sail between Belfast and **Cairnryan** on the Stena Line ferry. A Rail Link coach connects the Cairnryan port to Ayr, where you'll catch a train to Glasgow Central station (6/day, 2.5 hours by ferry plus 2.5 hours by bus and train, tel. 028/9074-7747, www.stenaline.co.uk). The P&O Ferry (tel. 01304/448-888, www.poferries.com) goes from **Larne,** 20 miles north of Belfast, to **Cairnryan** (6/day, 2 hours), with bus or rail connections from there to Glasgow and Edinburgh. There are hourly trains between Belfast and Larne (1-hour trip, Larne TI tel. 028/2826-2495).

To England: You can sail from Belfast to **Liverpool** (generally 2/day, 8 hours, arrives in port of Birkenhead—10 minutes from Liverpool, tel. 028/9074-7747, www.stenaline.co.uk).

Bangor

To stay in a laid-back seaside hometown—with more comfort per pound—sleep 12 miles east of Belfast in Bangor (BANG-grr). With elegant old homes facing its spruced-up harbor and not even a hint of big-city Belfast, this town has appeal, and it's a handy alternative for travelers who find Belfast booked up by occasional conventions and conferences.

Formerly a Victorian resort and seaside escape from the big city nearby, Bangor now has a sleepy residential feeling. To visit two worthwhile sights near Bangor—the Somme Museum and Mount Stewart House—consider renting a car for the day at nearby George Best Belfast City Airport, a 15-minute train trip from Bangor.

GETTING THERE

Catch the train to Bangor from either Lanyon Place/Central or Great Victoria Street stations (2/hour, 30 minutes, go to the end of the line—don't get off at Bangor West). Consider stopping en route at Cultra (Ulster Folk Park and Transport Museum; see page 513). The journey gives you a good close-up look at the giant Belfast harbor cranes.

Orientation to Bangor

Tourist Information: Bangor's TI is in a stone tower house (from 1637) on the harborfront, a 10-minute walk from the train station (Mon-Fri 9:15-17:00, Sat from 10:00, Sun from 13:00 except closed Sun Sept-April, 34 Quay Street, tel. 028/9127-0069, www. discovernorthernireland.com, search for "Bangor Visitor Information Centre").

Helpful Hints: You'll find **Laundry Chute** at 2 Market Square, a block east of the train station, hidden next to a parking lot behind the post office—easiest access is from Main Street and up Market Street (Mon-Fri 9:00-17:30, Sat until 15:30, closed Sun, tel. 028/9146-5900). **Kare Cabs** provides local taxi service (tel. 028/9145-6777). So does **Bangor Cabs** (tel. 028/9145-6456).

Sights in Bangor

Walks

For sightseeing, your time is better spent in Belfast. But if you have time to burn in Bangor, enjoy a walk beside the water on the **Coastal Path,** which leads west out of town from the marina. A pleasant three-mile level walk along the water leads you to Crawfordsburn Country Park in the suburb of Helen's Bay. Hidden in the trees above Helen's Bay beach is Grey Point Fort, with its two WWI artillery bunkers guarding the shore (generally Sat-Sun 12:00-16:00, tel. 028/9082-3247). Allow 1.5 hours each way as you share the easy-to-follow and mostly paved trail with local joggers, dog walkers, and bikers.

For a shorter walk with views of the marina, head to the end of the **North Pier,** where you'll find a mosaic honoring a portion of the D-Day fleet that rendezvoused offshore in 1944, far from Nazi reconnaissance aircraft. Keep an eye out in the marina for Rose the seal. Little kids may enjoy the **Pickie Fun Park** next to the marina, with paddleboat swan rides and miniature golf. The **Bangor Castle** grounds are good for picnics, and include a peaceful walled garden (free, Mon-Thu 10:00-17:00, Fri-Sun until 18:00).

North Down Museum

This small museum covers local history, from monastic days to Viking raids to Victorian splendor. It's hidden on the grassy grounds behind City Hall, uphill and opposite from the train station.

Cost and Hours: Free, July-Aug daily 10:00-16:30; Sept-June

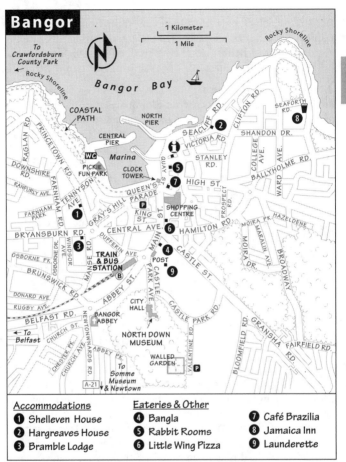

Bangor

1 Kilometer

1 Mile

To Crawfordsburn County Park

← Rocky Shoreline

Rocky Shoreline

Bangor Bay

BELFAST

COASTAL PATH

NORTH PIER

SEACLIFF RD.

CLIFTON RD.

SEAFORTH RD.

❽

CENTRAL PIER

❷

VICTORIA RD.

SHANDON DR.

RAGLAN RD.

PRINCETOWN RD.

WC

Marina

❶

STANLEY RD.

COLLEGE AVE.

WARD AVE.

BALLYHOLME RD.

PICKIE FUN PARK

CLOCK TOWER

❺

HIGH ST.

PROSPECT RD.

DOWNSHIRE RD.

FARNHAM RD.

TENNYSON AVE.

QUEEN'S PARADE

❼

QUAY ST.

MOIRA PK.

HAZELDENE

RANFURLY AVE.

FARNHAM PARK

GRAY'S HILL

P

KING ST.

SHOPPING CENTRE

MAIN ST.

HAMILTON RD.

MOIRA DR.

MARALIN AVE.

BROADWAY

BRYANSBURN RD.

WINDSOR RD.

❸

CENTRAL AVE.

DUFFERIN AVE.

❻

❹

CASTLE ST.

OSBORNE PK.

GOODWOOD AVE.

MANSE RD.

TRAIN & BUS STATION

POST

❾

CASTLE PARK AVE.

CASTLE PARK RD.

BLOOMFIELD RD.

GRANSHA RD.

FAIRFIELD RD.

BRUNSWICK RD.

Ⓑ

ABBEY ST.

DONARD AVE.

RUGBY AVE.

CITY HALL

VALENTINE RD.

BELFAST RD.

NEWTOWNARDS RD.

BANGOR ABBEY

NORTH DOWN MUSEUM

← To Belfast

CHURCH ST.

CHESTER PK.

CHURCH AVE.

ABBEY RD.

WALLED GARDEN

P

To Somme Museum & Newtown

A-21

Accommodations
❶ Shelleven House
❷ Hargreaves House
❸ Bramble Lodge

Eateries & Other
❹ Bangla
❺ Rabbit Rooms
❻ Little Wing Pizza

❼ Café Brazilia
❽ Jamaica Inn
❾ Launderette

Tue-Sat 10:00-16:30, Sun from 12:00, closed Mon; tel. 028/9127-1200, www.northdownmuseum.com.

NEAR BANGOR

The eastern fringe of Northern Ireland is populated mostly by people who consider themselves true-blue British citizens with a history of loyalty to the Crown that goes back more than 400 years. Two sights within reach by car from Bangor highlight this area's firm roots in British culture: the Somme Museum and Mount Stewart House. Call ahead to confirm sight opening hours.

Getting There: Bus service from Bangor is patchy (15 minutes to Somme Museum, one hour to Mount Stewart House with transfer, best to check schedule with Bangor TI or www.translink.co.uk). I'd rent a car instead at nearby George Best Belfast City

Airport, which is only 15 minutes by train from Bangor or 10 minutes from Belfast's Lanyon Place/Central Station. Because the airport is east of Belfast, your drive to these rural sights skips the headache of urban Belfast.

▲Mount Stewart House

No manor house in Ireland better illuminates the affluent lifestyle of the Protestant ascendancy than this lush estate. After the de-

feat of James II (the last Catholic king of England) at the Battle of the Boyne in 1690, the Protestant monarchy was in control—and the privileged status of landowners of the same faith was assured. In the 1700s, Ireland's many Catholic rebellions seemed finally to be squashed, so Anglican landlords felt safe flaunting their wealth in manor houses surrounded by utterly perfect gardens. The Mount Stewart House in particular was designed to dazzle.

Cost and Hours: £10.45 for house and gardens; house open daily 11:00-17:00, gardens from 10:00, closed Nov-Feb; 8 miles south of Bangor, just off A-20 beside Strangford Lough, tel. 028/4278-8387, www.nationaltrust.org.uk/mount-stewart.

Visiting the House: In the **manor house,** you'll glimpse the cushy life led by the Marquess of Londonderry and his heirs over the past three centuries. The main entry hall is a stunner, with a black-and-white checkerboard tile floor, marble columns, classical statues, and pink walls supporting a balcony with a domed ceiling and a fine chandelier. In the dining room, you'll see the original seats occupied by the rears of European heads of state, brought back from the Congress of Vienna after Napoleon's 1815 defeat.

A huge painting of Hambletonian, a prize-winning racehorse, hangs above the grand staircase, dwarfing a portrait of the Duke of Wellington in a hall nearby. The heroic duke (worried that his Irish birth would be seen as lower class by British blue bloods) once quipped in Parliament, "Just because one is born in a stable does not make him a horse." Irish emancipator Daniel O'Connell retorted, "Yes, but it could make you an ass."

Afterward, wander the expansive manicured **gardens.** The fantasy life of parasol-toting, upper-crust Victorian society seems to ooze from every viewpoint. Fanciful sculptures of extinct dodo birds and monkeys holding vases on their heads set off predictably classic Italian and Spanish sections. An Irish harp has been trimmed out of a hedge a few feet from a flowerbed shaped like the Red Hand of Ulster. Swans glide serenely among the lily pads on a small lake.

Somme Museum

World War I's trench warfare was a meat grinder. More British soldiers died in the last year of that war than in all of World War II. Northern Ireland's men were not spared—especially during the bloody Battle of the Somme in France, starting in July 1916 (see the "1916" sidebar on page 494). Among the Allied forces was the British Army's 36th Ulster Division, which drew heavily from this loyal heartland of Northern Ireland. The 36th Ulster Division suffered brutal losses at the Battle of the Somme—of the 760 men recruited from the Shankill Road area in Belfast, only 10 percent survived.

Exhibits portray the battle experience through a mix of military artifacts, photos, historical newsreels, and life-size figures posed in trench warfare re-creations. To access the majority of the exhibits, it's essential to take the one-hour guided tour (leaving hourly, on the hour). Visiting this place is a moving experience, but it can only hint at the horrific conditions endured by these soldiers.

Cost and Hours: £7; July-Aug Mon-Fri 10:00-17:00, Sat from 11:00, last tour one hour before closing, closed Fri Sept-June and Sun year-round; 3 miles south of Bangor just off A-21 at 233 Bangor Road, tel. 028/9182-3202, www.irishsoldier.org. A coffee shop is located at the center.

Sleeping in Bangor

Visitors arriving in Bangor (by train) come down Main Street, a 10-minute (mostly downhill) walk to reach the harbor marina. You'll find Hargreaves House up the east side of the harbor to the right, along the waterfront on Seacliff Road. The other two listings are to the left, closer to the train station and farther from the water. Take the first immediate left out of the station onto steeply downhill Dufferin Avenue; both are near the roundabout at the bottom.

$$$ Shelleven House is an old-fashioned, well-kept, stately place with 13 prim rooms on the quiet corner of Princetown Road and Tennyson Avenue (RS%, family rooms, parking, 61 Princetown Road, tel. 028/9127-1777, www.shellevenhouse.com, info@shellevenhouse.com, Sue and Paul Toner).

$$ Hargreaves House, a homey Victorian waterfront refuge with three cozy, refurbished rooms, is Bangor's best value, run by ever-helpful Pauline (RS%—use code "HHRS18," ocean views, parking, 15-minute walk from train station but worth it, 78 Seacliff Road, tel. 028/9146-4071, mobile 079-8058-5047, www. hargreaveshouse.com, info@hargreaveshouse.com).

$ Bramble Lodge is closest to the train station (10-minute walk), offering three inviting and spotless rooms (1 Bryansburn Road, tel. 028/9145-7924, mobile 077-9262-8001, jacquihanna_bramblelodge@yahoo.co.uk, Jacquiline Hanna).

Eating in Bangor

Most restaurants in town stop seating at about 20:30.

$$$ Bangla serves fine Indian cuisine with attentive service and a good-value early-bird option before 19:00 (daily 12:00-14:00 & 16:30-23:00, 115 Main Street, tel. 028/9127-1272).

$$ The **Rabbit Rooms** serves hearty Irish food to local crowds with live music after the dinner service several nights a week (daily 12:00-21:00, music Mon and Thu-Sat, near the harbor at 33 Quay Street, tel. 028/9146-7699).

$ Little Wing Pizza is a friendly joint serving tasty pizza, pasta, and salads. Grab your food to go and munch by the marina. It's also one of the few places in town that serves food later at night (daily 11:00-22:00, 37 Main Street, tel. 028/9147-2777).

$ Café Brazilia, a popular locals' lunch hangout with a simple menu, is across from the stubby clock tower (Mon-Sat 8:00-16:30, Sun from 10:00, 13 Bridge Street, tel. 028/9127-2763).

The **$$ Jamaica Inn** offers pleasant pub grub and a breezy waterfront porch (food served about 12:00-21:00, 10-minute walk east of the TI, 188 Seacliff Road, tel. 028/9147-1610).

IRELAND: PAST & PRESENT

Ireland is rich with history, culture, and language. The country continues to transform and grow today, making progress toward peace and reexamining some of its long-held social customs as it addresses new challenges.

Irish History

PREHISTORY

Ireland became an island when rising seas covered the last land bridge (7000 BC), a separation from Britain that the Irish would fight to maintain for the next 9,000 years. (Snakes were too slow to migrate before the seas cut Ireland off, despite later legends about St. Patrick banishing them.) By 6000 BC, Stone Age hunter-fishers had settled on the east coast, followed by Neolithic farmers from the island of Britain. These early inhabitants left behind impressive but mysterious funeral mounds (passage graves) and large Stonehenge-type stone circles.

THE CELTS (500 BC-AD 450)

More an invasion of ideas than of armies, the Celtic culture from Central Europe settled in Ireland, where it would dominate for a thousand years. There were more than 300 *tuatha* (kingdoms) in Ireland, each with its own *rí* (king), who would've happily chopped the legs off anyone who called him "petty." The island was nominally ruled by a single *Ard Rí* (high king) at the **Hill of Tara** (north of Dublin), though there was no centralized nation.

In 55 BC, the Romans conquered the Celts in England, but they never invaded Ireland. Irish history forever skewed in a different direction—Gaelic, not Latin. The Romans called Ireland

Hibernia, meaning Land of Winter; it was apparently too cold and bleak to merit an attempt at colonization.

THE AGE OF SAINTS AND SCHOLARS (AD 450-800)

When Ancient Rome fell and took the Continent—and many of the achievements of Roman culture—with it, Gaelic Ireland was unaffected. There was no Dark Age here, and the island was a beacon of culture for the rest of Europe. Ireland (population c. 750,000) was still a land of many feuding kings, but the culture was stable.

Christianity and Latin culture arrived first as a trickle from trading contacts with Christian Gaul (France), then more emphatically in AD 432 with **St. Patrick,** who persuasively converted the sun- and nature-worshipping Celts. Legends say he drove Ireland's snakes (symbolic of pagan beliefs) into the sea and explained the Trinity with a shamrock—three leaves on one stem.

Later monks continued Christianizing the island. They flocked to scattered, isolated monasteries, living in stone igloo beehive huts, translating and illustrating manuscripts. Perhaps the greatest works of art from all of Dark Age Europe are these manuscripts, particularly the ninth-century Book of Kells (in Dublin).

By 800, **Charlemagne** was importing educated and literate Irish monks to help organize and run his Frankish kingdom. Meanwhile, Ireland remained a relatively cohesive society based on monastic settlements rather than cities. Impressive round towers from those settlements still dot the Irish landscape—silent reminders of this scholarly age.

VIKING INVASION AND DEFEAT (800-1100)

In 795, Viking pirates from Norway invaded, first testing isolated island monasteries, then boldly sailing up Irish rivers into the country's interior. The many raids wreaked havoc on the monasteries and continued to shake Irish civilization for two chaotic centuries. In 841, a conquering Viking band decided to winter in Ireland. The idea caught on as subsequent raiders eventually built the island's first permanent walled cities, Dublin and Waterford. The Viking raiders slowly evolved into Viking traders. They were the first to introduce urban life and commerce to Ireland.

ANGLO-NORMAN ARRIVAL (1100-1500)

The Normans were Ireland's next aggressive guests. In 1169, a small army of well-armed soldiers of fortune invaded Ireland under the pretense of helping a deposed Irish king regain his lands. This was the spearhead of a century-long invasion by the so-called Anglo-Normans—the French-speaking rulers of England, descended from William the Conqueror and his troops.

By 1250, the Anglo-Normans occupied two-thirds of the island. But when the **Black Death** came in 1348, it spread rapidly and fatally in the tightly packed Norman settlements. The plague, along with Normans intermarrying with Gaels, eventually diluted Norman identity and shrank English control. But even as Anglo-Norman power eroded, the English kings considered Ireland theirs.

THE END OF GAELIC RULE (1500s)

Martin Luther's **Reformation** split the Christian churches into Catholic and Protestant, making Catholic Ireland a hot potato for newly Protestant England to handle. In 1534, angered by **Henry VIII** and his break with Catholicism, the **earls of Kildare** (father, then son) led a rebellion. Henry crushed the revolt, executed the earls, and confiscated their land. Henry's daughter, **Elizabeth I,** gave the land to English Protestant colonists (called "planters"). The next four centuries would see a series of rebellions by Gaelic-speaking Irish-Catholic farmers fighting to free themselves from rule by English-speaking Protestant landowners.

Hugh O'Neill (1540-1616), a Gaelic chieftain angered by planters and English abuses, led a Gaelic revolt in 1595. At the Battle of Yellow Ford (1598), guerrilla tactics brought about an initial Irish victory. But after the disastrous **Battle of Kinsale** (1601), O'Neill ceded a half-million acres to England, signaling the end of Gaelic Irish rule.

ENGLISH COLONIZATION AND IRISH REBELLIONS (1600s)

By 1641, 25,000 Protestant English and Scottish planters had settled into the confiscated land, making Ulster (in the northeast) the most English area of the island.

Then, **Oliver Cromwell**—who had pulled off a *coup d'état* in England—invaded and conquered Ireland (1649-1650) with a Puritanical, anti-Catholic zeal. Cromwell confiscated 11 million

Stone Circles: The Riddle of the Rocks

Ireland is home to more than 200 evocative stone circles. These jaggedly sparse boulder rings are rudimentary in comparison to Britain's more famous Stonehenge. But their misty, mossy settings provide curious travelers with a glimpse of the mysterious people who lived in Ireland before the Celts.

Late Bronze Age communities put considerable time and effort into moving huge rocks into ring formations. Scholars believe that these circles may have been used as solar observatories, to calculate solstices and equinoxes as they planned life-sustaining seasonal crop-planting cycles. Without any written records, we can only surmise their exact purpose.

In the Middle Ages, superstitious people believed that the stones had been arranged by an earlier race of giants. Later, some thought that at least one circle was made up of petrified partiers who had dared to dance on the Sabbath. A nearby standing stone was supposed to have been the piper who had been playing the tunes.

Two main regional clusters hold more than a hundred circles each: central Ulster, in the North (radiocarbon-dated 1500-700 BC); and County Cork and County Kerry, in the south (radiocarbon-dated 1000-700 BC). The remaining dozen circles are scattered across central Ireland. Some circles have only recently been rediscovered, having been buried over the centuries by rapidly accumulating bog growth.

Dedicated travelers seeking stone circles will find them marked in the Ordnance Survey atlas and signposted along rural roads. Ask a local farmer for directions—and savor the experience (wear shoes impervious to grass dew and sheep doo).

My favorite stone circles are all within a druid's dance of other destinations mentioned in this book:

Kenmare is in County Kerry, on the western fringe of Kenmare town. It's the most easily accessible of the circles listed here.

Drombeg is in County Cork, 35 miles (56 km) southwest of Kinsale, up a narrow winding lane just south of the R-597 coastal road.

Glebe is in County Mayo, two miles (3 km) east of Cong and 100 yards south of the R-345 road to Neale (across a minefield of sheep droppings).

Beltany is in County Donegal, 10 miles (16 km) southeast of Letterkenny, straight south of Raphoe.

Beaghmore is in County Tyrone, 20 miles (32 km) east of Omagh, north off A-505 (Cookstown Road).

additional acres of land from Catholic Irish landowners to give to English Protestants.

In 1688-1689, Irish rebels rallied around Catholic **King James II,** who had been deposed by the English Parliament. He wound up in Ireland, where he formed an army to retake the crown. The showdown came at the massive **Battle of the Boyne** (1690), north of Dublin. James and his 25,000 men were defeated by the troops of Protestant **King William III** of Orange. From this point on, the color orange became a symbol in Ireland for pro-English, pro-Protestant forces.

PAST & PRESENT

PROTESTANT RULE (1700s)

During the 18th century, urban Ireland thrived economically, and even culturally, under the English. Dublin in the 1700s (pop. 50,000) was Britain's second city, and one of Europe's wealthiest and most sophisticated.

But beyond Dublin, rebellion continued to brew. Irish nationalists were inspired by budding democratic revolutions in America (1776) and France (1789). Increasingly, the issue of Irish independence was less a religious question than a political one.

England tried to solve the Irish problem politically by forcing Ireland into a "Union" with England as part of a "United Kingdom" (**Act of Union,** 1801). The 500-year-old Irish Parliament was dissolved, with its members becoming part of England's Parliament in London. From then on, "Unionists" have been those who oppose Irish independence, wanting to preserve the country's union with England.

VOTES, VIOLENCE, AND THE FAMINE (1800s)

Irish politicians lobbied in the British Parliament for Catholic rights, reform of absentee-landlordism, and for **Home Rule.** But any hope of an Irish revival was soon snuffed out by the biggest catastrophe in Irish history: the **Great Potato Famine** (1845-1849). Legions of people (between 500,000 and 1.1 million) starved to

Typical Castle Architecture

Castles were fortified residences for medieval nobles. In Ireland, Norman (evolving into English) warlords introduced them in the late 1100s. Castles come in all shapes and sizes, but knowing a few general terms will help you understand them.

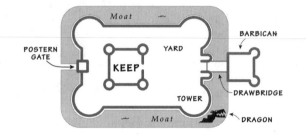

Barbican: A fortified gatehouse, sometimes a stand-alone building located outside the main walls.

Crenellation: A gap-toothed pattern of stones atop the parapet.

Drawbridge: A bridge that could be raised or lowered, using counterweights or a chain-and-winch.

Great Hall: The largest room in the castle, serving as throne room, conference center, and dining hall.

Hoardings (or Gallery or Brattice): Wooden huts built onto the upper parts of the stone walls. They served as watchtowers, living quarters, and fighting platforms.

Keep (or Donjon): A high, strong stone tower in the center of the complex; the lord's home and refuge of last resort.

Loopholes (or Embrasures): Narrow wall slits through which soldiers could shoot arrows.

Machicolation: A stone ledge jutting out from the wall, with holes through which soldiers could drop rocks or boiling liquid onto wall-scaling enemies below.

Moat: A ditch encircling the wall, sometimes filled with water.

Parapet: Outer railing of the wall walk.

Portcullis: An iron grille that could be lowered across the entrance.

Postern Gate: A small, unfortified side or rear entrance. In wartime, it became a "sally-port" used to launch surprise attacks, or as an escape route.

Towers: Square or round structures with crenellated tops or conical roofs serving as lookouts, chapels, living quarters, or the dungeon.

Turret: A small lookout tower rising from the top of the wall.

Wall Walk (or Allure): A pathway atop the wall where guards could patrol and where soldiers stood to fire at the enemy.

Yard (or Bailey): An open courtyard inside the castle walls.

Typical Church Architecture

The oldest stone churches that survive in Ireland were designed and built by religious orders (Cistercians, Benedictines, Franciscans, and Dominicans) that came to Ireland from the Continent in the mid-1100s, and were supported by the Norman invaders who soon followed. Even if you wouldn't know your apse from a hole in the ground, learning a few simple terms will enrich your experience.

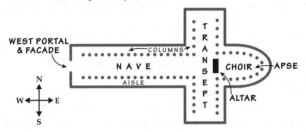

Aisles: The long, generally low-ceilinged arcades that flank the nave.

Altar: The raised area with a ceremonial table (often adorned with candles or a crucifix), where the priest prepares and serves the bread and wine for Communion.

Apse: The space beyond the altar, often bordered with small chapels.

Barrel Vault: A continuous round-arched ceiling that resembles an extended upside-down U.

Choir: A cozy area, often screened off, located within the church nave and near the high altar where services are sung in a more intimate setting.

Cloister: Covered hallways bordering a square or rectangular open-air courtyard, traditionally where monks and nuns got fresh air.

Facade: The front exterior of the church's main (west) entrance, generally highly decorated.

Groin Vault: An arched ceiling formed where two equal barrel vaults meet at right angles. Less common usage: term for a medieval jock strap.

Narthex: The area (portico or foyer) between the main entry and the nave.

Nave: The long, central section of the church (running west to east, from the entrance to the altar) where the congregation sits or stands through the service.

Transept: In a traditional cross-shaped floor plan, the transept is one of the two parts forming the "arms" of the cross. The transepts run north-south, perpendicularly crossing the east-west nave.

West Portal: The main entry to the church (on the west end, opposite the main altar).

death or died of related dis-
eases. Another 1 to 2 million
emigrated.

Ireland was ruined. Many
of the best and brightest fled, and
the island's economy—and spirit—took generations to recover.
And culturally, old Gaelic, rural
Ireland was being crushed under
the Industrial Revolution and
the political control wielded by Protestant England.

EASTER RISING AND WAR OF INDEPENDENCE (1900-1920)

As the century turned, Ireland prepared for the inevitable showdown with Britain. On Easter Monday, April 24, 1916, Irish nationalists marched on Dublin and proclaimed Ireland an independent republic. British troops struck back and in a week suppressed
the insurrection. When the British government swiftly executed
the ringleaders, Ireland resolved to win its independence at all
costs.

In the 1918 elections, the separatist Sinn Féin party (meaning "Ourselves") won big, but these new members of Parliament
refused to go to London. Instead, they formed their own independent Irish Parliament in Dublin. Then Irish rebels began ambushing policemen—seen as the eyes and ears of British control—
sparking the **War of Independence** in 1919. The fledgling Irish
Republican Army faced 40,000 British troops. A thousand people
died in this multiyear guerrilla war of street fighting, sniper fire,
jailhouse beatings, terrorist bombs, and reprisals.

PARTITION AND CIVIL WAR (1920-1950)

Finally, Britain agreed to Irish independence. But Ireland itself was
a divided nation—the southern three-quarters of the island was
mostly Catholic, Gaelic, rural, and for Home Rule; the northern
quarter was Protestant, English, industrial, and Unionist. The solution? In 1921, the British Parliament partitioned the island into
two independent, self-governing
countries within the British
Commonwealth: **Northern Ireland** and the **Irish Free State.**

Ireland's various politi-
cal factions wrestled with this
compromise solution, and the
island plunged into a **Civil War**
(1922-1923). The hardline IRA

opposed the partition. Dublin and the southeast were ravaged in a year of bitter fighting before the Irish Free State emerged victorious. The IRA went underground, moving its fight north and trying for the rest of the century to topple the government of Northern Ireland.

In 1949, the Irish Free State left the Commonwealth and officially became the **Republic of Ireland.**

TROUBLES IN THE NORTH (1950-2000)

The Republic moved toward prosperity in the second half of the century, but Northern Ireland—with a slight Protestant majority and a large, disaffected Catholic minority—was plagued by the **Troubles.** In 1967, organized marches and demonstrations demanded equal treatment for Catholics. Protestant **Unionist Orangemen** countered by marching through Catholic neighborhoods, provoking riots. In 1969, Britain sent troops to help Northern Ireland keep the peace.

From the 1970s to the 1990s, the North was a low-level battlefield, with the IRA using terrorist tactics to advance their political agenda. The Troubles, which claimed some 3,000 lives, continued with bombings, marches, hunger strikes, rock-throwing, and riots (notably Derry's **Bloody Sunday** in 1972).

Finally, after a string of failed peace agreements, came the watershed 1998 settlement known as the **Good Friday Accord** (to pro-Irish Nationalists) or the **Belfast Agreement** (to pro-British Unionists).

GLOBAL NATIONS (2000 AND BEYOND)

After years of negotiation, in 2005 the IRA formally announced an end to its armed campaign, promising to pursue peaceful, democratic means. In 2007, London returned control of Northern Ireland to the popularly elected Northern Ireland Assembly. Perhaps most important, after almost 40 years, the British Army withdrew 90 percent of its forces from Northern Ireland that summer.

Now it's up to Northern Ireland to keep the peace. The 1998 peace accord gives Northern Ireland the freedom to leave the UK if ever the majority of the population approves a referendum to do so. At the same time, the Republic of Ireland withdrew its constitutional claim to the entire island of Ireland. Northern Ireland now has limited autonomy from London, with its own democratically elected, power-sharing government.

PAST & PRESENT

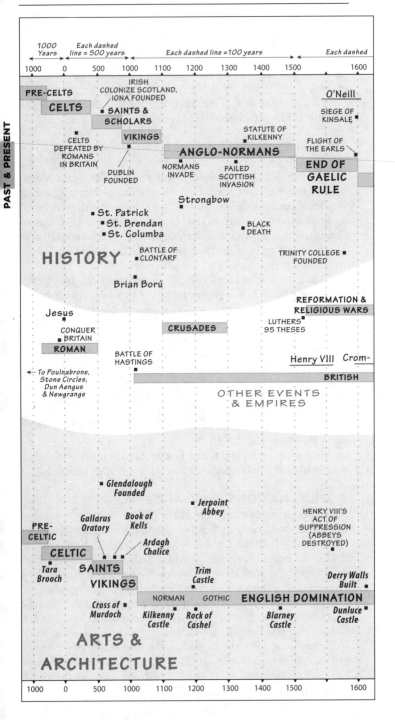

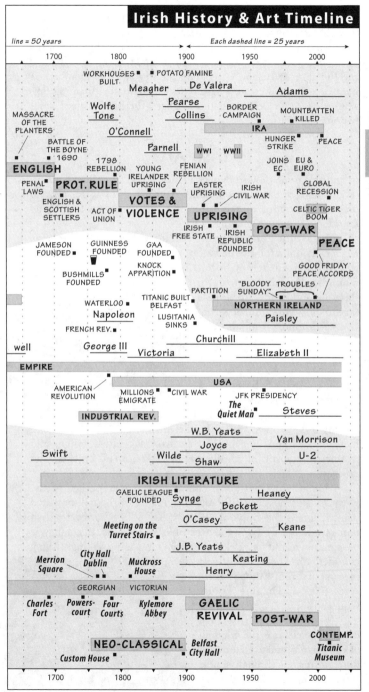

Irish History & Art Timeline

line = 50 years | Each dashed line = 25 years

1700 — 1800 — 1900 — 1950 — 2000

PAST & PRESENT

WORKHOUSES BUILT ■ ■ POTATO FAMINE

Meagher — De Valera

Adams

MASSACRE OF THE PLANTERS ■

Wolfe Tone

Pearse

Collins

BORDER CAMPAIGN

MOUNTBATTEN ■ KILLED

O'Connell

IRA

HUNGER STRIKE

PEACE

BATTLE OF THE BOYNE ■ 1690

Parnell

WWI WWII

1798 REBELLION

ENGLISH

JOINS EC

EU & EURO

YOUNG IRELANDER UPRISING

FENIAN REBELLION

PENAL LAWS ■

PROT. RULE

EASTER UPRISING

GLOBAL RECESSION

ENGLISH & SCOTTISH SETTLERS

ACT OF UNION

VOTES & VIOLENCE

IRISH CIVIL WAR

CELTIC TIGER BOOM

UPRISING

IRISH FREE STATE

IRISH REPUBLIC FOUNDED

POST-WAR

PEACE

JAMESON FOUNDED ■

GUINNESS FOUNDED ■

GAA FOUNDED ■

KNOCK APPARITION ■

GOOD FRIDAY PEACE ACCORDS

BUSHMILLS FOUNDED ■

"BLOODY SUNDAY" TROUBLES

PARTITION ■

WATERLOO ■

TITANIC BUILT BELFAST ■

NORTHERN IRELAND

Napoleon

LUSITANIA SINKS ■

Paisley

FRENCH REV. ■

Churchill

well

George III

Victoria

Elizabeth II

EMPIRE

USA

AMERICAN REVOLUTION

MILLIONS EMIGRATE ■

■CIVIL WAR

JFK PRESIDENCY ■

INDUSTRIAL REV.

The Quiet Man

Steves

W.B. Yeats

Joyce

Van Morrison

Swift

Wilde

U-2

Shaw

IRISH LITERATURE

GAELIC LEAGUE FOUNDED ■

Synge

Heaney

Beckett

O'Casey

Keane

Meeting on the Turret Stairs ■

J.B. Yeats

Merrion Square ■

City Hall Dublin ■

Muckross House ■

Keating

Henry

GEORGIAN VICTORIAN

Charles Fort ■

Powers-court ■

Four Courts ■

Kylemore Abbey ■

GAELIC REVIVAL

POST-WAR

NEO-CLASSICAL

Belfast City Hall ■

CONTEMP.

Custom House ■

Titanic Museum ■

1700 — 1800 — 1900 — 1950 — 2000

Britain's decision to leave the European Union (Brexit) has brought new uncertainties to Ireland. The stakes are high: The fragile peace that ended the Troubles works in part because of the EU's open border between Northern Ireland (part of the UK) and the Republic of Ireland (a separate country and EU member). A hard Brexit would create a hard border, potentially inflaming tensions in these divided communities. (See "The Brexit Effect" sidebar on page 431 for more.)

Irish Art

Megalithic tombs, ancient gold and metalwork, illuminated manuscripts, high crosses carved in stone, paintings of rural Ireland, and provocative political murals—Ireland comes with some fascinating art. Here are a few highlights.

Megalithic Period: During the Stone Age, 5,000 years ago, farmers living in the **Boyne Valley,** north of Dublin, built a "cemetery" of approximately 40 **burial mounds.** The most famous of these mound tombs is the passage tomb at Newgrange, part of Brú na Bóinne, which also features some of Europe's best examples of megalithic (big rock) art.

The Age of Saints and Scholars: Christianity grew in Ireland from St. Patrick's first efforts in the fifth century AD. During this "Golden Age" of Irish civilization, monks, along with metalworkers and stonemasons, created imaginative designs and distinctive stylistic motifs for **manuscripts, metal objects,** and **crosses.**

Monks wrote out and richly decorated manuscripts of the Gospels. The most beautiful and imaginative of these illuminated manuscripts is the **Book of Kells** (c. AD 800). Crafted by Irish monks at a monastery on the Scottish island of Iona, the book was brought to Ireland for safekeeping from rampaging Vikings. Many consider this book the finest piece of art from Europe's Dark Ages (now at Dublin's Trinity College Library).

The monks used Irish high crosses to celebrate the triumph of Christianity and to educate the illiterate masses through simple stone carvings of biblical themes.

The **Cross of Murdock** (Muiredach's Cross, AD 923) is 18 feet tall, towering over the remains of the monastic settlement at Monasterboice. It is but one of many monumental crosses in Ireland.

Native Irish Art: The English suppressed Celtic Irish culture, replacing native styles with English traditions in architecture, painting, and literature. But in the late 19th century, revivals in Irish language, folklore, music, and art began to surface. **Jack B. Yeats** (1871-1957, brother of the poet W. B. Yeats), Belfast-born painter **Paul Henry** (1876-1958), and **Sean Keating** (1889-1977) were among the painters who looked to traditional Irish subjects for inspiration, focusing on Ireland's people, the country's rugged beauty, and its struggle for independence.

To learn more about Irish history, consider *Europe 101: History and Art for the Traveler*, written by Rick Steves and Gene Openshaw (available at www.ricksteves.com).

Irish Literature

Since the Book of Kells, Ireland's greatest contributions to the world of art have been through words. After Christianity transformed Ireland into a refuge of literacy (while the rest of Europe crumbled into the Dark Ages), Charlemagne's imported Irish monks invented "minuscule," which became the basis of the lowercase letters we use in our alphabet today. The cultural importance placed on the word (spoken, and, for the past 1,500 years, written) is today reflected in the rich output of modern Irish writers.

William Butler Yeats' early poems and plays are filled with fairies and idyllic rural innocence, while his later poems reflect Ireland's painful transition to independence. Yeats' Nobel Prize for literature (1923) was eventually matched by three later, Nobel-winning Irish authors: **George Bernard Shaw** (1925), **Samuel Beckett** (1969), and **Seamus Heaney** (1995).

Dublin-born **Oscar Wilde** wowed London with his quick wit, outrageous clothes, and flamboyant personality. Wilde wrote the darkly fascinating *Picture of Dorian Gray* (1890) and skewered upper-class Victorian society in witty comedic plays such as *The Importance of Being Earnest* (1895). Meanwhile, **Bram Stoker** was conjuring up a Gothic thriller called *Dracula* (1897). Most inventive of all, perhaps, was **James Joyce,** who captured literary lightning in a bottle with his modern, stream-of-consciousness *Ulysses,* set on a single day in Dublin (June 16, 1904).

In recent decades, the bittersweet Irish literary parade has been inhabited by tragically volcanic characters like **Brendan Behan,** who exclaimed, "I'm a drinker with a writing problem." Bleak poverty experienced in childhood was the catalyst for **Frank McCourt**'s memorable *Angela's Ashes.* Among the most celebrated of today's Irish writers is **Roddy Doyle,** whose feel for working-class Dublin resonates in his novels of contemporary life (such as *The Commitments*).

Irish Language

The Irish have a rich oral tradition that goes back to their ancient fireside storytelling days. Part of the fun of traveling here is getting an ear for the way locals express themselves.

Irish Gaelic is one of four surviving Celtic languages, along with Scottish Gaelic, Welsh, and Breton. Some proud Irish choose to call their native tongue "Irish" instead of "Gaelic" to ensure that there is no confusion with the language spoken in parts of Scotland.

Only 165 years ago, the majority of the Irish population spoke Irish Gaelic. But most of the speakers were of the poor laborer class that either died or emigrated during the famine. After the famine, parents and teachers understood that their children would be better off speaking English if they emigrated to the US, Canada, Australia, or England. Children in schools wore a tally stick around their necks, and teachers cut a notch each time a child was caught speaking Irish. At the end of the day, the child received a whack for each notch in the stick. It wasn't until a resurgence of cultural pride in the late 19th century that an attempt was made to promote the language again.

These days, less than 5 percent of the Irish population is fluent in their native tongue. However, it's taken seriously enough that all national laws must first be written in Irish, then translated into English. Irish Gaelic can be heard most often in the western counties of Kerry, Galway, Mayo, and Donegal. You'll know you're en-

Gaeltacht Regions

N. IRE. BELFAST

GALWAY

DINGLE
(AN DAINGEAN)

REP. OF IRELAND

DUBLIN

CORK

AREAS SHOWN IN GREY
ARE PART OF THE GAELTACHT

tering an Irish Gaelic-speaking area when you see a sign saying Gaeltacht (GAIL-takt).

Irish Gaelic has no "th" sound—which you can hear today when an Irish person says something like "turdy-tree" (thirty-three). There are also no equivalents of the simple words "yes" and "no." Instead, answers are given in an affirmative or negative rephrasing of the question. For example, a question like "Did you mail the letter today?" would be answered with "I did (mail the letter)," rather than a simple "yes." Or "It's a nice day today, isn't it?" would be answered with "It is," or "'Tis."

IRISH PLACE NAMES

Here are a few words that appear in Irish place names. You'll see these on road signs or at tourist sights.

Irish	English
alt (ahlt)	cliff
an lár (ahn lar)	city center
ard (ard)	high, height, hillock
baile (BALL-yah)	town, town land
beag (beg)	little
bearna (bar-na)	gap
boireann (burr-en)	large rock, rocky area
bóthar (boh-er)	road
bun (bun)	end, bottom
caiseal (CASH-el)	circular stone fort
caisleán (cash-LAWN)	castle
cathair (CAHT-her)	circular stone fort, city
cill (kill)	church
cloch (clockh)	stone
doire (dih-ruh)	oak
droichead (DROCKH-ed)	bridge
drumlin (DRUM-lin)	small hill
dún (doon)	fort
fionn (fi-UN)	white, fair-haired person
gaeltacht (GAIL-takt)	Irish language district
gall (gaul)	foreigner
garda (gar-dah)	police officer
gort (gort)	field

Irish	English
inis (in-ish)	island
mileac (MIL-yach)	low marshy ground
mór (mor)	large
muck (muck)	pig
oifig an phoist (UFF-ig un fusht)	post office
poll (poll)	hole, cave
rath (rath)	ancient earthen fort
ros (ross)	wood or headland
sí (shee)	fairy mound, bewitching
slí (slee)	route, way
sliabh (sleeve)	mountain
sráid (shrayd)	street
teach (chockh)	house
trá (traw)	beach, strand

IRISH PLEASANTRIES

When you reach the more remote western fringe of Ireland, you're likely to hear folks speaking Irish. Although locals can readily converse with you in English, it's fascinating to hear their ancient Celtic language spoken. Here are some basic Irish phrases:

Irish	English
Fáilte. (FAHLT-chuh or FAHLT-uh)	Welcome.
Conas tá tú? (CONN-us A-ta too)	How are you?
Go raibh maith agat. (guh rov mah UG-ut)	Thank you.
Slán. (slawn)	Bye.
Dia dhuit. (DEA-gwitch)	God be with you.

IRISH POLITICS

Politics is a popular topic of conversation here. Whether you pick up a local newspaper or turn on your car radio, you're likely to encounter these Irish political terms in the media:

Irish	English
Taoiseach (TEE-shock)	prime minister of Irish Republic
Seanad (SHAN-ud)	Irish Senate
Dáil (DOY-ill)	Irish House of Representatives
Teachta Dála (TD) (TALK-tah DOLL-ah)	member of Irish Parliament
Fine Gael (FEE-nuh GWAIL)	political party "Clan of the Gaels"
Fine Fáil (FEE-nuh FOIL)	political party "Soldiers of Destiny"
Sinn Féin (shin-FAIN)	political party "We Ourselves"

IRISH PUB AND MUSIC WORDS

The Irish love to socialize. Pubs are like public living rooms, where friends gather in a corner to play tunes and anyone is a welcome guest. Here are some useful pub and music words:

Irish	English
poitín (po-CHEEN)	moonshine, homemade liquor
craic (crack)	fun atmosphere, good conversation
bodhrán (BO-run)	traditional drum
uilleann (ILL-in)	elbow (*uilleann* pipes are elbow bagpipes)
trad (trad)	traditional Irish music
ceilidh (KAY-lee)	Irish dance gathering
fleadh (flah)	music festival
Slainte! (SLAWN-chuh)	Cheers! (To your health!)
Táim súgach! (taw im SOO-gakh)	I'm tipsy!
lei thras (LEH-hrass)	toilets
mná (min-AW)	women's room
fír (fear)	men's room

IRISH NAMES

Here are some of the most common Celtic first names. Amaze your new Irish friends by pronouncing them correctly, or at least not mangling them.

Irish	English
Aoife (EE-fuh)	Ava
Áine (ON-yuh)	Anna
Eammon (A-mun)	Edmond
Liam (LEE-um)	William
Mairéad (mahr-AID)	Margaret
Michael (ME-hall)	Michael
Niall (NILE)	Neil
Pádraig (POD-rig)	Patrick
Peadar (PAD-er)	Peter
Roisín (ROW-sheen)	Rosaleen
Seamus (SHAME-us)	James
Sean (SHAWN)	John
Sinéad (shin-AID)	Jane
Siobhán (shiv-AWN)	Joan

Irish-Yankee Vocabulary

If some of these words seem more British than Irish, those are ones you're likely to hear more often in Northern Ireland (part of the UK).

advert: advertisement
anticlockwise: counterclockwise
aubergine: eggplant
banger: sausage
bang on: correct
banjaxed: messed up
bank holiday: government holiday
bar: except
beer mat: coaster
bespoke: custom
billion: a thousand of our billions (a trillion)
biro: ballpoint pen
biscuit: cookie
Black Mariah: police van
black pudding: sausage made from pig's blood
black stuff: Guinness
blather: rambling, empty talk
blinkered: narrow-minded
bloody: damn (from medieval blasphemy: "Christ's blood")
blow off: fart
boffin: nerd
bog: slang for toilet
boho: bohemian
bolshy: argumentative
bonnet: car hood
boot: car trunk
braces: suspenders
bridle way: path for walkers, bikers, and horse riders
brilliant: cool
bum: bottom or "backside"
busker: street musician
cacks: trousers, underpants
candy floss: cotton candy
caravan: trailer
car boot sale: temporary flea market, often for charity
car park: parking lot
carry on: nonsense
casualty: emergency room
cat's eyes: road reflectors
ceilidh (pronounced "KAY-lee"): dance, party
champ: mashed potatoes and onions

chemist: pharmacist
chicory: endive
chipper: fish-and-chips shop
chips: french fries
chock-a-block: jam-packed
chuffed: pleased
cider: alcoholic apple cider
clearway: road where you can't stop
coach: long-distance bus
concession: discounted admission
cos: romaine lettuce
cotton buds: cotton swabs
courgette: zucchini
craic (pronounced "crack"): fun, good conversation
crèche (pronounced "creesh"): preschool
crisps: potato chips
Croker: Croke Park (GAA Dublin sports stadium)
crusties: New Age hippies
culchie: hick, country yokel
cuppa: cup of tea
CV: résumé (curriculum vitae)
Da: father
deadly: really good
dear: expensive
digestives: round graham crackers
dinner: lunch or dinner
diversion: detour
dodgy: iffy, risky
dole: welfare
done and dusted: completed
donkey's years: until the cows come home, forever
draughts (pronounced "drafts"): checkers
draw: marijuana
dual carriageway: divided highway (four lanes)
Dubs: people from Dublin
Dutch courage: alcohol-induced bravery
eejit: moron
Emergency, The: World War II
en suite: bathroom attached to room
face flannel: washcloth
fair play (to you): well done, good job
fanny: vagina
fiddler's fart: worthless thing
first floor: second floor (one floor above ground)
fiver: five-euro note
flat: apartment

fluthered: drunk
flutter: a bet
football: Gaelic football
fortnight: two weeks
full monty: the whole shebang, everything
GAA: Gaelic Athletic Association
gallery: balcony
gammon: ham
gangway: aisle
gaol: jail (same pronunciation)
Garda: police
gargle: to have an alcoholic drink
gasman: the life of the party
give way: yield
giving out: chewing out, yelling at
glen: valley
gob: mouth
gobsmacked: astounded
grand: good, well ("How are you?" "I'm grand, thanks")
guards: police *(Garda)*
gurrier: hooligan
half eight: 8:30 (not 7:30)
hen night: bachelorette party
holiday: vacation
homely: likable or cozy
hooley: party or informal shindig
hoover: vacuum cleaner
hurling: Irish field hockey
iced lolly: popsicle
interval: intermission
ironmonger: hardware store
jacket potato: baked potato
jacks: toilet
jars: drinks (alcohol)
jelly: Jell-O
Joe Soap: dim stranger
jumble: sale, rummage sale
jumper: sweater
just a tick: just a second
kipper: smoked herring
knackered: exhausted
knickers: ladies' panties
knocked: torn down (buildings)
knocking shop: brothel
knock up: wake up or visit
ladybird: ladybug

lash: a try ("give it a lash")
left luggage: baggage check
let: rent
lift: elevator
listed: protected historic building
lorry: truck
Ma, Mam, Mammy: mother
mac: mackintosh (trench) coat
mangetout: snow peas
mate: buddy (boy or girl)
mean: stingy
mental: crazy
minced meat: hamburger
minerals: soft drinks
mobile (MOH-bile): cellphone
mod cons: modern conveniences (not convicts in bell-bottoms)
naff: dorky, tacky
nappy: diaper
natter: talk and talk
"Norn Iron": Northern Ireland
nought: zero
noughties: the decade from 2000-2009
noughts & crosses: tic-tac-toe
OAP: old-age pensioner (qualified for senior discounts)
off-license: liquor store
Oirish: exaggerated Irish accent
on offer: for sale
paddywhackery: exaggerated Irish accent
paralytic: passed-out drunk
pasty (PASS-tee): crusted savory (usually meat) pie
pavement: sidewalk
pear-shaped: messed up, gone wrong
petrol: gas
pissed (rude), paralytic, bevvied, wellied, popped up, ratted, pissed as a newt: drunk
pitch: playing field
plaster: Band-Aid
publican: pub manager
pull: to attract romantic attention
punter: partygoer, customer
put a sock in it: shut up
quay (pronounced "key"): waterside street, ship offloading area
queue: line
queue up: line up
quick smart: immediately
quid: pound (currency in Northern Ireland, worth about $1.40)

ramps: speed bumps
randy: horny
rat run: shortcut
redundant, made: laid off
return ticket: round-trip
ride: have sex with
ring up: call (telephone)
ROI: Republic of Ireland
roundabout: traffic circle
RTE: Irish Republic's broadcast network
rubber: eraser
runners: tennis shoes
sanitary towel: sanitary pad
sat-nav: satellite navigation technology
sausage roll: sausage wrapped in a flaky pastry (like a pig in a blanket)
scarlet: embarrassed
Scotch egg: hard-boiled egg wrapped in sausage meat
self-catering: apartment with kitchen
sellotape: Scotch tape
serviette: napkin
session: musical evening
shag: have sex with
shag all: hardly any
shebeen: illegal drinking hole
single ticket: one-way ticket
skint: broke, poor
skip: Dumpster
slag: to ridicule, tease
smalls: underwear
snogging: kissing, making out
solicitor: lawyer
sort out: figure out, organize
spanner: wrench
spend a penny: urinate
splash out: splurge
stag night: bachelor party
starkers: buck naked
starters: appetizers
stick: criticism
stone: 14 pounds (weight)
strand: beach
stroppy: bad-tempered
subway: underground pedestrian passageway
sultanas: golden raisins
surgical spirit: rubbing alcohol

swede: rutabaga
take the mickey: tease
tatty: worn out or tacky
taxi rank: taxi stand
tenner: 10-euro note
theatre: live stage
tick: a check mark
tight as a Scotsman (derogatory): cheapskate
tights: panty hose
Tipp: County Tipperary
tipper lorry: dump truck
tin: can
to let: for rent
top up: refill a drink or your mobile-phone credit
torch: flashlight
towpath: path along a river
trad: traditional music
Travellers: itinerants, once known as Tinkers
turf accountant: bookie
twee: corny, too cute
twitcher: bird-watcher
verge: grassy edge of road
victualler: butcher
wain: small child
way out: exit
wee (v.): urinate
wee (n.): tiny (in the North)
Wellingtons, wellies: rubber boots
whacked: exhausted
whinge (rhymes with hinge): whine
witter on: gab and gab
woolies: warm clothes
your man: that guy, this guy
zebra crossing: crosswalk
zed: the letter Z

R460

PRACTICALITIES

This chapter covers the practical skills of European travel: how to get tourist information, pay for things, sightsee efficiently, find good-value accommodations, eat affordably but well, use technology wisely, and get between destinations smoothly. For more information on these topics, see www.ricksteves.com/travel-tips.

Tourist Information

Ireland's two government-funded tourist offices (one for the Republic and one for the North) offer a wealth of information. **Before your trip,** scan their websites. For the Republic of Ireland, visit www.discoverireland.ie. For Northern Ireland, use www. discovernorthernireland.com. At either site, you can download brochures and maps, ask questions, and request that information be mailed to you (such as a free vacation-planning packet, regional and city maps, walking routes, and festival schedules).

In Ireland, a good first stop in any town is generally the tourist information office (abbreviated **TI** in this book). Avoid ad agencies masquerading as TIs, especially in Dublin—use the official

TI. Fáilte Ireland TIs are information dispensaries with trained staff that don't sell anything or take commissions. I make a point to swing by to pick up a city map and get information on public transit, walking tours, special events, and nightlife. Anticipating a harried front-line staffer, prepare a list of questions and a proposed plan to double-check. Many TIs have information on the entire country or at least the region, so try to pick up maps and printed information for destinations you'll be visiting later in your trip. Be aware that TI phone numbers for some towns often simply connect you to a centralized national tourist office, with staff that may not have the "local" knowledge you are seeking.

In Dublin, try to get everything you'll need for all of Ireland in one stop at the TI (see page 38). The general nationwide tourist-information phone number for travelers calling from within Ireland is 1-850-230-330 (office open Mon-Sat 9:00-17:00, closed Sun).

Travel Tips

Travel Advisories: For updated health and safety conditions, including any restrictions for your destination, consult the US State Department's international travel website (travel.state.gov).

Emergency and Medical Help: For any emergency service—ambulance, police, or fire—call **112** from a mobile phone or landline. Operators will deal with your request or route you to the right emergency service. If you get sick, do as the locals do and go to a pharmacist for advice. Or ask at your hotel for help—they'll know the nearest medical and emergency services.

Theft or Loss: To replace a passport, you'll need to go in person to an embassy (see next). If your credit and debit cards disappear, cancel and replace them (see "Damage Control for Lost Cards" on page 558). File a police report, either on the spot or within a day or two; you'll need it to submit an insurance claim for lost or stolen rail passes or electronics, and it can help with replacing your passport or credit and debit cards. For more information, see www.ricksteves.com/help.

US Embassies: In **Dublin**—by appointment only Mon-Fri 7:30-16:30, closed Sat-Sun, 42 Elgin Road, tel. 01/668-8777, http://ie.usembassy.gov; in **Belfast**—by appointment only Mon-Fri 8:30-17:00, closed Sat-Sun, Danesfort House, 223 Stranmillis Road, tel. 028/9038-6100, after-hours emergency mobile 012-5350-1106, http://uk.usembassy.gov/embassy-consulates/belfast.

Canadian Embassies and Consulates: In **Dublin**—by appointment only Mon-Fri 9:00-13:00 & 14:00-16:30, consular and passport services Mon-Fri 9:00-12:00, closed Sat-Sun, 7 Wilton Terrace, tel. 01/234-4000, www.canada.ie; in **Belfast**—Honorary Consul, tel. 028/9754-2405. This office does not offer passport services; instead contact the Canadian High Commission in London (www.unitedkingdom.gc.ca).

Time Zones: Ireland is five/eight hours ahead of the East/West coasts of the US—and one hour earlier than most of continental Europe. The exceptions are the beginning and end of Daylight Saving Time: Europe "springs forward" the last Sunday in March (two weeks after most of North America) and "falls back" the last Sunday in October (one week before North America). For a handy time converter, use the world clock app on your phone or download one (see www.timeanddate.com).

Business Hours: In Ireland, most stores are open Monday through Saturday from roughly 10:00 to 17:30, with a late night on Wednesday or Thursday (until 19:00 or 20:00), depending on the neighborhood. Saturdays are virtually weekdays, with earlier closing hours and no rush hour (though transportation connections can be less frequent than on weekdays). Sundays have the same pros and cons as they do for travelers in the US: Sightseeing attractions are generally open (with limited hours), while banks and many shops are closed. You'll notice special events, limited public transportation, no rush hours, and street markets lively with shoppers. Friday and Saturday evenings are rowdy; Sunday evenings are quiet.

Watt's Up? Europe's electrical system is 220 volts, instead of North America's 110 volts. Most electronics (laptops, phones, cameras) and newer hairdryers convert automatically, so you won't need a converter, but you will need an adapter plug with three square prongs, sold inexpensively at travel stores in the US. Avoid bringing older appliances that don't automatically convert voltage; instead, buy a cheap replacement in Europe.

Discounts: Discounts for sights (called "concessions" in Ireland) are generally not listed in this book. However, seniors (age 60 and over), youths under 18, and students and teachers with proper identification cards (obtain from www.isic.org) can get discounts at many sights—always ask. Some discounts are available only to European citizens.

Money

Here's my basic strategy for using money in Europe:
- Upon arrival, head for a cash machine (ATM) at the airport and withdraw some local currency, using a debit card with low international transaction fees.

- In general, pay for bigger expenses with a credit card and use cash for smaller purchases. Use a debit card only for cash withdrawals.
- Keep your cards and cash safe in a money belt.

PLASTIC VERSUS CASH

Although credit cards are widely accepted in Europe, cash is sometimes the only way to pay for cheap food, taxis, tips, and local guides. Some businesses (especially smaller ones, such as B&Bs and mom-and-pop cafés and shops) may charge you extra for using a credit card—or might not accept credit cards at all. Having cash on hand helps you out of a jam if your card randomly doesn't work.

I use my credit card to book and pay for hotel reservations, to buy advance tickets for events or sights, and to cover most other expenses. It can also be smart to use plastic near the end of your trip, to avoid another visit to the ATM.

WHAT TO BRING

I pack the following and keep it all safe in my money belt.

Debit Card: Use this at ATMs to withdraw local cash.

Credit Card: Handy for bigger transactions (at hotels, shops, restaurants, travel agencies, car-rental agencies, and so on), payment machines, and online purchases.

Backup Card: Some travelers carry a third card (debit or credit; ideally from a different bank), in case one gets lost, demagnetized, eaten by a temperamental machine, or simply doesn't work.

A Stash of Cash: I carry $100-200 US dollars as a cash backup, which comes in handy in an emergency (such as if your ATM card gets eaten by the machine).

What NOT to Bring: Resist the urge to buy euros and pounds before your trip or you'll pay the price in bad stateside exchange rates. Wait until you arrive to withdraw money. I've yet to see a European airport that didn't have plenty of ATMs.

BEFORE YOU GO

Use this pre-trip checklist.

Know your cards. Debit cards from any major US bank will work in any standard European bank's ATM (ideally, use a debit card with a Visa or MasterCard logo). As for credit cards, Visa and

Exchange Rates

I've priced things throughout this book in the local currencies. The Republic of Ireland uses the euro currency. Northern Ireland, which is part of the United Kingdom, has retained its traditional currency, the British pound sterling. Border towns in the North might take euros, but at a lousy exchange rate. (Check www.oanda.com for the latest exchange rates.)

1 euro (€) = about $1.20

1 British pound (£) = about $1.30

Republic of Ireland: To convert prices in euros to dollars, add about 20 percent: €20 = about $24, €50 = about $60. Like the dollar, one euro is broken down into 100 cents. Coins range from €0.01 to €2, and bills from €5 to €200 (bills over €50 are rarely used).

Northern Ireland: To convert prices in pounds to dollars, add 30 percent: £20 = about $26, £50 = about $65. The British pound (£, also called a "quid") is broken into 100 pence (p). Pence means "cents." Coins range from 1p to £2 and bills from £5 to £50. Fake pound coins are easy to spot (real coins have an inscription on their outside rims; the edges of fakes resemble tree bark).

Northern Ireland issues its own currency, which is worth the same as an English pound. If you're traveling on to Great Britain, note that Britain's and Northern Ireland's Ulster pounds are technically interchangeable in both regions, although Ulster pounds are "undesirable" in Britain. Banks in either region will convert your Ulster pounds into English pounds at no charge. Don't worry about the coins, which are accepted throughout Great Britain and Northern Ireland.

MasterCard are universal, American Express is less common, and Discover is unknown in Europe.

Know your PIN. Make sure you know the numeric, four-digit PIN for all of your cards, both debit and credit. Request it if you don't have one, as it may be required for some purchases in Europe (see "Using Credit Cards," later), and allow time to receive the information by mail.

Report your travel dates. Let your bank know that you'll be using your debit and credit cards in Europe, and when and where you're headed.

Adjust your ATM withdrawal limit. Find out how much you can take out daily and ask for a higher daily withdrawal limit if you want to get more cash at once. Note that European ATMs will withdraw funds only from checking accounts; you're unlikely to have access to your savings account.

Ask about fees. For any purchase or withdrawal made with a card, you may be charged a currency conversion fee (1-3 percent) and/or a Visa or MasterCard international transaction fee (less than 1 percent). If you're getting a bad deal, consider getting a new debit or credit card. Reputable no-fee cards include those from Capital One, as well as Charles Schwab debit cards. Most credit unions and some airline loyalty cards have low or no international transaction fees.

IN EUROPE
Using Cash Machines
European cash machines work just like they do at home—except they spit out local currency instead of dollars, calculated at the day's standard bank-to-bank rate.

In most places, ATMs are easy to locate. When possible, withdraw cash from a bank-run ATM located just outside that bank. Ideally, use the machine during the bank's opening hours, so you can go inside for help if your card is munched.

If your debit card doesn't work, try a lower amount—your request may have exceeded your withdrawal limit or the ATM's limit. If you still have a problem, try a different ATM or come back later—your bank's network may be temporarily down.

Avoid "independent" ATMs, such as Travelex, Euronet, Moneybox, Your Cash, Cardpoint, and Cashzone. These have high fees, can be less secure than a bank ATM, and may try to trick users with "dynamic currency conversion" (see next page).

Exchanging Cash
Avoid exchanging money in Europe; it's a big rip-off. Irish banks do not exchange money unless you have an account with them. In most Irish countryside towns, the post office will be your only option. In a pinch you can always find exchange desks at major train stations or airports—convenient but with crummy rates. Anything over 5 percent for a transaction is piracy.

Using Credit Cards
Despite some differences between European and US cards, there's little to worry about: US credit cards generally work fine in Europe. I've been inconvenienced a few times by self-service payment machines that wouldn't accept my card, but it's never caused me serious trouble (I carry cash just in case).

European cards use chip-and-PIN technology; most chip cards issued in the US instead have a signature option. Some European card readers will accept your card as-is while others may generate a receipt for you to sign or prompt you to enter your PIN (so it's important to know the code for each of your cards). If a cashier is present, you should have no problems.

At self-service payment machines (transit-ticket kiosks, parking, etc.), results are mixed, as US cards may not work in some unattended transactions. If your card won't work, look for a cashier who can process your card manually—or pay in cash.

Drivers Beware: Be aware of potential problems using a US card to fill up at an unattended gas station, enter a parking garage, or exit a toll road. Always carry cash as a backup and be prepared to move on to the next gas station if necessary. When approaching a toll plaza, use the "cash" lane.

Dynamic Currency Conversion

If merchants offer to convert your purchase price into dollars (called dynamic currency conversion, or DCC), refuse this "service." You'll pay extra for the expensive convenience of seeing your charge in dollars. If an ATM offers to "lock in" or "guarantee" your conversion rate, choose "proceed without conversion." Other prompts might state, "You can be charged in dollars: Press YES for dollars, NO for euros or pounds." Always choose the local currency.

Security Tips

Pickpockets target tourists. Keep your cash, credit cards, and passport secure in your money belt, and carry only a day's spending money in your front pocket or wallet.

Before inserting your card into an ATM, inspect the front. If anything looks crooked, loose, or damaged, it could be a sign of a card-skimming device. When entering your PIN, carefully block other people's view of the keypad.

Don't use a debit card for purchases. Because a debit card pulls funds directly from your bank account, potential charges incurred by a thief will stay on your account while the fraudulent use is investigated by your bank.

While traveling, to access your accounts online, be sure to use a secure connection (see the "Tips on Internet Security" sidebar, later).

Damage Control for Lost Cards

If you lose your credit or debit card, report the loss immediately to the respective global customer-assistance centers. With a mobile phone, call these 24-hour US numbers: Visa (tel. +1 303/967-1096), MasterCard (tel. +1 636/722-7111), and American Express (tel. +1 336/393-1111). From a landline, you can call these US numbers collect by going through a local operator. European toll-free numbers (listed by country) can be found at the websites for Visa and MasterCard.

You'll need to provide the primary cardholder's identification-verification details (such as birth date, mother's maiden name, or Social Security number). You can generally receive a tempo-

rary card within two or three business days in Europe (see www.
ricksteves.com/help for more).

If you report your loss within two days, you typically won't
be responsible for unauthorized transactions on your account, although many banks charge a liability fee.

TIPPING

Tipping in Ireland is appreciated, but not expected. As in the US,
the proper amount depends on your resources, tipping philosophy,
and the circumstances, but some general guidelines apply.

Restaurants: At a pub or restaurant with waitstaff, check the
menu or your bill to see if the service is included; if not, tip about
10 percent. At pubs where you order food at the counter, a tip is not
expected but is appreciated.

Taxis: For a typical ride, round up your fare a bit (for instance,
if the fare is €9, give €10). If the cabbie hauls your bags and zips you
to the airport to help you catch your flight, you might want to toss
in a little more. But if you feel like you're being driven in circles or
otherwise ripped off, skip the tip.

Services: In general, if someone in the tourism or service industry does a super job for you, a small tip of a euro/pound or two
is appropriate...but not required. If you're not sure whether (or how
much) to tip, ask a local for advice.

GETTING A VAT REFUND

Wrapped into the purchase price of your Irish souvenirs is a value-
added tax (VAT); it's 23 percent in the Republic and 20 percent in
Northern Ireland. You're entitled to get most of that tax back if you
purchase more than €30/£30 (about $36/$42) worth of goods at a
store that participates in the VAT-refund scheme. Typically, you
must ring up the minimum at a single retailer—you can't add up
your purchases from various shops to reach the required amount.
(If the store ships the goods to your US home, VAT is not assessed
on your purchase.)

Getting your refund is straightforward...and worthwhile if
you spend a significant amount on souvenirs.

Get the paperwork. Have the merchant completely fill out the
necessary refund document. You'll have to present your passport.
Get the paperwork done before you leave the store to ensure you'll
have everything you need (including your original sales receipt).

Get your stamp at the border or airport. Process your VAT
document at your last stop in the European Union (such as at the
airport) with the customs agent who deals with VAT refunds. Arrive an additional hour before you need to check in to allow time
to find the customs office—and wait. Some customs desks are po-

sitioned before airport security; confirm the location before going through security.

It's best to keep your purchases in your carry-on. If your item isn't allowed in your carry-on (such as a knife), pack it in your checked bag and alert the check-in agent. You'll be sent (with your tagged bag) to a customs desk outside security; someone will examine your bag, stamp your paperwork, and put your bag on the belt. You're not supposed to use your purchased goods before you leave. If you show up at customs wearing your new Irish sweater, officials might look the other way—or deny you a refund.

Collect your refund. You can claim your VAT refund from refund companies such as Global Blue or Planet with offices at major airports, ports, or border crossings (either before or after security, probably strategically located near a duty-free shop). These services (which extract a 4 percent fee) can refund your money in cash immediately or credit your card. Otherwise, mail the stamped refund documents to the address given by the shop where you made your purchase.

CUSTOMS FOR AMERICAN SHOPPERS

You can take home $800 worth of items per person duty-free, once every 31 days. Many processed and packaged foods are allowed, including vacuum-packed cheeses, dried herbs, jams, baked goods, candy, chocolate, oil, vinegar, mustard, and honey. Fresh fruits and vegetables and most meats are not allowed, with exceptions for some canned items. As for alcohol, you can bring in one liter duty-free (it can be packed securely in your checked luggage, along with any other liquid-containing items).

To bring alcohol (or liquid-packed foods) in your carry-on bag on your flight home, buy it at a duty-free shop at the airport. You'll increase your odds of getting it onto a connecting flight if it's packaged in a "STEB"—a secure, tamper-evident bag. But stay away from liquids in opaque, ceramic, or metallic containers, which usually cannot be successfully screened (STEB or no STEB).

For details on allowable goods, customs rules, and duty rates, visit http://help.cbp.gov.

Sightseeing

Sightseeing can be hard work. Use these tips to make your visits to Ireland's finest sights meaningful, fun, efficient, and painless.

MAPS AND NAVIGATION TOOLS

A good map is essential for efficient navigation while sightseeing. The maps in this book are concise and simple, designed to help you locate recommended destinations, sights, and local TIs, where you can pick up more in-depth maps. Maps with even more detail are sold at newsstands and bookstores.

Train travelers do fine with a simple rail map (available as part of the free Intercity Timetable found at Irish train stations) and city maps from the TI offices. (You can get free maps of Dublin and Ireland from the national tourist-office websites before you go; see "Tourist Information" at the beginning of this chapter.)

You can also use a mapping app on your mobile device. Be aware that pulling up maps or looking up turn-by-turn walking directions on the fly requires a data connection: To use this feature, it's smart to get an international data plan. With Google Maps or City Maps 2Go, it's possible to download a map while online, then go offline and navigate without incurring data-roaming charges, though you can't search for an address or get real-time walking directions. A handful of other apps—including Apple Maps and Navmii—also allow you to use maps offline.

PLAN AHEAD

Set up an itinerary that allows you to fit in all your must-see sights. For a one-stop look at opening hours, see this book's "At a Glance" sidebars for cities (Dublin, Dingle, and Belfast). Most sights keep stable hours, but you can easily confirm the latest by checking with the TI or visiting museum websites.

Don't put off visiting a must-see sight—you never know when a place will close unexpectedly for a holiday, strike, or restoration. Many museums are closed or have reduced hours at least a few days a year, especially on holidays such as Christmas, New Year's, and Labor Day (first Monday in May). A list of holidays is in the appendix; check for possible closures during your trip. In summer, some sights may stay open late. In the off-season, hours may be shorter.

Going at the right time helps avoid crowds. This book offers tips on the best times to see specific sights. Try visiting popular sights very early or very late—late morning is usually the worst time to visit. Evening visits (when possible) are usually peaceful, with fewer crowds.

If you plan to hire a local guide, reserve ahead by email. Popular guides can get booked up.

Study up. To get the most out of the self-guided walks and sight descriptions in this book, read them before you visit.

RESERVATIONS, ADVANCE TICKETS, AND PASSES

Given how precious your vacation time is, I recommend getting reservations for any must-see sight that offers them (see page 25). And a sightseeing pass can offer significant cost-savings.

Reservations and Advance Tickets

To deal with lines, many popular sights sell advance tickets that guarantee admission at a certain time of day, or that allow you to skip entry lines. Either way, it's worth giving up some spontaneity to book in advance. While hundreds of tourists sweat in long ticket-buying lines, those who've booked ahead are assured of getting in. In some cases, getting a ticket in advance simply means buying your ticket earlier on the same day. But for other sights, you may need to book weeks or even months in advance. As soon as you're ready to commit to a certain date, book it.

The advance-purchase price is often less expensive than what you would pay on-site (my listings include the online price, if available). And many museums offer convenient mobile ticketing. Simply buy your ticket online and send it to your phone, eliminating the need for a paper ticket.

Passes

Ireland offers two passes (each covering a different set of sights) that can save you money. Both are smart.

Heritage Card: This pass gets you into nearly 100 historical monuments, gardens, and parks maintained by the Office of Public Works (OPW) in the Republic of Ireland. It pays off if you visit at least eight included sights (€40; seniors age 60 and older—€30, students—€10, families—€90, valid one year, includes handy map and list of sights' hours and prices, purchase at first Heritage sight you visit, some sights take cash only,

tel. 01/647-6592, www.heritageireland.ie, heritagecard@opw.ie). Those traveling by car are most likely to get their money's worth out of the card.

To help you determine if the pass is right for you, use the following list to add up entry fees. An energetic sightseer with three weeks in Ireland will probably pay to see nearly all of the following sights.

- Dublin Castle-€12
- Kilmainham Gaol-€8 (Dublin; advance reservations recommended)
- Brú na Bóinne (Knowth and Newgrange tombs and Visitors Centre Museum-€18—Boyne Valley; advance reservations recommended)
- Battle of the Boyne-€5
- Hill of Tara-€5 (Boyne Valley)

PRACTICALITIES

- Old Mellifont Abbey-€5 (Boyne Valley)
- Trim Castle-€5 (Boyne Valley)
- Glendalough Visitors Centre-€5 (Wicklow Mountains)
- Kilkenny Castle-€8
- Rock of Cashel-€8
- Reginald's Tower-€5 (Waterford)
- Charles Fort-€5 (Kinsale)
- Muckross House-€9.25 (near Killarney)
- Derrynane House-€5 (Ring of Kerry)
- Garnish Island Gardens-€5 (near Kenmare)
- Great Blasket Centre-€5 (near Dingle)
- Ennis Friary-€5 (Ennis)
- Dun Aengus-€5 (Inishmore, Aran Islands)
- Glenveagh Castle and National Park-€7 (Donegal)

Together these sights total €130.25; a pass saves €90.25 per person over paying individual entrance fees. Note that scheduled tours given by OPW guides at these sights are included in the price of admission—regardless of whether you have the Heritage Card. The card covers no sights in Northern Ireland.

Heritage Island Visitor Attraction Map: This free map adorned with coupons—mostly two-for-one entries, some 10-25 percent discounts—is worth seeking out, particularly for couples (at TIs or participating sights; tel. 01/775-3870, www.heritageisland. com; skip the accompanying booklet sold online). The coupons cover 90 sights in both the Republic of Ireland and Northern Ireland. At sights with free admission, you may get discounts at their shop or café.

Discounted sights on this map typically include:

- Trinity College Library (Book of Kells, Dublin; advance tickets recommended)
- Chester Beatty Library (Dublin)
- EPIC: The Irish Emigration Museum (Dublin)
- Guinness Storehouse (Dublin)
- National Gallery of Ireland (Dublin)
- Dublinia
- National Museum: Decorative Arts and History (Dublin)
- Gaelic Athletic Association Museum (Dublin)
- Dublin City Hall
- Irish National Stud (Kildare)
- Powerscourt Gardens (Enniskerry)
- *Dunbrody* Famine Ship (New Ross)
- Waterford Crystal Visitor Centre
- Blarney Castle (County Cork)
- Aillwee Cave (Burren)
- Clare Museum (Ennis)
- Kylemore Abbey (Letterfrack)

PRACTICALITIES

- Mount Stewart House (near Bangor)
- Titanic Belfast Museum (Belfast; advance tickets recommended)
- Ulster Museum (Belfast)
- Ulster Folk Park and Transport Museum (Cultra)
- Belleek Pottery Visitors Centre (Belleek)
- Ulster American Folk Park (Omagh)

AT SIGHTS

Here's what you can typically expect:

Entering: You may not be allowed to enter if you arrive too close to closing time. And guards start ushering people out well before the actual closing time, so don't save the best for last.

Many sights have a security check. Allow extra time for these lines. Some sights require you to check daypacks and coats. (If you'd rather not check your daypack, try carrying it tucked under your arm like a purse as you enter.)

Photography: If the museum's photo policy isn't clearly posted, ask a guard. Generally, taking photos without a flash or tripod is allowed. Some sights ban selfie sticks; others ban photos altogether.

Audioguides and Apps: Many sights rent audioguides with recorded descriptions. If you bring your own earbuds, you can often enjoy better sound. If you don't mind being tethered to your travel partner, you'll save money by bringing a Y-jack and sharing one audioguide. Museums and sights often offer free apps that you can download to your mobile device (check their websites).

Temporary Exhibits: Museums may show special exhibits in addition to their permanent collection. Some exhibits are included in the entry price, while others come at an extra cost (which you may have to pay even if you don't want to see the exhibit).

Expect Changes: Artwork can be on tour, on loan, out sick, or shifted at the whim of the curator. Pick up a floor plan as you enter, and ask museum staff if you can't find a particular item.

Services: Important sights usually have a reasonably priced on-site café or cafeteria (handy places to rejuvenate during a long visit). The WCs at sights are free and generally clean.

Before Leaving: At the gift shop, scan the postcard rack or thumb through a guidebook to be sure you haven't overlooked something that you'd like to see. Every sight or museum offers more than what is covered in this book. Use the information I provide as an introduction—not the final word.

Sleeping

Outside of Dublin you can expect to find good doubles for $100-150, including tax and a cooked breakfast.

Extensive and opinionated listings of good-value rooms are a major feature of this book's Sleeping sections. Rather than list accommodations scattered throughout a town, I choose hotels in my favorite neighborhoods that are convenient to your sightseeing.

My recommendations run the gamut, from dorm beds to fancy rooms with all the comforts. I like places that are clean, central, relatively quiet at night, reasonably priced, friendly, small enough to have a hands-on owner or manager, and run with a respect for Irish traditions. I'm more impressed by a handy location and a fun-loving philosophy than flat-screen TVs and a fancy gym. Most of my recommendations fall short of perfection. But if I can find a place with most of these features, it's a keeper.

Book your accommodations as soon as your itinerary is set, especially if you want to stay at one of my top listings or if you'll be traveling during busy times. Also reserve in advance for Dublin for any weekend, for Galway during its many peak-season events, and for Dingle throughout July and August. See the appendix for a list of major holidays and festivals throughout Ireland.

Some people make reservations as they travel, calling or emailing ahead a few days to a week before their arrival. If you're trying for a same-day reservation, it's best to call hotels at about 9:00 or 10:00, when the receptionist knows which rooms will be available. Some apps—such as HotelTonight—specialize in last-minute rooms, often at boutique or business-class hotels in big cities.

The Republic of Ireland and Northern Ireland have banned smoking in the workplace (pubs, offices, taxicabs, etc.), but some hotels still have a floor or two of rooms where guests are allowed to smoke. If you don't want a room that a smoker might have occupied before you, let the hotelier know when you make your reservation. All of my recommended B&Bs prohibit smoking. Even in places that allow smoking in the sleeping rooms, breakfast rooms are nearly always smoke-free.

Loud and rowdy Irish stag/hen (bachelor/bachelorette) parties are plentiful on weekends. If you're a light sleeper, bring earplugs and think twice before booking a weekend room in a hotel with a pub on the ground floor. Steer clear of establishments that trumpet "stags and hens welcome" on their websites.

RATES AND DEALS

I've categorized my recommended accommodations based on price, indicated with a dollar-sign rating (see sidebar). The price ranges suggest an estimated cost for a one-night stay in high season in a standard double room with a private toilet and shower, include a hearty breakfast, and assume you're booking directly with the hotel (not through a booking site, which extracts a commission). Room prices can fluctuate significantly with demand and amenities (size, views, room class, and so on), but these relative price categories remain constant.

Room rates are especially volatile at hotels that use "dynamic pricing" to set rates. Prices can skyrocket during festivals and conventions, while business hotels can have deep discounts on weekends when demand plummets. Of the many hotels I recommend, it's difficult to say which will be the best value on a given day—until you do your homework.

Booking Direct: Once your dates are set, compare prices at several hotels. You can do this by checking Hotels.com, Booking.com, and hotel websites. Then book directly with the hotel itself. Contact small family-run hotels directly by phone or email. When you go direct, the owner avoids the commission paid to booking sites, thereby leaving enough wiggle room to offer you a discount, a nicer room, or a free breakfast (if it's not already included). If you prefer to book online or are considering a hotel chain, it's to your advantage to use the hotel's website. When establishing prices, confirm if the charge is per person or per room (if a price is too good to be true, it's probably per person).

Booking directly also increases the chances that the hotelier will be able to accommodate any special needs or requests (such as shifting your reservation). Going through a middleman makes it more difficult for the hotel to adjust your booking.

Getting a Discount: Some hotels extend a discount to those who pay cash or stay longer than three nights. And some accommodations offer a special discount for Rick Steves readers, indicated in this guidebook by the abbreviation **"RS%."** Discounts vary: Ask for details when you reserve. Generally, to qualify for this discount, you must book direct (not through a booking site), mention this book when you reserve, show this book upon arrival, and sometimes pay cash or stay a certain number of nights. In some cases, you may need to enter a discount code (which I've provided in the listing) in the booking form on the hotel's website. Rick Steves discounts apply to readers with either print or digital books. Understandably, discounts do not apply to promotional rates.

LODGING VOUCHERS

Many US travel agents sell vouchers for lodging in Ireland. In essence, you're paying ahead of time for your lodging, with the assurance that you'll be staying in B&Bs and guesthouses that live up to certain standards. I don't recommend buying these, since your choices will be limited to only the places in Ireland that accept

Sleep Code

Hotels in this book are categorized according to the average price of a standard en suite double room with breakfast in high season.

$$$$	**Splurge:**	Most rooms over €170/£140
$$$	**Pricier:**	€130-170/£110-140
$$	**Moderate:**	€90-130/£80-110
$	**Budget:**	€50-90/£50-80
¢	**Backpacker:**	Under €50/£50
RS%	**Rick Steves discount**	

Unless otherwise noted, credit cards are accepted and free Wi-Fi is available. Comparison-shop by checking prices at several hotels (on each hotel's own website, on a booking site, or by email). For the best deal, *book directly with the hotel*. Ask for a discount if paying in cash; if the listing includes **RS%**, request a Rick Steves discount.

PRACTICALITIES

vouchers. Sure, there are hundreds in the program to choose from. But in this guidebook, I list any place that offers a good value—a useful location, nice hosts, and a comfortable and clean room—regardless of what club they do or don't belong to. Lots of great B&Bs choose not to participate in the voucher program because they have to pay to be part of it, slicing into their already thin profit. And many Irish B&B owners lament the long wait between the date a traveler stays with them and the date the voucher company reimburses them. In short, skip it. The voucher program is just an expensive middleman between you and the innkeeper.

TYPES OF ACCOMMODATIONS

Ireland has a rating system for hotels and B&Bs. These stars and shamrocks are supposed to imply quality, but I find that they mean only that the place sporting symbols is paying dues to the tourist board. These rating systems often have little to do with value: One of my favorite Irish B&Bs (also loved by readers) will never be tourist-board approved because it has no dedicated breakfast room (a strict requirement in the eyes of the board). Instead, guests sit around a large kitchen table and enjoy a lively chat with the friendly hosts as they cook breakfast 10 feet away.

Hotels

Note that to be called a "hotel" in Ireland, a place must have certain amenities, including a 24-hour reception (though this rule is loosely applied). Know the terminology: "Twin" means two single beds, "double" means one double bed. If you'll take either one, let the hotelier know, or you might be needlessly turned away. An

PRACTICALITIES

Making Hotel Reservations

Reserve your rooms as soon as you've pinned down your travel dates. For busy national holidays, it's wise to reserve far in advance (see the appendix).

Requesting a Reservation: For family-run hotels, it's generally best to book your room directly via email or phone. For business-class and chain hotels, or if you'd rather book online, reserve directly through the hotel's official website (not a booking website).

Here's what the hotelier wants to know:
- Type(s) of rooms you want and size of your party
- Number of nights you'll stay
- Your arrival and departure dates, written European-style as day/month/year (for example, 18/06/22 or 18 June 2022)
- Special requests (en suite bathroom, cheapest room, twin beds vs. double bed, quiet room)
- Applicable discounts (such as a Rick Steves reader discount, cash discount, or promotional rate).

Confirming a Reservation: Most places will request a credit-card number to hold your room. If you're using an online reservation form, make sure it's secure by looking for the *https* or a lock icon at the top of your browser. If the hotel's website doesn't have a secure form where you can enter the number directly, it's best to share that confidential info via a phone call.

Canceling a Reservation: If you must cancel, it's courteous—and smart—to do so with as much notice as possible, especially for smaller family-run places. Cancellation policies can be strict; read

"en suite" room has a bathroom (toilet and shower/tub) inside the room; a room with a "private bathroom" can mean that the bathroom is all yours, but it's across the hall; and a "standard" room has access to a bathroom down the hall that's shared with other rooms. Figuring there's little difference between "en suite" and "private" rooms, some places charge the same for both. If you want your own bathroom inside the room, request "en suite." If money's tight, ask for a standard room. You'll almost always have a sink in your room, and as more rooms go "en suite," the hallway bathroom is shared with fewer standard rooms.

Some hotels can add an extra bed (for a small charge) to turn a double into a triple; some offer larger rooms for four or more people (I call these "family rooms" in the listings). If there's space for an extra cot, they'll cram it in for you. In general, a triple room is cheaper than the cost of a double and a single. Three or four people can economize by requesting one big room.

Most hotels offer family deals, which means that parents with young children can easily get a room with an extra child's bed or a

From:	rick@ricksteves.com
Sent:	Today
To:	info@hotelcentral.com
Subject:	Reservation request for 19-22 July

Dear Hotel Central,

I would like to stay at your hotel. Please let me know if you have a room available and the price for:
- 2 people
- Double bed and en suite bathroom in a quiet room
- Arriving 19 July, departing 22 July (3 nights)

Thank you!
Rick Steves

the fine print before you book. Many discount deals require pre-payment, with no cancellation refunds.

Reconfirming a Reservation: Always call or email to reconfirm your room reservation a few days in advance. For B&Bs or very small hotels, I call again on my day of arrival to tell my host what time to expect me (especially important if arriving late—after 17:00).

Phoning: For tips on calling hotels overseas, see page 584.

discount for a larger room. Call to negotiate the price. Teenagers are generally charged as adults. Kids under five sleep almost free.

Arrival and Check-In: Hotels and B&Bs are sometimes located on the higher floors of a multipurpose building with a secured door. In that case, look for your hotel's name on the buttons by the main entrance. When you ring the bell, you'll be buzzed in.

Hotel elevators are common, though some older buildings still lack them. You may have to climb a flight of stairs to reach the elevator (if so, you can ask the front desk for help carrying your bags up). Elevators are typically very small—pack light, or you may need to send your bags up without you.

The EU requires that hotels collect your name, nationality, and ID number. When you check in, the receptionist will normally ask for your passport and may keep it for anywhere from a couple of minutes to a couple of hours. If you're not comfortable leaving your passport at the desk for a long time, ask when you can pick it up. Or, if you packed a color copy of your passport, you can generally leave that rather than the original.

If you're arriving in the morning, your room probably won't be ready. Drop your bag safely at the hotel and dive right into sightseeing.

In Your Room: Most hotel rooms have a TV, telephone, and free Wi-Fi (although in old buildings with thick walls, the Wi-Fi signal might be available only in the lobby). Simpler places rarely have a room phone, but often have free Wi-Fi.

More pillows and blankets are usually in the closet or available on request. Towels and linens aren't always replaced every day.

Breakfast and Meals: Small hotels and B&Bs serve a hearty "Irish fry" breakfast (more about B&B breakfasts later). Because B&Bs owners are often also the cook, there's usually a limited time span when breakfast is served (typically about an hour, starting at about 8:00). Modern hotels usually have an attached restaurant.

Checking Out: While it's customary to pay for your room upon departure, it can be a good idea to settle your bill the day before, when you're not in a hurry and while the manager's in.

Hotelier Help: Hoteliers can be a good source of advice. Most know their city well, and can assist you with everything from public transit and airport connections to finding a good restaurant, the nearest launderette, or a late-night pharmacy.

Hotel Hassles: Even at the best places, mechanical breakdowns occur: Sinks leak, hot water turns cold, toilets may gurgle or smell, the Wi-Fi goes out, or the air-conditioning dies when you need it most. Report your concerns clearly and calmly at the front desk.

If you find that night noise is a problem (if, for instance, your room is over a rowdy pub or facing a busy street), ask for a quieter room in the back or on an upper floor. Pubs are plentiful and packed with revelers on weekend nights.

To guard against theft in your room, keep valuables out of sight. Some rooms come with a safe, and other hotels have safes at the front desk. I've never bothered using one and in a lifetime of travel, I've never had anything stolen from my room.

For more complicated problems, don't expect instant results. Above all, keep a positive attitude. Remember, you're on vacation. If your hotel or B&B is a disappointment, spend more time out enjoying the place you came to see.

Small Hotels and B&Bs

Compared to hotels, bed-and-breakfast places give you double the cultural intimacy for half the price. While you may lose some of the conveniences of a hotel—such as frequent bed-sheet changes and being able to pay with a credit card—I happily make the trade-off for the lower rates and personal touches. The amount of coziness, doilies, tea, and biscuits tossed in varies tremendously.

B&Bs range from large guesthouses with 10-15 rooms to small homes renting out a couple of spare bedrooms, but typically have six rooms or fewer. A "townhouse" or "house" is like a big B&B or a small family-run hotel—with fewer

amenities but more character than a hotel. The philosophy of the management determines the character of a place more than its size and amenities. I avoid places run as a business by absentee owners. My top listings are run by people who enjoy welcoming the world to their breakfast table.

I've tried to list which B&Bs have pets, but if you're allergic, ask about pets when you reserve.

Rules and Etiquette: Small hotels and B&Bs come with their own etiquette and quirks. Keep in mind that B&B own-

ers are subject to the whims of their guests—if you're getting up early, so are they; and if you check in late, they'll wait up for you. It's polite to call ahead to confirm your reservation the day before and give them a rough estimate of your arrival time. This allows your hosts to plan their day...and also allows them to

give you specific directions for driving or walking to their place. If you are arriving past the agreed time, call and let them know.

B&Bs are not hotels. Think of your host as a friendly acquaintance who's invited you to stay in her home, rather than someone you're paying to wait on you. At some B&Bs, children or people booking just a single night are not welcome.

Most B&Bs often come with thin walls and doors, and sometimes creaky floorboards, which can make for a noisy night. If you're a light sleeper, bring earplugs. And please be quiet in the halls and in your rooms at night...those of us getting up early will thank you for it.

B&Bs serve a hearty "Irish fry" breakfast (see "Eating," later in this chapter). Let you host know which parts of the "fry" you don't want. If you arrive at the last minute for breakfast (or if you need to leave before breakfast is served), don't expect a full cooked breakfast; most B&B hosts will let you help yourself to

In the Room: Some B&Bs stock rooms with an electric kettle,

Using Online Services to Your Advantage

From booking services to user reviews, online businesses play a greater role in travelers' planning than ever before. Take advantage of their pluses—and be wise to their downsides.

Booking Sites

Booking websites such as Booking.com and Hotels.com offer one-stop shopping for hotels. While convenient for travelers, they present a real problem for independent, family-run hotels. Without a presence on these sites, small hotels become almost invisible. But to be listed, a hotel must pay a sizeable commission... and promise that its own website won't undercut the price on the booking-service site.

Here's the work-around: Use the big sites to research what's out there, then book directly with the hotel by email or phone, in which case hotel owners are free to give you whatever price they like. Ask for a room without the commission mark-up (or ask for a free breakfast if not included, or a free upgrade). If you do book online, be sure to use the hotel's website. The price will likely be the same as via a booking site, but your money goes to the hotel, not agency commissions.

As a savvy consumer, remember: When you book with an online booking service, you're adding a middleman who takes roughly 20 percent. To support small, family-run hotels whose world is more difficult than ever, book direct.

Short-Term Rental Sites

Rental juggernaut Airbnb (along with other short-term rental sites) allows travelers to rent rooms and apartments directly from locals, often providing more value than a cookie-cutter hotel. Airbnb fans appreciate feeling part of a real neighborhood and getting into a daily routine as "temporary Europeans." Depending on the host, Airbnb can provide an opportunity to get to know a local person, while keeping the money spent on your accommo-

along with cups, tea bags, and coffee packets (if you prefer decaf, buy a jar at a grocery, and dump the contents into a baggie for easy packing).

Hang towels up to dry and reuse. Many Irish B&Bs don't provide washcloths. If your electrical appliance isn't working, flip the switch at the outlet to turn on the current.

Virtually all rooms have sinks. You'll likely encounter unusual bathroom fixtures. The "pump toilet" has a flushing handle that doesn't kick in unless you push it just right: too hard or too soft, and it won't go. (Be decisive but not ruthless.) There's also the "dial-a-shower," an electronic box under the showerhead where you'll turn a dial to select the heat of the water, and (sometimes with a separate dial or button) turn on or shut off the flow of water. If you can't dations in the community.

Critics view Airbnb as a threat to "traditional Europe," saying it creates unfair, unqualified competition for established guesthouse owners. In some places, the lucrative Airbnb market has forced traditional guesthouses out of business and is driving property values out of range for locals. Some cities have cracked down, requiring owners to occupy rental properties part of the year (and staging disruptive "inspections" that inconvenience guests).

As a lover of Europe, I share the worry of those who see residents nudged aside by tourists. But as an advocate for travelers, I appreciate the value and cultural intimacy Airbnb provides.

User Reviews

User-generated review sites and apps such as Yelp and TripAdvisor can give you a consensus of opinions about everything from hotels and restaurants to sights and nightlife. If you scan reviews of a restaurant or hotel and see several complaints about noise or a rotten location, you've gained insight that can help in your decision-making.

But as a guidebook writer, my sense is that there is a big difference between the uncurated information on a review site and the vetted listings in a guidebook. A user-generated review is based on the limited experience of one person, who stayed at just one hotel in a given city and ate at a few restaurants there. A guidebook is the work of a trained researcher who forms a well-developed basis for comparison by visiting many restaurants and hotels year after year.

Both types of information have their place, and in many ways, they're complementary. If something is well reviewed in a guidebook and it also gets good online reviews, it's likely a winner.

find the switch to turn on the shower, it may be just outside the bathroom.

Your bedroom probably won't include a phone, but nearly every B&B has free W-Wi; you may need to sit in the lounge or breakfast room to access it.

Paying: Many B&Bs take credit cards, but may add the card service fee to your bill (about 3 percent). If you do need to pay cash for your room, plan ahead so you have enough on hand when you check out.

Big, Cheap, Modern Hotels

Hotel chains—popular with budget tour groups—offer predictably comfortable, no-frills accommodations at reasonable prices. These

PRACTICALITIES

hotels are popping up in big cities in Ireland. They can be located near the train station, in the city center, on major arterials, and outside the city center. What you lose in charm, you gain in savings.

I can't stress this enough: Check online for the cheapest deals. But be sure to go through the hotel's website rather than an online middleman.

Chain hotels are ideal for families, offering simple, clean, and modern rooms for up to four people (two adults/two children) for €150-225, depending on the location. Note that couples often pay the same price for a room as families (up to four). Most rooms have a double bed, single bed, five-foot trundle bed, private shower, WC, TV, and Wi-Fi. Hotels usually have an attached restaurant, good security, an elevator, and a 24-hour staffed reception desk. Of course, they're as cozy as a Motel 6, but many travelers love them. You can book online (be sure to check their websites for deals) or over the phone with a credit card, then pay when you check in. When you check out, just drop off the key, Lee.

The biggies are **Jurys Inn** (call their hotels directly or book online at www.jurysinns.com), **Comfort/Quality Inns** (Republic of Ireland tel. 1-800-500-600, Northern Ireland tel. 0800-444-444, US tel. 877-424-6423, www.choicehotels.com), and **Travelodge** (also has freeway locations for tired drivers, reservation center in Britain tel. 08700-850-950, www.travelodge.co.uk).

Short-Term Rentals

A short-term rental—whether an apartment, house, or room in a local's home—is an increasingly popular alternative, especially if you plan to settle in one location for several nights. For stays longer than a few days, you can usually find a rental that's comparable to—and cheaper than—a hotel room with similar amenities. Plus, you'll get a behind-the-scenes peek into how locals live.

Many places require a minimum stay and have strict cancellation policies. And you're generally on your own: There's no hotel reception desk, breakfast, or daily cleaning service.

Finding Accommodations: Websites such as Airbnb, FlipKey, Booking.com, and the HomeAway family of sites (HomeAway, VRBO, and VacationRentals) let you browse a wide range of properties. Alternatively, rental agencies such as InterhomeUSA.com or RentaVilla.com, which list more carefully selected accommodations that might cost more, can provide more personalized service. Both of Ireland's tourism websites (www.discoverireland.ie and www. discovernorthernireland.com) are reliable sources.

Before you commit, be clear on the location. I like to virtually "explore" the neighborhood using the Street View feature on Google Maps. Also consider the proximity to public transportation, and how well connected the property is to the rest of the city. Ask about amenities (elevator, air-conditioning, laundry, Wi-Fi, parking, etc.). Reviews from previous guests can help identify trouble spots.

Think about the kind of experience you want: just a key and an affordable bed...or a chance to get to know a local? There are typically two kinds of hosts: those who want minimal interaction with their guests, and hosts who are friendly and may want to interact with you. Read the promotional text and online reviews to help shape your decision.

Confirming and Paying: Many places require you to pay the entire balance before your trip. It's easiest and safest to pay through the site where you found the listing. Be wary of owners who want to take your transaction offline; this gives you no recourse if things go awry. Never agree to wire money (a key indicator of a fraudulent transaction).

Apartments or Houses: If you're staying in one place for four or more nights, it's worth considering an apartment—sometimes called a "flat" in Ireland—or rental house (shorter stays aren't worth the hassle of arranging key pickup, buying groceries, etc.). Apartment or house rentals can be especially cost-effective for groups and families. European apartments, like hotel rooms, tend to be small by US standards. But they often come with laundry facilities and small, equipped kitchens, making it easier and cheaper to dine in.

Rooms in Private Homes: Renting a room in someone's home is a good option for those traveling alone, as you're more likely to find true single rooms—with just one single bed, and a price to match. These can range from air-mattress-in-living-room basic to plush-B&B-suite posh. Some places allow you to book for a single night; if staying for several nights, you can buy groceries just as you would in a rental house. While you can't expect your host to also be your tour guide—or even to provide you with much info—some may be interested in getting to know the travelers who come through their home.

Other Options: Swapping homes with a local works for people with an appealing place to offer (don't assume where you live is not interesting to Europeans). Good places to start are HomeExchange.com and LoveHomeSwap.com. To sleep for free, Couchsurfing.com is a vagabond's alternative to Airbnb. It lists millions of outgoing members, who host fellow "surfers" in their homes.

Hostels

Ireland has hundreds of hostels of all shapes and sizes. Choose yours selectively; hostels can be historic castles or depressing tenements, serene and comfy or overrun by noisy school groups.

A hostel provides cheap beds in dorms where you sleep alongside strangers for about €30 per night. Travelers of any age are welcome if they don't mind dorm-style accommodations and meeting

PRACTICALITIES

Irish Castle Lodging

The stone castles that dot the Irish landscape are some of the most famous and evocative in the world. Built in the 11th to the 16th centuries, they were the fortified homes of Anglo-Norman settlers and Irish chieftains, designed for defense. Modern-day visitors can get an intimate feel for medieval Irish life by spending the night in one of these fortresses of yore.

These are not the modern, boxy hotels with cheesy crenellated rooflines that call themselves "castles," but the real thing (or in some instances a heavily modified version). The true-to-history castle lodgings are rustic, isolated tower houses, while the modified ones amount to fancy mansion splurges. Be honest about how much cushiness you need and don't be swept away with frilly Camelot film-set expectations.

Rustic

For an authentic experience, search out a real tower-house castle built by native Gaelic lords in the 1400s. Usually four to six stories high, these age-old fortifications sleep from 8 to 12 (3-night minimum stay). A visiting cook may prepare meals, but all have self-catering kitchens.

Authenticity comes with surprises, such as the occasional spider, drafty windowsill, or flake of medieval dust sprinkling down from original wicker-imprinted ceilings. Canopy beds protect you as you sleep...just like the lord and lady 600 years ago. You'll carry your bags up tight stone stairways and may have to share a bathroom. Wi-Fi can't handle the three-foot-thick walls, so unplug for a few days. However, floor heating and electric lights take the edge off "roughing it."

These remote castles don't come with fancy landscaping—your windows will likely overlook bogs or grazing land. Get clear directions and be sure to arrive in daylight. Prices vary wildly depending on number of nights and time of year (and require 50% advance deposit). Figure €1,800 for three nights and up to €4,000 for a week (give or take a crown jewel). Split that cost by 10 friends and you've got the recipe for a unique, good-value evening à la the 15th century. Light the candles, stoke up the fire-

other travelers. Most hostels offer kitchen facilities, guest computers, Wi-Fi, and a self-service laundry. Hostels almost always provide bedding, but the towel's up to you (though you can usually rent one for a small fee). Family and private rooms are often available.

Independent hostels tend to be easygoing, colorful, and in-place, and uncork the wine—a convivial night in a castle can be truly magical. Three well worth considering can be found at www. celticcastles.com.

Ballyportry Castle (10 miles north of Ennis in County Clare, www. ballyportry.ie) was built by a branch of the O'Brien family in the 15th century.

Turin Castle (9 miles east of Cong in County Mayo, turincastle. com) was built by the locally powerful De Burgo family in the 13th century.

Ballybur Castle (5 miles south of Kilkenny town in County Kilkenny, www.ballyburcastle.com) was built in the 16th century as the seat of the Comerford clan.

Fancy

Despite their castle-like exteriors, these fancy versions are plush, pampered estates with spas and adjacent golf courses. They have all the comforts and then some. The current structure may indeed include a smaller fortified castle that once stood alone hundreds of years ago. But then wealthy Romantic-age Anglo-Irish aristocrats built luxurious additions and surrounded them with lush gardens and gurgling fountains. Real fortified castles would never have had the vulnerable ground-floor bay windows you see on these palaces today.

These dolled-up dream houses are a fanciful indulgence: In summer, don't expect basic room prices below €500 per night. The upside? A chance to live like a privileged character in a Victorian novel for a day or two. A couple to consider:

Dromoland Castle (8 miles south of Ennis or 9 miles north of Shannon Airport, www.dromoland.ie) once secretly hosted Beatles John and George as they attempted to hide out during the height of "Beatlemania."

Ashford Castle (28 miles north of Galway near the town of Cong, www.ashfordcastle.com) has hosted Ron and Nancy Reagan, John Wayne, Maureen O'Hara, and the weddings of both former 007 Pierce Brosnan and champion golfer Rory McIlroy.

formal (no membership required, www.hostelworld.com). You may pay slightly less by booking directly with the hostel. Ireland's Independent Holiday Hostels (www.hostels-ireland.com) is a network of independent hostels, requiring no membership and welcoming all ages. All IHH hostels are approved by Fáilte Ireland.

Official hostels are part of Hostelling International (HI) and share an online booking site (www.hihostels.com). HI hostels typically require that you be a member or else pay a bit more per night.

Eating

Denis Leary once quipped, "Irish food isn't cuisine...it's penance." For years, Irish food was something you ate to survive rather than to savor. In this country, long considered the "land of potatoes," the diet reflected the economic circumstances. But times have changed. You'll find modern Irish cuisine delicious and varied. Expatriate chefs have come home with newly refined tastes, and immigrants have added a world of interesting flavors.

Modern cuisine is skillfully prepared with fresh, local ingredients. Irish beef, lamb, and dairy products are among the EU's best. And there are streams full of trout and salmon and a rich ocean of fish and shellfish right offshore. While potatoes remain staples, they're often replaced with rice or pasta in many dishes. Modern foodie places almost always have a serious vegetarian main dish. Try the local specialties wherever you happen to be eating.

For listings in this guidebook, I look for restaurants that are convenient to your hotel and sightseeing. When restaurant-hunting, choose a spot filled with locals, not tourists. Venturing even a block or two off the main drag leads to higher-quality food for a better price.

Tipping: At a sit-down place with table service, tip about 10 percent—unless the service charge is already listed on the bill. If you order at a counter, there's no need to tip.

RESTAURANT PRICING

I've categorized my recommended eateries based on the average price of a typical main course, indicated with a dollar-sign rating (see sidebar). Obviously, expensive specialties, fine wine, appetizers, and dessert can significantly increase your final bill.

The categories also indicate the personality of a place: **Budget** eateries include street food, takeaway, order-at-the-counter shops, basic cafeterias, and bakeries selling sandwiches. **Moderate** eateries are nice (but not fancy) sit-down restaurants, ideal for a straightforward, fill-the-tank meal. Most of my listings fall in this category—great for getting a good taste of the local cuisine at a reasonable price.

Pricier eateries are a notch up, with more attention paid to the

Restaurant Code

Eateries in this book are categorized according to the average cost of a typical main course. Drinks, desserts, and splurge items can raise the price considerably.

$$$$	**Splurge:** Most main courses over €25/£20
$$$	**Pricier:** €20-25/£15-20
$$	**Moderate:** €15-20/£10-15
$	**Budget:** Under €15/£10

In the Republic of Ireland, carryout fish-and-chips and other takeout food is **$**, a basic pub or sit-down eatery is **$$**, a gastropub or casual but more upscale restaurant is **$$$**, and a swanky splurge is **$$$$**.

setting, presentation, and (often inventive) cuisine. **Splurge** eateries are dress-up-for-a-special-occasion swanky—typically with an elegant setting, polished service, and pricey and intricate cuisine.

At classier restaurants, look for "early-bird specials," which allow you to eat well and affordably, but early (about 17:30-19:00).

BREAKFAST

The traditional breakfast, the "Irish Fry" (known in the North as the "Ulster Fry"), is a hearty way to start the day—with juice, tea or coffee, cereal, eggs, bacon, sausage, a grilled tomato, sautéed mushrooms, and optional black pudding (made from pigs' blood). Toast is served with butter and marmalade. Home-baked Irish soda bread can be an ambrosial eye-opener for those of us raised on Wonder Bread. This meal tides many travelers over until dinner. But there's nothing un-Irish about skipping the "fry"—few locals actually start their day with this heavy traditional breakfast. You can simply skip the heavier fare and enjoy the cereal, juice, toast, and tea (surprisingly, the Irish drink more tea per capita than the British).

PICNICS

Picnicking saves time and money. Try boxes of orange juice (pure, by the liter), fresh bread (especially Irish soda bread), tasty Cashel blue cheese, meat, a tube of mustard, local-eatin' apples, bananas, small tomatoes, a small tub of yogurt (it's drinkable), rice crackers, trail mix or nuts, plain digestive biscuits (the chocolate-covered ones melt), and any local specialties. At open-air markets and supermarkets, you can get produce in small quantities. Supermarkets often have good deli sections, packaged sandwiches, and sometimes salad bars. Hang on to the half-liter mineral-water bottles (sold everywhere for about €1.50). Buy juice in cheap liter boxes, then drink some and store the extra in your water bottle. I often munch a relaxed "meal on wheels" in a car, train, or bus to save 30 precious minutes for sightseeing.

If you're driving, pull over and grab a healthy snack at a road-side stand (Ireland's climate is ideal for strawberries...County Wexford claims the best spring/summer crop).

PUBS

Pubs are a basic part of the Irish social scene, and whether you're a teetotaler or a beer-guzzler, they should be a part of your Ireland experience. Whether in rural villages or busy Dublin, a pub (short for "public house") is an extended living room where, if you don't mind the stickiness, you can feel the pulse of Ireland. Unfortunately, many city pubs have been afflicted with an excess of brass, ferns, and video games; you'll find the most traditional and atmospheric pubs in Ireland's countryside and smaller towns.

Smart travelers use pubs to eat, drink, get out of the rain, watch the latest sporting event, and make new friends. You're a guest on your first night; after that, you're a regular. A wise Irishman once said, "It never rains in a pub." The relaxed, informal atmosphere feels like a refuge from daily cares. Women traveling alone need not worry—you'll become part of the pub family in no time.

Craic (pronounced "crack"), Irish for "fun" or "a good laugh," is the sport that accompanies drinking in a pub. People are there to talk. To encourage conversation, stand or sit at the bar, not at a table.

It's a tradition to buy your table a round, and then for each person to reciprocate. If an Irishman buys you a drink, thank him by saying, *"Go raibh maith agat"* (guh rov mah UG-ut). Offer him a toast in Irish—*"Slainte"* (SLAWN-chuh, the equivalent of "cheers"). A good excuse for a conversation is to ask to be taught a few words of Irish Gaelic.

Pubs are generally open daily from 11:00 to 23:30 and Sunday from noon to 22:30. Children are generally welcome before 20:00 (sometimes in specific sections). You must be at least 18 to order a beer.

There's seldom table service in Irish pubs. Order drinks and meals at the bar. Pay as you order, and only tip (by rounding up to avoid excess coinage) if you like the service.

Don't expect every pub to offer grub. Some only have peanuts and potato chips. All pubs in the Republic are smoke-free, but have covered smoking patios.

Pub Grub: Pub grub gets better every year—it's Ireland's best eating value. Pubs that are attached to restaurants, advertise their food, and are crowded with locals are more likely to have fresh,

made-to-order food. But don't expect high cuisine; this is, after all, comfort food. For about $20, you'll get a basic meal.

Pub menus offer a hearty assortment of traditional dishes, such as Irish stew (mutton with mashed potatoes, onions, carrots, and herbs), soups and chowders, coddle (bacon, pork sausages, potatoes, and onions stewed in layers), fish-and-chips, collar and cabbage (boiled bacon coated in bread crumbs and brown sugar, then baked and served with cabbage), boxty (potato pancake filled with fish, meat, or vegetables), and champ (potato mashed with milk and onions). Irish soda bread nicely rounds out a meal. In coastal areas, try seafood, such as mackerel, mussels, and Atlantic salmon.

Beer: When you say "a beer, please" in an Irish pub, you'll get a pint of Guinness (the tall blonde in a black dress). If you want a small beer, ask for a glass, which is a half-pint. Never rush your bartender when he's pour-

ing a Guinness. It's an almost sacred two-step process that requires time for the beer to settle.

The Irish take great pride in their beer. Popular with connoisseurs are the real ales, which are fermented naturally, vary from sweet to bitter, and often have a hoppy or nutty flavor. Experiment with obscure local microbrews (a small but growing presence on the Irish beer scene). Stout is dark and more bitter, like Guinness. If you think you don't like Guinness, try it in Ireland. It doesn't travel well and is better in its homeland. Murphy's is a very good Guinness-like stout, but a bit smoother and milder. For a cold, refreshing, basic, American-style beer, ask for a lager, such as Harp. Ale drinkers swear by Smithwick's (I know I do). Caffrey's is a satisfying cross between stout and ale. Craft beer microbrews are making inroads in Ireland (check www.beoir.org for options). Try the draft cider (sweet or dry)...carefully. The most common spirit is triple-distilled Irish whiskey. Teetotalers can order a soft drink.

"My Goodness, My Guinness!"

Every year on March 17, bars around the US serve pint after pint of green beer. But if you go to Ireland on Saint Patrick's Day, the beer is never green. It's black—or actually "dark ruby," according to the Guinness Brewery.

In 1759, Arthur Guinness signed an astounding 9,000-year lease on a dilapidated Dublin brewery. The rent: £45 a year. Competition was fierce among Dublin brewers, and friends of the 34-year-old entrepreneur thought his idea was ridiculous. He began pumping out two varieties of beer—an ale, and a darker "stout porter," so named because it was popular among porters in London. Against big odds, his dark beer thrived. By 1868, Guinness had the largest brewery in the world.

Today, Guinness remains one of the world's largest beer producers, with breweries in 50 countries. Around the world, 10 million pints of Guinness stout are consumed each day (with a few extra on St. Patrick's Day).

Over the years, a clever ad campaign has helped fuel the beer's success. In the 1930s, the brewery was known for its animal cartoons that featured simple but catchy slogans such as, "Guinness is good for you," "My goodness, my Guinness!" and "Have a Guinness when you're tired." Whether or not it's a good idea to drink alcohol when you're fighting fatigue, the slogan certainly helped sell beer.

Guinness stout is known for its dark color and creamy white head. The color and slightly burnt flavor come from roasting the barley before the beer is brewed. The beer is carbonated with nitrous oxide in addition to the usual carbon dioxide, producing the thick white foam on top. Traditionally, Guinness is served at a slightly warmer temperature than most ales and lagers.

Because of the high carbonation, pouring a Guinness takes skill, and ordering one takes patience. To tap a perfect pint, Guinness instructs bartenders to use a "two-part pour." The glass should be tilted at a 45-degree angle and filled to three-quarters capacity. Then you must wait for the surge of bubbles beneath the foam to settle before the glass is filled to the brim. The overall process takes about two minutes.

Several years ago, a Dublin company worked on developing a process to cut down the pouring-and-settling time without disrupting the beer's quality...but Guinness aficionados weren't impressed. A bartender at one of Dublin's oldest pubs told CNN, "Our customers will certainly not go for that. Guinness is a traditional drink and I don't think people will sacrifice that for a little extra speed and efficiency."

Staying Connected

One of the most common questions I hear from travelers is, "How can I stay connected in Europe?" The short answer is: more easily and cheaply than you might think.

The simplest solution is to bring your own device—mobile phone, tablet, or laptop—and use it just as you would at home (following the money-saving tips below, such as getting an international plan or connecting to free Wi-Fi whenever possible). Another option is to buy a European SIM card for your US mobile phone. Or you can use European landlines and computers to connect. Each of these options is described next, and more details are at www.ricksteves.com/phoning. For a very practical one-hour talk covering tech issues for travelers, see www.ricksteves.com/mobile-travel-skills.

Because dialing instructions vary between the Republic and Northern Ireland, carefully read "How to Dial," on the next page.

USING A MOBILE PHONE IN EUROPE

Here are some budget tips and options.

Sign up for an international plan. To stay connected at a lower cost, sign up for an international service plan through your carrier. Most providers offer a simple bundle that includes calling, messaging, and data. Your normal plan may already include international coverage (T-Mobile's does).

Before your trip, call your provider or check online to confirm that your phone will work in Europe, and research your provider's international rates. Activate the plan a day or two before you leave, then remember to cancel it when your trip's over.

Use free Wi-Fi whenever possible. Unless you have an unlimited-data plan, you're best off saving most of your online tasks for Wi-Fi. You can access the internet, send texts, and even make voice calls over Wi-Fi.

Most accommodations in Europe offer free Wi-Fi, but some—especially expensive hotels—charge a fee. Many cafés (including Starbucks and McDonald's) have free hotspots for customers; look for signs offering it and ask for the Wi-Fi password when you buy something. You'll also often find Wi-Fi at TIs, city squares, major museums, public-transit hubs, and airports, and aboard trains and buses.

Minimize the use of your cellular network. The best way to make sure you're not accidentally burning through data is to put your device in "airplane" mode (which also disables phone calls and texts), turn your Wi-Fi back on, and connect to networks as needed. When you need to get online but can't find Wi-Fi, simply

How to Dial

International Calls

Whether phoning from a US landline or mobile phone, or from a number in another European country, here's how to make an international call. I've used recommended hotels in Dublin (tel. 01/679-6500) and in Belfast (tel. 028/9027-1066) as examples.

Initial Zero: Drop the initial zero from international phone numbers—except when calling Italy.

Mobile Tip: If using a mobile phone, the "+" sign can replace the international access code (for a "+" sign, press and hold "0").

US/Canada to Europe

Dial 011 (US/Canada international access code), country code (353 for the Republic of Ireland, 44 for Northern Ireland), and phone number.

▸ To call the Dublin hotel from home, dial 011-353-1-679-6500.

▸ To call the Belfast hotel, dial 011-44-28-9027-1066.

Country to Country Within Europe

Dial 00 (Europe international access code), country code, and phone number.

▸ To call the Dublin hotel, whether from Northern Ireland or elsewhere in Europe, dial 00-353-1-679-6500.

▸ To call the Belfast hotel from the Republic of Ireland or elsewhere in Europe, dial 00-44-28-9027-1066.

Europe to the US/Canada

Dial 00, country code (1 for US/Canada), and phone number.

▸ To call from Europe to my office in Edmonds, Washington, dial 00-1-425-771-8303.

Domestic Calls

To call within the Republic of Ireland or within Northern Ireland (from one Irish landline or mobile phone to another), simply dial the phone number, including the initial 0 if there is one.

▸ To call the Dublin hotel from Wexford, dial 01/679-6500.

▸ To call the Belfast hotel from Derry, dial 028/9027-1066.

More Dialing Tips

Republic of Ireland to Northern Ireland: To avoid international rates when calling from any Republic of Ireland phone number to a landline in Northern Ireland (prefix 028), you can dial 048, then the local number (skipping the access code, country code, and Northern Ireland's area code).

▸ To call the Belfast hotel from a Dublin landline, dial 048-9027-1066.

PRACTICALITIES

Dialing from Northern Ireland to Republic of Ireland
From a Northern Ireland phone number, dial 00-353, then the area code without its initial 0, and then the local number.

▸ To call the Dublin hotel from a Belfast number,
dial 00-353-1-679-6500.

Irish Phone Numbers: Phone numbers in both the Republic and Northern Ireland can vary in length. I keep things simple by always dialing the full number (including the area code or prefix). Mobile phone numbers in the Republic start with 083, 085, 086, 087, and 089. Mobile phone numbers in Northern Ireland (and the rest of the UK) start with 07. Note that calls to a European mobile phone are more expensive than calls to a landline.

Toll and Toll-Free Numbers: It's generally not possible to dial Irish toll or toll-free numbers from a US mobile or landline (although you can sometimes get through using Skype). Look for a direct-dial number instead.

More Phoning Help: See www.howtocallabroad.com.

European Country Codes		Ireland & N. Ireland	353 / 44
Austria	43	Italy	39
Belgium	32	Latvia	371
Bosnia-Herzegovina	387	Montenegro	382
Croatia	385	Morocco	212
Czech Republic	420	Netherlands	31
Denmark	45	Norway	47
Estonia	372	Poland	48
Finland	358	Portugal	351
France	33	Russia	7
Germany	49	Slovakia	421
Gibraltar	350	Slovenia	386
Great Britain	44	Spain	34
Greece	30	Sweden	46
Hungary	36	Switzerland	41
Iceland	354	Turkey	90

turn on your cellular network (or turn off airplane mode) just long enough for the task at hand.

Even with an international data plan, wait until you're on Wi-Fi to Skype, download apps, stream videos, or do other mega-byte-greedy tasks. Using a navigation app such as Google Maps over a cellular network can take lots of data, so do this sparingly or offline.

Limit automatic updates. By default, your device constantly checks for a data connection and updates apps. It's smart to disable these features so your apps will only update when you're on Wi-Fi. Also change your device's email settings from "auto-retrieve" to "manual" (or from "push" to "fetch").

Use Wi-Fi calling and messaging apps. Skype, WhatsApp, FaceTime, and Google Hangouts are great for making free or low-cost calls or sending texts over Wi-Fi worldwide. Just log on to a Wi-Fi network, then connect with any of your friends or family members who use the same service. If you buy credit in advance, with some of these services you can call or text anywhere for just pennies.

Some apps, such as Apple's iMessage, will use the cellular net-work for texts if Wi-Fi isn't available: To avoid this possibility, turn off the "Send as SMS" feature.

Buy a European SIM card. If you anticipate making a lot of local calls, need a local phone number, or your provider's inter-national data rates are expensive, consider buying a SIM card in Europe to replace the one in your (unlocked) US phone or tablet.

SIM cards are sold at department-store electronics counters, some newsstands, and vending machines. If you need help setting it up, buy one at a mobile-phone shop (you may need to show your passport).

There are no roaming charges when using a European SIM card in other EU countries, though to be sure you get this "roam-like-at-home" pricing, buy your SIM card at a mobile-phone shop and ask if this feature is included.

WITHOUT A MOBILE PHONE

It's less convenient but possible to travel in Europe without a mo-bile device. You can make calls from your hotel and check email or get online using public computers.

Most **hotels** charge a fee for placing calls—ask for rates before you dial. You can use a prepaid international phone card (usually available at newsstands, tobacco shops, and train stations) to call out from your hotel. Dial the toll-free access number, enter the card's PIN code, then dial the number.

Phones are rare in **B&Bs;** if there's no phone in your room,

Tips on Internet Security

Make sure that your device is running the latest versions of its operating system, security software, and apps. Next, ensure that your device and key programs (like email) are password-protected. On the road, use only secure, password-protected Wi-Fi hotspots. Ask the hotel or café staff for the specific name of their Wi-Fi network, and make sure you log on to that exact one.

If you must access your financial info online, use a banking app rather than accessing your account via a browser. A cellular connection is more secure than Wi-Fi. Avoid logging onto personal finance sites on a public computer.

Never share your credit-card number (or any other sensitive information) online unless you know that the site is secure. A secure site displays a little padlock icon, and the URL begins with *https* (instead of the usual *http*).

PRACTICALITIES

and you have an important, brief call to make, politely ask your hosts if you can use their personal phone.

Public pay phones are hard to find in Northern Ireland, and they're expensive. To use one, you'll pay with a major credit card (which you insert into the phone—minimum charge for a credit-card call is £1.20) or coins (have a bunch handy; minimum fee is £0.60). Only unused coins are returned, so put in biggies with caution.

Some hotels have **public computers** in their lobbies for guests to use; otherwise you may find them at public libraries (ask your hotelier or the TI for the nearest location).

On a European keyboard, use the "Alt Gr" key to the right of the space bar to insert the extra symbol that appears on some keys. If you can't locate a special character (such as @), simply copy it from a web page.

MAIL

You can mail one package per day to yourself worth up to $200 duty-free from Europe to the US (mark it "personal purchases"). If you're sending a gift to someone, mark it "unsolicited gift." For details, visit www.cbp.gov, select "Travel," and search for "Know Before You Visit." The Irish postal service works fine, but for quick transatlantic delivery (in either direction), consider services such as DHL (www.dhl.com). Get stamps at the neighborhood post office, newsstands within fancy hotels, and some minimarts and card shops. Don't use stamps from the Republic of Ireland on postcards mailed in Northern Ireland (part of the UK), and vice versa.

Transportation

Figuring out how to get around in Europe is one of your biggest trip decisions. **Cars** work well for two or more traveling together (especially families with small kids), those packing heavy, and those delving into the countryside. **Trains** and **buses** are best for solo travelers, blitz tourists, city-to-city travelers, and those who want to leave the driving to others. Smart travelers can use short-hop **flights** within Europe to creatively connect the dots on their itineraries. Just be aware of the potential downside of each option: A car is an expensive headache in any major city; with trains and buses you're at the mercy of a timetable; and flying entails a trek to and from a usually distant airport.

To see all of Ireland, especially the sights with far-flung rural charm, I prefer the freedom of a rental car. Connemara, the Ring of Kerry, the Antrim Coast, County Donegal, County Wexford, and the Boyne Valley are really only worth it if you have wheels.

If your itinerary mixes cities and countryside, my advice is to connect cities by train (or bus) and to explore rural areas by rental car. Arrange to pick up your car in the last big city you'll visit, then use it to lace together small towns and explore the countryside.

Ireland has a good train-and-bus system, though departures are not as frequent as the European norm. Most rail lines spoke outward from Dublin, so you'll need to mix in bus transportation to bridge the gaps. Buses pick you up when the trains let you down.

Given the choice of either a bus or a train between the same two towns, I prefer trains, which are sometimes faster and are not subject to the vehicle traffic that can delay buses (although bus travel can be more direct). Also, unlike bus travel, on a train you can get up and walk around, and your bags ride with you in the main compartment (rather than under the bus).

The best overall source of schedules for public transportation in the Republic of Ireland as well as Northern Ireland—including rail, cross-country and city buses, and Dublin's LUAS transit—is the Republic of Ireland's domestic website: www.discoverireland.ie (select "Getting Around" near the bottom of the home page).

I've included a sample itinerary for drivers (with tips and tweaks for those using public transportation) to help you explore Ireland smoothly; you'll find it on page 20. For more detailed information on transportation throughout Europe, see www.ricksteves.com/transportation.

TRAINS

To research Irish rail connections online, you need to access two sites. For the Republic of Ireland, use www.irishrail.ie. For Northern Ireland, use www.translink.co.uk. The only city pair both web-

Rail Pass or Point-to-Point Tickets?

Will you be better off buying a rail pass or point-to-point tickets? It pays to know your options and choose what's best for your itinerary.

Rail Passes

A Eurail Ireland Pass lets you travel by train in Ireland for three to eight days (north or south, consecutively or not) within a one-month period. Ireland is also covered (along with Britain and most of Europe) by the classic Eurail Global Pass. Discounted rates are offered for seniors (age 60 and up) and youths (ages 12-27). Up to two kids (ages 4-11) can travel free with each adult-rate pass (but not with senior rates). All passes offer a choice of first or second class for all ages.

In addition, Irish Rail sells a rail pass that's good for four consecutive days or five days of train travel in the Republic of Ireland within a 15-day period. This pass can be purchased at rail ticket offices in Ireland.

Eurail passes are best purchased outside Europe (through travel agents or Rick Steves' Europe). For more on rail passes, including current prices, visit RickSteves.com/rail.

Point-to-Point Tickets

In Ireland, buying tickets as you go works fine for both rail and bus. Use this map to add up approximate fares for your itinerary, and compare that to the price of a rail pass. The rates here require purchase online; additional discounts may be available with advance purchase.

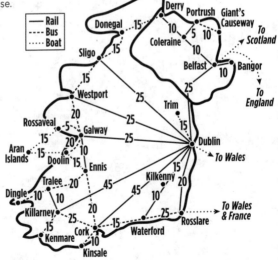

Map shows approximate costs, in US dollars, for one-way, second-class tickets purchased online at least 90 minutes before departure.

PRACTICALITIES

Ireland's Public Transportation

- - - - - Rail
- - - - Bus (not all lines shown)
· · · · · · · · · Boat

25 Kilometers
25 Miles

Dunfanaghy
Bunbeg
Burtonport
Letterkenny
Donegal
Enniskillen
Belmullet
Sligo
Ballina
Ballymote
Foxford
Carrick-on-Shannon
Castlebar
Boyle
Westport
Knock
Strokestown
Dromod
Claremorris
Roscommon
Longford
Letterfrack
Cong
Clifden
Ballinasloe
Athlone
Galway
Rossaveal
Athenry
Kilronan
Aran Islands
REPUBLIC OF IRELAND
Doolin
Cliffs of Moher
Ennis
Nenagh
Atlantic Ocean
Killimer
Thurles
Shannon
Tarbert
Limerick
Cashel
Limerick Junction
Tralee
Charleville
Tipperary
Cahir
Dingle
Clonmel
Kerry
Farranfore
Mallow
Killarney
Midleton
Cahersiveen
Blarney
Cork
Youghal
Kenmare
Cobh
Waterville
Ringaskiddy
Ardgroom
Bantry
Kinsale
Skibbereen
To Cherbourg, France

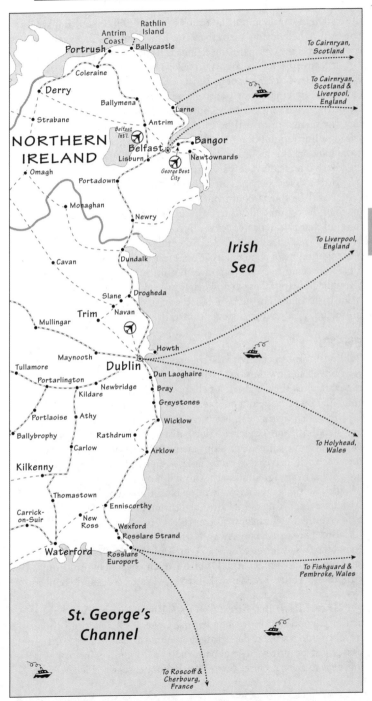

sites share in common are the trains between Dublin and Belfast. For train schedules on the rest of the European continent, check www.bahn.com (Germany's excellent Europe-wide timetable).

It really pays to buy your train tickets online ahead of time. Advance-purchase discounts of up to 50 percent are not unheard of, but online fares fluctuate widely and unpredictably. Online and off, fares are often higher for peak travel on Fridays and Sundays. Remember that the quoted price will be in euros or British pounds. Booking ahead online (up to 90 minutes before departure) can also help you avoid long ticket lines in Dublin and elsewhere at busy times.

Be aware that very few Irish train stations have storage lockers.

Rail Passes: For most travelers in Ireland, a rail pass is not very useful. Trains fan out from Dublin to major cities but neglect much of the countryside. But if a pass works for your itinerary, keep in mind that Eurail passes cover all trains in both the Republic and Northern Ireland, and give a 30 percent discount on standard foot-passenger fares for some international ferries. Irish Rail also offers a pass covering five days of travel within a 15-day period in the Republic only (purchase at any major rail station in Ireland, http://www.irishrail.ie). For more detailed advice on train travel options in Ireland, visit www.ricksteves.com/rail.

BUSES

Public transit (especially cross-country Irish buses) will likely put your travels in slow motion. Although buses are about a third slower than trains, they're also a lot cheaper, and can be more direct. A combination of train and bus works best for many routes.

The Irish distinguish between "buses" (for in-city travel with lots of stops) and "coaches" (long-distance cross-country runs). Note that some rural coach stops are by "request only." This means the coach will drive right on by unless you flag it down by extending your arm straight out, with your palm open.

Bus stations are normally at or near train stations. On some Irish buses, sporting events are piped throughout the bus; have earplugs handy if you prefer a quieter ride.

Bus Éireann Expressway is the main bus company in the Republic (www.buseireann.ie); **Translink** serves Northern Ireland (www.translink.co.uk). **Dublin Coach** covers Dublin, Ennis, Killarney, Tralee, Kildare, Kilkenny, Waterford, and Belfast (www.dublincoach.ie).

Travel Pass: Bus Éireann's **Open Road** tourist travel passes can be a good option for nondrivers. Coverage starts from three travel days in a six-day period and goes up to 15 days out of 30. The passes can be pricey, so compare the cost of your point-to-point journeys to the pass price (www.buseireann.ie, select "Tickets" and then "Tourist Travel Passes").

Discounts: Students can use their ISIC (international student identity card, www.isic.org) to get up to 50 percent discounts on cross-country coaches. Children 5-15 pay half-price on trains, and wee ones under age 5 go free.

Backpacker Bus Circuits: For a hop-on, hop-off bus ride geared to thrifty hostelers, **Paddy Wagon** offers three- to nine-day "tours" of each half of Ireland (north and south) that can be combined into a comprehensive trip connecting Dublin, Cork, Killarney, Dingle, Galway, Westport, Donegal, Derry, and Belfast (May-Oct, 5 Beresford Palace, Dublin, tel. 01/823-0822, toll-free from UK tel. 0800-783-4191, www.paddywagontours.com). They also offer day tours to the Giant's Causeway, Belfast, Cliffs of Moher, Glendalough, and Kilkenny.

TAXIS AND RIDE-BOOKING SERVICES

Most European taxis are reliable and cheap. In many cities, two people can travel short distances by cab for little more than the cost of bus or subway tickets. If you like ride-booking services such as Uber, their apps usually work in Europe just like they do in the US: Request a car on your mobile phone (connected to Wi-Fi or data), and the fare is automatically charged to your credit card.

PRIVATE DRIVER

While not cheap, hiring a private driver can make sense, particularly if you're traveling with a group. One solid outfit worth considering is **Fitzpatrick Coaches,** based in Monaghan but available to drive anywhere in Ireland (tel. 047/82331, mobile 087/273-1396, www.fitzpatrickcoaches.com). The three main vehicle size choices are SUV (3 passengers), van (up to 7 passengers), or small coach (up to 17 passengers).

RENTING A CAR

Travelers from North America are understandably hesitant when they consider driving in Ireland, where you must drive on the left side of the road. The Irish government statistics say that 10 percent of all car accidents on Irish soil involve a foreign tourist. But careful drivers—with the patient support of an alert navigator—usually get the hang of it by the end of the first day.

It's cheaper to arrange most car rentals from the US, so research and compare rates before you go. Most of the major US rental agencies (including Avis, Budget, Enterprise, Hertz, and Thrifty) have offices throughout Europe. Also consider the two major Europe-based agencies, Europcar and Sixt. Consolidators such as Auto Europe (www.autoeurope.com—or the sometimes cheaper www.autoeurope.eu) compare rates at several companies to get you the best deal.

PRACTICALITIES

Driving in Ireland

m = miles
h = hours
...... = ferry

Note: Your times may vary based on traffic, construction, and sheep on road.

Wherever you book, always read the fine print. Check for add-on charges—such as one-way drop-off fees, airport surcharges, or mandatory insurance policies—that aren't included in the "total price."

Rental Costs and Considerations

In midsummer expect to pay at least $250 for a one-week rental of a basic compact-size car with minimum insurance (not including fuel, tolls, and parking). You'll pay more for an automatic or for supplemental insurance. Smaller economy-size cars cost about $50 less per week. Minibuses are a good, budget way to go for larger groups (five to nine people). To save money on fuel, request a diesel car.

Manual vs. Automatic: Almost all rental cars in Europe are manual by default—and cars with a stick shift are generally cheaper. If you need an automatic, request one in advance. An automatic

The Wild Atlantic Way

This Irish tourism marketing initiative offers drivers "the world's longest defined touring route." Stretching 1,550 miles (2,500 km) from Kinsale in the south to Derry in the North, the Wild Atlantic Way snakes along the inlets and outcrops of Ireland's west coast, passing through nine counties and bagging some of the best coastal views along the way. This is the scenic, long-way-around route for travelers not in a hurry. You'll frequently see signs with a large blue "WW" meant to symbolize waves, which tells you that you're driving on a section of the route (www.wildatlanticway.com).

PRACTICALITIES

makes sense for most American drivers: With a manual transmission in Ireland, you'll be sitting on the right side of the car and shifting with your left hand...while driving on the left side of the road. When selecting a car, don't be tempted by a larger model, as it won't be as maneuverable on narrow, winding roads or when squeezing into tight parking lots.

Age Restrictions: Some rental companies impose minimum and maximum age limits. Young drivers (25 and under) and seniors (69 and up) should check the rental policies and rules section of car-rental websites. In the Republic of Ireland, you generally can't rent a car if you're 75 or older, and you'll usually pay an extra €25 per day insurance surcharge if you're 70-74. Some companies in Northern Ireland won't rent to anyone over 69.

Choosing Pickup/Drop-off Locations: Always check the hours of the locations you choose: Many rental offices close from midday Saturday until Monday morning and, in smaller towns, at lunchtime. When selecting an office, plug the address into a mapping website to confirm the location, and make sure your rental company has offices on both ends of your itinerary. A downtown site is generally cheaper—and might seem more convenient than the airport. But pedestrianized and one-way streets can make navigation tricky when returning a car at a big-city office or urban train station. Wherever you select, get precise details on the location and allow ample time to find it.

Crossing Borders in a Rental Car: If your trip covers both Ireland and Great Britain (Scotland, England, and Wales), you're better off with two separate car rentals, rather than paying to

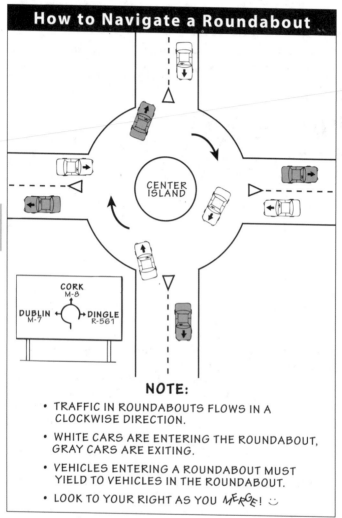

How to Navigate a Roundabout

CENTER ISLAND

CORK
M-8

DUBLIN ← →DINGLE
M-7   R-561

NOTE:

- TRAFFIC IN ROUNDABOUTS FLOWS IN A CLOCKWISE DIRECTION.

- WHITE CARS ARE ENTERING THE ROUNDABOUT, GRAY CARS ARE EXITING.

- VEHICLES ENTERING A ROUNDABOUT MUST YIELD TO VEHICLES IN THE ROUNDABOUT.

- LOOK TO YOUR RIGHT AS YOU MERGE! ☺

transport your car via ferry between the two islands. On an all-Ireland trip, you can drive your rental car from the Republic of Ireland into Northern Ireland, but will pay a drop-off charge (as much as $200) if you return it in the North. You'll pay a smaller drop-off charge (as much as $100) for picking up and returning the car from different locations, even within the same city. If you pick up the car in a smaller city, you'll more likely survive your first day on the Irish roads. If you drop the car off early or keep it longer, you'll be credited or charged at a fair, prorated price.

Picking Up Your Car: Before driving off in your rental car, check it thoroughly and make sure any damage is noted on your rental agreement. Rental agencies in Europe tend to charge for even minor damage, so be sure to mark everything. Find out how your car's gearshift, lights, turn signals, wipers, radio, and fuel cap function, and know what kind of fuel the car takes (diesel vs. unleaded). When you return the car, make sure the agent verifies its condition with you. Some drivers take pictures of the returned vehicle as proof of its condition.

Car Insurance Options

When you rent a car in Europe, the price typically includes liability insurance, which covers harm to other cars or motorists—but not the rental car itself. To limit your financial risk in case of damage to the rental, choose one of these options: Buy a Collision Damage Waiver (CDW) with a low or zero deductible from the car-rental company (roughly 30-40 percent extra), get coverage through your credit card (more complicated, and few credit cards now offer free coverage in Ireland), or get collision insurance as part of a larger travel-insurance policy.

Basic **CDW** costs $15-30 a day and typically comes with a $1,000-2,000 deductible, reducing but not eliminating your financial responsibility. Tires and wheel rims are usually excluded from this coverage. When you reserve or pick up the car, you'll be offered the chance to "buy down" the basic deductible to zero (for an additional $10-30/day; this is sometimes called "super CDW" or "zero-deductible coverage").

If you opt for **credit-card coverage** (and your credit card is one of the few accepted for this type of coverage in Ireland), there's a catch. You must decline all coverage offered by the car-rental company, which means they can place a hold on your card for up to the full value of the car. In case of damage, it can be time-consuming to resolve the charges. Before relying on this option, quiz your credit-card company about how it works.

For more on car-rental insurance, see www.ricksteves.com/cdw.

Navigation Options

If you'll be navigating using your phone or a GPS unit from home, remember to bring a car charger and device mount.

Your Mobile Phone: The mapping app on your phone works fine for navigating Europe's roads, but for real-time turn-by-turn directions and traffic updates, you'll need mobile data access. And driving all day can burn through a lot of very expensive data. The economical work-around is to use map apps that work offline. By downloading in advance from Google Maps, City Maps 2Go,

PRACTICALITIES

Driving Tips

Driving gives you access to the most rural sights and is my favorite mode of transportation in Ireland. In addition to our general driving advice within this chapter, here's what I've learned in the school of hard brakes and adrenaline rushes:

Prepare Ahead

Study your map before taking off. Get a sense of the areas you'll be visiting, as road numbers are inconsistent. The shortest distance between any two points is usually the motorway (highway). But miss a motorway exit and you can lose 20 minutes.

Estimate an average speed of 40 mph (1 km per minute). Find distances and driving times on the driving map (see the chart in this chapter) or online (www.google.com/maps or www.viamichelin.com).

In the Republic, the speed limit is in kilometers per hour, unleaded costs about €1.30/liter ($5.50/gallon), and the roads can be bumpy, narrow, and winding. In Northern Ireland, the speed limit is in miles per hour, unleaded costs about £1.30/liter ($7.30/gallon), and roads are better maintained.

Adjust and use your side-view mirrors. Get comfortable with the sound of vegetation whisking the side of your car on narrow roads.

Diesel fuel pumps (which are usually green in the US) are black in Ireland. Mixing them up while fueling is a sure way to ruin your

Apple Maps, Here WeGo, or Navmii, you can still have turn-by-turn voice directions and maps that recalibrate even though they're offline.

You must download your maps before you go offline—and it's smart to select large regions. Then turn off your data connection so you're not charged for roaming. Call up the map, enter your destination, and you're on your way. Even if you don't have to pay extra for data roaming, this option is great for navigating in areas with poor connectivity.

GPS Devices: If you want the convenience of a dedicated GPS unit, consider renting one with your car ($10-30/day). These units offer real-time turn-by-turn directions and traffic without the data requirements of an app. The unit may come loaded only with maps for its home country; if you need additional maps, ask.

A less-expensive option is to bring a GPS device from home.

day. Insurance doesn't cover this mistake.

If you have a disabled parking card, bring it. For information on disabled parking, call the Irish Wheelchair Association at tel. 045/893-094 (from the US, dial 011-353-45-893-094).

On the Road

Get an early start. Rushing makes you miss turns, which causes you stress, which makes your trip feel less like a vacation.

Enlist passengers to help navigate: Road signs can be confusing, too little, and too late.

Get used to shifting with your left hand. Find reverse...before you need it. (I love the smell of burnt clutch in the morning.)

Avoid driving in big cities; use ring roads to skirt the congestion. Real-time traffic conditions are updated on www.aa.ie.

On narrow rural roads, pull over against a hedgerow and blink your headlights to signal faster drivers to pass.

Expect a slow tractor, a flock of sheep, a one-lane bridge, and a baby stroller to lurk around blind turns. Honk when approaching blind corners to alert approaching drivers.

Buses have the right of way on rural roads.

Don't drink and drive. The Garda (police) set up random checkpoints. If you've had more than one pint, you're legally drunk in Ireland.

Enjoying the Ride

Tune in to RTE Radio 1, the national radio station (89 FM), for an education in Irish culture (see page 34). The same goes for BBC Ulster (94.5 FM) in Northern Ireland.

Be sure to buy and install the European maps you'll need before your trip.

Paper Maps and Atlases: Even when navigating primarily with a mobile app or GPS, I always make it a point to have a paper map, ideally with a big, detailed regional road map. It's invaluable for getting the big picture, understanding alternate routes, and filling in if my phone runs out of juice. The free maps you get from your car-rental company usually don't have enough detail. It's smart to buy a road atlas that covers all of Ireland. Ordnance Survey atlases are best (€11 in gas stations and bookstores). Drivers, hikers, and cyclists may want more detailed maps for Dingle, Connemara, Donegal, Wexford, the Antrim Coast, the Ring of Kerry, and the Boyne Valley (easy to buy locally at bookstores or gas stations).

Driving

Ireland's new motorways have vastly improved the cross-country driving experience and now link most major cities (Dublin, Belfast, Cork, Waterford, Limerick, and Galway). But many sights require driving on narrow country lanes. For using credit cards at gas pumps and garages, see "Using Credit Cards," on page 557.

An Irish Automobile Association membership comes with most rentals (www.theaa.ie). Understand its towing and emergency road-service benefits.

Road Rules: Driving in Ireland is basically wonderful—once you remember to stay on the left and have mastered the roundabouts. Don't let a roundabout spook you. After all, you routinely merge into much faster traffic with cars slipping into your blind spot on American highways back home. The traffic in a roundabout has the right-of-way; entering traffic yields (look to your right as you merge). It helps to remember that the driver is always in the center of the road. As you approach bigger roundabouts, look for instructions on the pavement that indicate which lane to be in for your destination.

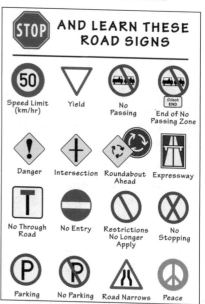

Spend a little time using Google's Street View option (www.google.com/maps) to actually see 360-degree views of the roads you'll be driving and how to access lodging or sightseeing you're considering. An advance peek online can settle the nerves of twitchy drivers and give you a heads-up on navigational issues you hadn't thought of yet.

Be warned: Every year I get a few emails from traveling readers advising me that, for them, trying to drive in Ireland was a nerve-racking and regrettable mistake. If you want to get a little slack on the roads, try to time your car rental to begin on a Sunday morning when you can acclimate to driving on less congested roads at a mellower pace.

Be aware of typical European road rules; for example, many countries require headlights to be turned on at all times, and nearly

PRACTICALITIES

Ferry Information

INTERNATIONAL FERRY CONNECTIONS

Ireland has good ferry connections with Britain and France. Check the websites listed per route below for specifics on price, frequency, and length of journey.

Republic of Ireland

Irish Port	To...	Web Site
Dublin	Liverpool (England)	www.poferries.com
Dublin	Holyhead (Wales)	www.irishferries.com and www.stenaline.com
Rosslare	Fishguard (Wales)	www.stenaline.com
Rosslare	Pembroke (Wales)	www.irishferries.com
Rosslare	Cherbourg (France)	www.stenaline.com
Ringaskiddy (near Cork)	Roscoff (France)	www.brittanyferries.ie

Northern Ireland

Belfast	Liverpool (England)	www.stenaline.com
Belfast	Cairnryan (Scotland)	www.stenaline.com
Larne	Cairnryan (Scotland)	www.poferries.com

all forbid handheld mobile phone use. In Ireland, you're not allowed to turn left on a red light unless a sign or signal specifically authorizes it, and on motorways it's illegal to pass drivers on the left. Seat belts are mandatory for all, and kids under 12 or under 1.5 meters tall (about 4 feet, 9 inches) must ride in a child-safety seat.

Ask your car-rental company about these rules, read the Department for Transport's *Highway Code* (www.gov.uk/highway-code), or check the "International Travel" section of the US State Department website (www.travel.state.gov, search for your country in the "Learn About Your Destination" box, then click "Travel and Transportation").

Speed Limits: Speed limits are 50 kilometers per hour (roughly 30 miles per hour) in towns, 80 kph (approximately 50 mph) on rural roads (such as R-257, R-600, etc.), 100 kph (about 60 mph) on national roads (N-8, N-30, etc.), and 120 kph (roughly 75 mph) on motorways (M-1, M-50, etc.). Note that road-surveillance cameras strictly enforce speed limits. Any driver (including foreigners renting cars) photographed speeding will get a nasty bill in the mail. (Cameras—you'll see the foreboding gray boxes—flash on your rear license plate in order not to invade the privacy of anyone sharing the front seat with someone they shouldn't be with.)

Tolls: Many rental-car companies automatically charge for an eFlow pass that electronically pays the toll for Dublin's M50 motorway—ask (see www.eflow.ie). Toll motorways are usually blue on maps and are shown with the letter "M" followed by the route number (toll prices and map: www.tii.ie/roads-tolling).

Parking: Parking is confusing. One yellow line marked on the pavement means no parking Monday through Saturday during business hours. Double yellow lines mean no parking at any time. Broken yellow lines mean short stops are OK, but you should always look for explicit signs or ask a passerby.

Even in small towns, rather than fight it, I just pull into the most central parking lot I can find. For street parking, signs along the street indicate whether an area uses pay-and-display (machines have a blue circle with white letter *P)* or parking-disks (sold at nearby shops; buy one disk for each hour you want to stay, scratch off the time you arrived on the disk and put it on your dashboard).

FLIGHTS

To compare flight costs and times, begin with an online travel search engine: Kayak is the top site for flights to and within Europe, easy-to-use Google Flights has price alerts, and Skyscanner includes many inexpensive flights within Europe. To avoid unpleasant surprises, before you book be sure to read the small print about refunds, changes, and the costs for "extras" such as reserving a seat, checking a bag, or printing a boarding pass.

Flights to Europe: Start looking for international flights about four to six months before your trip, especially for peak-season travel. Depending on your itinerary, it can be efficient and no more expensive to fly into one city and out of another. If your flight requires a connection in Europe, see my hints on navigating Europe's top hub airports at www.ricksteves.com/hub-airports.

Flights Within Europe: Flying between European cities is surprisingly affordable. Before buying a long-distance train or bus ticket, check the cost of a flight on one of Europe's airlines, whether a major carrier or a no-frills outfit like Easyjet, Aer Lingus, Flybe, and Ryanair. For flights within Ireland, try Aer Arann, a regional subsidiary of Aer Lingus. Be aware that flying with a discount airline can have drawbacks, such as minimal customer service and time-consuming treks to secondary airports.

Flying to the US and Canada: Because security is extra tight for flights to the US, be sure to give yourself plenty of time at the airport. Charge your electronic devices before you board in case security checks require you to turn them on (see www.tsa.gov for the latest rules).

Ireland's Airports: There are four major airports planted in the four corners of the island of Ireland: Dublin (east), Cork (south), Shannon (west), and Belfast (north). If you only have a few days and are focused mainly on one region, investigate flying into that airport to save valuable time (rather than assuming Dublin is best because it's biggest, then wasting half a day driving).

Direct flights from the US land in Dublin, Shannon, or Belfast. Cork has become a handy arrival point as well (via connecting flights from London). If you're offered a choice and have no interest in sightseeing in busy, congested Dublin, you'll find Shannon Airport to be a far less stressful entry or exit point into or out of Ireland. Drivers will especially appreciate getting used to the "other side of the road" around rural Shannon, as compared to urban Dublin. Be aware that smaller regional airports may have fewer car-rental offices.

Resources from Rick Steves

Begin Your Trip at RickSteves.com

My mobile-friendly **website** is *the* place to explore Europe in preparation for your trip. You'll find thousands of fun articles, videos, and radio interviews; a wealth of money-saving tips for planning your dream trip; travel news dispatches; a video library of my travel talks; my travel blog; my latest guidebook updates (www.ricksteves.com/update); and my free Rick Steves Audio Europe app. You can also follow me on Facebook, Instagram, and Twitter.

Our **Travel Forum** is a well-groomed collection of message boards where our travel-savvy community answers questions and shares their personal travel experiences—and our well-traveled staff chimes in when they can be helpful (www.ricksteves.com/forums).

Our **online Travel Store** offers bags and accessories that I've designed to help you travel smarter and lighter. These include my popular carry-on bags (which I live out of four months a year), money belts, totes, toiletries kits, adapters, guidebooks, and planning maps (www.ricksteves.com/shop).

Our website can also help you find the perfect **rail pass** for your itinerary and your budget, with easy, one-stop shopping for rail passes, seat reservations, and point-to-point tickets (www.ricksteves.com/rail).

PRACTICALITIES

Rick Steves' Tours, Guidebooks, TV Shows, and More

Small Group Tours: Want to travel with greater efficiency and less stress? We offer more than 40 itineraries reaching the best destinations in this book...and beyond. Each year about 30,000 travelers join us on about 1,000 Rick Steves bus tours. You'll enjoy great guides and a fun bunch of travel partners (with small groups of 24 to 28 travelers). You'll find European adventures to fit every vacation length. For all the details, and to get our tour catalog, visit www.ricksteves.com/tours or call us at 425/608-4217.

Books: This book is just one of many books in my series on European travel, which includes country and city guidebooks, Snapshots (excerpted chapters from bigger guides), Pocket Guides (full-color little books on big cities), "Best Of" guidebooks (condensed, full-color country guides), and my budget-travel skills handbook, *Rick Steves Europe Through the Back Door*. A complete list of my titles—including phrase books; cruising guides; travelogues on European art, history, and culture; and more—appears near the end of this book.

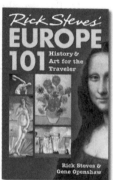

TV Shows and Travel Talks: My public television series, *Rick Steves' Europe*, covers Europe from top to bottom with over 100 half-hour episodes—and we're working on new shows every year (watch full episodes at my website for free). My free online video library, Rick Steves Classroom Europe, offers a searchable database of short video clips on European history, culture, and geography (http://classroom.ricksteves.com). And to raise your travel I.Q., check out the video versions of our popular classes (covering most European countries as well as travel skills, packing smart, cruising, tech for travelers, European art, and travel as a political act—www.ricksteves.com/travel-talks).

Audio Tours on My Free App: I've produced dozens of free, self-guided audio tours of the top sights in Europe. For those tours and other audio content, get my free **Rick Steves Audio Europe** app, an extensive online library organized by destination. For more on my app, see page 26.

Radio: My weekly public radio show, *Travel with Rick Steves*, features interviews with travel experts from around the world. It airs on 400 public radio stations across the US. An archive of programs is available at RickSteves.com/radio.

Podcasts: You can enjoy my travel content via several free pod-casts. The podcast version of my radio show brings you a weekly, hour-long travel conversation. My other podcasts include a weekly selection of video clips from my public television show, my audio tours of Europe's top sights, and live recordings of my travel classes (RickSteves.com/watch-read-listen/audio/podcasts).

APPENDIX

Holidays and Festivals

This list includes select festivals in major cities, plus national holidays observed throughout Ireland. Many sights and banks close on national holidays—keep this in mind when planning your itinerary. Before planning a trip around a festival, verify the dates with the festival website, TI sites (www.discoverireland.ie and www.discovernorthernireland.com), or my "Upcoming Holidays and Festivals in Ireland" web page (www.ricksteves.com/europe/ireland/festivals).

Jan 1	New Year's Day
Jan 27-31	Temple Bar Trad, Dublin (Irish music and culture festival, http://templebartrad.com)
March 17	St. Patrick's Day
Mid-March	St. Patrick's Day celebration throughout Ireland (parades, drunkenness, 5-day festival in Dublin, www.stpatricksday.ie)
April 2	Good Friday
April 4-5	Easter Sunday and Monday
Mid-April	International Pan Celtic Festival
May 3	May Day/Labor Day; Early May Bank Holiday, Ireland and UK

Late May	Fleadh Nua, Ennis (traditional music and dance festival, www.fleadhnua.com)
May 31	Spring Bank Holiday, UK
June 7	June Bank Holiday, Ireland
Mid-June	Bloomsday, Dublin (James Joyce festival, www.jamesjoyce.ie)
Late June	Patrún Festival, Kilronan (*currach* boat races)
Late June	St. John's Eve Bonfire Night (Kilronan)
July 12	Battle of the Boyne anniversary, Northern Ireland (Protestant marches, protests)
Mid- to Late July	Galway Arts Festival
Late July/Early Aug	Galway Races (horse races, www.galwayraces.com)
Aug 2	August Bank Holiday, Ireland
Early Aug	Dingle Races (horse races, www.dingleraces.ie)
Early-Mid-Aug	Dingle Regatta (boat races)
Early-Mid-Aug	Puck Fair, Killorglin, Kerry ("Ireland's Oldest Fair" and drink-fest, www.puckfair.ie)
Early-Mid-Aug	Féile an Phobail, West Belfast (Irish cultural festival, www.feilebelfast.com)
Mid-Aug	Fleadh Cheoil, Drogheda (traditional music festival, www.fleadhcheoil.ie)
Aug 30	Summer Bank Holiday, UK
Late Aug	Rose of Tralee International Festival, Tralee (http://roseoftralee.ie)
Late Aug/Early Sept	Blessing of the Boats, Dingle (maritime festival)
Mid-Sept/Late Oct	Galway Races (www.galwayraces.com)
Late Sept	Galway Oyster Festival (4 days, www.galwayoysterfest.com)
Late Sept/Early Oct	Dingle Food Festival (www.dinglefood.com)
Oct 25	October Bank Holiday, Ireland
Dec 25	Christmas, Ireland and UK
Dec 26	St. Stephen's Day, Ireland (religious festival); Boxing Day, UK
Dec 31	New Year's Eve

Books and Films

To learn more about Ireland past and present, check out a few of these books or films:

Nonfiction

Angela's Ashes (Frank McCourt, 1996). This evocative memoir documents an Irish family's struggles during the Great Depression.

Are You Somebody? The Accidental Memoir of a Dublin Woman (Nuala O'Faolain, 1996). A woman steps out of the traditional shoes she was always told to fill.

The Back of Beyond: A Search for the Soul of Ireland (James Charles Roy, 2002). Roy, an authority on Irish history, leads a group of Americans on an unconventional tour through the byways of Ireland.

How the Irish Saved Civilization (Thomas Cahill, 1995). Cahill explains how the "island of saints and scholars" changed the course of world history.

The Immortal Irishman (Timothy Egan, 2016). This well-written biography spans three continents to describe the incredible, passionate, and short life of Thomas Francis Meagher.

Ireland: A Concise History (Máire and Conor Cruise O'Brien, 1972). This is a riveting account of Irish history from pre-Christian Ireland to the Northern Irish civil rights movement.

O Come Ye Back to Ireland (Niall Williams and Christine Breen, 1987). Two New Yorkers adjust to life in a tiny Irish village after leaving their careers for a simpler life.

Round Ireland with a Fridge (Tony Hawks, 1997). For a humorous jaunt through the countryside, read Hawks' account of his attempt to hitchhike around Ireland with a fridge.

A Short History of Ireland (Richard Killeen, 1994). Killeen's well-illustrated book is among the most accessible introductions to Irish history.

To School Through the Fields (Alice Taylor, 1988). In one of the best-selling Irish memoirs of all time, Taylor fondly remembers growing up in a rural Irish town.

Fiction

The Barrytown Trilogy (Roddy Doyle, 1992). This trilogy includes Doyle's first three novels—*The Commitments, The Snapper,* and *The Van*—each capturing the day-to-day lives of working-class Dubliners.

The Bódhran Makers (John B. Keane, 1986). Keane documents the struggles of hard-living farmers in 1950s Ireland.

Circle of Friends (Maeve Binchy, 1990). One of Binchy's many soapy novels, *Circle of Friends* tells the story of a group of friends starting college in Dublin.

Dublin Saga (Edward Rutherfurd, 2004). Rutherfurd's historical saga traces the lives of rich and poor families through key events in Irish history, from AD 430 to the fight for independence.

Dubliners (James Joyce, 1914). Joyce's classic short-story collection describes Irish life in the 1900s, told through the experiences of 15 ordinary Dubliners.

Finbar's Hotel and *Ladies' Night at Finbar's Hotel* (Dermot Bolger, 1997/1999). These novels, about a collection of guests at a Dublin hotel, were collaboratively written, with each chapter penned by a different modern Irish author.

Ireland (Frank Delaney, 2004). Delaney's historical epic follows Ronan O'Mara on his journey to find a beloved Irish storyteller.

The Last Prince of Ireland (Morgan Llywelyn, 1992). An Irishman and his clan are determined to hold on to their homeland following the 1601 Battle of Kinsale, in which the Gaelic nobility were defeated by English invaders.

Long Lankin (John Banville, 1970). This collection of short stories by the Man Booker Prize-winning Irish author explores themes of alienation, jealousy, and love lost.

A Star Called Henry (Roddy Doyle, 1999). Doyle's political thriller, set in Ireland during the 1916 Easter Rising, is narrated by the young Henry Smart, a soldier in the Irish Citizen Army.

Trinity (Leon Uris, 1976). Uris dramatizes the sectarian struggles in the decades just prior to modern Irish independence.

Film and TV

Cal (1984). This complicated love story centers on a widow who must cope when her lover is hunted by the Irish Republican Army.

The Commitments (1991). Working-class Dubliners form a soul band in this adaption of Roddy Doyle's popular novel. Other film adaptions of Doyle's books include *The Snapper* (1993) and *The Van* (1996).

Dancing at Lughnasa (1998). This drama following five unmarried sisters in 1930s rural Ireland is based on a play that first opened in Dublin and then on Broadway.

Derry Girls (2018). This sitcom about a group of high-school girls in Northern Ireland during the early 1990s brings out a lighter side of the Troubles.

Evelyn (2002). Single dad Pierce Brosnan must fight the Irish courts to keep his kids after being abandoned by his wife.

Far and Away (1992). Tom Cruise and Nicole Kidman star as penniless Irish immigrants seeking their fortune in late-19th-century America.

The Field (1990). A farmer fights to keep his land in 1930s Ireland.

Fifty Dead Men Walking (2008). Director Kari Skogland's crime thriller features an IRA informer navigating a brutal world during the Troubles.

In the Name of the Father (1993). Daniel Day-Lewis plays wrongly accused IRA bomber Gerry Conlon in this biopic.

Into the West (1992). Two boys hide their beloved horse in urban Dublin before fleeing cross-country with it in this film written by Jim Sheridan, director of *My Left Foot*.

Leap Year (2009). In this movie set in Dingle (but filmed on the island of Inishmore), Amy Adams plays a woman who travels to Dublin to propose to her boyfriend.

The Magdalene Sisters (2003). Director Peter Mullan tells the story of three unwed Irish mothers struggling to survive an abusive 1960s nunnery.

Man of Aran (1934). Directed by Robert J. Flaherty, this haunting, near-silent documentary about life on the Aran Islands in the early 20th century is a classic.

Michael Collins (1996). Director Neil Jordan's biopic stars Liam Neeson as the famous Irish patriot and revolutionary who was killed in the Irish Civil War.

My Left Foot (1989). Daniel Day-Lewis plays an Irishman with cerebral palsy who learns to write and paint with his left foot.

Odd Man Out (1947). This British film noir, about the early IRA, is set in Northern Ireland with a great scene filmed in Belfast's Crown Bar.

Omagh (2004). "Best Drama" winner of the 2005 British Academy of Film and Television awards, *Omagh* recounts the deadly 1998 IRA bombing that killed 29 people in Northern Ireland.

Once (2006). An Irish street musician joins a Czech classical musician to compose heartfelt melodies in a sensitive tale set in gritty modern Dublin.

Philomena (2013). This poignant but clear-eyed story centers on an Irish woman's search for the son she had to give up.

The Quiet Man (1952). John Wayne plays a disgraced boxer who returns to the Irish village where he was born.

Ryan's Daughter (1970). David Lean's epic WWI love story documents an affair between a married Irish woman and a British officer.

The Secret of Roan Inish (1995). This whimsical and sensitive film explores the Irish and Orcadian folklores of selkies—seals that can shed their skins to become human.

71 (2015). In this true story, a solitary British Army soldier flees on foot through hostile IRA-controlled territory at the height of the Troubles in 1971.

Some Mother's Son (1996). Helen Mirren stars in this movie about families of IRA hunger strikers.

Titanic Town (1998). A brave mother tries to protect her family while living on the bleak front lines of sectarian Belfast during the Troubles.

Veronica Guerin (2003). Cate Blanchett stars as Veronica, an Irish journalist who exposes Dublin's drug lords—and pays the price.

Waking Ned Devine (1998). A deceased villager wins the lottery in this funnier-than-it-sounds comedy that showcases the wit of the Irish people.

The Wind That Shakes the Barley (2006). Two brothers fight in the Irish Republican Army during the country's struggle for independence from Britain.

Conversions and Climate

Numbers and Stumblers

- In Europe, dates appear as day/month/year, so Christmas 2022 is 25/12/22.
- What Americans call the second floor of a building is the first floor in Europe.
- On escalators and moving sidewalks, Europeans keep the left "lane" open for passing. Keep to the right.

Metric Conversions

Both the Republic of Ireland and Northern Ireland use the metric system (except for driving signage in Northern Ireland). Weight and volume are typically calculated in metric: A kilogram is 2.2 pounds, and a liter is about a quart. The weight of a person is measured by "stone" (one stone equals 14 pounds). Temperatures are generally given in both Celsius and Fahrenheit.

On the road, the Republic of Ireland is still converting from miles to kilometers, and you'll likely see signs in both (especially in rural destinations). Northern Ireland uses miles and posts speed limits in miles per hour.

1 foot = 0.3 meter	1 square yard = 0.8 square meter
1 yard = 0.9 meter	1 square mile = 2.6 square kilometers
1 mile = 1.6 kilometers	1 ounce = 28 grams
1 centimeter = 0.4 inch	1 quart = 0.95 liter
1 meter = 39.4 inches	1 kilogram = 2.2 pounds
1 kilometer = 0.62 mile	32°F = 0°C

Clothing Sizes

When shopping for clothing, use these US-to-Ireland comparisons as general guidelines (but note that no conversion is perfect).

Women: For pants and dresses, add 4 (US 10 = UK 14). For blouses and sweaters, add 2. For shoes, subtract 2.5 (US size 8 = UK size 5.5)

Men: For clothing, US and UK sizes are the same. For shoes, subtract about 0.5 (US size 9 = UK size 8.5)

Children: Clothing is sized similarly to the US. UK kids' shoe sizes are about one size smaller (US size 6 = UK size 5).

Ireland's Climate

First line, average daily high; second line, average daily low; third line, average days without rain. For more detailed weather statistics for destinations in this book (as well as the rest of the world), check www.wunderground.com.

	J	F	M	A	M	J	J	A	S	O	N	D
Dublin												
	46°	47°	51°	55°	60°	65°	67°	67°	63°	57°	51°	47°
	34°	35°	37°	39°	43°	48°	52°	51°	48°	43°	39°	37°
	18	18	21	19	21	19	18	19	18	20	18	17

Fahrenheit and Celsius Conversion

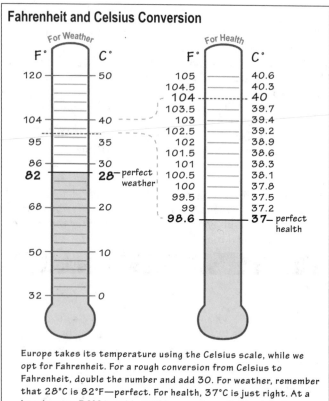

Europe takes its temperature using the Celsius scale, while we opt for Fahrenheit. For a rough conversion from Celsius to Fahrenheit, double the number and add 30. For weather, remember that 28°C is 82°F—perfect. For health, 37°C is just right. At a launderette, 30°C is cold, 40°C is warm (usually the default setting), 60°C is hot, and 95°C is boiling. Your air-conditioner should be set at about 20°C.

Packing Checklist

Whether you're traveling for five days or five weeks, you won't need more than this. Pack light to enjoy the sweet freedom of true mobility.

Clothing

- ❑ 5 shirts: long- & short-sleeve
- ❑ 2 pairs pants (or skirts/capris)
- ❑ 1 pair shorts
- ❑ 5 pairs underwear & socks
- ❑ 1 pair walking shoes
- ❑ Sweater or warm layer
- ❑ Rainproof jacket with hood
- ❑ Tie, scarf, belt, and/or hat
- ❑ Swimsuit
- ❑ Sleepwear/loungewear

Money

- ❑ Debit card(s)
- ❑ Credit card(s)
- ❑ Hard cash (US $100-200)
- ❑ Money belt

Documents

- ❑ Passport
- ❑ Tickets & confirmations: flights, hotels, trains, rail pass, car rental, sight entries
- ❑ Driver's license
- ❑ Student ID, hostel card, etc.
- ❑ Photocopies of important documents
- ❑ Insurance details
- ❑ Guidebooks & maps

Toiletries Kit

- ❑ Basics: soap, shampoo, toothbrush, toothpaste, floss, deodorant, sunscreen, brush/comb, etc.
- ❑ Medicines & vitamins
- ❑ First-aid kit
- ❑ Glasses/contacts/sunglasses
- ❑ Sewing kit
- ❑ Packet of tissues (for WC)
- ❑ Earplugs

Electronics

- ❑ Mobile phone
- ❑ Camera & related gear
- ❑ Tablet/ebook reader/laptop
- ❑ Headphones/earbuds
- ❑ Chargers & batteries
- ❑ Phone car charger & mount (or GPS device)
- ❑ Plug adapters

Miscellaneous

- ❑ Daypack
- ❑ Sealable plastic baggies
- ❑ Laundry supplies: soap, laundry bag, clothesline, spot remover
- ❑ Small umbrella
- ❑ Travel alarm/watch
- ❑ Notepad & pen
- ❑ Journal

Optional Extras

- ❑ Second pair of shoes (flip-flops, sandals, tennis shoes, boots)
- ❑ Travel hairdryer
- ❑ Picnic supplies
- ❑ Water bottle
- ❑ Fold-up tote bag
- ❑ Small flashlight
- ❑ Mini binoculars
- ❑ Small towel or washcloth
- ❑ Inflatable pillow/neck rest
- ❑ Tiny lock
- ❑ Address list (to mail postcards)
- ❑ Extra passport photos

INDEX

INDEX

INDEX

MAP INDEX

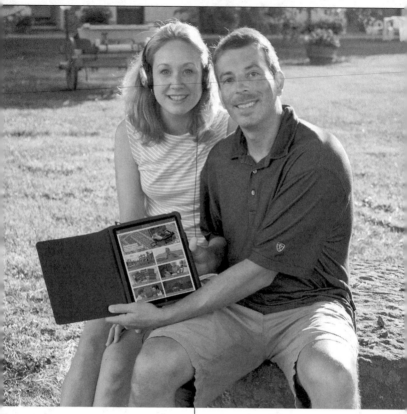

Explore Europe

At ricksteves.com you can browse through thousands of articles, videos, photos and radio interviews, plus find a wealth of money-saving travel tips for planning your dream trip. And with our mobile-friendly website, you can easily access all this great travel information anywhere you go.

TV Shows

Preview the places you'll visit by watching entire half-hour episodes of *Rick Steves' Europe* (choose from all 100 shows) on-demand, for free.

your travel dreams into affordable reality

Radio Interviews

Enjoy ready access to Rick's vast library of radio interviews covering travel tips and cultural insights that relate specifically to your Europe travel plans.

Travel Forums

Learn, ask, share! Our online community of savvy travelers is a great resource for first-time travelers to Europe, as well as seasoned pros.

Travel News

Subscribe to our free Travel News e-newsletter, and get monthly updates from Rick on what's happening in Europe.

Classroom Europe

Check out our free resource for educators with 400+ short video clips from the *Rick Steves' Europe* TV show.

Rick's Free Travel App

Get your FREE **Rick Steves Audio Europe**™ app to enjoy...

- Dozens of self-guided tours of Europe's top museums, sights and historic walks
- Hundreds of tracks filled with cultural insights and sightseeing tips from Rick's radio interviews
- All organized into handy geographic playlists
- For Apple and Android

With Rick whispering in your ear, Europe gets even better.

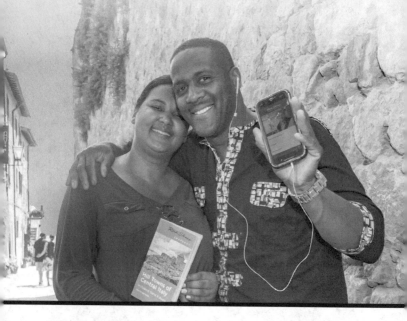

Find out more at ricksteves.com

Gear up for your next adventure at ricksteves.com

Light Luggage

Pack light and right with Rick Steves' affordable, custom-designed rolling carry-on bags, backpacks, day packs and shoulder bags.

Accessories

From packing cubes to moneybelts and beyond, Rick has personally selected the travel goodies that will help your trip go smoother.

Save time and energy

This guidebook is your independent-travel toolkit. But for all it delivers, it's still up to you to devote the time and energy it takes to manage the preparation and logistics that are essential for a happy trip. If that's a hassle, there's a solution.

Rick Steves Tours

A Rick Steves tour takes you to Europe's most interesting places with great

with minimum stress

guides and small groups of 28 or less. We follow Rick's favorite itineraries, ride in comfy buses, stay in family-run hotels, and bring you intimately close to the Europe you've traveled so far to see. Most importantly, we take away the logistical headaches so you can focus on the fun.

Join the fun

This year we'll take 33,000 free-spirited travelers— nearly half of them repeat customers—along with us on 50 different itineraries, from Athens to Istanbul. Is a Rick Steves tour the right fit for your travel dreams?

Find out at ricksteves.com, where you can also request Rick's latest tour catalog. Europe is best experienced with happy travel partners. We hope you can join us.

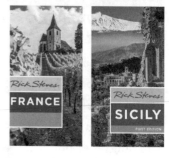

BEST OF GUIDES

Full-color guides in an easy-to-scan format. Focused on top sights and experiences in the most popular European destinations

Best of England
Best of Europe
Best of France
Best of Germany
Best of Ireland
Best of Italy
Best of Scotland
Best of Spain

COMPREHENSIVE GUIDES

City, country, and regional guides printed on Bible-thin paper. Packed with detailed coverage for a multi-week trip exploring iconic sights and venturing off the beaten path

Amsterdam & the Netherlands
Barcelona
Belgium: Bruges, Brussels,
  Antwerp & Ghent
Berlin
Budapest
Croatia & Slovenia
Eastern Europe
England
Florence & Tuscany
France
Germany
Great Britain
Greece: Athens & the Peloponnese
Iceland
Ireland
Istanbul
Italy
London
Paris
Portugal
Prague & the Czech Republic
Provence & the French Riviera
Rome
Scandinavia
Scotland
Sicily
Spain
Switzerland
Venice
Vienna, Salzburg & Tirol

E BEST OF ROME

, Italy's capital, is studded with
n remnants and floodlit-fountain
s. From the Vatican to the Colos-
with crazy traffic in between, Rome
erful, huge, and exhausting. The
the heat, and the weighty history

of the Eternal City where Caesars walked
can make tourists wilt. Recharge by taking siestas, gelato breaks, and after-dark
walks, strolling from one atmospheric
square to another in the refreshing evening air.

*Pantheon—which
done until the
3,000 years old
over 1,500).*

*Athens in the Vat-
the humanistic*

*diators fought
her, entertaining*

*ome ristorante.
t St. Peter's*

Rick Steves books are available from your favorite bookseller.
Many guides are available as ebooks.

POCKET GUIDES

Compact color guides for shorter trips

Amsterdam
Athens
Barcelona
Florence
Italy's Cinque Terre
London
Munich & Salzburg

Paris
Prague
Rome
Venice
Vienna

SNAPSHOT GUIDES

Focused single-destination coverage

Basque Country: Spain & France
Copenhagen & the Best of Denmark
Dublin
Dubrovnik
Edinburgh
Hill Towns of Central Italy
Krakow, Warsaw & Gdansk
Lisbon
Loire Valley
Madrid & Toledo
Milan & the Italian Lakes District
Naples & the Amalfi Coast
Nice & the French Riviera
Normandy
Northern Ireland
Norway
Reykjavík
Rothenburg & the Rhine
Scottish Highlands
Sevilla, Granada & Southern Spain
St. Petersburg, Helsinki & Tallinn
Stockholm

CRUISE PORTS GUIDES

Reference for cruise ports of call

Mediterranean Cruise Ports
Scandinavian & Northern European
  Cruise Ports

Complete your library with...

TRAVEL SKILLS & CULTURE

*Study up on travel skills and gain
insight on history and culture*

Europe 101
Europe Through the Back Door
Europe's Top 100 Masterpieces
European Christmas
European Easter
European Festivals
For the Love of Europe
Travel as a Political Act

PHRASE BOOKS & DICTIONARIES

French
French, Italian & German
German
Italian
Portuguese
Spanish

PLANNING MAPS

Britain, Ireland & London
Europe
France & Paris
Germany, Austria & Switzerland
Iceland
Ireland
Italy
Spain & Portugal

Credits

CONTRIBUTOR

Gene Openshaw

Gene has co-authored more than a dozen Rick Steves books, specializing in writing walks and tours of Europe's cities, museums, and cultural sights. He also writes for to Rick's public television series, produces tours for Rick Steves Audio Europe, and is a regular guest on Rick's public radio show. As a composer, Gene has written a full-length opera called *Matter*, a violin sonata, and dozens of songs. He lives near Seattle, where he enjoys giving presentations on art and history, and roots for the Mariners in good times and bad.

ACKNOWLEDGMENTS

Thank you to Risa Laib for her 25-plus years of dedication to the Rick Steves guidebook series. Thanks to Rozanne Stringer for her writing on the Celts, the Celtic Tiger, St. Brendan, and Irish art. Thanks also to Dave Fox of Globejotting.com for his writing on Guinness beer.

PHOTO CREDITS

Front Cover Photo: Skellig Michael, Ireland, © Marco Bottigelli / Sime / eStock Photo

Back Cover Photos: from left: Blarney Castle © Madrugadaverde; Inisheer village, Aran Islands © Graphicjet; pub in Dublin © Uta Scholl, Dreamstime.com

Title Page: Irish musician © Dominic Arizona Bonuccelli

Additional Photography: Dominic Arizona Bonuccelli, Rich Earl, Trish Feaster, David C. Hoerlein, Pat O'Connor, Rick Steves, Wikimedia Commons (PD-Art/PD-US). Photos are used by permission and are the property of the original copyright owners.

Avalon Travel
Hachette Book Group
1700 Fourth Street
Berkeley, CA 94710

Text © 2021 by Rick Steves' Europe, Inc. All rights reserved.
Maps © 2021 by Rick Steves' Europe, Inc. All rights reserved.

Printed in Canada by Friesens.
20th Edition. First printing January 2021.

ISBN 978-1-64171-278-1

For the latest on Rick's talks, guidebooks, tours, public television series, and public radio show, contact Rick Steves' Europe, 130 Fourth Avenue North, Edmonds, WA 98020, tel. 425/771-8303, www.ricksteves.com, rick@ricksteves.com.

Rick Steves' Europe
Managing Editor: Jennifer Madison Davis
Assistant Managing Editor: Cathy Lu
Editors: Glenn Eriksen, Suzanne Kotz, Rosie Leutzinger, Teresa Nemeth, Jessica Shaw, Carrie Shepherd, Meg Sneeringer
Editorial & Production Assistant: Megan Simms
Contributor: Gene Openshaw
Graphic Content Director: Sandra Hundacker
Maps & Graphics: David C. Hoerlein, Lauren Mills, Mary Rostad
Digital Asset Coordinator: Orin Dubrow

Avalon Travel
Senior Editor and Series Manager: Madhu Prasher
Associate Managing Editors: Jamie Andrade, Sierra Machado
Copy Editor: Maggie Ryan
Proofreader: Kelly Lydick
Indexer: Stephen Callahan
Production & Typesetting: Lisi Baldwin, Rue Flaherty
Cover Design: Kimberly Glyder Design
Maps & Graphics: Kat Bennett

Although every effort was made to ensure that the information was correct at the time of going to press, the author and publisher do not assume and hereby disclaim any liability to any party for any loss or damage caused by errors, omissions, loathsome leprechauns, or any potential travel disruption due to labor or financial difficulty, whether such errors or omissions result from negligence, accident, or any other cause.

COLOR MAPS

Ireland • Dublin • Dingle & "Ring of Kerry" Peninsulas

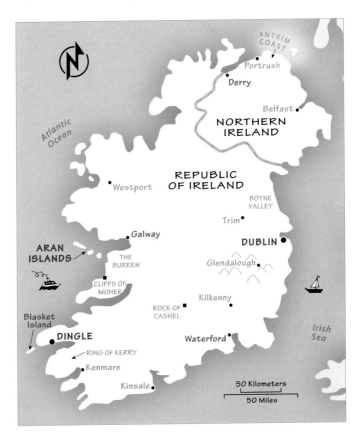

ANTRIM COAST

Portrush

Derry

Belfast

NORTHERN IRELAND

Atlantic Ocean

REPUBLIC OF IRELAND

Westport

BOYNE VALLEY

Trim

Galway

DUBLIN

ARAN ISLANDS

THE BURREN

Glendalough

CLIFFS OF MOHER

ROCK OF CASHEL

Kilkenny

Blasket Island

DINGLE

RING OF KERRY

Kenmare

Waterford

Irish Sea

Kinsale

50 Kilometers

50 Miles

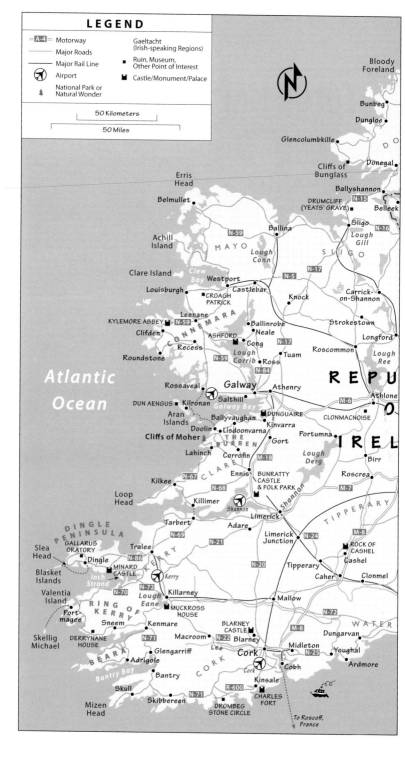

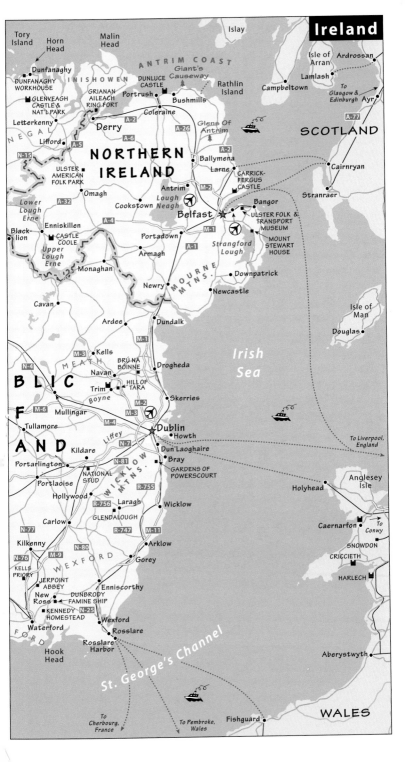

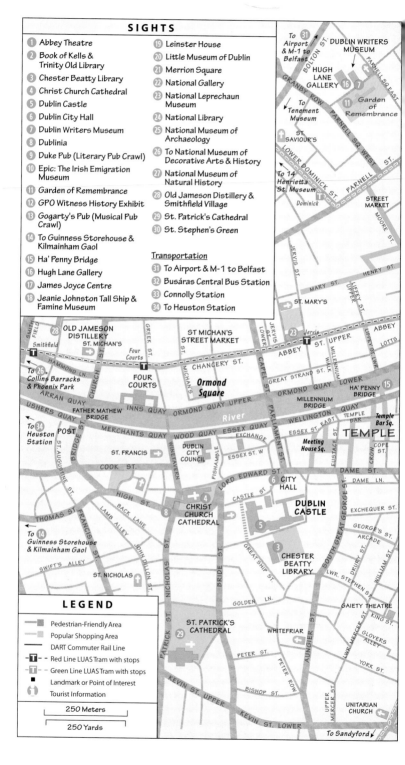

SIGHTS

1. Abbey Theatre
2. Book of Kells & Trinity Old Library
3. Chester Beatty Library
4. Christ Church Cathedral
5. Dublin Castle
6. Dublin City Hall
7. Dublin Writers Museum
8. Dublinia
9. Duke Pub (Literary Pub Crawl)
10. Epic: The Irish Emigration Museum
11. Garden of Remembrance
12. GPO Witness History Exhibit
13. Gogarty's Pub (Musical Pub Crawl)
14. To Guinness Storehouse & Kilmainham Gaol
15. Ha' Penny Bridge
16. Hugh Lane Gallery
17. James Joyce Centre
18. Jeanie Johnston Tall Ship & Famine Museum
19. Leinster House
20. Little Museum of Dublin
21. Merrion Square
22. National Gallery
23. National Leprechaun Museum
24. National Library
25. National Museum of Archaeology
26. To National Museum of Decorative Arts & History
27. National Museum of Natural History
28. Old Jameson Distillery & Smithfield Village
29. St. Patrick's Cathedral
30. St. Stephen's Green

Transportation

31. To Airport & M-1 to Belfast
32. Busáras Central Bus Station
33. Connolly Station
34. To Heuston Station

LEGEND

- Pedestrian-Friendly Area
- Popular Shopping Area
- DART Commuter Rail Line
- Red Line LUAS Tram with stops
- Green Line LUAS Tram with stops
- Landmark or Point of Interest
- Tourist Information

250 Meters
250 Yards

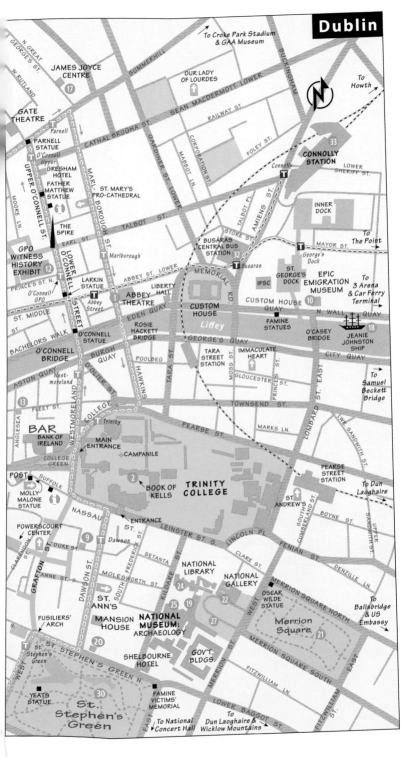

Dublin

To Croke Park Stadium & GAA Museum

To Howth

N. GREAT GEORGE'S ST.
W. RUTLAND ST.

JAMES JOYCE CENTRE (17)

SUMMERHILL

OUR LADY OF LOURDES

SEAN MACDERMOTT LOWER

BUCKINGHAM

GATE THEATRE

Parnell

PARNELL STATUE

O'Connell Upper

GRESHAM HOTEL

FATHER MATTHEW STATUE

THE SPIRE

CATHAL BRUGHA ST.

GARDINER ST. LOWER

RAILWAY ST.

FOLEY ST.

CONNOLLY STATION (33)

Connolly

LOWER SHERIFF ST.

ST. MARY'S PRO-CATHEDRAL

TALBOT ST.

MABBOT LN.

TALBOT PL.

AMIENS ST.

STORE ST.

INNER DOCK

To The Point

MAYOR ST.

GPO WITNESS HISTORY EXHIBIT (12)

UPPER O'CONNELL ST.

MOORE LN.

EARL ST.

Marlborough

ABBEY ST. LOWER

O'CONNELL GPO

PRINCE'S ST. N.

LARKIN STATUE

Abbey Street

ABBEY THEATRE (1)

LIBERTY HALL

BUSÁRAS CENTRAL BUS STATION (32)

Busáras

George's Dock

IFSC

ST. GEORGE'S DOCK

EPIC EMIGRATION MUSEUM

To 3 Arena & Car Ferry Terminal

ST. MIDDLE ST.

O'CONNELL STATUE

EDEN QUAY

MEMORIAL RD.

CUSTOM HOUSE

CUSTOM HOUSE QUAY (10)

FAMINE STATUES

O'CASEY BRIDGE

N. WALL QUAY

JEANIE JOHNSTON SHIP (18)

BACHELORS WALK

O'CONNELL BRIDGE

ROSIE HACKETT BRIDGE

Liffey

ASTON QUAY

Westmoreland

BURGH QUAY

GEORGE'S QUAY

POOLBEG

TARA STREET STATION

IMMACULATE HEART

CITY QUAY

To Samuel Beckett Bridge

D'OLIER ST.

HAWKINS ST.

TARA ST.

MOSS ST.

GLOUCESTER ST.

PRINCES ST.

LOMBARD ST. EAST

LWR. SANDWITH ST.

FLEET ST. (13)

ANGLESEA

BAR

WESTMORELAND

COLLEGE ST.

Trinity

PEARSE ST.

MARKS LN.

TOWNSEND ST.

UPPER SANDWITH ST.

BANK OF IRELAND

COLLEGE GREEN

MAIN ENTRANCE

CAMPANILE

PEARSE STREET STATION

POST

SUFFOLK ST.

MOLLY MALONE STATUE

BOOK OF KELLS (2)

TRINITY COLLEGE

ST. ANDREW'S

To Dun Laoghaire

SOUTH CUMBERLAND ST.

BOYNE ST.

NASSAU ST.

ENTRANCE ST.

LEINSTER ST. S.

LINCOLN PL.

FENIAN ST.

DENZILLE LN.

POWERSCOURT CENTER

GRAFTON ST.

CLARENDON ST.

ST. DUKE ST. (9)

Dawson

SETANTA ST.

SOUTH FREDERICK ST.

MOLESWORTH ST.

KILDARE ST.

NATIONAL LIBRARY (24)

CLARE ST.

NATIONAL GALLERY (22)

OSCAR WILDE STATUE

MERRION SQUARE NORTH

To Ballsbridge & US Embassy

ANNE ST. S.

DAWSON ST.

ST. ANN'S

MANSION HOUSE

(25) (19)

NATIONAL MUSEUM: ARCHAEOLOGY

(27)

WEST MERRION ST.

Merrion Square (21)

FUSILIERS' ARCH

ST. STEPHEN'S GREEN N.

SHELBOURNE HOTEL

GOV'T. BLDGS.

MERRION SQUARE SOUTH

St. Stephen's Green (20)

(30)

YEATS STATUE

FAMINE VICTIMS' MEMORIAL

FITZWILLIAM LN.

To National Concert Hall

LOWER BAGGOT ST.

To Dun Laoghaire & Wicklow Mountains

FITZWILLIAM ST.

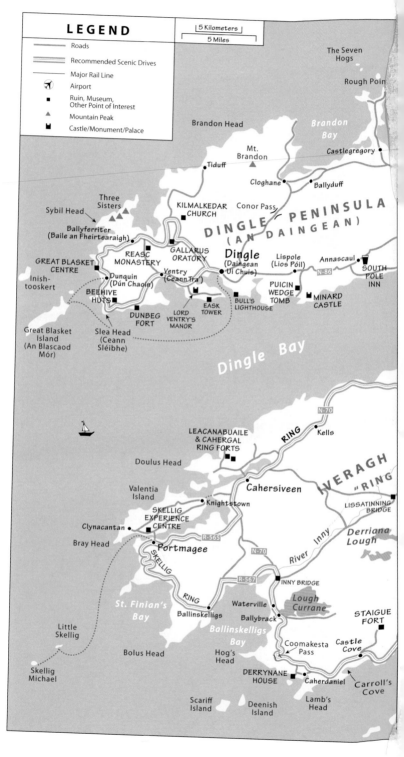

LEGEND

	Roads
	Recommended Scenic Drives
✈	Major Rail Line
	Airport
■	Ruin, Museum, Other Point of Interest
▲	Mountain Peak
▉	Castle/Monument/Palace

5 Kilometers
5 Miles

The Seven Hogs

Rough Poin

Brandon Head

Brandon Bay

Mt. Brandon ▲

Castlegregory

Tiduff

Cloghane

Ballyduff

Three Sisters ▲

KILMALKEDAR CHURCH

Conor Pass

Sybil Head

Ballyferriter (Baile an Fheirtearaigh)

DINGLE PENINSULA (AN DAINGEAN)

REASC MONASTERY

GALLARUS ORATORY

Dingle (Daingean Ui Chuis)

Lispole (Lios Póil)

Annascaul

SOUTH POLE INN

N-86

GREAT BLASKET CENTRE

Inishtooskert

Dunquin (Dún Chaoin)

Ventry (Ceann Trá)

PUICIN WEDGE TOMB

MINARD CASTLE

BEEHIVE HUTS

DUNBEG FORT

LORD VENTRY'S MANOR

EASK TOWER

BULL'S LIGHTHOUSE

Great Blasket Island (An Blascaod Mór)

Slea Head (Ceann Sléibhe)

Dingle Bay

RING

N-70

Kells

LEACANABUAILE & CAHERGAL RING FORTS

Doulus Head

IVERAGH "RING"

Cahersiveen

LISSATINNING BRIDGE

Valentia Island

SKELLIG EXPERIENCE CENTRE

Knightstown

R-565

N-70

River Inny

Derriana Lough

Clynacantan

Bray Head

Portmagee

SKELLIG

RING

R-567

INNY BRIDGE

St. Finian's Bay

Ballinskelligs

Waterville

Ballybrack

Lough Currane

STAIGUE FORT

Little Skellig

Bolus Head

Hog's Head

Ballinskelligs Bay

Coomakesta Pass

Castle Cove

Skellig Michael

Scariff Island

Deenish Island

DERRYNANE HOUSE

Caherdaniel

Carroll's Cove

Lamb's Head

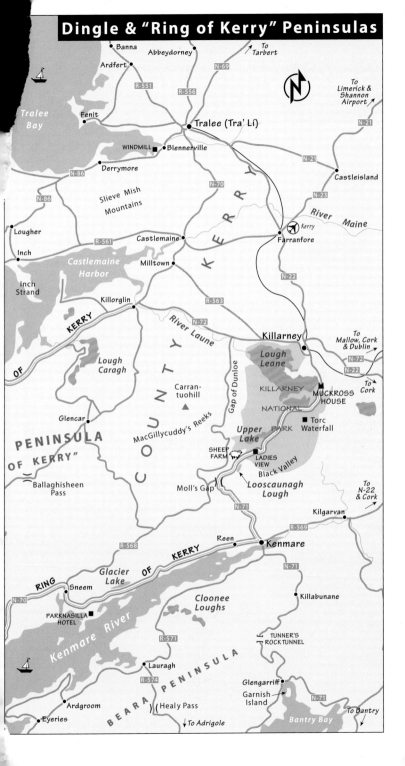

Dingle & "Ring of Kerry" Peninsulas